Books by John Lehmann

ଏଽ ଽଡ

THE WHISPERING GALLERY
(*Autobiography I*)

I AM MY BROTHER
(*Autobiography II*)

THE OPEN NIGHT

ANCESTORS AND FRIENDS

COLLECTED POEMS

THE AMPLE PROPOSITION
(*Autobiography III*)

CHRIST THE HUNTER

SELECTED POEMS OF EDITH SITWELL

A NEST OF TIGERS

IN MY OWN TIME
Memoirs of a Literary Life

IN MY OWN TIME

IN MY OWN TIME

Memoirs of a Literary Life

by JOHN LEHMANN

An Atlantic Monthly Press Book

LITTLE, BROWN AND COMPANY · BOSTON · TORONTO

ATLANTIC–LITTLE, BROWN BOOKS
ARE PUBLISHED BY
LITTLE, BROWN AND COMPANY
IN ASSOCIATION WITH
THE ATLANTIC MONTHLY PRESS

Published simultaneously in Canada
by Little, Brown & Company (Canada) Limited

PRINTED IN THE UNITED STATES OF AMERICA

Foreword

FOR the readers of this book, the following explanations may be of value.

My autobiography was originally published in Great Britain in three separate volumes: *The Whispering Gallery* (1955), *I Am My Brother* (1960), and *The Ample Proposition* (1966). *In My Own Time* brings the three together in a single volume for the first time, occasionally revised and with many passages omitted, but with the essential elements of the story left intact. The revisions in the text were made with the sole intention of providing the reader with a continuous and coherent narrative.

My decision to write my autobiography was prompted by several quite different motives. I wanted, first of all, to tell a story I believed to be interesting to many others beside myself, before the traces of it should be even more difficult to recover than they are already. I wanted, in that story, to re-create as far as possible the living forms of lovable and remarkable people I have known, who are now dead; and at the same time to give my own account of certain happenings and endeavors in which I was intimately involved, and which seem to me likely to be a matter of curiosity in the future, even if only for the studious explorers of literary history. Above all, I had come to the point when I wanted to understand myself by analysing my past, and perhaps in so doing to help others who had followed the same bents to understand their own selves.

Reflecting on all the difficulties, in fact the impossibility of digging everything up in one's own experience and arranging it in coherent and interesting shape, what I decided to do was to follow certain dominant themes through my life as far as I could. Poetry has always been an absorbing passion with me: the reading of it, the study of the lives of the poets, and the attempt to write it myself. I do not think one

needs to estimate one's own contribution to a particular art very highly
to believe that the story of how one came to love it and practise it, and
explore the secrets of its nature, may have some significance and may
even be stimulating to others who have the capacity to do something
very much better. One theme, therefore, that I have tried to follow
through, is my education in poetry. And that leads naturally to another theme: the story of how my love for the spirit of poetry led
me — by paths already marked by my ancestry, by impulses in the
blood and influences of early environment — to assume the role of
impresario to the creative work of others, both as editor and publisher.

In the second section, *I Am My Brother*, continuing the same pattern as in *The Whispering Gallery*, I tried to tell the story of the war
years in Britain from the point of view of an author who was at the
same time deeply involved in the literary scene from many other
angles. The war kept me, a civilian, from many of the activities and
adventures that varied my life both before and after. The adventures
I had were chiefly of the mind; and I beg the reader's pardon that it
contains no descriptions of hair-raising exploits in exotic theatres of
war.

And yet, humdrum as that may sound, life in London was extraordinarily enthralling during those years, not merely because we were
under siege in the essential stronghold the enemy had to take if his
plans for world conquest were to succeed, but also because of the
revolution that was taking place in men's minds while this struggle
went on. Under the extreme pressure of total war, one saw English
life, as conservative and traditional as any way of life in the world,
changing and yet resisting change in a ferment that released unsuspected energies in every layer of the population. I believe this ferment showed itself more in the records of the thoughts and experiences
men tried to give shape to in the more permanent and imaginative
forms of poetry, stories and novels than in the speeches, newspaper
reports and articles of the time; and as editor of *New Writing* — as
this section of my book will, I believe, show — I was especially fortunately placed to read and to evoke these records, often from young
people who had never thought of using words in this way before.

The third section, *The Ample Proposition*, is concerned, without
break in sequence or plan, with the years immediately following the
war, during which I built up a publishing house of my own, and lost
it at the height of its success; saw my *Penguin New Writing* reach
its peak of popularity and interest, fall away as more humdrum peace-

time conditions reasserted themselves, and come to an end; launched my experimental literary magazine on the air, *New Soundings*, and lost it, like my publishing house, just when its name and reputation were fully established; and after these reverses was enabled to found another literary periodical, the *London Magazine*, which still exists in different hands. During these years I also travelled and lectured extensively in Europe and America, wrote poems and literary essays and reviews, broadcast all over the world and made more friends in almost every country of Europe and America than ever before or since.

These years were therefore a period of the fullest and most exciting achievement in my life, and also of the most corroding disaster. The afflatus which drove me in full sail through all these experiences has, inevitably, died down. From a life devoted to different pursuits (even if in the same field of literature), I look back on it, short though the distance may be in the actual count of years, with surprise that is sometimes perilously near self-congratulation, with sorrow sometimes and bitter regret for opportunities missed and chances thwarted; and with a strange kind of almost detached curiosity, as one might look back on the life of a twin brother who had been very close to oneself and had been killed at the height of his self-realization.

Acknowledgements

IN the front of each of the three original volumes from which these memoirs are composed, I expressed my thanks to many friends and relations who had given me advice and assistance, stimulated my memory, corrected its lapses, and improved my prose before they were published. I wish now to repeat those thanks, with ever warm gratitude, knowing that they will forgive me if I do not set out their names once more.

I wish also to make appreciative acknowledgements again to the following authors for quotations I have used from poems, letters, and other writings: Mr. W. H. Auden, Mr. George Barker, Mr. John Betjeman, Mr. Paul Bowles, Mr. Cyril Connolly, Mr. Odysseus Elytis, Mr. E. M. Forster, Mr. Roy Fuller, Mr. David Gascoyne, Mr. Robert Graves, Mr. Christopher Isherwood, my sister Rosamond Lehmann, Mr. V. S. Pritchett, Mr. Henry Reed, Sir Michael Redgrave, Mr. John Sommerfield, Mr. Stephen Spender, Mr. Tennessee Williams and Mr. Henry Yorke (Green); and to the heirs and literary executors of Julian Bell, John Cornford, Keith Douglas, Lord Inverchapel (Sir Archibald Clark-Kerr), Sidney Keyes, John Lepper, Alun Lewis, Edwin Muir, George Orwell, Dame Edith Sitwell, Dylan Thomas, Sir Hugh Walpole, Denton Welch, Rollo Wooley and Virginia Woolf.

Finally, I must express my deep gratitude to Mr. William Abrahams of the Atlantic Monthly Press for his endlessly patient collaboration in the cutting and editing of the book, and to Mr. Patrick Gregory for his skillful assistance in seeing the work through the presses. Without their enthusiasm this book would never have appeared.

Contents

Illustrations

John Lehmann (*photo by Harrods*)   *frontispiece*

BOOK ONE

The Whispering Gallery

There is that whispering gallery where
A dark population of the air
Gives back to us these vocables
We dare not robe in syllables

I speak of the whispering gallery
Of all Dionysian poetry
Within whose precincts I have heard
An apotheosis of the word. . . .
    — George Barker, *Letter to a Young Poet*

I

Jewels in a Cave

I was born to this house:
The joys, the terrors, groping thoughts and dreams,
Unconfined apprehensions of the world
That lie in childhood like jewels in a cave
Half in the light, half in unmeasured dark,
Had their scene here for me.

WHEN I try to remember where my education in poetry began, the first image that comes to mind is of my father's library at our old family home of Fieldhead, on the Thames. It is an autumn or winter evening after tea, for James the butler has been in to draw the blinds and close the curtains, and my father is reading under a green-shaded lamp. He is sitting in his big arm-chair, drawn up towards the fire blazing in the dark-tiled fireplace; and I am sitting opposite to him on a sofa, with a large red cushion on my lap. On the cushion is a heavy blue-bound volume of *Punch* — perhaps of 1871 or 1898 or 1907, the last having a special fascination for me as being the year of my birth, and therefore surely containing some mysterious presages of destiny — and I am completely absorbed in it, not for the first time nor probably for the second or third time, for a great part of my childhood seems to have been spent in looking through the long series of *Punch* volumes. We were all of us — Helen, Rosamond, Beatrix and myself — immensely proud of our father's connection with it. When he retired in 1919 he had been a member of the "Table" — on which his initials are still to be seen, carved close to those of Thackeray — for just on thirty years, and nearly every week until his last illness some prose sketch or verses had appeared above the familiar initials of R.C.L. in its pages. Our pride stimulated our interest in the past of *Punch*, and I think I learnt more of the social and political history

[3]

of England by going through the bound volumes over and over again as a child than years of later schooling taught me.

Let me try to describe the library. My father had had it built on to the house after his marriage, when he also built the children's wing in which we grew up, thus transforming a bachelor's establishment, designed for a life devoted to the pleasures of the river, into a roomy family home. It had a high ceiling like a college hall, which made it seem of vast proportions to a small boy coming down from his nursery for the enchanted hours before bed-time. The effect of height was enhanced by the row of windows running above the book-cases which covered the entire north wall. Up there, on the inaccessible sills, my father had put some of his athletic medals and cups and a bronze statue of a rather limp-looking youth in modest nineteenth-century rowing costume, which had been presented to him for coaching the *Berliner Ruder Klub* many years before I was born. I remember considering it with feelings of anxiety, tinged even with shame, during the first war, when it was bad enough for a boy in his first year at a private school to bear a German name, and being glad that it was out of reach — its inscription perhaps out of sight.

The south wall, broken by the big fireplace and the door, was also covered with book-cases, and above them, in ornate gilt frames, some large and rather lifeless portraits in oils by my great-uncle Rudolf: my father as a young man, my grandfather in a jaunty sombrero with folded arms, Wilkie Collins, and James Payn, the witty and much-loved editor of *The Cornhill*. To me they were as awe-inspiring as they were remote; but more awe-inspiring and more remote was the portrait, also by my great-uncle, of a smartly-dressed, white-bearded Robert Browning, which was hung high up above the carved screen that opened on to the eastern window-embrasure. Appropriately facing the bard, who looked in his portrait more like the successful chairman of a city finance company, at the other end of the room and above the french windows that gave on to the garden, was an outsize picture of a genial French abbé sipping his wine and reading a book: a terrible picture, but it had been painted by Pen Browning, and my grandfather had bought it for 150 guineas in 1876, more I believe to please his friend, the artist's father, who wrote him an enthusiastic letter of thanks for the encouragement he had given Pen, than because he found any special merit in it. Another much-treasured Browning relic stood in its frame on the mantelpiece: a piece of notepaper from my grandfather's house at 15 Berkeley Square, on which Browning had written a few lines in 1886 in the most diminutive handwriting imaginable, to prove to an assembled dinner-party that his eyesight was still perfect. Even as a boy I found difficulty in deciphering the four lines in English, let alone the two exquisitely neat quotations from the Greek, without a magnifying glass.

The special atmosphere of the library, which I can recall to mind with the utmost vividness at any time, wherever I may be, came partly from the high beam-striped roof without ceiling, but chiefly from the books in all the darkly glowing colours of their gold-printed leather bindings. The main part of the collection had been bought and bound by my grandfather, and was almost entirely contemporary to his own day, except for some early nineteenth-century editions of the Elizabethan dramatists; my father had added some sets, old and new, of his favourite seventeenth- and eighteenth-century authors, and had very much increased the proportion of historical works — history being a taste that he shared with my mother. The accent of the collection, however, still seemed to lie on the Victorian novelists and poets; my grandparents had been the close friends of many of them, and glimpses of Dickens, George Eliot, Wilkie Collins, Bulwer Lytton and Browning were among my father's earliest boyhood memories. Out-topping all, Dickens was the hero of the library. There were at least three editions of the novels, two of them with the original illustrations, which rise as vividly to me out of my childhood as the pictures in *Punch*. Almost as soon as we could read a book at all we were started on Dickens, and if it was not a volume of *Punch* that lay on the red cushions in our laps during those still evenings of reading, it was *David Copperfield* or *Great Expectations* or *Nicholas Nickleby* or *Bleak House:* so that David's first visit to Peggotty's cabin on the sea-shore and Lady Dedlock's flight through the snow and Nicholas's arrival at Dotheboys Hall are among the earliest events I can remember, almost as if they had been part of my own experience. Indeed, the description of Dotheboys Hall caused a dread of the inevitable day when I should have to leave for boarding-school, which was only partly alleviated by my parents' assurance that things were no longer as bad as all that. After all, to judge from the *Magnet*, they *were;* and, my imagination played on by the sinister tales of older boys in the neighbourhood, I refused to be taken in by the farcical customs, taboos, striped caps and esoteric language that appeared to have invaded the world of school since Nicholas's day. The reality, when it came, was so strangely different, that in spite of the fact that I lay awake night after night for weeks in misery at being cast out from the paradise of home, I soon learnt to find happiness there, and to believe that, since schools had improved so miraculously since Dotheboys Hall, we must be living in an age of miraculous humane progress — that only the Kaiser had spoiled.

« 2 »

My father's desk was beside the french windows, and behind it, in the lowest shelves of the book-cases, only to be reached by crawling on all fours, were some of the books that fascinated me most: several very old volumes of natural history, astronomy and geology with engraved plates foxed at the edges, some large, heavy, illustrated books on Japan which my grandfather had brought back from a far-away tour to the East, and all the books associated with my great-grandfather, Robert Chambers. Every edition of the *Vestiges of Creation* (the immediate forerunner of Darwin's *Origin of Species*) was there, *The Traditions of Edinburgh*, *Chambers's Cyclopaedia of Literature*, and the complete *Encyclopaedia* itself in calf binding.

Scotland was very remote from the Thames Valley existence of my childhood, and it was only later that I gradually became aware how much I owed, how much we all owed, in our tastes and capacities, to the Scottish side of the family. If one's destiny lies in one's heredity as well as in one's environment, then my interest in editing and publishing as well as my impulse to be a writer are clearly derived from the Chamberses. And how they came into the book world is a story in which chance played a surprisingly large part; to be precise, the behaviour of certain French prisoners of war in the little town of Peebles just before the Battle of Waterloo.

Even in such a distant part of Britain the French wars caused enough commotion. According to my great-grandfather's account there were militia regiments stationed in the town and in the surrounding country, and there was a constant demand for recruits to fill their ranks and those of the regular army. Soldiers marched to and fro with drums beating and colours flying to inspire the sleepy inhabitants with martial enthusiasm, rumours of defeats and victories were brought by excited travellers who galloped in from over the border, and illuminations were staged to celebrate the most famous feats of arms. Peebles, however, was sufficiently out of the way to be considered a suitable place by the Government for the residence of prisoners of war on parole. The first to come, a couple of dozen or so, were sailors caught off the coast of the Netherlands, simple folk who quickly learnt some handicraft to supplement the small official allowances they received.

They settled into the life of the place without too much repining, hated by no one and with no malice in themselves towards the hosts they had never intended to visit. A few years later they were followed by a different class of prisoners, naval and military officers who had been captured in the Peninsula by Wellington's men. None of these officers is known to have broken parole, and they soon became welcome guests in the households of the better-off citizens of Peebles. They were, however, the cause of a serious calamity in the life of one of these citizens, who happened to be my great-great-grandfather.

James Chambers came of a family that had been living in Peebles for centuries. The earliest ancestor of which there is record was one William de la Chambre, "Bailif e Burgois de Peebles" in the list of those who signed bonds of allegiance to Edward I at Berwick-on-Tweed in 1296. James had inherited a small cotton-manufacturing concern which prospered reasonably; but being of an easy disposition, he extended credit to the prisoners to purchase cloth from him far beyond the bounds of prudence and in spite of the frequent remonstrances of his canny wife, Jean Gibson. The inevitable blow fell suddenly: one day the Government ordered the prisoners to be moved to Dumfries, and a few days later they were all gone. Loud were their protestations that they would discharge their debts the moment they returned to their homes at the end of the war; but never a penny of his money did my great-great-grandfather see.

He was ruined. And from that ruin came the family migration to Edinburgh. His two young sons, William and Robert, set out ahead, without a sixpence in their pockets, to earn their living there in the humblest way that offered itself. They began with copying and job-printing; a lucky break made it possible for them to start second-hand bookselling; and after years of struggle and cautious Scottish thrift, they had the idea of founding a magazine for popular education, afterwards to be known as *Chambers's Journal*. An immediate success rewarded them, and they went on to the founding of the publishing firm of W. & R. Chambers, from which eventually issued the famous *Encyclopaedia*. Soon Robert became well known as author as well as publisher, and his house the meeting-place of many of the most learned and gifted people in Edinburgh society of the time. Among these visitors happened to be two German brothers, whose father had been a portrait-painter in the Free City of Hamburg: Frederick and Rudolf Lehmann. Frederick had established himself as a merchant in Leith; Rudolf, like his elder brother Henri, who had settled in France, was an artist, destined to be a fashionable portrait-painter to whom "every-

[7]

one" sat in the London of the 'eighties; and within a few years each of them had married one of the daughters of Robert Chambers. Frederick migrated with his wife, Nina Chambers, to Sheffield, where he had interests in steel; and there my father, the eldest of a family of four, was born in January 1856.

« 3 »

THE most magical place in the house for me was the window-embrasure half-way up the front stairs, where they turned by the grandfather clock. The windows were of opaque coloured glass which shut out the view of the garden below, but allowed the hot afternoon sun of summer to stream through in wandering splashes of red and green and gold on to the banisters. On the ledge below the windows were some Chinese bowls and covered dishes, the bowls always filled with lavender, and the dishes, when one lifted the lids, giving forth the delicious aroma of dried rose-leaves.

These scents seemed to steam off the ledge on sunny days all through the summer, and I was drawn there to let the lavender sift through my fingers and to put my face into the rose-leaves and inhale, deep and long. And then I would open one of the windows to get my favourite glimpse of the garden: the paved circle in front of the french windows of the library, planted all through the year with the season's flowers, and to the right beyond it, festooned with climbing roses, the archway which divided the two bosky plantations of flowering trees and shrubs, lilac, laburnum, Japanese cherry and chestnut soaring above them, and to the left the old walnut-tree with the vista below its wide-spreading branches through the apple- and cherry-trees to the long herbaceous border that lay under the walls of the kitchen garden. Directly below, behind a high hedge, was the entrance to the boiler-room which always seemed to me, peering cautiously but not venturing into the forbidden darkness, a danger-fraught entrance to mysterious nether regions.

My memory of the earliest years of my life, before time was an adversary one was always conscious of, just behind one or just ahead in a race that was not of one's choosing, is cloudy, with erratic rifts in the clouds. As I try to imagine myself then, sitting in the window-embrasure over the garden, I can see certain pictures very clearly, and the rest scarcely at all. The pictures I see are nearly all of ritual events that took place year after year: tea under the walnut-tree, with James bringing out the tray with cucumber sandwiches and Fuller's cake and

[8]

the silver urn over which my mother would preside, or the deck-chairs under the laburnum-tree in June, with my father reading the newspapers and my mother a book, or the dogs sitting on the library steps under the red-and-white-striped sun-blinds and drowsily watching the birds hopping about the lawn. I can hear the calling of doves and chorus of blackbirds and thrushes in all the trees at sundown, and I can hear the mowing-machine as it makes its alternate strips of light and dark green over the grass in a massacre of daisies' heads. I can hear the murmur of talk as my parents take their guests slowly across the lawn down to the river: I am waiting for the coast to be clear, to slip down myself into the garden without getting involved, perhaps to look for my tortoise in the long grass of the lower orchard, perhaps to try to catch the orange-bellied newts in the lily-pool, lying on the edge with my sleeves rolled back, quite hidden, but knowing that I would answer when I heard my nurse Julia calling for me. I can even catch rare glimpses of particular happenings; my mother, for instance, lining us up with our American cousins, her nephews and nieces, to be photographed by the paved circle, or the Great Dane, Lufra, bounding up to me and nearly knocking me over. Little else swims out of the mist with any clarity, except one incident when I was three years old: the first glimpses of a strange machine I was told was an aeroplane, which had come down in a chalk-pit behind the Tennyson Downs in the Isle of Wight — of that more later. Even fading prints in the family photograph album, of myself, ridiculously chubby and curly-haired, looking aggressively out of my pram, or peering shamelessly between the curtains of a stranger's bathing-tent at the sea-side, stir no response. The password is still to be found.

The window-embrasure on the stairs has other associations of childhood joys and fears for me. I was put to sleep in my parents' bedroom, but even the moon-like glow of a night-light in its little white china cage could not allay the terrors that assailed me before they came up to bed themselves. There were huge ornate wardrobes in the room, and soon after my nurse had left me, possessed by a spirit of active malevolence they began to creak and crack. I was convinced some monster would suddenly open one of the big doors and advance upon me, and very soon — almost every night — I was in tears. I had made promises, of course, not to believe in these monsters, and not to forsake my bed in search of consolation; but they were all too often impossible to keep. I would get up and creep to the top of the stairs, then a few steps down towards the embrasure, in the hope of hearing the echoes of conversation from the dining-room or drawing-room to reassure me.

These terrors did not cease for years; and then I found an antidote to them in — of all books — Black's *Medical Dictionary*. I had discovered it one night beside my mother's bed, and my eye caught by the weird diagrams of internal organs, began to read the accompanying articles. For a long while it was my nightly companion, much to the amusement of the rest of the family, and my parents when they came up would find it beside my bed as it had fallen from my hands as I sank into sleep. How much I understood of it, I do not know; but it did not make me morbid, nor, alas, did it make me an expert on human ills and their cures. Even by the time I went to my preparatory school, I had forgotten nearly all of it.

But it was not only to escape the bogeys of the night that I used to creep down the stairs after going to bed. There were the evenings when my parents gave dinner-parties, and my sister Beatrix and I would wait for the guests to cross the hall on the way to the dining-room when we heard the gong boom out down below. As noiselessly as we could, we would hide behind the banisters and peer through, to catch a glimpse of the glittering brocaded dresses and the jewels, the fabulous world of grown-ups *en fête*. Then, about half an hour later, Beatrix would creep down into the corridor behind the green baize door, and hiding in the telephone-room, wait until Ernest the footman brought her the choicest left-over tit-bits, which she would bring back triumphantly in her soap-dish. And sometimes I would go down by myself, for a special treat: to hear my sister Rosamond playing the piano in the drawing-room. I revelled in a tune called "Holy Night" which she had just mastered; she knew how it carried me away on wings of voluptuous bliss, and would even play it specially for me. Then I would go back to bed perfectly happy, and even Black's *Medical Dictionary* had no further charms that night.

« 4 »

AN artist can have no greater luck than to be brought up in surroundings of natural beauty which he is free to explore at his own will: by the sea-coast away from the towns, in a mountain setting of lakes and forests, a lush river-valley or a garden cunningly planned for surprise and pleasure at all seasons of the year. There he may learn to know, and assimilate into himself, the rhythms and mysterious harmonies of the year, the multitudinous everyday miracles of plant, insect, animal life, the unaccountable empathies, intertwinings and transformations in which he comes to feel that he himself takes part with powers that are not in his conscious direction; thus images are invisibly laid up in his mind rather as precious pictures are stored in mountain caves in wartime, out of which the secret agencies of the imagination can summon them as symbols and correspondences that never fail. What poverty an artist must feel who has never had this luck: for me it was the garden of Fieldhead and the reach of the Thames between Marlow and Cookham that flowed by its western edge.

The extraordinary thing about the garden was that no situation could have been more unpromising, less likely to reflect an image of romantic perfection in a child's mind. Originally, when my father bought it, it had been a big field leading down to an old ferry with an inn that stood beside the landing-place. To round it off, he had bought up some old cottages on the south side, and pulled them down: all that remained of them were the gnarled apple-trees of unknown age that grew on the lawn between the house and the kitchen garden. At the time when he first made his home in Bourne End the village scarcely existed. There were a couple of shops, a post-office in one of them, that served the few big houses along the river-side, and a boat-building establishment a little further up. Then the railway arrived, crossed the river exactly at the bottom of the garden, and built its station and shunting yard all along the north side. My father planted a long line of poplars to shut it out; but he could not shut out the smell of what the goods-trucks contained, nor the ricochetting clatter they made as they were being shunted about. And yet the presence of the railway at our back-gate provided an extra element of romance when I grew old enough to be interested in trains and engine-numbers; and before that I remember how comforting it was to me, sleepless in the inhuman vacancy of night, to hear the last train rumble over the bridge soon after midnight, and hiss as it drew up in the station, its mission accomplished with a firm daylight dependability, its human load safely delivered.

The house itself, as I realized only later, in my teens, was badly sited in the grounds and awkwardly built; so that except for the library, my mother's drawing-room beside it and the three bedrooms directly above, the choice of views was either looking over the garden, cold and north, or south and warm but looking directly over the lane where a row of ugly workmen's cottages had been built, ineffectively screened by some dank shrubs, cypresses and a yew-hedge. To this day I cannot understand why the architect planned it in that way, or why my father agreed. My own nursery looked over the lane; and from my window I used to watch the antics of the children who abounded in the cottages, half-repelled but also half-fascinated by this close-up view of the incomprehensible lives of the poor. They seemed cheerful, noisy and vigorous enough in spite of their dishevelled clothes; and ready to shout gleefully rude remarks at us too, though my parents, declared radicals and full of kind works, were popular and respected in the village. The cottages were only one manifestation of the graceless, straggling village that had grown up round Fieldhead since my father had built it. It really had nothing to recommend it except the smiling Buckinghamshire faces of its inhabitants: everywhere ugly brick cottages scattered over what was once one of the prettiest parts of the valley below the line of the Chilterns, a new and hideous little church almost directly opposite our front-gate, an even worse Methodist chapel, and a row of featureless modern shops along a road on the other side of the railway, that had been absurdly and pompously named The Parade. It was given its raison d'être partly by the holiday attractions of the river as movement into and out of London became easier and faster, but much more by the paper-mills that lay just beyond it on the road to Woburn Green. The nearest unspoilt village was Little Marlow, a few miles up-river, where the church, the manor-house and the vicarage had remained the core of the community and in the same classic relationship to one another as for hundreds of years past. Further downstream Cookham, set against the romantic dark cliff of Cliveden Woods with the weir plunging just below the bridge, had much of the charm of Little Marlow, though it had grown bigger — a favourite riverside spot of an earlier generation. Only Bourne End disfigured the scene; and yet it was not till long after I had gone away to school that I became properly aware of its ugliness, so permeated was it for me with the overflow of Fieldhead's enchantments.

The garden had almost everything that a child could want to make him happy. Above all, it had the quality of making one feel one had never fully explored it. I always imagined that I would suddenly come upon some secret corner, hidden in the bushes or among the potting-sheds, or along one of the little overgrown paths: there, perhaps, I would discover a rusty old pump over a disused well, or a forgotten sundial long enveloped in undergrowth and overshadowed by the growth of poplars and chestnuts, or a storeroom of treasures from a time before I was born, or a rare shrub that I had never seen in flower, a fig-tree bearing fruit behind a brick archway I had never gone through. No formal garden, more elegantly and elaborately planned, could have given this impression.

The lily-pool, hidden in its cypresses and bamboos, with its teeming life of gold-fish, newts, water-beetles and tadpoles, all lurking under the reddish-green mats of the leaves, was one of the secret places of the garden for which I had a particular love; but there were others that drew me almost as strongly. Between the lower orchard and the railway line, hidden by pine-trees and branches of hazel-nut, was a little path that led down to the back-gate of the kitchen garden, with a dump of leaf-mould on one side under the pines and some gardeners' sheds and dog-kennels on the other. This was a favourite area of concealment in the games of hide-and-seek and "clumps" we were always playing, and to which the garden lent itself so well; when I heard the "coo-ee!" it was one of the first places I would make for, imagining I saw the corner of a jersey or skirt or a flattened hand behind every branch and pile of logs. The dog-kennels were the source of one of the bitterest, most terrible disappointments of my whole childhood. They had been constructed for Great Danes and St. Bernards, for which my father, a fanatical dog-lover, had a special liking. They were large, more than tall enough for a child to stand upright in and roomy enough to lie down in, and each had a long fenced yard in front of it. My sisters decided to make "homes" of them — they had long been disused — and with my parents' amused encouragement each took over one of the three kennels, and filled it with articles of individual preciousness; Beatrix, inspired as she was at the time by Boy Scout dreams of adventure and camping on the veldt, installing herself with even greater enthusiasm and thoroughness than Helen or Rosamond. Three: but where was the fourth? What my sisters had, I had to have too. Envy and the sense of being shut out from the enjoyments of others, to which as the baby of the family I was keenly sensitive, began to sour my days. Finally my mother promised that I should have something just as good for myself, and went into consultation with Mr. Goodman, the head-gardener. My spirits rose, as my mother told me that my own "home" would be arriving any day. At last the great moment came: a bulky object, I was told, had been delivered by goods-train the night before. I rushed down the garden, to find Goodman hammering away at — a packing-case of moderate size, far, far smaller than any of the kennels. I was appalled: I stared at it incredulously, and then burst into tears of rage and disillusionment.

Not far off, at the edge of the lawn, stood the Pavilion, which my father had built out of the bricks of the cottages he had pulled down. It was really a good deal bigger than what a garden pavilion suggests, consisting of a large hall with various smaller rooms leading off it, and could quite easily have been made into a pleasant home for a moderate-sized family. For many years, while we were growing up, it was used as a schoolroom: my parents had had the idea of engaging two or three teachers for ourselves and proposing to friends that they should share them with us. The scheme turned out a success, and many years of my childhood were dominated by the presence of the day-school in the garden and the friends I made there when I eventually joined it myself. The boys stayed until they left for preparatory school, but the girls much longer; Helen and Rosamond, in fact, until they went to Cambridge. It was well fitted for this purpose, not only because of its size but also because of the big lawn that stretched in front of it, a lawn on which games of tennis, croquet, Tom Tiddler's ground, grandmother's steps and hide-and-seek could all be played at the same time. Inside the Pavilion, ranged all down one side, was a series of lockers which contained relics of my father's sporting past: old dumb-bells, weird Japanese fencing-masks and boxing-gloves with the stuffing bursting out of them. There always seemed to be something in those lockers I had not discovered before, something I often did not understand the use of. The Pavilion was lit by popping gas chandeliers which hung down between the rafters and provided a flickering illumination for the children's dances that were sometimes held there: I can remember very little of them, but I can still faintly hear, at the bottom of a deep well of my mind, the strains of a polka, and the lancers, and Sir Roger de Coverley.

Just behind the Pavilion, surrounded by a miniature box-hedge, were three little flower-beds which had been presented to my sisters as gardens of their own, where they could grow the flowers they chose for themselves out of penny packets. It seems odd that, in so vast a garden, with flowers of every sort abounding wherever one looked, we should have thought it necessary to have planting space of our own; but everything else except those rather obscure and overshadowed plots was under the Olympian control of the head-gardener, and was hardly ever to be touched without incurring his displeasure, and therefore they were prized beyond measure. A sweet-william or a canterbury bell that flowered there, after weeks of eager tending with one's own small green watering-can, was a joy and triumph quite eclipsing the great pageantry of the herbaceous border spread out in the full sun only a few yards away. Needless to say, as soon as I was old enough to be moved by the same ambition, I demanded a plot too; and as there was no more room alongside the other three, I was allotted one on the other side in an angle of the Pavilion walls. It was almost totally deprived of sun, but I suppose that Goodman had slyly advocated it because the disorder he expected could not be seen from any main vantage point in the garden. I felt slightly cheated, as I had over the kennel-houses, but became — for a season or two — an ardent gardener, enrolling all grown-ups who could be persuaded to aid me at any hour of the day, though the coloured pictures on the seed-packets were apt to remain much more satisfying to me than the flowers when they came up (if they did).

My sisters' gardens were at the opening to the woodland path that was known as the Lovers' Walk. And just inside, behind the St. John's wort, and shadowed by the overhanging branches, was the most hallowed spot in the whole garden: the dogs' cemetery, a cluster of weather-stained tombstones standing over sad little hummocks in the ground. Engraved on the stones were the names of dogs that had had their day before I was born, known to me only by life-size paintings that were hung upstairs or in back corridors, stiff photographs of weekend groups in which they were clustered on the library steps or sprawled over my father's feet, or by the legends that were sometimes told when my father had old family or rowing friends to stay. There was buried Ben, the black Labrador of uncanny intelligence who guarded my mother whenever my father was away for long periods, barking on the stair-landing every night at 10 P.M. until she came to bed, and in the middle of the night with equal regularity putting his soft muzzle on to her bed to make certain she was still there; and Rufus, most beloved of all my father's dogs, a spaniel to whom he wrote some famous and much-anthologized pieces. These, the oldest stones, were almost obliterated by rain and lichen; others, more clearly legible, had been wept over by my sisters when they were first put up, and could stir an occasional fading memory for me out of my perambulator days. The first that I can myself at all clearly remember being put up was for a Pekinese called Tai-Tai, really the property of E. V. Lucas, for whom we were keeping her: she had been run over by a cart as she scampered across a country lane while we were all out on a walk together. The burial was performed by the gardeners, as it was unendurable for any of us children to attend after having witnessed her death agonies, and storms of tears flowed whenever we approached the new grave. The deaths of animals were the raw, unassuageable sorrows of our childhood, and it seems impossible that I shall ever weep again as much as I did over those earliest tragedies.

I loved the great flower-beds in the garden; I loved the rose-covered arbours, the lily-pool, the clumps of chestnut-trees with their pink-and-white candelabras of blossom; I loved the grey stone ornamentation of sundial and bird-bath and flower urns; I loved the smoothly striped expanses of lawn after mowing and the unkempt lawn with its daisies and buttercups and clover; but above all I think I loved the kitchen garden. The feathery green forest of the uncut asparagus, hung with orange bobbles at midsummer; the purple lines of beetroot, the plumes of the carrots, the light-green curly luxuriance of the lettuces, the ribbed blue-green Chinese boxes of the cabbages where the white butterflies flopped and dallied, the arching stakes that carried the twinings of the runner-beans with their winged flowers; all spoke of the rich and infinitely varied fruitfulness of the earth and appealed to taste as well as to sight and smell. I would watch the hairy green globes of the gooseberries turn golden-yellow and sticky, relishing the moment of bursting between my teeth; I would creep under the raspberry nets, more secure but scarcely less furtive than the starlings and blackbirds, to pull the just ripe berries off their hard green holders, or prowling on all fours among the straw that cosseted the strawberries, turn up the leaves to discover an occasional scarlet-pitted monster lurking underneath. More wonderful to me even than the netted rows of the berries, were the red-brick walls just behind the greenhouses and the frames for the violets, where the peaches, nectarines and figs grew. How often I climbed up on to the wall, to discover a hidden fig that had hitherto eluded picking, all purple and soft and juicy. How many mornings and evenings I would slip down to see whether a nectarine had ripened and would yield to a gently pressing thumb, whether a peach had fallen, lawful booty, into the grass below. Over the wall, where the gardeners' wheelbarrows, spades, forks and rakes leaned in their sheds against the piled flower-pots, a bonfire was smouldering with sweet drifts of smoke that wandered towards me; I could hear the splashing of oars from the invisible river, or the hurdy-gurdy tune played on a steamer passing under the railway bridge, while shouts and laughter echoed from bathers among the reeds.

« 5 »

ALWAYS at Fieldhead, though it was nowhere visible from the house, one was conscious of the river. This was partly the result of our upbringing as children of a father for whom water sports had been the passion of his life, and who had originally built the house in order to be able to indulge this passion with the friends of his bachelordom; but the river had an irresistible mysteriously indefinable attraction apart

from that. The garden was not a paradise in itself, but only in association with the river; its beauty was heightened and given meaning by
the fact that the river ran at the bottom of it, and not merely because
the presence of the river changed the quality of the air and the quality
of the light. The garden was a dallying place on the way to the river,
and the river was the real purpose of the people who refreshed themselves there. For the river not only provided the joys of punting, canoe-
ing, sculling, rowing, picnicking and bathing, but more than that, was
a magic highway of the great world, transfiguring the traffic that
passed along it. There were evenings of glittering, illusive light in
summer and misty mornings of mirror-still reflections and mingled
rainbow colours in early autumn, when the barges, the pleasure-boats,
the racing craft that slid into view round the up-river bend beyond the
sailing club, and passed, and dropped out of sight at the other end of
the great sweeping S-curve the river's course described through
Bourne End, seemed hardly real, but the symbols in some poem or
song — for music certainly seemed to emanate from it. All this, of
course, was not to be analysed or consciously apprehended by me at
that time, as I sat in my sailor suit by the bank and watched it all as
from a private garlanded box or balcony, but felt in the heart, where it
set in motion a tune, a dance of words for images that all the years of
adult life have failed completely to recapture or translate.

As one walked down from the french windows of the library, past
the walnut-tree and between the old apple-trees on the lawn, one came
to the gates into the kitchen garden, through which a long tunnel of
roses, honeysuckle, clematis and vines, whose grapes never fully ripened, led to the dark laurel boskage of the garden's end and another
gate. The river-garden was divided from the rest of the garden by a
right-of-way; one shook open another wooden gate on the other side of
the path — and immediately the play of light off water was in one's
eyes, the familiar faint smell of river-water and weeds was in one's
nostrils. Perhaps at that moment a string of barges was passing under
the dark-green bridge, the tug lowering its funnel as it chugged
through, or a motor-boat with silent, smartly dressed occupants gazing royally to left and to right, or a skiff with noisy country-folk getting into a tangle with their oars; and immediately after, as the ripples
reached the banks, one heard the slapping of the water against the
camp-shedding, and the raft heaved, pulling at the ring that moored it
to the creaking post and scattering the shoals of sticklebacks I used to
try to catch with the old tin bailer.

The Boat-House, built to accommodate any eight — Leander,

Cambridge or Oxford — that my father might be coaching, was of noble proportions and contained all sorts of craft, some in active use and some more ageing memorials of exploits in the past. It had a curious musty river smell, delicious to me as jonquils or ripe apples as I pushed back the heavy roller doors after an absence from home, a smell compounded of water-weeds drying on paddles, greased rowlocks, sheepskins, cobwebs and varnished timber. The punt always lay in the water, except in flood time, ready for an expedition or a crossing of the river at a moment's notice; but inside the Boat-House were a canoe and a skiff which belonged to my mother and in which we were all taught to scull, both boats well to the front and handy for a quick launching; further back in the gloom, dappled with the quivering light reflected off the river, lay the more serious uncompromising craft of the sport, a light double-sculler, a racing four often used in local regattas when my father with some of his old companions of the oar competed under the colours of his own club, and a neat single-sculler, with outriggers but rather too heavy for racing, known as the rum-tum. There was also a huge family boat, technically known as a randan and called "The Water-Baby," complete with enormous picnic baskets, crockery and plate. My father rowed it down from Henley one summer's day with my mother and myself to steer him, an astonishing feat for a man of over fifty which made him feel, as he said at the time, as if he were harnessed to a motor-bus. It was the most memorable expedition of my childhood, lasting the whole afternoon till dinnertime: at every lock he was recognized and entered into long conversations with the lock-keepers as we slowly sank away from the neat little gardens of roses and geraniums on the falling water. Up above these giants, supported on cross-bar shelves, were the two most exotic denizens of the Boat-House. One was a catamaran, a genuine South Sea craft, which consisted of a very narrow punt balanced by a huge boom, reputed to be very fast but seldom risked — only perhaps by the intrepid Beatrix. It had been given to my father by an admirer, as had the even more singular racing sculler of antique design that lay on the opposite side. This had been built in Australia in the eighteen-sixties, and was entirely round, shaped like a cigar with murderous sharp points at either end, and had outriggers (of doubtful advantage), but a fixed seat. My father kept it, I think, really as a joke, a museum exhibit: some of us did try to go out in it — but only in a bathing-suit.

High up, on the topmost tier of the struts, near the nests of the swallows, lay a quantity of oars, some with the Fieldhead colours on them, some designed for an eight which was no longer there. These unused oars evoked as nothing else, not the old Leander caps, the medals in the library, the challenge cups that adorned our dining-table on festive occasions, or the innumerable photographs of eights and fours which my father had coached, or in which he had rowed himself — these strong and slender oars called out of a legendary past for me my father's rowing fame and a picture far more human and vital than the "Spy" cartoon that hung in the bedroom corridor, of a man supple, athletic, radiant in the confidence of his strength and the love that all who knew him bore towards him. That man, alas, I scarcely knew: when the mists of childhood clear he is already beyond the fullness of his powers and soon to be afflicted with the illness that kept him an invalid for the last ten years of his life.

Attached to the Boat-House were two other rooms, one which had become a lumber-room and was turned by me into a place for the construction of weird and useless steel objects with my Meccano set, for my first experiments in carpentering and for the sawing out of horrible arty flowered designs in wood with my treadle fretwork machine — which I used to present with a glow of triumph to my mother or one of my sisters. The other was a changing-room, also hung with pictures of famous rowing events of ancient times, with an unpredictable shower-bath behind a canvas curtain — it worked when one least expected it and as soon as one had clothed oneself, but never when one was naked and awaiting. Dimly also I remember some pairs of old white flannel rowing-shorts, so long out of use and untouched that one day a robin was observed to fly out of one of them, which revealed on inspection a nest with three eggs. Here we changed for our bathing on summer evenings before dinner about six o'clock, when the falling sun lay on the reddening Virginia creeper that covered the Boat-House walls, and our parents sat in their deck-chairs in the shade of the chestnut-tree with the dogs beside them panting from the heat. We were all taught to swim at the earliest possible moment, one of our parents supporting us with a belt suspended from a pole that went round our middles, while we kicked and splashed and swallowed a great deal of river-water alongside the raft. Thus we learnt to feel at home in water before our teens, and our father could safely entrust us with any kind of boat.

Very often a dip off the raft came at the end of a picnic down-river for tea. Picnics were the most exciting of all river events: the thick jam sandwiches in their thin paper coverings and the tea in the Thermos flask were far more thrilling when safely stowed in a basket in the punt than in the nursery or drawing-room. The wooden backs were put up facing one another, the cushions arranged on them, paddles laid alongside, and there my mother, perhaps my nurse Julia, and sometimes my Aunt Nina or my Aunt Amelia would settle themselves in, and my sisters and I would jump in after them and push off. Two of my sisters would sit on the back seat and paddle — until I was old enough to take a hand myself — aided intermittently by one of the grown-ups. I would let my hand trail in the water, trying to catch at weeds as we passed, sometimes dislodging one from its root, when it would float up to the surface astonishingly long and pale like an invalid emerging from his sick-room. The big riverside houses slipped by, with their urns of roses and geraniums by the water's edge and their smooth lawns leading down to the landing-stages where a punt or a motor-launch was moored and men in white flannels and straw hats handed their ladies, in wide floppy hats and bright long dresses, into their seats. We had our favourite spot for picnics, under a line of willows between two lawns only a quarter of a mile down; but sometimes we would go further, to the Cookham bend, where there was another shaded spot that seemed to belong to no one; the swans paddled slowly up and gobbled the crusts we threw in, hissed at the eagerly watching dogs beside us and paddled away again; a river steamer passed with somebody thumping merrily at the piano and somebody pouring slops over the side; I buried myself in my copy of *Tiger Tim's Weekly* as the punt rocked in the wash, and my parents went on talking about their boring grown-up problems.

At last the picnic was over, the bathing was over; we had gone up for our supper and came down again as twilight gathered and the orange flush went out of the sky across the river; Bourne End regatta had been held, and on the last night the illuminations began. We hung up Chinese lanterns over the raft, and sat on the camp-shedding to watch the punts and skiffs going by, each decorated with its own Chinese lanterns, reflections of red and yellow and green splintered in the dull steel of the river. A band was playing away to our right, somewhere near Townsend's boat-houses; fish plopped every now and then in the reeds before us, and bats flitted over our heads; my father looked at the gold watch he took out of his waistcoat pocket; and then, remembered as bursting stars of colour against the sky of an innocent world, the fireworks began.

« 6 »

My father had a reputation for a certain intolerant brusqueness of manner and sudden moods of stern displeasure that would transform his more characteristic charm and humour; but he was indulgent and easy-going towards his children, and I cannot remember any occasion on which he was seriously angry with me. There was a kind of affectionate detachment about his attitude which made it difficult for him to see our misdemeanours as anything but absurd and entertaining. He could afford detachment, because he took the view that our upbringing was the responsibility of our nurses, governesses and mother; as far as we were concerned, we were there to amuse him. I don't think he showed anger even when it was discovered that I had been secretly ransacking the drawer of his other writing-table in the little back room known as the "Den." My stamp-collecting craze had started, and one day, opening one of the drawers out of curiosity, I saw bundles of old letters all with early Victorian penny stamps on them. It was as exciting for me as if I had lit on a cave of diamonds, and for some weeks, whenever I could steal down to the Den unobserved, I went through the bundles with hurrying fingers, tearing off every stamp that had been left in good condition by the postmark. How I hoped to conceal the haul I don't know; but I was overwhelmed with guilt when, inevitably, the theft was revealed, and the joys of stamp-collecting were dimmed for some time. The letters, most of which had passed between my grandfather and grandmother, were precious to my father, but I had, after all, not torn them, only the envelopes, and I daresay the chilliness that resulted was more on account of the furtive side of my character that had been shown up, than of the damage done.

His influence on us was indirect, by encouragement rather than by prohibition, and perhaps all the stronger for that. He left us to invent our own games, to make our own discoveries, but if it was anything in any way creative, if we were suddenly smitten with an urge to draw, or to paint, or to carpenter, or to write, he never openly laughed at us, but always gently encouraged and fed the urge. I don't think he ever tried to make us tackle a book when we were reluctant. He wanted us to have the freedom of his library, would answer our questions as we rummaged among the volumes, and would take out one for us if we asked what we should read next. Our taste was formed by his taste, simply by the choice of books available. Only on one occasion can I remember that he went further than that. I think he must have feared that my reading was too much influenced by what my sisters read and by nursery taste for it to be healthy for a boy; one day he returned from London with an old, blue cloth-bound set of Captain Marryat's novels, which he had obviously enjoyed himself when he was my age, and encouraged me to embark on them. I still have the very worn copy of *Jacob Faithful* out of this set, the pages covered with large greasy stains which fell on them as I ate my bread and dripping at tea-time and followed the appalling moral tale of Jacob's mother who burst into flames through drinking too much gin. *Mr. Midshipman Easy* and *Peter Simple* were more to my taste; but the swashbuckling adventures of midshipmen in the Napoleonic Wars failed to stir me as David Copperfield's adventures had, or E. Nesbit's stories which I was in process of discovering, or the yarns of the night-watchman in the orange volumes of W. W. Jacobs's stories that stood on the highest shelf of the book-case in the hall, and the experiment was not an out-and-out success.

My father, however, fed my imagination by the stories he told me. He would come in last thing, when I was tucked up in my nursery for the night, and for a few spellbound minutes produce the next instalment of a story he had begun many nights before. His invention never failed, and I never wanted the stories to end, and had to have them told again as soon as possible. He used to take me with him when he went out with the dogs in the morning, and as he walked up-river past the Sailing Club and the meadows, or crossed the river in the punt and struck out for Winter Hill and the water-logged land that lay at its foot, known as Cockmarsh, I would demand another instalment, another story, perhaps from the series *Richard and the Wishing Cap*, and ply him with endless questions about the extraordinary things he told me. One story in particular caught my imagination: he pretended that Winter Hill — a bare, steep chalk ridge that offered very little cover for anything, let alone fabulous monsters — harboured a genuine dragon. My father's stories seemed better, more satisfying than the stories in Andrew Lang's fairy-books, because they always had something to do with the world I lived in; but I appear nevertheless to have developed a slightly sceptical turn of mind fairly early, and I could never be quite certain that my father wasn't having me on. I waited anxiously for the dragon to manifest itself, but still not even a puff of smoke came out of gorse-thicket or blackberry bush. And then one day the cat was let out of the bag, literally, when I read my father's ballad on the subject, which appeared in *Punch:* the dragon was nothing but

A cat, a tortoiseshell mother-cat!
And a very diminutive cat at that!

It was typical of my father's attitude towards his family that he used us all quite shamelessly, and to the delight of his large circle of readers, as material for the verses, and sometimes even for the prose pieces, which appeared every week in *Punch*. For some weeks he encouraged Beatrix to tell him stories on their walks together, which he would then rearrange a little and, imitating her own highly individual spelling, serve up to *Punch* under the title of *Stories for Uncles*. The game was finally given away by one of the uncles, who told Beatrix of the plagiarism that was going on, and suggested she should be sharing in the proceeds; my father, however, turned away her wrath by pleading a hard-working author's poverty and the difficulty of paying for all the animals' dinners. I have reason to remember one example of this habit of his very vividly myself. During the first war he had started a series of sketches in which we all appeared under aliases but in very familiar surroundings. In one of the sketches he described how he took me up to London one day — I must have been nine years old — to buy some rare stamps for my collection at Mr. Gibbons's famous stamp shop. He embroidered a little, but the story was substantially as it had happened, and his readers guessed it. During the course of the next few months, in spite of the fact that it was wartime, stamps poured in for me from all over the world, beginning with the Fiji Islands, then from Australia, Africa, India, Barbados, Dominica and the Falkland Islands. I was overwhelmed by this stroke of luck far exceeding my most heated dreams, and became so spoilt by it that I was thoroughly disappointed when a week passed without more packets of long-desired exotic specimens rolling in. Perhaps, too, the episode sowed in me the seeds of a dangerous belief: that the printed word can work miracles.

The fact that our childish adventures and imaginings, and the antics of our dogs and cats, were so frequently written about made us feel that we lived a privileged life, on an enchanted island of which my father was Prospero; a feeling that continued into my school days, for several of the masters at my preparatory school, Summer Fields, were fans of R.C.L. Nothing could exceed my own boundless admiration for his works. There were two sketches in his book *Sportsmen and Others* which I read over and over again before I reached my teens, convulsed with noiseless merriment on the nursery floor or in the bathroom where I had locked myself. They were called *The St. Bernard*

Puppy and *The Black Kitten:* I doubt if a father has ever given his son more pleasure than I derived from these two sketches. He had, however, made his name as a writer of light verse, chiefly with his rowing poems, but later also with his animal poems. Nearly all the rowing poems belong to an earlier period in his life, before his marriage, when he was already a legend on the tow-paths of university rivers, when he founded *The Granta* at Cambridge and edited it for seven years as a nursery of talent which later blossomed forth in *Punch* and elsewhere, boxed, fenced, travelled as a special correspondent to distant Balkan wars, went to America to coach the Harvard crew and changed the whole atmosphere of amateur sport in that country,* and made himself that enormous circle of devoted friends by the magic of his personality which long after he was dead I would see reflected in the eyes of strangers who, having discovered that I was my father's son, came up to tell me of the memories they cherished.

When I took up rowing at Eton, my father was beyond giving me any practical example or coaching advice, confined as he was increasingly to his chair and limited in his exercise to the very shortest outings with his beloved dogs. He had, however, given me my first lessons in sculling in the skiff — lessons I should have known how to profit by if the same ambition had stirred in me as had fired him in the days of his youth. At least he infected me, as he infected all of us at Fieldhead, with the regularly recurrent leaping fever of excitement about the Boat Race. Every year we grew more and more tense as the day approached, listening as if our lives depended on it to the prognostications of the experts at the breakfast table. I really believe it was the most important day of the year for my father, a great spring festival and consulting of omens: if Cambridge won, the crops would grow; if Oxford beat them, the future seemed dangerous and dark, only to be redeemed perhaps by the triumph of a Trinity or Leander crew at Henley later on. My father had also loved boxing, and believed that every boy should know how to defend himself scientifically with his fists. I tried dutifully to follow his advice at school, but after a few furious bouts in the gym it was evident that as far as the science of fighting went I was unteachable, and the plan was dropped. As far as

* There is an amusing echo of this in *The Personal Letters* of the late President (F. D.) Roosevelt. In 1897, at the age of fifteen, he wrote to his parents from Groton: "Dear Papa and Mama, last night Mr. Lehmann, the English coach, gave us an informal talk on rowing. He went to Cambridge with Mr. Peabody, and, as you probably know, he is about the greatest authority on rowing in the world."

rowing went, it was not only that the dreamier pleasures of the river appealed to me rather than the arduous, and that when I reached Cambridge I found that rowing must be a wholetime devotion to which learning and poetry had inevitably to take second place; but also that my father's reputation as oar and coach was so overshadowing a legend that I felt deep down that I could not possibly compete with it.

I may have given the impression that my father was the spoilt son of a prosperous family, indulging himself throughout his life in all he liked best, without any other thought or responsibility. He certainly lacked the driving ambition that might have brought him, with his manifold gifts, to more serious fame as an author or as a public figure in the professions; and that easy-going side of his nature was a constant source of annoyance to my mother, with her strong New England sense of the importance of career in a man's life. This impression, however, would be wrong. He was keenly interested in politics from his early youth, became a fervent admirer of Gladstone, and had already stood for Parliament, though unsuccessfully, before he married. With his instinctive sympathy for the victim and the underdog, his belief in fair play and his ever-present awareness of social ills in the mid-Victorian England in which he grew up, it was natural that he should become a Liberal; one of those radical Liberals who in our own time have found their political home in the Labour Party, but are never quite easy about the dogmatic side of Socialism or the inevitable conservatism of the Trade Unions within the new pattern of society. In his day all, or almost all, was still to be won; and I believe that a small voice of conscience was always urging him to do more to push reforms through, to justify his own full and fortunate life.

In all this he found a strong ally in my mother, whom he had met in America during his trip to coach the Harvard crew, at the home of his old Trinity friend, Frank Peabody. She came of the most independent puritan New England stock — on her mother's side descended from John Wentworth, Lieutenant-Governor of New Hampshire between 1717 and 1727, and on her father's from the English family of Burnham — and was of decidedly liberal outlook. She and my father clashed at their first meeting over votes for women, but evidently her forthright progressive views as well as her charm and looks conquered him, and on his next visit he persuaded her to marry him. In those days notabilities received favours that seem almost unbelievable in our egalitarian society: my parents found a special suite had been reserved for them on the Cunard liner in which they returned to England, and a special private coach was attached to the train from Paddington to Bourne End by which they completed their honeymoon journey, all without any intervention on their part.

Very soon after they had settled into their married life at Fieldhead, the Boer War broke out. My father had found the brash imperialism of the end of the century very little to his liking, and in common with most of his political friends, who had long suspected the motives of Cecil Rhodes and the financiers with whom he was associated, thought the Boers were being very shoddily treated, in a way that did no credit at all to England's name. He stood against the war, and many of his most eloquent and impressive speeches at the time were devoted to a destructive criticism of the war party. My mother remembered stormy political meetings in which the audience got completely out of hand. Though the anti-war party had far greater popular support in the Boer War than in either of the world wars that followed it, it needed some courage to speak publicly in sympathy with the Boers while the fighting was going on, and there were occasions, notably one at Brighton, when he and my mother and others on the platform with them were obliged to make hurried and rather undignified exits to avoid rough handling. During this period Lloyd George offered him the editorship of the *Daily News*, when it changed hands and reverted to its former radical and anti-jingo course from which it had been deflected by the policy of E. T. Cook. He became a director with a financial stake in the new set-up, and accepted the editorship, but only for a short period which he found exhausting physically and nervously. There was continual tension under the surface, and finally, after a series of intrigues behind his back, he threw it up on a point of principle: he was determined that nothing should go into the paper of which he had not approved himself — but the manager thought otherwise. Curiously enough, he had as his assistant editor Harold Spender, brother of J. A. Spender and father of Stephen Spender, with whom I myself was to become so closely associated in the literary world.

These rankling disappointments were finally medicined by the landslide of 1905–6, in which he was at last returned as Liberal member for the Market Harborough Division of Leicestershire. He was popular, he was held in some esteem by Sir Henry Campbell-Bannerman, and everything seemed to point to a distinguished political career; but unfortunately he was already fifty, and his unceasing athletic exertions had been more of a strain on his physique than he realized. He contested the election at the beginning of 1910, and was again returned, but in the crisis of the Parliament Bill and the election that followed so soon after, he decided he could no longer stand the pace and withdrew. More practically, he had to consider the expense — no small matter in those days before M.P.s were paid. Only a year after his first election to Parliament he had suffered a serious financial disaster. Always generous and rather careless about money, he had entrusted his affairs to a stockbroker friend who was unfortunately more of a gambler than he realized. One day in 1907 he came back to Fieldhead from London to break the news to my mother that this man's speculations had failed, and that they were — at any rate at first sight — all but ruined. The shock to my mother was overwhelming: she was expecting another child, and a few hours later I was born.

My father's political life was thus more or less over by the time I was old enough to be aware of it. But the whole atmosphere of Fieldhead in my childhood was impregnated with political feeling. I saw my father as a crusader for the destruction of intolerable woes: it seemed to me, unconsciously influenced by the strong radicalism of the early days of *Punch*, and already beginning my reading of Dickens and troubled even more by another book I discovered in the library, Charles Reade's *It's Never Too Late to Mend*, impossible that a right-minded person should be anything but a reforming Liberal. Little enough comes back to me now of the two elections in 1910, when I was only three years old, apart from the fever of canvassing which infected all of us children; but I do remember the Liberal rosette I wore in my tubby brown overcoat during a local by-election a couple of years later, and the pang of misery and disbelief I experienced when we heard that the rival Conservative candidate had been elected in spite of all our efforts. I retired, baffled, to the *Children's Encyclopaedia*, which so eloquently taught the march of progress and justice throughout the centuries.

On more than one occasion between 1910 and 1914 my father was urged by his Liberal friends, officially and unofficially, to return to the fray, but he always refused, even when it was suggested that he should stand again for Market Harborough. His name, though I doubt if he knew it at the time, was on the list of those Liberals who were to be made peers if the House of Lords remained immovable about the Parliament Bill in 1911, and I think it possible he might have accepted this honour, with the less arduous political duties attaching to it, if it had come to the point. One day in July 1912, as he was waiting at Paddington to catch his usual late train home after a *Punch* dinner, he ran into Winston Churchill, who was off to join the Fleet by the midnight express. Churchill had been brought close to him in the work of the Liberal Association in earlier days, and had, when at the Home Office, appointed him to a departmental committee which looked into the way aliens were treated on their arrival in England. They chatted together on the platform for some time, Churchill enlarging on the pleasure he derived from his association with the Navy. "Why don't you come back?" he asked my father. "You ought to be in the House; come back to us. We're doing very well, *very* well! I think — a strong policy at home and abroad."

The truth was that my father valued too highly the freedom he had found to devote himself to his growing family, his rowing interests and rowing friends, and his work for *Punch*. Not that the weekly dinners at 10 Bouverie Street were always as merry as outsiders might have imagined. The real business of the dinners was to settle the political cartoons, and the Liberals were very much in a minority. "A very stodgy discussion," "very sticky last night" are phrases that continually recur in my father's diary, and on one occasion "all of us became quite intolerable." Nevertheless the cartoons were agreed on and friendships were maintained — by a hair's breadth.

I was never really able to discover what my father's religious beliefs had been in the past, but neither he nor my mother ever tried very hard to make us devout Christians. We were, it seems to me now as I look back on it, left to make up our own minds about the metaphysical side of Christianity, but encouraged to recognize Christ as the greatest and wisest of ethical teachers. Strict, old-fashioned church-going, in a Liberal household, and especially in a family descended from the author of *Vestiges of Creation*, carried with it a slight stigma of an ultra-conservative squirearchy. At the same time, by a curious contradiction, my parents were anxious that we should put in an appearance in church as often as possible on Sunday mornings, though they scarcely ever went themselves; I fancy this may have been more a social gesture of kindness towards the succession of nervous young curates who came to Bourne End, and the vicar we were all so fond of over at Woburn Green, Mr. Unsworth, a fine classical scholar admired by my father as much for his learning as for his human qualities. They did not, however, stand actively in the way of some of their zealously religious friends in the neighbourhood, who showed some concern that we should not stray too far from the flock; but it was my father's attitude of gentle teasing towards them, sharing the joke with us sometimes in secret winks, that I fear won us, and not their missionary endeavours. On one occasion, however, my mother joined forces with them to put on a Christmas Nativity play: my sisters were attired as angels behind and beside the crib, and I had to play the cock in a curious costume with wing attachments for me to flap as the curtain went up. I flapped them; but the "cock-a-doodle-do" that was supposed to come out at the same time went wrong in my desperate stage-fright, to the immense delight of the audience and my own shame.

My father was Beatrix's adored hero, while I (there was always some rivalry between us) was unbreakably attached to my mother and rushed to her as my champion in any crisis. I was haunted by the fear that I might lose her in some way, and one of the most terrible moments in my childhood was when she slipped on an icy front-door step as she was about to enter the car one Christmas Eve, and fell in a dead faint. I can still remember the scene: the servants and my sisters rushing towards her, the coachman helplessly twiddling his thumbs and exclaiming "She's a goner," and myself lingering paralysed with trembling lips in the background. But my anxiety about her did not need any such dramatic disaster to reach crisis point. She often used to take me with her in the Cadillac when she went for a fitting at her dressmaker's in Maidenhead, Myra Salter. . . . There was even something strange and sinister to me in the name. More sinister were the dressmaker's assistants in their tightly corsetted black dresses, who came out to greet her as we arrived. She disappeared within, and I was left alone in the car with the chauffeur. I could endure ten or fifteen minutes of her absence, though with difficulty; but after that my fears began to mount, and with every further minute that passed became more and more out of control. I pictured the most lurid things happening to her: the innocent, hard-working assistants turned into fiends who had trapped her in their den, torturing her, dancing indescribable rites of obscene triumph over her dying body in their black dresses, with Myra Salter herself directing the operation with my mother's long hat-pin in her grip. Perhaps she had even been turned into a rolypoly pudding, like the unfortunate Tom Kitten in Beatrix Potter's story. By the time she came out again, if the fitting had been a particularly long one, I was in paroxysms and beyond consolation.

It must, I think, have been these Maidenhead ordeals that made me dislike shopping with grown-ups so violently, and inspired my first poem, written at the age of three or four in a little book my nurse had helped me to thread together out of cartridge paper. I unearthed it as I was looking through a drawer of childhood remains before starting this book, and found on the first page, in a large uncertain hand, the following terse and simple lines:

SHOPPING
SHOPPING
NEVER
STOPING

The spelling may be faulty, but I do not think I could ever write a poem of more concentrated expression, of more naked emotion.

« 7 »

A FOUR-YEAR gap separated me from Beatrix, the youngest of my sisters, and I was very conscious during my childhood of being the baby of the family. My sisters had parties, expeditions and mysterious occupations from which I was excluded, another world which loomed large in my imagination and made me determined to compensate for with a private world of my own. Thus I became rather a solitary, and grew even to welcome the days when my parents took all three sisters to London to see a play or for some other special occasion; it was an adventure I enjoyed to the last crumb to eat with Julia and the staff in the servants' hall, munching a large slice of the caraway seed cake that always appeared on the table there; and I had the garden to myself and could wander up and down the flower border and lavender beds talking to myself, as I looked for my favourite butterflies and bumblebees, without anyone coming to laugh at me or tear me away.

My pleasure in my own company did not, however, go very deep; I could easily be shaken into a rage of resentment at not being asked to take part in all the exciting things my sisters did, and for the sake of peace I was sometimes allowed to be present, though my childish ways must have been very tiresome to them. I remember there were great sweet-making sessions, presided over by Helen, and I was sometimes allowed to help mix the ingredients, and got myself into a gloriously sticky mess, even though I didn't produce many sweets. More thrilling still were the literary sessions, when my sisters retired with pencil and exercise book to write poems and stories, and met afterwards to read them aloud to one another. I couldn't hope to compete, but I minded terribly if I was not allowed in at the final recitation. In my father's diary for May 22, 1910 I find the following entry:

The three girls became afflicted with literature this morning. I had to make composition books for them and they then set to work, Helen to write a story, Rosie a poem and Peggy a fairy-tale. John distinguished himself by getting lost after lunch. I found him reclining on two chairs on the Boat-House lawn. He had wandered down on his own and had taken his cart with him. . . .

I have no recollection of this precise incident, but I think it quite possible that alone on the Boat-House lawn that afternoon I was suffering silently from my incapacity to emulate my sisters, and resolving that I too would one day have a composition-book and write something in it of which my father could be proud. Perhaps the poem I have just described was born that day.

My sisters also founded a Fieldhead Debating Society, at the inaugural meeting of which Beatrix distinguished herself by a passionate and tearful defence of Mary Queen of Scots, arguing that her execution was especially heinous because it left her dogs and cats without a mistress. From those sessions also I was excluded; but the worst exclusion of all was connected with one of my father's great friends and fellow-Liberals, Wedgwood Benn (later Viscount Stansgate). He was adored by my sisters, and whenever he arrived to stay was dragged off by them at once to take part in their games and to hear their confidences. Only a week after they became "afflicted with literature," as my father describes, they hatched a momentous plot with him. He invented for them a secret society called The Butterfly League, for which butterfly badges were devised and even writing paper printed with a butterfly design on it. Once a year they went to visit him at the House of Commons, had tea on the Terrace and then retired to one of the rooms to conduct their impenetrable business. As soon as I got wind of this — everything was cloaked in the utmost hush-hush and my sisters were remote and tight-lipped when I tried to find out — it appeared to me unbearable that I wasn't a member myself. I made such a fuss, even shouting at night in my dreams about it, that eventually, it may even have been a year or two years later, it was decided that I should be allowed to join. A special initiation ceremony was invented, which consisted of a kind of ritual tickling of my leg and removal of my shoe while Wedgwood Benn and my sisters chanted a doggerel rhyme together. If I had not been made so nervous by all the mysterious hints of the ceremony beforehand, I might have taken it in good part; but I suddenly felt they were all enjoying themselves far too much at my expense and that it was not a true initiation at all. My soul was pierced by the realization that in spite of the hideous ritual I should never, never know what went on in The Butterfly League, and instead of the gurgles and chuckles they expected, to their horror I turned paler and paler and almost fainted away. For years after, the sight of a piece of the League writing paper aroused in me anxious thoughts of failure and outlawry.

In spite of this, I sometimes got even with my sisters, as when one April Fool's Day I managed to substitute hollow eggshells for their real eggs on the breakfast table; and I was always ready to be the most fervent admirer of what they did, provided I wasn't kept at arm's length. They were particularly fond of dressing-up and acting, and plays to which parents, staff and whatever visitors happened to be in the house were summoned succeeded one another with hectic frequency. To me these plays, when I was allowed to stay up to see them, were the supreme thrills, and no one in the audience took them more seriously, was more utterly purged by pity and terror than I. In fact while the rest were doing their best to suppress mirth, I would be silent, tense and wide-eyed.

The time came when I staged shows for myself, in my own nursery. Someone had given me a box of conjuring tricks, after a visit with my father to Maskelyne and Devant which had inflamed my ambition, and I remember an evening when the long-suffering staff was persuaded to form an audience yet again, this time for a display of my skill in the conjuror's art. I was suitably attired in a red dressing-gown and a sugar-loaf magician's hat which Beatrix had prepared for me; but it proved a terrible occasion. Over-confident, impatient to prove my ability to put on a performance as good as any of my sisters', I had hopelessly misjudged my proficiency and my understanding of the instructions. Trick after trick went wrong, I grew more and more flustered and incompetent, and when I could no longer disguise from myself that the under-housemaid was giggling hysterically, the footman purple in the face with suppressed laughter, and old Dickie, my grandmother's lady's-maid, enjoying herself hugely with a commentary that became more and more cockneyishly caustic, I broke down and abandoned the stage.

Looking back on my relations with my three sisters, I am amused to see how guilelessly, in my devotion, I opened myself to their teasing and the traps they laid for me. This persisted even after I had gone to my preparatory school, and I remember one morning at breakfast during the holidays when they teased me so much that I fled the room, scarlet in the face, shouting "Sirens! sirens!" Nothing, of course, could have delighted them more than this romantic cry of anguish. The teasing came mainly from Rosamond and Beatrix; Helen was always a little remote, not in the least snubbing or unkind, but just too far perhaps on the further side of a gulf of years quite to belong to my country. I think also that Helen preferred the real world to the world of imagination in which the rest of us spent so much of our time, and actually wanted to be grown-up as soon as possible — a thing incredible to me at the age of six or seven. Rosamond I idolized. She was well aware of this, and took cruel advantage on one occasion. All three of them were having a tea-party one day to which Dolly, the head-gardener's daughter, had been invited. As usual, I was excluded, but hung about the stairs irresistibly drawn and longing to know what they were doing. Suddenly the door of the day nursery opened, and a solemn cortège emerged, Beatrix and Dolly carrying Rosamond, who had her hands folded over her breast and her eyes closed in the attitude of death. Gloomily they marched past me: I tried hard not to believe that Rosamond had just died, but it all seemed too convincing even for my scepticism, and I bolted downstairs in despair to tell the terrible tale to my parents. I had hardly got to the baize door below when loud peals of demon laughter from Beatrix up above made me realize that I had been had again; but my heart went on thumping loudly for a long time.

Rosamond's early literary efforts filled me with enthusiasm: I was peculiarly susceptible to her high romantic manner, and wallowed in the doomful emotions and mystic intimations with which she filled her copybooks, listening spellbound to her thrilling tones as she read out poem after poem. All through my time at my private school I continued to think these poems the most marvellous I had ever known; and I possess a thin book carefully bound by myself, in which I copied out in Indian ink, in what I thought the most elaborately beautiful of scripts, three of her poems, illustrated in gold and coloured with illuminated titles and initials, an achievement on which I lavished hours and hours of devoted labour. The titles of the poems are *Defiance*, *Epitaph* and *Enchantment*, the last-named the most highly wrought and embellished with a black, red and gold butterfly and a spider web for the opening verse, which reads as follows:

> Come fearfully among these forest trees;
> Prithee, look not behind; enchantment creeps
> Among the stealthy shadows with the breeze,
> And cloud on purple cloud, in swaying deeps

The noiseless branches sweep around us — swing
　　To blind our eyes: beware!
See how the dank, dead-scented brambles cling
The crawling grass would have us in a snare. . . .

My fanatical belief in her work was rewarded later on when I began to write poetry myself, by her unfailing willingness to read and judge, with the most gently critical encouragement, my own adolescent renunciations and soul-awakenings. But I never achieved anything as lush as *Enchantment*, though I often wished I could; indeed, I think that until I was about sixteen it was my supreme model.

My relations with Beatrix have already appeared in various incidents: though we both had decidedly independent natures we were very much together, and I could rarely resist acquiescing in her leadership in all kinds of daring and mischievous exploits, inspired partly by her reading of boys' adventure stories, but also by her extremely fertile imagination. Beatrix — or Peggy as she was always called, at her own desire, and after a pony we kept — was also the comedian of the family, with a gift that developed early for making extremely funny drawings of everyone we knew and everything that went on in our family circle, and a knack of burlesquing all the village characters. Her imitations were ruthless. I loved any kind of comedy played before me, and I think I must have been the ideal audience: much of my childhood seems to have been spent in entranced amusement at the comic performances of others. My "Aunt" Amelia, sister of our cousin Liza Lehmann, the composer, had a genius for impersonation and ludicrous invention, and Beatrix had clearly inherited the same family strain.

Beatrix liked to score off me with my dreamy ways and innocent gullibility; but I don't think that, apart from sudden fits of rage and bitter vows to get even, I bore her any malice. In fact I was a willing slave to the fantasy life she led. On one occasion she built a "shop" in the bushes, carrying about fifty bricks two by two across the garden for the purpose, and stocking it with all sorts of sweets, ribbons, buttons and odds and ends: and it even had a bell, hung on the berberis bush, which one rang as one came in. I became an eager customer, and my father having presented me with a sixpence, I rushed to the "shop" with it and was given in exchange exactly one acid-drop. As the price of a bag of acid-drops (my favourite sweets) in those days was about a penny, I was grossly swindled; but so delighted was I with the "shop" that this did not occur to me at all. On another occasion, during the war, she built a "field-kitchen" in a great pile of earth in the Lovers' Walk. I followed the construction of this marvel with hypnotized admiration, and was promised the first soldier's meal that came out of it. At last one evening a plate appeared of roast potatoes: they were dry, shrivelled, blackened, smeared with ash and heaven knows what else, but I gobbled them up with pure enjoyment, as if they had been produced by the finest chef in the world. Helen's sweets; Rosamond's poems; Beatrix's roast potatoes; what in grown-up life has ever seemed so unflawed by any fault as these master-creations of my sisters to childhood's eye of faith?

« 8 »

My godmother, Violet Hammersley, played an important part in the childhood of all of us, and never forgot a birthday or a Christmas. She was the mistress of Abney, the romantic riverside house behind its high walls next door, to which she had come as Arthur Hammersley's second wife soon after my mother's arrival from America. With the raven hair and features of the classic ballerina, a dark musical voice and a strong natural sympathy with the dramatic and passionate, she might, we always thought, have made a famous career on the stage. As it was, all her artistic feeling went into her private life and the entertainment of her friends. Her imitations and impersonations at a moment's notice — sometimes in charades with my sisters or my Aunt Amelia — were transformations, displays of utter possession by the part she had adopted, that left me open-mouthed, and sometimes even a little frightened. She had an immense knowledge of French and English literature, and had, I believe, a considerable influence in forming the taste of all of us. Wonderful above all were the evenings when she read aloud. Reading aloud has always seemed to me a more difficult art than most people imagine, perhaps because in my estimation no one, excellent though my father and mother were, has ever approached the skill of my godmother. Never for a moment could my attention wander as she read chapter after chapter of some famous novel or biography, with just the right variation of tone and the right amount of dramatization and voice-change for the dialogue. If LeFanu's *In a Glass Darkly* and De Quincey's *Murder as a Fine Art* have always haunted me, it has been her doing. A little later a lasting love of Max Beerbohm was implanted in me by her performance — which I obliged her to repeat again and again — of *No. 2 The Pines* and *Going out for a Walk* from *And Even Now*. Her children — tall

Christopher with the look of a romantic Italian nobleman; mischievous David, with whom I was later at Eton, and my own special intimate, Monica, the youngest — were our constant playmates in every kind of game of hiding and pursuing and dressing-up; David in particular leading us on in wild games of Red Indians, building wigwams on the lawn, from which he and Beatrix would emerge, feathered and painted and uttering blood-curdling whoops. There were also rare, exotic trips in the gondola and the sandolo, which were kept in the Abney Boat-House; for Arthur Hammersley had a Venetian gondolier, Giulio, who came every year for the summer months. As a wedding present, he gave my mother four of those brass sea-dragons that one sees on the sides of gondolas in Venice, to be used as supports for fire-irons; two of them are at this moment serving the same purpose in my London house.

« 9 »

IN the years before 1914 my father ran Fieldhead lavishly, with an ample staff which lived in a busy territory of its own behind the green baize door downstairs and the swing-door at the end of the bedroom corridor upstairs. As so often happened in big country houses in the old days, the children were freemen of both front and back territories, and it was inevitable that the leading personages of the staff should loom large in my world. Besides, there were many lumber-rooms, store-cupboards and cellars at the back that had the most exotic attraction for me. For instance, leading out of the kitchen there was a dark little room where the cook kept all her stores: icing sugar, preserved cherries, candied peel, cooking chocolate, and the labelled tins of sultanas, currants and raisins — a cave of inexhaustible delights, all the more alluring because of the shadowy depths into which it stretched. Nearly as good was the larder on the other side of the tiled passage, even more jealously guarded, into which I would sometimes tiptoe to survey the long rows of bottled fruits and jams on the higher shelves, the Virginia hams of which my parents were particularly fond and the remains of cold joints, stewed fruits, jellies and puddings of the day before. It was a risky business, gaining entry into that larder; there had to be an especially active bustle in the kitchen before one could feel certain that one's stealthy turning of the handle would not be heard, but the risk seemed worth taking, not for any quick gobbling of delicious tit-bits, but rather for the aesthetic pleasure of contemplating all those cool and waiting joys of future meals. Further down the passage, the cellar was marvellous to me, not for the rows of dusty wine-bottles, but because it housed Helen's model railway, powered by a tiny engine which gave vent to a shrill whistle when the water boiled and set off on its always catastrophic journey with hectic speed; and the magic-lantern which under my father's control had brought terror to my earliest years with all too convincingly coloured slides of the history of Bluebeard. But most compelling of all was the telephone-room, so called because it had a huge, immovable early box machine in it beside the cupboards where extra crockery and glass were kept; it was not, however, the telephone on which my imagination feasted, but the safe, which took up the whole of one side of the high, dark room. Whenever I knew that James was putting silver back there, I would rush down to get a glimpse of the inside of the fabulous treasure-house before he pushed the heavy door back into place with the muffled "whoof" of escaping air. On the baize-covered shelves I could see all sorts of leather boxes for the knives and forks and spoons; beside them silver and gold salt-cellars, sweet-dishes and cream-jugs, boxes that were never opened and I felt certain contained glittering marvels beyond price, and on the shelves that were far out of reach of my small arms all manner of inscribed trays, challenge cups, goblets and bowls, some of them wedding presents to my parents, but most of them trophies that my father had accumulated as oar and coach through all that vista of mythical years before I was born.

The pantry in which James lorded it was at the foot of the back stairs. I liked to slip into it as often as I could to peer into the drawer which contained hammers, screwdrivers, clippers and piles of nails and screws of every sort and to watch James polishing the silver under the old Parliament Clock; but my welcome was uncertain, depending on James's temper, which generally in its turn depended on the amount of work he had to do, and I would often creep out again abashed and spend my time instead gazing at the system of bells just outside. In general James was kind, indulgent and sentimental; and he would often give me a penny to run off to the sweet-shop and buy myself a bag of acid-drops. His large, bald, humpty-dumpty head emphasized his pomposity when he was in an authoritative mood; it was not, however, the children who suffered from these moods so much as the young footmen and the cook, who had to listen while he droned on instructing them, laying down the law through the kitchen hatch, and reminiscing about the exalted past of Fieldhead before *they* had appeared on the scene. He was my father's oldest servant, except one, and with that one a long, jealous feud was maintained: my grandmother's lady's-maid, Dickie, who used to come down from London to spend several months with us every year. Though very old, she was the cleverest and neatest of needlewomen, and my mother was always anxious to have her in the house. She also sometimes accompanied the family on its migrations, whether to Brighton or to Paris, as the most experienced, the most widely travelled, the most reliable and most cuttingly amusing of retainers and companions.

Dickie had a room reserved for her, right at the top of the house, with perhaps the most attractive view of all the rooms overlooking the garden. In my memory it is always there that I discover her, though glimpses come back of her brushing my mother's hair under the lamplight in the boudoir, of my going to see her off at the station at the end of her visits, where I would find her settled in the little tin-roofed waiting-room at least half an hour before the train was due, and of her proceeding slowly round the garden paths on a summer afternoon, very small, very sedate, and enveloped in her black, bugle-covered dress and black bonnet. Perhaps I remember her best in her own room, because she kept there a little bag of sweets and would offer me one on my visits. While I sucked the toffee or acid-drop beside her, her head slightly nodding, bent over her needlework, she would talk to me, asking me about my own pursuits with a grave and delicate attention, occasionally slipping in a mocking remark about Julia or James as quick as the flickering tongue of an adder, or telling me long stories about my grandparents and the house in Berkeley Square, my father's youth and his exploits in the years before his marriage. How I wish I could remember those stories, for with her sharp cockney eye she had missed nothing in those days, and in her mind, so clear and retentive even in her old age, were stored all the lost chapters of the family past, which after her death I realized too late should have been written down. She would also tell me about her own life, and into her voice there would often come a note of great sadness. She was called "Dickie" because her first husband's name had been Dickinson: he had been the father of a boy, the apple of her eye, who had died in childhood long, long before. After Dickinson's death she had married a cabinet-maker from Bohemia called Martin Slezina, and she had actually gone over to Austria-Hungary to share his life. It was only later, after he too died, that she returned to London and entered our family life again. She had outlived all her own people, and was entirely alone: her sister Louisa, who had for a time acted as cook and who, like some other great artists, could not face supreme tests of her skill without the almost incapacitating support of the gin bottle, had also died before my time; but in addition to her old-world dignity and exquisite manners Dickie had astonishing courage, and lived out her last years in determined independence. She really preferred, I think, her solitary existence in London to Fieldhead, and her visits had to be most carefully negotiated by my mother: only during the Zeppelin raids of the First World War would she suddenly descend upon us by train and reoccupy her room upstairs without any preparation.

The tension between her and James was at its greatest in the servants' hall. She despised him for being woolly-minded and slow in the uptake, for she herself was quick and clever and could never be caught out; but she was also jealous of him for being so close to my father, and in addition, so to speak, the president or chairman of the staff. He sat at the head of the table and officiated with the joint, while the cook sat at the other end. On those days of happy exile when I had my meals with them, I can remember that her remarks, in the very formal atmosphere of a servants' hall of those days, were always brief and tart, slightly frightening to the housemaids and kitchenmaids, and often puncturing James's ponderous harangues with a neat and scathing efficiency that confused but did not deflect him.

James himself did not live in the house: he had the back part of the little red-brick lodge by the gate at the end of the drive, a mysterious region which seemed rather forbidding: it was, I believe, only after James's death that I penetrated upstairs to his bedroom, and found, to my surprise, a large and well-filled book-case in which many of the books written by my father's friends — and therefore James's friends also — were prominent. I think this book-case was his secret compensation for Dickie's thrusts, for she did not, as far as I know, read at all, and I can imagine that when worsted in some wordy contest with her, he might retire to this room and turn over the pages of a book written by one of the guests he had looked after at Fieldhead, and reflect with satisfaction that all this was beyond her world.

The front part of the lodge was inhabited by Mr. Goodman, the head-gardener, and his family. He was a remarkable man, of far too keen an intelligence to have spent his life in such a position. Nowadays a man of his mental energy and understanding of the world would be bound to have a proper schooling and rise to a position of wider and more important responsibility. Goodman, however, had learnt all he knew of literature, politics and science from books he had bought or borrowed from the house, from newspapers and conversations with my father and his friends; he was tied, too, by a patient devotion to an ailing wife rather older than himself and very much his intellectual inferior. He was a man of independent thought, a natural philosopher. In my childhood a zealous churchman, always keen to assist the local curate in his work, the mass cruelties of the First World War made him feel that something was wrong at the root with conventional religious teaching; gradually he turned against religion altogether, with a violence in proportion to the fervour of his former conviction, and no one in clerical garb dared to approach him. In the 'thirties, when he was already over seventy but displaying a vigour that many men of fifty might envy, he had gone so far that it was only one step more for him, dismayed by the collapse of the Liberal Party, to become a Socialist. He read the productions of the Left Book Club avidly, and followed the fortunes of the Republicans in Spain with fervent attention. At dusk sometimes he might be encountered crossing the lawn after locking-up the Boat-House and the potting-sheds, simmering with a murderous rage against the established order of things and prophesying rivers of blood; which did not prevent him remaining an excellent gardener and on the best of terms with all of us. In his old age, after the Second World War, when he had crossed the border of ninety, I think he had seen through the apocalyptic pretences of Communistic Socialism as well; the story of the growth and changes in his views and the reasons for them would have been an unique document.

On the last day before we left Fieldhead for good I went over to his cottage, and while we sat in his front parlour he called to mind his own early days and my father's early days at the house. He had come up from Somerset as a boy, and told me that there were men in his family who could remember the bad old times of the press-gangs, and how the rumour would spread through the villages of their approach and all the able young men would take to the hills and the woods. He had been employed first of all at Abney, next door; the hours were long and he was always expected to be available, Sundays as well as week-days, so when he was courting he used to slip off at dusk and walk many miles up-river to where his girl lived, and come back at dawn; and one day he came back with the girl herself. It was a hard life, he said, but "we were a stronger lot in those days." He was skilful and knowledgeable as a gardener, with a little more than the usual head-gardener's strain of independent obstinacy in his make-up, and a considerable pride in the garden, which he often reminded me had originally been laid out by one of the chief men from Kew. He liked to be consulted about garden fêtes and functions and put in charge of them, but he was quick to feel that the neighbourhood was imposing on my parents with incessant requests for every kind of dance, old folks' tea-party, jumble-sale, raffle and sports gathering to be held in the Pavilion or on the lawn. He would be found muttering about "a herd of elephants" and "litter everywhere" and "two-legged birds having got into the strawberry beds," and I used to think sometimes that he would gladly have wrung the necks of some of the most persistent charity-planners — as he wrung the necks of any unfortunate starlings or blackbirds that were caught trespassing under his nets. He seemed rather a daunting figure in my earliest childhood, ever watchful to see that small fingers were not surreptitiously closing round too many ripe figs and nectarines; but he could be wheedled to relent, and would lead me to a special monster strawberry that he had spied lurking under its leaf, or produce an extra-juicy fig he had just plucked from the top of the tree. And on autumn and winter mornings my garden explorations always led me in the end towards his potting-sheds, through the archway in the nectarine wall to the yard where the rubbish-heaps were. Perhaps in the sheds the three other gardeners — old Stacey and young Bob and Godden, who wore his Boer War medal-ribbons on Sundays — were drinking their tea and munching their bread and cheese among the spades and forks and trowels. I would peer through the cobwebbed window of Goodman's own special shed and, finding him there, tap on the window and beg for apples; then he would lead me into the store-room beyond, and I would gaze with wonder at the heaped tiers of apples of every sort, yellow and red and greeny-red and huge ones striped like a dahlia and the little hard, sweet russet ones, and go away triumphant with two or three stuffed into bulging pockets. His special domain, however, always seemed to me the greenhouses; and when I think of him now, the characteristic picture that comes to my mind is of his spare, erect form of medium height, with straw hat slightly tipped over his forehead, busy with his potted bulbs, his tomatoes or his chrysanthemums in one of the two contiguous greenhouses. As I grew older, we became firm friends, and on my way back from a walk along the river with the dogs I would look in on him there: he would tilt his straw hat back and his eyes would twinkle, and we would discuss the latest family news or the political events of the moment, or the prospects of peace and war, and he would make his shrewd comments and his dark prophecies; and with doom ringing in my ears, but stimulated and amused, I would leave him again to his pruning and potting and watering. And I am also haunted by an image of him shadowy in the late summer twilight, with the darkening mirror of the water behind him, locking up the changing-rooms and the big roller doors of the Boat-House, suggesting to my imagina-

[41]

tion some imperishable country god in humble disguise as in the oldest legends, and the river beside him flowing like Time into the night.

« 10 »

MUCH of my boyhood seems to have been spent taking Great Danes, spaniels, mastiffs, sealyhams and Pekinese dogs for walks. It became, in fact, an accepted thing that whenever everyone else was busy, or pretending to be busy, it was my duty, whatever I was doing, to take the dogs for this exercise. I grumbled that I was becoming nothing else but a kennel-boy, but most of the time I enjoyed it, not merely for the walking itself, but also for the stimulus I found in it for a dreaming mind. I must admit that there is something in Max Beerbohm's criticism of inveterate walkers, that the further they go the more inane they become; but taken in a leisurely fashion, alone, and for the first hour at any rate, there is nothing like a walk for stirring those obscure processes of the mind out of which poems and stories are born. When the urge to write was on me, a long walk by the river or into the woods would plunge me deep into a fantasy life, where whole trilogies of novels, epics in twenty-four books and poetic dramas in vast cycles would hover cloudily before me; dreams only to be disturbed when a swan was seen angrily bearing down on an astonished Pekinese, or a Great Dane rushed off to battle with a bristling enemy dog descried in the distance.

I was never a bird's-nester, though I remember Beatrix leading me in hushed excitement to some thrush's or blackbird's nest she had found in a remote part of the garden; but as I grew older, perhaps between my sixth and ninth year, butterflies, moths and insects of every sort became an absorbing passion with me. I grew to have an expert knowledge of the differences between the species and the peculiarities of each one's life-habits. I learnt to distinguish every kind of caterpillar and knew the plants it was likely to be found on; I kept several varieties in boxes, the furry ones giving me rashes all over my hands; I bred silkworms feeding them on the leaves from the mulberry-tree behind the Pavilion, and unwound the delicate golden thread of their cocoons on Heath Robinson machines constructed from old cotton bobbins. On walks over the hills with my sisters, while they were looking for wild flowers, I would spot from several yards away a rare blue butterfly or even a chrysalis hanging under a branch; I dreamt of a farm of giant caterpillars of the emperor moth, death's-head hawk moth and privet hawk moth, but somehow my parents guilefully managed to prevent me filling my nursery with these monsters. Nothing intrigued me more than the mystery of their changes, and sometimes when guests were present at luncheon or tea I would break into the conversation and volunteer embarrassing information about the number of thousand eggs a particular kind of butterfly could lay in a minute, or describe its mating habits with an innocence that had entirely failed to relate them to the appearance of babies in human families. Second only to butterflies and moths, bees, dragon-flies and beetles fascinated me. At an early age I was given several volumes of J. H. Fabre's works translated into English, and I read them over and over again; I got hold of a copy of Maeterlinck's *Life of the Bee*, and my thoughts obsessed by his description of the nuptial flight of the queen bee, began to look for queen bees everywhere, with lamentable results in multiple stings and dashes to the bottle of Pond's Extract in the bathroom cupboard; I kept water-beetles in large, weed-filled bowls in the night nursery, but this had to be stopped because the housemaids were terrified by the way the beetles, lifting the handkerchief with which I had covered the bowl for the night, would suddenly take flight from the water when the blinds were undrawn and zoom noisily round the room — one old char-woman who had come in to help with the spring-cleaning went off into a dead faint one day when this happened. I persuaded my father to give me a microscope, and for hours together would explore the strange ornamentation of moths' eggs and the minute jewelled scales that came off the wings of red admirals and peacock butterflies. I think my parents began to regret that they had encouraged me to take an interest in Nature; but when my schooling at Summer Fields began, this interest gradually faded and died out, and the volumes of *Butterflies and Moths of the British Isles*, with their ever-marvellous colour plates, lay neglected at last on the nursery shelves.

While this passion was raging, other inevitable passions of boyhood awoke in me: the bicycling craze, the stamp craze, the Meccano craze, the fretwork craze and the electricity craze. I mastered a bicycle early — in my fifth year — impatient to join my sisters in the sport of accelerating round and round the outer paths of the garden until one came to the final free-wheel past the flower-border, "Bicyclists' Dashing Hill" as it was named by us; so intoxicated did I become with this pleasure that at one time scarcely a day passed without my returning to the house and my disgusted nurse or mother with bleeding and scratched knees after yet one more spill. I have already described how the stamp craze landed me in one bad scrape and gave me one unexpected transport of delight. The collecting of stamps is always supposed to be an education in geography and history, and I think it did teach me quite a lot of miscellaneous and moderately useful information; my favourite stamps, for instance, from the point of view of romantic pictorial beauty, were those issued by the Austrian Government for Bosnia-Herzegovina, and I thus had a clear idea at once of the part of the world where the tragedy of Sarajevo occurred. Stamps also opened inviting windows on to the immense variety of foreign landscapes, jungles with elephants and tigers charging out of them, gigantic rushing rivers and mountain waterfalls, totem poles grinning by wigwams, weird-plumed birds perching in tropical surroundings, and savages waving spears below the well-known profiles of King Edward and King George. I gazed with wanderlust waking in me at the stars over the deep blue sea-coast view, with its sombre mountains and full-rigged sailing-ship, inscribed Correos de Costa Rica, at the improbable river steamers on the stamps of the Sudan Postage Tax and the weird sea-craft of Labuan; I repeated over and over again the romantic names of Afrique Occidentale Française, Sénégal, Mauretanie, Côte d'Ivoire, Oubangui-Chari-Tchad, Chamba State and Nicaragua of the wild desert mountains; but looking back on it now that the passion has entirely subsided — it was long dead before I left Eton — what astonishes me is the unpredictably fickle and irrational nature of the lust for possession. When stamps were the rage, the supremely desirable treasure, to be coveted above all other possessions, was a dull little three-cornered stamp without perforation from the Cape of Good Hope, which entered my day-dreams suffused with mysterious glamour and kept me awake at night; yet only a short while before, the same glamour had attached to a fat and ugly caterpillar with an absurd spiky tail, which if I could only find it would evolve for me into that beauty of all beauties, the privet hawk moth; and I was conscious that for some of my friends a rare bird's egg, totally useless and not necessarily among the most pleasing aesthetically, exercised the same immeasurable attraction. Now that I care nothing at all for the spikytailed caterpillars or for the little three-cornered pieces of paper, I am left bewildered by the meaning of it all. And yet I wonder whether I have really become very different, for I have to admit that a rare first edition of some famous author excites my desire to possess with almost as great a violence; and as any book-collector knows, the mysterious glamour has nothing to do with beauty of typography or elegance of format.

My adventures with electrical bells, lamps, magnets and batteries and coils within coils were fired by the presence of the machines in the woodshed, where we made our own electricity in the days before the local system arrived. I can remember watching it at work, rather awe-inspired at its humming and chugging, while Bob or Stacey sat beside it and chopped the logs in the semi-darkness; and I can remember the lights suddenly dimming in the house when it went wrong, and James hurrying to the telephone-room to fetch the green-shaded oil-lamps that were always kept in reserve. They were also stimulated by the magazine *Hobbies*, which, derided by my sisters, nevertheless seemed to me the guide to endless possibilities of power and miraculous achievement. Reading *Hobbies*, and the more lurid *Scientific American*, bundles of which were sometimes sent over by my New England cousins (who became real engineers and real inventors), I began to experiment with all sorts of chemicals and test-tubes; pieces of Meccano littered the floor, still refusing to make the cranes, bridges and dynamos that the pictures promised me; toy trains came to disastrous collisions in tunnels painted outside to imitate a mossy bank while boiling water spilled all over the linoleum; boxes and brackets laboriously prepared with blunt carpentering tools failed to stick together and stuck to my shorts instead, and at last the fatal fretsaw, first a hand one and then, joy of joys, a big treadle machine worked with furious zeal by my short legs, began its busy, footling activity, transforming beautiful pieces of satin-smooth wood into hideous imitations of crude lace.

And yet all this messing and making and collecting, all these attempts to perform simple magic and to foster the magic of nature, left me unsatisfied. I wanted to do more, I did not know what; there was an itch in my hands, in my mind, to shape and change and discover in ways far beyond what I had already attempted; I wanted to master and make use of everything around me for some end that was never plain to me; all the sights and sounds and smells of nature urged me to possess them, to preserve them, to transform them into myself; I kept nature note-books and laboriously described in them my minute observations about hips and haws and oak-apples and bumble-bees and newts and frog-spawn, but I always abandoned them, feeling that they were an inadequate substitute for some art of communion or transmutation that still eluded me. The Meccano nuts and bolts rolled away under the chest of drawers, never to be retrieved, the fretsaw snapped for the last time and was not repaired, the bits of string dangling in strange solutions with crystals collecting round them were thrown out of the window, the beetles were returned to the pond and the female red underwings laid their myriad eggs uncounted by my scientific eye. Perhaps books were the answer; all this was a long process, spreading over many years and stretching into the first holidays from Summer Fields; but books, words, gradually seemed more and more to be what it was all tending towards.

« 11 »

WHEN I was six years old, we made our first trip abroad together, to Château d'Oex in the mountains above Montreux. I remember very little of the journey, for the good reason that I was fast asleep nearly the whole time. I even slept through the arrival in Paris, where Mother broke the journey with Rosamond and Beatrix while the others went on by sleeping car. I slept a deep sleep of the abysm brought about by all the excitement that had preceded the journey; I was shaken, I was stood on my head, I was shouted at, but nothing would wake me up. The only picture that comes out of the depths is of a huge lake stretching away into the peaks of the sunset, and dwindling below us as the funicular slowly grinds up the mountain-side. It cannot refer to any other time, and the lake must have been Lac Leman; but it is strangely dissociated from anything else in my mind, and is nearly all that remains of that summer in the Alpine valleys.

Far more clearly remembered, because so often visited, with layer after layer of memories superimposed one on another, are our holidays in the Isle of Wight. We went to Totland Bay for the first time as a family in 1910. My father had not been on that side of the island for twenty years or more: he found it more delightful than he remembered, and as the visit was such a success with all of us he decided to make it an annual event. An absurd name, Totland Bay, a new little red-brick village without any charm, that had grown up, rather like Bourne End, round a few old houses; but it had everything to make the perfect holiday for children, and from the very first year it established itself in our mythology as a dream island of enjoyment. Every time we went there, we felt we were discovering it for ourselves: it existed only on privileged maps (our maps), it sprang into life only during the months of July and August, and sank back into the sea again the moment we had all left. And there was nothing of the tidy and spick-and-span plage about it: there was always more to find out, new explorations to be made, new treasure-trove to be revealed on that high corner of land facing the sunset that broke abruptly all round in steep cliffs to the sea.

[46]

To begin with, it was approached by a little paddle-steamer, sufficient romance in itself for a small boy. We used to make a cross-country journey from Bourne End to Lymington Pier, to avoid the business of taxi-ing with all our luggage from station to station in London, and changed three times — at Maidenhead, at Basingstoke and at Brockenhurst. It took only about three hours; but to me it was like crossing Africa. I thought about it for weeks before the day arrived, I laid in a store of acid-drops and caramels, I saved up my copies of the *Children's Magazine* and *Tiger Tim's Weekly* and as many other comics as my small funds would run to, and packed them all together with *Jemima Puddleduck* and *The Wizard of Oz* to be read and re-read during the long hours while our trains roared us across the vast stretches of Berkshire and Hampshire; and still it didn't seem enough. Of course I was so absorbed in everything that was to be seen from the carriage window, and the journey was over so much more quickly than it ought to have been, that I never got through more than a quarter of my travelling library; but I never learnt, and did exactly the same thing the following year.

And then suddenly we had slipped on to a new plane of existence, when the little train chugged down from Lymington Pier and the sea-breeze brought us smells at last of salt and seaweed, and we could see the sea-gulls perched on the stakes in the estuary. Everything from that moment on was of fabulous interest: would it be *The Solent* or *The Spithead* that was waiting for us at the landing-steps, with the friendly sailors in their dark-blue jerseys to help us aboard? I ran at once to the place amidships where I could peer down into the oily-smelling, hissing marvels of the engine-room and watch the big pistons beginning to revolve; then up on deck again so as not to miss the familiar landmarks emerging as we gained the sea: the long spit of land to the right on which Hurst Castle was built like a fortress in the desert, and beyond that the jagged advancing rocks of the Needles with the lighthouse at the end, dark and sinister against the falling sun. In those days the pier at Totland Bay was still in use, and after the stop at Yarmouth, where the sailing-boats spread their white wings about us, we went on in the paddle-boat round the point: abandoning buns and cups of strong tea in the saloon below, clasping pails and spades and rain-coats and handbags, we watched the delectable land approach. We could hardly bear not to run down on to the sands at once, seeing all the other children at play there in the golden light, building sand-castles and paddling and trying out their earliest whirling strokes as swimmers; but first our lodgings had to be occupied, with Mrs. Scovell waiting at the door to greet us, beds chosen and bounced on, sand-shoes unpacked and laced up as fast as possible; and then, then at last the wild rush began for a crowded hour of glorious sea-side life before supper, down the cliff through the ragwort and brambles and on to the beach, where the red-haired young man in charge of the bathing-cabins remembered and welcomed us, and our toes first felt the soft yield of the wet sand under them, the foam frothing up round them and sliding away again.

There was something to do every hour of the day at Totland Bay. There was the regular morning bathe, with *petit beurre* biscuits to nibble as soon as we had dried ourselves; the afternoon walk, either over the fields to lonely Colwell Bay that somehow looked so old-fashioned and as if a lady in a crinoline bathing-suit might at any moment emerge from one of the derelict huts, or up the downs and on to the heather, or along the road to Freshwater Bay on the other side; and then after tea a shrimping expedition on the wilder part of the beach where the downs came plunging in irregular weed-grown terraces and gullies towards the sea, and the tide left its mystery-filled pools under the rocks with their wet drooping hair of rubbery seaweed. Each of us had a shrimping-net, mine the smallest and most frequently broken, and would concentrate on separate portions of the beach. Sometimes there would be a shout from Rosamond, summoning us to observe a particularly beautiful sea-anemone she had discovered, or Beatrix would come running to show me a diminutive crab that had caught in the meshes of her net; we pushed the nets through the sand right up on to the ledges concealed by the seaweed, withdrawing them in tense expectation of the transparent little creatures left twisting and skipping in them as the sand and water drained out, with the rare excitement of bigger prawns. Gradually the sun would sink and the light grow more golden, the turning tide begin to swallow up the outer pools, and then the call would come from Julia or Mother to pack up and carry our loaded pails, with constant glances at our prizes on the way, up the long haul of the cliffs and back to our lodgings.

Bathing was a shivering, laughing ordeal; shrimping was as exciting as the pursuit of buried treasure; but perhaps most marvellous of all were the long picnic afternoons on the heather-downs. It was a stiff climb; but when at last the heather was all round us and the great vistas exposed before us on every side, we felt we were on top of the world. Away to the north, across a Solent grown absurdly small compared with our experience in crossing on the paddle-boat, lay the wooded mainland coast — the coast of England, as we liked to say —

with Hurst Castle diminished to the size of a nursery toy, stretching away past Bournemouth distinguishable only at nightfall, when its promenade lights made a winking diamond chain in the darkness, to a misty outline by Poole. If we were lucky, we would see a blurred shape coming out of that haze, and grow slowly larger until it could be distinguished as a Union Castle liner home from South Africa, or one of the smaller Cunard liners that had put in at Cherbourg and could navigate the Solent; then we would hear the deep echoing throb of the pilot-boat start up and see it set out for its meeting with the liner, which would pause in all its majesty almost, it seemed to us up there on our balcony of heather, within swimming distance. It was a tricky channel to navigate, and the biggest liners went round by Spithead entirely out of our view; there was a shifting sandbank in the middle, which in some years disappeared altogether, but one memorable summer had the wreck of a trawler or cargo-boat leaning over it in melancholy dereliction. Then as we followed the sandy paths across the top, where the bees seemed to be blown by the sweet-smelling wind rather than flying over it, marking out a hollow covered with the purple springy cushions of heather for our picnic later on, gradually the silvery line of the Needles would come into view and Alum Bay all sparkling in the shelter of their spears. Up there, on the furthest western edge of the heights, Beatrix, peering into the remains of some old forts built during the Napoleonic Wars, difficult of access, half blocked up, dreamt of tense dawns waiting beside her cannon for Boney's armada to show up over the horizon; while Rosamond with a far-away gaze stood immersed in fantasies of poetry which poured into her mind in floods as purple as the heather that surrounded her. I, meanwhile, was on the look-out for rare caterpillars, particularly for the furry brown caterpillar of the black-and-red cinnabar moth that chewed its way through the lacy leaves of the ragwort; but in later years the scene had much the same effect on me as on Rosamond. I longed to make something of it, to marry it to myself by a poem, or a painting, or a tale of mystery and adventure, to capture everything it seemed to be saying to me, the humming in my senses and imagination, before the experience faded.

The holidays were not complete without at least one pilgrimage across the downs to Alum Bay. In those days the old blackened pier still stood for *The Duchess of Fife* (my favourite paddle-boat) to land trippers from Bournemouth, and sometimes we went in it ourselves. Generally, however, we came over the downs, clutching our jam-jars for the supreme operation of the holidays: the gathering of the col-

oured sands from the towering, crumbly cliffs with their strange mingling of reds and purples and golden-brown. We were busily at work
as soon as we arrived, rubbing the fragments of rock we detached until
they sifted into the jam-jars in strata of our fantasy. Nothing, I realize,
when I look back on it, could be more boring than these jars of sand;
but to us at that time they were miracles of achievement, beautiful
beyond price, and we carried our booty home with loving care, to
stand on the mantelpieces of our bedrooms beside the shells and the
green and purple jewels the waves had made out of broken pieces of
bottle, that gleamed with the effulgence of emerald and sapphire in
our eyes.

Sometimes we bathed at Alum Bay before returning home, with a
sense of danger created by the near presence of the Needles and the
lighthouse, with the sea-gulls for ever screaming round them, and
the tiny figure of the coastguard coming out of his cabin on the edge
of the cliff. And sometimes, sitting among the decaying lobster-pots
and the dried seaweed and the fragments of spars and planks from
some forgotten wreck, my father would sing popular songs and Beatrix would dance to them, dances invented on the spur of the moment,
while we gathered round and applauded. Then back home again, perhaps taking the road instead of the scrambling path over the heather.
This road ran alongside the fields at the foot of the green Tennyson
Downs: another of our favourite expeditions was up to the Cross,
where we could see the cliffs of the whole southern coastline stretching
away to the east, and creeping cautiously forward on hands and knees,
we could peer over the sheer edge and watch the waves boiling and
battering far below at the base of the chalky rampart, with a thunder-
ous roar that echoed on and on whether the sea was calm or rough.

It was only many years later that Tennyson began to mean something to me, and the expeditions to the Cross at the top of the downs to
have something sacred about them. Before Farringford was sold to
become a hikers' guest-house, I had visited it in reverence and love; I
had stood by the Cross and, facing the sea all alone, I had shouted out
loud to the gulls and the grasses as much as I could remember of
Ulysses and *Break, Break, Break*. By that time Totland Bay had already become a half-buried history of childhood; I could no longer remember the features of Mrs. Scovell, that earliest landlady who had
once seemed so formidable and so fascinating, nor remember the name
of the tall, fair-haired boy in his teens who had given me his pet rabbit
to fondle on top of a wall (until I met him twenty years later in Berlin
just as Hitler was seizing power); even the summer soon after the war

when we brought Father there for the last time and shared a house with the Somerset Maughams and played with his daughter Liza, was growing remote. Still, so strangely, the downs and the rocky shore where I had gone shrimping as a child stirred in me that feeling of something undiscovered, something I might understand and penetrate at last with deep concentration and lonely communion, a secret behind the heathery hollows, the cold phantom shapes of the Needles, the mouldering Napoleonic forts and all the wildness beyond the black runway of the lifeboat house, the ponk-ponk of the pilot-boat at night and the myriad twinkling lights of the liner approaching in the darkness.

« 12 »

WE were at Totland Bay in the August when the war came. I can just remember my father opening the papers that morning of the 4th and saying in a rather grim, resigned way: "So it's come, after all . . ."

Immediately the wildest rumours ran through the island, and — to judge from a gently satirical article which my father wrote the following week in *Punch* — the German Fleet was expected to steam up over the horizon any moment, leaving the British Fleet at the bottom of the North Sea. The islanders, having a very high opinion of themselves, were convinced that they would be blockaded and cut off from the mainland, a special naval expedition having of course set out from Bremerhaven to sink *The Spithead*, *The Solent* and *The Duchess of Fife*. Dire famine was prophesied, and almost all of the holiday-makers left at once. We stayed on, however, my father having kept his sense of humour and his sense of proportion, though he was a man of peace and had personal reasons for especially regretting a war between England and Germany; we battled with the authorities over Maria, the kind, black-haired German maid who was with us and whom we eventually got back to her own country through the United States; and we even came again the next year and the year after that. The island changed: there were detectives to watch people going on the boats, barbed wire sprouted everywhere, and the military took over the old Napoleonic forts — which made them even more exciting to Beatrix and myself. Both of us, in fact, had a fine Buchan-ish time during those war summers, as the island was reputed to be infested with spies, and we conceived that Britannia, incarnate to us in the heroic figure of Bernard Partridge's cartoons, had given us the special mission of tracking them down by our own unaided cunning and

[51]

watchfulness. We never, alas, caught one, but we pursued several harmless gentlemen we found walking over the downs alone, creeping through the heather and coming up as close as we dared whenever they stopped or sat down. Everyone in Totland Bay saw the periscope of at least one German submarine popping up in mid-Solent every day, and we waited breathlessly for the stranger to produce a heliograph out of his pocket and start signalling; but we never saw any of our victims make as much as a code-sketch on a piece of paper produced from the lining of his straw hat.

It was only gradually that the war began to make its changes in our life at Fieldhead. My father was too old to join up, though he over-exerted himself with the volunteers, and thereby hastened his final ill-ness, and I had no elder brothers. Beatrix's scouting ardours as Lone Scout White Owl (she had passed herself off as a boy) were intensi-fied when Helen and Rosamond joined the local troop of Girl Guides, and we all felt that Bob, the under-gardener, had become a hero when he was drafted out to France with the Guards. Sometimes Goodman would claim that when the wind was in the right quarter he could hear the guns booming over the Channel; mornings came when my father looked particularly tense and drawn, having heard of the death of a friend or the son of a friend, and a cold gust blew suddenly closer when the news came that first one and then another of the Grenfell boys had been killed. Copies of Hilaire Belloc's *Land and Water* were piled up in the library: they meant very little to me, though I gradu-ally became aware that things were not going at all well and that the cheerfulness of *Punch* was beginning to seem rather forced in the face of the mounting casualty lists. Lady Astor organized a big hospital for the Canadians up at Cliveden, and my mother went to work there as a V.A.D., returning with stories that puzzled and frightened me when I overheard them. She also organized a garden-party at Fieldhead for those of the wounded who were well enough to move about, and one afternoon the garden was filled with young men, speaking much more like my American relations than I expected, in hospital blue with bandaged arms, feet or heads, who grinned at me and applauded me when I won in a raffle a piece of a Zeppelin that had been shot down over the Thames. It was not till the last year that I began to under-stand what was really happening; meanwhile, I thought there was something rather adventurous about the shifts we were put to in order to find enough food, the beet we grew to make sugar, the potato cakes and the maize bread made out of the indian corn my mother had al-ways insisted on having in the kitchen garden. If everyone else made rather a face at the appearance of each substitute novelty, I devoured it eagerly. Like everyone else in the country, we kept hens, and came to long for the day when we could get rid of the intolerable birds; we also made the experiment of keeping two pigs, Marmaduke and Millicent, who were housed in the old dog-kennels. The result could have been prophesied: we became so fond of them that we could not bear the idea of slaughtering them when the moment came. We would gladly have kept them as pets; but with cowardly patriotism we sold them to the local farmer, an act of treachery that disturbed me for many years.

By imperceptible stages only, the war drew everything that had happened before it away to a great distance. Only one event occurred, quite early on, that caused a minor revolution in our lives: the arrival of Belgian refugees to stay with us. Jealous as always of "outsiders," my sisters and I were dismayed at first, but our impulses to plot malice against the new-comers were checked by frequent reminders from our parents that we must be kind to the unfortunates who had been driven out of their homeland by the wicked Huns. We were good, by a great effort, and in the end settled down to accept the sweet and graceful Madame L. and her two small boys, Serge and Fred, as part of our lives. The boys were a little younger than Beatrix and myself in the count of years, but far older in knowledge of the shamelessness of the world. There were games down in the laurels, accompanied by giggles and conspiratorial whispers in which taboos were daringly broken and mutual inspection made of our small bodies. These games were not, as far as I remember, connected with any conscious knowledge or stirrings of sex, and derived their excitement simply from the sense that what we were doing was forbidden, what we were showing was normally veiled, except from our parents and nurses. They even made Beatrix and me recoil rather prudishly in the end and decide that Belgians were altogether too shocking for the likes of us.

When I was about seven I first fell in love. I have a vivid recollection of walking down the front stairs at Fieldhead to breakfast one morning, and announcing the fact with fatuous pride to my sisters, who didn't take it nearly as seriously as I had hoped. The object of my precocious affections was a girl of my own age called Margaret, whom I met every day at school and dreamt of every night at home. How disappointing to have forgotten so much of one's first passion: all I can remember is that we spent a great deal of time in secret conversation with one another, that as often as possible I asked her to tea with me or went to tea with her at the big house in Marlow, summoned by urgent postcards covered with kisses. We talked nearly all the time about the kind of house we should have when we grew up — I pictured it as a glorified dog-kennel or wigwam — what we should put in it, how many children we should have, and what we should grow in the garden. The truth is that the whole affair was not so much a passion as a very serious and practical contract of marriage, based on affinity of soul and mutual interests, as the best marriages should be. Romantic emotion was far from us; but now I come to a startling feature of my development in my eighth and ninth years. Romantic emotion I did experience: but it was for another girl, and at the same time, and without the slightest twinge of conscience or sense of disloyalty. Alas, it was the story of the houses of Montagu and Capulet all over again, and I dared not approach her: for Marjorie's father was the local Conservative M.P. Over the invisible gulf I watched her every movement in the schoolroom with calf eyes of hopeless adoration: she was slim and pretty, with a high colour in her cheeks, and she stuttered. This impediment seemed to me, in some mysterious way, to heighten her preciousness; I longed to come to her rescue when a word, thick with the prickles of impossible consonants, stuck in her throat; I yearned to stretch out a soothing hand to stroke her hair and cheek; but Mr. Gladstone's portrait in the library with ghostly power forbade.

Romantic emotion then boiled over in another direction. Perhaps my passion for Marjorie had made me unconsciously feel that the more impossible the longing the more wonderful it could be; for I fell in love with the young mother of one of the boys who had just joined the school. How it started I cannot remember; but she used to come and fetch this boy at lunch-time, and I have a perfectly clear picture of myself lying in wait to watch her pass. The little paved path from the station-gate ran alongside the upper orchard, which was screened by a hedge of hazels. Behind the hazels in early summer the cow-parsley grew tall and thick; and among the light-green stalks I would crouch, invisible to the object of my devotion, just for the happiness of that one moment when she walked by. When she returned with *him*, it was not the same, for they were obviously too pleased with one another's company, and I would slink out of the cow-parsley to avoid this moment of humiliation. I was late for luncheon, but my eyes had feasted. Her glance had not fallen upon me, nor would she have understood if she had glimpsed the son of the house in his curious lair. She might have laughed — terrible thought — and I came morbidly to treasure the pain that her total indifference gave me.

And then came the day when my bags were packed, my mother standing by checking over again the list of clothes that the matron of

Summer Fields had sent her, and I left home for the first time in my life. And the whole web of childish friendships, passions and dreams was torn away to become as if it had never existed, as I plunged into the strange and frightening element of boarding-school that was to be mine for the next nine years.

« 13 »

I HAD had a fortunate childhood. I had not lacked parental love, I had grown up in the midst of a happy family, even though I sometimes wished I had had a brother; I had had all the playmates and playthings I wanted, and I do not think I had been unduly spoilt. I had learnt to exercise my mind in absolute freedom, and my imagination had been richly nourished by books and pictures and beautiful surroundings, by the story-telling gifts of my elders and their love of music and comic invention. If my father sometimes regretted that I so exclusively preferred reading and nature-walks and mooning about by myself in the garden or in a boat on the river to boxing or any other form of athletic endeavour, he was pleased, I know, to see me growing up so imaginative, so fond of animals and so interested in books and the power of words. Before he died, I had shown at school that I could enjoy games like any other boy and be proficient at them too, even drive a powerful oar through the water and feather it cleanly. At the age of ten I had none of the bruises that sensitive children are sometimes unable to get rid of all their lives, and if the gods had missed out gifts at my fortunate birth, I had yet to discover what they were.

It was too good, of course, in view of what the century that promised so fairly was so soon to turn into, was already turning into outside the magic walls of Fieldhead before I left them. And yet, if it was a lucky life for us in money and love and all the opportunities to develop what was growing inside us, it was not a selfish life: my parents' radicalism was not fortuitous or self-interested, but came from deep conviction and deep compassionate awareness of the social injustices of the time and the suffering of others. We were brought up with the sense that if we were fortunate ourselves, we could justify that good fortune only by helping others, in one way or another, to share it, and to diminish the wrongs that still flourished so rankly in other places and other lives. That sense might lead us, at various times in our lives, to espouse false or foolish causes; it might burn with fitful intensity and show itself in obscure ways; but it was always there, as inescapable as a birthmark.

But even when I have said that, I have perhaps left out the most important thing my childhood gave me. I can only describe it as the conception of a complete order of things; a full world. I have sometimes tried to imagine what it would be like to be the only son of divorced parents, living with one parent, perhaps, with the other parent dead, without books or pictures or the immediately available instruments of every kind of pastime or sport, and isolated from the contemporary stream of life; but I cannot, for it is something too completely the opposite of what I experienced myself. My parents' united life, their well-ordered household and contented staff, of whom we were all so fond; the continual visits of aunts and uncles and cousins, some of them from Scotland and America and Germany; one cousin already in the diplomatic service, one making the Army his career, another going into the Navy; governesses from France and Austria to teach us, and a school for all our friends' children in our own gardens; the week-end arrival of heroes of the rowing world, of writers who were famous in the pages of *Punch*, of artists and musicians and political personalities who had fought beside my father in Parliament for the Liberal cause we held so sacred — all this made our family life seem the perfect pattern of earthly arrangements and Fieldhead the very hub of the world, and for a long time I found it difficult to believe that any other real centre of intense life could exist, or that happiness might have to be fought for jealously and ruthlessly; that there could be people who took any sport but rowing seriously, that men of goodwill could be anything but Liberals of my father's persuasion, that the world could honour any writers more highly than my father's friends or that *Punch* was anything but the greatest magazine in the world. This illusion was the cause of some disturbing shocks in the next decade of my life, and held me back from many experiences I might have enjoyed or profited from; but looking back now I believe it to have been a small price to pay for having swum in so clear a pool of contentment. Fieldhead was indeed a microcosm if not the only one in the universe; and when it all broke up, I knew at least what was lacking, and in many devious ways the impulse, not always understood, has risen from childhood depths in my life, to restore, to re-create a focus of harmony and order, a walled garden of meeting and making.

For break up it did. The old life went on in the holidays, but it was never the same. To begin with, I was not the same: from the very first encounter, school began to change me, developing me in some ways and giving me new horizons, but distorting me in others. And my sisters grew up, Helen and Rosamond going to Girton and Beatrix at her own urgent request to a girls' boarding-school, so that the old al-most conspiratorial intimacy as princes and princesses of a private kingdom could never revive — though it was never entirely destroyed. The war had changed the basis of our lives, had undermined the old river fraternity and confused the old political allegiances; most deci-sive of all, it had finally broken my father's health, and the social life of which Fieldhead had been the centre would not survive against the long years of his illness, and my mother's preoccupation with nursing him and looking after our affairs in his place.

It is strange to pause now, to try to recapture it in the middle years of one's life, to enter a world one had always imagined was securely preserved in memory and to find it is too late, that the picture has faded at the edges, that some of the figures are indistinguishable and later stains have blotted out details of vital importance. On the hills up above Cores End, where we sometimes went for a walk, was an over-grown field in which opened a mysterious deep shaft, the relic of some bygone mine-working of which no record seemed to exist. We would creep through the grass to the edge of this shaft, and throw a stone down: it was several seconds before we heard it strike hollowly on the bottom, which when we peered over was all shadowy darkness. So when I peer into the pit of memory, it is too deep for me to see what lies below with any clear certainty; I can only throw the pebble of an image, word or scent down into the depths and wait for the reverbera-tion it may make. And I cannot be sure that memories which echo up are all of one season or re-composed from fragments of many moments that a mood united. So it is with this final picture that comes to mind and may serve as a tail-piece to the memories of my childhood: I can-not be certain that it has the truth of an instantaneous photograph, but I do know that it has another kind of truth, the truth of symbols. It is the end of summer, and the last dahlias, orange and deep-crimson and yellow, are flaming in their showy clumps in the borders. Down in the kitchen garden the little apple-tree with the earliest crop has been stripped of its load of soft apples with their red-veined flesh, the yellow apples are wind-strewn under the oldest tree on the lawn, and the wasps are prodding their way into the bruises. I am sitting on the dark-green bench under the walnut-tree, which we climbed yesterday to reach the walnuts just bursting from their pungent cases, but now I am good as gold, dressed in my sailor suit, for my Aunt Amelia is telling me one of her funny stories. We are alone there, among the debris of tea, which everyone has finished: James is coming from the back door to carry away the silver tea-urn, and Goodman passes him with a basket full of nectarines for the dinner-table tonight. I can hear the click of croquet-balls from over by the Pavilion, where Rosamond and Helen are playing with cousin Eva, Aunt Amelia's daughter. Under the striped sun-blind of the drawing-room I can just see my mother sitting at her desk and writing letters; and up through the pergola comes my father, wearing his straw hat with the Leander ribbon, accompanied by Lufra the Great Dane and a flushed triumphant Beatrix — for he has just been giving her a sculling lesson. Very soon, for the girls, he will propose a bathe before the cool of the evening; but I shall not bathe. I am still too young. I shall only watch with Aunt Amelia from the raft. I should like to watch and listen all my life.

Lupton's Tower

WHEN I was sixteen years old one of William Morris's early poems, *The Blue Closet*, kept running in my head. I would mutter it to myself on country walks, intone it in my bath and chant it to my friends when the mood came and we were all reciting poetry to one another:

> Lady Alice, Lady Louise,
> Between the wash of the tumbling seas
> We are ready to sing, if so ye please;
> So lay your long hands on the keys;
>   Sing "*Laudate pueri.*"
>
> *And ever the great bell overhead*
> *Boom'd in the wind a knell for the dead,*
> *Though no one toll'd it, a knell for the dead . . .*

I never found any poem of Morris's maturity, no passage even among the vast epics and word-tapestry weavings, that achieved the same quality of pure evocative magic. My secret ear was haunted by the sound of the great bell "between the wash of the tumbling seas" tolling by itself in the wind; for bells have always had this power over me, of piercing through to the most sensitive layers of the mind. The sound of the bells of Cookham Church, floating up-river on Sundays across the cowslip meadows, can still bring memories of my childhood that start up out of the darkness, like nesting birds in the church's own ivy-covered tower, with a swoop and flutter of wings. Tears were in my eyes that wartime Sunday when, after so many years of silence, the bells began to ring again far and near, all over London: nothing could have conjured up more poignantly the sense of mortal danger averted and England returning to her ancient island peace and strength.

The clanging of the bells in Lupton's Tower at Eton also has this deep evocative power over me. Since it brings happiness to mind, I now find it a beautiful sound, though it is really rather harsh and ugly if considered without the interference of sentimental associations; in fact I disliked it quite vehemently at first. My earliest room in College at Eton, which by a strange turn of the wheel was next door to my last room, was in what was known as Sixth Form Passage: my "Election" was so large in 1921 that we spilled out of Chamber, the long room divided into oak cubicles which had housed the newly arriving King's Scholars for centuries, into the august precincts of the boys at the top of the school. I was thrilled to be so close to the bloods and stars and heroes, with their stick-up collars and spangled fancy waistcoats and lounging masterful walk, and thrilled to be in a room so large and (to me) so noble; but there was a fly in the ointment, and that fly was precisely the chiming of the hours in Lupton's Tower. The rooms on that side of Chamber and Sixth Form Passage looked out on School Yard and the long, northern flank of Henry VI's unfinished chapel that joins the classical façade of Upper School at one end and at the other stops just short of the older buildings of College Hall and College kitchens and the Provost's Lodge, in the centre of which stands Lupton's Tower — really twin bell-towers with the Great Window surmounted by the clock face in between; and in my own room I was nearer to the chimes than anyone else of my Election. They were terrible: every quarter of an hour they broke out remorselessly, unmusically, deafeningly loud. My letters home were full of plaints about the difficulty of getting to sleep. I was a light sleeper, and I worried about getting to sleep: it sometimes seemed to me that only a miracle could submerge my consciousness between the brazen quarters. If I was not asleep at the end of ten minutes, I began to anticipate the clanging that would start five minutes ahead, and as soon as that happened of course I was awake and waiting for it. Sometimes, in the end, I would climb up on to my high window-sill and breathe the night air for a few minutes, and try to penetrate the shadows of the dark-green statue, mottled and marked as if it had been dredged up from the ocean bed, of the pious, luckless King, our founder, in the middle of the Yard; until I felt refreshed for a new bout in my battle with sleeplessness.

This sleeplessness might lead to the conclusion that I was a nervy, overwrought boy at that time. I was certainly introspective and imaginative, but I seem nevertheless to have found enormous enjoyment in the extrovert existence of a young Etonian in his first year. At the end of October 1921 — I had been at Eton about six weeks — I wrote to my father:

Chamber Singing is over!! O Heavens! Now I feel more secure and peaceful. But it wasn't nearly as bad as anticipation, in fact when one's first two verses were over, it was rather fun. But the last two days or so have been rather full of excitement, so I'll start at the beginning. On Friday it was a whole holiday and I played the Wall Game after 12. We had the best game we've ever had, mainly because the sides were so evenly balanced. But another good reason was that the "Wall caps" — the things we wear to protect our heads and ears from being rubbed to nothing against the wall — were new and so didn't smell bad. I'm sorry to use the expression, but really that is the drawback of the Wall Game sometimes, the caps smell so foully of sweat. But you needn't repeat that, though it is the bare truth. Then in the afternoon I played fives and in the evening I boxed: so I had rather a good day of it. As I am Senior Fag the evenings are rather full . . .

As I have never been able to sing, the ordeal of Chamber Singing, when the new scholars had to get up and sing a song of their own choosing alone in front of the rest of College assembled round the big fire in Chamber, was grim indeed. The dreaded day had been even more eventful for me than the Friday. Some of my Campbell cousins had turned up without warning and given me an enormous lunch at Rowland's; and I had witnessed that extremely rare event, a goal scored in the Wall Game, and to make it more exciting for me it had been scored by my fag-master Bobbie Longden with the aid of Eric Blair, later famous as George Orwell. "Wasn't it wonderful?" I wrote in the same letter, and added, as if to make sure my parents assented to the proper view of the matter, "It was perfectly splendid. . . . Then as the fateful hour of Chamber Singing drew nearer, I grew more and more nervous, consoling myself with muffins." That I really rather liked it when it took place is proof to me now, as I look back on it, that the romantic charm of College was already working on me; a charm derived to a large extent from the sense of living in history, in a nest of ancient buildings, surrounded by the vestiges of crudely cut names of predecessors long departed and dead in vanished centuries, the sense of belonging to a select body of seventy young people who traced their tradition back through five hundred years to the Wars of the Roses, who had been at Eton long before any parvenu interloping Oppidans appeared, attracted by the fame of the new school and its situation so near London and just across the river from Windsor Castle. Had not each of us had the special privilege of kneeling before the Provost to be "gowned," while he took our folded hands in his and adjured us in the ancient Latin formula to be good, gentle and true? We were proud of our separateness from the thousand-odd other boys in their Houses, and gloried in being thought bookworms, in never having had to pass through the indignity of Lower School, in trailing about in our gowns like bedraggled jackdaws, in having our own privileges and honours, our special places in Chapel, our own inscrutably ancient game in the Wall Game, and — in spite of the fact that the top Collegers always made friends with the most intelligent and socially-minded Oppidans of their own age — in having a kind of brotherhood of intellectual apartness that united the boys at the head with the boys at the bottom of College far more closely than in any of the Houses. Perhaps it was not always so; perhaps it is not so any longer; but I arrived at a fortunate moment. As Cyril Connolly (who was a year or two older than I was and had suffered under the earlier *wicked* régime) has described in *Enemies of Promise*, a revolution had just taken place, and a group of boys had risen to the positions of power who thought the rigid tribal disciplines and taboos of the past were ridiculous, who didn't see why intelligent conversation and friendliness between an older and younger boy should be limited to the brief exchanges between a fag-master and his fag, who thought beatings were barbarous and used the cane only in cases of extreme provocation; who wanted, in fact, to make College a model of civilized society rather than an imitation penal settlement. The Master in College of the moment accepted this rather than welcomed it, I believe; in any case he had, under the Eton system, to work through his Sixth Form and the Captain of the School. It was the latter who was the trouble: a tall, blond, good-looking boy without humour, he was a devotee of the old régime, and it was a fascinating education in politics to see the tug-of-war between the Dictator and his openly anti-totalitarian Senate. Though he managed to devise some pathetic little reigns of terror that collapsed almost as soon as they started, he was thwarted at every turn, to the delight of the rest of College and particularly of the "plebs" in Chamber. Later, when a new Master in College was installed, an attempt was made with his active encouragement to revive the old system; but it never fully succeeded, for too many of us had tasted the sweets of the Golden Age and had learnt to assume that when it came to the point *we* ruled College.

Curiously enough, I became a martinet myself for a very brief period under this benevolent régime in which I intensely believed. I was the top scholar of my year, "head of my Election," and a year later was made Captain of Chamber, in which position I was responsible for law and order and invested with certain minor powers of punishment. I took these responsibilities very seriously, far too seriously — but how can a boy of fourteen or fifteen have the necessary experience and judgement? — and struggled with fanatical obstinacy to keep the larkier spirits among my subjects in check. I was, I think, just, but severe because I did not see how I could keep control if I was not. I was working against my nature and sustained only by this quite unsubtle conviction of being in the right. The result was, of course, that as soon as I laid my duties down I suffered a reaction and became an extreme anti-spartan for the rest of my time at Eton. Saul on the road to Damascus could not have had a more complete conversion.

It was at this time, when I was battling prematurely with the eternal problem of order and repression in society, that I had my first encounter with Cyril Connolly. He occupied an isolated room on the other side of the corridor from my own first room: it was notorious amongst us, dangerous, shocking and exciting at the same time. The perfume of Sin that seemed to rise from it was compounded in my imagination from the curling smoke of Turkish cigarettes, powerful liqueurs produced from secret hiding-places, risqué discussion of avant-garde books that one could never imagine finding in College Library, and lurid stories of the forbidden world of cabarets, night-clubs and dancing girls. Cyril was already fairly high in the school, and under the tolerant College régime of the time did more or less as he liked: one of the things he liked was to invite one or two boys from my Election to come to his study and join the privileged circle of his friends in emancipation. I was appalled by this; I felt responsible for the boys — as Captain of Chamber a certain respect was due to me, but my authority was rather like that of the Paramount Chief of a small African tribe under British colonial rule, and I could in fact do nothing — and I was convinced they were being corrupted by an evilly cynical worldliness, a tone one associated with the faster and more disreputable Oppidans, only worse because much more intellectually sophisticated. No doubt this feeling cloaked a longing to be one of the initiated myself, and Cyril divined it. In any case he was much amused at my studied disapproval: he would stand at the door of his room, slim, self-assured, smartly attired, with a teasing look on his puggish face, and when I passed would say, in a tone which made the simple greeting heavy with malice and mockery, "Well, Johnny Lehmann, how are *you* this afternoon?" How could I answer this provocation from the Devil's emissary? I passed on, head in air, a blush stealing to my cheeks, with as much dignity as I could muster, back to the seat of my miserable authority.

In his book Cyril speaks of Godfrey Meynell as one of the worst of his bullies, though changed later by a severe illness. His claws had certainly been drawn by the time I appeared on the scene, and to me he was a figure of pure splendour, epitome of the Olympian world of Sixth Form and "Liberty." He used to "mess" during my first half in the room next to mine, and would come to borrow my chair every evening for the occasion. I thought of this as a sublime privilege, the chair seemed to glow with some sacred invisible fire, and I could not bear not to be there when he arrived, not to be able to beg him to accept it when he asked in his off-hand lordly way. One evening I was a little late in getting away from a rather more distant classroom, ran all the way and thundered up the stairs to lean gasping against the wall just as he was helping himself to the chair. I could not blurt out my joy, but it was written plain on my face: I think he was slightly embarrassed as well as flattered by this evidence of insensate devotion from one who, though much younger, was already rather larger than he was.

The drama of the chair added its tints to the romance with which the new world of College was suffused for me during those early days. The light of autumn evenings falls with peculiar beauty on the older buildings of Eton: under the darkening rose-and-flame-coloured skies, with the yellow leaves drifting from the elms, the boys returning from practice at the Wall Game, mud spattered on their striped stockings and shirts, huge coloured woollen scarves wrapped round their necks, might have been the young Greek warriors seen through the eyes of a medieval chronicler, as they returned from one more day's heroic assault on the walls of Troy. . . . Then the sound of the shower-baths and padding feet filled the corridors, lights were turned on, meals zealously prepared for fag-masters, schoolbooks brought out and abandoned as friends came in to talk and tease and fantasticate. Two or three times every half we gathered before bed-time in the Master in College's rooms for what was known as Secular Singing. There we sang our favourite songs: "Green grow the rushes o," with its mysterious symbolic presences that had such a hold on my boyish imagination, "Little Brown Jug," which in some curious way I managed to associate with my hopeless hero-worship of Godfrey, the song in which Britons, instead of vowing never, never to be slaves, vowed never to be "marr-i-ed to a merma-i-d at the bottom of the deep blue sea," and the solemn and hauntingly beautiful Agincourt Song, which always sent shivers down my spine as I imagined the victor of Agincourt's mild, unwarlike son looking up towards us from his pedestal in the darkness outside. With him, too, was associated another event that stands out in my memory as part of the troubling poetry of that time. It was the custom that on the eve of Founder's Day, which falls on December 6, the two top boys of the new Election should carry a sheaf of lilies up to King Henry's tomb in St. George's Chapel and attend the evening service there. It was Freddy Coleridge who went with me, and in our top hats and gowns, tenderly holding the bouquet, we trudged up over the river to Windsor, feeling very proud, very young and rather awestruck, to perform our ceremonial act of piety among the flowering stone arches and the tattered banners, the tarnished colours of which we could only dimly make out above the soft golden candle-stars of the choir. I remember that the Chapel was being repaired that winter, and we had to dodge through the scaffolding to find the tomb, which happened at that moment to be covered by a huge packing-case. The same evening King Henry's statue had the traditional wreath put over it; and twenty-four hours later the senior scholars walked in illuminated procession round the Cloisters before removing it. We were back in the Middle Ages: the evening concluded with a great banquet in Hall, and we were allowed to attend the speeches afterwards, and watch from the Gallery while the Pageant of St. Nicholas was played by the Lower Chapel Choir. . . . Years later, I was to think of this while attending the "Krampus" festivals in Austria on the same evening, when St. Nicholas (whom we in England have turned into Father Christmas) appeared, to give presents to the good boys, and the Devil to thrust diminutive birch-rods, painted all over with gold, on the bad boys.

The expedition to St. George's Chapel gave us a strange feeling of escaping from enclosing barriers of school life into a timeless symbolism, a moment in the sky. Another escape we prized was an invitation to breakfast with the Provost, M. R. James: it was an escape into the spacious dignity of the eighteenth century, and it seemed extraordinary that by walking a few steps across School Yard and into the Cloisters one could be translated out of the struggle so completely and be treated as a friend and a gentleman — instead of an ignorant fag who must buck up and learn the rules — not by a kindly visiting relation, but by the highest dignitary of Eton. The spirit of Dr. Arnold, it seemed, had not touched the Provost: the whole modern development of the competitive, tribal public-school system might never have been as one sat at the table of this genial and amusing super-uncle, who gave the impression of thinking all the dreaded paraphernalia of rules and taboos and marks and examinations rather ridiculous; for surely a young eighteenth-century gentleman would know how to behave himself without all that dragooning and denouncing, and would *naturally* want to be proficient in the Classics? . . . The faces of the beautiful young eighteenth-century gentlemen looked out of their treasured canvases on the walls, and smiled their silent "of course." And one knew that one could say anything one liked, provided it was not mean or illbred, about anything or anyone in the school, beaks included, with complete impunity and in complete confidence: the Provost would chuckle, and offer one another helping of bacon and eggs. And then we admired him, too, for his wonderful ghost stories; he enjoyed a discussion of these, and I remember telling him at my first breakfast of the ghost of the nun who had been walled up at the Manor-House (once a priory) at Little Marlow. Above all he preferred to talk about detective stories, and had the reputation amongst us of reading one a day, photographing a whole page on his mind in the time it takes an ordinary mortal to read two lines. And then the clanging of the bell in Lupton's Tower would break in on the conversation, harshly reminding us that it was time to return to earth and the forfeits of the present.

All that was in the early enchanted days at Eton: they were like the upper reaches of a river among delightful and fertile valleys. All too soon the mountains gave way to the plains, and for years one navigated through a flat and dreary landscape, sometimes feeling the floods rise and carry one violently away from one's course amongst the treacherous sandbanks, sometimes baling desperately to keep from sinking as cracks opened wide in the timbers, and still the waters came in; far off in the distance shimmered the famous cities of the delta: achievement, understanding, control; and then the reeds closed in again and the flood sank, and one was lost. I think I disliked myself more than Eton during those years. I suffered miserably from the bewildering stresses of adolescence, from an exhaustion that accumulated out of having worked too hard for my scholarship and then too hard to keep my place at the top of my Election. I suffered too from a philosophic darkness that swallowed me up, in which nothing seemed to have any secure meaning, no beginning or purpose or end, the darkness being filled with relentless questioning voices. But it was not all like that, not all the time; there were compensations, and the begin-

nings of new solidity, the happiness of friendships, and the excitement
of new discoveries in the world of books and the world of art.

I was editing my first literary magazine — unless a mysterious
production, unprinted, called *The Pagoda* at Summer Fields can be
counted — with Dennis Wrangham as co-editor. *College Days* had
been started soon after the war, one number appearing every half or
two during the year. There had been ten by the time the departing
editors handed over to us, and we produced the eleventh in time for St.
Andrew's Day. It was a simple racket. One wrote round to all the well-
known authors one could by the furthest stretch of one's imagination
claim to be acquainted with, and begged them for a contribution; and
they, out of the goodness of their hearts and touched by the schoolboy
pathos of it all, generally found something to send. One then wrote to
all the firms one could think of which might be interested in an advertising appeal to Eton boys and their relations, and, pointing out how
many distinguished authors there would be among the contributors
and how many influential visitors would be reading it on St. Andrew's
Day, or the Fourth of June, suggested they should buy space. To our
never-failing astonishment a large number did, and even bought it
again on the next occasion. The result was that if one displayed
enough energy and a moderate amount of canny business sense, one
made money, more money than we had ever dreamt of falling into our
laps at that time, making possible the purchase of many long-desired
books and pictures, new cushions for our ancient wicker arm-chairs,
new ties for the holidays at Devereux or New & Lingwood and a round
or two of banana messes for our friends. It all went quickly enough,
but it was a heady excitement while it lasted. As far as I remember, the
contributors did *not* share in these profits. At the same time, to be fair
to myself, I must add that it would still have been exciting if we had
made only sixpence — or even lost sixpence. Nearly all intelligent
boys, I imagine, enjoy the chance of making a magazine of their own,
but to me there was the special stimulus of at last achieving something
that I had longed to do since childhood: the beaver had built its dam,
the tom-tit had found its letter-box to build a nest in. But I have to
admit we did not do well enough by *College Days*. Our first number
was a gallant attempt to produce a kind of Eton *Punch*, with contributions from my father's old friends Barry Pain, Archie Marshall and
Alfred Noyes. I think it went down well enough; but I am dismayed to
find that by the fourteenth number, produced in my last year, the
proportion of outside contributions had increased. The names were
splendid feathers in our cap — John Buchan, Rose Macaulay, Eva

Gore-Booth and even the Headmaster himself, C. A. Alington — and significantly enough we had stopped trying to be *Punch*. But why had we not done more ourselves? Our work looks very tame beside *The Eton Candle*, that outsize avant-garde chapbook, bound in boards of the purest Brighton-rock pink, with a postage-stamp area of elegant type to an acre of page, with which Brian Howard, Alan Clutton-Brock and Harold Acton had made the mortar-boards of the staider beaks dance on their heads only a short time before; and tame, too, beside what Peter Fleming was simultaneously making of the official weekly *Eton Chronicle* in a different vein. The truth was that since the departure of Cyril Connolly, Peter Loxley, Alan Clutton-Brock, Noel Blakiston, George Orwell and their friends, the literary stew had gone off the boil in College, the moment of discovery was past.

The chance to buy long-desired books meant for me at that time the works of Bernard Shaw and Lytton Strachey, which I read till late into the night under the bed-clothes with a torch, my mind in a whirl of over-stimulation with all the revolutionary ideas propounded in Shaw's prefaces, and receiving a shock of almost sensual pleasure from Lytton Strachey's style. I lusted grossly after Hakluyt's *Voyages and Discoveries*, having had my imagination inflamed by an early nineteenth-century compilation of ancient voyages — with a delicious musty fragrance of old paper — which I had found tucked away in the library at home; but I was never able to run to Hakluyt, nor to any of the really interesting old maps of which I bought catalogues at the same time, in spite of the super-profits of *College Days*.

Long-desired pictures meant at that time colour reproductions of the works of the Early Flemish painters. I cannot remember exactly how this craze started, but it must have had its germ in a little book we were once given as holiday reading, Arthur Clutton-Brock's Home University Library study of William Morris. I still think it a remarkable work, for its skilful compression and presentation, for its eloquence and clarity of style, and for its imaginative insight; but at that time Clutton-Brock's exposition of William Morris's criticism of modern industrial society and the death of pleasure in good craftsmanship, opened entirely new vistas to me. The effects were profound and long lasting, with many ramifications, leading to the love of printing and the making of books that was as much as anything else the origin of my publishing career.

I bought one day as a prize (the admirable Eton system was to give the prize-winner a book-plate signed by the Headmaster and a chit with which he could choose his own book up to a certain value) a book called *The Early Northern Painters*, an introduction to the Flemish, Dutch and German painters of the fifteenth and sixteenth centuries as they could be studied in the National Gallery. I had discovered a world utterly unknown to me before, as unknown as Australia to Captain Cook when he first sighted its shores: the world of Jan Van Eyck, Robert Campin, Dirk Bouts, Roger van der Weyden, Hans Memlinc, Gerard David, the Master of St. Hubert, the Master of St. Giles, Joachim Patinir — names that gleamed in my imagination with all the brilliance of those exotic birds and flowers and beasts the early explorers of the antipodes found on their unknown shores. I spent long mornings during the holidays in the National Gallery, and bought all the reproductions I could afford at the Medici Galleries and Pulman's shop in the Marylebone Road, collected them in folders and had some of them framed to hang in my room at Fieldhead as well as at Eton.

What seems to me extraordinary when I look back at this craze is that while it lasted I found more to satisfy me in the more obscure and indifferently gifted of these Early Flemish painters than in almost any of the great masters of other schools. To come upon a small and dubiously attributed work by Petrus Christus, or a follower of Geertgen tot Sint Jans or the Master of the Death of the Virgin in a foreign gallery was a fulfilment for me incomparably greater than the first sight of a famous Giotto or Rubens. Standing now in front of some of the most crudely painted of these panels, I am at a loss to understand how this taste had developed so violently in my teens — though my love of the greatest pictures of the school has persisted ever since. I can only try to distinguish the various elements in it. Above all, I believe, I was seduced by the delight Van Eyck and his followers show in landscape and the outdoor view before they had come into their own as independent branches of painting, by foregrounds of lovingly painted flowers and grasses — not a blurred outline or tone among them — and by the exquisite views of medieval towns and river-valleys glimpsed through open windows or between the pillars of porches and arcades in a smokeless air, moments of long-vanished time arrested with such fidelity to nature that I was almost surprised to find the figures in the same places when I looked again, and yet transformed and purified by an artist's vision. I could never have enough of the tiny medieval town one sees through the casement behind Robert Campin's "Virgin and Child," the workmen mending the roof, the woman standing in a shop doorway, the gaily clad horseman and the road winding over the hill beyond the church spire, past the white farmhouse and into the blue-green distance; nor of the landscape of "The Legend of

St. Giles," the misty castles with their pale-red roofs in the folds of the green-hazed mountain distance, and the clump of purple-blue irises and the yellow mullein in the foreground. The wonderful Van Eyck "Madonna and Child" (the Rolin Madonna) in the Louvre seemed to me one of the greatest pictures in the world, not for the important figures that dominate the foreground but for the river view on to which the hall opens beyond, a view so dazzling in its jewelled light and atmosphere, composed with a million precise touches of drawing and colour, that it is like a hymn to the beauty of the world. Today, looking into it again, I see it, with its delight in the world made by man as well as the natural world, as an achievement that would be all but impossible in our alienated modern age, not an irrelevant exercise with which the artist could not resist transforming a solemn subject which bored him, but in fact the *meaning* of the picture, an image of the joy of creation in the birth of its Saviour.

I wanted to express — I did not know what. I wanted to write — I did not know whether in verse or prose, in stories or novels; but words fascinated me, and what they could evoke when cunningly chosen and ordered in the rhythms of a sentence, a paragraph. Learning Latin and Greek, careful construing of Lucretius and Vergil and Catullus (my favourite Roman authors) and Homer and Euripides (my favourite Greek authors), and being obliged to write verses myself in these languages had taught me to narrow the focus of my response and care more and more for the colour and sound and texture (I did not call it that until I read Edith Sitwell a few years later) of each individual word. I had also been greatly influenced by Robert Graves's little book *On English Poetry*, which first introduced me to the ideas of overtones and "under-patterns" in poetry, the manipulation of the letter 's' and the psychotherapeutic theory of imaginative literature. It explained to me, in a novel and stimulating way, why I liked certain passages of poetry and was bored by others; and at the same time inhibited me — from writing reams of bad verse. In fiction I had grown increasingly interested in the descriptive passages: a landscape, a storm, a walk through the woods described with sensitive feeling came alive to me as nothing else on the page. I began to write stories and sketches, but the real object of them was always to paint some natural scene or effect, and my problem more often than not was to fit some plausible story round these passages, to give them a point which was not the real point at all. They were influenced by Walter de la Mare's stories in *The Riddle*, a book which I especially prized at the time for its fastidious prose and the poetic evocation in its descriptions. To his poetry I had been introduced even earlier, while I was still at Summer Fields, by Rosamond, who was always gently trying to draw me away from the *Oxford Book of English Verse* to contemporary poetry. *The Listener* was the first volume of his poems I read, and I can still remember the pleasure I had in the discovery that poetry could make so vivid an appeal to the eye and the ear by such simple means — by a vocabulary where no word seemed to be without its sensuous content and its imaginative overtones.

Besides Rosamond, I had had another unofficial teacher of contemporary literature before I came to Eton, and it was not until I went to Cambridge that I met anyone again to direct my reading and awaken my sensibility with such discriminating sympathy. Leonard Strong became an assistant master at Summer Fields soon after my arrival there. He did not teach English literature, though a poet himself, but I think he soon spotted my greed for reading and my imaginative inflammability. I had also become a kind of story-teller to the school, and in our dormitories at night, assuming my role of "Great White Chief" or "Sosoko" (I cannot any longer think why I chose that name), I spun endless tales of terror and romance to the listening beds. This must have tickled his fancy; I on my side was intrigued to find that he wrote poetry, and, as usual, I was at the feet of anyone who could tell me funny stories and make comic drawings and caricatures for me. When I discovered these gifts in him, I accepted him at once into the sacred company of entertainers which included my father, my Aunt Amelia and my sister Beatrix. I talked to him for hours during our free time on Sundays, and would sit beside him in the playing-fields in summer while waiting to go in to bat, listening to his persistent coaxing that I should get beyond *The Hound of the Baskervilles*, *Prester John* and *She* and learn something of writers who were trying to create a new literature and express a modern sensibility. It was all done very gradually, over several years; but by the time I left Summer Fields he had introduced me to Yeats, Housman, Flecker, Synge, Robert Graves, Rupert Brooke, W. H. Davies, had made me understand something of the mood of the young poets who had been in the war, and of the reasons why one writer was good and another bad. When I protested that he didn't think much of the *Punch* gods of my childhood, he told me that there were people who didn't think much of the gods he had introduced me to either, that there were even more advanced modern writers he hadn't mentioned; a reply which stunned me into silence. For many years after I left he was a shrewd and encouraging critic of my own earliest efforts, and I came to regret that I never found his equivalent at Eton.

Of course I wrote poetry as well as plays and stories at Eton; but though the longing was desperate, the achievement was nil. I could not find myself, even in the precocious imitativeness with which some of my contemporaries managed to fill the pages of Oppidan rivals to *College Days*. Actual verse-making seemed to me appallingly hard, and I got stuck emotionally in the inevitable sentimental nostalgia for romantic friendships, the futility of which I took far too seriously. In addition, I read too much Shelley, not only because the mood of his last poems chimed in with my mood but also because I had become particularly interested in the poets who had been at Eton and in whose work I found a feeling for the familiar and so well-loved landscape of river and lush river-valleys. I used to read over parts of *The Revolt of Islam*, *The Question*, *Spirit of Night*, and *O World O Life O Time* to myself night after night: what more fatal models could there be for a young man trying to write in 1925? Nevertheless, I cannot regret the hours I spent getting to know one of the greatest poets in our language, nor that the fact that Swinburne was also an Etonian drew me to *Poems and Ballads* and *Atalanta in Calydon*. I selected Atalanta's speech beginning "Men and the chosen of all this people" for my own contribution to speeches on the Fourth of June in the year I left; I have re-read the poem again and again in succeeding years, and the better I know it the more beautiful it seems to me, a more astonishing work of genius the more I understand the harmony of its parts, and the problems Swinburne overcame in writing it.

My last year at Eton was also important for two new worlds of aesthetic enjoyment into which I entered. I had become a member of the Shakespeare Society, which was run by Henry Luxmoore. He had long retired from his House and from teaching, but he still kept his home behind the Chapel and also his exquisite garden on a little island in the river just opposite, where I spent many afternoons of peaceful contemplation, reading a book, dropping it to talk to a friend who had also come to enjoy the garden's seclusion, taking up the book again, and brooding on what I was going to do when I left Eton. It was Luxmoore, I think, who was responsible for the strong pre-Raphaelite note that had crept into Chapel and was so formidably challenged by the genuine medieval wall-paintings that were uncovered while I was there; a bent, impressive old man with a sepulchral voice and flowing white hair, he had little humour but great kindness, a passionate devotion to the traditions of Eton and a sincere love of art and literature; I remember him telling me how much he objected to being described as "ring-bedizened" in Shane Leslie's *The Oppidan,* but if his rings were actually few, it is curious how strongly he suggested that impression. The Shakespeare Society was recruited from the top layer of Collegers and Oppidans, and met once a week in his house. He chose the plays we were to read, and allotted the parts; the day before we met an envelope would arrive for each member, which contained a small slip of paper on which was written in a spiky, gothic hand the character to be impersonated. He seldom took a leading part himself, generally confining himself to reading the stage instructions in his slow and ponderous voice, with results that were sometimes too much for us. He did not at all like merriment in the wrong places, as in some of Shakespeare's more salacious innuendos, but as he was growing rather deaf and kept his eyes glued to the text, he was not always aware of it; when, however, we were reading *The Winter's Tale* and he pronounced, with the solemnity of a judge passing sentence of death, *Exit pursued by a bear,* the explosion of giggles that followed was too violent for him to ignore and we were in bad odour for the rest of the session. But we all enjoyed the play-reading evenings, and I certainly benefited from them. It helped me to lift Shakespeare out of that fatal classroom atmosphere — there is something intolerable to the junior British schoolboy about the Forest of Arden and Ophelia floating in the brook — in which for many he remains gassed for ever.

The other world I discovered was that of classical art and its revival in the Italian Renaissance. The flash-point was a trip in a private yacht in the Mediterranean at Easter; but obviously the train had been fired long before, in the gradual growth of my feeling for Greek literature and the civilization of Athens. I remember being rather surprised during my first half at Eton to find that nearly all the emphasis was on Greek and so little on Latin; I was lucky, for in the thirty years since then Greek has gradually been fading out of the schoolboy's curriculum and will soon no doubt be extinct altogether; it is true that I came to feel by the end of my time at Eton that one could have too much of it if it excluded modern history and one's own literature, but I have nevertheless remained unrepentantly of the opinion that without a knowledge of the Classics no one can call himself properly civilized or acquire that finer sense of distinction between the creative and meretricious in his own literature. Weeks, months, years of boredom with Livy, Cicero and Xenophon had not prevented me responding to the Greek and Latin poets and dramatists; and suddenly, in the light and

colour of the Mediterranean and the great Italian museums, it all burst
into meaning and joy.

My sister Rosamond had married Leslie Runciman, and I became
very attached to him. I was invited to join the family on the *Sunbeam*,
which was then in the possession of Leslie's grandfather, the old sea-
dog Lord Runciman, in a trip down the Italian coast from Genoa to
Naples. In the end I went on board at Portofino: the next evening, in
the still, velvety darkness, unseen by us, a little boatful of musicians
and singers slipped out from the harbour to our moorings, and suddenly began to play. The surprise, the warm Italian voices rising from
the obscure water, the gaiety and southern nostalgia of "Santa Lucia"
and "O Sole Mio" cast a spell on me that lasted to the end of the trip.
We put in at Elba, explored the flower-grown ruins of Napoleon's miniature summer palace and made an expedition into the mountains to
see the old farmstead where he lodged for the night when engaged in
secret signal communication with his partisans in Corsica. When we
finally reached Naples, I spent a long day looking over Pompeii and
another in the museums. The statues, the bas-reliefs, the mosaics were
a revelation to me of poetry and harmony, of the world as it can be
dreamt separated only by the hair's breadth of unclouded inspiration
from the world as it is. I fell in love in particular with the marble bas-
relief of Paris and mighty-winged Cupid before Aphrodite and Helen,
and with two mosaic bas-reliefs, one of the young Mercury with a
ram and the other of a draped figure of a young girl called Hope. Unfortunately, very soon after we reached Rome I fell a victim to "Roman
tummy," and was stuck in bed while Lord Runciman was received in
audience by Mussolini, an experience from which he emerged to praise
Fascism, the disciplined ardour of youth and the punctuality of the
trains in the once so happily insouciant land of music, art and wine.
Nevertheless, I managed to see the Sistine Chapel, and returned home
with Michelangelo's sybils, prophets and heroic male figures whirling
in my head amongst the statues and the bas-reliefs.

My state of mind during my last summer half was curiously divided and troubled. The cities of the delta had at last been reached,
but they had an unsubstantial and disappointing look — at least in
certain lights. The charm of Eton persisted, though showing to me
others of its many facets than those I had been so aware of during my
first year. The sense of living in history, of becoming a part of very
ancient traditions, had to some extent faded. It was rather of Eton as a
beautiful setting to grow up in that I thought continually at that time;
of Eton as a place where boyhood friendships were made that one

dreamt of lasting far into one's life beyond its walls; and above all, now that many of the friends of my first year had already gone out into the world and at the same time I had reached the point where I had come to know the most interesting among the Oppidans of my own age, as a place where one was trained to make history, which naturally led into the council chambers where the world was governed and fate was decided. Some people may think of this as a hang-over from the eighteenth century, when Etonians — as the names carved on the walls of Upper School and all those smiling, assured young faces that look out of the canvases in the Provost's gallery prove — ruled England, made its Empire and saw themselves as the inheritors of Rome. It is nevertheless an interesting fact that all through the last hundred and fifty years during which the opportunities of rule have been spread far beyond the jealously guarded circle of the eighteenth-century aristocracy, Etonians have remained prominent, not only in the seats of power as cabinet ministers, governors-general, ambassadors, field-marshals and captains of industry, but also in the arts. It is not easy to give a simple explanation of the discovery that was made during the Festival of Britain, that of the "Hundred Best Books" chosen to represent English literature of this century, more than one in ten were by Etonians. During the brief five years of my own career at Eton, among my contemporaries were a surprisingly large company who were to make distinguished names for themselves in the world of books, including Cyril Connolly, Anthony Powell, Eric Blair (George Orwell), Henry Yorke (Henry Green), Harold Acton, Rupert Hart-Davis, the Fleming brothers Peter and Ian, Alan Pryce-Jones and Freddie Ayer.

My own dissatisfaction was to some extent due to the feeling that I was less well equipped to make a fitting contribution to this tradition in my last year than I had been during my first. I was proud, and could not bear the idea of being second-rate in anything I took up, but the introspective side of my character had for the time being the ascendancy over the aggressive, and I was haunted by the conviction of being a failure. I was in Sixth Form, my reports were good, but I had kept my place at the top of my Election only by the skin of my teeth and an all-round ability rather than exceptional gifts in any one subject. I had got my "Upper Boats" — I was in the *Prince of Wales* — but the Eight was definitely not within my reach. All during my years at Eton the desire to be a poet had grown, but I knew that I had produced nothing that was of any value or even promise; it was all inchoate, and I could not find my proper means of expression. This was as true of my "real" career as of my literary ambitions; I knew I had to have a career while I learnt to be a writer, but the idea of becoming a diplomatist like my Uncle Ernest and my cousin Ronald, a project favoured by my parents at the time, left me cold — though certainly not as icily cold as the idea of going into business.

This conviction of failure was at the same time, of course, largely subjective, an aftermath of adolescence, which is rather like an infectious disease attacking some victims extremely severely and letting others off with hardly a rise in temperature. I believed at the time — and on looking back I still believe I was right — that I had outgrown Eton, and I was full of restless impulses to go to sea for a year — to spend six months as a dock-hand — to be trained as a compositor in a printing-house. I wanted to work with my hands, to rough it and to get to know another kind of life. These impulses may have been laughable, but they were symptoms of a real malady. I do not think my experience was unique. A public school is designed for young boys, but by the time one is seventeen or eighteen the restrictions and limitations of experience (even in such a broad-minded school as Eton) that are suitable for a boy of fourteen or fifteen have become absurdly inhibiting. I feel more than ever convinced now that after the age of sixteen a boy should begin to live the kind of life that he will lead at Oxford or Cambridge, and it seems to me as warping to his nature to be still in monkish segregation and under narrow discipline as to be allowed to exercise that discipline over boys a few years younger than himself. Sex is not the only problem, but it is one of the most obtrusive. The sex-problem in the public schools has been written about again and again, statistically, prudishly, sensationally and sentimentally, and has become rather boring; but it is still there. Two stories may illustrate the absurdly distorted perspective into which sex is thrown for a public-school boy. The first did not occur at Eton, but was told me by a friend at another school later on. He was caught making some rather salacious drawings of naked women. This was of course the most ghastly type of offence. He was solemnly denounced before the whole school, and then flogged. That was the result of a normal sexual impulse seeking a mild, frustrated outlet. If instead his sex had found an abnormal outlet towards his own schoolfellows, he would have been expelled. If in despair he had turned in on himself, he would have suffered appalling guilt and anxiety, with the warnings of his elders and masters that madness and imbecility would rapidly overtake him echoing in his ears. And this at an age when, we are told, male sexual energy is approaching its height. . . . The other story shows the tension generated by the inevitable tendency towards inversion in a society which excludes females and at the same time throws young men of eighteen together with boys of fourteen, worships athletics, and holds up the civilization of Greece and Rome for boundless admiration. The Headmaster, Cyril Alington, a man who delighted in intellectual surprises and paradox, took as the text of his sermon one day in Chapel Oscar Wilde's story of the Happy Prince. When the name of the prisoner of Reading Gaol boomed forth in those hallowed surroundings one could immediately sense the change in the atmosphere. Scarcely any boy dared to look at the opposite pews except in a glazed, rigid way; jaws were clenched, and blushes mounted involuntarily to innumerable cheeks. It was a moment of horror and panic: no one knew what was coming next, and everyone was thinking exactly the same thing. Luxmoore cleared his throat like a thunder-clap, and the ancient Dames in their traditional pews bowed their heads — as if about to be executed. Only Sir Galahad continued to look soulfully out of Watt's picture up near the altar, with a gentle feminine innocence.

One of the most pleasant aspects of Eton for me was that I was never completely cut off from home. Fieldhead was only ten miles away and linked by the river. My mother, and my sisters when they were staying there — for both Helen and Rosamond were now married and Beatrix had started her life as an actress — would often motor over on a Sunday or a half-holiday afternoon and take me out with them; and I managed to get permission to pay many brief visits home in between "absences," and was sometimes even motored over by Marsden himself. This proximity also had its disadvantages: my relatives were apt to appear without due warning, and, growing to feel familiar with Eton, would ignorantly flout some of the most sacred taboos. There was a terrible afternoon when my mother brought Helen's eldest child, my dear niece Maureen, then a small baby, over with her nurse. She came in to find me, and left nurse and child outside with the car parked by the low wall that runs between the yard outside Upper School and the road. No one was allowed to sit on this wall except the members of Pop: an electric wire of privilege, of the highest voltage but visible only to the Etonian eye, ran along it. As I emerged through the gateway of Upper School with my mother, a shock of the utmost consternation and dismay went through me. I would rather have sunk into the ground than see what I did see, and desperate plans of immediate escape and renunciation of my family for ever ran through my head: for Maureen's nurse had taken her out of the car and was encouraging her, with cooing baby noises, to toddle along the top of the holy wall. Nearly all schoolboys are, I believe, hyper-sensitive about the appearance and behaviour of their relatives, but perhaps I was peculiarly so: I remember how I boasted at Summer Fields about the beauty of my sisters and the smartness of the world they already moved in, and the disgrace I felt when Helen came to visit me soon after her marriage with her husband, Mountie, who was wearing — an old deer-stalker hat. But the disgrace about Pop Wall was far worse and far more profoundly disturbing.

Few Etonians enjoyed my special kind of luck in having their homes so near; but all of us as we grew older, with London so accessible and Windsor just across the river, had the agreeable feeling of easy contact with the outside world. And yet we were curiously insulated at the same time. Of the 'twenties as the 'twenties we were scarcely conscious, and I look with wonder at the satires and caricatures of the period which are done nowadays, as at something I cannot have lived through. Monsieur Coué made an almost State visit to Eton and attended Chapel, and everyone went about muttering "*ça passe, ça passe, ça passe*" for some days after, without any noticeable effect on their conduct or nerves. I thought Noel Coward's *Hay Fever* the most glorious play I had ever seen, quite outclassing *Chu Chin Chow*, and fell in love with Marie Tempest. . . . There was a wild evening at the Café de Paris at Bray with Beatrix and Tallulah Bankhead, but I found I was temperamentally unsuited to keep up the pace when the husky-voiced beauty from the Deep South began to be surrounded by smashed glasses. One of my more spirited aunts suddenly took to a one-man, or rather one-woman jazz-band, which she carted about with her everywhere and played with hideous verve — but not at Eton.

The rage for Shakespeare in modern dress had a curious freak progeny at Eton, where, at the end of the Christmas half in 1925, we put on a production of *Androcles and the Lion* in modern dress, in School Hall, with the Matron in College, Miss Oughterson, as producer. I played the Captain in topee and khaki shorts, Rupert Hart-Davis a frighteningly convincing Ferrovius, Peter Fleming doubled Spintho and the Lion, and Quintin Hogg, Megaera and the Editor of the Gladiators.

I went back for my last summer half at Eton reluctantly, having tried to persuade parents and tutors to let me leave. I knew I couldn't get into the Eight, I had won my Exhibition at Trinity, and I felt that the old round of exams in Latin and Greek was a waste of time for me. They won me over by flattering hints of my being a "good influence" in College and of the need of my juniors to be coached by me in the fledgling stage of their rowing careers; also by arranging that I should join the History specialists for half my time, which was at least a novel experience. As a matter of fact I enjoyed it, though I felt that I was marking time in everything except the strengthening of many friendships. I was oppressed by the strange, despairing feeling of having been through huge cycles of experience without getting anywhere at all; but the cycles were in my own thinking and the experience was of the void. In that void neither conventional religion nor social attitudes nor moral values seemed to make any sense at all. If I was still an unhesitating Liberal in practice it was because I hated to see or hear of other human beings in either physical or mental pain. That still rang solid in the darkness, as did the experience of friendship and the experience of beauty. All the aims in life so passionately pursued by so many millions of people seemed to me extraordinary illusions; all except one, the writing of poetry or painting of pictures, because in art there was something that stayed real, resistant to the remorseless inner questioning, when everything else that man made or did was dissolving. It was to art, therefore, that I was drawn more and more, and the conviction was growing in me that Cambridge and the future would be tolerable only if the pursuit of imaginative art took the chief place in my life, if necessary ousting everything else except the need to earn my bread and butter.

And yet that summer itself was experienced as a kind of poetry, and was happy for me because it escaped from the time-pressure and competitive struggles of the last few years almost into an absolute air of its own. Luxmoore's garden epitomized the feeling: one had reached an island garden out of the hurly-burly where one could pause for a precious moment, and through one's melancholy savour something in the circle of one's friends that the past had been secretly distilling inside one, drop by drop. And the garden too was against the background of the river, surrounded by the river, as the whole of that summer was suffused with light off the water. It trembled in reeds and willows and swallowed our limbs and the arrows of the light racing-boats in which we rode into its own substance, as we paused on a cloudless afternoon to gather breath in midstream on our way from Monkey Island or Queen's Eyot, or to rise and fall on the roaring sluices of a rose-festooned lock.

Never had Henley seemed more magical, a poem of rambler roses and ripe strawberries and dark leaves of elms reflected in the ripples of a punt-crowded reach: in the state of one listening to romantic music I watched the eights and the pairs and the scullers flash by to the cheers from Phyllis Court and the Steward's Enclosure, which did not quite drown the hurdy-gurdy tunes of the fairground behind, while the gold of afternoon turned into the copper of evening and the old rowing heroes in their Leander caps climbed out of the launches and conferred together, comparing the battles of the day with the battles of long ago. Never had the Fourth of June seemed more like an echoing ballad, as we dressed self-consciously in our white ducks and our striped vests and little jackets of old-time sailors and tipped our flower-festooned straw hats with their gold-lettered ribbons on the backs of our heads and *Monarch* and *Victory* and *Prince of Wales*, followed by *Britannia*, *Dreadnought*, *Thetis*, *Hibernia*, *St. George*, *Alexandra* and *Defiance*, like the roll-call of a fleet Nelson might have commanded, passed under Windsor Bridge in procession and rowed out of sight downriver to the feast spread out in the meadows.

In the gathering twilight Windsor Castle loomed behind us, dominated by the silhouette of the Round Tower, and we thought of the old, mad king, George III, who had loved Etonians so much and in honour of whose birthday it all took place as it had taken place when he could watch it from his terrace. And then when darkness fell we climbed into our boats again for the great ordeal and triumph, returning for the densely packed rows of friends and relations on Fellows' Eyot suddenly to be revealed to us, a strange sea of motionless illuminated faces in the ruddy glare of the fireworks as we floated by, standing erect in our boats; and the catherine wheels beginning to turn and the rockets and star-shells soaring up above the elms to make their soft twin explosions in sky and river, reminded one young oarsman, holding his breath for anxious balance as he rose to his feet with his seven companions and cox, of regattas long ago when he had watched with his father on the river-bank at Fieldhead for the dance of the coloured stars to begin.

The Dilemma Itself

MANY were the vows that the Lehmann children had made to themselves at Fieldhead to find fame and honour by their deeds in the world of art, music and literature; and now at last, in my first year at Cambridge, a vow was to be accomplished, a dream fulfilled. Rosamond had for some years past abandoned poetry for prose. She wrote several sketches and *nouvelles*, and, with a determination worthy of Althaea, mother of Meleager, cast them on the flames as juvenilia. And then, with Girton behind her, and a new sense of what it was all about and how it was all to be done, she began to write a novel into which she was pouring all the treasures that had accumulated in the bulging trunks of memory and imagination. When report reached us that some of her new literary friends, to whom she had showed her work in progress, thought very well of it indeed, we were gripped with a dread excitement. I identified myself with her to such an extent in her career as an author, that I was as tense, alternating between wild hopes and anxious fears, as if I were writing the book myself; and when Chatto & Windus finally accepted her manuscript, I was as happy as on the day when I won my top scholarship at Eton — indeed far happier, because then I had had a nervous collapse. Rosamond's success was somehow a triumph for all of us, *Dusty Answer* was our book, and not merely because so much of it was an imaginative transposition of the world we had grown up in together.

Encouraged by the acceptance, Rosamond began a new book before *Dusty Answer* was actually published in the spring of 1927. The new novel was *A Note in Music*. Meanwhile proofs arrived of *Dusty Answer*, but I was only able to snatch a few glimpses of them, and had to wait for advance copies to read the whole book. As the day of publication approached, I could scarcely control my impatience to know what everyone else would think of it. Waiting for reviews was an agony: and some of the earliest were lukewarm or even hostile.

A few days later a review of the utmost enthusiasm, written by my father's old friend Alfred Noyes, appeared in the *Sunday Times*. News of the result came to me from Rosamond very soon after:

A letter from Chatto this morning says the Noyes review has swept them off their feet. All the first edition (1,500) is gone, the second (2,000) is ready and they've even ordered paper for a third. The Times B. Club took 300 in 3 days and can't cope with the demand. For the *first* time this morning I had a faint passing thrill.

If Rosamond found it difficult to be thrilled, I was bursting with pride myself, and I think the whole of that summer I walked on air, the world transformed for me by Rosamond's success, our success, our justification. I read the book again and again, and then read it in the miraculous French translation by Jean Talva, and once more in the American edition. I was beginning avidly to assimilate contemporary novels at that time, looking for something that would make articulate and put into perspective the experience and feelings of our own generation, our sense of being cut off from the past by the war and endowed with unique sensibility and revolutionized values we did not expect our parents' generation to understand; and everything else seemed cold, artificial or sententious when I had read *Dusty Answer*. Evidently, to judge from the reviews and the sales and the letters Rosamond was getting, a large slice of the English and American public — and perhaps even more the French public — agreed with me and found that Rosamond had spoken for them as no else had. Cynics who do not know the book world intimately may be inclined to say that this extraordinary international success of a first novel by an unknown writer only proves that readers will believe anything they are told to believe by a critic they are prepared to follow. The truth, however, is that no amount of praise, even of the most hysterical kind, will move the public to read a book they find they do not like: it is the combination of the right praise at the right time with the *right book* that causes the avalanche at the lending libraries.

All during my Cambridge period Rosamond remained the most patient and understanding critic of my own writing, especially of my poetry, in which I was at last beginning to find out what was worth saying in what I wanted to say, and how to say it. She would spot at once when I was using someone else's poetic style (generally Walter de la Mare's) and when my adjectives and metaphors were second-hand or "thought" rather than felt or seen. "You suffer," she wrote to me on one occasion, "as I always did, from a fatal facility. It is so *easy* for us to write. Don't you find that? I personally am only just beginning to find it terribly difficult, and feel a little more hopeful." And again, a little later, when I was in one of my recurrent glooms of indecision about my future career:

I *don't* want you to go into the Diplomatic. I can't bear you to go on being inwardly torn. . . . I am confident that you can make a success of a literary career. It may be struggle, and it may mean never being rich — but you don't mind that. . . . If I can help in any way you know I always will. The great thing is to have confidence in oneself — and I think you have. The *London Mercury* success is a great encouragement. What you'd do well would be to edit a paper. . . .

The little "*London Mercury* success" she referred to was that I had had a poem illustrated by myself accepted by that magazine. I had begun to do wood-engravings; and my first efforts so surprised all my friends, who had never thought of me as having even a glimmering of a draughtsman's instinct, that they urged me to go on. It was a curious sudden outcrop of a vein that failed to prove very rich, but it had a remarkably satisfying and soothing effect on me at a time when my prevalent mood was rather tense and morbid. I acquired a set of linocut materials, found that I enjoyed playing about with them, and quickly went on to wood-engravings, encouraged by Wogan Philipps, who helped me to buy the right instruments and an assorted pile of the little highly polished box-wood blocks on which the engravings are done. Nobody was more astonished than myself to discover that I could make designs and patterns that pleased within the diminutive dimensions of the blocks. I studied everything that I could find about the history of wood-engraving, unearthed in the library of Fieldhead old copies of Bewick's *British Birds* and *Quadrupeds* that had been given to my father when he was a boy, and developed a passion for the eccentric old Northumbrian illustrator's work that all the years of deepening knowledge and appreciation of art and artists have done nothing to destroy. Bewick's vignettes of the life he observed round his Newcastle home, in which he managed in a space no larger than a couple of square inches to convey so subtly the feel of the countryside in all its moods of winter snow, spring rain and wind, and leafy summer sunshine, the melancholy of a troupe of ragged musicians strumming outside the walls of an elegant garden, or the joy of children playing at soldiers in the mud, set me an impossible standard of technical skill; but I also studied the works of modern artists in the medium, which was enjoying a sudden popular revival at this time, and began to see how to adapt their favourite techniques of rich sensuous blacks and fine white cross-hatching to my own ideas. I strained my eyes at it in the end, and had, after several years, to give it up; but not before I had designed book-plates for many of my friends, made a number of patterns for end-papers and cover-papers that I never exploited, and produced a set of broadsheets of my own early poems (of which the *London Mercury* poem was one) with an engraved block at the top and the bottom of the page. I even had a vision of myself, in a moment of manic optimism, as a new William Blake, developing my poetry and engraving side by side in an artistic marriage where each enhanced the interest of the other. Of course I really had no notion at all; as I had had no artistic training, the whole thing was a flash in the pan; but I still sometimes wish that I could pick up my old engraving tools and design tail-pieces for my own and other people's stories — as I commissioned many genuine artists to do when I was editing *Penguin New Writing* and *Orpheus*.

Already at that time my feeling that I could be an artist as well as a writer was starting to fade, and the letters exchanged between Rosamond and myself were more and more occupied with my poetry and her novels. She sometimes told me, after reading the book reviews and the articles I was beginning to get published, that she wondered whether perhaps I ought not to concentrate on prose more exclusively; but the knot of my will had formed round the desire to make poetry. If only I could one day write one lyric that would take its place in English literature — that seemed to me worth more as an achievement than any fame prose could bring me; and in any case I felt that Rosamond had established novels as her territory in a way that I could never possibly rival. It was not only my own admiration for her books that taught me that; but her fans and fan-mail, in which letters of perceptive, heart-warming praise from shrewd critics were mixed up with bedlamite outpourings of hysteria, reckless intimate confidences from unknown pilgrims of eternity of both sexes, proposals of marriage from the Colonies, unsolicited illegible manuscripts from aspiring authors who saw her as soul-mate and star disclosed by Heaven to guide them, demands for immediate cash support and love-sonnets from remote Alpine monasteries. She used to keep the plums for me, and we passed hours of innocent enjoyment in reading (and acting) them over to one another. No prose I could write would ever, I knew, evoke such a response, and it was not only from the fan-mail that I learnt this. Strangers had once come up to me to declare that they had known my father, to lavish on me for a moment a devotion that had started perhaps long before I was born; now began another experience of adulation by proxy, but this time the worshippers were more often very little older than myself. "Are you any relation of the author of *Dusty Answer?*" — "You are the *brother?*" — the fanatical light would kindle in the eye, I would feel as if a bucket of something warm, sweet and frothing were about to be emptied over my head, I was transfixed like St. Sebastian by flying arrows of passion meant for another — "*Ach, wie wunderbar!*" — "*Comme vous êtes heureux, je rêve chaque nuit à votre sœur!*" — "Say, Mr. Lehmann, you sure are the luckiest man in the whole world; when I think that I've shaken hands with Rosamond Lehmann's brother!" And then the identifications would start, and I would be reminded of the little boy in this or that novel who had been sitting up in bed doing his knitting, who had been trundled across the lawn in his pram, who had been danced up and down in the waves by his mother at the sea-side while his teeth chattered, and I would do my best to join in the general merriment and ecstasy. It was hard; but I reminded myself that it was far, far harder for Rosamond; and even when I acquired a little modest and special-ized fame for myself, I believe the pang of pleasure remained in the midst of embarrassment and wounded conceit. But by then I had grown a kind of sixth sense, and could detect in the front rows of a lecture-hall even while I was speaking the harpy who would pounce at the end, and would plan evasive action. I pictured Rosamond's dismay if she had been present herself; and resolved that to be a lightning-conductor of all this emotion was the least I could do.

« 2 »

CAMBRIDGE was for me a great release and new beginning. I floun-dered badly during my first term, broke away, and came back, and must have been a spectacle for my friends of overwrought nerves and spiritual confusion. By the winter, however, I had seen that it was impossible for my University life to be a continuation of my Eton life. I finally abandoned Classics and turned, not to English, which I deter-mined should be my private rather than my official subject, but to History and Modern Languages. And I made the discovery that if I was to be a successful rowing man, closely watched by many an older pair of eyes on the tow-path for signs of my father's flair, I could not devote my leisure to anything else at all. Not without sentimental regret, but with a profound feeling of a burden at last slipped off the shoulders, I gave it up, though at home I still continued to find enjoyment sculling along the familiar reaches in the deliciously light and speedy racing-craft Claude Goldie had presented me with. Alone in a "whiff" I could dream about poetry; walking and bicycling with friends I could talk about it; but it shows the extraordinary hold that the idea of violent competitive exercise has on a boy who has been through an English public school, that I felt I was being rather daring and laying myself open to almost moral criticism in abandoning in one reckless *seisachtheia* rowing, fives, football, tennis, boxing, the hundred yards, the high jump and even the egg-and-spoon race for ever.

With the attempt to be a model public-school boy now finally behind me, I plunged myself with impatient zest into all the intellectual and aesthetic experiences that Cambridge offered. One of the chief of these was the Festival Theatre, which had recently been opened under the eccentric and stimulating direction of Terence Gray. Week after week, and often two or three times a week, I would trudge up the hill with a friend to revel in the modernistic decoration of the three bars, programmes on transparent paper that could be read in the dark, multiple sets, illuminated cycloramas, austerely plain back-cloths with melodramatic spotlighting playing on them, scene-shifters doing their work in full view of the audience, and the continuous bombardment of ideas and contrasts in dramatic style from all countries and periods provided by Terence Gray's bill of fare. Ninette de Valois, with the founding of a British school of ballet still in the impossible future, was choreographic director and produced from time to time a programme of "Dance Cameos" of her own invention. Sophocles, Congreve, Chekhov, Wilde, Ibsen, Shaw, Yeats, Synge, Maeterlinck, Strindberg, Kaiser, Dunsany, Elmer Rice, Capek, C. K. Munro, Flecker and Victorian melodrama were all in the repertoire; and as the theatre's success and self-confidence grew, many young actors were introduced who were later to become world-famous, notably Flora Robson and Robert Donat.

One of the plays that stirred me most was C. K. Munro's *The Rumour*, that bitter, disillusioned play of two Ruritanian states that are precipitated into war with one another by the machinations of sinister political and commercial interests behind the scenes. The atmosphere of intellectual Cambridge at that time was strongly pacifist, there were many younger dons who had been through the war or had had some of their dearest friends killed in it, and admiration of Cambridge's darling poet, Rupert Brooke, was at a low ebb: the memory of horror and the sense of futility and waste were uppermost. I had read C. E. Montague's *Disenchantment*, and I was ploughing through Goldie Lowes Dickinson's study of international diplomatic intrigues in the years immediately preceding the war, *The International Anarchy*. *The Rumour* completed the revolution in my thought against the conventional judgements about war-guilt that I had shared until then; not as yet towards Socialism, which was by no means the implication of Lowes Dickinson or Munro, but to the ideals of the League of Nations. I suddenly saw, or seemed to see, that war might come about, not because one nation deliberately planned it, but because of the anarchy that was inherent in the idea of sovereignty and the unchecked competition of great industrial interests, national in scope and repercussion but controlled by private individuals or groups. Not the Kaiser and the German General Staff plotting to master the world, but the industrial kings instigating armament races and fomenting old hatreds and jealousies became for me the villains of the world political scene. From that time I realized that what had happened in 1914 might happen again at any moment, and became permanently haunted with wardread. I discovered Wilfred Owen, a revelation to me as much for expressing the mood of disillusionment and human pity transcending frontiers that was antidote to Rupert Brooke, as for his experiments in the technical devices of poetry. I devoured R. H. Mottram's *The Spanish Farm*, Zweig's *Sergeant Grischa*, Edmund Blunden's *Undertones of War*, Edward Thompson's *These Men My Friends;* it seemed to me that Joe Ackerley's *The Prisoners of War* led to unanswerable conclusions against modern war; I was deeply moved, even without seeing it on the stage. I tried to get anyone I knew who had been through the war to tell me about his experiences. My chief source was Pitson, a reserved, rugged-faced mechanic and chauffeur who had taken over our old stables and coach-houses at Fieldhead to transform them into a garage and petrol filling station. He used to come to fetch me at the end of term in my mother's Morris. Stimulated by my continual questions, he would describe the Western Front as he had seen it as an army lorry-driver: a steady flow of reminiscences, all the grimmer for being uttered in his habitual undertone and without any dramatic heightening or trace of personal emotion, gradually built up in my mind the picture of that blasted landscape of massacre. I tried not to believe it; I tried even harder to believe that it could not present itself again; but in my heart I knew that I was fooling myself.

I have always hated a passive attitude in the face of imminent danger, and I determined to associate myself with the only immediate kind of positive action that seemed feasible: the exposure of armaments intrigues and the building of a supra-national society through the League of Nations. Such a reaction, however, was out of tune with the mood of that powerful side of intellectual Cambridge which formed a kind of Bloomsbury-by-the-Cam. I do not think that Goldie himself had much hope; but many of his younger friends and colleagues adopted a far more defeatist attitude, treating enthusiasm for the League of Nations as slightly absurd, like putting on shorts and scouting with the boys in middle age. When I look back on it, it seems to me that the Cambridge I knew was haunted inescapably by the old war; it was always there in the background conditioning the prevalent sensibility, with its preference for tragedy and bitter wit, its rejection of cosy pretences and its refusal to accept any criterion of behaviour except one: does your action cause suffering to another?

King's was my spiritual home in the new phase of my life, but I retreated gladly when the gay, stimulating, malicious parties were over to the ample, dignified bosom of my own College. Trinity was too large for the complex web of gossip and scandal that was spun so closely over the denizens of King's, and seemed spiritually as far distant from that animated world as a stately country house in the eighteenth century from the coffee-houses of the capital. Of George (Dadie) Rylands, one of the youngest dons of King's, I saw a great deal. He had long been a friend of Rosamond's and took an incredible amount of trouble to direct my reading in English literature and to give advice about the poetry I was writing. I owe more than I can say to his coaxing, teasing sympathy; when he praised I knew it was because he sincerely admired, when he found fault he did it so gently but with so pure a precision of analysis that it was impossible for me not to be convinced. His *Words and Poetry* was just the book I needed to read at the time: with its emphasis on the importance to a line of the weight, colour and overtones of every single word, it brought me down to the earth of craftsmanship and truth — truth of eye and heart — from some of my windier cloud-wanderings among abstractions and emotional clichés. We used to go for walks together, discussing every poet under the sun, E. M. Forster's and Virginia Woolf's novels and Lytton Strachey's biographies and the works of all the other authors I envied him for knowing in London; and I found that he shared my interest in printing and wanted, as I did, to own a press of his own.

Eddie Playfair was one of the Eton friends who had come up with me at the same time, and gone to King's. Through Eddie, in my second or third year, I came to know the young poet with whom I struck up the most intimate intellectual friendship of my Cambridge years. Julian Bell was the elder son of Clive and Vanessa Bell, a nephew of Virginia Woolf, and one of the most gifted of that fortunate second generation of the Bloomsbury giants who inherited the well-laid-out gardens of ideas their elders had created, and basked in the sunshine of their artistic achievements. Julian was a great, untidy, sprawling figure of a young man, awkward in manner and dressed always in dishevelled clothes with buttons rarely meeting button-holes at the neck and wrists. He imposed, nevertheless, by charm of expression in the smiling, intelligent face under the curly tangled hair, by natural force of temperament and by an obstinate persistence of intellectual curiosity — to which was added a conviction that the arguments he defended had the authority of graven tablets of the law: the tablets of Bloomsbury. He had had a Quaker schooling, followed by a period in France, but Bloomsbury had been his real education. An instinctual power, as strongly growing as a wild thicket of hawthorn and briar rose, was at war in him and never completely tamed by the rationalist ideas that his father Clive Bell, Roger Fry and their friends represented. To act from reasonable motives that were clear to oneself and to avoid confused irrational emotions; to treat chastity and the sense of sin in sexual matters as relics of the barbarous dark, as uncivilized as religious superstition or any of the fashionable mumbo-jumbo mysticisms; to be a pacifist because war was futile and absurd as well as painful and destructive of beauty — all these principles were already inscribed on his banner, which he waved demonstratively in one's face during his first year at King's. And yet he had a passion for nature at its wildest, and the poetry he was writing at that time was remarkable because it was an attempt to let the countryside, the moods of wind and weather and life outside the cultivated human pale, speak for themselves without any interference of the poet's own moralizing thoughts. "We receive but what we give" — perhaps; but if so it was the non-rational intuitive side of his temperament that Julian was finding in nature. As time went on, the struggle in his mind was almost completely resolved in favour of the eighteenth century, in my opinion much to the detriment of his poetry; but I am convinced that if he had lived there would have been a new turn in the struggle and a new creative phase. No one who knew him at all intimately could doubt that he was born to lead in some intellectual sphere: I remember that a French poet who stayed at Cambridge for some time was so struck by him that he exclaimed, "Julian Bell is not a young man like other young men, he is a force of nature."

A letter he wrote to me in the spring of 1929 shows in an amusing way the conflict in his mind between his poetic sensibility and his fear of being found guilty of romantic emotions. He was staying at the Bells' villa, La Bergère, at Cassis:

I am leading a thoroughly primitive and simple life here, which means one has too much of those commodities of civilization of which one has no need, and one has to walk ten miles to get a nail or a box of matches — which is not strictly true, but at any rate near enough.

I asked Michael to let you have *Winter Movement* when he had finished with it: I hope you have it safely. I find it very hard to do any work here. I get conscience stricken about staying indoors, and then in the evenings I become sleepy. However I'm getting my hand in again by translating one or two of Ronsard's sonnets. He is a poet for whom I have suddenly developed an absolute passion. I hope you like him, for I foresee I shall be boring everyone about him next term. I feel half tempted to write you a short essay about him but refrain. Meanwhile the country here is delightful. Spring has just begun, the almonds are in blossom — so pretty that one suspects them of being dressed for the occasion, and of making up on the sly — wild purple anemones and grape hyacinths, with endless birds singing and a most Shelleyan Aziola — which I stalked last evening and, to my great joy, identified as Scop's owl — hooting in a melancholy manner to the sunset, whilst Aristophanes' frogs — but I'm really getting too literary — sing choruses all down the valley. And the most incredibly romantic views, with hills, pines, sea, sunsets and distant mountains. Yet the whole affair done in the best grave, sober, French classical style, laid out by Cézanne, with the ghost of Racine at his elbow. So I get the best of both worlds, to say nothing of first-rate French cooking and red wine. Or rather of all three, for I don't believe that even in Greece itself would one be more likely to come on Pan and the Dryads — or my classical prototype, Silenus. Indeed, I discovered Parnassus only the other day, the most enchanting deserted oliveyards, high up in the hills, with open grassy lawns under the trees and a tiny stream falling from terrace to terrace.

Lord, what an appalling rhapsody. I shall have to take to writing shilling shockers in mock-Stevenson next. Appalling!

If he had not allowed himself to grow fat (though he was certainly not a Silenus), Julian would have been strikingly good-looking. An impish smile lurked about his lips when he was engaged in the arguments he loved to pursue; if someone else put forward a point of view that seemed to him difficult to refute the smile would momentarily fade, and one was conscious only of the intent clear gaze of the reflective eyes. He was a hesitant but obstinate debater, never voluble or overbearing; he was too anxious to discover the truth and too conscious of the importance of good manners in argument to want to gain a victory by the tricks of rhetoric. And yet strong emotions were held in uneasy control under the smile, and his nature was more complex than these discussions at first revealed. At one moment he seemed full of indolent charm, a sensualist who cared only for the good things of life; at the next one saw an entirely different side emerge: ascetic, hardworking, ruthless and battlesome. We kept up an enormous correspondence for years, mostly concerned with problems of poetic technique and the philosophy of poetry. Writing in an untidy, sloping, almost illegible hand, he would one day attack my own poems for woolly romanticism; another day he would declare that I would still be read in three hundred years' time, a compliment I ill deserved, but typical of his sudden spurts of generous appreciation of somebody working on lines he could not entirely approve. As his career at Cambridge progressed, and he felt his ideals challenged by the followers of Eliot and Pound or the surrealists among his contemporaries, or one of the anti-Bloomsbury pundits, his letters became full of malicious cracks and angry verse-satire in the best eighteenth-century manner with no holds barred. At the same time the challenge, the furious wrangles in which he involved himself, accentuated his rationalist stand and drove him even further away from the kind of imaginative writing with which in reality he had a strong instinctive sympathy. He finally reached the point where he would have liked to blot out the whole of the romantic movement and the century and a half of poetry that followed it. "Altogether," he wrote to me in the autumn of 1930, "I'm beginning an education whose end is to be the full enjoyment of classical poetry — not because of its romantic beauty, but for a beauty of its own. When I shall really be able to read it as if I had been born before 1798, I don't know — but I feel that it may not after all be too long." Pope was finally established as his god of poetry, and his rage descended, with ludicrous and wilful exaggeration, on Shakespeare. "Talking of the grand simplicities," he wrote during one long vacation, at the end of a terrific diatribe about common sense, precision and the eighteenth-century virtues, "I am obeying Peter's instructions and reading all Shakespeare's plays. I am astonished to find how right I am about them. What can be said at this time of day for a person so utterly lacking in all notions of construction, half whose lines mean nothing at all, and who has only the vaguest notions of metre. An intelligent earwig with a gift for blank verse could do as well." At this I blew up (perhaps I was meant to). I was staying with a French family at Fontainebleau at the time, as part of my vaguely sketched education for becoming a diplomatist, and nearly choked over my breakfast croissant when his provocation reached me. I wrote in answer one of the longest letters I have ever dispatched to anyone. I told him how fatal I thought it to try to resurrect the eighteenth-century mentality in our own time, how monotonous and inadequate the end-stopped couplet must become for a modern poet if indulged in to the exclusion of everything else; and then in refuting his criticisms of Shakespeare called to my aid two of his favourite modern critics, Lytton Strachey and Charles Mauron, and flung at him as many quotations from his own seventeenth- and eighteenth-century authors — Dryden, Dr. Johnson, and even Pope — as I could remember, all praising Shakespeare for the qualities Julian denied him. The result was typical and comic. Another long letter arrived, written in even more illegible pencil all up and down several sheets of crumpled notepaper, with an even longer tirade about the advantages of a course of the pre-romantic poets for a modern who wanted to learn his craft, but ending, almost as an afterthought, "But the greater part of your argument remains unanswerable."

The book by Lytton Strachey from which I took my ammunition was the luminous little masterpiece of interpretative criticism he wrote for the Home University Library, *Landmarks in French Literature*. I had already met him by then, through Dadie Rylands and my sister Rosamond, and I think it was he himself who suggested that I might find the book of use, as I was embarking on a deeper study of French literature. It taught me, as no other book could have, how to find excellence in the French tradition even if one were a devoted believer in the English tradition, and why Racine was a great poet and dramatist even though his greatness was so totally different from Shakespeare's. My enthusiasm for the book was the origin of an amusing occurrence that very summer. I was deep in it on the boat-train on my way back to England; and I noticed that a distinguished-looking lady dressed in black, who was sitting next to me, was unusually interested in me and the book. Finally she leaned over and asked me what I thought of it. She looked French, and yet she spoke perfect English without any trace of accent: I was intrigued, and immediately launched into a rhapsody about the book, adding, with all the naïve vanity and pride of youth, "You see, I *know* Lytton Strachey personally." This seemed to delight the unknown lady, who proceeded gently and skilfully to draw me out on the subject of the author. . . . It was only when we reached Calais that she revealed, to my total confusion, that she was in fact his sister, Dorothy, married to the French painter Simon Bussy, the *traductrice accreditée* of Gide, and many years later famous as the author of *Olivia*.

Paradoxically enough, in the same letter in which Julian had written so unpardonably about Shakespeare, he told me he had thoroughly enjoyed *Wuthering Heights*. It was rare for him to like or even read a novel at all. He admired his Aunt Virginia's work with strong Bloomsbury loyalty, and yet he was made uneasy by it. It was a surprise to me, therefore, a year later, to find that he had been reading Rosamond's just published novel, *A Note in Music*, and evidently *Dusty Answer* as well. He wrote to me from Charleston:

The fifth symphony is going on, much against Clive's will, but really just now Beethoven is the only musician I can endure, for I'm suffering from — not melancholy but black blood, the black blood of the Stephens, I suppose, that Virginia talks of, and only hardness, strength, tragedy are endurable. In fact I've had an overdose of romance and beauty. Cures: Beethoven and ten-mile walks in big boots, and the slaughter of innocent birds. . . . I've just finished your sister's book — which happened, heaven knows why, to fit into my mood so just now I am confident it is a work of indubitable genius. My opinion on novels, tho', isn't worth very much. But it must really be pretty good to have affected me at all. You know, you're rather alike in imagination . . . you've both got a same quality, midsummer in gardens — trees — water and parties I should label it — which is fascinating.

When I read over today the letters that Julian and I exchanged in such numbers at that time, I find them full of the most detailed arguments and theories about couplets, quatrains, blank verse, free verse, caesuras, rhythm and counter-rhythm, realism and romanticism, dialogue in verse and description in verse, clarity, obscurity, ambiguity and all the other subjects that two eager apprentice craftsmen in poetry can find to discuss with one another. The light has faded from them, the ashes are dead. And yet it was the most exciting colloquy in the world: the whole future of poetry, we felt, depended on these arguments; we were remoulding English literature nearer to our own hearts, and even our great differences of approach seemed to promise a spark of fusion out of which the new way of writing, the completely modern poem would be made. In the release of Cambridge life I gradually found new energies in myself, and began for the first time to write poetry that gave pleasure to others whose opinion I respected, that disturbed, however slightly, the common pool of the creative imagination. I have experienced only three or four such periods in my life; and this, the first, was inevitably the most exhilarating. I began to drain off the romantic excess of my dreamings and to be far more successfully what every poet or novelist must learn to be: the critical objective spectator as well as the actor, discovering thus how to give words and images a newly charged life and significance. I read all Eddie Marsh's volumes of *Georgian Poetry* through, and Squire's fat volumes of selections from the Georgian poets again and again in order, not merely to find the real and nourishing food I wanted, but to purge myself, by surfeit, of all contemporary clichés of attitude and metaphor and phrase-making. Of course I cannot pretend that I did completely purge myself, but many years later, when I found so many young poets ardently returning to all the stale poeticizings of the 'twenties and believing that the dew of dawn was upon their writings, I wished I could have persuaded them to take the same course. Inevitably my poems were colder and more impersonally dry for a time than the norm of temperature I knew I had one day to reach; but joyfully exploring modern French literature I longed to blend the complexity and vision of Rimbaud with the passion of Baudelaire and the pictorial power of Heredia. I urged Julian in my letters to read La Fontaine rather than Boileau, and Valéry on the subject of La Fontaine, and Peter Quennell's all-too-slender volume of poems to see how a gifted poet could be modern as well as traditional, a symbolist and a classicist at the same time. I dreamed of writing poems beyond those I was at work on then, which would have the intensity and packed imaginative richness of Yeats, Wilfred Owen, Valéry's *Charmes* and Gerard Manley Hopkins's shorter poems (which I had just discovered).

Julian and I used to carry on endless discussions whenever we were together as well as by letter: walking along the Backs, in his room at King's or in mine overlooking the Great Court of Trinity. I lured him during the vacation to Fieldhead, and I visited him in return at Charleston. Life at Fieldhead in those days was not very formal, but nevertheless a sense of the formality of big country houses in Edwardian times still lingered about the softly carpeted corridors and the dining-room with its silver candlesticks on polished tables and its ring of onlooking family portraits; even though the occasions were rare when we dressed for dinner, and old James with his serio-comic grand manner and jingling keys was no longer there to carve the joint on the sideboard. The contrast of Charleston's bohemian atmosphere was an agreeable stimulus to me. I have always enjoyed being able to be the citizen of several worlds at the same time, and found a special pleasure a few years later in being accepted intimately in the working-class life of Vienna and the literary life of London. It amused me at this time to move between Charleston and Fieldhead and the even more traditional atmosphere of my sister Helen's comfortable home in Northamptonshire, from where I wrote to Julian: "I'm here in the middle of the hunting country," when I would sometimes find myself, inexplicably, discussing the merits of the various Hunts in the Southern Midlands with one of the grooms. There were no grooms touching their caps on the porch at Charleston, nor pink coats hanging up in the cupboards, and the discussion was about *The Nature of Beauty*, *Vision and Design* and *The Ego and the Id* rather than the way in which the Grafton or the Bicester was run by the latest M.F.H. or the impact of rich American horsey enthusiasts on the ancient pattern of country life. The half-finished canvases by Duncan Grant, or Julian's mother Vanessa, or his brother Quentin, piled carelessly in the studios, and the doors and fireplaces of the old farmhouse transformed by decorations of fruit and flowers and opulent nudes by the same hands, the low square tables made of tiles fired in Roger Fry's Omega workshops, and the harmony created all through the house by the free, brightly coloured post-impressionist style that one encountered in everything from the huge breakfast cup one drank one's coffee from to the bedroom curtains that were drawn in the morning, not by a silent-footed valet or housemaid but by one's own hand to let in the Sussex sunshine, excited the suppressed painter that lurked in my breast. They seemed to suggest how easily life could be restored to a paradise of the senses if one simply ignored the conventions that still gripped one in the most absurd ways, clinging from a past that had been superseded in the minds of people of clear intelligence and unspoilt imagination.

Julian was often alone in the house while his parents were in London or down at La Bergère. "My own life is utterly monastic," he warned me before my first visit, "except for letters. I work three hours a day, walk four, and get meals, make fires and bathe in two." But this was just what I looked forward to, an ideal way of life and perfect surroundings if one wanted to write and think about writing. We went for long walks over the downs with their distant views of a hazy sea, accompanied by — for Julian, like all sensible bachelors, possessed, or rather was privileged to enjoy the company of a spaniel bitch — Clinker, who at that time was carrying on a protracted and embarrassing love-affair with a fine gentleman from the neighbouring farm at Tilton, where Maynard Keynes and Lydia Lopokova lived. "Clinker is with child by the Keynes's cur, what a life!" grumbled Julian in a letter to me after I left. Clinker would return from her distant trysts in a state of the wildest elation, running round the kitchen and barking at the top of her voice, while Julian cooked me delicious ham omelettes. After dinner we both laid our pens down, and took up again the endless argument of Pope versus Shakespeare, Herrick versus Keats and Shelley, and plotted a magazine of our own which Julian saw as a counterblast to the crimes committed in the name of Eliot and Dr. Leavis by his contemporaries. . . . I had a dream one night that Edmund Blunden (who had recently accepted a poem of mine for the *New Statesman*) was going to speak about this magazine through a megaphone, and that I had been given, as a great favour, the post of Editor-for-Scotland. . . . But we were both already deeply involved with other, real magazines in Cambridge.

« 3 »

THE "Michael" of Julian's letter from La Bergère was Michael Redgrave, and the paper for which he was holding Julian's long poem *Winter Movement* was *The Venture*, a magazine edited by himself, Robin Fedden and Anthony Blunt. It was during the long vacation of 1928 that I received a letter from Anthony, who was already establishing a reputation for himself in Cambridge as a formidable and disputatious art critic, informing me that a new magazine was being planned and inviting me to contribute, not poems but woodcuts.

The first number of *The Venture* appeared in November, and from that moment till I went down it occupied a central place in my interests. Many of Julian's best poems appeared in it, some poems of mine (most of which I had the good sense to tear up later), and nearly all the passable woodcuts I designed in my freak career as engraver. It was, I think one might say, a magazine of the "centre" in what was already being called a Cambridge poetic renaissance. The extreme left started its rival magazine at exactly the same time, and for the next two years a furious battle raged (in our minds at any rate) between the protagonists of the two magazines. *Experiment* disdained wood or lino-cuts, but had reproductions of paintings by abstract and surrealist artists. There were surrealist and imagist poems, many pieces in which the influence of Eliot was glaringly evident, and nearly all of them offended against Julian's canons of clarity, concrete imagery and common sense. In spite of the rivalry, a number of contributors managed to live comfortably in both camps, and were contemptuously dubbed by Julian "the Mercenaries." By far the most interesting of all the contributions were those by William Empson, including the extraordinary early poem *Camping Out*, which begins, "And now she cleans her teeth into the lake." Nothing more original was produced in our time, and yet these rare blooms had poison in the stalk for those who plucked them. I was fascinated by their formal skill, the poetic discipline which controlled the off-hand conversational manner, giving it a subtle texture and music; not, however, having received, as Empson had, a training in mathematics or science, I was all too often baffled by the extended specialist metaphors which he carried through with sure cunning; and I looked with a suspicious and unbelieving eye on those of my friends who claimed that they understood them. No such frustrations arose about the extracts which Empson also allowed to appear in *Experiment* from the book on which he was at work, *Seven Types of Ambiguity*, which I still consider one of the cardinal books of my initiation into the deeper mysteries of poetry, as important for me then as Robert Graves's *On English Poetry* had been at an earlier stage.

In spite of Empson, *The Venture* remained my spiritual home; and through *The Venture* I became a close friend of Michael Redgrave, the most versatile in his talents of the group of gifted young men at Magdalene at that time. Tall, slim, with curly chestnut hair and a romantic profile, he was an engaging embodiment of the ideal conception of what a young poet should look like and how he should behave; but the stage was in his blood — and would out.

The perishable nature of play production being what it is, and the impossibility of comparing one production with another, as one can compare one picture or even one film with another, making all judgements highly uncertain, I can only record my subjective conviction that the *King Lear* which Dadie Rylands produced for the Marlowe Society in the early spring of 1929 was one of the most moving and beautiful of our time and without much doubt the one truest to the spirit of the poetry. Michael's playing of Edgar revealed a quality that put most clever undergraduates' acting in the shade: it was easy — at least it seemed so to me — to prophesy a brilliant stage career for him after that experience.

Michael pursued his triple career as poet, player and editor with astonishing verve. In the winter he was in another production of

Dadie's, Milton's *Comus*, for which his beautiful speaking voice was well suited. He wrote to me just after Christmas, to tell me of its success at the end of term, and added:

We did it again on the 19th at the Keynes', with Duncan Grant scenery, and *all* Bloomsbury in the auditorium — including Shaw, Sickert and Strachey. Lydia spoke an epilogue and danced, and she and Maynard did a pas-de-deux which brought things to an end uproariously. Afterwards sausages and beer in the supper-room, where Robert and I wanted to examine the Sickerts, Seurats, Derains, Frys and Grants which hung on the walls, but thought it would be impertinent, with all those famous people paying full attention only to their sausages. Miss Matheson of the B.B.C. was there, and I have since received an invitation to "try the Microphone" with a view to broadcasting poetry. I should like you to tell me what I ought to broadcast, if I am allowed to do so.

Some of his poems appeared in the volume of *Cambridge Poetry* which was published by the Hogarth Press the next year. And yet, for all the pleasure they gave those readers who were attuned to them, I find it difficult to doubt that he made the right decision in devoting his mature energies to the theatre, where the peculiar originality and force of his temperament found a far more unimpeded outlet.

« 4 »

I HAD chosen History and Modern Languages when I gave up Classics, chiefly because I still had my eye on a diplomatic career, but also because I felt I could take care of English literature by myself while learning something about French and German literature. My appetite reached out in all directions, and dictated a meal more gigantic than any supervisor would have dared to set me. Volume after volume of the Mermaid Series of Elizabethan and Jacobean dramatists was swallowed to the last morsel, one century after another of English poetry was cleared off my plate as a hungry dog licks its bowl clean of the crumbs. I found a special delight in the prose of the seventeenth century, from *Urn Burial* and *Centuries of Meditation* to Dryden's essays; and when I came to the novel, exploring huge territories my boyhood reading in the library at Fieldhead had left untrodden, I looked more and more for what was distinguished by a poet's fastidious sense of style and care for the individual word. I carried home from Bowes & Bowes every volume or anthology of modern poetry I could afford to purchase. I made my first serious explorations into the world of the contemporary novel: at Eton, only Conrad had been added to my reading pleasures. D. H. Lawrence, Aldous Huxley, E. M. Forster and Virginia Woolf had been entirely unknown, and excited me by their ingenuities of approach and artistry to a whole new series of ambitious dreams of revolutionary novel-writing. In addition, I had my long reading list of French and German books, and was trying to swallow Tolstoi and Chekhov at the same time. I also began to read some books of Shakespearean criticism, stirred by Wilson Knight's *The Wheel of Fire*. The more I read the more interested I became. I began to feel I wanted to master the huge scholarly and interpretative literature in an orderly fashion; but I realized at the same time that to do this I needed a discipline and an objective I could not find in any higgledy-piggledy private reading. I therefore welcomed Dadie Rylands's suggestion that I should spend one long vacation working for the Charles Oldham Shakespeare scholarship. Generally this scholarship attracted very few entrants, as the prize was not great and the time involved in preparation might swallow up a whole summer; but for that very reason the few were keen, hard-working, would-be experts, and it was not at all an easy plum to shake from the tree. This was not really the point in my mind: my instinct was that I must *know* Shakespeare through and through, and if at the end I could say I did, that would be reward enough for having "stayed in after school" during three holiday months of summer.

I stayed in. And I have seldom enjoyed anything so much, or felt so deeply satisfied with the results of an effort made, even though I only achieved the position of runner-up to the winner. The whole Shakespeare panorama unfolded before me, like a new landscape or the further side of a mountain pass — new because, though many details were already familiar enough to me, I had never seen it as a whole before — and my mind was changed by the experience. In no other way could I have understood that Shakespeare was the key to the whole of English literature, the master mind that determined its course and depth and vitality so fundamentally that we can hardly conceive what our imaginative life — perhaps even our moral values — would be like without him. The pedants and witch-doctors moped and mowed round him in ever-thickening hordes, but if one raised one's eyes and ignored their mumblings and dervish howls, he towered still above them, a figure striking a rock: and the whole of our civilization since his day fertilized by the streams that came gushing out. What excited me as much as anything else was the discovery that even those minds which seemed most unlike his — Dryden's or Dr. Johnson's — were not only compelled into admiration in the study of his work, but were also brought to know themselves more deeply — as if his genius were radio-active, penetrating immediately beneath the surface layers of varying historical circumstances and fashion. No one had prepared me for this experience before Cambridge, nor would I, with my sceptical turn of mind, have been ready to believe what the necessity of reading every play (and every apocryphal play as well) two or three times in the order of writing — and following step by step how that order had been established — so miraculously presented to me: the incredible flowering of his genius and the immeasurable amplitude that flowering reached. Even if there had not been this revelation, which was almost like the revelation of a new dimension to existence, the summer would not have been lost. On the contrary, it was transformed into one of the most memorable summers of my life, because the whole of my surroundings seemed to exist within Shakespeare's vision. I spent a great deal of it at Kidlington, near Oxford, where Rosamond, now married to Wogan Philipps, had taken the old grey-stone manor-house, and from there we used often to motor over to Stratford. Even in those days, before the great revival of Shakespearean production and acting we have enjoyed in the last twenty years, one could see productions that never lacked something to delight or illuminate a student at the height of his passion for his subject. And the delight I found in the ripening orchards and golden cornfields of the countryside between the Chilterns and the Cotswolds, the sheep-farms on the slopes and the water-meadows below, the old villages huddled round their Crusader churches and the little towns basking in the afternoon sunshine of July, with their inn-signs swinging a welcome as ancient as the Wars of the Roses, the towering umbrage of oak and elm in the parklands and the lanes so deeply furred with wild flowers leading up to the beechwoods on the horizon, were enhanced and consecrated by Justice Shallow and Hotspur and Falstaff and the music that haunted a wood near Athens. It was a time in my life when the identification of poet and landscape was one of the greatest sources of imaginative pleasure to me. My eye blotted out the pylons and ribbon development that encroached apace on the "russet lawns and fallows gray" of Buckinghamshire, and I saw them with the vision of the young Milton:

> Meadows trim with Daisies pide,
> Shallow Brooks, and Rivers wide.

Towers, and Battlements it sees
Boosom'd high in tufted Trees. . . .

The river and the wooded slopes round Marlow were filled with the presence of Shelley composing *The Revolt of Islam*, and his magic boats sailed under the willows, reducing to ghostly vanishing point the spooning spivs with their raucous portable gramophones oozing sentimental jazz. On the downs of the Isle of Wight the rhythms of *Maud* and *Crossing the Bar* were what sounded in my ears, and not the backfiring, the honking and brake-screeching of the char-a-bancs that carried their loads of trippers on the daily advertised tours down lanes that were made for shepherd and farmer's cart. I lived in a timeless England of ideal presences, where all the centuries joined hands to praise; and learnt to understand the meaning of that *absence* which poets have lamented in countries like New Zealand, so dazzlingly beautiful but so entirely (as yet) without spiritual significance.

In my third year at Trinity, my father died, after ten years of illness bravely borne, but tragic for his family and friends to watch, who could remember the man so devoted to active pursuits, so surrounded by health and energy and the hope of youth. Strangely enough, as I stood by his bedside — I had failed to arrive from Cambridge in time to see him in his last moments — though the face before me seemed infinitely remote, centuries and the space of stars distant, some element that his illness had obscured and confused for so long reigned there again, giving an unforgettable impression of triumphant resolution and the calm that comes from having won through all obstacles and sufferings; something I had never expected to see on a dead man's face, which pierced me to the heart with a sense of communication. We were alone; I had never felt so close to him, nor so strongly the archetypal power of the bond between father and son, at the very instant when it had been broken — for me — for ever.

My wanderings about Europe had now started in my vacations. I stayed with a family at Munich to learn German, which I still found a difficult and ugly language (and only discovered the beauty of a year or two later when I could read Rilke's poems in the original), and fell in love with Nymphenberg but *not* with the family or the Bavarian character even in that pre-Nazi period. Incautiously one morning at breakfast I made an approving remark about the League of Nations, which provoked a terrifying explosion about the wickedness of the

Versailles *Diktat* from the cropped-headed ogre of a paterfamilias, backed up by his dour student son of lean and sallow countenance already slashed by duelling. A peace was patched up by the mother, and we were all courtesy again at lunch-time, though the conversation did not flow. I had learnt something, that did not quite square with the idealistic beliefs I had acquired at Cambridge, about the causes of modern war. On another occasion I was taken round Nuremberg by a young student, who spent the whole day trying to persuade me that the French had no lavatories and never washed. This seemed rather a caricature of the great bidet-loving nation over the frontier which he himself had never crossed, and I tried shyly to say so. A fatal move. When he saw me off on the train in the evening there was a look of despairing contempt underlying his polite smile. I also stayed with a French family at their home in Fontainebleau and in their lodgings on the sea-coast at La Baule, to steep myself again in a French atmosphere while studying French poetry. Michel, the son of my own age, was a pleasant companion, but the family was grimly *petite bourgeoise*, and I felt constrained all the time. One day the news arrived of the death of a child relation, a distant cousin of the mother. I saw her open the letter and discuss the news with the rest of the family without any sign of great distress, before leaving the table. A few hours later Michel came into my room and told me she would like to see me. I was astonished to find her in her room with her hair carefully disarrayed, her rouge very obviously wiped off her lips on to a handkerchief with which she was dabbing her remarkably dry eyes. I had been called in to witness a conventional scene of mourning and to offer conventional condolences. I knew by then what genuine grief was like in the presence of death, and the episode left a disagreeable taste in my mouth. But I had learnt something again; and whenever I come up against the extraordinary, undying English legend of the frivolous, loose-living "frogs," cocking a snook at those rules of conventional decency that keep John Bull so superior, I think of that scene in Madame's room.

I had scarcely finished this round of Europe when Violet Hammersley reported that she had heard of a vacancy in the Prints and Drawings Department of the British Museum: would I be interested to try for it? We had often discussed together what I was going to do, and she knew that my thoughts were turning increasingly towards something more closely connected with the arts than diplomacy. The views of her friends in the Foreign Office milieu were discouraging: a diplomatist had become nothing but a letter-box since the war, they asserted, but at the same time much harder work was expected of him than in the days when he had a genuinely influential role in international affairs. Unlike the Quai d'Orsay, the Foreign Office did not seem to favour literary creation, at least until the conventional book of memoirs appeared, like an egg in an elderly hen's nesting-box, out of ambassadorial retirement. I was fascinated by the world of diplomacy, but I had a passion for art, and surely in a career at the British Museum I should find sympathetic surroundings and time to write my poetry. So the argument ran, and I found it persuasive. The job seemed interesting and well paid, and the people who interviewed me charming, even if the whole atmosphere had for me, faintly, the dusty smell of a mausoleum. Off I went, therefore, on their advice, on another round of Europe, this time chiefly to study the great foreign collections of prints and drawings, in the Louvre, the Kaiser Friedrich Museum in Berlin and the Albertina in Vienna. By natural inclination I specialized in the drawings of the Early Flemish school, but I found new delights in the work of Tiepolo, Guardi and other Venetian artists of the eighteenth century, an affection that began to grow and rival my early love of Van Eyck and his followers. In the Albertina I encountered for the first time the attractive but thoroughly formidable Fräulein Spitzmüller. She ruled the room in which we studied the drawings from the dazzling collection under her care as firmly as any schoolmaster dealing with an unruly class of small boys: an invisible cane seemed sometimes to rattle on her desk. I was sensible of her Viennese charm, but rather frightened of her, reduced to awful guilt when it was discovered that I was trying to introduce a magnifying glass into the room and a pencil not previously approved. Fifteen years later, with two Austrian revolutions and a world war between, she was reinstalled at her bomb-battered desk by the British, and brought over to England on a visit; and I was amused to find that a faint sensation of alarm mingled with my pleasure at seeing her again.

I lived rather a solitary life during these visits; by choice as much as by the way things fell out. I read a great deal of poetry; I liked to think of myself in the guise of the imaginary figure Dickens invented for *Household Words*, "The Shadow," moving invisibly through the great cities, learning the pulse of their life, the aura of their history and literature and art that encircled them, trying to find the European mood and to see them in the perspective of the tragedy they had just been through, the tragedies that yet threatened them. How could one individual help to avert those tragedies? This problem was always present in my mind, baffled by the growing feeling that politics were impure and diplomacy powerless. At least one could raise a voice, and give "*un sens plus pur aux mots de la tribu* . . ." I spent long after-noons in the parks of Schönbrunn, Nymphenberg, Chambord, letting myself be invaded by the nostalgia they exhaled, feeling for the begin-ning of poems into which these inchoate intimations might crystallize. Poems did slowly emerge from all the false starts and scratchings out, a few in which emotion and observation seemed at last to be matched by words and technique; but only a fraction of the vast series that struggled within me for expression. These poems were affirmations wrung with endless struggle out of the void that still oppressed me, little islets with a single palm-tree on each pushing out of a fathomless ocean. Still I could write in my note-book: "A day of utter self-torment — leading nowhere, NOWHERE!" And then suddenly, with pencil and paper before me, the dance of the words would start, and the solidity of the impalpable envelop and assuage me.

Home again, I began to spend more time in London, browsing among the bookshops in the Charing Cross Road and buying more books than I could ever read. Beatrix had been launched some years before on her theatrical career, to our great excitement; she played for several seasons at the Gate Theatre, where I remember she made a deep and characteristic impression as Blazes in Robert Nichols's *Twenty Below;* and at the little Royal Court Theatre in Sloane Square played in *All God's Chillun Got Wings*, her first appearance in a play by Eugene O'Neill — who was to be the playwright of her greatest triumphs. I was a frequent visitor, renewing thus the pleasures I had first tasted, at the Festival Theatre, in Cambridge, of the experimental modern theatre. In fact, I had come to the point where I could scarcely bear to see any play in an ordinary West End theatre with conven-tional production — unless Noel Coward was the author or Marie Tempest the actress. My godmother had now taken Sargent's house in Tite Street, and in the great studio which she had converted into the most sumptuous and elegant of living-rooms she gave parties at which, shy but keyed up, I was introduced to some of the notable literary figures of London, including Arnold Bennett, Somerset Maugham, Desmond MacCarthy — whose daughter Rachel, soon to be married to Lord David Cecil, had been a fellow-guest at Charleston — Osbert Sitwell and Raymond Mortimer. There also I met Lord Esher, who, with his ceaseless behind-the-scenes devotion to English literary and artistic life, was at that time supporting *Life and Letters* under Desmond MacCarthy's editorship. *Life and Letters* often had a wayward and unfinished air about it, but with only the rarest editorial comments or contributions from Desmond MacCarthy himself, nevertheless succeeded in being impregnated with his personality, his standards of taste and style, and his enormous range of literary enjoyment. I spent hours brooding on the problem of how the magic worked: my uncertainty at that time about my own literary gifts had not killed the strange dream that persisted, like a vision of cabbage-leaves in a common or garden-white butterfly's brain as it emerges from the chrysalis, of an editor's chair, a telephone at the elbow, a pile of manuscripts and a blue pencil. The first cabbage-leaf was nearer than I knew.

« 5 »

DURING my travels in late summer of 1930, after I had come down from Trinity, I was deeply preoccupied in my inner self with the preparation of a book of poems. At last it seemed in sight: the gradual adding of poem to poem had been a painfully slow process, but now, as I anxiously sifted through and re-wrote lines and stanzas, I could begin to imagine that the total had passed the absolute minimum for a young poet's first, very slender volume. It hovered before me in fantasy with all the effulgence of an impossible apple from the Garden of the Hesperides. Gusts of hope and despair swept through me with alternate violence, rising to gale force when Julian's book, *Winter Movement*, was published by Chatto & Windus. On my return to Fieldhead from Paris at the beginning of November, I wrote to him:

Here I am, immensely glad to be back, in time to see the last act of an English Autumn. *And* in time to see the publication of *Winter Movement:* I have seen a copy, and I think it looks admirable — Chatto have not failed you. I re-read the first twenty-six pages — to which I am deeply devoted — on the spot. You must let me know what reviews there are — keep them for me. I have not seen anything myself yet, but the Lords of Reviewdom take their time about poetry — if they condescend to notice it at all. I must say I think in some ways Keats was rather lucky to have so many important pages of abuse devoted to him. . . .

Julian himself, flushed with triumph though he was that autumn at getting his book out, did not cease to coax and encourage me to try my luck as well. He considered that my poems to a large extent vindicated his own principles in his crusade for the "eighteenth-century virtues" against the technical licence and intellectual obscurities of the school of Eliot that continued to excite his bellicose derision, just as they had when he turned the pages of the undergraduate magazines at Cambridge. I was an ally, perhaps a disciple; but the ally, alas, was slipping, for in the same letter I made the dangerous admission that after re-reading his poems I was beginning to believe that the imitation of Pope was a wrong turning for him. "The couplet pieces," I wrote, "seem small beside the splendour of the earlier pieces." In fact, this treasonable thought had never been far from my mind, and when I re-read Julian's poems after his death I felt convinced that amusing and stimulating though the whole campaign had been, he was never meant to write couplets or even satiric verse at all. There was something untidy and untameable about his deeper nature that was wounded by this forceful grafting on of alien stock for the formal garden; his instinctual power seemed never to be as strong again as it had been in the early poems, which were unlike any nature poetry written before or since in their precise and loving observation and absolute lack of any prettification or poetic sentimentality. They created, I thought, a new kind of poetic "stuff," the precipitate of an unusual and difficult but exciting way of experiencing the objective world.

Julian's belief in me buoyed me up, as did my sister Rosamond's, in that last lap before the almost unbelievable goal; and great was my joy when, the finally winnowed pieces having been carefully typed out and sent to be scrutinized by my most exacting and sensitive judge, Dadie Rylands, the verdict was favourable. What was more, Dadie promised to show them to Leonard and Virginia Woolf.

Then began the rapid sequence of events that was, as it turned out, to determine the course of my life for many years to come. Dadie had worked in earlier days under Leonard in the Hogarth Press, and shared the interest in printing that had woken in me when I first began to read about William Morris. He had helped the Woolfs print some of their booklets of poetry on their own hand-press, and for a long time we had schemed to have a printing press together. We had even gone to see a manufacturer about machinery and type. He guessed that I was really more interested in printing and publishing than in prints and drawings and diplomacy, and when the Woolfs told him that they were again looking for a manager who could run the Press under their supervision and eventually become a partner, he immediately suggested that the young poet whose work he was bringing them (and about whom they already knew quite a lot from their nephew Julian) might fill the bill.

The result was that one morning I received a letter from Leonard, which informed me not only that he and Virginia liked my poems very much and wanted to publish them, but also that they had heard that I might be interested in working in the Hogarth Press, and would I come and discuss it with them? I wrote off triumphantly to Julian:

I have heard from the Woolfs, and they say they will be glad to publish my poems. Bless them. I'm cheered, I don't mind saying. It won't be till the autumn — I'd rather it were the spring — but it scarcely matters, will be an admirable experience in patience for myself, and I'm grateful to have them published at all. I gather they are now being inspected by Lady G. Whether, if she disapproves of them, they'll publish them on their own, I know not. But I suppose having said they'll publish them, they will. Bear with my selfish pleasure.

"Lady G." — Dorothy Wellesley (later the Duchess of Wellington), to whose patronage the series of Hogarth Living Poets owed its existence — announced her approval in spite of my fears. Gone at once were the rather sobering visions of a lifetime dedicated to etching and aquatint in the dusty recesses of the British Museum, banished for ever the idea of following my uncles and cousins into the service of His Britannic Majesty, as I rushed off to see the Woolfs in 52 Tavistock Square at the beginning of January. Immediately I sent a report to Julian:

I would have written to you before about your poems, if the end of last week had not been so hectic — interviews — consultations — calculations. I expect you know substantially what the offer of the Woolves was going to be: I was surprised when they made it to me — on Friday, at tea, when I met them both for the first time, and thought them most charming, Virginia very beautiful — and not a little excited. I've now decided I'm going to make every effort to accept the offer. . . . I really can't imagine any work that would interest me more, and to be a partner with them, with a voice in what's to be published (and how) and what isn't — it seems an almost unbelievable stroke of luck.

The consultations and calculations continued intensively for the next few days. There were problems to be solved about raising the money, but I found my mother sympathetic in general and pleased to see me launched on something that I obviously cared about so much. Looking back on it now, it seems to me that everything was settled with astonishing speed, for only six days later I could announce to Julian:

This week has been a fevered one — I emerge with an agreement in my pocket, by which I become Manager of the Hogarth Press in October — if not fired after eight months of apprenticeship. And I have the option of becoming a partner in a year or two. And I start in on Wednesday as ever is! Your advice was just what I wanted — very welcome. As a matter of fact Leonard had lost confidence in his first proposition even before my Trustee turned a dubious eye on it, so I think both parties feel better under the present agreement that we argued out in a series of interviews. I pray that I shall be a success: hard work, but congenial . . . and Leonard is giving me good holidays, long enough to get some writing done, I hope. But there's so much I want to say, that I can't say it all in a letter, and must wait till I see you. I was charmed by both Leonard and Virginia, and hope they liked me.

« 6 »

THE year before, I had been staying in London with my sister Beatrix in St. George's Square. Now I moved into the house in Heathcote Street, just off the Gray's Inn Road, that was occupied by Douglas Davidson, the painter, and his brother Angus, skilled translator from the Italian and author of an excellent book on Edward Lear. There the room which had previously been occupied by Dadie was made over to me. The advantage of Heathcote Street was that it was only a few minutes' walk from Tavistock Square. Every morning I set out to reach the Woolfs' house at 9:15 A.M., passing through a disused graveyard filled with ancient tombstones of the seventeenth and eighteenth centuries, its half-effaced inscriptions and funeral ornaments dappled with moss and lichen. The Burial Ground of St. George-the-Martyr had become a quiet garden, and some old people used to sit there all day when the sun was shining: I would see the same faces on my return after work as I had observed on my setting out.

At No. 52 the Press occupied the basement, formerly the kitchen and servants' quarters; a friendly firm of solicitors were installed on the ground and first floors, while on the top two floors Leonard and Virginia had their own living quarters. The basement was cold and draughty and ramshackle. My own office, as apprentice manager, was a small back room that had once been a pantry and cupboard room — the cupboards were piled high with the dusty files of the activities of the Press ever since it had started in 1917. It was badly in need of redecorating, it had a jammed window that looked out on a narrow outside passage and a gloomy wall, and a decrepit gas-fire in front of which Leonard would attempt, without any striking success, to warm his hands when he came in to see me with the day's correspondence soon after my arrival. My mother was appalled when she first visited

me there; but to me nevertheless it was sacred ground. I was at last
part of a publishing firm, and the one that seemed to me the most
glamorous of all; I was associated every day with the — to me — legendary Leonard and Virginia Woolf; in the former scullery up the
passage an actual printing-machine was installed, with its trays of
type beside it, and there on many an afternoon Leonard could be found
rolling off the firm's stationery, writing paper, invoices, royalty forms
and review slips; while every now and then Virginia herself could be
glimpsed setting the type for one of the small books of poetry that the
Press still produced at home — at that time it was, I think, Vita Sackville-West's *Sissinghurst* — in spite of the fact that it had grown into
a large business dealing with many of the biggest printers and
binders. All round me, in all the rooms and down the dark corridors,
were the piled packages of finished books as delivered from the
binders. It gave me a special pleasure to explore among them, noting
on the labels the names of books that were already precious to me,
such as Virginia's *Monday or Tuesday* (not many of these) and *To
the Lighthouse* in their original editions, and occasionally coming
across a single, opened package of some early publication that had
long been famous, Ivan Bunin's *The Gentleman from San Francisco*,
or E. M. Forster's *Pharos and Pharillon*, or *The Notebooks of Anton
Chekhov*, though not, alas, Katherine Mansfield's *The Prelude* or T. S.
Eliot's *The Waste Land*, long out of print but tantalizingly advertised at the back of some of the other books. And I persuaded Leonard
to allow me to make a collection of the early hand-set volumes of poetry, all different shapes and sizes in their prettily decorated paper
covers. By far the largest piles were in the studio room at the back
where (as I have described elsewhere) Virginia had her work-desk;
and I would slip in, with carefully controlled eagerness and as silently
as possible, to hunt out some books that were suddenly needed on the
packing-table in the front room, feeling that I was entering the holiest
part of the house, the inmost ark of its presiding deity. I was even
allowed, later, to work at the desk when they were both away.

No one could have been a kinder or more sympathetic teacher than
Leonard. There was no nonsense of formal "business relations" in the
Press, and he would explain to me how to prepare estimates and contracts (on his own highly individual patterns), how to design a book-
page and an advertisement and how to organize the flow of books to
the shops, with steady patience and an assumption of intimate interest
in everything we published. He described the authors, the printers'
and paper-makers' travellers and all the other people with whom I was

to have to deal, including the persistent and unsnubbable bores, at length and with characteristically caustic comment. The absurd conventions of the trade, the prejudices of certain important booksellers and reviewers, the inexplicably chancy ups and downs of success and failure in the fortunes of books, would rouse him at all times to exasperated and withering wit; and it was due to his teaching that I learnt early on to face with a certain detached philosophy the irrational behaviour that almost everyone who has to do with books is so frequently capable of. In fact I learnt the essentials of publishing in the most agreeable way possible: from a man who had created his own business, had never allowed it to grow so big that it fell into departments sealed off from one another, and who saw it all as much from the point of view of an author and amateur printer as of someone who had to make his living by it. If Leonard had a fault, it was in allowing detail to loom too large at times. A small item that could not be accounted for in the books, a misunderstanding about a point of production would, without apparent reason, irritate him suddenly to the extreme, he would worry it like a dog worrying a rat, until indeed he seemed to be the rat and the detail the dog; and betray, I felt after one or two such experiences, the long nervous tension he had lived under in caring so devotedly for the genius of his wife.

My relations with Virginia began with an ardent youthful hero-worship; but gradually, as I got to know her better, this turned into a feeling of real affection as well as respect. At first she was irradiated in my eyes with the halo of having written *Jacob's Room*, *To the Lighthouse* and *Mrs. Dalloway*. No other books seemed to me to express with anything like the same penetration and beauty the sensibility of our age; it was not merely the conception that underlay those works, of time and sorrow and human longing, but also the way she expressed it, the paramount importance in her writing of technical change and experiment; almost everything else seemed, after I had read them, utterly wide of the target and inadequately aware of what was needed. I was influenced, of course, as a poet, by the skill with which she managed to transform the material of poetry into the prose-form of the novel; but that in itself seemed to me one of the major artistic problems of our time, arising out of the terror and tension, the phantasmagoria of modern life. I devoured the three novels again and again, and always with fresh delight, valuing them far higher than *The Common Reader*, *A Room of One's Own*, *Orlando* and even *Flush*, which, much as I enjoyed them and popular as they were, seemed to me of far less significance. In those early days I revered Virginia as the sacred centre, the most gifted and adored (and sometimes feared) of the Bloomsbury circle. But, as time went on, the feeling she inspired in me was more one of happy release than of reverence. I found her the most enchanting of friends, full of sympathy and understanding for my own personal problems and the problems I was up against in my job, with an intense curiosity about my own life and the lives of my friends in my generation (many of whom were, of course, known and even related to her). She liked to hear all about what we wanted to do in poetry, in painting, in novel-writing. She would stimulate me to talk, she had an unique gift for encouraging one to be indiscreet, and would listen with absorption and occasionally intersperse pointed and witty comments. Some of the happiest times I can remember in those years were the luncheons and teas I would be invited up to in the Woolfs' part of the house, where the walls were painted with frescoes by Duncan Grant and Virginia's sister Vanessa Bell, discussing the plans of the Press, the books submitted to us, and all the histories and personalities involved. She was always bubbling with ideas, longing to launch new schemes and produce books that no one had thought of before, that would startle the conventional business minds of the book world. She found an all-too-ready response in me, and had sometimes quietly to be checked on the rein by Leonard.

There were days, however, when she seemed withdrawn behind a veil, and it was hard to draw out her interest in the activities of the Press or ignite the gaiety which at other times was so characteristic of her. Sometimes this veil concealed her preoccupation with the problems of whatever she was writing at the moment; at other times it was darker and more opaque, bringing an uneasy atmosphere of strain and misery to the house. It is not for me to explain or explore the moods of fathomless melancholy that overcame Virginia Woolf at various periods during her life, and nearly always began with a series of acute headaches; I can only record the anxiety and distress they caused me for her own sake and for Leonard, who had fought them with her for so long, and my wonder that she managed to achieve so much with that perpetual threat hanging over her, always dropping nearer when she was in the throes of her finest creative achievement.

One of the worst of these fits of melancholy attacked her in the last stages of her work on *The Waves*, and Leonard decided that she must abandon it altogether for a time. The crisis passed, and she was able to get the book, to me the most daring if not the most successful of all her experiments, ready for press in the late summer. I could hardly contain my impatience to read it; it was for me the great event of the year, even though my own first book of poems was coming out in September. At last, at the beginning of the month, the advance copies arrived, just after I had spent a week-end with her and Leonard at Rodmell, and in writing to thank her I mentioned that I was in the middle of reading it. She immediately sent me a note insisting that I should write down for her exactly what I thought about it. I was deeply stirred by the book, and wrote her a long letter in which I tried, no doubt naïvely, to describe the impression it had made on me. In the same letter I suggested that it was high time for her to define her views about modern poetry, which we had discussed so often together. I received the following letter in reply, dated September 17:

Dear John, I'm most grateful to you for your letter. It made me happy all yesterday. I had become firmly convinced that *The Waves* was a failure, in the sense that it wouldn't convey anything to anybody. And now you've been so perceptive, and gone so much further and deeper in understanding my drift than I thought possible that I'm immensely relieved. Not that I expect many such readers. And I'm rather dismayed to hear we've printed 7,000: for I'm sure 3,000 will feed all appetites; and then the other 4 will sit round me like decaying corpses for ever in the studio (I cleared up the table — for you, not the corpses). I agree that it's very difficult — bristling with horrors, though I've never worked so hard as I did here, to smooth them out. But it was, I think, a difficult attempt — I wanted to eliminate all detail; all fact; & analysis; & myself; & yet not be frigid and rhetorical; & not monotonous (which I am) & to keep the swiftness of prose & yet strike one or two sparks, & not write poetical, but pure-bred prose, & keep the elements of character; & yet that there should be many characters & only one; & also an infinity, a background behind — well, I admit I was biting off too much.

But enough, as the poets say. If I live another 50 years I think I shall put this method to some use, but as in 50 years I shall be under the pond, with the goldfish swimming over me, I daresay these vast ambitions are a little foolish, & will ruin the press. That reminds me — I think your idea of a Letter most brilliant — "To a young Poet" — because I'm seething with immature & ill considered & wild & annoying ideas about prose & poetry. So lend me your name — (& let me sketch a character of you by way of frontispiece) — & then I'll pour forth all I can think of about you young, & we old, & novels — how damned they are — & poetry, how dead. But I must take a look into the subject, & you must reply, "To an Old Novelist" — I must read Auden, whom I've not read, & Spender (his novel I swear I will tackle tonight). The whole subject is crying out for letters — flocks, volleys of them, from every side. Why not get Spender

& Auden & Day Lewis to join? But you must go to Miss Belsher, and I must go to my luncheon.

This is only a scribble to say how grateful I am for your letter.

Yrs
Virginia Woolf.

Virginia need not have been so anxious about the sales of *The Waves*, for it was an immediate success; I find myself complaining in the middle of October to Julian that an accident to my hand was "all very unfortunate with your Aunt's book booming and high pressure of work in the office, the public apparently having decided that to be IT one must have *The Waves* on the drawing-room table." Naturally, in the excitement of the preparation for the book's publication and the first public reactions to it, the idea of a *Letter to a Young Poet* did not get very much further; but Virginia was turning it over in her mind all the time, and was changing her views about the "deadness" of poetry, for when I sent her a copy of my own *A Garden Revisited*, she wrote:

I am a wretch not to have thanked you for your book, which will not only stand on my shelf as you suggest but lie beneath the scrutiny of my aged eyes. I want to read it with some attention, & also Auden, & Day Lewis — I don't suppose there's anything for me to say about modern poetry, but I daresay I shall plunge, at your bidding. We must talk about it. I don't know what your difficulties are. Why should poetry be dead? etc. etc. But I won't run on, because then I shall spurt out my wild theories, & I've had not a moment to read for days, days — everybody in the whole world has been here — the Easdales in cartloads etc. etc. And now I should be packing. And then we go back. And then there'll be all the books fluttering about us; alas: it's going to be a bad season, I'm afraid.

But I want to go into the question of poetry all the same. . . .

« 7 »

THE publication of my first book of poems had a further unexpected consequence, which, like one bowl hitting another bowl that in its turn knocks all the other bowls into different places, was to set a series of events into motion not without historic interest for the curious student of literary movements and associations in England between the wars. One of the letters I received was from someone I had never heard of before, called Michael Roberts. He wrote that he admired the poems, had been watching my work for some time, and asked if I would care to come in to see him in his flat one evening to discuss them. An irresistibly flattering call for a young author: a few days later, after dinner, I knocked at his door, and found myself in the presence of a tall young man in glasses who reminded me at once of a giraffe that had taken to the serious life of learning, a University don of a giraffe. The presence was solemn as well as freakish, but the rare, contracted smile that played across the sharp and concentrated gaze was sympathetic. We plunged into talk about modern poetry at once, and I discovered that he had read all my contemporaries, and what was more had an idea that they belonged together more closely, in spite of the wide apparent differences, than I, in the middle of the mêlée which Julian made so dramatic, had detected. The more he talked, the more flattered I felt at the thought of belonging to a revolutionary movement in the arts, and the more my fresh publishing ardour was inflamed by the possibility, which began to grow in my mind, of presenting all of us in some way as a *front*, so that the public, notoriously sluggish in its appreciation of individual poets, should be obliged to sit up and take notice. I went home with many ideas humming in my mind. During the spring and summer we had endeavoured to get a Cambridge Miscellany together, but the project had collapsed at the last moment: out of Michael Roberts's theories I saw an admirable substitute, with far more possibilities, emerging. During the next few days I talked it over with Leonard and Virginia, proposed an anthology of poetry by all the young writers whose names had been mentioned that evening, got their sympathy and provisional support, and then wrote to Michael Roberts and suggested he should edit it for us and write an introduction.

The project that was eventually to take shape as *New Signatures* was on. It was not meant to be a presentation of entirely new poets, but rather the tracing of a pattern, between a number of young and recently published poets, which had escaped notice before, which was in fact becoming clearer, under the gathering winds of the epoch, all the time. The three "Oxford" poets who roused Julian's bristling suspicion — Cecil Day Lewis, Wystan Auden and Stephen Spender — were to be in it; Julian and William Empson (who was in Japan at the time) and Richard Eberhart and myself from Cambridge; and two writers I had got to know since I came to London, A.S.J. Tessimond and William Plomer. When I was being frank with myself, I had to admit that the links that joined us seemed rather frail; but Michael Roberts stoutly maintained that in spite of what I might say in my moments of misgiving, they were real. Three Cambridge poets, leading lights of *Experiment*, he excluded because he thought them too close to T. S. Eliot and to the French surrealists Eluard and Tzara. In his view, however estimable their aims might be, we were on a different tack that he was convinced would in the long run prove more important. We all represented a reaction against the poetry that had been fashionable hitherto, we were united by a desire to assimilate the imagery of modern life, and even when we wrote, as Julian did, of country life, we meant something very different from what he described as the sentimental country clichés of our predecessors. The precision of thought and expression characteristic of the eighteenth century reappeared in our work, he said; and we were trying to make a new intellectual and imaginative synthesis that would be positive, not negative and pessimistic in its attitude to the problem of living in the twentieth century. Only the slightest hint, in all this, of the radical politics which so very soon after were to appear as the label attached to most of us.

Julian, battlesome to the last, did not at first like the idea at all of appearing under the same label as the "Oxford" poets. In reply to my invitation to contribute, he wrote me a long, growling letter about what we had stood for hitherto and the danger of condoning the heresies of Spender and Auden. As the poets of *New Signatures* have so often been assumed to have started off as a "school," or to have imagined themselves a "school," it is perhaps worth quoting my retort to Julian, written on Christmas Eve, 1931:

Thank you for your damned intransigient and intractable letter. I enclose a copy of the blurb for the book which will show you how deeply you will commit yourself if you offer any poems to it. The net is meant to be wide, and naturally the poets are not meant to form a *School* — an idea totally ludicrous. Are we to expunge your name from that provisional list? I hope not — but your letter in tone might have been that of a French General arriving in the Ruhr, 1923.

Cecil Day Lewis was already one of the poets published in the Hogarth Living Poets, so to recruit him was easy. His volume, *From Feathers to Iron*, had appeared at the same time as my own volume, and the interest it roused in inner literary circles was enormously magnified by an approving remark from T. E. Lawrence, which managed to get into the papers. It is perhaps unfair to a remarkable book to say that it was one of the first to show the strong current of Auden's influence; but *From Feathers to Iron* marked a decisive change in Cecil

Day Lewis's poetry from what he had written before, and the new imagery of mysterious skirmishes in a landscape of industrial decay, railheads, frontiers and escapes across them came unmistakably from the bursting warehouse which Auden had thrown open. Auden's first book, *Poems,* had come out only the year before, but because it focused the growing restlessness and dissatisfaction of his generation coming to manhood in a world erupting with economic crisis after crisis and heading for another war, and focused it with dramatic imagery in poetry that already had its own distinctive rhythmic life and tone of voice, because in fact with the arrow aim of genius it exactly touched the nerve that no one had touched before, it had an overwhelming effect. All of us were to show the marks of it in the next few years.

I had met Stephen Spender for the first time during the Christmas holidays of 1930, when my sister Rosamond had brought him over from Ipsden. We went for a long walk together by the river in the direction of Marlow: I found him the most rapidly self-revealing person I had ever met, in fact he seemed to be devoured by a passion for presenting his *cœur mis à nu.* Very tall and slim, with a huge head of curls, he loped along beside me in the mild winter landscape, pouring out his views on the world, on how to find fulfilment and how to write, and graphically described the life he had adopted in Germany, where he spent most of his time. My father and his (as I have already related) had been colleagues in the old heyday of Liberalism, in both politics and journalism, and everything he said struck uncomfortably home: we came from the same matrix, we both had a blood connection with Hamburg, and his so very different solution to our common problems was bound to have a violently disturbing effect on me. In his view Germany, because of defeat and ruin, had escaped from the mortal sickness of Western civilization, and there youth had started to live again, free of the shackles of the past, a life without inhibition, inspired by hope, natural humanity and brotherhood in the springs of being. In England we were chained still by guilt, ossifying bourgeois conventions, and philistinism. If only I came out to Germany I would see the beginnings of the new world for myself. . . . He talked a great deal about Auden, who shared (and indeed had inspired) so many of his views, and also about a certain young novelist called Christopher Isherwood, who, he told me, had settled in Berlin in stark poverty and was an even greater rebel against the England we lived in than he was, and had been closely associated from the beginning with himself and Auden.

[116]

Since that first meeting we had exchanged letters from time to time, and had met abroad, and I had read and admired his early poems in spite of the large difference which I felt existed between what he was trying to do in poetry and what I wanted myself. He was enthusiastic about the idea of the anthology, and he wrote to me in January of 1932, from Berlin, to tell me that he and Christopher Isherwood had sent Auden a joint letter urging him to contribute as well. In the same letter he said that he hoped I would stay at the Hogarth Press, as one or two intelligent young publishers were badly needed; but he realized that his and Christopher's eagerness for me to stay put was purely selfish, and if I felt the work was seriously interfering with my writing, I ought to go. How familiar this note was to become in my life: like a slowly tolling bell, I was to hear it for the next twenty-one years, and indeed still hear it. Rung by one or other of my friends, or by some friendly reviewer or critic, always it reminded me of the unresolved dilemma of my life: was I to be the impresario of other people's creative work, or a creative writer myself? Each time I had some success in the one direction, I was to feel the need of effort in the other; and perhaps one day I shall discover that the dilemma itself was all the time the real pattern, the figure uniquely my own I had to write on the sand before the tide washed it away for ever.

So it was that *New Signatures* took shape, with surprising ease and an exciting cumulative impetus. But even as its outlines emerged, the stream was changing course, and with extraordinary rapidity. Ever since Cambridge I had been turning gradually away from the Liberalism of my upbringing, towards Socialism. My arrival at the Hogarth Press hastened the process. Leonard Woolf was a convinced and proselytizing Socialist and anti-Imperialist, active in the inner councils of the Labour Party, and many of the non-literary publications of the Press, especially the pamphlets, were propaganda for the Socialist point of view and exposures of the wrongs due to British Imperialist exploitation of other races. My conversion was partly the result of my deep-seated horror at human injustice and cruelty, a feeling that none of us brought up in the atmosphere of Fieldhead could ever escape, quickened into new life by these luridly documented cases for the prosecution, revealing how our Empire-builders and their followers had behaved in India and in Africa; and partly the effect of the more abstract economic theories of the intellectuals of the *New Statesman*, with whom Leonard and most of the leading lights of Bloomsbury were so intimately associated, theories which seemed to prove conclusively that social injustice and economic crisis and the wars of colony-grabbing Great Powers could be abolished only by the triumph of Socialism. By the time of the General Election in 1931 I was already sufficiently converted to share to the full the consternation and gloom that settled on all our circle at the collapse of the Labour Government. I remember a party on Election night, where faces grew longer and longer and prophecies of doom more and more despairing as the results came in, and the impenetrable, evil-tasting, olive-green fog that had blotted London out during the whole day seemed to me a symbol of the ominous obscurity of our future. But even as I reached this point of intellectual conviction, I began to move away from it, further to the left. The discredit of Labour made even staunch supporters of the Party in Bloomsbury mutter that perhaps far more radical measures of Marxism were necessary to defeat reaction and stop the drift towards a new war.

It was under the first wave of this disillusionment that work on *New Signatures* began; and Stephen Spender's contributions were portents of what was to come. In Germany of the Weimar Republic, in the last spasms before it gave birth to the Third Reich, the class-war that we felt was now approaching so much faster in our own country was far more nakedly apparent; the Communist Party was a great force, engaged in actual, ceaseless battle with its opponents; and from living with the ordinary working people of Berlin and Hamburg, Stephen's so fine and sensitive poetic intuition had penetrated to the purest elements of the hope and idealism that underlay the Communist faith in action at that time. I was deeply impressed and moved by the poems he sent us, the now-famous exhortation beginning "Oh young men, oh young comrades," the Lawrence-like *I think continually*, and the celebration of a Communist funeral, *Death is another milestone on their way*. They had a visionary ardour and sincerity that could not fail to quicken the turbulence of thoughts and emotions that had already been stirred up in my mind — and in the minds of many others moving along the same lines in my generation; though, as Stephen insisted, they were the issue of *poetic* sympathy, and in no way proof that the poet himself had assented to the whole Communist faith or wished to become an active political worker. In fact, he made it quite clear (in letters) that he thought it essential for an artist not to commit himself in that way. Now, many years later, when Stephen and I have long come to see how unscrupulous and ruthless the power-urge was beneath the idealism, and how cynically the realities of Stalinist Communism contradicted the hope, these poems still seem to me to retain their poetic validity; in fact I find them even more poignant because of the disappointed dream that haunts them today.

It was part of the romantic mythology in which Stephen delighted to cloak his contemporaries, to present himself as a learner at the feet of Auden, the great prophet, but to suggest that behind both of them stood an even greater Socratic prophet, cool in the centre of the stormy drama of remote Berlin: Christopher Isherwood. When he had first mentioned him to me during our winter walk by the river, he had told me that after his disappointment about the way his first novel *All the Conspirators* was received, he had abandoned England, written another novel, failed to get it published, and thrown it into a bottom drawer in despair and disgust. He talked about this unknown novel with enthusiasm: it was called *The Memorial*, and was, Stephen said, an extremely important work for our generation. My curiosity was aroused, and when I joined the Hogarth Press I persuaded Stephen — who in fact needed very little persuading — to write to Christopher and ask him to let me see it. In due course the manuscript arrived; I can still remember the eagerness with which I took it home with me to read. I was completely won over by it, and immediately decided to hand it on to Leonard and Virginia with a very urgent plea that we should accept it for publication.

During the course of the next few years Christopher became such an intimate personal friend and also such a close associate in my publishing and editing activities, that I find it very difficult to recover the impression he made on me when he first came to see me in my back room at the Hogarth Press. Much shorter than myself, he nevertheless had a power of dominating which small people of outstanding intellectual or imaginative equipment often possess. One of my favourite private fancies has always been that the most ruthless war that underlies our civilized existence, more ancient than the opposition of Teuton and Slav or Moslem and Christian, more ruthless even than the sex war, a war never to be concluded or halted by any but the most temporary and contemptuous of truces, is the war between the tall and the short. Does not example after example of conqueror and dictator in modern history — Napoleon, Dollfuss, Stalin among the foremost — demonstrate how unassuageable and remorseless is the lust for power when it wakes in a breast only four feet from the ground? Has it not been proved again and again that the small man on the war-path regards nearly all tall people as amiable loons with their heads in the mist, incapable, in the state of mushy good nature and confidence which their inches give them, of discerning in time the small foot put out so cunningly to trip them? There were moments when a look crossed Christopher's face which seemed to suggest the stirrings of this ancient and implacable urge. . . . And then, immediately after, a smile of extraordinary breadth and charm would flash across it and the deep-set eyes below the high forehead would twinkle with tenderness and fun, with that sense of the total absurdity of everything in the world which has always broken in irresistibly even on his most serious and passionate discourses, and led him away without warning on recklessly unbridled comic fantastifications: an element intoxicating to breathe with him, and entirely belying the formidable authority of his imperial nose.

It was impossible not to be drawn to him: I was attracted by the warmth of his nature, and by the quality which appealed to me so much in *The Memorial*, an exact feeling for the deeper moods of our generation with its delayed war-shock and conviction of the futility of the old pattern of social life and convention; his capacity — the pressure he was under in his imagination — to invent the most extravagant dream-situations of comedy for everyone he knew, evoked a response at once in that part of me that had produced the dotty fantasy plays at Eton; and at the same time I had fallen under the spell of his Berlin legend. And yet for some months after our first meeting, in fact until I actually joined him in Berlin after the break with the Hogarth Press, our relations remained rather formal: perhaps it was the sense of alarm that seemed to hang in the air when his smile was switched off, a suspicion he seemed to radiate that one might after all be in league with the "enemy," a phrase which covered everything he had, with a pure hatred, cut himself off from in English life, or even a mutual shyness that took quite a different form for each of us. In any case, the bonds between us were not yet very close: one mutual friend, and my enthusiasm for his work. A fruitful enthusiasm: Leonard and Virginia had decided, after some hesitation, to publish *The Memorial*, and early in 1932 it came out. The book made a deep impression on our circle, and one or two of the critics were quick enough to spot a future winner; but it did not sell more than a few hundred copies. Christopher took its financial failure with a philosophy uncommon among young authors. When I sent him a report on the sales in the summer, he wrote back: "Please don't suppose that I'm disappointed by the sales of *The Memorial*. They are actually £1 more than I'd reckoned." Some years later, of course, when he'd made his name on both sides of the Atlantic as the creator of Mr. Norris and Sally Bowles, the edition sold out and even became a rarity.

Meanwhile, *New Signatures* had come out and had an unexpected success. The reviewers were impressed, the public bought it and there was a general feeling in the air that Something had happened in poetry. We even had to print a second impression within a few weeks. Several of the poets were already known individually; but the little book was like a searchlight suddenly switched on to reveal that, without anyone noticing it, a group of skirmishers had been creeping up in a concerted movement of attack. Some of us were, perhaps, as surprised as the public to find that we formed part of a secret foray; Michael Roberts himself felt that one or two of his contributors had let him down by failing to provide poems that quite came up to his dramatic billing of them, and that his preface was inadequate and imperfectly worked out. As so often happens, however, an impression had been made on the public that no amount of reservations or protestations on the part of individual contributors could efface, and from that moment we were all lumped together as the *"New Signatures* poets." In retrospect, what surprises me is that while much was made of the sense of social shifting and upheaval in the poems, so little notice was taken of the sense of menacing war, implicit or explicit in so many of the contributions.

The success gave me confidence as a poet, more confidence than the rather soggy reception *A Garden Revisited* had the year before. More important at that time, I think it gave Leonard and Virginia confidence in me, and made them feel that whatever private criticisms they might have of the aims and achievements of the new writers, their works were worth publishing. They were also shrewd enough, I believe, to divine a success to come behind the partial flop of *The Memorial;* and they saw that our joint enterprise, the Hogarth Letters, was turning out lively and popular. At the same time they had observed with approval, if also with a certain amusement, the avidity with which I had learnt all the details of the publishing business, the possessive passion I displayed for all Hogarth authors, and the enthusiasm with which I launched myself into every new development, undaunted by the cobwebs of my basement and the continuing need to save pennies. They decided they would be able to do something that had seemed too difficult for years: to take a long holiday abroad while I looked after the Press for them.

They set out for Greece in the spring, with Roger and Margery

Fry. It was by no means unwillingly that I was left in charge, even though the trusty Miss Belsher, head of the front office, was absent much of the time. The omens for the future might have seemed as good as could be when Virginia wrote to me from Athens:

I have written to you several times (in imagination) a full account of our travels, with a masterly description of Byzantine and Greek art (Roger is all for Byzantine) but I'm afraid you never got it. The truth is it's almost impossible to put pen to paper. Here am I balanced on the edge of a hotel bed, with Marjorie and Roger popping in and out to suggest excursions, and Leonard ranging the sponge-bags with a view to packing.

I'm afraid you've had the devil of a time, with Belsher away, and the doors standing open to bores of every feather. I've often thought of you with sympathy when one wheel of the car has been trembling over a precipice 2,000 feet deep, and vultures wheeling round our heads as if settling which to begin on. This refers to the road into the Peloponnesus. Then we went to Delphi, to Nauplia, to Mycenae — it's all in the letter I never wrote. I can assure you Greece is more beautiful than 20 dozen Cambridges all in May Week. It blazes with heat too, and there are no bugs, no inconveniences — the peasants are far nicer than the company we keep in London — it's true we can't understand a word they say. In short I'm setting on foot a plan to remove the Hogarth Press to Crete. Roger is the greatest fun — as mild as milk, but if you've ever seen milk that is also quicksilver you'll know what I mean. He disposes of whole museums with one brush of his tail. He plays chess when the dust is sweeping the pawns from the board. He writes articles with one hand, and carries on violent arguments with the other. It has been far the best holiday we've had for years, and I feel deeply grateful to you, for sitting in your doghole so stalwartly meanwhile. Excuse scribble. Love from us both.

Virginia.

« 8 »

THE two years of my apprenticeship at the Hogarth Press were so entirely absorbed into the zealous learning of my trade, into reading up the past publications of the proud little firm and ploughing through the manuscripts that came to us, into planning and preparing and discussing with the Woolfs and my poet friends, that when I search my mind for images of the period, I see all the time the house in Tavistock Square and the short walk across Southampton Row and through the old graveyard that connected it with the studio flat, a little further down Heathcote Street from the Davidsons, into which I had moved. The first year was a very busy and happy time, in fact, and like so many times of contentment has left very few detailed traces behind it in memory.

And yet during those active months I was meeting a great number of people in the artistic and literary London of those days, and getting to know better many others I had originally met in my Cambridge days, in Cambridge itself or with Rosamond or at my godmother Violet Hammersley's house. There were evening parties at the Woolfs', where I was introduced to Roger Fry, eagerly spinning his theories about painting and poetry and discarding them again with the greatest good humour when Leonard exclaimed that they were "grotesque" and began to pick holes in them; Aldous Huxley, a tall, rather willowy figure who struck me as a little austere and remote as he leaned against the painted mantelpiece in his horn-rim spectacles and discoursed learnedly about everything under the sun — though, as a devotee of *Crome Yellow* and *Antic Hay*, I listened in fascinated awe; and the formidable and legendary Lady Ottoline Morrell, whose strangely garbed figure, deep voice, predatory smile and aristocratically ruthless "attack" in her manner towards young poets she was meeting for the first time, conquered but terrified me. After my first encounter with her, I wrote to Julian: "Do you know Ford's lines, something like 'not like the ruins of his youth, but like the ruins of those ruins'? — She made me think of that." This was not very gallant, but implied, nevertheless, wonder and awe; and whenever she summoned me to her famous salon in Gower Street I hastened thither, drawn by her powerful personality and the expectation of meeting some of the great men of letters who had frequented it so long, above all W. B. Yeats.

There were also parties which Ottoline definitely did not attend and into which Leonard and Virginia were rarely drawn, late-night parties at the studios in Fitzroy Street or elsewhere in the neighbourhood, where the younger members of Bloomsbury predominated, danced, dressed up for charades and skits on their elders — of which Angelica, Julian's sister, was more often than not the leading spirit — and argued, glass in hand, into the dawn. No one, I firmly believe, has ever succeeded in retaining a coherent recollection of such a party, or has been able in after-years to distinguish one party from another that followed it a few weeks later, unless some ineffaceably awful disaster or crisis occurred at one of them; even falling in love does not make a party memorable, for one only remembers a blur of faceless figures behind the chosen, the unique face; and because they were happy parties, and I happily rode on the crest of the wave, I remember them only as if they were a series of tapestries, in which many of the same figures are repeated again and again against a background that varies only in detail, tapestries woven out of the bright colours of our life at the time, before Hitler and another war changed everything, and all of us moving to a rhythm that seems now broken for good and part of the history that no one ever discovers again, a tune unique and beyond all exact evocation, even of the most brilliant pen.

In the middle of this brotherhood of two generations of poets, critics and painters, linked together by an easy community of artistic beliefs and ethical values, by an athletic intellectual curiosity and a passionate faith in the sensuous world, a tragic gap was soon to be torn. I had continued to see Lytton Strachey since my arrival in London, and egged him on to tell me many fond and malicious stories of Leonard, one of his oldest Cambridge friends: in those early days at the Press everything that could add to my knowledge of my two employers and future partners was vitally important to me. We used to meet in his rooms at 51 Gordon Square, or at his club. I was in a glow of pleasure and amusement as Lytton, in his high, thin but authoritative voice, ordered an excellent wine and we settled down to a long discussion about the past of Bloomsbury and Lytton's Cambridge days, about poetry (which Lytton wrote copiously, though modestly and in secret), or modern French literature, in which he sadly found all the vices of German literature and very few of the great traditional French virtues. I also visited him at Ham Spray, and explored endlessly in his library while he worked, and afterwards would go for walks with him, during which we renewed our discussion — or rather I renewed my eager questioning and he his judicious and witty answers to the ever-unsatisfied disciple.

During the late autumn of 1931, however, he fell seriously ill, and nobody quite knew what was the matter. At Christmas he rallied, and Rosamond, who with her husband Wogan Philipps was a constant visitor to Ham Spray, wrote to me describing the Christmas celebrations at Ipsden:

That evening was the first for a week when the feeling of being in a bad dream lifted a bit — as we had just heard that a miracle had happened and Lytton had pulled round after being given up by everybody. I feel now he will live, though the danger is still acute. The bottom would fall out of the world for us if Ham Spray was no more.

But the danger was more acute than anyone guessed, and he began to sink again. Towards the end of January he died: the post-mortem revealed that he had been suffering from cancer of the stomach, that all the diagnoses had been wrong and that nothing could have helped him. It was a shock and great sorrow to me, but more for what might have been than for what had already matured between us in the way of friendship. Others among my intimate circle felt the true sharpness of a blow that oppressed the whole of Bloomsbury.

One of the most interesting sides of my work at the Hogarth Press was meeting the authors who were already published by the Woolfs. One of the first books that Leonard urged me to acquaint myself with was a short novel called *Turbott Wolfe* by William Plomer, which they had published five or six years before. I was impressed when I read it: I felt that the emotional design was more chaotic, the execution a great deal rougher and more haphazard than appealed to my rather orderly taste; but how I envied the passion that swept through it, the ferocity of its rejection of prejudices and conventions that stand in the way of human justice and the natural flowering of human feeling.

The opportunity to meet him came very soon, as the Press was at that time preparing to publish his novel of Japan, *Sado*, and his book of poems, *The Fivefold Screen.* What struck me at once about the rather burly figure with the deep voice who came into my office one morning, was the shrewdly observant look behind the spectacles, the sensitive mouth and the humour that would leap into the whole expression of his face at the slightest lead from whoever was talking with him. As I got to know him, I found his delight in anything eccentric or fantastic, the continuous bubble of crazy commentary that he would keep up in responsive company, completely irresistible. I noticed, too, that when I was with him things would happen, people would appear, that were exactly the right food for this kind of foolery: as he approached the ticker-tape news in the Athenaeum, the machine would make a misprint that reduced the whole sentence to absurdity; as one went out into the street with him a woman would pass wearing a hat that looked as if it had been lifted entire from an amorous nook in the parrot-house in the Zoo. Like so many other people of lively personality, he seemed to create his own surroundings. Or is it simply that one doesn't notice them in that particular light until such a person points them out?

Poetry has informed the best of his novels and stories, and if in the medium of verse his control of formal design has not always been so sure, some of his poems achieve that absolute rightness of concen-

trated effect that only a true poet can bring off. By far the most remarkable sections of *The Fivefold Screen* were those groups of poems
inspired by Africa and Greece. They owed their success, I believe, to
William Plomer's direct response to what is primitive, vivid and elemental, so that his gifts have always seemed to me by comparison
muffled and uncertain of themselves in the mists and half-tones, the
temperateness of England — all his gifts, that is, except his gift for
satire and comic portraiture.

Even in his humorous ballads, with their violent resolutions in
which the grotesque and the terrible so oddly mingle, one feels the
same response at work. And yet it would be unfair to stress this side
too much; William Plomer is a writer of deep compassion, and no one
of his generation has shown a more emphatic respect for the civilized
virtues of scepticism, tolerance and patient understanding. As with
other writers who owe a great debt to E. M. Forster, he takes seriously
the poet's and novelist's role of philosopher and interpreter of life, and
it came to be of increasing importance to him after the early books.

« 9 »

IN those first few months of 1932, when the fruits of my entry into the
Press were beginning to show, when our worldly fortunes looked
bright enough with a Book Society Choice in the shape of William
Plomer's new novel *The Case Is Altered*, and a second volume of *The
Common Reader* to follow the success of *The Waves*, when I was
beginning to feel an entirely new self-confidence in practical affairs as
well as a new hope for myself as a poet, all should have been well. I
had great ambitions already to draw all the new writers to the Press, I
wanted Stephen's prose if I could not have his poetry, I was jealous
that the magnet of T. S. Eliot and *The Criterion* had drawn Auden to
Faber & Faber, I worked as hard as I could to persuade the Woolfs and
Dorothy Wellesley to take on Louis MacNeice's poetry, and I heard
with the tremor of excitement that an entomologist feels at the news of
an unknown butterfly sighted in the depths of a forest, that behind
Auden and Spender and Isherwood stood the even more legendary figure of an unknown writer, Edward Upward. I determined to catch
him in the Hogarth net. And yet even while Virginia was writing so
happily from Athens and I was sitting in my "doghole" revolving these
schemes, things were beginning to go wrong. Under the surface my
restlessness was increasing, and as the time loomed nearer for the decision about my partnership with the Woolfs to be taken, difficulties

and doubts began to arise on both sides. Leonard and Virginia might approve in general of the new authors I was bringing to the Press, and encourage the new schemes I was so eager to propose; but their sober check on all this youthful foisoning of ideas would, it was clear, be much less effective when I was an equal partner — in an enterprise which was their own child and had never been shared so far with anybody.

Very soon after Leonard and Virginia returned from Greece, I left for my own holiday abroad: it was a trip that did nothing to lessen my growing doubts about the harmony of future relations at 52 Tavistock Square, and did much to increase my restlessness. My plan was to go through France into Austria, and then up from Salzburg through Germany to Hamburg and Berlin, and end with a visit to Stephen Spender (and Christopher Isherwood if he was there) on Ruegen Island on the Baltic coast. I stayed only a few days in Paris, and then went on by the Arlberg Express to St. Anton in Tirol. Even though I was alone, the sense of release and exhilaration I felt at getting into Austrian Alpine surroundings was extraordinary, all the more so as I had no interest in ski-ing or mountaineering (and have never been bitten by either sport). Even today I am not quite sure why Austria became a passion for me, was in fact already a passion before this, though I had visited Vienna only once, two years before, on my tour of the Prints and Drawings departments of the great European museums. Was it an obscure recollection of the summer we all spent at Château d'Oex just before the war, the sunset over Lac Leman a small boy caught for ever in his sleepy eye as the funicular ground slowly up the mountain-side? Had all this been stirred again by the story of the ruined Empire, that was bound to draw the children of those who had fought on the other side? Perhaps it was Rilke's poetry, which I had come to know since I had joined the Hogarth Press, a poetry so evocative in itself and so intensely redolent of the old Austria, that had quickened all these seeds lying deep in my mind; that had created the illusion that the country itself was more beautiful than any other, the inhabitants more sympathetic, more deeply civilized and yet closer to the natural rhythms of life than anywhere else in Europe. Whatever it was, illusion or reality or childhood haunting, it grew into an infatuation strong enough to turn the whole direction of my life, that survived the knowledge that came to me later of poverty and squalor in a discarded metropolis, of social dissension and a fecklessness that made the Austrians the easy prey of their powerful and pushing northern neighbours — a people to whom I was more closely allied in blood.

[127]

My first morning in St. Anton the mist blew away and I saw blazing snow-peaks against the blue sky, and slopes of fresh green below the dark pine-woods. I spent the day climbing up through the high meadows, following the roaring, narrow torrent full of spring's melted snow, while the arch of sapphire above me seemed to grow deeper, more incandescent in the purity of its tone: only on the topmost peaks little clouds were still clinging like attendant spirits, like Ariel to Prospero. Next morning, in Innsbruck, I looked out of my window to see a sheer wall of mountain rising straight up behind the houses; the white-powdered rock-face shot clear above the freshly opened buds on the chestnut-trees in the town's park spaces, where I sat at midday with a Baudelaire unread in my hand and watched the beautiful Tirolean young men and girls saunter past with their strong mountaineers' placing of foot on ground, laughing and chattering together. I was keyed up by the pure air, and I felt for a moment as if I had always been in Innsbruck, as if the bells I heard begin to ring called back innumerable such days in years gone by: my happiness was so great, I felt an urgent need to gather and store the emotion, as if I could make a reservoir of it strong enough to drive a mill-wheel, a turbine. Then the train took me twisting down through Alpine meadows so thickly woven with spring flowers they seemed to me like Bokhara carpets or the glittering fragmentations of light in the medieval rose-windows of the great cathedrals, dazzling harmonies of deep-violet and silver-yellow and pure cloud-white and every shade of coral and rose; and landed me in Salzburg, a crystal city of sun and open spaces and towering architecture so white in the sun it might have been made of snow.

Everyone seemed burnt and transformed by sunlight in Salzburg, with a fiery warmth in sharpest contrast to the pale faces I had left behind me emerging pastily from a London winter. The handsome features of the Salzburgers seemed open with the openness of sunlight, their fair hair had the glint of the sun, the ruddy darkness of their cheeks, their necks, their sturdy legs and arms was like a honey extracted from the huge flower of the sun, as they whirled recklessly through the streets and over the bridges ringing their bicycle bells, or leant against the pillars of a white baroque colonnade, laughing together in the sun, or lay on the edge of the baths (but not bathing) luxuriating in the rays that poured down ceaselessly out of a sky without a cloud. In the evenings I wandered into the Mirabel Gardens, where a concert was being held and all the statues were illuminated and the fountains changed from green to red to purple and back to flashing silver; and watched the people strolling in and out of the focus of light, standing quietly listening round the band with absorbed faces, or talking under the trees in groups of three or four, or leaning over the balustrades and chaffing one another. I was a spellbound watcher of a conjured scene, and my imagination began to weave patterns of poems out of them, to invent stories of their lives that would capture as if by accident something of the magic element in which they seemed to exist.

I began to think again of the poetry I wanted to write. For a long time I had intended it to become more personal, following more fluid rhythms of thought, my thought, responding to and in harmony with the nervous, complex, unmonumental awareness of my own European generation, the tunes that travelling, that watching and brooding on the lives of strange people in new countries started up in my mind; a mingling of outer and inner, of the beleaguered past and the dissolving present, of the conscious mind with the irruptions of the unknown rain-maker in the deeper intuitive mind, that the couplets and quatrains I had been writing at Cambridge disciplined too rigidly — though the discipline had been necessary. I felt that my wanderings — and they had essentially to be undertaken alone for this purpose — released springs that I had instinctively known to be welling up inside me for some time; I wanted, as it were, to travel light in my search for whatever the truth was that I craved, and poetry to be as simple and informal as marching songs, and yet, like the sublime lyrics that suddenly break out of the prose in Rimbaud's *A Season in Hell*, or Yeats's *Words for Music Perhaps*, to concentrate experience and vision in a few lines. That, in an age when prose was staking claims all over the lazy ancient lands of poetry, was surely poetry's proper destiny and technique for survival. I was haunted by the words that Rilke puts into the mouth of Malte Laurids Brigge in the famous *Notebook:*

In order to write a single verse, one must see many cities, and men and things; one must get to know animals and the flight of birds, and the gestures that the small flowers make when they open out to the morning. One must be able to return in thought to roads in unknown regions, to unexpected encounters, and to partings that had long been foreseen; to days of childhood that are still indistinct . . . and to mornings by the sea, to the sea itself, to oceans, to nights of travel that rushed along loftily and flew with all the stars. . . .

Only then, it seemed to me, as the train followed the swirling, opaque ochre-yellow waters of the Danube on the way to Passau, when one had trained one's imagination to turn one's life, one's experience into legend in that way, could one write a truly modern poetry.

And yet it was not enough merely to be a watcher of other people's lives from the outside. One must, I thought, be able somehow to enter into them, to lose oneself in them until one could hear inside one's own heart the rhythms and music to which they moved, until their hope and dismay touched one on the quick of one's own nerve. And then the poetry that was still out of reach would lean out towards you and take you and create itself through you. Of all places, the Austrian provinces I had just been through inspired me with the greatest longing to accomplish this act of self-loss and self-renewal. "Towards the heart of the fire" — that was a phrase that kept repeating itself in my mind, and the fire was the suffering, tension and bitterness the ordinary working men and women of the world were enduring, the creative despair and the revolutionary ferment that seemed to increase like a hammer beating louder and louder in the economic crisis of the 'thirties. A poet, if he was to accept all the implications of being a poet in our age, could not run away from that, but must set out towards it. When I reached Hamburg (where I made a pilgrimage to discover the paintings of my great-grandfather in the museum), the sight of the masts of all the ships in the harbour that had been lying up for so long unused, and the clusters of unemployed sailors and port-workers who slouched round the quays in their dark-blue caps dully watching those masts and funnels, stirred these thoughts violently again. And I remembered that in Vienna an experiment was being made by the Socialist Municipal Government to prove what had become so doubtful to us in London: that the working masses could find welfare and civilized conditions of life without a Communist revolution. Another reason to know Austria intimately — another magnet pulling me into the heart of Europe.

For some time I had been telling Stephen and Christopher in my letters that I was beginning to wonder whether my life as a publisher in London was compatible with the life of a poet, as I now felt it should, in the world and at the time in which we lived, be ordered. Our debates about the nature of modern poetry, the way the poet should prepare himself to create it, began again as soon as I reached Stephen on Ruegen Island. While I had been travelling, Leonard and I had exchanged letters about the future, half-exasperated with one another, half-unwilling to break up what had started so promisingly. Stephen was sympathetic to my desire to be more completely a poet, but also clearly believed that there was much to be said — from the point of view of all of us — for having me planted in the centre of publishing and editing in London. Sensibly, he preferred not to influence me too strongly, and in spite of the turn my thoughts had been taking and in spite of the living example Stephen himself was, in so many ways, of my idea of "travelling light" as a poet, I might even then have plumped for the back pantry; but, alas, there was more to it than just my restlessness.

We went for long walks through the gently sloping, wooded landscape of the island, where fields of barley alternated with pastures of black-and-white Friesian cattle and water-meadows full of yellow irises and yellow mustard. We climbed the high cliffs on the northern edge of the land and came down to sand dunes and a cobalt sea stretching out towards invisible Scandinavia. Stephen, who always went about with an open collar to his shirt and was often without a shirt at all, was now burnt a deep brick-red, which, contrasting with his large, deep-set, bluish eyes, gave him a demoniac look, particularly when his face was split by a huge pantomime grin at some absurd recollection. We talked all through the walks, about poetry, about politics and what was happening in Germany, about his friends in Berlin and the way they lived, about Bloomsbury and our mutual circle in London, about a magazine I wanted to launch, to carry on what *New Signatures* had started. Stephen did not exactly monopolize the conversation, but he had the lion's share. When he was excited, perhaps about some opinion he thought outrageous on politics or poetry, his words would pour out, grating on the ear like pumice-stone; and then suddenly he would check himself and fall into a gentler, more receptive, almost diffident mood, and his expression would soften as his voice became more harmonious. In the evenings we would go on talking in the local café where the German sailors danced with their girls, or in his room, where, in a sudden outburst of confidence and intimacy, he would rummage wildly in the chaos of his work-table and the wardrobe, and out of the jumble of pens, papers, ties, torn shirts, unpolished shoes and undarned socks would fish up poems, photographs and letters, all to be heaped upon me for my admiration or critical inspection.

Christopher was not on Ruegen, nor in Berlin when I passed through, and I returned to London without seeing him. The situation between myself and the Woolfs seemed to have got worse since I left, and it continued to deteriorate during the remainder of the summer, some weeks of which I spent in convalescence, after a persistent fever, at Fieldhead. It seemed impossible to find a compromise that would satisfy Leonard and myself, and thinking it all over again during my rest, I saw only too clearly that if I stayed, my relationship with him and Virginia would almost certainly be poisoned for good; and I did not want that. I was far too happy in my relationship with them as a literary beginner sitting at their feet; and this relationship did indeed continue to the end as if nothing else were growing up between us. The *Letter to a Young Poet* had come out, and Virginia and I had many discussions about it. Our chief point of difference was over "Mrs. Gape," the symbolic char-woman figure she took to represent the intractable realistic material we were trying to use in our poetry. I felt that this was the weakest part of a brilliant piece of work: Mrs. Gape was a fantasy of Virginia's, who corresponded to nothing we were trying to assimilate, and her idea of "beauty" was oddly conventional. In her reply (in a letter to me at the end of July), she admitted she had chosen quotations that were weak for her argument, but returned — and I think effectively — to the attack by saying that her complaint was that the poet, in tackling this new material,

doesn't dig himself in deep enough; wakes up in the middle; his imagination goes off the boil; he doesn't reach the unconscious, automatic state — hence the spasmodic, jerky, self-conscious effect of his realistic language. But I may be transferring to him some of the ill effects of my own struggles the other way round — with poetry in prose. Tom Eliot I think succeeds; but then he is much more violent; and I think by being violent, limits himself so that he only attacks a minute province of the imagination; whereas you younger and happier spirits should, partly owing to him, have a greater range and be able to devise a less steep and precipitous technique. But this is mere guesswork, of course. . . .

In spite of these absorbing exchanges, I knew that an impossible situation was approaching. So it was that, impelled partly by disappointment and bitterness, partly by a need to prove to myself whether I was a poet or not, partly by currents that ran too deeply under the surface of the time for me to be entirely aware of them, currents that were affecting in greater or lesser degree all our friends and all our world, I finally decided to make the break. I knew it meant abandoning all my hubristic schemes to make the Press the centre of literary publishing for my generation, and, more particularly, abandoning the chance of having a share in the book to follow *New Signatures*, which I was already discussing with Michael Roberts (and which was published the following year as *New Country*, with some of my poems in it). I minded bitterly. I thought I was leaving the Hogarth Press for good. It would have appeared fantastic to me if someone had suggested that six years later I should be back, better friends than ever with Leonard and Virginia, and in a stronger position as a publisher, with the enterprise of *New Writing* successfully under way.

◆§ IV §◆

Towards the Fire

DURING my first autumn in Vienna in 1932 I was feeling my way towards a new life, trying to learn to be the poet that Rilke had ideally imagined in *The Notebook of Malte Laurids Brigge*. That book, Yeats's last poems, Arthur Waley's translations from the Chinese, a collection of Rimbaud's works in prose and poetry and Wilfred Owen's poems were, I think, my most constant companions: books I wanted to absorb into my bloodstream and be the food of the poetry I planned to write. I used to settle in a café for an hour, morning and evening, with my lexicon beside me, and struggle to understand the jargon of the Austrian newspapers, adding about twelve hideous words to my vocabulary every day. In between, I went out to learn the ordinary speech of the Viennese, and whenever I visited the park of Schönbrunn or the Belvedere, or took a trip up to the Kahlenberg or to the *Heurigen* of Grinzing, endeavoured to get into conversation with Viennese people who looked as if they would *not* be able to speak even the most pidgin English. So little by little, as the golden, dusty days of that perfect September slipped away and the piles of grapes on the fruit-stalls in the streets grew scarcer, I made my first steps into intimacy with the city that had fascinated my imagination for so long. At last I managed to penetrate to the outer circles of habitation, discovered the Karl Marx Hof, and made friends with a family that occupied one of the flats. The young son, Karl, was an electrician and a fervent member of the Schutzbund, the armed defensive organization that the Social-Democrat Government of Vienna, knowing itself surrounded by enemies who had already shown their teeth, had created after coming to power. He showed me all over the beautiful tenement, the only one I had ever seen that did not remind me in one sense of a barracks, and proudly described the achievements of his Party in social welfare and education. He was absolutely confident in their power to resist any attacks of the Austrian fascists; confident, too, in their natural leadership of the civilized forces of progressive Socialism — which seemed more like radical Liberalism to me — throughout Europe.

It was Karl who, flashing his gold tooth at me, first brought home to me the reality, the increasing desolation of unemployment in the little Republic. It was difficult to believe, in that beautiful country, with the sun laying its benediction day after day on baroque domes and dahlia-filled parks, that anything could be wrong: even the bands of young singers and musicians with their accordions, who wandered all day through the streets picking up a few groschen here and there, seemed to be more part of a sad, timeless pageant at first than raw human evidence of the same urgent tragedy that had overtaken the unemployed in England, who seemed so much more denatured, plunged so much deeper in squalor.

Those autumn months convinced me, nevertheless, that in the life I envisaged in Austria I could not only find the food I needed for my poetry but also that close-up view and understanding of the human and social problems of the time that had become so important for me. Towards the heart of the fire . . . There, in Vienna, I should find the way. In the new year, I decided, after returning to England for Christmas, I would look for a more permanent abode in Vienna. But another, unexpected card was to be dealt me before that, rearranging the whole outlook I had so carefully planned for myself.

Christopher Isherwood was still in Berlin, and again invited me to visit him there. I decided that it would be a good plan if I stayed for a few weeks on my way back to Vienna. I arrived at the end of January, and within a very short time found myself in the midst of the last agony of the Weimar Republic. In my lodgings off the Nollendorfplatz, stung by Christopher's claim to be able to write a thousand words a day and give English lessons to earn his bread and butter as well as live an agreeable social life, I laid out my exercise book and my pens every morning. It was not much use: what was going on in Berlin was too novel for me, too tense and too ominous. The crucial elections were approaching, and bloody conflicts between the Nazis, the Communists and the Social-Democrats were taking place almost every day in some part of the ice-bound city that was laid out like a patient about to undergo an operation without any anaesthetic at all. Now that I was close at hand to the battle I had read about and heard so much about from Christopher and Stephen, I noticed something that I had not foreseen, an element, puzzling and disturbing, that had been left out of the reporters' reckonings of Right versus Left, reactionary capitalism versus the working-class movement, and so on. All over Berlin, especially in the middle-class shopping and residential districts, huge pictures of Hitler were displayed at night in windows illuminated by devout candles. As I wandered along the streets with Christopher, muffled up to the eyes against the flaying wind, the crude likenesses of the Man of Germany's Destiny, row upon row above us, were like altars dedicated to some primitive demon-cult, and seemed to menace far more terror than had been conceivable in the rational, easy-going atmosphere of London.

A few nights later I was in a bar near the Zoo, when a friend who had been to a cinema came in, and said, "The Reichstag's on fire!" I followed him outside, and could see the glow of flames eastwards against the black sky. . . . It is not my intention to tell again here the story that is known so well, of the Nazi *putsch* that followed the trumped-up crime and Hitler's inevitable triumph and appointment as Chancellor after the hollow voting had taken place; only to describe some results it had for me. For the events of the next few days, until I left Berlin for Prague and Vienna about a week after the elections, laid a searing mark across my mind. Christopher, who so skilfully managed to have friends or acquaintances in all the warring camps, had of course a number of friends among the Communists and their sympathizers: they were in immediate danger of arrest, exile in concentration camps and death. Their plight in hiding, their sudden disappearances never to be explained, the tales they told of the brutality that the victorious Nazis were indulging in towards their opponents in the secrecy of barracks and prisons, the ruses that had to be invented to remove them to some kind of temporary safety, the Jew-baiting, sabre-rattling, hysterical tone of the Press — all this illuminated for me the hour that had struck in Europe with blinding clarity, and keyed me up to one of those rare moments of vision when I could almost have broken into prophecy. Indeed, when a broadcast by Vernon Bartlett on the new Germany was reprinted in *The Listener*, I wrote a letter in which I denied all his hopeful and comforting conclusions and said roundly that Hitler's success meant war sooner or later and we should very quickly find all the treaties torn up in our faces. From that moment it seemed to me desperately urgent to do all in one's power to help build some kind of dam against this torrent that was sweeping down towards war, and in spite of governments if governments were half-hearted about it. From that moment, too, I was obsessed by the political terror that had broken out: it was almost as if I had been a victim myself, so keenly, on the raw of my nerves, did I feel the abomination of it and the need to prevent it breaking out in other countries. And I experienced for the first time the strange paradox of life maintaining its smooth and smiling surface while out of sight thousands were being tortured and broken, and edifices of political liberty that had taken generations to build up were being sent crashing to the ground.

I spent several months of 1933 in Vienna, where I eventually found a small flat in a modern block off the Arenberg Park. I lived there in rather absurd austerity, with little more than a bed, a few chairs and a table built for me by an out-of-work carpenter of the district. The austerity was not the result of principle, or really of poverty, but of the restlessness and uncertainty that the *putsch* in Germany had so enormously increased in me: in Prague and in Paris I met again some of those who had been fortunate enough to escape from the new Third Reich, and their tension and gloomy forebodings deflected me even further into the political anti-fascist movement that was now beginning to gain an international impetus. The dream of making myself into Rilke's poet seemed shattered: the dangers of the future had taken such a huge bound nearer, I found myself, with my own friends and Christopher's friends, so deeply involved, plunged so far into the swirl of refugee, underground and above-ground, anti-war and anti-fascist activities, that I could only fitfully recapture the mood of the previous autumn — rare little islands that would suddenly be overwhelmed by a gigantic wave of alarming news. Christopher, exiled from the Germany he had made his home, suffered acutely from now on from traumatic anxiety about the explosive state of Europe. He pitched his tent in various European cities — Lisbon, Copenhagen, Brussels, Amsterdam — never staying very long, listening to the darkest prognostications of the refugee friends from Berlin who nosed him out, prostrated every seven days by the grisly international low-down that Claude Cockburn served up in his skilful little news-letter *The Week*. The burden of his letters was always the same. "What do you think of Europe?" he wrote from Copenhagen. "I am utterly unable to judge, having lapsed even deeper into a state of utter inert horror. I read all the newspapers and listen in to the wireless in all languages, even those I don't understand; hoping somehow I shall get a clue from the peculiar intonation with which the Lettish announcer pronounces the word Alexander. . . ." And again from Greece: "Is there going to be a war? This question may well be answered before you read it. Anyhow, I can't judge anything from the scrappy paragraphs at the back of the Athens *Messenger*, whose leading articles are generally about Lord Byron, 'Sir Codrington' or a French poet's impressions of the Ægean. . . ." Or from Tenerife: "I read the most alarming reports. When and where will the war start? K—— has ceased to write to me, and his silence is more terrifying than his worst prophecies. Wasn't there an Oracle which foretold disaster and then suddenly shut up altogether — and the Assyrians arrived and killed everybody? But perhaps I am getting mixed. . . ." It was a mood that only the Spanish War was to make intelligible to most of our contemporaries in England, and even then only in the most gradual stages. And yet during these years Christopher was writing his first plays in collaboration with Auden, and working at the material in his Berlin diaries which was soon to make his name known far outside the small circle that had admired *The Memorial*.

The ominous year passed with ever-growing anxiety in Austria. The Austrian clerical-fascists and their Heimwehr, with the picturesque but adolescent throw-back Prince Starhemberg, at their head, seemed to derive as much comfort from the change in Germany as the Pan-German Austrian Nazis. No wonder the morale of the Social-Democrats trickled away: they continued to make brave gestures and statements in public, but being above all men of peace, they allowed their outer fortifications to be taken piecemeal and without a struggle as autumn deepened into winter. I had espoused their cause emotionally, and tried hard not to look the future in the face. Again and again there came up before my inner eye memories of Berlin: a patrol of S.A. men breaking into a bar one night, and young Jews being taken away while one Nazi stood at the door covering us with a revolver — lorries full of political suspects driving top-speed towards the Alexanderplatz — the monstrous effigies of Hitler candlelit at night. . . . No, this could not happen in Vienna, it would require too violent a reorientation of one's thinking, too horrible a menace to all one had already grown to be so fond of and to admire in Austria. . . . At the beginning of February 1934, stopping off in Paris on my way back from Vienna to London, gloomily convinced that the Social-Democrats in Austria would in the end surrender without a fight, I found myself jammed one evening in a huge, excited crowd by the Madeleine, the bells of the ambulances ringing incessantly as they tried to nose their way through: at the bottom of the Rue Royale in the distance I could hear the roar of the rioting demonstrators in the Place de la Concorde, while near me in the shadows the blue-cloaked police reserves shifted and muttered uneasily. I did not then realize that this upheaval in

Paris would have almost immediate results in Vienna; but the last inhibition that restrained the Austrian fascists from the coup de grâce
they had so long prepared to give the Socialists, was anxiety about the
reaction of the French Radicals. This inhibition was now suddenly
lifted, while Parisian politics were in turmoil. Only a few days later I
was agitatedly telephoning through from London to find out if my
Viennese friends were safe, while the guns were bombarding Floridsdorf and the Karl Marx Hof, and Schutzbundler Karl's dream was
smashed for ever into the rubble.

For the time being the experience seemed to create an irrecoverable
and widening distance between myself and those of my friends in England who had not been through it, who had not learnt the mysteries I
had learnt. I felt as if I was looking through the observation car at the
end of a train that was gathering speed, making familiar landmarks
diminish and bringing mountains to light beyond them on the horizon,
mountains I had not known before existed. I tried to explain the why
and whence of my new extremism in my letters, especially to Julian,
who had remained sturdily by his belief in the Labour Party and the
gradual revolution, and anyway had a deep suspicion of almost everything that emanated from beyond the Rhine. I wrote sometimes plead-
ingly, sometimes priggishly and intolerably: underneath it all lurked
an unhappiness that events should be separating me from the friend
who had been closest to me in the life of poetry — the most real life of
all hitherto. I think Julian sensed this, for he wrote to me in December
1934:

. . . All your old Cambridge friends are asking after you and hoping to
see you. When we met we didn't find much chance to talk about poetry,
which was a pity, because I feel that it's probably our best subject of
agreement now. It's very hard for me to share your feelings about politics
because we live in such different worlds. . . . But I've always felt that
there's a certain intimacy between us as poets that should be able to last
through any other difficulties of communication. Incidentally, do remember this difference in our lives when you feel that I'm unsympathetic. None
of my friends are in danger or hardship, and it's hard for me to imagine
what I should feel if they were.

A strange perplexity overcomes me as I reach this point in my
story; for the seven years of the war and its aftermath so completely
buried my life in Vienna, that it is as if I needed superhuman strength
to lift up the stone slab that presses on it. How can it be that so many

years of one's life, so full of varied and intense experiences and discovery, in human relations as in intellectual exploration, should be as completely cut off from oneself as an arm or a leg left on the battlefield? The total loss of even small details is curiously bewildering: my telephone number in Vienna, or the registration number of my car, which seemed somehow to symbolize the solidity of my day-to-day life. Why should I have cared so passionately to scour so many papers every day for information that would piece together into some kind of coherent picture of the international situation, to know so much about it and to have forgotten and to care so little about those dramatic details today? How is it possible that people in the centre of one's happiness in those years should have vanished without a trace, and one's life go on, still so busily and so urgently? The great biographies and the great novels give the impression that every character and every experience in the first act of one's life will play a part in the last act, bringing all to harvest and meaning; but in this again we discover how dangerous it is to mistake art for life.

It is, then, with a kind of agonized detachment that I find myself exploring the six years during which Vienna was the centre of my life; wondering whether there really are fortunate people who have never experienced such obliterations on the path they have trodden. It dismays me not to be able to remember in clear sequence how my thinking changed, not to be able to disentangle all the threads that contributed to the emotional texture of that time, which gave certain kinds of action an imperative necessity and made others unthinkable; for these things are more complex than most people in their recollections are willing to admit — far more complex than the critics of a generation that comes after, who judge by the result in the present and not the possibility in the past, are ever likely to see.

In the reasoning that between 1933 and 1934 led me, not alone among my contemporaries, to believe that the solution to the troubles and dangers with which we were faced lay in Marxism, and even in Moscow, I can still, nevertheless, distinguish the strongest of the intertwining strands. First, we had seen three successive and cumulative failures of ostensibly radical régimes, but reforming rather than revolutionary, to survive against the counter-offensive organized by the privileged and the possessors in the economic crisis: the collapse of the Labour Government in England in the face of (what we at any rate believed was) the trick-scare of the "your savings are in danger!" election; the elimination of all liberal and social-reforming parties in Hitler's triumph in Germany; and now the inch-by-inch encirclement of

Vienna's Democratic Government by the reactionary forces which had
gathered in the provinces, with their private armies and their cynical
use, in the final thrust, of heavy artillery smuggled in from abroad to
crush the last struggles of a régime that had been too civilized — and
too hopeful of civilized behaviour in its opponents — to take the offensive while it was still possible. These three defeats seemed to point
to one conclusion: that if it was in serious danger, capitalism would
stop at nothing to turn back the wheels of democratic progress and
social justice and establish its puppets in power.

Another essential strand in our reasoning, an inference to which the
combination of all these events all too easily led, was the belief that the
attacks were part of an international conspiracy in which all capitalist
countries acted in secret concert; and that out of fear of the propaganda value of the sheer existence of the "one Socialist country," even
more than from a perception that rearmament and only rearmament
offered an easy solution to the economic crisis, all capitalist countries
were preparing to launch a war against the Soviet Union. This inference was reinforced, for a generation that had been brought up on the
idea that it was primarily the wicked intrigues of arms manufacturers,
oil companies and banks that had been responsible for the First World
War, by the continual uncovering of international armament deals and
what appeared to be the connivance of the Western Powers behind the
scenes in the flouting of the rearmament clauses of the peace treaties
by the Central Powers; and then, at a later stage, by the Abyssinian
and Spanish wars. Society was sick, it was sick unto death: it had
called in the thugs as doctors: the thugs were preparing to sweep
away all the traditional liberties of Western civilization and use force
to destroy the one country that was not in the grip of economic crisis.
That was one part of the argument in which we saw the trend of the
times summed up and exposed; and the other was: society is sick because it is organized on capitalist lines; every crisis will be succeeded
eventually by an even worse one, because that is the nature of capitalism; the only country that is not subject to these crises is the Soviet
Union, because it has gone the Marxist whole-hog, and totally eliminated capitalism. Those two parts of our argument came to form our
intellectual climate, as we searched for a means to make an end of the
horror of recurrent unemployment and a way of escape from the narrow tunnel that we knew was leading to war. It was the climate of
Auden's *The Dance of Death*, that witty, brilliantly simplified and
partisan "picture of the decline of a class, of how its members dream of
a new life, but secretly desire the old, for there is death inside them,"

which ends with the entry of Karl Marx (with two young Communists) announcing: "The instruments of production have been too much for him. He is liquidated."

What completed the change in our thinking was the apparent supineness of our own Government in the face of the fascist menace, even its collusion with the fascists in the hope of deflecting this dynamic away from itself and against the Soviet Union. We were deeply suspicious of the motives of Whitehall; and everything that happened, up to and above all including the Munich agreement, confirmed our suspicions. Not all of us pretended to superior wisdom about the international chessboard, but with Eden's eventual resignation and Winston Churchill campaigning against the policy of Whitehall, we felt that honest men "in the know" supported our case.

Of course there was another side to the story, and factors we missed; but it wasn't particularly easy to see them in the conditions of the 'thirties. The *bona fides* of so many of those who presented the other side seemed suspect. The factors we missed were missed by thousands who did not hold our views. It did not occur to us that the dynamic released by Hitler's revolution might be more anti-rational than anti-Russian, or that Wotan and Marx were capable, at a given moment, of finding the democrats and imperialists of the West more contemptible than one another. We never imagined, having seen the reforming régimes collapse, that a solution to the endemic crisis of monopoly capitalism other than Marx's revolution might be found. We missed the absurdity of the apocalyptic nature of the Communist doctrine — an absurdity that had long become clear to such canny and cynical dictators as Stalin. None of us, not even George Orwell, had as yet grasped the fact that in the proletarian paradise all citizens might be equal in theory — but some were "more equal than others." And we astonishingly deluded ourselves into believing that Moscow had not only established all those liberties and opportunities that were the breath of our being, but had established them beyond the possibility of destruction.

The delusion that "Moscow, of all places, was the sole source of light" came partly from wish-dreaming; partly from the absence of adequate facts on which to base our views (the facts were to come thick and fast in the next decade for those who had eyes open enough to see them); and partly from the extremely skilful and widely ramified propaganda emanating from Moscow. In Russia itself, one might have thought, one would see the facts for what they were; but once across the border at Negoreloye the propaganda was non-stop and exclusive, and so intense that it was difficult to remain in a frame of mind where one could coolly question; besides, there was much to be applauded and much that was absorbingly interesting, and on these features one's visitor-eyes were carefully directed. What one saw was a welfare state being built up with heady Slavonic enthusiasm. What one did not see then were the moral and intellectual conditions of the material progress: the total absence of political freedom, the fatal lack of open critical check in bureaucratic one-party government, the concealed poisoning of truth and corruption of values, the paralysing power of the secret police which produced one kind of life for those who were not suspect to the régime, and another of the most cruel and unjust order for those who were. In 1934, when I made my first trip to Russia, there was an impetus and zest to Socialist planning in such marked contrast to the economic stagnation and political despair of the Austria from which I had come, that it was impossible not to feel there was "something in it." This active optimism excused for me spectacles of poverty in the outskirts of the big cities as squalid as any in Vienna; the development of a privileged class one couldn't fail to notice in the course of long journeys in trains with their sharply distinguished levels of comfort; and the electric-light switches that didn't work, the plugs that didn't pull, and the taps that came away in one's hands in the new hotels into which one was ushered with such a flourish of pride. In the future lay the Trials, the new terror (old terror admitted as soon as a new one started), the betrayal of the Spanish War and the Nazi-Soviet pact, not to be guessed at that time. I had seen the Schutzbundler, who had fled to Russia after the February Risings, marching in the formidable May Day parades and dedicating themselves to fight fascism until they could return to a liberated Austria. It was a heartwarming sight if one had been personally involved in the Austrian tragedy; and though half-formulated questions were already stirring uneasily at the back of my mind, I came home feeling that there was more than "something in it." I decided that in some way or other I must myself be identified with the same cause.

Recurrent as malaria, a serious bout of rentier-guilt, the characteristic malady of my class and generation, laid me low. I began to feel that even my poetry was a frivolity unless in some way it was *useful* to the anti-fascist and anti-war cause. Already, after the Hitler *putsch* in Berlin, I had come into contact with a new international movement, Communist-controlled, though trying (with only varying success) to pretend that it was not, that held its baptismal congress in Amsterdam and called on all who were opposed to war and fascism, from whatever class they came, to unite under its banner. I had been introduced to its Paris offices, where I tried to persuade the dishevelled, overburdened political workers as they struggled with bursting files, broken-down typewriters and a dozen different languages, *gauloises* for ever drooping from their mouths and nerves for ever on edge, of the sincerity and ardour of my wish to help. I doubt if they quite knew how to take this strange six-foot animal from unpredictable England, who loomed up through the tobacco-smoke into the focus of their horn-rimmed spectacles; a poet talking enthusiastically in unidiomatic French of revolutionary English poets they had never heard of (and would not have understood if they had), an Old Etonian with public-school manners and a copy of *L'Humanité* in his pocket, as persistent as he was shy. I was suspected of being an agent of the famed *Intelligence Service Britannique*, an adventurer in search of cash, or just an eccentric nuisance; but one Polish girl believed in me, and I was eventually taken in to the inner sanctum to shake hands with Henri Barbusse, who had been persuaded to be the movement's figure-head, and received his blessing to act as their secret correspondent in Vienna. For I had determined that the best way I could serve was by making myself a channel of information from all the underground parties and sects in Austria (even of the Nazis if their news proved valuable) to their friends in the outside world. The idea of this work acted like an aspirin on the rentier-guilt: I felt I could pursue my literary activities and enjoy my life in Austria far more happily if I had this matter-of-fact association with the new movement, working in a way for which I intended specially to equip myself and in which I already had certain obvious advantages. Besides, the triangular struggle in Austria, between the so-called clerical-fascists, the underground Social-Democrats and Communists, and the underground Nazis had begun to fascinate me in itself; and I had been seized by the wild ambition to explore all through the countries of the old Habsburg Empire and make myself an expert on Danubian affairs.

With all this in mind, and feeling, after the collapse of the Nazi insurrection in Austria in the summer of 1934, that the struggle would be of longer duration than had seemed likely even three months before, I made up my mind to look for a more permanent home in Vienna. So it was that, when one of my friends introduced me to a young Viennese architect, an apostle of the neo-Viennese *Wohnkultur* but intelligent enough to listen to a client who did not want cacti sprouting all over the place from cosy little plywood cupboards that turned into dinette-tables or extra beds for midgets at night, I decided to enlist his help to find an old studio or attic that could be converted into a flat to live in, and entertain in, and work in: a proper headquarters, and not just a waiting-room at a station in transit.

The place I eventually found was at the top of a big building in the Invalidenstrasse, that belonged to a rich Czech mining concern. It had originally been used for offices, and I was told that the room which took my fancy had served, oddly enough, as the directors' dining-room. The great feature was a wide semi-circle of tall windows, from which one could see all over Vienna as far as the heights of Kahlenberg. Herr Grünbaum spotted its potentialities in a flash, and carried the day by his eloquently persuasive description of what it would look like when he had waved his (not extravagantly expensive) wand over it.

A few months later it was ready, and I moved in, to remain there for the rest of my years in Vienna. At the window end of the room a raised platform had been built to make it possible to sit in a chair and enjoy the view. On this platform a large desk jutted out from one wall, and above this desk I arranged a wall-paper of maps: large-scale maps of Vienna, Austria and the surrounding countries, smaller ones of England, France and the Caucasus. Down below the platform there was a bedroom on one side, closed by a curtain, and a big L-shaped settee on the other with table and chairs and a massive Austrian stove: the whole had been ingeniously arranged by Herr Grünbaum to give the impression of three rooms in one. There was more than a touch of *Wohnkultur* about it, but the transformation was not fussy or affected and marvellously improved the amenities. The door at the end led on to the hallway with a new built-in cupboard; through that to the kitchen and the shower-bath, and out to the back, where there was a terrace which we surrounded with a trellis and boxes of plants to make a screen from the other roof-tops in summer and autumn.

I was lucky enough to find a paragon of a housekeeper in a plump, cheerful-faced woman of Czech blood by the name of Frau Chval, who plunged into her work like a high-powered tank going straight across country through copses, hedges and spinneys. There was never a speck of dirt in the flat, nor a hole in a sock, nor a button missing from a shirt, and I never had to remind her about these things. She arrived on the dot in the morning, and produced delicious breakfasts, *Jausen* and luncheons, which I would dread to face now, with their fattening Viennese delicacies, all manner of *torten, nockerln, nudel-suppen, zwetschken-knödel, palatschinken* and so on. Mysteriously, I thrived on them then, and my weight remained steady. Her son Toni became a sort of secretary-chauffeur to me, and when there was anything to be done — a job of painting, plumbing, carpentering, shoemaking, repairs to the car or provision of wines — he immediately produced a friend from the district to quote what I was assured was a bargain price. Unemployment was by then diminishing from the worst, but very few of these young men had regular work, and I was glad enough to give them the jobs and thus, as they were friends of Frau Chval's family, extend my knowledge of the working people of Vienna.

Toni also had a near relation of his own age, whose plight was an epitome of the worst that had happened to a generation that seemed to have been simply struck out from the roll of human fortune. He had *never* had proper work: after training as apprentice to a shoemaker, he was flung on to the streets as soon as his time was up to earn a schilling or two here and there by any odd job he could scrounge, no matter how squalid or sweated. Sometimes he had no more than a few hours' work in a month, and would sit in the cheapest and most villainous cafés smoking an occasional cigarette made out of ends picked up from the gutter, and paying for a malt-coffee and a roll — sometimes his whole food for a day — with a few groschen he had wheedled out of Toni or his parents, who were extremely poor themselves and lived in a tumbledown shack in the Lobau. He had grown moody, bitter, unemployable and felt permanently ill. He had made several attempts at suicide and had long gashes on one of his wrists; he would often involve himself in brawls with the police solely in order to get into prison and have a few days' prison food. There were thousands like Heini in Vienna. As the iron winter of Central Europe closed down, the desperate, rotting horror of their existence, without adequate food or heating or clothes, seemed to me to reach its climax; as I watched the first snow falling on the roofs and domes of the city from the windows of my new eyrie, only prison thoughts came to me, a clenching of the fists to live through this evil time, for all those I knew and loved in Vienna to survive to better days; and yet, paradoxically, the arrival of the snow was a moment of relief and opportunity, for the Municipality had sudden need of an army of auxiliary street-sweepers, into which Heini and his unemployed friends were all likely to be enrolled for a few days.

It was not only in the cities that unemployment had made its ravages. One winter I went up to Puchenstuben in the foothills of the Alps; and I remember walking down from the inn one day to the village, through the utter stillness of the sparkling untrodden white, the branches of the tall pine-trees loaded down with lumps of snow that looked like whipped cream in the afternoon light, and having a long discussion with the young man who ran the general store. Most of the inhabitants of the surrounding country, he told me, earned their living in the timber industry, and conditions had gone from bad to desperate, and some of the peasants had had no work at all for months; in the farms it was just as bad, costs of transport were high and to compete with foreign produce in the Viennese market was almost impossible. Hundreds of lean, hollow-eyed young peasants came down from the mountains to join the ranks of the "*ausgesteuerten*" in the Viennese doss-houses.

When the work of converting my new home was completed, Toni produced a young student from art school, a friend of his girl-friend (whom he eventually married), an amusing boy of irrepressibly comic vein called Richard, who decorated the back wall of the house giving on to the terrace with fantastic pictures of jungle life — some of which were certainly not for the shockable eye. When he had finished them, I remember, we all celebrated with several bottles of Gumpoldskirchner on the terrace on a sunny afternoon; we were like a pack of cards for Happy Families, with Frau Chval beaming, arms akimbo, in the background. . . . How few years later war had sundered us and carried us away to opposing destinies: some, like Richard, who disappeared into the hell of Stalingrad, for ever.

Far away, out in the Atlantic, his movements made more and more eccentric by loyalty to *émigré* German friends and their passport difficulties, Christopher Isherwood was also trying to make a home and a plan of work for himself.

Here, amidst the flowers, our Rousseau life goes on [he wrote from the Canaries]. This place is a sort of monastery. It is run by a German of the Göring – Roman Emperor type and an Englishman who dyes his hair. The Englishman loathes women so much that he has put up a barbed wire entanglement across an opening in the garden wall, to keep them out. . . . My novel is exactly three quarters done. I hope to finish it on the day war was declared in 1914. It is a sort of glorified shocker; not unlike the productions of my cousin Graham Greene. . . . I am very happy here, and then, because I am happy, I feel sad. As long as we stay on this island, or somewhere equally remote, life is so charming and pleasant and calm; but nowadays a retreat seems artificial and wrong. As long as I work on a book my conscience is partially relieved, because I feel I'm doing a job to the best of my ability and helping in my tiny way. But I wish I were you. . . . I admire passionately the people who are standing up now and telling the truth; especially I find myself warming to Cockburn — I get *The Week* regularly. Misinformed or not, he does slash out at these crooks and murderers, and he's so inexhaustibly cocky and funny; like a street-boy throwing stones at pompous windows. . . . It is Sunday, and the moron Englishman and his guests are playing the gramophone in the bar, effectively sabotaging my attempts to work. ". . . What does it matter?" says the Englishman, when I expostulate: ". . . In fifty years we'll all be dead. . . ."

Now that I had a real home in Vienna, I felt much more settled and in harmony with myself; and though I still used to spend several months in every year in England, I was always glad to get back to my big desk with the wonderful panorama of the city I had become so infatuated with. In the rainy winds of late winter the line of hills, washed of their habitual mist, stood out behind the Stephansdom and the Karlskirche in sharp, blue outline all round the horizon; as spring advanced I could see the trees in the Stadtpark filling out with the fresh green of new leaves; and as evening came, I would raise my head from my work to see the falling sun had covered the maps on the wall with a dull, red glow. Here I worked on my book about the Caucasus, *Prometheus and the Bolsheviks*, on my novel with a Viennese setting, *Evil Was Abroad*, and on the articles about Vienna under the Dollfuss-Schuschnigg régime and about Danubian problems which were to form the basis of my book, published in the autumn war broke out, *Down River*. Here, too, I collected and sorted all the news that came to me from the underground parties, that reached me by word of mouth from people who arrived in my flat for a few hours and then vanished again, and by the innumerable little forbidden newspapers and pamphlets disguised as catalogues, religious appeals and medical advice that were thrust into my letter-box by invisible hands.

Sometimes, while I was away in England, friends would take the flat over: Stephen Spender, who had become deeply interested in Viennese underground politics since he had written his poem *Vienna*, was installed one summer, and his travel-shattered wardrobe was transformed and made new — "as if by a miracle," he exclaimed — by Frau Chval's furiously busy hands in a couple of weeks. Various members of my family arrived to stay, and we would go off to the Salzkammergut lakes, scattered round which many of one's London acquaintances could be found at one time or another during the season of the Salzburg Festival.

I was so deeply absorbed in Austria in the life of the hounded and the unemployed, all those living on the furthest outskirts of fortune, that when, on these summer expeditions, I moved again amongst the personalities of English social life, familiar acquaintances from the world of London salons and country houses, I sometimes had the curious sensation of visiting a country I had known only in a vivid dream. There, in the Austrian lakes, bringing with them their money, their jokes and the gossip of their class — the class to which I belonged by birth and education — the difference from their surroundings not obliterated but made only more striking by the adoption of a dirndl or a pair of lederhosen, they moved in a kind of protective cellophane, insulated from the deep, troubled, transforming currents of Austrian life, that roared with only the faintest of echoes beneath the confidence of their holidaying feet. I knew I must find the connection; but I felt often like an actor who cannot remember which is play and which is reality of the two existences he leads.

One of the channels through which I tried to make the connection was *New Writing;* but that story belongs to another chapter.

The Constant Element

IN 1935 my restless, confused plans for a magazine, which had haunted me ever since the success of *New Signatures*, began to crystallize. I think it was bound to happen: no one can be so obsessed by a craving without taking steps to satisfy it. Indeed, I had been obsessed for so long, and had fed myself on so many fantasies about it, and devised it in imagination in so many different ways, that I can no longer remember exactly when the precise seed that was to grow into *New Writing* was sown.

I had talked it over, in one way or another, with my sister Rosamond, with Stephen Spender, with William Plomer and many of my friends abroad; and above all with Christopher Isherwood. Since the days of *New Signatures* a great many changes had taken place in my life. My *Wanderjahre* had begun; I had come to know a side of life in the big European cities that was entirely new to me. I had seen popular uprisings and counter-revolutionary repressions, and I had even made a pilgrimage to Moscow with the reasonable intention of trying to understand the other side of the picture. I had made the acquaintance of many strange figures in the revolutionary ferment that called itself anti-fascism, idealists like Henri Barbusse and mysterious agents of the Comintern like Bramson, who was probably known by a dozen different names to other people and who had a habit of sitting down at the next table to one in Paris just when one had heard for a fact that he had been arrested in Berlin.

Like so many of my contemporaries, I was haunted by the feeling that time was running out before a new world war. "How to get out of this trap?" I noted in a journal at the time. "How to find sanity and a clear thought again? How to defend oneself, to be active, not to crouch paralysed as the hawk descends? But there must be hundreds, thousands like myself in every town in Europe, wrestling with this nightmare." And I was bewitched by the idea that writers and artists had a large role to play in the struggle to prevent it. The literary side of Barbusse's anti-war movement fascinated me; *Monde* and *Vendredi*, where the politics were interspersed with stories and reportage by a group of clever young writers, including André Chamson, Paul Nizan, Jean Giono and Louis Guilloux, seemed to reach a far higher literary level than *Left Review* in England, which had certainly not attracted many of the younger writers of parts. Why should there not be a magazine in England round which people who held the same ideas about fascism and war could assemble without having to prove their doctrinaire Marxist purity? Why not a magazine to which the writers of *New Signatures* and *New Country* could contribute, side by side with writers like Chamson and Guilloux, and other "anti-fascist" writers from other countries? In *Left Review* the politics came, fatally, first; I wanted a magazine in which literature came first, with the politics only as an undertone. I believed it would serve the triple purpose of providing a platform for the *New Country* writers that *The Criterion*, the *London Mercury* and *Life and Letters* could not provide; of introducing foreign writers, who had excited my interest during my travels, to an English audience; and of serving as a rallying point for the so rapidly growing anti-fascist and anti-war sympathies in my intellectual generation.

It was natural that it should be with Christopher that the first schemes should be sorted out, the first steps taken. He was living in Amsterdam at the time, and invited me to visit him on my way back to England from Vienna. We had talked it over vaguely before, we had written about it in our letters, but during that visit I suddenly felt that it was no longer a pleasant day-dream, but something about to become real. He promised me his own collaboration, which seemed to me essential, and agreed to help me in getting the active support of Wystan Auden and Edward Upward. One point which had nothing to do with the aims I have already mentioned was also, I think, settled on this visit: the magazine should, if possible, provide an outlet for short stories longer than most magazines were prepared to take, and also for all forms of imaginative writing in prose that were rather too unconventional in style or approach to find a home easily elsewhere. We both admired the *novelle*-length short novel that was so popular in Europe, and Christopher had in mind to write several himself; and at the back of our minds was also the possibility of publishing some of the Mortmere fantasies that Christopher was later to describe in *Lions and Shadows*. And where in England could one publish prose-poems of the sort that so many of my poet friends admired in the work of Rilke and Rimbaud and other, living, French writers? I dreamed confusedly of our magazine growing famous for publishing modern English equivalents of *Les Illuminations* and *The Notebook of Malte Laurids Brigge*. . . . I dreamed, too, of being the author of some of them myself.

For a long time we could not settle on a good name. We called it originally our *Chapbook;* and then for a while it became *The Bridge*, as a symbol of the work we wanted it to do in bringing together writers of our own class and writers from the working-class, writers of our own country and writers from abroad. At this distance I cannot remember what finally decided us to choose *New Writing*, a name that had been mooted early on and then abandoned for a time; perhaps the publishers. I had had fairly close relations with The Bodley Head over *The Year's Poetry*, which I edited for 1934 and 1935 with Denys Kilham Roberts of the Authors' Society; and it was he who suggested that Allen Lane and Lindsay Drummond of that firm might be interested in my plans. To begin with, I put up the suggestion of a quarterly of about 160 pages at a fairly cheap price, 3s. 6d. or less, but Lane and Drummond found when they worked out their estimates that this was impracticable, if there was to be a provision for editorial expenses as well as payment to contributors at even the smallest reasonable fee. The letter containing this dismal news was sent to me in Vienna early in September 1935. I had been so certain that The Bodley Head were sold on the idea that I had told Christopher that we were all set to go. I was therefore appalled at the letter, and realized that unless fairly vigorous action was taken at once all our plans would collapse. So I packed up and returned to London as fast as I could; and by the end of the month we had come to an agreement, and the project emerged as a book in stiff covers which was to appear twice a year with a guarantee of three numbers. I was given £60 a number, to cover editorial expenses (roughly estimated at £15) and all contributors' and translators' fees. Needless to say that sum was always exceeded by me, though I believe that it was as much as The Bodley Head could risk on such a venture in those days; and if it had not been for the indulgent sympathy and provision of my mother — whom I was able to pay back in full many years later — *New Writing* would have been on the rocks in a very short time indeed.

The moment the agreement was in the bag, I wrote round with the news to the authors who had provisionally promised to contribute, and in triumph to Christopher:

Your own contribution can be anything between 3,000 and 12,000 words long. However deeply Wystan A. may have involved himself with the Empire-builders and their film-hacks, he must not be allowed to leave for our far-flung territories without producing something. He will probably write it while you stand over him one evening. My homage to him when he comes. I think the moment has arrived for me to write to Edward Upward myself, now you have prepared the way. Can you give me his address? And will you find out from Stephen whether his contribution is finished, or nearly finished? Put the pen in his hand if not. I'm reckoning to be able to pay each contributor (of prose more than 3,000 words in length) at least £4 on account of royalties.

At first I had wanted him and some others of our friends to form a sort of advisory committee to be announced beside my name. He was against this, and had written:

Certainly I will be most honoured to act on the advisory committee, if you don't think my absence from England disqualifies me? But let me urge you, once more, to take as little notice of us all as possible and be very autocratic. I'm *sure* it's better. Need you, in fact, have a formal committee at all? Why not just consult people informally, whenever you want an outside opinion?

The idea of a committee was dropped. Christopher's advice was, in the circumstances, with so many of us scattered so far from each other across Europe, sound; but I am inclined to think that, apart from the ideal aspects of the matter, he had, with his usual quick perception, divined that I was likely to prove an autocrat anyway.

Gradually the manuscripts accumulated from all the sources that were available to me. I sifted a huge pile of French and German magazines and books of short stories to find works suitable for translation and authors to write to for the future. If you have rather strong ideas about the character you want your magazine to have, the first number is bound to be the most difficult. So many of the authors whose natural home it will be are still invisible to you, and will appear only when they have read or heard about your first number: the magazine then quickly acquires its own impetus, bowling along with little more needed than a firm hand on the steering-wheel, an alert eye to avoid the pot-holes and interpret the confusing sign-posts, and a hard heart to refuse to slow down for the shady individuals thumbing a lift. Even so, before make-up time arrived I found many more contributions in my hands than I could get into the limits to which The Bodley Head were sensibly determined to keep me. My suit-cases were full of them as I travelled between Vienna, Paris and London, and my mind contentedly revolved scheme after scheme of selection and arrangement for the first volume. I think those were some of the most happy-anxious months I have ever spent.

In spite of having abandoned the idea of an advisory board, it seemed to me extremely important to get the magazine's Manifesto accepted beforehand by all the people who had formed the "shadow committee" in my mind: apart from Christopher, Stephen, Rosamond, William Plomer and Ralph Fox — who had promised to help over modern Russian literature (about which he knew a great deal more than any of us) and to introduce me to some of the French contributors to *Monde* and *Vendredi*. When it came to putting our aims into words, I found the problem a good deal trickier than I had envisaged. Almost everyone had objections and suggestions about the draft I made, and rightly; in the end, deciding that some definition, some pointer to the direction in which I intended to go, was better than none, not satisfied, but hoping that controversy over the Manifesto would be more likely to stimulate interest than choke off potential readers or future contributors, I put this on a page by itself at the head of the first number:

NEW WRITING will appear twice yearly, and will be devoted to imaginative writing, mainly of young authors. It does not intend to concern itself with literary theory, or the criticism of contemporaries.

NEW WRITING aims at providing an outlet for those prose writers, among others, whose work is too unorthodox in length or style to be suitable for the established monthly and quarterly magazines. While prose will form the main bulk of the contributions, poetry will also be included.

NEW WRITING is first and foremost interested in literature, and though it does not intend to open its pages to writers of reactionary or fascist sentiments, it is independent of any political party.

NEW WRITING also hopes to represent the work of writers from colonial and foreign countries.

The third paragraph, I see now, was all too imperfectly expressed, and only indirectly contained my intention, which was to appeal to all those writers to whom, in the catastrophic impasse of the 'thirties, Keats's famous lines applied:

Those to whom the miseries of the world
Are misery, and will not let them rest.

It brought me some sharp raps over the knuckles when the reviews began to come in; but the Manifesto as a whole succeeded in arousing the controversy I had looked for.

« 2 »

FAR more abundantly than any of us had hoped, *New Writing* was a success. In its ingenious, multi-coloured poster-jacket devised by Edward Young, it began to sell, it was talked about, it was reviewed at length, more often than not with an enthusiasm that surprised us, though there were slaps and buffets too. Nevertheless, most of the critics agreed that *New Writing* had avoided the crudities of propaganda and justified its claim to be interested in imaginative writing before politics. I longed to offer the minority who did not agree a copy of the Russian *Internationalnaya Literatura,* or one or other of the continental magazines of the same sort, to show them what happened when the order of priorities was reversed.

Looking through the early press-cutting books we kept for *New Writing,* I have felt as if I had suddenly found myself back in a room where a babble of discussion was going on; discussion that was still interesting for the light it threw on the times and for the effect it had on the fortunes of an enterprise that was to last, in one transformation after another, through the next fifteen years. Of course *The Nowaks,* as it justly deserved, received bouquets from everyone; but there were many strands woven together in the book, and it gratified us to see one critic seizing on the opportunity it provided for long short stories as the most interesting thing about it, another on the inclusion of so large a proportion of foreign writers, one on the realism he found to be the keynote of many of the contributions, another on the imaginative intensity that struck him in other contributions. What encouraged us most was the recognition, in so many of these reviews, that we had succeeded in our object of making our readers realize that there was a new awareness among imaginative writers which transcended frontiers, an awakened conscience and interest that impelled them to look for their material in new fields, and produce, as Ifor Evans said in the *Manchester Guardian,* "a literature arising from the violent conflicts of human life in our time."

We were lucky on the whole in our reviews, especially at the beginning, and those which showed an imaginative sympathy with what we were aiming at gave me confidence even when they were critical. I have an obstinate nature, and I doubt if I was often deflected by its public critics to one side or other of the path I thought *New Writing* should take; I made my own discoveries of faults in my own time, and I was more likely to be swayed by the private advice of those whose judgement I respected and solicited; but I remained inordinately sensitive to the tone of the reviews nevertheless. A thoroughly hostile review, and I began at once to wonder whether it would not be better to give the whole thing up after all; a praising review followed, and my needle swung back to *Set Fair* in an instant.

Sometimes when a batch of reviews had arrived by the morning post in Vienna, I would take them with the rest of my mail to the café round the corner, and study them with manic-depressive anxiety over a *mokka.* "We should ask ourselves, for the sake of lucidity and order, whether this documented fiction is fiction at all, or a red herring trying to pass itself off as a grilled sole." *Down. . . .* "*New Writing* sets itself apart; it does not describe the bright and easy world of the successful magazine tale. These, rather, are stories in which the authors' teeth have been set on edge." *Up. . . .* "The temporary amorality of the junior fictionists makes their work strangely juiceless." *Down (though a trifle bewildered). . . .* "The outspoken or imaginative author has, today, about as much chance of getting into the average editorial fortress as a convict has of getting out of Parkhurst; and my only criticism of *New Writing* is that its appearances are absurdly infrequent." *Up again, strongly. . . .* "New in what sense? The total effect is one of sprawling." *Down, down. . . .* I was anxious, too, for the individual authors, as much as for the volume as a whole. When a critic in *The Criterion* said: "Mr. Auden's fable was probably thrown off over a meal or in his bath, but bears traces of his genial sadism," I felt low again. I began to wonder whether authors blamed editors for the reviews they got, casting back in my own experience (I have since learnt how strong the impulse to blame publishers is, if a book is badly received). I held on to a letter that had just come in from one author: "I think you are my patron saint. Since you published my story, people publish as much as I write. . . ." The faint halo of a patron saint banished the doubts about Auden, the gloom caused by that nasty word "sprawling." I felt strong enough to go back to that pile of manuscripts upstairs in my flat, and polish off a dozen of them before luncheon.

LOOKING back through the early volumes, it seems to me that the reputation I gained for introducing entirely new names was not altogether justified. I did publish some first poems and stories by unknown writers (though many more later, during the war); but my success, such as it was, lay rather in creating a kind of magnetized area round the magazine which attracted the best from young writers who had already begun to be known, and manuscripts that had failed to find a home but were destined, when published in *New Writing*, to bring their authors fame. I still think *The Nowaks* (which was too long for any other magazine and was written specially for me out of the fragments of the great unfinished Berlin novel, *The Lost*, left over when *Mr. Norris Changes Trains* had been made into a separate novel) is one of the best things Christopher Isherwood ever wrote. I felt that I had brought off a small coup in landing André Chamson's *My Enemy* for the first number: everyone praised it, E. M. Forster remarking that "when the French do remember their boyhood it can be quite extraordinary," and Christopher that it "makes one feel that a real artist can write about absolutely anything and still produce all the correct reflections about fascism, nationalism, etc. in the reader's mind, a trite observation but it always comes as a fresh surprise." The fun, however, really began when No. 1 had been widely read and discussed. Encouraged by the opportunity *New Writing* gave him, Christopher had started to work as hard as he could on turning the remainder of the wreckage of *The Lost* into stories. "There is another section of *The Lost* ready," he wrote before he had seen more than the contents list of No. 1, "about an English girl who sings in a Berlin cabaret, but I hardly think it would suit the serious tone of *New Writing*. It is rather like Anthony Hope: *The Dolly Dialogues*. It is an attempt to satirize the romance-of-prostitution racket." It was not, however, till the end of October that *Sally Bowles* reached me, and though I was enthusiastic and did not agree in the least that it was too frivolous for *New Writing*, there was a difficulty about its length. Some futile proposals for cutting it were discussed and (luckily) abandoned, and in the end I published instead the first part of the *Berlin Diary*, which Christopher described as "only mildly dirty": *Goodbye to Berlin* was slowly taking shape.

Meanwhile, other contributions were being brought in by the wave *New Writing*'s publication had created. It was an exciting morning when George Orwell sent me a short piece, which has since become as famous as anything he wrote, called *Shooting an Elephant*. Urged on by Christopher, and full of admiration for *Burmese Day*, I had written asking him to contribute (I do not know whether he remembered the ardent fan of his football prowess fifteen years before), and he wrote to me in answer:

I waited before answering your letter, as a friend in London was endeavouring to get me a copy of *New Writing*, but evidently she hasn't succeeded yet. What I was going to say was, I am writing a book at present and the only other thing I have in mind is a sketch, (it would be about 2,000–3,000 words), describing the shooting of an elephant. It all came back to me very vividly the other day and I would like to write it, but it may be that it is quite out of your line. I mean it might be too low-brow for your paper and I doubt whether there is anything anti-Fascist in the shooting of an elephant! Of course you can't say in advance that you would like it, but perhaps you could say tentatively whether it is at all likely to be in your line or not. If not, then I won't write it; if you think it might interest you I will do it and send it along for you to consider. I am sorry to be so vague but without seeing a copy of *New Writing* I can't tell what sort of stuff it uses.

Encouraged by this letter, I sent him a copy of the first number of *New Writing* at once. It found favour with him, and a fortnight later the typescript of *Shooting an Elephant* was in my hands. Equally rewarding was the morning when V. S. Pritchett, who had written a generous and perceptive review of No. 1, offered to send me a story which he told me had no hope of being accepted by other editors:

I've got a story I want to send you for *New Writing* but I'm not sure whether you want to see unsolicited MSS. It's about 7,000 words long and this and either its manner or its subject or both, give it little chance as far as I can see with the monthly reviews. May I send it to you? We met, if you remember, at the *New Statesman* the other week. I was covered in books and bottles. If you are this way come in and have a drink one evening. Give me a ring. I've just been reviewing your book in the *Fortnightly Review* and I liked it immensely. Thank God, no editorial notes!

The story arrived, and I immediately wrote Pritchett an enthusiastic letter of acceptance. I apologized that I could only offer him a fee of three guineas, a miserable payment by today's standards but all I could provide out of what my publishers gave me. There was also a problem about the title, as another contributor had already staked a claim in his original title. He wrote back:

I'm very glad you liked "The Commercial Traveller" and that you are going to put it into *New Writing*. The fee is all right — that is to say, it's damn little for weeks of hard work, but the people who pay me 15 and 20 guineas for stories would certainly not publish this one; and then I don't like their magazines as well as I like *New Writing!* So go ahead. And call it "Sense of Humour," if the other chap sticks to his title. This is perhaps more acutely descriptive. When does the next number appear?

After that, Pritchett became a close friend and collaborator, and we published several of his most remarkable short stories, including his masterpiece *The Sailor*, which was not only greatly admired when it appeared in *New Writing*, but seemed as fresh as ever, and almost completely stole the applause in many reviews when it was reprinted in *English Stories from New Writing* after the war. But it was not only such "realism" I was after, though to break with the "mandarin" style, to support bold experiments in the "vernacular," was one of our chief aims. When I went to see Cecil Day Lewis at his country home, to persuade him to write for us, he told me that his friend Rex Warner had written a novel, *The Wild Goose Chase*, in a fantastical or allegorical manner, and was finding great difficulty in getting anyone interested in it. We persuaded Rex — whom I did not meet personally for some years — to pick out one or two more or less self-explanatory episodes for *New Writing*, and I remember feeling, when they came in, that an entirely new event, comparable with Edward Upward's *Journey to the Border*, was taking place in the imaginative writing of our time. Upward was trying, by the use of shifting images of reality, to present an upheaval of thought occurring within the mind; Rex Warner, by the use of even more highly charged dramatic symbols, to work out an allegory of contemporary politics in action outside the mind; taken together they seemed to add a new dimension to the novel. *The Football-Match* was printed in No. 2 with Pritchett's *Sense of Humour* and Orwell's *Shooting an Elephant*, and soon after, under the impetus of this acceptance, the whole novel was bought and published by Boriswood. When it came out, this novel, which, like *The Memorial*, had had so much difficulty in pushing to the light, was treated by the Press, and *The Times* in particular, as a work of the most disturbing significance. I can still remember the extreme surprise

— and equal satisfaction — I felt, as I sat in a Viennese café one morning and read the long review, almost a whole column, which *The Times* devoted to it.

« 4 »

THE success of *New Writing* was crucial for me. I felt that I had at last justified my decision in breaking with the Hogarth Press, at last fulfilled a life-long ambition, and had also done something which was specifically mine in the common effort we felt we were all engaged in towards a solution of the crisis and tragedy of the 'thirties. Since leaving London I had not only continued to review for *The Listener*, *The Adelphi* (then under Richard Rees's sympathetic editorship) and other literary periodicals, but I had also begun to write a great many articles for various papers on Austrian and Central European affairs: I had wanted the outside world to know what it felt like to be in the desperate situation of the Viennese after the collapse of the February Rising, and turned myself into a journalist to make my own contribution to this missionary work. This was the "open" side of the work which had its "underground" side in the information I collected from the political agents hunted by the police. I happened to feel very strongly about it, and believed I knew more intimately what was going on below the surface than most other writers; but while journalism was the job of many others more efficiently trained for it and experienced at it than I was, *New Writing* came out of my own special capacities and interests. It also seemed to me that it could do more than any poem — any poem that I could write — in the short time still left to us. The fatal error made by so many thinkers from Plato to Wells, Edward Sackville-West once observed when discussing *New Writing* in a sympathetic review, is to imagine there is anything better to be than a poet. Deep down, in my heart, I knew this to be true; yet I felt that poetry was a channel through which only part of my energies could flow, for the channel was not broad enough; and I sometimes reminded myself of Thomas Lovell Beddoes's remark: "Apollo defend us from brewing all our lives at a quintessential pot of the smallest ale Parnassian." When the preparations for *New Writing* were being made I remember feeling a curious sense of repose and relief at the broad channel being at last discovered. And the success filled me with an extraordinary sense of explosive power; but a power that used me rather than a power I had developed myself. Always at the back of my mind was what was perhaps the most important discovery of all those

I had made in my years of turning myself into "the Shadow" among the submerged masses of Central Europe. Talking with Karl and his friends of the Social-Democrat movement, and with the unpolitical younger generation I came to know through Toni and his family, again and again I was struck by their eagerness to understand, to take part, to rifle the honeycombs of civilization's knowledge and power, to learn to enjoy in art and literature what we of the fortunate educated classes enjoyed as our birthright. There were times when it seemed to me like an irresistible force of water slowly piling up against a dam, and filled me with feelings of alarm and wonder at the same time: alarm because of the power it gave to false prophets and self-seekers to deflect it for their own evil purposes, wonder for the sheer beauty of the instinct and desire behind it, the potentialities of creative renovation that stirred in its darkness.

For the next few years, *New Writing* controlled my movements; when I journeyed across Europe I was in search of new contributors or new collaborators, whether in Paris, or Prague, or Amsterdam, or Moscow, or Tiflis, whether working in London or Vienna, the two poles of my wanderings. My earlier ambitions still remained, but rather, now, as an undertone to all this editorial activity. The political idea, however, continued to be strong; and I was to make many mistakes, when I failed at first to see that an author whose political attitude was exactly what I sympathized with was not, from the point of view of creative power, a good author. And yet, I believe, I was constantly saved from the worst excesses of "political literature," which flourished so rankly in many periodicals of the time, by a deeper instinct — or perhaps a deeper wish — to be pleased rather than to be edified. My response to imaginative literature has always been more instinctive than intellectual; and confronted with some new poem or story that bothered me ideologically, I could never resist it in the end if it excited me, if it seemed to me to break new ground imaginatively; though I would sometimes invent farcical pieces of casuistry to justify my ideological qualms. When I first read the stories of Jean-Paul Sartre (whom Ralph Fox had mentioned to me), the impact on my imagination was terrific and I felt it was absolutely necessary to enrol him as a contributor; we eventually published *La Chambre* in John Rodker's translation; but I remember one morning in Paris, saying rather anxiously to Paul Nizan, his great friend: "I suppose one could call Sartre a humanist?" — and Nizan, with a grin spreading over his face, flashing back: "If you do, you'd better not tell him!" I remained suspect, therefore, and capable of flagrant heresy, to the exponents of the pure doctrine of Socialist (or Proletarian) Realism; inarticulately aware as I was all the time — though this practical experience was helping me gradually towards a formulation — of the difference between a literature that is an interpretation of its time, and one that transforms it.

« 5 »

SOON after I left the Hogarth Press in 1932, I had given up my studio flat in Heathcote Street, and transferred my books and furniture to Fieldhead, where I eventually converted one of the old nurseries at the back of the house into a *New Writing* work-room. I had, therefore, no place of my own in London, and being too awed in my early years as a member of the Athenaeum to introduce my bohemian literary friends into its solemn archiepiscopal atmosphere, I used to meet them in Bloomsbury cafés, Soho restaurants and also in the little avant-garde Parton Street bookshop run by the ever-welcoming but tongue-tied David Archer. There I bought the first slim green collections of poems by Dylan Thomas and George Barker long before I met either of them, and was taken by Ralph Fox next door to visit the publishing offices of Lawrence and Wishart, where the poet Edgell Rickword (whose *Invocations to Angels*, since sadly neglected, I had long known and admired) was always to be found sunk in profound and almost wordless gloom.

Archer's bookshop was also the rendezvous where I at last came together with Rex Warner, who looked — to my first, surprised but admiring glance — more like one of the powerful three-quarters in his own *Football-Match* than the author of it, as I had imagined him; and with David Gascoyne, in whose company, after a shy, rather limp hand had been offered me with an almost inaudible mutter, I retired for tea over the road. David was at that time only twenty or so, but was already the author of a novel and a number of poems that had been published in various London papers. He was particularly interested in the French surrealists and wanted to prepare some translations for us from that phase of surrealism where it suddenly embraced revolutionary doctrines. We had planned a surrealist section, but it all came to nothing. Unlike English painting (though even there only to a small degree), English poetry never took kindly to surrealism, in spite of the strong "nonsense" tradition in the nineteenth century; David's own poems of that period have remained an almost completely isolated "sport." His first contribution to *New Writing* was his short poem *Snow in Europe:* a beautiful and imaginative piece of work, but which only faintly foreshadowed the philosophical and mystical preoccupations that were to give his poetry its extremely rare and individual flavour. David himself, tall, broad-shouldered but excessively slim and slightly bowed, with his beautifully regular oval face and large, greenish-grey eyes in which sparks of light flickered as the tumble of his conversation gathered speed, following his thoughts like the spray of a fountain tossed by contrary gusts of wind, gave me the impression at one moment of an ultra-aesthetic poet as imagined by the cartoonists of the 'nineties, at another of a hunted hare. The introspective suffering of a highly strung sensibility was in his expression when in repose (and how rarely it was in repose), but would suddenly give place to a look of darting, malicious humour — an element that emerged in his poetry only at a later date. His hands attracted one's attention at once, with their long, elegantly articulated fingers. He has described them himself in his poem *The Writer's Hand:*

> . . . See my hand
> The only army to enforce your claims
> Upon life's hostile land: five pale, effete
> Aesthetic-looking fingers, whose chief feat
> Is to trace lines like these across the page:
> What small relief can they bring to your siege!

When I launched *New Writing*, I believed prose to be much more important for my purpose than poetry. It was in prose that the idea of "an effective brotherhood born between victims of oppression" and the "sense of broader comradeships" was most clearly to be traced, especially in its international parallels; modern English poetry, at that moment, seemed to me to be following a more complex ideal, in which the champion influences of Eliot, Hopkins and Rilke fought against the transparency I looked for (and found) in prose, and the ideas of Freud and Lawrence — and perhaps Groddeck and Homer Lane as well — were as important as the new "revolutionary" awareness that had been the theme-song of *New Signatures.* Privately, in my capacity of poet, I found this complexity and "density" of supreme interest, but I did not think them compatible — at any rate on the rather narrow front I proposed to break through on — with the intention of the prose. Later, as *New Writing* acquired its own momentum and became more broadly representative of all my generation's ideas, and at the same time their poetry itself performed an evolution towards the spirit of the prose, poetry was to come into its own. But the domination of prose at the beginning was also due to the fact that the poetry of my contemporaries already had its own magazine, Geoffrey Grigson's *New Verse*. Its aim was entirely non-political; but it is an amusing comment on the mood of the times that so large a proportion of the poems sent in for the first number were so unequivocally revolutionary in tone (including Wystan Auden's *Poem* and Cecil Day Lewis's extracts from *The Magnetic Mountain*) that Grigson was obliged in his second number to insist that "if there must be attitudes, a reasoned attitude of toryism is welcomed no less than a communist attitude."

Nevertheless, by the time I was preparing the third volume for press, more poetry had come my way and more poets who felt strongly that they belonged to the world of *New Writing*. No. 3 presented seven poets, including three Spaniards and a Pole; and from that time on poetry played an essential part. Some of the best poems by Stephen Spender, Cecil Day Lewis, Louis MacNeice (including his beautiful *June Thunder* and *Meeting Point*) appeared in the eight volumes that had been published by the time the war broke out; but by far the largest number of poems by any single author were from Wystan Auden. I had started with what many people (myself included) still think one of his most beautiful and original poems, *Lay your sleeping head, my love*, in No. 3; and in No. 4 came *Under the fronds of life* and the extraordinary ballads *Miss Gee* and *Victor* — perhaps a little too much of the "genial sadism" in the former, but the latter would have made any poet's name immediately and sensationally if he had written nothing else: in Wystan's case it showed only another extension of the scope and inexhaustible fertility of his genius. All these poems came to me copied out on long foolscap sheets in Wystan's minute, squashed handwriting, more like the recordings of a highly sensitive seismograph while a road-drill was breaking up the street outside than an attempt at human communication. We rose to a bumper harvest of eight in the seventh volume, and from America he sent me three, including the famous *In Memoriam Ernst Toller* and *Refugee Blues*, for the eighth and last volume of the new series, published only when the war had already broken out.

Reading through these poems of Wystan's again, I am even more impressed than I was then by their variety, their intellectual power and formal skill. By the time he started contributing to *New Writing* he had outgrown the arcane doom-laden telegraphese of his first book and *Paid on Both Sides;* had passed very rapidly through the phase of the bullying, Marxist bogey-man exhortations and emerged unscathed

into the clear sunlight — so clear that it is only necessary to recite two
or three of them to silence anyone who complains that modern poetry
is too obscure and esoteric to bother about — the midsummer's day of
his genius. In that full-flowering moment, feeling, thought and technical mastery were, it seems to me, in perfect balance; before his passion
for rhetorical personification of abstractions like "glory," "desire,"
"hunger," "the will," began to devour his invention, and the transplantation to America dried up the sensuous sap and made his utterances
for a time seem more like the delphic riddling of a disembodied mind.
Each of these astonishing poems was a new discovery about the world
we lived in, and seemed to illuminate whole stretches of experience
that had lain in a kind of twilight confusion before; disturbing, as all
good poetry must be, to accepted ideas and habitual sentiments, by the
unexpectedness of its psychological insight — not merely into the behaviour of individuals but also of classes and nations — and the images it brought together to act as symbols for that insight. There was
a kind of dismay mixed with my delight as the foolscap sheets came
in: I envied as well as admired the smoothness with which the cylin-
ders of his poetic engines worked, compared with the pinking, backfiring and sudden total non-functioning of my own — even though I
knew I was after something rather different. Other poets of this century may have shown more fastidious care in the polishing of the texture of their poems, line by line, and the proportioning of the architecture of the whole, than Wystan with his Byron-like exuberance and
fluency; some may have penetrated deeper into their specialized areas
of experience; but none, I believe, has shown such an extraordinary
capacity to speak through poetry, with a poet's vision, about the whole
of life. The vision of his generation was, in fact, largely formed by
him; and if one has been more often than not disappointed in the poets
who have come after him it is, I think, because they have lacked this
particular power that every generation needs to find in its imaginative
creators, and have seemed, by comparison, for those who had lived in
the age of Auden's great poetic outflowing, to be little more than neat
annotators on the margin of life — and art. Auden has his weaknesses, as his critics are never tired of pointing out: his occasional slap-
dash, his adolescent lapses of taste, his obsessive ideas, a fondness for
the sententiousness of the pulpit that is apt to overcome him; but when
I turn, in the pages of the old volumes of *New Writing*, from the lyric
sublimity of *Lay your sleeping head, my love*, with the wit that coun-
terpoints the ecstasy, to *Victor*, that transforms old ballad forms so
skilfully to modern uses and contrives to extract tragic passion out of

grotesque case-history, and then to the emblematic reflections of *Under the fronds of life;* from the folk-song rhythms of *Refugee Blues* that so poignantly accent the despair of the theme, to the sonnets on *The Novelist, Rimbaud* and *A. E. Housman* that illuminate with such unforced economy and apt symbolism, in fourteen lines, the whole complexity of difficult lives; it seems to me that each mode would be a respectable achievement for a modern poet by itself, might even be thought to be by different poets in an age that expects no miracles, if all were not united by the peculiar unmistakeable cast of Wystan's imagination.

Reflecting on all these triumphant poems of Auden's, on Louis MacNeice's effortlessly airborne songs, with their colloquial freedom and gaiety — a tone of voice that he alone has discovered and no one can imitate — that carry the subtle metaphysical probings of his mind with such easy assurance, and on George Barker's highly wrought coruscating elegies; hearing the strange, half-muffled music of David Gascoyne's philosophical meditations, and delighting in the wit of William Plomer's *French Lisette;* I am struck not only by the range of achievement but also by the absence of that "naïve radicalism" of which the poets of the 'thirties have so often been accused by those who argue from undiscriminating general impressions or, less disinterestedly, wish to conjure away awkwardly formidable presences before they present their own shadow-shows. If you want to condemn people wholesale, it is an excellent principle to lump them together under some slogan, some half-truth that obliterates individual differences. It would be easy to compile a dunce's anthology of foolish and shallow and affected effusions by the poets of these years (one could compile a similar one from the off-moments of most of the outstanding poets of former ages), and they would sound especially ridiculous in the entirely altered conditions of today; but every artist has the right to be judged by his best, as the scientific explorer is judged by the experiments that come off, and not by the hundreds which go astray before or after; and the best that Auden and MacNeice and their contemporaries contributed to *New Writing* and *New Verse* in the brief, agitated, exciting and tragic period between Hitler's rise to power and the outbreak of the Second World War, stands for judgment as art independently of all topical considerations. "Occasional verse," said Dr. Johnson, "must be content with occasional praise"; but I firmly believe that when their occasional verses have long been lost in the turbulently running waters of our time, the poets of the 'thirties will still be remembered by poems that for imaginative vitality, intellectual backbone and innovating technical resourcefulness — for the creative power of the word — have certainly not been excelled, and only rarely equalled, by their successors.

« 6 »

THE British contributors who met in the pages of *New Writing* could be roughly divided into two teams: those who, like Christopher, Stephen, Wystan, George Orwell and James Stern, had a background of middle-class education (though not necessarily public school followed by University), and already moved to some extent in metropolitan intellectual circles; and those who when they wrote of mines, seamen, factory workers or East End tailors, were writing from the inside, out of their own experiences. These I was particularly interested to encourage; it was, in my view, one of the main reasons for the existence of *New Writing* to break down the barrier between these and the other team, to provide a place of cross-fertilization of their talents.

The way was hard, and the harvest was not abundant. One of the chief difficulties was, of course, money. Very few of these writers had anyone who could support them, even with the most meagre weekly subsidy, in fact the older ones among them generally had families which looked to them; they at all events could not afford to devote more time to learning their craft as writers than a few hours after work in the evenings, with children squealing and romping around in the clatter of dishes being washed and all the other noises and smells that cannot be escaped in crowded tenement flats with thin dividing walls. Sometimes the writer was on the dole: this provided more time all right, but made the purchase of even such minor instruments of the trade as note-books and pens an almost impossible extravagance. I tried to devise all kinds of stratagems to get round the difficulties when I believed that the writer really had "got something"; but I had not the means at my disposal to do more than occasionally produce a tiny allowance, as advance on a remotely envisaged fee, for a limited number of weeks. One wrote to me, with savage despair, that if he didn't get a job, or a promise of acceptance from a publisher in two or three weeks' time, he knew it would be impossible to go on; that on twenty-five shillings a week he could only produce a twenty-five-shilling job, and he knew it wasn't good enough; and that anyway he could not go on doing all the "taking" without any "giving" in return. Another told me that not only did he have five small boys of his own, but that next door there was a family of eight children, and above him a family of nine;

and that through the ceiling and the walls he could hear not only the normal noises of boisterous tenement children, but also roller-skates, marbles, coal-breaking, firewood-chopping, the roar of the lavatories being flushed, and worst of all the piano being played out of tune. If he tried to write during the few blessed hours — being out of work — when most of the children were at school, there was a constant stream of callers, canvassers, pedlars, hawkers, rag-and-bone men, coalmen, buyers of old gold, and equally unemployed neighbours coming to pass the time of day; if he told them he was trying to write, he would merely become an object of special curiosity, and they would come all the more. If he tried to do his writing in the early hours, when everyone had gone to bed, he was too exhausted the next morning to cope with the household chores and necessary visits to the U.A.B.

The "About the Contributors" pages of each volume were a catalogue, often, of trades extraordinary for writers: leaving school at fourteen or fifteen, they had been carpenters, die-sinkers, tool-makers, railway-men, dock-hands, plasterers, metal-turners, racing tipsters and sewer cleaners. Glamorous indeed these origins beside the humdrum acknowledgement of vain years as a private-school teacher or hack reviewer or clerk in an advertising agency, that came from the other side. There were the keen political workers, too; one young author, a dockyard apprentice, described to me his struggle to find an evening or two a week for writing against the claims of political study-circles and organizing the Labour League of Youth, door-to-door collections for "Arms for Spain," making speeches at the Co-operative Guild and running a stall at the Labour Party Christmas Fair. It was *not* a good programme for an intending author; but he had endless courage and energy to obscure for many years the impossibility of running three careers at the same time.

There were, of course, those who made it, in spite of all obstacles. Most remarkable of these, to my mind, most significant of the moment in English history in which he lived, was B. L. Coombes. This small, hard-bitten miner, with his small, square head, his pale, rough-hewn, serious face, was the son of a Herefordshire farmer; he had set off for Wales at the age of seventeen to work in the mines, and in his thirties had decided to take up his pen and describe, for the world to know, the life in the lost country of the coal-face, where

> Many hearts with coal are charred
> And few remember.

He had a wide experience to draw on: he had worked in almost every type of mine, had narrowly escaped death or mutilation many times himself, had seen others escaping — and some fail to escape. He had been in charge of the installation and working of the new coal-cutting machinery, and when I first came into contact with him was responsible for dealing with accidents underground. A man of quite unusual gifts, but above all the gift of imagination, which perhaps worked so freshly and vividly in him because he had come as a young countryman to the mines, his senses attuned to the clean air and green fields and slow, natural rhythms of the Herefordshire farmlands, he was plunged into the darkness of the tunnels deep below the earth where men worked in continual danger for a wage that had no relation to the endurance and skill demanded of them. After many years crowded into a squalid miner's lodging with his wife and children, forced to type in the bedroom in any odd half-hour he could snatch, he had at last got a room of his own for writing, in a lodge which belonged to an old castle. Later, when he had made his name and sold many stories and articles, and had had his autobiography *These Poor Hands* made a Left Book Club Choice by Victor Gollancz, he bought a small farm and there returned, happily, to the life from which he had started.

What struck me at once about *The Flame*, the first sketch he sent me late in 1936, was the simplicity and unforced, quiet movement of the writing with its occasional small touches that revealed the natural way of talking of the West of England. This rare quality — for men who have had no formal education beyond elementary school too often use the jargon of newspapers and the lurid style of cheap novelettes when they try to write — was allied, as story after story showed, with a capacity to make you feel exactly what it was like to be alone in a mine and see "a thin flame — dancing and blue as the flame that one sees on a coal fire" suddenly flicker out of the darkness and approach the end of a fuse one had just laid; or to have to gather with your mates round an obstruction in a gallery where twenty tons of coal had fallen, knowing that when you had moved it you would find the broken body of a friend underneath it.

One of the chief pleasures of editing *New Writing* was the discovery, not simply of individual writers, but of pockets or fertile valleys of them hitherto unsuspected. We were disappointed that so little had as yet developed in Scotland from the impulse that Hugh MacDiarmid and Lewis Grassic Gibbon had given to a local literary revival —

many years were to pass before it was obligatory for a literary critic to assume familiarity with Lallans. It was surely absurd that I expected so much so suddenly, but nothing could quench my faith: I was like a water-diviner walking over country where springs and wells had always been few and far between, absolutely convinced that his rod would twitch again and again. In the mines, on the sea, there was something to quicken the imagination, it was natural to look for young writers in those directions; least of all did I expect that my rod would twitch over industrial Birmingham and the ants' nest home of the Austin Seven. Yet there, centred on the University where Louis MacNeice had been teaching, a group of local writers had appeared, all the more interesting and significant to me because they were outside the magic (and tyrannical) triangle of London-Oxford-Cambridge. John Hampson — who helped to lead me to this discovery — I already knew from Hogarth days; Walter Allen, whose first novel Michael Joseph were to publish a few months after I got in touch with him, had already had one or two of his stories published in *New Stories;* Leslie Halward, who had also appeared in *New Stories*, was to send me one of the best "proletarian" stories I ever published, *Arch Anderson;* and there were other promising talents, many of them contributors to *The Mermaid*, the University magazine, in which later on, at the beginning of the war, I came for the first time on the work of Henry Reed, who had written a skilful and penetrating review of Auden's work.

No one, I believe, has ever satisfactorily explained how these sudden flowerings occur. It is, of course, no more mysterious that a group of people with exceptional imaginative gifts should suddenly emerge in Birmingham or Aberystwyth than in the older universities. Uncommon teachers, extraordinary books, processes of influence and opportunity too complex to unravel to the end of the skein produce a moment when Auden, Spender, Day Lewis, MacNeice, Warner, Bell, Isherwood and Empson all appear together at Oxford and Cambridge; but there, because of their centrality, and because one has the habitual expectation of an almost annual crop of talent, it seems less remarkable — at any rate until many years later. Once the process starts, however, wherever it starts, it appears to generate its own momentum, and more and more people come forward who might never have thought it worth-while to develop those particular gifts in themselves — or perhaps even realized they possessed them. We had welcomed Mulk Raj Anand and Ahmed Ali as young Indian writers who held the same ideals as ourselves; we had found one or two writers of unusual gifts in the West Indies; but the British Empire is vast, and was a great deal vaster when I began to edit *New Writing*, covering in fact a quarter of the world's land surface. Why was it then that out of all the hundreds of towns and universities in the English-speaking lands scattered over the seven seas, only one should at the time act as a focus of creative activity in literature of more than local significance, that it should be in Christchurch, New Zealand, that a group of young writers had appeared, who were eager to assimilate the pioneer developments in style and technique that were being made in England and America since the beginning of the century, to explore the world of the dispossessed and under-privileged for their material and to give their country a new conscience and spiritual perspectice? It was William Plomer who had first drawn my attention to a little pamphlet called *Conversation with My Uncle*, which had been sent to him by an admirer in New Zealand by the name of Frank Sargeson; and I was struck at once by the wit and the style of the short pieces, the skilful use of the vernacular idiom, and the tension between rebellion and acceptance underneath which lay an extraordinary warmth of feeling for the New Zealand scene: miles away in its attitude to the world from Katherine Mansfield, and yet unmistakably out of the same orchard.

I got in touch with Sargeson at once, and he soon became a frequent contributor to *New Writing*, as well as a delightful correspondent, his letters full of illuminating and entertaining news about his own country and lively comments about literature in England, which were especially stimulating because they came from so far outside the fashionable judgements of the metropolis. Through him I learnt a great deal about the circle of young writers of like mind who found a generous and enthusiastic patron in Denis Glover of the Caxton Press; and I eventually published poems and stories by several of them — Charles Brasch, Roderick Finlayson, Allen Curnow and A.R.D. Fairburn.

It gratified me immensely to print the New Zealanders; for not only did I want to make *New Writing* world-wide in its scope, but I was also obsessed by the conviction, based more on faith than on reason, that the climate which had produced our English, French and German writers had spread all over the world, and therefore should be ripening talents of the same flavour wherever literature was alive at all. There are, of course, several fallacies in this view, which I see more clearly now than I did then; but the New Zealanders were at any rate a proof for me that I was not altogether mistaken in my faith, or entirely foolish in my desire to be without metropolitan exclusiveness and snobbery in my responsibility as an editor. I was less successful in my search for American contributors (though Americans were often included), partly, I think, because at that time I did not know the American scene well enough to look in the right places, partly also because so many of the American writers who were in the same line of business as my other contributors — the Hemingways, Steinbecks and Caldwells — were already famous and earning big money for whatever short stories they produced. It was a particular disappointment, because Alfred and Blanche Knopf had been interested enough to take sheets of some of the early volumes, and they had been well received. I longed to be able to mobilize the Americans round the standard of *New Writing;* and I can well remember the stab of pleasure it gave me when a spy reported that Hemingway had been observed in the Place de l'Odéon deeply engrossed in the first volume.

« 7 »

THE five years before the outbreak of Hitler's war was a time, fantastic in retrospect, of innumerable international writers' conferences. They were summoned to prepare a plan for a new international encyclopaedia, to proclaim the solidarity of the world's writers against fascism, or with their exiled German, Austrian and Czech colleagues, or in favour of the Spanish Republicans; conferences full of dust and fury, of remorseless quarrels behind the scenes as well as upon the rostrum, which gave the opportunity to pour out a vast flood of rhetoric to those who had a fancy for making exhibitions of themselves in that way, and to weave the most elaborate and entangled intrigues behind the scenes to those who had suddenly found an outlet in them for long-suppressed political ambitions. How few of all the hundreds of thousands of words that the overworked multi-lingual stenographers recorded can have any validity or interest today — how devoutly many must hope that those records are lost for ever. These conferences, exciting to some, painfully boring to others who nevertheless felt it was their duty to attend and associate themselves with the declared aims, effectively kept creative writers from creating; I never heard of a good poem or story inspired by any one of them; but they did nevertheless give heart to those who were suffering and fighting, and often collected money for them; they sometimes resulted in surprising attacks on the pro-Communist line to which their organizers, or the political wire-pullers behind them, tried to keep them attached; and above all they gave writers a wonderful opportunity, in more intimate gatherings outside the conference-room, to meet interesting writers from other countries. I treated them, I must confess, from a purely practical point of view: they made excellent opportunities for me to intensify my search for contributors to *New Writing*, and, keeping my mouth shut during the speeches and the squabbles, feeling rather ignoble and unheroically inarticulate, I would mark my prey down and stalk him (or her) through the jungles of recrimination that followed among the cafés and restaurants. Wystan and Christopher managed to keep away from most of these orgies, but Stephen was an ardent and popular figure, always commanding respect by his illuminated Shelleyan look: he had the gift of taking the whole thing extremely seriously, and at the same time seeing and exposing the comic or pretentious side with a ruthless sudden perspicacity that astonished and confused the targets of his laughter.

One of the earliest of these conferences took place in London, rather too hastily organized to be a success, and abstained from by most of the Distinguished Literary Figures of England (someone had trodden heavily on their toes), except H. G. Wells, who arrived at the end, hailed as a prize acquisition by the unsuspecting organizers: he proceeded to dynamite the whole affair with an angry, contemptuous speech. I remember it chiefly for my first sight of André Malraux, his pale, tense, unsmiling face with long nose and pointed chin, the downward droop to the lips, holding all eyes as he delivered his scorpion-like attacks on fuddled thinking and muddled personalities; and of British-hating Ilya Ehrenburg in action, a large, untidy figure with scowling features who made a biting speech in his characteristically humourless, sardonic vein.

Paris, as the centre not only of French intellectual life but also of the *émigré* activity of all the exiled writers from Italy, Germany, Austria, Poland, Hungary and later from Czechoslovakia as well, was the scene of many more of these conferences; and in Paris I would always make a stop of a week or so on my way to and from Vienna, in order to gather material from books and magazines and look up my *copains* and *chers collègues* on *Monde* and *Vendredi* for news of new writers and new literary projects. I made great friends with André Chamson, whose watchdog pugnacity, ever ready to defend 1789 revolutionary ideals, had been aroused by the fascist riots of 1934, to make him a leading spirit among the intellectual supporters of the Front Populaire and the editor-who-mattered on *Vendredi*. "*On les aura!*" was the dominant motive of his thought and action at the time, and by "them" he meant all the rats gnawing away behind the arras, all the death-watch beetles at work in the great rafters of the Republic, financial swindlers, fascist plotters, the sly and secret friends of Hitler and Mussolini who invisibly made their influence felt through social and political contacts in the Army, the police and the "two hundred families." His pale, narrow, penknife face with its jutting, forceful chin seemed to grow tense with passion as he talked of the dangers that threatened his beloved France; his eyes gleamed dangerously under the high, intelligent forehead as he clenched his fist and broke into a grin: "*On les aura!*," leaving one with a vivid picture in one's imagination of what he would do to "them" if they fell into his hands.

Nothing, at first sight, seemed more unlikely than the friendship that united him with André Malraux, nothing more opposed to his own extrovert nature than Malraux's brooding, introspective obsession with destiny and spiritual fulfilment. And yet, in spite of these fundamental differences, and beyond a common love of art, they have always shared a profound feeling for the importance of what St. Exupéry called, in his famous *Letter to a Hostage*, "the most precious fruit of our civilization — human respect" and the need to champion that cause not merely by words but by action when the occasion arose. I felt powerfully drawn towards Malraux, and though problems of timing and other technical obstacles always prevented me from using in the volumes of *New Writing* any advance portion of *Le Temps du Mépris* or *L'Espoir* which he freely offered me, I had many long talks with him during these visits to Paris, fascinated by the flow of his political and philosophical disquisitions, the mythopoeic power with which contemporary events were transformed in his passionate words.

Malraux seems to me one of the key writers of our time, and a man to whom, when one considers his activities as a whole, one cannot refuse the title of genius. And yet I was aware, almost from the first, that if one was to judge him strictly as a novelist, there was something dissatisfying, some flaw or limitation the importance of which I could not easily assess. I had long debates with myself, which ran something like this:

Prosecution: Can you really call a novelist great, who appears to have no sense of humour? Isn't Malraux a glaring example of the tendency Lytton Strachey observed in so many modern French writers — their loss of the classic French virtues of clarity and wit, their acquisition of the worst Teutonic faults of turgidity and inflated pseudo-philosophizing?

Defence: I am not sure that Dostoevsky shows very much sense of humour in his major novels, either; but he is made great by other qualities that outbalance that particular lack. Malraux has irony: his sense of tragic irony is one of his most impressive gifts. No one can really be found guilty of solemn word-flummery who has this rare sense so power-fully developed.

P.: But isn't your taste offended by the constant use of such words as Destiny, Fate, Death and Man, all (in effect) with capital first letters?

D.: I must admit that I find it rather overpowering sometimes; but I suspect that's because I am reacting from too careless a use of these words by second-rate writers. Malraux never uses them carelessly or shallowly: he gives them their full content. He is not an arm-chair philosopher, he has tested the meaning of thought in action, in the successive labours of his own legend.

P.: That may make him an interesting philosopher, but not a good novelist. His power of creating character seems fatally limited; the main characters in *L'Espoir*, for instance, are simply various aspects of Mal-raux's own thought, of his own endless debate with himself. They don't begin to wear that illusory garment of flesh-and-blood reality that makes us feel that we know Mr. Micawber, or Natasha, or Raskolnikov per-sonally.

D.: I am not sure that Malraux *is* a good novelist, pure and simple. He is perhaps something less — but he is also something more. And a great imaginative creator does not always show his genius through his charac-ters. What one remembers first from Malraux's novels are certain supreme scenes of crucial significance: the prison hall scene at the end of *La Con-dition Humaine*, the scene in the San Carlos hospital in *L'Espoir*, the gas attack in *Les Noyers de l'Altenburg*.

P.: All the scenes you have mentioned are moments of great terror and physical agony. Isn't that another proof of Malraux's limitations? Wouldn't we think Shakespeare a lesser artist if we had not got Falstaff in his cups and Romeo in his ecstasy of happy love as well as Lear in his agony?

D.: I am not suggesting that Malraux has Shakespeare's stature. There are great geniuses and lesser geniuses. I think Malraux a genius partly because he is a writer who has imposed his own legend upon his age, as Byron and Rimbaud did — as Malraux's own favourite Lawrence of Arabia did in another way. And partly because of a belief which is in-extricably involved with the scenes I chose. Malraux believes profoundly in individualism, in the individual's value and right to develop his own potentialities. But he also believes in the meaning that is given to life by the experience of human comradeship in the supreme tests — against the worst that circumstances can do.

P.: I'm not sure that those two faiths aren't mutually exclusive.

D.: On the contrary, I believe they are one of the few real hopes for our age, if they exist together: belief in individualism alone is as destructive as the belief that nothing matters except the shared experience of the mass. Malraux sees, as Wilfred Owen saw, that men realize their common human destiny, their brotherhood through suffering and endurance; but he wants that sense of brotherhood to result in a kind of society in which every man has his human dignity. And there, to my mind, is the basis of a faith, the only dynamic with which the West can challenge the East in the transformations of the twentieth century. And what writer in our time has searched more profoundly and more illuminatingly into the roots of art and its meaning for civilization? His belief that art is a means of man possessing his own destiny says so much more for me than the old classical idea of art, drama being a "catharsis," which has always seemed to me rather coldly clinical. . . .

Always, as this debate went on in my mind, I could see Malraux before me, his greenish, sea-creature's eyes fixed upon me under the falling lock of black hair, while a nervous twitch and sniff punctuated the electric outpouring of argument. Malraux shares with Silone, we see now that the cycle has been completed, the distinction of being one of the few European writers of the first class who acted in their own person the whole drama of modern Communist faith, and whose final disillusionment and rejection of that faith are all the more impressive and significant for the fullness of their experience. Thinking over their work in the perspective of a quarter of a century, one is, indeed, drawn to the conclusion that the experience of that cycle may have been *necessary* to make the greatest writers of our age (as a similar cycle made Wordsworth in a previous age), for it has been in the centre of the whole human and social dynamic of a generation.

Silone's perception of something being wrong, fundamentally, with Communist idealism in practice was already evident in *Bread and Wine*. In fact, Silone had been much more closely identified with the Communist movement than Malraux, and from earliest youth, and his disillusionment ante-dated Malraux's. In *Bread and Wine*, Spina's realization that the Party line has nothing to do with the realities of peasant life and his growing fear that the end is being lost sight of in the pursuit of the means, are at the heart of the action. But before *Bread and Wine* appeared, I had accepted his incomparable short story, *The Fox*, brought to my notice by Gwenda David and Eric Mosbacher, the translators of *Fontamara*, and *The Journey to Paris*, less satisfactorily realized as a work of art but full of extraordinary flashes of imagination. It is an odd quirk of fate that has cheated Silone of the recognition he deserved in his own country. As he was living in exile in Switzerland, *Bread and Wine* was published in translation in the Anglo-Saxon countries before the Italians could read it in Italian, and after the war he seems to have reminded his compatriots

Fieldhead

Fieldhead — The Lily Pond

J. L. at an early age, with friend

J. L. at Eton, 1926, in Fourth of June boating dress

Michael Redgrave, circa 1930; photo by the author

Julian Bell, circa 1930; photo by the author

Rosamond Lehmann, J. L., and Lytton Strachey, circa 1930

*J. L. and
Rosamond Lehmann,
circa 1930*

J. L. in the Austrian Alps,
circa 1935

The flat in the Invalidenstrasse

Beatrix, Rosamond and John Lehmann

too much of something they wanted to forget to receive his due honour.

In Paris I also used to see Louis Aragon, whose great gifts seem to me to have remained unfulfilled because he failed to go through the spiritual evolution of Malraux and Silone. Perhaps the itch for political intrigue and combination was always too strong in him: he certainly had a remarkable flair for it, and seemed, when one visited him in his newspaper office, to be the spider controlling all the lines of the web of anti-fascist and Popular Front activity among the intellectuals. A spider of the utmost charm, sensibility and intelligence: a smile of great delicacy would illuminate his sensitive features as he talked of modern English literature, which he appeared to know as well as he spoke the English language. He had an immense admiration for Rosamond and her works, and used his subtlest powers of persuasion upon me to bring her into his web, to become a member of the Presidium of the anti-fascist writers' association, and to speak at one of the congresses in Paris. "You must give the lie," he would say again and again, "to the legend that has such a hold on continental writers, that English writers are too individualist to act with their colleagues in defence of all we care about. It's nonsense — I know it to be a lie — but you must help me to prove it to the doubters." The keen but gentle face, the beautiful grey eyes, the fine artistic hands gave little inkling of the demon of energy that drove him, that plunged him into the immense, complex and exhausting political labours of the movement, that made articles flow from his pen, rhetoric pour from his lips without cease while he was at the same time writing his gigantic novels. His cleverness was phenomenal: observing his myriad activities, reading his Communist poems of the time, one could not doubt that; and yet the poems were little more than poster-stuff, and one felt that he was too lacking in that essential artist's inner repose, repose at a deeper level, ever to create anything of the first order. When repose came, during the war, he produced at last, in his beautiful *Crève-Coeur* volume, something worthy of his gifts; while the demon, for all too brief a space of time, was in chains. The *trahison des clercs* can act both ways; and a poet can be a traitor to his social responsibilities by neglecting poetry for politics and the vanity of the limelight of topical importance. Malraux has performed the miracle of being a politician and a creative writer at the same time, because his political action issued out of the same deeply reflected philosophical vision as his art, and because he has always possessed the artist's inmost repose and integrity.

« 8 »

IT was only a few months after the first volume of *New Writing* had appeared that the Spanish Civil War broke out; and everything, all our fears, our confused hopes and beliefs, our half-formulated theories and imaginings, veered and converged towards its testing and its opportunity, like steel filings that slide towards a magnet suddenly put near them. For, as Stephen Spender wrote in the introduction to the anthology of *Poems for Spain* which we produced together two years later, what all felt was that "the long, crushing, and confused process of defeat, which the democratic process has been undergoing, has been challenged in Spain, and this challenge has aroused hope all over the world." It is almost impossible to convey the strength of this feeling to anyone who was not subjected to the pressures that preceded the summer of 1936, the mixture of relief and apocalyptic hope that flared up as the struggle began, and made one poet, Rex Warner, write that "Spain has torn the veil of Europe," and another, Wystan Auden, in the most famous poem of the period:

> On that tableland scored by rivers,
> Our thoughts have bodies, the menacing shapes of our fever
> Are precise and alive. . . .

I was in Paris when the first news came through of the officers' revolt against the Republic. I knew nothing of Iberian politics, and did not see any cause for special alarm. But I happened, the next day, to go and see a Spanish writer then living in Paris, and found him in a state of the utmost agitation, with tears in his eyes. "Surely everything's going to be all right?" I said, fumbling to offer comfort. "The Government'll have this under control in a few days — the news is already better." "O no, no!" he cried. "You're making a great mistake. It's extremely serious. And it's going to be serious for everyone, for the whole of Europe. You'll see, you'll see." Very soon after, this young poet returned home to fight. He was captured by the fascists, and before the year was over I learnt that he had been shot.

When the full significance of what was happening in Spain gradually became apparent, and all the political parties, organizations, the unattached liberals, intellectuals and artists who had become aware that their own fate was deeply involved in the battles developing in front of Madrid and Barcelona, had banded themselves together to organize the International Brigade and the Spanish Medical Aid, I think every young writer began seriously to debate with himself how he could best be of use, by joining the Brigade, or driving an ambulance, or helping the active committees in England or France, or in some other way. The pull was terrific: the pull of an international crusade to the ideals and aims of which all intellectuals (except those of strong Catholic attachment) who had been stirred by the fascist danger felt they could, in that hour of apocalypse, whole-heartedly assent. It is strange, in retrospect, to see how the pattern of 1914 repeated itself, as it were in a different key. In 1914 the emotion had been the most idealistic patriotism identifying itself with a crusade against tyranny; which gradually succumbed to disillusionment as the war proceeded, as the realities of the carnage became known and doubts about the purity of the motives of the Allies mingled with the soldiers' feeling of fraternity with the soldiers in the opposite trenches. Rupert Brooke to Wilfred Owen: and the intellectuals, seeing the end lost sight of in the prosecution of the means, determined they would never be had in that way again. And yet when, in 1936, the emotion was anti-fascist idealism, identifying itself with an international crusade against tyranny, tyranny of class rather than race or nation, there was the same almost unquestioning, tragic acceptance of the purity of motive of "our" side. It was no question of defending "the bad against the worse" — that more sombre, realistic mood was to come later, in 1939 — and the problem of means and ends was again lost sight of while the necessity seemed, in the words of Garcia in Malraux's *Days of Hope*, "to organize the apocalypse"; until the realities of the Communist struggle for power underneath the struggle of the Republic for its life became apparent, and people were ready to admit that the cruelties of one side had been matched by the cruelties and stupidities of the other. From Auden's *Spain* to George Orwell's *Homage to Catalonia:* the same parabola had been described.

Nearly all those who volunteered for Spain were either Communists (and it is doubtful if one can talk of volunteering in this case) or victims of this idealism; there were, however, exceptions, and one of them was Julian Bell. He had never been more than moderately sympathetic to the poetry of Auden, Spender and Day Lewis — a reservation that had been one of the causes of the friendly estrangement between us after I left the Hogarth Press. Believing as he did that poetry should be reasonable, masculine and public in the eighteenth-century manner, he disliked the esoteric jokes and the enthusiastic "Boy Scout" element in the poems they wrote during the early 'thirties. This temperamental hostility blinded him to the strength and originality of Wystan's work below the superficial topical flourishes. Cecil Day Lewis's work he found more to his liking, and to him he addressed a long *Open Letter* on "The Proletariat and Poetry" (reprinted in the memorial volume), criticizing the "movement" for disguising personal neurotic malaise under Marxist ideology, and for sentimentalizing the proletariat. "The myth of the proletarian saviour. is an inheritance from D. H. Lawrence and the early days of your movement," he wrote. "But the search for him is surely another symptom of softness and enthusiasm." He also attacked them for pretending that what to Julian was an obvious good — the leisured cultured life with its ethos of freedom and tolerance that bourgeois conditions provided for intellectuals in the West — was bad in itself: "The business of intelligence is to recognize that we are confronted by an essentially tragic situation. We have to abandon what is good, a free, tolerant, humane culture, and follow what is evil, violence, compulsion, cruelty." He was making his criticisms, he declared, "from the left-centre: from the position of a social-democrat"; but it was certainly a social democracy of an unusual sort, an essentially Bloomsbury sort.

Underneath the surface, however, he was much more divided and distressed than the *Open Letter* revealed. He had always hated war, and yet something drew him towards it. He still, theoretically, disliked emotion in art, but the poetry he was writing had become strongly nostalgic, almost sentimental. He was restless in England, and jumped at the opportunity in 1935 to be appointed Professor of English in the University of Hankow. Before that, he had written to me:

I *can't, can't* get clear about politics. Again, there's an emotional contradiction, or set of contradictions. I'm Left by tradition, and I'm an intellectual of the governing classes by tradition, and I can neither quite make up my mind to trying to get an economically intelligent Roosevelt "Social Fascism" nor give way to "the Party" with its fanatical war mentality. . . . I don't mind war as killing, nor as pain, nor utterly as destruction. But it means turning our minds and feelings downwards, growing hard (well, no harm, perhaps) but also savage and stupid and revengeful. You know, the Russians haven't escaped: spies and suspicion and tyranny, and no joke if your "class origins" aren't above suspicion. That's war — far more than the battlefields, even, tho' I think I shall live to see the people who talk about "the masses" in peace using those same masses like Haig and Wilson, until you've knocked the heart out of them. . . . As you'll see, I'm not yet clear, and pretty near despair either way. I believe one of the differences in our points of view comes from the circumstances of our private lives. I don't know at all, but I fancy you don't hit back when you're hurt. I do. When one has seen the extent of human beastliness and cruelty in oneself as well as outside one hesitates to let loose devils. There's nothing in the world fouler than enthusiasm, the enthusiasm of a fighting group, not even jealousy or suspicion, not even open-eyed causing of misery.

Julian saw pretty clearly, clearer than most of his generation, as this letter shows, the danger in any war, whether revolutionary or national, of ends being lost in means. In China, at first, his gloom and indecision deepened, though the mood may have arisen partly from a prostrating illness. In October 1935 he wrote to me:

At times I get homesick for the secure familiar English background. I suppose I may harden and get able to do without it, but having been ill is very weakening. I want to have the untroubled bourgeois holiday again. I suppose I shan't get it for long, ever. You know, I'm not going to be really good at the new world.

As time went on, however, and he made more Chinese friends, this mood began to change. He made a long journey with one of his students, Yeh (who later came to England during the war), through some territory which had recently been held by the Chinese Red Army. "Their record is extremely formidable, and I suspect that at the moment they're the best-led army in the world," he wrote at the end of September 1936. While he was away, the Spanish War had broken out.

What a show, Gods, what a show [he wrote in the same letter]. Better, really, than Germany or Vienna, but still — Not even the satisfaction of seeing the facts prove that revolutions don't occur and civil wars do, as I've always held, really compensates, even at this distance. It all happened while we were away from news; in Chengtu we had a Chinese paper talking about some kind of revolt in Ma Shan, which we eventually concluded was a Riff rising in Morocco. Then we got back — I by air to Peking — after three weeks, and it was in full swing. The Press here is wildly reactionary, as you might suppose, and it's hard to know what is happening.

I think his journey, and the news from Spain, brought Julian's desire to be involved in action, if possible violent action, never very deeply buried in his psychology, up to the surface again. He seemed more self-confident and settled; but he did not go further than saying he had made up his mind to get a job in politics on his return. When he did get home, however, in 1937, he decided almost at once to join the Spanish Medical Aid, and went out to Cordoba as a driver with an ambulance unit. We had missed one another, by ill-chance, before he left for China, and we were to miss one another again on this occasion. To my everlasting regret; for only a month later, on July 18, he was killed by a bomb from one of Franco's aeroplanes on the Brunete front. His letters from Spain gave the impression that he was amazingly happy and fulfilled in what he had undertaken; and in spite of his high intellectual ambitions, he had once written to his mother, Vanessa, that he would rather be killed violently than die any other way.

For me, it is as hard to forgive the killing of Julian as the killing of Lorca, wanton and deliberate as the murder of the young Spanish genius was compared with Julian's death; and I have been unable to find it in my heart to visit Spain as long as Franco's régime lasts.

The Spanish War presented *New Writing* with an opportunity that appeared at the same time as an imperative. I wanted, I felt it absolutely necessary, to make *New Writing* mirror this latest, crucial phase of "a new life breathing through the old," and become the place where whatever imaginative writing came out of the Spanish experience should naturally be published; the poems and stories from writers of our class appearing side by side with poems and stories I believed would come from new, inexperienced writers thrown up by the popular upheaval out of the darkness of the masses. I soon began to hear not only of what famous authors such as Sender, Alberti and Bergamin were writing, but also of the *Romances of the Civil War*, that extraordinary outburst of lyrics on themes of the day, which poets all over Republican Spain were writing. I wanted to get the best of these translated as soon as possible, but in this case it was rather a question of choosing between a host of eager volunteer translators: almost every English writer whose sympathies were engaged on the Republican side seemed to be burning to tackle them. Not knowing Spanish myself, I was presented even more urgently with the problem that had already become familiar in connection with Russian translations: to discover, when a poem or draft of a poem in its English version appeared to me weak or trite, how much was due to the translator and how much to the original poet. My files of the time are full of letters about translations, selecting, checking, suggesting emendations and polishing. By the time the third volume of *New Writing* had to go to press I had managed to include some of the *Romances*, as well as contributions by Alberti and Arconada, and the first personal story of an

English volunteer to the International Brigade, John Sommerfield's *To Madrid*.

Ironically, however, in this volume, which was dedicated to Ralph Fox, who had been killed in action a few months before, and in which it seems to me now I rather lost my judgement in the enthusiasm of the hour and included too much for "political" reasons and too little for literary merit, the outstanding contributions, those which have best stood the test of time, had nothing whatever to do with the war and little enough with political events. And yet Jose Herrera Petere's *Against the Cold in the Mountains* and Gonzalez Tunon's *Long Live the Revolution*, both from the *Romances*, have, like many similar poems that were written during the French Resistance in the next decade, a poignancy that can still be felt though their worth as poetry can scarcely be said to survive. For, as Stephen justly wrote in the Introduction to our *Poems for Spain*, which I have already quoted:

The fact that these poems should have been written at all has a literary significance parallel to the existence of the International Brigade. For some of these poems, and many more which we have not been able to publish, were written by men for whom poetry scarcely existed before the Spanish War. Some of these writers, first awakened to poetry by Spain, died before they had the opportunity to cultivate their talent.

Some of them, I believe, did achieve something greater than topical significance. I have always had an affection for such spontaneous, untaught writings, when, by a lucky chance, they escape the laboured struggle with what their authors fondly imagine to be correct and cultured diction; and to me one of the most moving poems that came out of the Spanish War is the eight lines that were found scribbled, anonymously, on the leaf of a note-book by a soldier in the International Brigade:

> Eyes of men running, falling, screaming
> Eyes of men shouting, sweating, bleeding
> The eyes of the fearful, those of the sad
> The eyes of exhaustion, and those of the mad.
>
> Eyes of men thinking, hoping, waiting
> Eyes of men loving, cursing, hating
> The eyes of the wounded sodden in red
> The eyes of the dying and those of the dead.

The Spanish War also demonstrated that there are occasions when poetry concerned entirely with a political creed and the action resulting from it can have an enduring poetic power: warmly applauded in the political surge of the moment, rejected when disillusionment sets in, they are later found to have some uranium content that still makes them impressive and valid as poetry. In the fourth volume of *New Writing* we published a group of poems by John Cornford (son of Frances Cornford), a Cambridge undergraduate of only twenty-one, who had been killed fighting with the International Brigade. I still find them, for all their faults, among the most remarkable poems that came out of the Spanish War: untainted even by the suspicion of rhetoric that clings to Auden's *Spain*, more directly moving than that magnificent virtuoso piece in the Newbolt vein, Cecil Day Lewis's *The Nabara*, they are a rare example of closely packed thought in verse that is yet entirely clear, without private riddles, and transformed into a hard-muscled poetry in which often brutally realistic images are used — not always, for Cornford was still finding his way, but surprisingly frequently — without destroying the harmony of the whole. They gain enormously from being written as part of the experience of action: Cornford seems sometimes to write of the battle for Communism as Donne wrote of love; and though the deeply touching love-lyric *Heart of the Heartless World* is the one that has had the widest appeal, I do not think it as important as the longer poems *Full Moon at Tierz* or *As Our Might Lessens*, in which the movement and tension come from the struggle against the fear of pain, the brooding about pain in the poet's mind:

> Now the same night falls over Germany
> And the impartial beauty of the stars
> Lights from the unfeeling sky
> Oranienburg and freedom's crooked scars.
> We can do nothing to ease that pain
> But prove the agony was not in vain. . . .

I do not know whether John Cornford would have seen the other side of the moon, the corruption of Stalinism, if he had lived; but I believe, on the evidence of the power of the few poems he left, in spite of their obvious moments of immaturity, that if he had written about El Alamein or the storming of Normandy as he wrote about the storming of Huesca, no other poet of action in the Second World War could have touched him: his name would be a household word today, with the more literary-minded statesmen quoting him in their speeches for solemn occasions.

In mood, as well as in the "feel" of the verse, nothing less like Cornford's work could be imagined than the poems Stephen Spender wrote during the Spanish War; but they have always deeply moved me because they were not written from the side-lines, but — like nearly all his best poems — they came freshly out of personal experience. In his autobiography Stephen has told the story of how he became involved in the human realities behind the rhetoric through the misfortunes of a friend; with the result that the poems were not the musical romantic apostrophes that might have been expected from the author of *Oh young men, Oh young comrades*, but troubled, disturbing and anti-heroic. Stephen's quick, imaginative perception had once more spotted a falsehood, and poems like *Regum Ultima Ratio*, with their echo of Wilfred Owen, were a reply which did not endear him to the Communists. His description of André Chamson at the International Writers' Congress in Madrid in the summer of 1937 (of which he wrote a personal account for *New Writing*) has stayed in my mind for the same reason:

Every morning I would go up to Chamson to enquire how he was and he would reply, "*Mal, mal, MAL!*" He would go on to say that the intellectual level of our Congress was appallingly low, that we were irresponsible, lighthearted, we did not *feel*. . . . Along paths which I can scarcely follow, Chamson had arrived at a truth which few of the Congress — fêted, banqueted, received enthusiastically, the women bridling with excitement at Ralph Bates's or Ludwig Renn's uniform — had even glimpsed, that the war is terrible, that the mind of Madrid, if it is sublime, like Shakespeare's, is also terrible, like Shakespeare's. I myself had learnt this through painful experiences some months before, not at the Congress. I applaud Chamson.

I did not attend this Congress, or go to Spain on any other delegation or weighty mission, like so many of my colleagues, nor as a reporter, nor as an ambulance driver. Christopher, with his insatiable passion for directing the destinies of his friends as if he were allotting the parts in a play (mock-serious melodrama generally), had immediately begun to invent roles for us; but I had already chosen mine. I had made up my mind that I was going to see the Austrian drama through to the end: I had created a home in Vienna, I had many friends who were deeply involved, and I believed that in a crisis I might be of help — of far more help than in a country I knew almost nothing about, where so many international experts of every sort had already gathered. But I realized, as we all realized in Vienna, that the fate of Austria depended not a little on the fate of Spain. Sometimes, as I sat at my desk by the big window and the hubbub of the city seemed for a few minutes to be stilled, the wind dropping as the clatter of trams and horses' hooves died out, it was as if all Vienna was listening for the echo of the guns in the far-away peninsula. . . . Every Franco victory sent Nazi hopes soaring, every Republican victory was secretly celebrated by the left-wing sympathizers meeting in cafés or private houses unsuspected by the police. A kind of underground railway was organized to get would-be volunteers for the International Brigade out of the country to the West, over the high mountain passes that could never be completely patrolled by the frontier guards. Absorbed as I was in the Central European scene, these movements in the darkness had an endless fascination for me; nevertheless, as the fortunes of the long-drawn-out war moved gradually against the Republicans, as news came of the deaths of Ralph Fox, and Julian, and John Cornford, I could not help feeling the pull of Spain more and more, and a sense of release when I travelled home every few months through Paris and London, a sense of returning to the centre of desperately urgent activities. The wall of civilization was falling, and I was doing so little, posted at one remote corner, to shore it up.

It was not particularly easy to pursue the editorial work for *New Writing* under these conditions, and yet the very fact that I was in Vienna, and not in Paris or Madrid, helped me, I believe, to maintain a balance against the encroachments of politics into literature. Curiously enough, the close censorship on foreign mail that Schuschnigg's Government kept up under the cloak of *devisenkontrolle* did not ever prevent me receiving the packets of MSS. from my assistants in London nor corresponding about them, nor correcting the proofs of many stories and poems that were concerned with the war. This work made me feel that, even at long range, I had some small if not particularly glorious part to play in the movement which was absorbing the energies of so many of my friends. Letters began to come in from contributors and fans of *New Writing* in Spain, which damped down the ever-smouldering fires of my guilt. Alfred Kantorowicz wrote from Madrid:

An English friend showed me here *New Writing* No. 4 containing my Madrid Diary. . . . We stormed together with the 15^e Brigade Villanueva de la Canada and Romanillos in the Brunete battle, always side by side with the English and American comrades; I had always to work with

Major Nathan, the English hero of the 15ᵉ Brigade. Two days before his death I was wounded. . . .

Rosamond kept up a long correspondence with me describing, with a sense of the phantasmagoric comedy as well as the tragic seriousness of the situation, what was going on in England and what it felt like to be the grass-widow of a volunteer hero in Spain. Right to the bitter end, when only the forlornest hopes remained, English intellectuals maintained their agitation for arms to be sent to the Republican Government, more I believe out of an unassuaged indignation at the farce of the Non-Intervention Committee and a still ineffaceable horror at the wiping out of Guernica by Nazi bombers (with all it promised for ourselves), than with any idea that the agitation could be effective. In January of 1939 Rosamond wrote me a description of what must have been the last of the official demonstrations:

Yesterday I took part in a deputation to the P.M., Attlee, Sinclair, Alfred Barnes. Attlee . . . spoke of "exploring every avenue" etc. etc. This roused a Welsh delegate to a fine frenzy of vituperation — and we all felt worse than ever. Sinclair, not having a party to lead, exhibited exceptional qualities of leadership. To my pained surprise I found myself committed to walking in a procession down Whitehall, holding a placard, with Dame Adelaide Livingstone in a fur toque and eyeveil in front of me, Amabel (Williams-Ellis) beside me, and various T.U.C. delegates at the back and before. 200 strong! We were stopped at No. 10, delivered a protest by letter to a flunkey, and were bidden to stand on the corner and shout "Arms for Spain!" — when I escaped, and jumped into a taxi and came home. The policeman on duty gently suggested we should all go home quietly, which no doubt we did.

In the same letter she revealed more of her true feelings when she added: "It's snowing here, and I await the fall of Barcelona with feelings to match the leaden skies."

« 9 »

WE were extremely anxious at the beginning not only that we should publish translations of Russian stories, but also that our aims should evoke sympathy and understanding in Moscow intellectual circles. This was to prove a much more complex business than in our political unlicked-ness we guessed at the outset, even though cultural contacts between Russia and the outside world were far easier then — easier than anyone could imagine who judged from the Tibetan conditions of the years following the war. I had already written a rather naïvely semi-Marxist study of modern English literature for the Russian magazine *Internationalnaya Literatura*, and had introduced myself to its editors during a visit to Moscow. When I finally had the contracts for *New Writing* in my pocket, I wrote eagerly off to *Internationalnaya Literatura* and asked for their help in getting Russian authors. The editors promptly made the most interested and sympathetic gestures; but somehow or other we never got much beyond that, and practically all the Soviet material — apart from what I later collected myself in Georgia — came from *New Writing* enthusiasts in England who could read Russian and had a good collection of modern Russian books. From time to time I would send an urgent, pleading letter to Moscow, reminding them of their promises to assemble stories for me. After a long, long interval, during which at least one more number of *New Writing* had been prepared and sent to press, a telegram would suddenly arrive: MATERIAL ON ITS WAY FRATERNAL GREETINGS. Keyed up by this, I would wait a few more weeks, until a letter from one of the chief editors' secretaries appeared, announcing, "I have to disappoint you, but I think truth is always better. The material was not and is not as yet being sent. . . ." What grim ideological battles lay behind this reversal I could not fathom then — indeed, I did not think to put it down to anything but Russian *schlamperei* (and I may well have been right). However, I tried again, with an obstinate refusal to admit defeat. The weeks passed, and no answer came. Suddenly the silence was broken by a telegram: EXTREMELY INTERESTED LATEST MOVEMENTS PEN CLUB PLEASE SEND FULL INFORMATION URGENT. After this stunning blow, I gave up and turned to my own English advisers and translators for Russian work, though I occasionally made a special search for Russian stories in French or German versions which I could read myself. And yet every now and then sudden signs were vouchsafed that *New Writing* was being closely watched in some mysterious Kremlin office. Our pathetic eagerness to win Russian sympathy and Russian readers had been shown by the discussion that went on over the title of Christopher's first story. Originally he wanted it called *The Kulaks*. Soon after the MS. reached me, however, he wrote:

About the Kulaks: it occurs to me that maybe, if the book is to be read at all in Russia, the title conveys quite a wrong impression. Do you think I should change the family name? I could do this, of course, in proof: or maybe it could be done before the MS. goes to press. What about Nowack? "The Nowacks" — Nowak, perhaps, is better? Yes: "The Nowaks". . . .

Christopher's instinct was sound, for one day a Russian girl, emissary of Moscow, suddenly arrived in my office, and carried off copies of No. 1 proofs, and any other material lying about, and a few months later a little Russian booklet appeared on my desk with the picture of a youthful down-and-out on the cover, and the superscription in cyrillic characters: HOBAKN. But I never heard what the Soviet public made of Otto and his ambiguous adventures.

When I eventually set out again for Russia, on a hunting expedition from which I was determined to bring back a few rare specimens of new writing from Transcaucasia at least — for my imagination had been fired by the Caucasus, and I wanted to explore it with a book mistily in view — I was armed with all sorts of introductions to Russians, Georgians and *émigré* German writers who, I hoped, might put me on the right scent. I felt that if I actually appeared on the spot, I might be able to circumvent the mysterious obstacles that had prevented me so far from ringing any bell in the Soviet Union. I also had an introduction to Ivy Low, the English wife of Foreign Minister Litvinov; and tried to get in touch with her by telephone from my hotel in Moscow. I rang up again and again, I enlisted the aid of my Intourist interpreter, of the handsome and efficient manageress, a former aristocrat who had "gone over" to the Bolsheviks, and various other friends; but always fruitlessly. The noise that came through the receiver reminded me of the confused humming, muttering and crackling that K., in Kafka's novel, hears when he tries to ring up the Castle. Occasionally a sombre voice broke in with a few angry but unintelligible words of Russian before cutting me off. I very much doubt if I got anywhere near Litvinov's office or home; the line was probably tapped half a dozen times between the hotel and him; and I very much doubt also whether my Russian helpers rang up the right number, in spite of all the screaming and shouting they were obliged to indulge in by the antiquity of the instrument and the state of the lines — it was probably extremely unwise for them to do more than make a show for my benefit. Once or twice they assured me that Mme. Litvinov was out but they had left messages. Then suddenly, an hour or two later, I would be called on the telephone, and an extraordinary thing would happen: through the confusion of sound a voice speaking broken American would suddenly emerge, and ask whether I would like to *see*

[189]

a circus. . . . This happened several times, and each time the demand was more urgent. It reduced me to a state of panic: "to see a circus," I felt sure, was a code phrase which meant entering into contact with a counter-revolutionary group, and either someone in the group had been detailed to watch me or the secret police were testing me; I pictured a nice little "circus" in one of the interrogation rooms of the Lubyanka prison, way underground, with myself as performing elephant.

It was the time of the Moscow Trials, and the look of confidence and optimism which I had thought to observe on the faces of people I passed in the streets during my first visit seemed to have gone. Strange things were happening under the surface, people were jumpy and preoccupied, and much less willing to talk in public than they had been a couple of years before: I was forced to admit this to myself, in spite of my wish to see everything through rose-coloured spectacles. One day, in Rostov, I found myself being tracked by a tall, hawk-faced man of middle age, who finally cornered me and began to speak to me in halting French. Visions of the circus rose before me again: I tried to throw him off, but in vain. He wanted to talk to me, he said; there were many things he could show me in Rostov I wouldn't otherwise see. He wormed the name of my hotel out of me, and the next day emerged from a clump of trees further up the avenue as I came out. He pressed his company upon me, and insisted that as I was interested in modern Russian writing there were many books he could show me if I would come to his flat. In a sort of hypnotized trance, dreading to offend rather than impelled by curiosity — for he had a formidable personality — I allowed myself to be taken up to his small abode, where vodka was offered me. Then, gradually, the talk came round to the point. . . . There was much dissatisfaction in the Soviet Union, particularly in the Ukraine. . . . Secret opposition groups were at work. . . . He himself planned to escape, and had already collected some English pound notes. . . . Panic gripped me again, I was even more convinced than I had been in Moscow that the secret police were testing me, and I desperately tried to keep my answers as colourlessly polite as possible. Finally he saw he was not getting anywhere, and with a sigh abandoned his attempt to interest me further. When I got back to the hotel I looked under the bed and into the cupboards with anxious care; but my innocent papers did not seem to have been disturbed, not one of my letters read.

My actual experience of two hours in the hands of the Ogpu, when it came, was rather an anti-climax. I was strolling alone round the

Batum water-front with my camera. Up the avenue, in the distance, a detachment of Soviet marines was approaching: the scene suddenly composed into an excellent picture, I lifted my Leica and pressed the shutter. Three minutes later, as I was wandering down to the sea's edge, I heard angry shouts behind me, and on turning round saw to my dismay that a naval lieutenant with drawn sword, accompanied by two of the marines hurriedly fixing their bayonets, was rushing towards me. I was placed under arrest in an instant, my stumbling expostulations in bad Russian were ignored by the lieutenant, who seemed beside himself with rage at the sight of my British passport, and I was marched off to Naval Headquarters down the road. I felt lucky not to have been put up against a wall and shot on the spot; but my constant repetition of the word "Intourist" had in the end the desired effect, my guide arrived half an hour later at the Headquarters, out of breath and very nervous, and persuaded the officers that I was harmless. Meanwhile, however, an Ogpu agent had also arrived, a little weasel-faced man in a cloth cap who grinned at me affably and explained that there was still one trifling formality before I could be freed: I must accompany him to a photographer in the town, where my film would be developed. My guide disappeared, and I found myself trying to explain to the Ogpu agent that the film was Panatomic and not even red light must be used in the developing room. Unfortunately, in the stress of the moment I could not remember the Russian word for light, and kept on saying *"Ne krasne, ne krasne!"* I noticed that the Ogpu man seemed to grow decidedly less affable at this, and refused to listen to me any longer. It was only too clear that he had mistaken my intention, when the film emerged from the developing room: one long roll entirely black, without a sign of a picture on it. Evidently some diabolical trick of the British Intelligence Service, to manage to obliterate all pictures at the moment of unmasking. . . . He released me rather reluctantly.

My hunt for new Soviet authors during the seven weeks of my visit was assiduous and single-minded, but not particularly rewarding. There were, however, other occasions of misunderstanding, less awkward for me personally, which have remained in memory as comic relief. I was taken one evening to the House of Writers in Moscow, where a celebration was being held to honour Berthold Brecht. After the speeches of welcome, a young Russian poet got up, to read a translation he had made of one of Brecht's famous longer poems: it was a fiery declamation; the young Russian lashed himself into a passion, gesticulating dramatically and turning purple in the face with the effort, and then sank back to his seat with bowed head. There were storms of applause. Then Brecht himself was asked to recite the same poem in his original German. He read it sitting down, with dead-pan face, in the totally flat, anti-rhetorical manner he had intended it. A look of bewilderment came into the young Russian poet's eyes; and embarrassed glances were exchanged among the other Russian writers there. At the end the applause was respectful rather than enthusiastic. I had a suspicion that Brecht was secretly deriving immense enjoyment from the episode.

I was told of another episode, in Tiflis, which amusingly spotlighted not only the ignorance and lack of sophistication of the younger Soviet officials and literary world, bemused by years of solemn Marxist distortion of reality, but also the absurdities that constantly arose from sudden changes in the Party line about friends and enemies abroad. It was the time when André Gide was the great hero, Exhibit Number One of the triumph of Soviet sympathies among the intellectuals of the West. A tremendous celebration was arranged for him when he visited Tiflis, including a banquet in which local writers poured forth eulogies of his work. When it was all over and Gide had departed, someone casually mentioned *Corydon*. The speechmakers had never heard of it; and on being told what it contained and what Gide's frankly avowed sexual preferences were, they were utterly appalled. Violent quarrels broke out and raged for weeks. Someone may even have been sent to Siberia.

I had the impression that in literature and in the theatre — where Kouchitashvili, the brilliant young Georgian producer who had worked in Paris for some years and had then decided to accept the Soviet invitation to return home, had a dominant influence — the Georgians, with their love of fun and the colour of life and their long romantic history, a tradition so entirely different from the Russian, did not take the earnest strivings of the Marxist purists very seriously, though they paid lip-service to the Party line and the necessity of Socialist optimism.

In painting, too, this saving grace still seemed to me happily apparent. As I wandered round the rooms of an exhibition of modern Georgian painting, every now and then I received an authentic shock of aesthetic pleasure — even if not of a very high voltage. Impossible in Moscow, where the official doctrines had extinguished life in the plastic arts as swiftly and completely as an old-fashioned snuffer clapped over a candle-flame: an obliteration only too painfully evident to one's hopeful gaze in the Soviet pavilion at the Paris Exhibition, even if one had not made the journey to Russia. Of this pavilion, and the monstrous twin figures of a Soviet worker and his lass which stood in front of it, E. M. Forster wrote, in the sad and witty description of the Exhibition he contributed to the number of *New Writing* which contained my first gathering of Georgian poems and stories:

Passing beneath their sealed up petticoats and trousers we enter a realm which is earnest cheerful instructive constructive and consistent, but which has had to blunt some of the vagrant sensibilities of mankind and is consequently not wholly alive. Statistics, maps and graphs preach a numerical triumph, but the art-stuff on the walls might just as well hang on the walls of the German pavilion opposite: the incidents and the uniforms in pictures are different, but the mentality of the artists is the same, and as tame.

He went on to say that the Soviet pavilion was nevertheless "a nudge to the blind," meaning those who could not see the corrupting effect of money values. It might also have been a nudge to the blind of another sort. . . . But André Gide's eyes had already been opened, and the waves of rage and indignation were lashing round his famous little book *Au Retour de l'U.R.S.S.*

In my Moscow hotel I used sometimes after dinner (which means round about midnight) to meet Prince Mirsky, whom I had known slightly in London before he made his gesture of returning to Russia. In spite of his conversion to Bolshevism, he could not rid himself entirely of the Old Adam: he used to give huge tips to the waiters (many of whom were themselves weary relics of the *ancien régime*) with an aristocratic disdain for the change, and conversed freely about literature in Bloomsbury terms. I remember talking with him one night about Zoschenko, Olyesha, and other Soviet writers who seemed not to care overmuch for the fatuous dictates of Socialist Realism. "Yes, it still goes on," he said in a rather gloomy undertone. "But I wouldn't like to say how long our political leaders will stand for it." When the wind changed to the north, Prince Mirski himself was one of those who vanished without trace: an ironic epilogue to his not uncourageous — and for the Bolsheviks politically useful — action.

« 10 »

IT was natural for me to have great expectations of finding writers from the working-class and from the anti-fascist underground in Vienna as well. I asked all my friends, in all the circles I knew; but to my surprise and chagrin, they had nothing, no one to suggest. My final, one and only discovery came by chance. The story of this young writer stands for me as an epitome of all the dignity and tragedy of the time of fascist triumph and threatening war.

After my early travels in Russia, I had made up my mind for future travels to get beyond the "*da*" and "*spasebo*" stage of Russian and learn it well enough to converse (when the Intourist guide wasn't looking) with chance encounters, and to get the drift of the newspapers. I looked round for a teacher in Vienna, and was recommended a young poet of Russian parentage who was eking out a living by giving lessons and by writing sketches for one of the many little café-cabarets which existed at that time in Vienna.

Yura Soyfer was a delicate-looking man, of just under average height, in his middle twenties. He had a soft voice, a gentle expression and great charm of manner; but under this mild exterior he concealed, as I was later to realize, not only a subtle understanding of his fellow-men but also a strong will and cool courage. His family was poor, and he earned far too little himself to live even an averagely comfortable life; but I never once heard him complain about it. His work as a poet and the pursuit of his political ideals absorbed him entirely.

I did learn some Russian from Yura; enough to understand the headlines in the newspapers and converse haltingly when I made my trips to the Caucasus; but I learnt far more about the literature of Austria and the secret political movements at my door. Yura, who had been a small child when his parents fled from the Bolshevik Revolution, had completely acclimatized himself to Viennese writing and art, and his great admirations were the three famous Austrian dramatists Raimund, Nestroy and Grillparzer, particularly the first two, so difficult to translate and interpret for anyone without an intimate knowledge of the Viennese background. He would talk for hours about these three and the history of the Austrian theatre; and I believe that if he had lived he might have made some notable contributions to it himself. Some of his cabaret plays have survived and have been published since the war in Vienna: they are clever, full of playful topical wit against the police-rulers of the country, but above all remarkable — to me — for their human warmth and the tenderness of their idealism. Yura was the poet of a ruined and dispossessed generation, the young men and women whose childhood had been the inflation and revolutionary aftermath of the war in Central Europe, and who had grown up to unemployment as a permanent condition of the life around them. He expressed their half-despairing longings, the gentleness that remained in the midst of the bitterness, the sense of civilized values so essentially Viennese (which penetrated right down through the educated working-classes), with such truth of feeling that I have only to read the opening lines of one of his sketches for the whole atmosphere of that melancholy time to come back to me.

In politics, Yura's case was typical of the younger Austrian intellectuals of those years. He began by being a fervent Socialist, full of the idealism of the Viennese movement that had accomplished such an extraordinary work of education and welfare during the decade and a half of its control of the city's government. But he belonged to that wing of it which believed that the movement needed to be armed and prepared to fight against the counter-revolutionary forces that were being organized on the one side by Starhemberg and on the other by the pan-German Nazis. I think Yura already belonged, before 1934, to the Schutzbund, and he certainly took part in some capacity in the final stand, the despairing all-too-late gesture of the out-manoeuvered party. The disillusionment and bewilderment that followed it are not easy to describe now, when we have become accustomed to far greater destruction and horror and have learnt disenchantment with so many ideologies that still had their appeal in those days. For Yura and his friends the answer seemed clear: war, with fascism as its driving force, was approaching fast, the Socialist parties of Europe were going to put up only a half-hearted fight against a movement that was entirely ruthless — they had seen what had happened in Germany the year before and knew that Austria, once Hitler and Mussolini came to terms, would be wide open to the Nazis — and more extreme solutions were called for. What remained in these circumstances but the Communists, now pointing with I-told-you-so contempt at the leaders of a party they had always despised, and offering a programme not only of militant counter-action but also the true and only interpretation of Socialism, the gospel according to St. Lenin and St. Stalin, which would, when the party was ready to seize power, avoid all such errors as had made the February debacle possible?

I did not learn that Yura had joined the Communist underground at once, but only gradually as I gained his confidence and he saw that my devouring interest in what was going on in Vienna under the surface could be put to good use. He became one of my chief sources of information, and also of supply of the illegal pamphlets and diminutive newspapers, printed in eye-teasing type on the flimsiest paper or duplicated, with crude but amusing cartoons. I had had a secret cupboard built into the new furniture of my flat, and there the copies of these extraordinary little productions, prepared with such devotion in conditions of considerable danger or smuggled across the frontier from Prague, were hidden until I could get them out of the country myself or send a digest of them with my own annotations to the papers which were interested.

When I told Yura about the *New Writing* project, he was immensely interested, and wanted to know all about the English writers who were contributing; most of the French, German and Russian authors in the first number he already knew of. He was excited by the idea of an international magazine that planned to reflect the revolutionary ferment of the time, and promised to see if he could find any suitable poems or stories by unknown writers among his acquaintances in Vienna. Looking over the first volume when it arrived in its bright colours, exclaiming with delight about some of the contributions ("the whole development of nineteenth-century philosophy is in this!" he cried of Upward's *The Border Line*), he shook his head dolefully and told me he didn't think there was anyone of his generation who cared enough about writing to qualify; almost all Austrian talent had been drained off to Germany in the days of the Weimar Republic, as soon as it had shown itself; and now, well, who could begin a literary career under the hopeless political conditions in which they had been living ever since Hitler came to power across the frontier? Then I remembered that a little time before he had, very diffidently, mentioned a book on which he himself was working, a novel in which he wanted to give the whole inner story of the Socialists and the Schutzbund in the last months before they were crushed. From the way he had talked about it I had formed the impression that it would be a work of art and not a crude propaganda effort or a disguised piece of journalist's reportage. Not without difficulty, I at last managed to persuade him to let me look at some chapters which he considered were in a sufficiently finished state to be seen by a critical eye.

As soon as I had read them, I felt certain that I had found the real thing. With my keen Schutzbund sympathies of the time, I was fascinated by the theme: but I was particularly struck by the sensitive skill Yura had shown in creating atmosphere and in conveying the erratic, psychological weather of a group of characters waiting for a battle to begin, waiting in a state of nervy tension for their leaders to tell them when skirmishes and patrols in force by the enemy — which little by little were robbing them of all their advantages — could be answered by a real offensive. Much to Yura's surprise and delight, I told him that I would publish a section of what he had showed me as soon as I could get it translated; and in the second number of *New Writing* it appeared as *In the Corner* under the pseudonym of Georg Anders.

Publication, impossible in his own country, gave Yura a much needed spur, and he set to work on the novel with renewed faith. I was convinced of its importance, and of the promise of Yura's gifts. I kept on urging him to greater speed as time went on, for like everyone else I felt the threat of a curtain falling, not merely on Yura's own illegal political activities in Austria but on the whole pattern of our lives. Yura, however, was a slow worker, he was writing under extremely difficult conditions, and he had to earn some kind of a living by his cabaret sketches and the lessons he gave. What was more, he had planned the novel on a large scale, and with his passion for the smallest significant details the further he worked into it the longer it seemed to him it would have to be. I wanted to publish more in *New Writing* — it was only after his death and after the outbreak of war, at Christmas, 1939, that another section appeared — but Yura realized as well as I did that, pleasant as it might be to have fragments published in translation abroad, he must find a publisher for the novel in German. He was actually in contact with one in Prague, when the first blow fell.

Schuschnigg's secret police did not lack efficiency, even though a strange paralysis often seemed to come over them when dealing with the Nazi underground, and in demoralized Vienna there were plenty of informers to be blackmailed or bought among the unemployed intellectuals and the working population. I took many precautions to conceal my activities as a collector of information about the hidden Socialist and Communist organizations; but I suppose that the privileged position any resident foreigner even of moderate means enjoyed in those days made me careless in the end; though I think it extremely unlikely that the first clue that brought the police on to the trail of myself and several of those who kept me in touch came from a slip of my own. I was remarkably foolish not to have reflected more about the fact that for some weeks there had always seemed to be a car starting up behind my own when I went out in the evenings; if I had not been so happy at that time in Vienna — it was, I think, the early summer of 1937 — I would have paid more attention to the fact that when I went out to dine in an open-air restaurant in Grinzing or in the Prater, a nearby table was so frequently occupied by two or three men who did not appear quite to fit the place or the occasion.

One morning, just after Frau Chval had arrived, there was a ring at the door. A moment later she parted the curtains of my bed-recess and hissed: *"Die Polizei!"* A glance at her horrified face, and I leapt out of bed, to find myself confronted by a youngish man of pleasant countenance and extremely courteous manner, who produced his secret-police badge and suggested that it was his regrettable duty to search the flat and put some tiresome questions to myself. He was accompanied by a decidedly less courteous acolyte.

I am, I believe, a person who is easily confused by the unexpected, but my good angel assuredly stood by my side that morning. In spite of my embarrassment, I decided in a flash to reveal all — or, to be strictly accurate, nearly all. I explained that I was a foreign journalist engaged in collecting every piece of information that might help to elucidate the real situation in Austria, and that I therefore kept as close contact as possible with the underground organizations. I opened the drawer of my desk for them to examine, pulled out several of the illegal pamphlets I happened to have been working on the day before, and invited them to explore further. Having got their assent to a quick shave and wash, I left them at their nosey work, and on my way to the shower-bath told Frau Chval in a whisper that the moment I was taken away by the detectives she was to ring up one or two of my friends among the Anglo-American journalists who might be able to pull strings for me. Feeling herself in passionate league with me against the hated police, she performed this mission with the utmost efficiency. Times have changed, but even so I would scruple to reveal this — governments come and go, but the police remain and have long memories — were it not that dear, brave, loyal, kind-hearted, hard-working Frau Chval, who burst into tears when, without warning, I knocked at her door one day after the war, is now dead and beyond all petty revenge or suspicion.

Having concluded their examination of the flat, without lighting on the secret cupboard, the detectives invited me down to their car, which was standing discreetly on the other side of the block, and suggested that the most agreeable place for us to continue our civilized conversation was the Police Headquarters. I soon found myself in that sombre fortress of seedy (but all-too-powerful) bureaucracy, and was ushered in to the presence of a high officer, who greeted me with politeness but without enthusiasm, and proceeded to fire some shrewd and pertinent questions at me, which showed how carefully my movements had been watched for some weeks. The odd pattern of the detectives who arrested me was repeated here: behind the comparatively urbane officer was standing another hefty individual of sinister aspect, who uttered his own commentary on the proceedings in furious hisses of indignation and disbelief. How this second act of the uncomfortable comedy would have concluded if it had run its course as the police intended, I do not know; for in the middle of it another detective hurried into the room and whispered something to the examining officer, the drift of which I was not slow to gather: Frau Chval had done her job, and my friends had begun to make inquiries. Reluctantly, but with a look that said "Don't worry, I'll get you in the end," the officer released me. Reflecting with nervous relief on the curious fact that I must be one of the few people in Europe at that time to have been arrested (and released) by both fascist and Communist police, I walked out into the free air of heaven.

It was all right for me; but very soon after — and here is my reason for the interpolation of my own story at this point — I heard that my arrest had been only part of a much wider swoop the police had organized that morning against the left-wing underground, and that several of my friends, including Yura, had fallen into their net. That was the beginning of the end for him. I cannot be sure of the details of what happened to him during the next two years, because I have lost all contact with those mutual friends who might be able to refresh my memory; as far as I can recollect, however, and as far as I was able to piece the story together from fragmentary reports that reached me during a time of dispersal and confusion, Yura was released by the Austrians just before the Anschluss in 1938, but promptly seized again by the Nazis when they overthrew Schuschnigg's Government. A former Schutzbundler, a convicted illegal worker for the Communists, and a Jew, he stood little chance: the way led to Dachau.

The epilogue was told me one day in my office at the Hogarth Press in Mecklenburgh Square, just after the outbreak of war. An unknown young Austrian came to see me, who informed me that he had known Yura in Buchenwald, whither he was transferred from Dachau. So far from being crushed by this disaster, the assassination of all his own hopes, and by all the horrors he had to witness, Yura, the gentle, smiling, fragile intellectual, had developed into a tower of physical strength and spiritual endurance. He worked miracles, his friend said, in keeping up the morale of his fellow-Austrians who were imprisoned with him, he even wrote — what must appear weirdest of all literary activities — cabaret pieces to be acted by the inmates of the concentration camp, and gained a grudging respect from the thugs who ruled it. They made him a sick-bay attendant; and then, in carrying out his duties during an epidemic of typhus, just as a visa for the United States reached him — the long-dreamed-of visa we had been working so hard for, that promised him a new start in a new country — he succumbed to the epidemic himself, and died.

Copies of Yura's Viennese cabaret sketches had been carried into the free world by friends before the war, and were published a few years ago in Austria in a memorial volume. Nothing remained of the novel except the fragments I had preserved. Nearly all his poems were also, I believe, destroyed, except his beautiful *Lied der Einfachen Menschen,* and another deeply moving song which he wrote in Dachau and which the friend who came to see me had memorized. Later I translated it and published it in *Folios of New Writing* under the title of *Song of the Austrians in Dachau.* It had as its ironic theme the words that stood over the entrance to the concentration camp, *ARBEIT MACHT FREI:*

Pitiless the barbed wire dealing
Death that round our prison runs,
And a sky that knows no feeling
Sends us ice and burning suns;
Lost to us the world of laughter,
Lost our homes, our loves, our all;
Through the dawns our thousands muster,
To their work in silence fall.
> *But the slogan of Dachau is burnt on our brains*
> *And unyielding as steel we shall be;*
> *Are we men, brother? Then we'll be men when they've done,*
> *Work on, we'll go through with the task we've begun,*
> *For work, brother, work makes us free.*

Haunted by the gun-mouths turning
All our days and nights are spent;
Toil is ours — the way we're learning
Harder than we ever dreamt;
Weeks and months we cease to reckon
Pass, and some forget the years,
And so many men are broken
And their faces changed with fears.
> *But the slogan of Dachau is burnt on our brains,* etc.

Heave the stone and drag the truck,
Let no load's oppression show,
In your days of youth and luck
You thought lightly: now you know.
Plunge your spade in earth and shovel

Pity where heart cannot feel,
Purged in your own sweat and trouble
Be yourself like stone and steel.
    But the slogan of Dachau is burnt on our brains, etc.

One day sirens will be shrieking
One more roll-call, but the last.
And the stations we'll be seeking —
Outside, brother, prison past!
Bright the eyes of freedom burning,
Worlds to build with joy and zest
And the work begun that morning,
Yes, that work will be our best!
    But the slogan of Dachau is burnt on our brains, etc.

« 11 »

EVERY new movement or impetus in literature sooner or later, if it has strength and direction, attempts to invade the theatre (if it is not born there). This still seems to remain true as a general rule even nowadays, when, paradoxically, literature itself, in the novel, has been so deeply influenced by the tempo, cutting, and visual primacy of the cinema. Christopher Isherwood's Berlin stories are one outstanding example (though very far from the only one) of this revolutionary influence; and Christopher, significantly, was one of those who led the way in the new theatrical movement of the 'thirties.

The lively, infuriating Unity Theatre was founded to present avowedly left-wing propagandist drama, such as was already being successfully played in little theatres in America, and specialized in witty, topical cabaret and revue sketches on political themes. Unity Theatre, like the Gate, was a *place;* you could find it in the back streets of North London and enjoy a totally different kind of evening there if you were bored with the West End theatre. The Group Theatre, however, which was launched in the autumn of 1935 under the fanatically single-minded direction of Rupert Doone, former Diaghilev dancer and choreographer, was a producing organization and used whatever theatre it could get.

Doone's first production was the first Auden-Isherwood play, *The Dog Beneath the Skin.* I was too much abroad to be in the swim of this adventure in experimental theatre, missed *Dog-Skin* (as Christopher always called it), but saw the next child of the famous and all-too-brief collaboration, *The Ascent of F6,* and Stephen Spender's *Trial of*

a Judge; and shared in the excitement that steadily rose as the Group
Theatre established itself as *the* avant-garde theatre movement of the
time. It even seemed possible that the everlasting, conventionally tai-
lored West End play with its neat three acts and superficial realism
was at last doomed. First the Gate; now the Group. . . . But the
walls of Shaftesbury Avenue did not fall at this blast of trumpets; and
it is melancholy now to reflect for how brief a spring the new poetic
drama ruled. *The Dog Beneath the Skin* and *The Ascent of F6* were
genuine attempts to break entirely new ground, and began an experimental movement behind which one could feel the youthful pressure of
new ideas and new notions of form; a movement that, in spite of a
certain debt in its origins to German Expressionism, was original to
England, taking an entirely different direction from either continental
or American avant-garde theatre, as much in its mixture of the styles
of cabaret sketch and charade with elements of Greek drama, as in its
philosophical content, its peculiarly Audenesque message, part Marx,
part Groddeck and Freud, on the sickness of civilization. The plays
have been criticized for the often slap-dash schoolboy impertinence of
the satire and a lack of subtlety in the drawing of the characters; but
these objections seem to me irrelevant to what they were trying to do
in a genre which deliberately aimed at preserving the speed and light-
ness of cabaret "attack." Christopher has told us that he had to keep a
sharp eye on Auden to prevent the characters flopping down on their
knees on the slightest pretext. . . . One would like to know more
about the way the collaboration worked. Who invented Destructive
Desmond, epitome of a philistine-fascist mentality not confined to totalitarian states? Who named Frustrax Abominum, that sinister
Freudian plant that had evidently strayed from Mortmere to the slopes
of F6?

By the time Stephen's *Trial of a Judge* was put on, the fame of the
Group Theatre had spread far beyond the original circle of enthusiasts.
Even cabinet ministers, it was reported, had been observed in the audience, had looked shaken as they went back to their desks and the
Munich agreement. Whatever statesmen might think, the drawing of
imaginary statesmen in these plays was scornfully judged in some
quarters. Soon after *On the Frontier* was put on, I encountered Guy
Burgess one evening in the Athenaeum, and with characteristic bois-
terousness he exclaimed: "The trouble about Wystan, Christopher
and Stephen is that they haven't got the foggiest notion what politicians are really like!" They certainly hadn't got a clue to what Guy
was really like.

Christopher had always been interested in the theatre, and it was inevitable that his close association with Auden should lead to the theatre. But, as he has described in *Lions and Shadows*, his interest in films had started even earlier, with a childhood passion for Westerns, and it was no surprising revolution that led him, just before the outbreak of war, to California and the studios of M.G.M. To that new life Berthold Viertel, the Viennese poet and producer, had obtained him entry. A close alliance, founded on a common love of theatre and cinema, had grown up between Berthold, Christopher and my sister Beatrix. Berthold had made a distinguished name for himself in Central Europe with his theatrical productions, and had come over to England as a film director: his best-known (though perhaps not best) production was *Rhodes of Africa*, with Oscar Homolka as Kruger. Physically he was small and stockily built, a small shaggy bear of a man, of enormous energy, much persuasive charm and finely perceptive intellect, capable of talking with brilliant wit and imagination for hours as he paced up and down his working-room in his dressing-gown, in and out of the huge piles of half-read books that always littered the floor; equally capable of changing his mood with the speed of lightning and growling with rage at some slight he detected, or imagined he detected, in the way he himself or one of his friends had been treated by the obtuser film-bosses with whom he had to work. A man of quite unusual, unshakeable integrity and loyalty; but not, I fancy, the easiest person, with his inflammable temperament, to be associated with professionally.

Christopher was an enthusiastic fan of Beatrix's art and a devoted admirer of Berthold, who believed in the genius of them both. When they were together, they were the most amusing and stimulating company imaginable: they struck sparks off one another and encouraged one another to the most grotesque imitations of famous actors and actresses and the most hilarious fantasies in film and play projects. But their ideas were, at bottom, serious enough: if Christopher and Berthold had stayed in Europe, if the war had not come, I believe that the alliance might have made theatrical — or film — history.

Beatrix was at a peak of her acting career at that time and had just scored her greatest triumph of all as Electra in Eugene O'Neill's *Mourning Becomes Electra*. No one who saw her performance will, I believe, ever be able to forget it. It had such an overwhelming effect on my mother when I took her to see it, that she fainted in the middle and had to be carried out of the theatre. I was away for the first night, but Berthold wrote me a long appreciation of it, as interesting as a revelation of his profound understanding of dramatic art as of Beatrix's performance. He had seen Beatrix for the first time as Hilda Wangel in *The Master Builder* four years before, and ever since had been convinced that London had in her "without being fully aware of it" (as he put it) "an actress of the highest degree. The soundness, the definition and purpose in every word and gesture were as extraordinary as the spiritualization, the transformation which happened at the end of the play." He had seen the Broadway production of *Mourning Becomes Electra*, and had thought it failed to make the supreme last change of character which gives the play its meaning. What he called the "uncontrolled exhibitionism" of the usual kind of star performance could never pass that test:

How Beatrix spans the inner space for the later development of the character, how she spans an enormous arch in order to reach the sphere of humanity in her ultimate renunciation (this last scene belonging to the few most beautiful scenes in art I ever saw); the inexorableness of her characterization, how she is not afraid to be antipathetic and even repulsive in order to complete her task: all that is admirable and of course is being admired. But I admire even more what she omits, what she skips, understatement as a dramatic means. It is a new kind of acting altogether in which every small gesture is of the greatest importance and where one has to follow the thought, the thinking process becoming transparent. In a play like this one, in which neurotic complexes, not individuals, are the heroes, only this kind of acting can do any good, so she makes the play. And London, taken by surprise, makes the partly bewildered, partly enthusiastic audience.

Beatrix was to make almost as powerful an impression later in *Desire under the Elms*, and to confound the managers and producers — without, alas, their ever properly grasping it — who believed that she could only play the macabre and the sinister-tragic. That winter, however, Christopher, driven by the demon of restlessness that had been at his back ever since Hitler's triumph in Germany, left for China with Wystan, with the idea of writing a book about the Japanese invasion; and the many schemes that he had hatched with Beatrix and Berthold had to be postponed — as it turned out, fatally postponed — once more.

It was a strange irony that led two more of my friends to China, about which they knew nothing, so soon after Julian, who knew so much more and might have played so effective a part in the war that had broken out, had left it to die in Spain, about which he knew so little. On February 24 Christopher wrote to me from Hongkong, describing their plans for making their way by slow river-boat to Canton, which the Japanese were bombarding every afternoon at that time (though apparently doing their best to stick to military objectives, especially the railway):

We plan to stay in Canton two or three days. Then we meet a rather sinister Colonel Lawrence sort of man, who drives a lorry backwards and forwards between Canton and Hankow for a cigarette firm. The road is rather problematical, floods, broken bridges etc., and the journey may take as much as ten days. Once at Hankow, we'll be in the middle of things. Most of the government is there, and we can get the necessary passes and introductions for a visit to one or other of the fronts. Also, we hope to see the new British Ambassador, whom we met for a few minutes while he was passing through here. He is a very live wire, and ready to be helpful. Also, he reads Auden and enjoyed Sally Bowles. . . . Hongkong is the ugliest town in the loveliest harbour I have ever seen. A cross between Manchester and Buxton. The view from the peak of the island is a real Chinese painting, with junks and little rock-garden crags embedded in a green plate-glass sea. Yesterday evening, we dined with the Governor, and Sir Victor Sassoon showed us a coloured film he had taken himself of the Governor's arrival in Hongkong. Wystan, who is having a Proust fit, enjoyed himself hugely. I was slightly more acid, as I am suffering from a mild local variety of dysentery known as "Hongkong Dog." Most of the big nobs here are inclined to be pro-Chinese; and you can talk about the Communist troops in even the most polite society without a shudder. So much for the ideology of Business when its interests are really threatened!

The British Ambassador who enjoyed *Sally Bowles* was Sir Archibald Clark-Kerr (afterwards Lord Inverchapel), whom I was to get to know very well some years later during the war, while he was occupying the key post of Ambassador at Moscow. He was a staunch supporter of *New Writing* and all the young authors associated with it, but when I met him in London under bombardment he was very much disappointed that the two whose company he had enjoyed so much in China, and for whom he had done so much, had opted for America. It was on their return journey from China that Christopher and Wystan travelled west-east through America, and took the decision, so totally unexpected by their friends (and to me so sad and discouraging at a time when I had hoped for their close collaboration), that the United States was the country of the future and the country for them.

« 12 »

ONE of the great hopes I had entertained when *New Writing* was transferred from John Lane to Lawrence & Wishart was that my new sponsors would be willing to publish a New Writing Library of novels, autobiographies and books of poems by the authors I had come across in my explorations for the magazine. So many opportunities had already come my way in the first eighteen months, so many books or projects for books had been there for the taking if I had been a publisher as well as an editor, that it was becoming unbearable to me to be unable to do anything about them. Some of them, I feared, might never find a publisher to believe in them as I did; and I also saw the issuing of books as a completion of the work the magazine had started.

I managed to persuade Lawrence & Wishart to be interested in the idea; Edward Upward's *Journey to the Border*, Christopher's *North-West Passage* (which eventually came out as *Lions and Shadows*) and books by James Stern, Willy Goldman, John Sommerfield, B. L. Coombes, André Chamson, Jean Giono and Jean-Paul Sartre were among those I had first in mind. Prospects looked so rosy at one moment in 1937 that I actually got to the point of writing to several of the authors that the project was on. Hardly had I done so when Lawrence & Wishart began to change their minds and even lost interest in *New Writing* itself, the contract for which was coming to an end. It was a bitter set-back at the time, though I realize now that a publishing house with the political ties that bound Lawrence & Wishart could never have carried the project through, or have continued to give me a free hand indefinitely.

Once more I had to take my child by the hand, and find a new home for us both. When they got wind of it, several intelligent publishers showed the liveliest interest; and I was actually on the point of signing an agreement with one of them — I am still grateful to Michael Joseph for the appreciation and enterprise he showed at that difficult moment — when an extraordinary thing happened. I almost believe that it was some sixth sense that led me to call on Leonard and Virginia, whom I had not seen for some years. Any ill-feelings that were generated by my abrupt departure five years earlier had blown away, and I found them not only full of friendliness but also very much interested in the fate of *New Writing*. It was not long before they showed their hand: they were both tired of the drudgery of the Hogarth Press and wanted to sell it; and in spite of all that had happened, they still felt that I was the person they would most like to take it over. They offered me, in fact, not only a home for *New Writing* but also a resumption of my publishing career in which I should at last be able (or so it appeared) to fulfil my dream of a New Writing Library.

The first scheme was that, after a two-year "trial" period, I should buy them both out. When I looked into the financial side of it, however, I realized that it was going to be rather difficult to find the money without embarrassing obligations; and in the end it was decided that I should buy only half of the Press — Virginia's half — and become after two years Leonard's full and equal partner as well as general manager. This seemed to me at the time almost incredible good luck; and I was particularly happy that I should again be working with Virginia. The agreement came into force in April 1938, and on the 22nd Virginia wrote to me:

I am ashamed not to have answered your very nice kind and by all means welcome letter before. Nor can I write suitably now, because I am being badgered . . . to write an obituary of Ottoline. I'm full of sanguinity about the future; and thankful to lift the burden on to your back. Nor can I see myself any reason why we should quarrel; or why we should drink the Toast in cold water. What about a good dinner (not English) at Boulestin or some such place? You are hereby invited to be the guest of Virginia Woolf's ghost — the Hogarth ghost: who rises let us hope elsewhere.

Let's arrange it. We come back on Sunday: and then there'll be the usual uproar.

Much warmth of feeling in the bitter evening (sitting over the fire) from us both. And Lord! When I die don't ask anyone to write a few words about me in *The Times*.

Yours ever
V. W.

This decision, of course, as I could see, involved the gradual liquidation of my life abroad; but the sorrow had already been, for only six weeks earlier Hitler had marched into Austria, and I knew that I could no longer continue to live my happy life in the flat in the Invalidenstrasse.

« 13 »

SATURDAY morning, March 12, 1938. The early express from Prague to Vienna slowly drew out of the shadows of the terminus, and I sat back in my compartment, trying to order my chaotic thoughts and emotions.

A few days before, I had left Vienna to spend a fortnight in Czechoslovakia and find out what the Czechs were thinking and doing about the sudden turn for the worse that the Austrian situation had taken since Schuschnigg's journey to Berchtesgaden. But I had hardly been there long enough to establish contact with my harassed and excited friends, when the news came through that Schuschnigg had made his move, a lightning last moment move: there was to be a plebiscite at once, on Sunday. I decided that, after all the years I had lived in Vienna and so passionately followed the underground struggle, the tightrope walk for independence, I could not miss the supreme trial of strength that the plebiscite was likely to be. I quickly cancelled the arrangements I had already made in Prague, and settled to return on Saturday afternoon. As a farewell fling, a group of Czech artists and poets asked me to come out with them on the Friday evening.

Our party must have started a little before seven. We were in high spirits, argued a lot, laughed a lot, drank a lot, wandered about the old town to explore out-of-the-way "dives" where there was reputed to be good music or good wine. We bought no papers and listened to no wireless. About midnight we were still discussing what chances Austria had of remaining independent, when a boy came into the bar with the first editions of the morning papers. There was an immediate commotion, and the music broke off. I grabbed a copy as the boy passed me, and read: Schuschnigg had thrown in his hand, and Germany's armed forces were already over the frontier. . . . The whole of a pattern of life collapsed. . . .

I do not think there were many passengers on that train actually destined for Vienna. Only a few foreigners on business or completing already planned tours and one or two Austrians who for some vitally urgent reason wanted to go *in* after the night's events. In my compartment there was an Egyptian who kept on praising the British Empire to me, a strange Englishwoman looking rather bewildered and desperate and not at all sure what she was meant to be doing entering German Austria that day, and a Czech business man hurrying down to get his daughter out of a Viennese school. The conversation consisted of each one of us in turn suddenly breaking out of a spell of anxious brooding and asking the others whether they thought we were going to be allowed in. The Englishwoman did not catch on at first; but when she realized that there was a real danger of our being turned back, she was thrown into a state of violently alternating indignation and panic. But all the time I was thinking of the Vienna I had left behind me a week before, the mood of hope that had suddenly swept the country at the last moment when Schuschnigg seemed to be coming out of his state of paralysed apathy. I had been told by intellectuals in his circle that for days after Berchtesgaden he had been practically unapproachable, sitting with his head in his hands, refusing or incapable of action. And a picture came back to my mind of a year or so before: I had taken Violet Hammersley to visit the exquisite little Lustschloss in the Prater, when suddenly out of the trees Schuschnigg had appeared on horseback, with his equerry mounted beside him. He looked, I had thought then, the perfect type of civilized upper-class Austrian, dignified, intelligent, gentle, and not in the least like that Prince of Stendhal's Parma, whom in his actions he so closely resembled, master of tortuous intrigue and repressive cruelty. . . . I also thought of a brief discussion I had had not long before with an intelligent official in the Austrian Foreign Office, who, while admitting to me that things were very critical and that Schuschnigg's Berchtesgaden interview "had not been at all a nice one," still put his faith in Mussolini and discounted the evidence from Italy that he was quite wrong as the work of a brash young "set" who would soon be called to order. . . . As the train rattled through Moravia, I wondered what had happened to that Foreign Office official. And I wondered whether Frau Chval, Toni and his friends had been swept up into the flood . . . whether my Jewish friends were still in their homes.

The frontier came at last. It looked extraordinarily quiet. When the passport official entered our compartment, the Czech business man hurried to ask him if we were going to be allowed in. "Everything is just as before," he replied with tight lips, putting his stamp into the purple inkpad, "only a slight change in the regulation about those who want to *leave* the country. . . ."

The Austrian countryside looked as peaceful and deserted as any day. Could there be some mistake? Had the Czech papers blundered? There were flags hanging here and there from farmhouses, but there were more Austrian red-and-white flags than swastikas, and nobody seemed in a hurry to pull them down. Perhaps there had been some intervention from London or Paris at the last moment that had compelled the German troops to halt?

It was at the Vienna terminus that we encountered the first real evidence of what had happened. As we got out of the train, we had to pass through two lines of young Nazis with swastika armlets and rifles, and police behind them. The newly revealed Nazis looked slightly comic with their callow excited faces, in yesterday's knickerbockers with steel helmets on their heads; but they watched our progress as if we had pockets bursting with bombs.

Out in the streets there was still little or nothing to see. But only an hour or two later the transformation began that was to wipe out the Vienna I had known as if with one sweep of a sponge. Soon after I got back to my flat, to my relief Frau Chval and Toni appeared, unharmed, dismayed but obviously infected by the excitement, and we watched from my window the arrival of the German bombers, roaring in from the north-west in ever-increasing numbers and circling low and repeatedly over all districts of the city. They were greeted with frenzied delight by the Nazi supporters who began to appear on the streets in jostling crowds; but it was easy to imagine that in many factories and apartment houses of the populous districts they provoked a different thought, precisely the thought they were there to provoke — that even the slightest resistance was useless. Later, Toni told me that when the workers had arrived in their factories that morning, they found that armed guards were already installed, and their leaders of the previous day, the day of false dawn for democratic hopes, had vanished. The confusion of the night before in proletarian Vienna must have been fantastic. As I walked through the streets in the afternoon a young garage-hand I knew ran up to me and told me one of the strangest stories of all. On Thursday evening the *Internationale* was being openly sung in hundreds of workers' meetings, and the old greeting of *Freiheit* was heard even on the Kaerntnerstrasse. Social-Democrat stalwarts who had lain low for years, he told me, suddenly began to draw people around them at the street corners and to harangue crowded tables in the beer and wine shops. Late on Friday afternoon he had gone with his friends to an appointed meeting-place where all the workers were to collect and demonstrate for the promised plebiscite and the independence of Austria. Just as Schuschnigg was making his broken farewell speech over the wireless, they formed up into a procession and set off for the main streets: they knew nothing of the speech. As they turned a corner they saw a mass of police facing them at the top of the road. The previous day such demonstrations had received police protection, and they imagined that they were there to clear a way for them. But before they could advance any further, the policemen were making a savage charge at their ranks, and only too late my friend saw the swastika armlets they were carrying — already, though Schuschniggs' speech had only gone over the air a few minutes earlier.

The bombers thickened like a plague of locusts all Saturday, and all Sunday and Monday their droning roar continued. The noise acted as a form of third degree peculiarly crushing to the impressionable and pacifist-minded Viennese. And soon another noise was added to it, the rumble of the Reichswehr lorries, the gun-carriages, the field-kitchens, the tanks that began to roll through all the main streets, advance guard of the weary-faced infantry and cavalry who grinned sheepishly or stared slightly bewildered at the cheering Nazi crowds. All Sunday this movement went on, and with the troops came busload after busload of German *Schupos* and German Frontier Police and German gendarmes and German S.S. By Sunday night all the biggest hotels had been cleared of their normal guests and were filled with German officers and their staffs. All except the Imperial, for which a higher honour was reserved, that of receiving Adolf Hitler himself. It was almost impossible to find a place in the restaurants of the Inner Town. I went to my favourite restaurant, and found it crowded out with German uniforms, the waiters, with an absolutely blank look on their faces, rushing to and fro and gasping *"Heil Hitler!"* whenever a word was spoken to them. In the residential districts housemaids and shop-girls were already swooning on the arms of their blond deliverers from the north, but I saw no scenes of demonstrative fraternization or enthusiasm outside the centre of the town; and plenty of Viennese were already beginning to feel a little uncomfortable about the nature of the liberation that had taken place. Walking down the Ring, one saw every evidence that the Germans considered themselves the masters of a conquered country. The Reichswehr flag waved over the sentry-guarded Grand Hotel, where the German General Staff was quartered, and still troops were thundering by in their camouflaged lorries and vans. Placed there suddenly without any knowledge of what had actually happened, one could only have imagined that war was already raging, with the front only a few score miles away. And if one did know, a single thought was in one's mind all the time: when will it begin? All during those days I walked and drove about Vienna half in a daze of confusion and misery, half-determined to see as much as I could as long as I could; wondering how long I had to get out, whether a bigger international explosion would follow, what would happen to my friends and my home, whether I should ever see them again.

Among the non-political masses, so deep had been the misery

through which they had gone for years, unemployment and shooting and repression, that the general feeling at the beginning, it seemed to me, in the dazed moment of the change-over, was that things couldn't be worse than they had been, that they must give the Nazis a chance and "see if Hitler gives us work." During the holidays that were celebrated directly after the Anschluss was formally proclaimed, the streets presented a weird caricature of what I had seen in the streets of Moscow on May Day. Students and workers were being whirled round in lorries, waving flags and cheering, while contingents of workers, ordered out from the factories, marched round carrying huge placards: WIR DANKEN DEM FUEHRER, and EIN VOLK — EIN REICH — EIN FUEHRER. At night there were torchlight processions: what struck me was that they were almost entirely composed of boys and girls under twenty, and a large proportion of them seemed scarcely older than sixteen. The culmination of the celebration was the long-delayed arrival in Vienna of Hitler himself. Young Nazis explained, when one asked why he was so slow in coming, that he wanted to see the joy of all the villages en route, that the crowds would not let him through, and so on; only afterwards did the truth trickle through, that the great German Army had broken down. Tanks and motorized columns were stranded all over the roads from the frontier to Vienna, and Hitler was in a rage with his generals. But at last he came, at last he made his triumphal entry into the Hotel Imperial, from which everyone had been bundled out at a moment's notice and without ceremony.

That evening I managed to get through to the Schwarzenbergplatz, and from there, as twilight fell, worm my way slowly through the congealing crowds to a place where I could see the front of the Imperial. There was a steady hum of loud and excited conversation, but above this every few minutes or seconds the frenzied Nazi chants would break out: "SIEG HEIL! SIEG HEIL! SIEG HEIL!" and in between "HITLER! — HITLER! — HITLER!" All eyes were turned towards the first-floor balcony, behind which the rooms were brilliantly lit. After some time, the brown-uniformed figure that I had never actually set eyes on before, but whose myth-magnified demon image had haunted me with intimations of violence and evil ever since I had seen the candles burning before it in frozen Berlin five years earlier, Adolf Hitler emerged; and immediately a battery of arc-lamps, mounted on a moving trolley in the road, was turned upon him. He came to the front of the balcony and raised his hand in Nazi salute. Then, very slowly, with the perfect instinct of an actor, he marched towards one end of the balcony and raised his arm again. His face was sombre and appeared, in the glare of the lights, to be tense with emotion. Then he marched to the other end of the balcony, and saluted again there. All the time the chanting and yelling went on, and the crowd swayed and struggled. At last he went in again, and after some more cheering, people began slowly to disperse.

That week in Vienna completed, I think, a decisive change in my thinking about the way the political movements of our time worked: the final turn came with a sudden imaginative illumination. For I became overwhelmingly aware of the strength of the non-rational impulse in National-Socialism. I had for a time had growing doubts about the adequacy of the rational left-wing interpretation of the fascist phenomenon as the popular mask worn by finance-capitalism to organize the peoples of Western Europe for war against the Soviet Union, with behind it the cool, calculating head of the cynical profit-grabber. What I had seen in the streets, what I had heard in the tales of extraordinary incidents passed from mouth to mouth, made it clear to me that the head was not so cool after all, the cynicism — if that was still the right word — not so calculated. Rational people were looking for rational villainy: but what I had witnessed, sensed, was much more like the outburst of some tremendous force from irrational depths. These were people who could not be fitted into any conventional diplomatic calculation of a balance of power and the satisfaction of "just aspirations": they were possessed, and much more frightening for that reason than for all the guns and tanks by themselves. I suddenly realized that not only the callow youths, but probably also the leaders themselves, the Himmlers and Streichers and their underlings, *believed* the fantastic nonsense they preached. That the Jews were not merely scapegoats in their eyes, to be sacrificed to the discontent of the masses, but really and truly authors of all evil and frustration that had befallen the noble Aryans. . . .

Now in Austria the Terror was on. With the Jews, all the enemies of National-Socialism, the Communists, the Monarchists, the politically active Catholics, were caught like rats in a trap: the impossible mirage of the plebiscite had held them from making their get-away in time. There were undoubtedly Austrians among the pace-makers, but I know that some of the young Viennese who had joined the S.A. or S.S. were so revolted by what they saw that they would have backed out if they had dared. The scenes of agonized farewell at the Vienna stations were followed by ghastlier scenes of arrest, indignity and plunder at the frontiers. Night after night in all districts the visitations went on. Hundreds, thousands were hauled off to prison, and were not heard of for weeks, some never again alive. Jewish shops were rifled, windows smashed, cars simply stolen from their owners and taken off for a drunken party with the proceeds of the raid. An eye-witness told me that in his district some boys dragged an old Jew out on to the streets, and, urging him on with plentiful kicks, forced him to wash out slogans painted on the cobbles. A crowd gathered, some in an hysteria of senseless hate, but others quite evidently revolted. The old man was trembling, and finally fainted and had to be dragged away. One Jew ran into a café near the Central Telegraph office, screaming "*Heil Hitler!*" and brandishing a knife with which he slashed at several people before cutting his own throat. Hundreds of others among Vienna's enormous Jewish population in those first days made a less spectacular end to a life grown intolerable and meaningless. Many foreigners who were present commented with bewilderment on the change that seemed to have come over the Austrians, whom they had always known as a peaceable and civilized people; but to be in a smart café — swept of its former Jewish guests — and see the fanaticism with which people jumped to their feet and sang when *Deutschland Über Alles* blared from the loudspeaker, was to catch a glimpse of what it had meant to be the impoverished citizen of a small, defeated and defenceless country for so long. The rumours and chatter that one heard in the shops and on the trams were fantastic. The return of South Tirol was being openly celebrated at one moment. I overheard one man explaining to another, after a jubilant description of how two Jewish stands in the big Market Hall had been sacked, that Slovenia would be the next addition to Greater Germany ("They're all Germans there!"), and that the Yugoslavs anyway had got hold of the country only because the priests had supplied them with rifles to shoot from the church towers. There was no limit to credulity or hate in those days, even though, before a week was out, many were frightened, bewildered in the midst of the excitement. "It can't last" — "This is the beginning of a war" — "It's all over with us Austrians now, and for good" — these remarks were to be heard, and not from Jews, nor Marxists, nor Monarchists, but ordinary business and working people. And Vienna's large Czech population kept their dark thoughts to themselves.

Fires were roaring all over Vienna the morning of the Anschluss and the smoke from innumerable compromising letters, reports and records was pouring out of the chimneys of politicians, journalists and secret agents. Soon after I reached Vienna five years before, I had made friends with G.E.R. Gedye, the brilliant journalist who had worked for the *Daily Telegraph* (and later for the *Daily Herald*) and the *New York Times*, and who eventually described the events of that week so graphically in *Fallen Bastions*. His personal sympathies had been strongly with the Social-Democrats, and in his dispatches after the February Rising he had made little effort to conceal either his contempt for the clerical-fascist régime or his hatred of the Nazis. Gedye's truculent wit and sanguine temperament were a tonic in the darkest days of foreboding and dismay. He took to a fight with the zest of a street-urchin, and had a terrier's nose for any dirty secret smooth politicians were trying to conceal. He was probably the best informed of all the members of the Anglo-American Press Association in Vienna about the underground activities of the Social-Democrat partisans. Dollfuss and Schuschnigg had handled foreign journalists with considerable caution, and left him alone, though they knew perfectly well where his sympathies lay. He had no reason to expect such respect from the Nazis, and that morning his stove was roaring more furiously than any other in Vienna: his face emerged from dense smoke as he cautiously opened a few inches of door in response to my ring at his bell. He was able to get his Jewish secretary, as attractive as she was efficient, out of Austria when he left for Czechoslovakia, only to meet another Nazi invasion there; but by that time she had married my own secretary, John Lepper, and had an English passport.

I think that every Englishman or American living in Vienna had at least one Jewish friend towards whom he felt he had a special responsibility, and for whom he tried to obtain an exit visa and a permit to enter his own country. It was an anxious business, a race against time as the process of despoiling and making outlaws or prisoners of the Jews went forward with relentless thoroughness. Yura was already beyond the reach of any help I could give him (or seemed to be at that time), and my own special care became Frau Schweiger, a plump, animated, amusing, violently Anglophile widow of considerable literary and musical accomplishments, to whose salon I had been introduced some years before, and who had given me inestimable help in getting to know the artistic life of Vienna. I kept in touch with her during those first few days of Nazi rule: she was putting up a very brave show, even forcing herself to believe (incredibly, like so many of her fellow Jews in Austria) that Austrian National-Socialism would be more tolerant and humane than the German version. These illusions did not last very long, and I remember that what eventually

broke her nerve was a series of anonymous telephone calls she began
to receive: day after day an unknown voice would threaten her, gloating over what it promised would be her end, and mixing the foulest
obscenities with the threats. Her beaming, kindly face had always reminded me of a large, red flower, perhaps a double begonia, full-blown
to the sun, and supported on a stalk too short for it. To see that face
now so transformed by apprehension and pain was tragic indeed. These
telephone calls, which were being received by Jews all over Vienna,
were of unspeakable cruelty: I do not believe they were systematic,
but the work of local Nazis, raw youths or disappointed wretches of
the shop-keeper class who were working off the long-accumulated
envy of their mean souls. Eventually we did manage to obtain the
necessary papers for Clothilde Schweiger and her daughter Hertha,
and after staying with us at Fieldhead for some months, in a state of
euphoria induced by all things English, she sailed for America a little
time before the war.

About ten days after the Anschluss, I left Vienna for Yugoslavia
with a friend. I had written as detailed notes as possible of everything
I had seen and heard, and collected eye-witness accounts of friends and
acquaintances. I planned to work all this up into one or two articles for
the English Press, but obviously could not send it all out from Vienna
itself: censorship of letters had been spasmodic and erratic under the
former régime, but under the Nazis it was rigorous. I therefore concealed my notes within the uncut folds of a large French novel, having
cut the first fifty pages or so. When we reached the frontier, I planned
to be reading the cut pages of the novel, and to hope for the best. At
the last station before the border a horde of young S.A. men and frontier police sent down from Germany invaded the train, and proceeded
to conduct an even more meticulous examination of everything and
everybody than I had expected. A Yugoslav couple, with a suspi-
ciously Jewish name, had all their suitcases emptied on to the floor of
the carriage, the linings ripped up and the coats they contained cut
open as well: the Nazis were ostensibly looking for jewels and valu-
ables being smuggled out, but I had the feeling they did it from wanton spite. While this was going on, one of the green-uniformed frontier police came in, looked at our passports, and then — to my horror
— took the books and magazines that my fellow-passengers were
reading, and shook them to see if they contained thousand-schilling or
other currency notes . . . the French novel was likewise seized and
shaken. Nothing, miraculously, fell out. . . . "What was the matter
with you?" said my friend, who had been standing in the corridor, as

the train steamed into sunny and carefree Yugoslavia; "I thought you were going to be sick, you looked so green in the face." I assured him that I was completely restored, bursting with health in fact, and invited him to explore the French novel himself.

« 14 »

LITERARY critics are sometimes accused of being disappointed authors, wreaking their spite on more creative poets and novelists for the poems and novels they themselves have failed to write. But why should they not once have written themselves? The spite is sometimes all too evident, the acid of disappointment running corrosively through everything a critic writes about his contemporaries; but these are rare cases, and in general I have always thought it a good thing that critics should also be creators, in however small a way. A reviewer who has written novels himself is likely to understand from the inside the problems a novelist faces, and write of his struggles with his material with imaginative sympathy: a sympathy that will save him from that far greater bane of academic classification mania, in which a critic treats authors as an entomologist treats dead butterflies.

An editor, too, may hide a frustrated author in his soul; and in his case I do not see why the secret influences should not act altogether beneficially. Nearly all my life I have harboured a straws-in-the-hair babbler in a corner of my brain, distracting me on walks and at concerts and keeping me awake at night with his impossible imaginings and inordinate ambitions for epics, song-cycles, sonnet-sequences, poetic dramas and novel series of modern life as long as the *Comédie Humaine*. Every new country I have visited, every new experience I have been involved in, every discovery I have made in human relationships, not to mention plays and films of genius I have seen, has set this babbler to his importunate demands on me. I could not carry out more than the tiniest fraction of his dizzy schemes: but he has made me look for their achievement in others, and know an excited satisfaction when I have come across authors whom I saw at once to be engaged on realizing in their art the new arrangement of life, the new music I had dreamt of myself, but knew to be beyond my powers.

It was this, I think, above all that made me find such pleasure in my work of editing *New Writing*. I enjoyed the arranging of every volume, grouping and contrasting contributions so that what was significant in them might be more effectively brought out and the reader's attention continually stimulated; and trying, by the mixture of different kinds of poetry and prose in a certain order to give the volume as a whole a vitality that might carry the weaker pieces along with it and add another dimension to the stronger. This of course was only an ideal, never to be realized entirely to my satisfaction; but as time went on I learnt not to try to impose an intention too rigidly or hastily, but to let the material that came to hand suggest its modification; and I learnt, too, to accept the disappointments, when promised contributions that I had thought essential failed to turn up, as a challenge to make my bricks with other straws, to create other combinations. And at the back of my mind was always the belief that the way I presented the contributions might not only stimulate readers but also the authors themselves. Nor could I have done any of this effectively if I had not endlessly enjoyed corresponding and talking with authors and making them think aloud for me about their projected work.

Nevertheless, during these years of building up *New Writing*, while part of my energies were absorbed in political journalism and in preparing my travel books *Prometheus and the Bolsheviks* and *Down River*, I was determined to keep my hand in as an imaginative writer, in however small a way. I wrote my (one and only) novel, *Evil Was Abroad*, and from time to time went on with my experiments in prose-poems. Poetry itself took a back place, but I did not altogether abandon it. The problem of writing poems that should express the overwhelming interest that I had acquired in the political struggle seemed to me more and more difficult as time went on. I could see plenty of examples around me, especially among the manuscripts that came in to *New Writing*, of how *not* to write it; I realized that some of the things I wanted to do were being done by *New Writing* poets with a skill that made me unwilling to compete; and I could also see that certain solutions which the more ingenious of my contemporaries had discovered, could never be my solutions. There was a kind of silent refusal to co-operate of some power in the inmost poetic chamber of my imagination; and as nearly all the pieces I began showed only too clearly the absence of this secret influence before I had gone very far, I tore them up. In fact, it was not until several years later, in the middle of the war, when I had abandoned the belief that topical passions and apocalyptic enthusiasms could ever be the stuff of *my* poetry, that the mysterious agency began to co-operate freely again.

In spite of this, some themes that haunted me continually entered deeply enough into my mind for me to feel that the poetry that arose from them had some authenticity, and made an original, if small, contribution to the poetic expression of the time. Chief of them, most persistent, was the feeling that war was approaching more certainly with every month that passed, while something in human nature refused to accept or be disturbed by the foreboding. Yet all the signs were gradually piling up in the years between Dollfuss and Hitler; they were too obvious to be missed by anyone who *wanted* to look as he walked about the streets and parks of Vienna in all their spring loveliness, bringing nearer step by step what still seemed incredible in its monstrosity, in contrast to the roaming couples and the chestnut blossoms and the carefree contentment of life with life that showed itself everywhere.

I was also continually coming back in my mind, and trying to make sense of the indifference of *nature;* of the smallness of the tremendous happenings, that hang the tattered banners in our chapels, in the scheme of the universe. This feeling came to me very strongly one day when I made an expedition in my car with some friends to those foothills of the Alps between the Semmering Pass and Vienna, with my thoughts continually returning to some phase of the international crisis that had filled the papers the day before:

These night-green masses in their scented air,
The frail snow-roses, clustering as they climb
  The cold slope's bouldered stair,

All this expanse of noiseless growth, and rock,
Would hardly stir or change, though just beyond
  World reeled in war's first shock;

Only perhaps the bombing planes would cross
Startling the eagles as they roared for towns,
  Vanish, like bees from moss. . . .

I remember hearing, during the war, how, after a bomb explosion in one of the parks in London, the birds would gather round the crater, with a calm eye to the main chance, looking for worms exposed by the upheaval; and what an extraordinary lift of the heart this gave me. I find it difficult to believe that, even in the atomic wars of the future, nature would not soon reassert itself — even over the ruins of Moscow or New York.

« 15 »

WHEN Leonard and Virginia had first suggested to me that I should buy them both out of the Hogarth Press, I had been fired with the idea that I could make of it a publishing centre for all the *New Writing* authors, with Christopher, Wystan and Stephen as my fellow-directors and literary advisers; but when it became clear that to buy a 50 per cent partnership was as much as I could reasonably manage, the idea had, to my great regret, to lapse. It would probably have lapsed anyway, because I was beginning to realize that Christopher's restlessness was too deep-seated for me ever to be able to count on him being at hand in London for any long period. In fact, he had scarcely returned from China before he left for Europe again. Nevertheless, he and Stephen agreed to appear as my advisory fellow-editors on the title-page of the New Series of *New Writing* that the Hogarth Press now began to publish; this was as much a recognition of all the advice they had given and suggestions they had made in the past as an ideal blueprint for the future.

It did not work out very well, because, as I had foreseen, editorial discussions conducted at long range by post are bound to be unsatisfactory, even if one is prepared to take the risk of sending precious manuscripts to and fro across frontiers. Stephen was more easily available; he had been especially helpful over Spanish contributors and Spanish translations, and continued to help in this direction; but even he was liable to disappear at five minutes' notice on some mysterious and urgent journey abroad. As neither Christopher nor Stephen had any stake in the new set-up, I had no right to expect them, individualists both and following obdurate lines of destiny on their own palms, to feel any particular obligations beyond those of friendship and general identity of literary interests. There were times, however, during the early months of the new phase at the Hogarth Press, when I bitterly wished it could have been otherwise. Adjustment was not easy at first: when I originally joined Leonard and Virginia in 1931, I was too young, too grateful and too enthusiastic to wish to do anything but take the lead from them; but I returned with a reputation of my own made by the success of *New Writing*, and a much clearer (and more obstinately held) idea of the kind of writers I wanted to encourage. There were inevitable checks and clashes. Leonard and I sometimes seemed to be skirmishing in a wood of incomprehension in the shadows of which I perhaps appeared to him like a bearded anarchist with a smouldering, black, European bomb I was scheming to lay at the foundations of the Hogarth Press, and he to me like an implacable Abraham with knife raised over Isaac, the promising young writer of my choice; though Virginia's presence helped to cool our fevers and bring us back to the understanding that really underlay our differences. I wrote rather dismally to Christopher in Brussels about these starting troubles and the burden of work in Mecklenburgh Square — whither the Press now emigrated.

I do think you could lighten your work [Christopher wrote back], and incidentally rub several people up the right way, if you threw the weight of more decisions on the shoulders of the advisory board. After all, we have our uses, if only as an alibi. For instance, you could send Wystan more poetry. And you could send me more novels. . . . You know we are only too glad to co-operate, and I sometimes feel that you wouldn't feel yourself so isolated . . . if you appealed to the board more often. Stephen, I'm sure, would respond to this policy very warmly. What he really wants is to feel that he's being useful.

Touched as I was by this offer, I felt a certain irritation too; Christopher was dreaming and pretending to me about the possibilities of us all working together. Ever since the return from China, he had seemed withdrawn into obscure preoccupations, which he shared only with Wystan. What were they hatching together, out there in Brussels, with their vague hints of another trip to America so soon after the first? I answered rather tartly:

How, may I ask, are you to lighten my work of reading at the Press, if you use England rather as I use my Club? A few weeks a year you seem to be available, and then off on the great trek again. But would-be Hogarth authors know no close season, nor do their beaters, the agents. . . . Of course I'd like you and Wystan and all to read and advise more, and you mustn't imagine for a moment it's because I don't trust you. Stephen, for instance, can do really brilliant poetry reports. The simple fact is, not merely that you're rarely to be found, but that people must (and most certainly should) be rewarded for reading work, and the H.P. just can't afford a heavy overhead on this item.

Nevertheless, manuscripts did from time to time go across the Channel. Poems were sent over to Wystan, and came back with shrewd comments. "I sometimes think that Hopkins ought to be kept on a special shelf like a dirty book, and only allowed to readers who won't be ruined by him," he wrote about one young poet's work. "I believe I've found a really first-class novel. I long for you to read it," I wrote to Christopher in December 1938. "L. hasn't pronounced yet." This was the manuscript of Henry Green's *Party Going*, which Rosamond and Goronwy Rees had persuaded the author to show me: discouraged by the failure of that youthful work of genius, *Living*, to obtain more than a moderate *succès d'estime*, he had let it lie in a drawer for some years without attempting to send it round the publishers after the first refusals. The story of Christopher and *The Memorial* was repeating itself; and I had not been so excited by any book by an author of my generation since then. "I'm longing to hear what you have to say about Henry Green's MS.," I wrote to Christopher a few weeks later, "which I have just sent you. I — and many others — think it is an amazing bit of work." Christopher was favourable; and after some hesitations by Leonard and Virginia it was accepted by the Press and published in 1939.

The arrival of Henry Green as a Hogarth author was really the beginning of a new phase. Henry had not been a *New Writing* author, he had not been connected with us before, in spite of the fact that *Living* was the solution to many of the problems that had exercised us about "proletarian" writing. His arrival gave me confidence in the future, I felt that a new momentum was gathering, forcing me to turn my lingering gaze from the backward scene to the discoveries that were to come.

By the time it came out Christopher and Wystan had already left on the second trip to America, though I was still unaware that they were going in on the "quota" and not merely as tourists. Perhaps Christopher feared too many reproachful looks from me, and plangent letters about the betrayal of all we had plotted together. He had, in fact, as I came to know later, already left Europe in spirit long before, rejecting at last the categories of its conflicts and dimly discerning that California might reveal itself as the home he had looked for in vain since the break-up of his Berlin life and German circle of friends. As I read the letter he sent to me at the beginning of May, I felt that our troubles were already taking on a far-away, wrong-end-of-the-telescope look:

As soon as I'm in Hollywood, I plan to write a piece for you, about New York. I have quite a lot to say about it. Oh God, what a city! The nervous breakdown expressed in terms of architecture. The skyscrapers are all Father-fixations. The police-cars are fitted with air-raid sirens, specially designed to promote paranoia. The elevated railway is the circular madness. The height of the buildings produces visions similar to those experienced by Ransom in F6. Which reminds me that F6 is being done, quite grandly, some time in August. We have written a new ending, and, altogether, I hope it may be a real success.

In the same letter, he made a startling confession:

I myself am in the most Goddamawful mess. I have discovered, what I didn't realize before, or what I wasn't till now, that I am a pacifist. That's one reason why I am going out to Hollywood, to talk to Gerald Heard and Huxley. Maybe I'll flatly disagree with them, but I have to hear their case, stated as expertly as possible. . . . What are you feeling? What are your plans? You sound so very unperturbed, amidst all the screaming we hear from the distant European shores.

That letter, that confession, I saw quite clearly and sadly, wrote the epitaph to our friendship as we had known it, as I had imagined it continuing into the future, a friendship that had been the pivot of my life as a writer and editor-publisher for nearly seven years. I remembered that in the late summer of the year before we had spent some days together in the Isle of Wight, territory almost as sacred to him as to the Lehmanns. On the way down in the car he had described chapter after chapter of a sequence of fantastic Mortmere novels to me, novels that never had been set down on paper nor, for their Rabelaisian eccentricity, ever could be: it was not so much a description as an actual reading aloud from a text that seemed clear in his mind to the last detail. The performance was repeated during the next forty-eight hours as we walked over the heather downs towards Alum Bay or up the chalk to the Tennyson Monument, but this time it was a description of a trilogy of novels, sequels to *The Lost*, the general theme of which was the fate of all the odd characters thrown out of Germany by the arrival of the Nazis and living a rootless, restless life, for ever struggling with the passport and permit nightmare, from one European capital to another. He talked them aloud to me so vividly, that I could almost have taken them down for a finished copy on the spot: all the plots, all the incidents seemed completely worked out in his mind, and they struck me as far more entertaining, more dramatic and more moving than *Sally Bowles* and *The Landauers*. It was a continuous performance, broken only when one of us pointed out a pier or a tree-clump or a lodging-house famous in the annals of my childhood or his early days with Wystan on the island; but this trilogy was never actually written either, not one chapter or paragraph. Christopher was changing too fast; and so was the world. It was not long before Munich, and a feeling of doom and menace hung over the island. The old forts were reoccupied by young soldiers, and the guns were pointing seawards again. We knew in our hearts that it was all over, the dream that the world could be transformed before it went down into war, and all our private dreams with it.

BOOK TWO

I Am My Brother

To the End of the River

O N September 1, 1939, when the news came through that **Hitler** had opened his attack on Poland, I had the feeling that I **was** slipping down into a pit, clutching at grass on the ledges but failing to stay the accelerating descent into darkness. This feeling must have been shared by many others. It was more than the knowledge that we should obviously be at war ourselves within a few days: listening to the broadcasts of Hitler's speeches, it seemed to me that the frightening irrational note in his voice, the lunatic evil that I had become more and more acutely conscious of since the invasion of Austria, had drowned everything else. It had led me deeply to distrust both the school of thought that held that he could be handled on traditional foreign-policy lines, and the other, that everything the Nazis did could be explained on orthodox Marxist lines as part of a shrewdly ruthless plan for capitalist expansion. Now it afflicted me like nausea; and I am certain that I knew from that moment, in spite of the hopes of last-minute withdrawal we all talked about during the tense forty-eight hours between the two decisions, that war to the ruinous end, until either Hitler was destroyed or we ourselves were finished for ever, had become inevitable.

And yet the upper part of our minds clung to straws: I remember during that morning Stephen Spender came in to see me, and like prisoners tapping every corner of a cellar into which they have been flung in the hope of finding a loose stone, we went through every tiniest possibility of escape we could imagine in the situation. He was oppressed with the same weight of foreboding as I was, and though we made our usual jokes to one another, melancholy kept falling on us like a fog. That night — the first night of black-out — I struggled out in the slithery rainy darkness to dine up in Highgate with Beatrix, who had just returned from a holiday abroad and the adventure of getting across France in the middle of the confusion of mobilization. Her experience had made her feel, as I felt, that it was only a matter of days or hours; and yet we fell to arguing whether the Chamberlain Government might not still try to put across a gigantic sell-out to the Nazis.

When the actual declaration of war came on the 3rd, the immediate uppermost sensation was, curiously enough, relief. The whole point, after all, of the movement I and my friends had belonged to and believed in was that Hitler must be thwarted and stopped by every means possible. War we dreaded, but war was better than giving in to Hitler if it came to that. It had not been prevented; but at least England was going to show that her — perhaps too tardy — threats were no bluff, and the whole nation was in it at last. We were not alone; and yet, ironically enough, the country we had so lightly thought to be the great champion and leader of our cause was not one of our allies. Even in those early days, before the partition of Poland, the attempt of the comrades to prove that what had broken out was just one more imperialist war was an eye-opener for those who were not too irremediably blinded to read the signs.

All the same, the blow was grim enough. Everyone, except possibly those who scented in the war the chance to infuse meaning into lives that had hitherto been meaningless, had his own hardships and disappointments to bear. For those who were younger than I was, there was the prospect of an early call-up, the unassessable danger of the front line and a sponge wiped right over the immediate hopes of their careers. During those September days I saw many of them, and was struck by the quiet, undemonstrative way they were taking it, haunted by the slightly dazed look that would come over their faces. For me, there seemed to be an end to many things: a new life had come, and almost everything that mattered in the old life had to be tied up like letters in bundles, and locked away in a drawer for the duration — or for ever. Irrevocably, I was cut off from all my friends and all that I had loved so much in Austria: my flat in Vienna would probably be taken over by the Reichswehr, and young people I had talked and laughed and drunk with as intimate friends up to only a few weeks ago would soon be marching — or flying — against my English friends. My career as a publisher seemed to be broken again, for in those days it was difficult to see how ordinary book-publishing could survive the transformation of civilian life that had already begun and the onslaught we expected any moment, even if I was not drafted into war work or put into uniform at once. *New Writing*, too, seemed utterly doomed. I felt I had lost everything.

About eighteen months before, when it had become clear to me that my centre of activities must once more be London, I had taken a flat on the north side of Mecklenburgh Square, only a few doors away from the new abode of the Hogarth Press, which had just emigrated from Tavistock Square. I had two big rooms on the second floor. From the window of the back room, which I made into a bed-workroom, pasting up maps just as I had in my Vienna flat, I looked over Heathcote Street, where I had started my London life nine years before; from the front room the view was over the tall, shadily spreading, pom-pom-hung plane-trees of the Square garden; to the right, across the Foundling Estate playground, I could just glimpse Lansdowne Terrace, where Stephen Spender had taken a ground-floor flat.

I had scarcely had time to make my flat feel like home when the war had come; but the flat in the Invalidenstrasse, occupied since the year before by my Viennese secretary Toni and his wife Gretl, was already slipping away from me. I had made two visits, one at the end of March and a longer one in the summer — returning only a few weeks before war broke out. I remembered how I had stood at the window and seen in the railway station below the troop trains filled with Reichswehr soldiers travelling eastwards, a sight that began to drain out of my heart the hopes I still entertained that war could be avoided. It was some comfort to me that I had at least left the flat in the hands of friends, with my furniture and a few of my books and pictures around them. It seemed to me then to make the break that was surely coming a little less total; and now I could envisage the life that was going on there, in a kind of secret code that passed over the angry frontiers of war. There had been a last reunion that Toni had organized, a dinner-party for the circle of friends he had introduced me to. One of them, a young carpenter who had never interested himself in politics before, disgusted by what he had already seen of Hitler in action since the Anschluss, had joined the illegal Communist Party at the most dangerous hour to do so. It was heart-rending to hear him speak of the blow to the hopes of himself and his friends that the German occupation of Czechoslovakia had been, to hear him saying: "I listen in to Moscow every night, and still the Russians say nothing. How much longer is this going to go on, when will a halt be called? When will England move? We are powerless unless England and the rest move at last —

[229]

you can at least still try to organize opposition to this monster, you can still say what you think, write the truth, denounce the crimes and point out the dangers, but all we can do here is to wait in silence and secrecy, and have our hopes broken down by the waiting." But Marabu had not long to wait before Russia spoke — before the Nazi-Soviet pact cleared the road for the invasion of Poland and the war for which the troops were already rolling eastwards, only a few hundred yards away from the inn where we were drinking our wine.

In my work-bedroom at the back of the flat, where I put the finishing touches to the last volume — so I imagined — of *New Writing*, the maps on the wall reminded me of another part of my life that was gone for good: the explorations I had made so happily through all the countries of the old Austro-Hungarian Monarchy, down the course of the Danube to the sea.

On the last trip I had made, only a few months before, to collect the final details for my book *Down River*, I had realized the ambition that had for so long tantalized me: one afternoon I had found myself within sight of the Danube's ultimate lighthouse. From the deck of the steamer, as it slid along the straight, rush-bordered canal that forms the middle arm of the Delta, the little port of Sulina appeared like a mirage, the wharves and buildings balanced on air and quivering. This unreal vision was the first sign of a bewitched quality that had haunted me all through the country of the Danube mouths: I had found myself continually thinking of *The Tempest* and the "insubstantial pageant" of Prospero's island. I had crossed the marshes from Sulina to Valcov, home of the famous Russian religious sect of the Lipovani, in a little buggy cart driven by a grumpy, bearded Russian and drawn by two horses who were followed by a long-legged foal. . . . The road ran in a straight line over a dead level waste of rushes, weeds and water. I say road; but as we advanced the pools deepened and closed together, until there was nothing but water under our wheels. The horses dropped from their swift trot to an amble, and splashed their way on ever more slowly, their heads plunging up and down with the effort of the pull. The little foal dawdled and got left behind, until a long anxious whinny from the mare brought it level again, leaping friskily in fountains of water and whinnying in answer. The rushes seemed to grow taller, and shut out the earlier glimpses I had had of the sea. Sulina lighthouse sank out of sight, the world seemed to consist of rushes, water and the wild life that emerged from them. Water-hens zig-zagged in and out of the lilies and white-flowering weed at the edge of the road; wild duck, curlews, snipe and many other kinds of bird I could not distinguish rose to left and right and vanished into the sky; occasionally a crane flapped heavily across, and settled invisibly in the reedy jungle. Later on, we began to move out of the water and into a forest of oaks and silver birches: nothing could have been more unexpected in the middle of the Delta, at the edge of the sea. We were soon deep in its silent, sedgy-smelling undergrowth. Huge dragon-flies, red as pillar-boxes, darted round us, bloodthirsty insects clotted in iridescent masses on the wretched horses' flanks. Brilliant blue birds flew among the branches: one glittering azure feather floated down just beside the buggy, and an extravagant regret for not having stopped to pick it up oppressed me for the rest of the journey. Once we lost ourselves, and went round and round in what I gradually recognized with dismay to be huge, slow circles. Light was rapidly failing by the time we found the overgrown track again. As if they knew the worst was over, the horses broke into a trot and the foal, unwearied by so many hours' wandering, galloped gaily ahead. In a few minutes we were out of the forest, and then suddenly the enormous lake-like river was in front of us: the northernmost arm of the Danube, spreading down to a confusion of dark islands in the west. A huge Russian Charon, with blazing eyes and matted beard, emerged as if from nowhere, bundled our luggage into the ferry-boat, and we pushed off for the lights of Valcov that could just be seen twinkling down below, in the shadow of the further bank.

On my way home I had stopped for a few days in Paris, where I had met Beatrix. Together we had gone out to Versailles to visit the Chamsons, and my mind often returned to the talk round the table that day.

André Chamson, fellow-editor, friend and admired author, represented for me, from old association, almost more than anyone else, the international side of *New Writing*, which now seemed broken beyond repair. And what else remained of the project at this time when the future was so obscure that no literary plans could be made? It looked as if it would soon become nothing more than a memory, especially as Christopher Isherwood and Wystan Auden were far away in America. The pattern, the impulse of the original conception no longer existed, and I had very few illusions about Christopher's optimistic suggestions that they would continue to contribute and collaborate from the other side of the Atlantic. How stupid I had been, I thought now, not to have seen what was coming the year before, at the time of Munich.

And now the last volume of the peacetime *New Writing*, posthu-

mous child of the collaboration that existed no more, was in the press
and about to be launched into a world at war and in which already
many of the beliefs and interests it reflected seemed extraordinarily
remote, overtaken by the roaring express of international events.
What a discouraging irony of time it was to re-read Marina Raskova's
account of a Russian airwoman's experiences flying in a May Day parade over the Red Square, while Russian bombers were preparing to
complete the destruction of our new ally, Poland. The next turn of the
wheel, by which two years later we were to be toasting the Red pilots
as comrades-in-arms in the common struggle against the Axis, was
entirely unimaginable, as much to the shocked and disillusioned Left
as to the contemptuously told-you-so Right. Better it seemed for the
moment, in the plight in which we found ourselves, to meditate the
paradoxes of John Tessimond's poem on *England*, still uncertain
whether its final lines described a past that had been outlived:

> England the snail that's shod with lightning. . . .
> Shall we laugh or shall we weep?

That was only one of many remarkable poems in the volume, a
harvest that saddened me as I passed the proofs for press. Wystan
Auden's *In Memoriam Ernst Toller* and *The Leaves of Life;* George
Barker's *Four Elegies;* Louis MacNeice's four poems, including the
beautiful *Meeting Point;* Stephen Spender's *The Vase of Tears* and
Ambitious Son; William Plomer's *French Lisette*, most skilful of all
his comic ballads, and the fragment from David Gascoyne's never-to-
be-finished narrative poem *The Conspirators;* they saddened me because I felt, in the ebb-tide mood of that autumn, that they represented
a high-water mark, a meeting of young talents at their best under a
common impetus that was now lost for ever. No doubt purely personal
regret entered more into this feeling than I realized at the time: these
poems, V. S. Pritchett's masterly story *The Sailor*, George Orwell's
savagely prophetic sketch *Marrakech*, and the scene from Rex Warner's work in progress (soon to be published as *The Aerodrome*)
seemed to me to make this number in many ways the best of all, and I
could not without some anguish relinquish the idea of its being a prelude to a long maturity rather than a final curtain-call.

In the same number was a section I had called "Workers All," a
symposium of short sketches and stories of the kind with which *New
Writing* was perhaps most immediately associated in the mind of the
public: stories of working-class life, of miners, factory-workers and

the unemployed, on the border-line between fiction and reportage. I had, I believed, made some real discoveries of writing talent whose natural material was working-class life, but the limitations of the genre had become gradually more obvious to me during the four years of *New Writing*'s life. Now, in any case, in a country where production would soon be going all out for war supplies and where most of the unemployed who were not absorbed into the newly humming factories would be putting on uniforms, the conditions that had brought this kind of writing to birth were fast disappearing. I did not at that moment see what future the old impulses could have under war conditions. I did not by any means feel that the effort had been entirely wasted, but I was saddened by the tiny proportion of authentic ore of literature that had been found in all the dross; and saddened, too, by the feeling that what I thought really worth-while as literature was so fragmentary. The decade we had been through seemed to me in retrospect a period where promising beginnings had failed again and again, among all the distractions of political causes and the continual earthquake tremors that had been shaking the old-established way of life, to come to *enough;* like a magnolia-tree in a cold spring that puts out a succession of blooms but each time gets them nipped by the frost. Christopher Isherwood's case was, I thought, the most spectacular example of an experience that was typical: *Mr. Norris Changes Trains* and the stories of *Goodbye to Berlin* seemed to me far too inadequate an *oeuvre* for someone who had been tipped, for every kind of good reason, as the most promising novelist of his generation.

One day — it must have been in the first week of the war — turning out the pockets of a summer jacket which I was putting away for the duration, I found an old, clipped railway ticket to St. Gilgen: it brought back with almost unbearable vividness the happiness of summer expeditions among the Austrian lakes and mountain forests. Such memories, after a time, began to hurt so much that I found myself trying to avoid them. And yet they refused entirely to be clamped away; objects as potent as the old railway ticket insinuated themselves under my fingers as I was looking through writing-table drawers, chests and wardrobes; photographs would fall out of books as if lying in wait for me. An Austrian *émigré* asked me if I could lend him certain specimens from my collection of illegal papers of the Dollfuss-Schuschnigg era; opening the box and fingering through them, *Volkssport, Arbeiter Zeitung, Der Rote Trommel,* and the little stickies with *Denkt an die Februaropfer!* and *Wir Kommen Wieder!* cyclostyled on them, I was stabbed by the recollection of the hope that had buoyed us up then against the degradation of unemployment, the insolence of the police, the constant sight of the bullet-scarred walls of the Floridsdorf tenement-houses, the rumble of tanks on the frontier — the hope that the dictatorships would be defeated before it was too late, and the insane destruction and the killing be staved off. My godmother, Violet Hammersley, reminded me that we had lunched one day together at the Lusthaus in the Prater, and afterwards had been strolling down the long alley when suddenly a mounted party had emerged from a side-path among the trees, among whom we recognized Chancellor Schuschnigg, accompanied by one of his A.D.C.s. Very erect and distinguished he looked, an Austrian aristocrat of the old school, embodiment of gentle and humane authority: it was hard to equate this figure with the monster master of repression who figured in the propaganda of the underground parties, Nazi, Communist and Socialist; hard to envisage him as the dictator of a police-state in the prisons of which so many of my friends had suffered; easier at that moment to think of the impossibly conflicting international forces at whose centre he found himself, and to feel even a stirring of pity for him. Often, since his régime had collapsed and the comparatively mild Austro-fascism had been swallowed up in the vaster, more demonic police-state of the swastika, that image had come back to me, and in spite of my allegiances pity had deepened as I pictured him in some prison prepared by his gloating and treacherous conqueror; where he still remained while the anti-aircraft guns ringed the Vienna I had loved so much, and my friends-transformed-into-enemies turned to their sleep behind blacked-out windows, and only the moon lit the Danube as it lit the Thames, where I was also turning to my sleep behind blacked-out windows under the guardian sentinel watch of our side's anti-aircraft guns.

◄§ I I §►

Transformation Scene

LONDON had suddenly become two cities: the one, the daytime city where we went about our business much as before, worked in our offices and discussed what plans we could make for the future, lunched with our friends, and visited the shops to lay in what stores our consciences told us were not so great as to be considered hoarding. Already before the declaration of war many had disappeared into the jobs in the war-machine which had been waiting for them ever since the Munich crisis of the year before; others, who had had some kind of training or experience in the regular forces or the Territorials in the past, began to be called up and were off at a few hours' notice after hurried telephone calls to their closest friends; but as that first feeling of stunned shock wore off and the days went by and the colossal air-raids we had braced ourselves to meet failed to materialize, the rhythm of life reasserted itself with a remarkable steadiness.

The other London was the new, symbolic city of the black-out, where one floundered about in the unaccustomed darkness of the streets, bumping into patrolling wardens or huddled strangers, hailing taxis that crept along learning their new element, admiring the gigantic criss-crossing arms of the searchlights as they lit up the sudden silver bellies of the far balloons or scurrying clouds on windy nights, and found new beauty, when it was fine and still, in the fall of moonlight on pavements and pillars and high window-embrasures. Torches, cigarette-lighters flashed their momentary, tiny illuminations; the shuttered slits of the traffic lights winked their way through red, amber, green; there were many accidents in the streets those first days — a man heard moaning but not seen — a tin-hatted policeman running into a pub to telephone for an ambulance — it seemed fantastic not to use light on such occasions, but the discipline held everyone in its grip. Strangest of all at night were the London terminus stations:

King's Cross appeared like some weird imagining of John Martin, the long trains waiting like prehistoric beasts, smoking and hissing under the huge, gloomy caverns of the glass roofing only discernible by the rows of faint blue lights far above. Shadowy figures of porters and policemen moved round the bales and packages heaped in dark corners, a gang of plate-layers worked at the rails in a narrow circle of concentrated light at the far end between two platforms, and beyond them, in the vast indistinguishable mouth, a twinkling of red-and-green signals was all that indicated the beginning of houses, bridges, repair-sheds. The whole city was in a great conspiracy of secrecy, confusing yet curiously stimulating; when one went into a club or restaurant or drinking-place, one felt one had reached some beleaguered subterranean den or cave in the mountains, and one was conscious as never in daytime of airmen waiting by their hangars and soldiers by their camouflaged anti-aircraft guns, on guard to protect.

And yet it was difficult to imagine the war as a reality of violence. The pompous French communiqués from the Maginot Line announcing nothing, the R.A.F. raids over Germany merely to drop leaflets, the soberly factual reports of the German radio, all seemed part of some inexplicable game of nations only pretending to be at one another's throats. One evening, just before sunset, I went down to Hyde Park Corner, and walked up through the Park. So much was changed: and yet so much was the same. There was still a crowd promenading to and fro along the paths, though all the soldiers were in battledress; the booths at Marble Arch still had their preachers with the rings of sceptical listeners surrounding them, soldiers and sailors cracking jokes at the girls on the outskirts and shabby shufflers moving aimlessly between the groups, though just behind them a space had been railed off where a silver balloon was anchored, guarded by an R.A.F. unit. This was more like the rehearsal for some tournament than the Real Thing we had been dreading for so long.

One morning, soon after half-past six, there was an air-raid warning. The minutes passed, and nothing happened. Finally, I left the shelter in the basement, and went to the door of the house to see what was going on. It was a hauntingly lovely September morning, with a clear mother-of-pearl sky: the alarm had brought almost dead silence, broken only by the echo of gunfire once, very faint and far away, and then a few minutes later by the muffled rumble of a train in the distance beyond King's Cross. The soldiers on the gun-site nearby stood motionless in their helmets and heavy greatcoats, watching the east. . . . Could this really portend death and destruction? Only the news from the other end of Europe, where the claws of the beast were tearing Poland into bloody shreds, brought one back again to the truth of one's place and time.

The mood of London was calmer than one had imagined possible: a sense of tragic disaster was dominant, without the slightest trace of terror or patriotic hysteria. Even the melancholy fading wail of the sirens, like a dog in the extremities of misery or agony, gradually ceased to stir a queasy feeling in the pit of the stomach. I tried to sum it all up in a letter to Christopher in California, describing the impression so many of us shared, that under the calm surface life was changing very fast, like one shot fading quickly into another in a silent film, that even if the war only lasted a few months it would never be the same again. . . . And if it lasted for years, how long would this mood of calm survive, against frayed nerves and the clatter of guns and bombs, and the swelling casualty lists? Meanwhile, until a finger beckoned from some window slit in the vast fortress of the war bureaucracy, try to piece together some of the fragments of one's old hopes and plans, peer into the fog, find long books to absorb one's thoughts, Gibbon or Proust or *Seven Pillars of Wisdom*.

It was inevitable that one of the questions that most deeply occupied those who had belonged to the pre-war anti-fascist movement was the attitude of the Soviet Union to our war against Hitler. Disillusionment had set in for most of us many months before the Nazi-Soviet pact, but even after that pact had blown a huge hole through the myth of an idealistic revolutionary Russia leading the forces of resistance to Hitler, desperate hopes kept on bobbing up like shipwrecked men clinging to spars on the edge of an engulfing vortex. I mean for those who were not hypnotized by the farcical clap-trap of the new "party line," who could still think for themselves; for the comrades, the war against Nazi Germany had suddenly become an imperialist war, with Russia in the role of far-sighted defender of peace, and now and then — incredible though it seemed — one actually came across sincere enthusiasts, fellow-travellers, who had made themselves believe this line. What fanatical twist in their minds made it possible for them to accept the topsy-turvy reasoning that found it suddenly respectable to shake hands with the Jew-baiters, the murderers of Guernica, the plunderers of Austria and Czechoslovakia? Certainly they got little or no support from the people whose interests they were supposed to be defending: Goronwy Rees, already transformed in battledress and forage cap, came in one evening to describe his job of guarding the docks, and confessed to us that all the dockers he had come across were for the war and dead against Hitler. Perhaps these dockers did not go all the way with Harold Nicolson, who declared that the British governing classes were committing suicide in the interests of humanity; but at least they had a sound view of the crucial moral question and of what national preservation implied. Nevertheless, the hopes still clung on, faint graspings at the idea that all might be well after all, and Hitler one morning be proved the biggest dupe of history. What happened one morning, however, was that we heard the shattering news that the Red Army had joined in the murder of Poland and was already sweeping across the Polish Ukraine to meet the victorious Reichswehr. It was little help to say that our own Government was reaping a well-deserved reward for seven years of bungled foreign policy, or that Stalin could not allow the Ukrainians to fall into Hitler's hands; both these reflections were true, but the inescapable fact remained that by cynical justification of aggression and violated contracts, the Soviet Union had lost in moral power what she had gained in material power. And yet, and yet, there were still pathetically obstinate hopes, castaways that refused to be sucked into the vortex: as the two armies approached one another, was it not possible to imagine that under the pretence of amity, Stalin was completing the first phase of a cunningly devised plan of *liberation?* . . . These last, icy-fingered hopes did not survive the Russian invasion of Finland.

The moral, it seemed, could not be evaded: I discussed it with Stephen Spender again and again during these weeks, and with many others who had been associated with us. Nothing that had happened made us feel that we had been wrong to stand openly for the ideas of liberty and justice, to show that we stood on the side of those parties and groups that appeared to be championing them most effectively in the political struggles of a political decade. Our general position, we still felt, had been right: poets and other creative artists cannot, if they are to remain fully living people, if they are to fulfil their function as interpreters of their time to their own generation, fail to interest themselves in the meaning behind political ideas and political power. It was our particular position that had probably been wrong: in the heat of the battle, to give our specific assent to a particular set of slogans, even if we did not actually join a particular party.

Nor was it pride and arrogance that made us want to distinguish ourselves from the contestants in the political arena: we did not think that creative artists are necessarily better (or for that matter worse) than politicians, but that it was their business to remain true to their *different*, highly specialized and difficult task.

That did not prove that all we had said and done was meaningless. Underneath even the most extreme political pamphleteering we had been guilty of remained the humanist impulse: to speak for justice, to reveal, through the power of imaginative sympathy, what the action of "impersonal historic forces" meant in terms of individual human experience. That impulse was at least as important as before; perhaps, in the agreed partial surrender of liberty that modern war-making involved in a democratic country, more important than ever. I felt myself that the purely human side of the war would be far the most interesting and significant to me; and I was aware of a growing need to understand the deeper pattern of what was happening in order to grasp that human side.

Meanwhile the practical problem remained of defending liberty in whatever way was still open to us. The immediate danger to guard against was censorship: the stifling, under cover of "military security," of opinions and attitudes that were unpopular with the war bureaucracy for political or narrow-mindedly patriotic reasons. Writers of every sort had their eyes fixed on the Ministry of Information, into which many of their kind had already disappeared to pursue impenetrable activities that seemed to have no obvious results. It did not, one thought, matter very much what they did provided they left the rest of their tribe alone. The "Big House in Bloomsbury" presented a façade of monolithic power, concentrated purpose and dignity to the mere denizens of neighbouring squares creeping beneath its pile; but inside, to judge from the stories that continually leaked out, and were passed on with relish in every pub, restaurant and office frequented by journalists and poets, chaos had come again. Making fun of the Min. of Inf. became the favourite intellectual pastime of the first year of the war; but the greater dangers never materialized, opinion remained officially free, books were not censored except by a voluntary — and eventually efficient — pre-publication system on security grounds. No poets, as far as I know, got into trouble with the civil authorities over the expression of alarming or gloomy sentiments, though when they donned uniform, commanding officers were known on certain occasions to have become apoplectic. The trouble, however, was not by any means only the bureaucracy; editors acting on their own hunch were often over-zealous, their directors overcome by scruples the Big House seemed never to have entertained.

The intellectuals of the 'thirties were by no means popular at that time with members of Parliament, influential civil servants and generals in authority. For some obscure reason we were held by many of these — or so it often seemed to us — to be responsible for the mess the country had got itself into, though in fact, of course, all our miserable efforts had been directed towards preventing the mess. One sensed an only just undivulged wish to put us in front of a firing squad, or at least to clap us into prison for the duration under regulation 18B. The suppressed emotions of hostility broke violently into the open over the "Auden-Isherwood affair." Christopher and Wystan were suddenly branded as traitors and cowards in a campaign that was waged with the utmost fury against them in dailies and weeklies, respectable as well as less respectable; questions were asked in Parliament, scathing judgements were passed on them under privilege by people who may never have more than glanced at their works. They had, these accusing voices thundered, called on their contemporaries to fight fascism, and now that we were in fact at war with Hitler they had run away to America and refused to return. Flocks of wish-dream white feathers winged their way across the Atlantic to them. It was in vain to try and point out that they had left long before the invasion of Poland or even of Czechoslovakia, that they had taken out papers for American citizenship but had nevertheless registered with the British Embassy in Washington and been told to stay put for the time being. Their friends were dismayed: their position was difficult, because though they knew the campaign was unfair and, privately, suspected that it was yet another, familiar outburst of British official philistinism and had little to do with the rights and wrongs of the victims' particular case, they themselves felt that their absence was painful. How often I was to think in the coming years of all that had been lost by their not sharing what the rest of us were experiencing in Britain under siege: what treasures there would have been for us to lighten the darkest days if the creator of *The Nowaks* and *Mr. Norris* had cast his compassionate and humorous eye upon the ardent follies of our wartime scene; if the spiritual physician of his generation had been able to write of what it felt like to be still alive after a night of heavy blitz, rather than offer us those impeccably above-the-battle sentiments that appear in his poem *September 1, 1939*.

During that first autumn of the war, most of the writers I knew, who had remained with us, seemed incapable of producing very much. Stunned by the catastrophe, oppressed by a deep melancholy, totally uncertain about the kind of future we were entering, their instinct was either to immerse themselves in journals, to try and make sense of the changed world around them and of their own thoughts in this pre-

Apocalyptic moment, or to plunge back into the past of childhood and youth, times which now stood out in memory with a strange insulated intensity, an hallucinatory effulgence. Out of this mood were to come such variously beautiful achievements as Henry Green's *Pack My Bag*, with its "cry of a huntsman on the hill a mile or more away"; my sister Rosamond's story *The Red-Haired Miss Daintreys*, with its closing, nightfall note, "there will be no more families in England like the Daintrey family"; Cecil Day Lewis's sonnet sequence *O Dreams, O Destinations*, and Stephen Spender's novel *The Backward Son*, with its centre-piece evocation of a childhood Christmas, hauntingly poetic and humorously, unsentimentally vivid at the same time, perhaps the most perfectly realized scene in all his prose.

At the very beginning of the war Stephen had decided that, until his call-up came, he must reduce expenditure to a minimum, live in the country and bury himself in his writing. Our meetings at first were half gloomy silences, half sudden bursts of nostalgic recollections and random guesses at the riddle in the crystal before us. Gradually, however, Stephen's natural buoyancy reasserted itself, his own private affairs resumed their place in the foreground of his thought and conversation, and the old spice of affectionate malice returned to his comments on the doings of friends and acquaintances. Christopher and Wystan were not spared; Christopher's reported plan to reappear in Europe with an American Ambulance Unit, to soothe our dying moments among the ruins, casued him spasms of irritation, as it did me; there was even an unguarded moment at lunch in the Athenaeum when, his grin seeming to spread right across the huge dining-room, he referred to "Christopher and Stalin, those great neutrals."

Virginia Woolf, too, was one of the writers who felt that the only thing that made sense was to devote oneself to one's work, to the inner world of order as the outer world collapsed in disorder. One day, in the first week, she and Leonard came up from the country, and, while we ate sandwiches despondently in my flat, she confessed that the only way she could find to dispel the restless visions of anxiety that continually oppressed her was to force herself to carry on with the biography of Roger Fry she was preparing, and to re-create herself in her diary.

From time to time I went down to Rodmell, to discuss Hogarth affairs with her and Leonard. In theory, I had bought Virgina out of the Press, but in fact she continued to be as keenly interested in all its activities as ever before, and every evening we would settle down in the little sitting-room upstairs, where the shelves were filled with books in Virginia's own binding and the tables and window-sills covered with the begonias, gloxinias and rare giant lilies that Leonard raised in his greenhouses, and we would discuss books and authors and the opportunities that were open to us in the new situation. Leonard stretched out his feet towards the fire in his arm-chair on one side, and puffed at his pipe; Virginia on the other lit another home-rolled cigarette in her long holder. Occasional visitor though I was, I had come to be very fond of Monk's House, the old village cottage they had bought just after the first war and rebuilt to make an ideal home for two authors to live and work in: I loved the untidy, warm, informal atmosphere of the house, with books and magazines littered about the rooms, logs piled up by the fireplaces, painted furniture and low tables of tiles designed by the Bloomsbury artists, and writing done in sunny, flower-filled, messy studios. A smell of wood smoke and ripe apples lingered about it, mixed with the fainter under-perfume of old bindings and old paper. We ate our meals always at the stove end of the long kitchen-scullery. I remember one autumn evening there, just after Leonard's book *Barbarians at the Gate* had come out: I had been moved by the persuasive force of the argument he developed, the lucidity of the style and the underlying warmth, and I told him so, and how important I felt his warning was at a time when people were all too easily allowing themselves to believe that any means were justified by the ends. Virginia was splashing gravy in large dollops over my plate as I talked, and joined in with her praise, "You know, Leo, it's a wonderful book," while Leonard himself sat in modest silence, with lowered eyes, like a schoolboy praised by the headmaster at an end-of-term prize-giving.

During those months Virginia alternated between cautious confidence and weary depression about the Roger Fry biography, very much as she always did when at work on a new book; but sometimes the depression seemed so deep that both Leonard and I encouraged her to leave it for a while, to put down on paper her objections to my generation of writers, and to prepare a third *Common Reader* collection of essays; the idea of a change nearly always lightened her mood. When *Roger Fry* was finished, however, just before Christmas, she was transformed: radiant and buoyant, full of teasing malice and the keenest interest in what her friends were doing, and finding a startling new beauty in London — the squares and side-streets in the black-out on a clear night — a transfigured look in the faces of the men and women she passed — the smartness of uniforms of every sort.

How grateful one was at that time for week-ends in the country; even before the air-raids one had a sense of escaping from an atmosphere of strain and tension, as the last suburbs gave way to the country fields and the yellowing autumn trees outside one's carriage-window. Country houses seemed like islands of the pre-war life; all else had been submerged, perhaps for ever, and even the islands were hard-pressed by the encroaching seas. Evacuees were, of course, the great problem and endurance test at the beginning: no one likes his house to be invaded suddenly by strangers of unknown habits and unpredictable demands, but the communal emotion, the sense of national duty, fortified hearts against the shock of privacy violated, squalor unmasked and property under siege. Only a sense of humour, however, could keep up the courage of their obligatory hosts until the grumbling hordes, who could never make themselves at home, began to trickle back to the still undamaged tenements they had expected to be reduced to rubble and ashes during the first few days of war. (The episode of the Connollys in Evelyn Waugh's *Put Out More Flags* remains the classic, unforgettable picture of this relationship.) My sister Rosamond had had her quota of evacuees at her Berkshire home, Ipsden — eleven ragamuffins, one of whom promptly developed scarlet fever — but told tales of their sayings and doings as fantastically comic as Beatrix's description of the porter's wife at the Highgate flats where she lived acting as "hostess" in the air-raid shelter. Rosamond had made up her mind, as Virginia had, to treat the whole situation as a challenge to her creative powers, and had settled to work at a series of short stories, the first of which was *The Red-Haired Miss Daintreys.*

My mother, though already in her middle sixties and given to chronic anxiety, especially about her children — nothing delighted her more than their successes, but there was always at least one she was convinced was on the road to ruin, in spite of the efforts of those of us who had happened momentarily to have escaped this sentence to persuade her to the contrary — showed a wonderful fortitude in the face of the war. She immersed herself at once in local Red Cross work as well as carrying on with her many duties connected with the County Council, of which she was an elected member, and the problems of the numerous schools of which she was a Governor. One of the first things she said to me was that she knew I would be confronted with very difficult decisions and she wanted me to know that she would be ready to help me in any way she could: I was not to think, even if I had to turn myself into a soldier or sailor, that it was all up with my career as a publisher, and if it were ever a question of expansion and more capital, even during the war, she might be able to suggest ways and means. She wanted me also to hold on to *New Writing*, to the foundation of which her help had contributed so much: don't be discouraged, don't lose heart, was her message to me, at a time when I felt she might well have been expected to want moral support herself from her children. Until her accident in the spring, when she fell in the library and broke her thigh, we used still to take walks together along the river, discussing her favourite subject of history and parallels out of the past with our own day, and the changing international situation. Contemptuous as she often was of brash American attitudes towards Europe, convinced that all too often ignorance and arrogance mingled fatally in American handling of diplomatic affairs, she nevertheless understood the deep moral currents that united the two peoples underneath all differences and disagreements, and had an unshakeable belief that her own countrymen would never let us in Britain starve or, in the last instance, allow our islands to be occupied by an enemy power. This belief fortified her through the darkest days of the Battle of Britain and the U-boat war: her comments, however, were on the scathing side when food parcels began to arrive from American relations who knew that the one thing Fieldhead had was a large, well-stocked kitchen garden, and were found to contain choice tins of concentrated onion-juice and other remedies for vegetable deficiency.

The house, the garden, was a haven of peace, where I settled blissfully, on Saturdays and Sundays, into the mysterious, sustaining compost of the happy past. Through the tangle of autumn colours, the red and yellow apples falling from the trees, Mr. Goodman the head-gardener passed on his way, prophesying, not without a certain exultation, black doom and crimson revolution.

« 2 »

No one, in the early days of the war, had the slightest idea what the future of writing and book-publishing would be. It is easy to be wise after the event, and to say that the boom that developed in the course of the 1914–18 war should have been a precedent to give authors, publishers and booksellers confidence; but in fact, if air-bombardments had started at once and the main cities of Britain had found themselves under siege before industry, commerce, communications had adapted themselves to war conditions, it is very doubtful if the book trade would have flourished as it eventually did; and immediate, overwhelming attack was what seemed to everyone at first extremely likely. The bookshops were empty; and publishers cancelled their plans or postponed them indefinitely, except for those with books already going through the press or preparing works of urgent topical significance. In the Hogarth Press basement in Mecklenburgh Square everything came to a standstill; all discussions about paper supplies and printing facilities seemed entirely academic, manuscripts lay on the shelves like orphans without prospects; and Leonard Woolf, coming in to work out an emergency skeleton scheme to keep the Press at least in being if raids came or if I were called up, commiserated with me on the ill-luck that seemed to dog my footsteps as a publisher.

Gradually, however, the lifeless body began to stir again; it was only concussion after all. After a few weeks, people began to feel that the German air-armadas were not coming just yet, perhaps had thought better of it, and to realize at the same time that they needed books and were going to have plenty of time to read them. Leonard and I began to look again at our stocks of the International Psycho-Analytical Library and Virginia's Uniform Edition, and to calculate how soon we should need reprints if the demand continued to recover. A little later, we brought out Henry Green's *Party Going*, which received an early batch of enthusiastic reviews, and began to sell fast. Something could be done after all; it was worth having a basic plan for the use of a paper ration which threatened to be minuscule. I put in a plea for poetry: if the 1914–18 war was any guide, I argued, people would eventually want to read poetry, and books of poetry consumed very little paper while keeping a flag flying over the Hogarth Press — a flag which told young authors that we were still keenly interested in them.

For me, however, the crucial question was still what was going to happen to *New Writing*. As I have already mentioned, I felt profoundly pessimistic about its future when the autumn number of the old *New Writing* came out: it did not seem to me likely that I should have either the money — for those packed volumes of 150,000 words each were becoming rather expensive to produce — or the paper, or the opportunity to go on with it as before; and it struck me as rather absurd to pretend that the "movement" had not been changed in certain decisive ways by the outbreak of war, quite apart from the fact that Wystan and Christopher had abdicated from it (from us), and the old foreign contributors were mostly beyond reach. Yet my natural obstinacy and dislike of giving anything up until it was finally proved to be hopeless, the little ember of optimism that burned still under the ashes, was fanned by the tone of the reviews. "One hopes that war will not demolish it," said the *Manchester Guardian;* "Now that the *Criterion* and the *London Mercury* have gone the way of all literary reviews, there is nothing left but *New Writing* to supply the demand for good prose, good verse and good criticism" was the opinion of *The Listener;* and the *New Statesman* even more reassuringly maintained that "the task which Mr. Lehmann undertook in 1935 is by no means finished or even interrupted by the war." At the same time letters from some of my old contributors began to reach me, in which there was a note almost of desperation at the idea that *New Writing* might come to an end. The book trade was beginning to pick up, people were gradually distinguishing shapes and directions more clearly in the darkness that had suddenly fallen. Perhaps after all there was a chance; perhaps it would be foolish not to keep something going, less extravagant of paper, time and finance, which would mean continuity and welcoming signals to the young men who still believed, who had transferred their fountain-pens and note-books to the pockets of their battledress.

It seemed to me that the spirit of *New Writing* was in fact very far from confined to the association of left-wing politics and literature, whatever might be said by the detractors and those who, silent in their hostility before, were now eagerly gathering round the burial ground they had marked out for it. The belief in literature as part of life, the belief in the power of the creative imagination to give meaning to life; these were surely going to be as important as ever in the times we were about to enter. The reviews and the letters and messages that were coming in hinted that once one had taken on a responsibility towards young writers, it was not so easy to put it down again without looking a little selfish, a little cowardly (though I was aware of the ambuscade of vanity in this argument). If *New Writing* was to go on, it must avoid the political, yes, but emphasize the human, be committed to the human scene even more completely; it could be a laboratory, an experimental ground for the development of a new consciousness; it would probably find itself moving towards something more lyrical and individual, burlesque and satire too of a kind that represented the revolt of the free human spirit against the prisons that the war with its imperatives and its bureaucratic impersonality threatened to build up round us. . . . So my thoughts went, as I walked about London's moonlit streets or leaned in pubs, deliberately alone, working out practical schemes at the same time as I tried to clear my mind about aims and values. I found the warmest support from Leonard and Virginia when I explained to them what I wanted to do; and it was not long before I had called for estimates from the printers and was settling down with Leonard to see if they worked out right.

It was during my preparation of this scheme that calamitous disagreements broke out between Stephen Spender and myself. They were connected with the birth of *Horizon*, which happy event had just taken place. Ridiculously unimportant though they may appear in retrospect, I find it difficult to pass them over as if they had never existed, as they gave rise to the quite unwarranted idea that some feud-to-the-death existed between *New Writing* and *Horizon*, that Cyril Connolly and I had snipers' guns trained on one another, as long as our two magazines existed side by side. Nothing could be further from the truth; a friendly rivalry certainly existed, which spurred us on (I hope) to greater efforts; I disagreed strongly with the "ivory tower" attitude Cyril appeared to adopt at first, his view that the only thing writers could do while the war was going on was to concentrate on technique and shut their ears; and I thought the sneers *Horizon* allowed to be printed in its first number against Wystan and Christopher were in bad taste; but I am quite prepared to believe that Cyril, on his side, had equally decided criticisms of *New Writing*'s policy and judgement. That did not prevent Cyril and myself remaining very good friends throughout the war. Which of us could swear on all he holds most sacred that a crack, edged with malice, did not escape his lips at the other's expense between 1940 and 1945? And yet, as the war became more embittered and destructive, and shortage of supplies threatened us both, we began, I believe, to hold one another's editorial existence as almost sacred. What caused the disagreements was quite simply my belief that Stephen, with whom I discussed all my plans in the frankest friendship from the first day of the war, had agreed to come in, as associate editor, on any scheme which I could realize for *New Writing*'s future. It was for that reason that my dismay was so acute when I heard one day, without any warning, that he was to be co-editor with Cyril and Peter Watson on a new literary magazine. No doubt I had assumed a great deal more than I had any right to assume; but in the end, of course, peace was made and sealed with the presentation to me by Stephen of an exceptionally splendid gift: the large, leather-bound ledger in which he had written the whole of his play, *Trial of a Judge*, and the greater number of the short lyrics composed at the same time.

One ironical result of this increased sense of competition was that I turned all my spare energies to the nourishment of my new baby, *Folios of New Writing*. Now, I said to myself, it must not fail. Just before, I had begun to feel the impulse to write poetry again; the contemplative, poetical-analysing side of my nature was uppermost in those early weeks of the war when the train of all one's pre-war activities was brought to a sudden halt as if by a landslide on the line. Poems were beginning to form in the back of my mind; but, as on so many other crucial occasions in my life, a renewed challenge to my career as editor-impresario made me turn away and leave the poems to sink back again into the darkness. One day I hope to understand whether this reaction was evidence of weakness or strength.

The first volume of *Folios* came out in the spring of 1940, and was followed, as in the pre-war days of *New Writing*, by another six months later. Many of the old names were still there, and yet I think the change of mood could immediately be felt. These volumes were more "miscellanies" than any of the pre-war volumes; yet they were given a certain unity by the fact that so many of the contributors had been moved by the slogans of passion and idealism of the 'thirties, and now found them inadequate. Only an undertone, or even less — the faintest of implications — in some of the contributions, it becomes more articulate in George Orwell's *My Country Right or Left*, where he reveals (with some contemptuous side-thrusts at the "boiled rabbits of the Left") that a dream on the night before the Russo-German pact was announced made him suddenly understand that he was patriotic at heart, if by patriotism was understood the "devotion to something that is changing but is felt to be mystically the same"; and in Stephen Spender's article on *The Creative Imagination in the World Today*. Stephen attacked at the same time the blinkered Marxist view that all writers must side with a political party in their writing and the philistine patriotic view that all poetry in wartime must sound a clarion-call of heroism and defiance to the enemy, and asserted, with a more effective marshalling of arguments than ever before, that the essential and genuinely revolutionary task of the poet is to discover what is true and what is living in his own time below what is assumed to be true and what is only pretending to be alive.

What gave me hope for the future was not so much that I saw, from what I had been able to collect for those first two volumes between the outbreak of war and the Battle of Britain, that fresh developments could be expected from the writers of my own generation, but that already new poets and story-writers were beginning to appear. In

the spring *Folios* I published some of the earliest poems of Terence
Tiller, who had just left Cambridge to take up an appointment in the
University of Cairo; and in the autumn a group of poems by Laurie
Lee, a new poet of twenty-six, whose lively Cotswold eye and vivid
appreciation of landscape and life in Spain gave his work an immediate appeal. The music and evocative imagery in Terence Tiller's
poems, the lyrical freshness of Laurie Lee's, gave the promise, I
thought, of still flowing springs of inspiration and a poetic response to
the life of war far more full of meaning than any Rupert Brooke-ish
"war poems" whose absence was so censoriously complained of by
some elderly pundits. And I had received from a young captain in the
Signals, Ralph Elwell-Sutton, the first story to reflect the mood of the
new conscript Army, *The Deserter*:

. . . We talked about him being plumb scared of war. We were all
plumb scared of war, we reckoned. But it seemed to be different with this
chap. He couldn't stand anything to do with war. He couldn't stand all
the men in uniforms and the routine and the rifles. It killed him inside
and he went about in misery and awful fear. Everything he saw and smelt
and heard made it worse, and some of us began to wonder if it would
slowly drive him mad.

To find out what the feeling about the future was among the booksellers outside London, I made a number of expeditions that autumn,
with Hogarth books and provisional lists in my bag, which gave me an
opportunity to see what was happening beyond the narrow frontiers of
my own existence. I remember in Cambridge, everything was looking
its most beautiful in the late October sunlight, the great golden chestnut half-obscuring the Senate House on King's Parade, and the yellow
tumbling leaves on the Backs glimpsed through the iron gates of a
newly scrubbed Neville's Court in Trinity. Confused and painful emotions troubled me, not so much nostalgia as regret that so large a
chunk of my life could slip away so easily, could seem so far away on
the other side of all that I had experienced in the cities of Europe
during the 'thirties. Did I really spend so many years of my life on this
Pacific island, which now appeared so extraordinarily blessed and remote from the stormier waters of life, even though the young R.A.F.
men hurrying through the streets suggested the encroaching reality of
war? Dining in King's, I had the odd feeling of being like a man who
had emigrated to Australia and built up a sheep-farm there: the nostalgia was checked by the consciousness of being planted, spiritually,

elsewhere. I kept on asking myself what I had learnt in Cambridge; a great deal about books and art, but almost nothing about life.

« 3 »

IN spite of the fact that I had begun to change the focal point of my life from Vienna back to London over a year before the war broke out, and in spite of my impulse, after the blow fell, to repress the too intimate, too painful memories, I could not altogether resist a hankering to keep in touch with the Danube world in some way or other, to do something, even if only of a symbolic nature, for my Austrian friends. I knew that the sympathies of most of them were far more with England than with the goose-stepping Third Reich that had absorbed Austria, but I also knew something of the power of the Nazi propaganda machine, and feared that gradually they might come to believe in the distorted mask with which Goebbels was concealing the true face of our country. I could not think of a single one who had ever expressed any bellicose sentiments or any appetite for the military life, and it was horrible to me to imagine them being trained to kill young Englishmen who — so it seemed to me from my own circle of friends — had just as little hatred of them and just as little zeal for killing.

No letters of course could get through, and I thought that even if I succeeded in sending something via America it might only cause them serious embarrassment with the Nazi authorities. I did ask an English friend in Italy, who had connections and acquaintances in many parts of South-Eastern Europe, to try and get news of my former secretary Toni, his wife and family, by devious means; but, not surprisingly, he failed. My life, that had grown its roots in two countries, thus brought home to me the cruel absurdity of modern war, the declaration of which immediately cuts off tens of millions of people on one side of the frontier from all contact with or knowledge of all the tens of millions of people on the other side of the frontier; and I thought with bitter envy of how in the past, right up to the Napoleonic Wars, the artists and writers of one country could visit the capital of another with which they were at war, and be received in dignity and respect.

After a while, I began to immerse myself in books that would at least partly assuage the ache for the world from which I was now totally excluded. I took down again Hassek's marvellous *Schweik*, preferring to think that the immortal dodger more truly represented the attitude of my Austrian friends to army life than the massed fanatical warriors with whose pictures the Austrian papers had been filled since the Anschluss; I embarked on Joseph Roth's *Radetskymarsch*, I re-read Schnitzler's haunting story *Spiel im Morgengrauen*, which I had often thought of translating, and an anthology of modern Austrian lyrics I carried about with me. From time to time I saw my friends among the Austrian *émigrés*, who depressingly reported a hardy survival of dissensions between Social-Democrats, Communists and Monarchists: in France I gathered that only the Monarchists were favoured by the Government, and even in England there seemed to be, in Foreign Office circles, a strong hankering after a Habsburg solution to Austrian problems in the event of victory. This, I knew from of old, could only produce violent opposition among the Czechs and Slovaks (if not among the Hungarians) whom we had good reason to count among our potential friends behind the façade of Hitler's empire.

Not unnaturally, my hope and aim was to be used by my country in some sphere in which my special knowledge of the Danubian countries would prove to be of some value. In the first few weeks of the war, I foolishly believed that my application of the previous year to be placed on the emergency register would result in a rapid call to service: I had visions of myself playing a small but crucial part in some military mission to a still neutral Balkan country, or being trained to be landed by submarine, my pockets stiff with false papers, on some Adriatic or Black Sea shore. It was not to be. Every week or so I would ring up the appropriate department of the Ministry of Information; every week the reply grew vaguer and more discouraging. I was finally told there was no hope: I was not told why, but the difficulties which some of my friends, who had been closely associated with the Spanish Republican cause, were experiencing in being taken on as volunteers led me to suspect that the same objections were working against me. By then, however, new suggestions and new ideas had come up, and at one moment possibilities were dangled before me of being taken on by three different outfits, one connected with the Foreign Office, one with the Ministry of Information and one with the European Commission of the Danube, which buoyed me up with the hope of being able to assuage my nostalgia for the countries I had left behind and serve my own country at the same time. The British Representative on the European Commission told me that he personally very much wanted me to join him in some capacity, and over luncheon at the Athenaeum we swapped stories of Danube politics and Danube travel: he made me laugh with his description of the fantastic situation he still found himself in of having to sit at the conference table in Rumania with the German delegate and shake hands with him in the Council Chamber.

In anticipation I saw the sunlit marshes of the Delta again more vividly than ever, I could almost smell the reeds and hear the cries of the
birds. . . . All this was but a mirage, for the weeks turned into
months, and still the fatal veto appeared to block my advance at all
doors.

Finally, I forget how, an idea took shape that I should start a British bookshop in Yugoslavia or Rumania. The co-operation of the British
Council with the Foreign Office appeared necessary for this project,
and one day I went for an interview with one of the Higher Execu-
tives of the former body. I am astonished, on looking back, at the
persistence which brought me to this point: my efforts by that time
had something feverish and hallucinated about them, and I was quite
unaware what a wild-goose-chase the whole scheme must have appeared in the eyes of a cautious and conventional civil servant. The
Higher Executive was very polite, very F.O. with me; but it was quite
clear he had no idea who I was or what my qualifications really were,
in spite of the briefing I was led to believe he had been given. He
seemed much reassured by observing that I wore an old Etonian tie,
but nevertheless betrayed acute anxiety as he posed *the* question: had
I been to a University? Immense relief flooded his face when he heard
the answer, but seeped away again as the desultory conversation proceeded. In desperation, and shamelessly, I managed to mention as if in
passing that my cousin happened to be Sir Ronald Campbell, who was
British Minister at Belgrade at the time: this provided a brief oasis of
cheer for the Higher Executive, but dismay reigned again when I
rather crossly explained that I wasn't looking for a job at all costs but
wanted to be of use, if I could, in a way for which I felt myself specially fitted. . . . Yes, of course, if there were a British Book Exhibition somewhere down in the Balkans. . . . Exactly. . . . Very
good of you, Mr. Lehmann. . . . Politely bowed out, I had the dubious satisfaction of knowing that I had been "put on their files," and the
half-acknowledged inner conviction that precisely nothing would come
of the interview.

Very soon after, however, while the idea of the Balkan bookshop
was still being considered by the authorities, Rumania fell under Hitler's control, and I realized that it was too late. Nevertheless, as I had
gathered that a large shipment of British books had arrived in Bucha-
rest, in the restless hours of the night I conceived an even more extraordinary scheme: that I should open and take charge of a British
cultural-propaganda centre, in the guise of a bookshop, in Moscow. I
bombarded the long-suffering Leigh Ashton at the Ministry of Infor-

mation with details of my latest project, proposing that the books in Rumania should be crated again and shipped to Odessa as a quick way of getting them into Russia; that as the Germans had staged a major cultural exhibition in Moscow we must do the same; and that special attention should be paid to the English classics and books about Shakespeare at the Old Vic, the Sadler's Wells Ballet, the Stratford Memorial Theatre and English documentary films. I had a freakish hope that as I had worked in the past for Sir Stafford Cripp's paper *Tribune* he would be sympathetic to my proposals. In the end I went to discuss them with the Northern Division of the Foreign Office, and Fitzroy Maclean, who interviewed me, suggested chillingly that though they could not officially back me, they would have no objection to my having a shot on my own. When I had recovered — some days later — from the blow this bewildering method of turning me down had dealt me, I realized that I had been losing touch with reality. I thought no more about it. I knew that no one else was thinking about it. So why should I?

Meanwhile, publishing was rapidly recovering from the sharp frost of the previous September, and I was more and more engrossed with the problems of book-production which I thought I had left behind me at least for the duration. And yet one didn't quite believe in it all: for how could it survive the plunge over the Niagara one knew must be approaching?

« 4 »

I TRY to reconstruct the everyday life of those months from winter to spring, before the German swoop westwards, but, as if it were shattered by what came after, I only find fragments and cannot put them together again.

Voices from far away, from the past of *New Writing* and old friends: Frank Sargeson writes from Takapuna: "I have only a dead sort of feeling about the war. I hear the intellectuals out here saying we'll have to let old man Europe just go to pot, and start culture all over again out here. But of course it wouldn't work. . . ." And Bertold Brecht from Sweden: "In the next few days I shall send you a copy of my *Svendberger Gedichte*, about which I've already written to you. One request: can't you send me regularly a copy of each number of *New Writing?* I'm always so pleased to see it, one gets so few good things now." And Anna Seghers from a Paris become immensely remote: "I go on with my literary work in spite of every kind of worry and interruption. . . . I've got to earn a living for myself and my children somehow."

Voices from nearer home: from my godmother Violet Hammersley in the Isle of Wight: "I agree with you that part of the pain of this war is an isolation from all one's accustomed human contacts. Here, you can imagine what it's like. On the Solent nowadays there's nothing to see save two or three small yachts, painted grey, and flying strange flags proclaiming them to be on scout duty of some kind. No other ships are ever seen. . . . I've been made very unhappy over various Polish friends. It's all too long to tell, but several I knew, who escaped from the Germans sought refuge in East Poland in a friend's house, and were horribly massacred by the Russians, one a boy of 17, the son of a very, very old friend who adored him." And from Victor Pritchett down in Berkshire, a glimpse of the absurd difficulty of arranging even the simplest meetings between friends in those days: "Your letter horrified me because it sounds as though, not having received mine, you must have sat in the Paddington snack bar hour after hour eating snack after snack. A fate I would not wish you. I'm sure I didn't call you a cad, but I wonder what the insult was? Was it Com? Short for Communist? I get waves of rage about the Party Line now and then, so perhaps I was wishing you are not of that persuasion; but like myself, a crypto-Tory anarchist free trade Liberal with strong Socialist bias. I'm not really any -ist because I don't like any good news that comes from On High straight from the lips of the Infallible. I'm a natural Protestant. . . . But I back myself to keep alive under any régime, even though I detested it — which is the nastiest kind of egoism, but it's like all the people you see going into the towns to get something cheap, on the country buses. Civilization was never built by people like me; we're the dead-weight, but sometimes an embellishment."

Voices from young men under arms, poets and lovers of poetry, cramped into the discomforts of the creaking, grinding military omnibus; voices overheard in pubs, confidences over glasses of mild and bitter; voices rise and are gone like clouds on a windy autumn day. Day-dreams, forebodings, meditations and visions . . . What is the prospect? A mad world after the war — or no end to the war because the world has already gone mad? Somehow or other, one must build a fortress for poetry, for art. I must behave, think as if I'd died (and indeed I truly feel like that sometimes). Signs begin to multiply that enormous slaughters may after all take place, by a sort of fatal diseased compulsion, and the war spread east, down the Danube, into Asia. Does anyone grasp that victory is as unlikely as defeat — victory in the old sense?

Images of regret: goodbye to John Lepper, who joined up one weekend without a word to me; John his usual unperturbed self, bringing out story after story over the bottle of champagne; but a sense for me of guilt and frustration, of not having done enough for him while he worked as my secretary. Christopher Isherwood's room in London, as his mother opens the door for me, with the windows closed, blinds half-down, and dust sheets over everything. A note-book filled with the beginnings of poems scribbled down in Austria, lines, half-finished stanzas; now impossible ever to complete.

Images of phantasmagoria: the centre of London on New Year's Eve. In some pubs there was little or no life, in others the Scots and the tarts between them were creating a pandemonium of sing-song; as one passed down the street outside, barbaric yells echoed from them; the dank streets, lightless in spite of the moon, chilly with thin, trailing fog. In the thickest darkness, in the thickest part of the crowds, at Piccadilly Circus where would-be revellers were grouped like swarming bees round the boxed lump that had taken the place of Eros, a group of Canadian soldiers suddenly began to shout at the tops of their voices, all faces indistinguishable. Later, as I walked home, two small sailor figures loomed up out of the blackness, and asked in obviously foreign accents where they were. I took them to the station, discovered they were Polish ratings on leave; a grin, a salute, and they were swallowed up again, leaving me with the strangeness of the war hanging in the air round me all of a sudden like a scent.

Images of pleasure: a visit to the Westminster Theatre, to see Beatrix in *Desire under the Elms*. One of her greatest performances: her unweakening intensity, her diamond-hard brilliance covered up the moments of melodrama, and made the love scenes an almost unbelievable discovery of joy and spring. An iron-cold winter night at the King's Theatre, Hammersmith, our fingers almost stick to the bars in the auditorium, the cold is so intense. The Three Arts Ballet: a new young Polish dancer from Paris, Alexis Rassine, showing in every movement the lyrical grace, the blood-sense of the dance that only the Slav peoples have. A world of pure art that still, incredibly, can exist in spite of the war.

Memories of parties run together: a last *New Writing* party, or was it more than one party? And then voices, dreams, images were swept away, drowned in a torrent that changed all our lives, that made them in a few weeks as remote, as historic as they are today.

Let the Journal I kept at the time take over. . . .

« 5 »

Friday evening, May 10, 1940

THE gathering storms of the Norway crisis dominated all minds, I think, this week. Everyone followed the debates in the House as never before; and as they reached their climax, people held their breath, scarcely believing it could be true that the outbreak of anger had come at last, that the Old Men of Munich were slipping after years of obstinate, seemingly unshakeable grip on power. . . . And then, the next morning, the invasion of the Low Countries. The stationmaster at Bourne End told me what had happened as I took my place in the 8:44. By the time I was in London and more and more news began to come through, I began to see what it meant, how enormous the danger was, how many plans must go by the board. By midday most people, I think, had a slightly sick feeling in the pit of their stomachs, with sudden visions reviving — after so many quiet months — of air-raids and even parachute invasion. Cuthbert Worsley and I discussed it anxiously at lunch; then began to laugh about it and find absurd ideas; by evening with the knowledge that the defence was working, there was a different feeling growing up, a feeling that, well, after all, it was a good thing if we could settle the beastly business this summer once and for all.

Tuesday, 14th

The strain of waiting on events becomes even greater, as the news comes through of the gigantic thrust the Germans are making. . . . It seemed impossible that the spring day in London could be so fresh and quiet and lovely, with death so mercilessly at work only two or three hundred miles away. . . . When one reads of the numbers of tanks and bombers employed the world seems utterly and finally mad. . . . Only here, in Southern England, one can refuse to believe it for just a little longer.

New appointments to the Cabinet come through every few hours. One can make all sorts of criticisms, but the decisive fact seems to be, without question, that a breach has at last been made in the concrete defences of the Old Gang. As the war intensifies, especially if danger becomes greater, can they ever recover the ground they've lost? Then at least it must prove to be the thin end of the wedge — of the power of the people.

Saturday, 18th

Still these glowing spring days, these pure moonlit nights; and still this horrible, gigantic battle on the other side of the Channel, with news that presses on one's brain like the beginning of madness. Leonard, coming up for the day to discuss urgent Hogarth business, tells me at lunch that hospital as well as refugee trains go through all day from the ports in the south. He insists that the news is worse than the papers say, but sticks to his belief that we must win in the end: he agrees that we have only to hold the thing now, and in a few months all the production and power of the Americans will be at our side. . . . But right now, there are moments when it seems like a matter of days, not months.

Friday, 24th

The Germans have taken Boulogne, and England has adopted her own peculiar brand of totalitarianism: these two salient features of the last twenty-four hours, more or less incredible if suggested a year ago, are today simply in the accepted stream of events, and there is not even a trace of hysteria, now that the shock of last week-end has passed. And what a shock it was, with only too many people considering how best they should take their lives if the imminent became the real. . . . Only submerge slowly enough, and you will hardly feel the change from breathing fresh air to the beginnings of drowning. . . . Standing on Maidenhead platform a few days ago, I saw an enormous train of scrap-iron and raw materials roar through westwards, and it seemed a symbol of the new set of men in the control room, men who are at last going to put up a fight, and with the weapons of 1940, not 1914.

Leonard lost his usual and wonderful poise on Wednesday morning after Reynaud's speech. The evening before, when I sat with them late into the night, Virginia and Tom Eliot and William Plomer, we had agreed to avoid the subject, but he had been unnaturally silent; and when we talked the next morning, he seemed overcome.

Saturday, 25th

A letter has arrived from Christopher in Santa Monica, in which he says:

[257]

The news from Europe makes one feel unspeakably wretched — especially as many people here regard it as an exciting football game, in which they would rather like to play. It is strange to live amongst these psychically virgin Californians, with their sound teeth and intact nerves. Partly it is very stimulating; partly it makes you feel lonely. Sometimes I think that I must return to Europe, anyhow, at any price. But I'm afraid I should feel myself just as much of an outcast there. There are few people I could honestly agree with, about this war. You would understand, I think. . . . Believing what I do, there's simply no place for me in existing society — even in the opposition. And, not being a prophet, like Wystan, I can't raise my voice in the wilderness. The way things look now, I shall most likely end up in prison — or, if I'm lucky, the Red Cross. But enough of all this.

Berthold has gone to New York, as you doubtless know, to produce a play by Terence Rattigan — "Grey Farm," or some such name. His departure was a scene of unspeakable excitement and confusion — after all these months of cloistered work and study — like a professor who is suddenly called upon to become Chancellor: a truly Austrian situation. . . . I am alone with the ocean, Gerald Heard and the Metro Lion. The weather is terrific — 94 in the shade — and all the beaches crowded. Money swirls around me like autumn leaves. I pick some of it up and throw it away again — there is really nothing to spend it on; except the books which remind me of England. I have quite a library. All the poets. I long to read Stephen's novel, and hope you'll send it in due course. . . . I saw Zorina the other day. She was wonderfully beautiful. Her face was pale violet. Rooney now looks like Hercules. He is so small you could get him into a large suitcase easily. This studio has just finished "The Mortal Storm" — which will probably be good, but terribly funny, because the nice Germans are played by Americans, and the nasty ones by German refugees. I am just about to start a picture about Chopin, who is to be whitewashed for Robert Donat. Actually, I think he was the most unpleasant of all geniuses. Georges Sand was much too good for him. . . . First line of our picture: "Hullo." Last line: "Let's hope and pray he is." You can guess the rest.

Today I'm on the last lap of *Seven Pillars of Wisdom.* All along, I have been finding it difficult to read (a difficulty increased by the page), but the moment Lawrence stops describing minutiae of movement or landscape, my interest quickens; and for all the strain of his style (the very opposite of what I should like to achieve myself), superb in his account of his own self-questioning, of the highlights of action (the first triumphant bridge demolitions, for instance), and of scenes of glittering colour such as gatherings of chiefs in the desert, of the passage through the Valley of Rumm.

Thursday, 30th

In every street in Bloomsbury one meets men and boys, whose slightly out-of-the-ordinary clothes and looks show them to be Belgian or Dutch refugees. One hears from people back from the south coast that they're pouring across the whole time in fishing smacks, row-boats — any kind of boat.

Every day the battle leaps nearer. Lying awake at night, I'm surprised I can't hear the guns and bombs: for it's as if one of the greatest battles in history were going on as near as Yorkshire. And yet I believe that to most English people the Channel is a magic barrier that makes everything beyond it almost infinitely distant.

How can one's life ever be the same, whatever the outcome of the war, after this slaughter that has been going on for more than a month, a slaughter that's beginning to engulf so many of one's friends? Perhaps it's a good thing that I can only faintly imagine what the trapped men of the British Army are going through; imagination is not a thing to have these days if one means to survive and be sane.

The attack on England must come, and soon, and it will be one of the biggest events in history. I suddenly realize this as a fact, and am no longer shocked.

June 2

And I wake this morning, and am still alive and thirty-three years old, and still in the lush summer peace of the house where I was born. And I think of Toni, and wonder all day where he can be, on this our common birthday, for I am certain that if he's alive he's thinking of me. Is he in Norway? Is he in the advance columns of motor-bicyclists sent into Flanders? Or is he somewhere in Austria, stationed as anti-aircraft gunner, still out of danger, but for how long?

A.L., sitting out in the garden for the first time, smiling and fresh and wonderfully recovered, tells me how often she has thought of him and his family.

I motored over to Ipsden for tea, and found that the emotion of the epic withdrawal from Dunkirk, now reaching its last and most terrible stages, had almost overcome Rosamond. She had come back from Cambridge in a dark state of confused anxiety and depression; but as usual, as we talked, her spirits and gaiety were on the up-curve. She said that her train had passed train-loads of the returning B.E.F., almost every man of them sunk in a stupor of sleep.

Tuesday, June 11

One has tried to prepare oneself during the last few days for severe reverses, even up to the capture of Paris; so Italy's entry into the war did not come as the shock it might have been. And the voice of Roosevelt over the wireless last night, a voice made symbolic by the roaring of the atmospherics, calling out the New World to our aid, was one of the most dramatic and hope-inspiring things I have ever heard.

I have forced myself to get ahead with my book this week. Each day I found it hard to get into it, but the work formed a sort of protective case around me once I was absorbed.

The soldiers from Dunkirk seem to be stirring up a violence of opinion in the country against the Old Men of Munich, that must burst soon: a more effective army of revolutionary agitators, penetrating to the furthest villages, could not be imagined — could not have been organized by the cleverest political party.

Last Friday night: London streets may be quiet nowadays, even in the growing light, but I have never seen such a scene of vigour and high spirits as in the pubs round Victoria way. Pay night, but even so: soldiers and sailors and civilians packed tight, a roar of conversation, animated groups and grins, some singing; and amongst all of them, soldiers deeply sun-tanned back from France, guardsmen still on London duties, sailors from the Low Countries, girls of every age and description, not a trace of despondency.

Saturday, 15th

A letter from John Lepper, now deep in his training up in Nottinghamshire: "We have left our camp, and for the past few weeks have been bivouacing 'somewhere in Lincolnshire,' sleeping in haystacks, barns and open fields. The whole regiment has to be ready at fifteen minutes' notice to rush off and deal with any paratroops who may decide to pay us a visit. Among our many duties is the task of providing a patrol to scour the countryside at night looking for lights flashed by Fifth Columnists. This is facetiously known as 'The Glowworm Patrol.'" He ends up: "Is it possible to obtain a second-hand copy of Garcia Lorca's poems (the recent translation)?"

As the Nazis go on pouring through France — and nothing seems to be able to stop them for long — the constriction of one's heart grows tighter and tighter. It is still possible to believe that not merely this island but also France will survive; but sometimes it's as if one couldn't breathe.

In Brighton to see Beatrix's play again. Her performance more polished even than before, deeply, terribly moving. Lifting the curtain in the morning, the hazy, unbroken expanse of the sea revealed, faintly blue in the rising sun: how impossible to think there's a war on. . . . That across that smiling water, only a few miles away, the Nazi Empire is already established, and Paris opening her gates to the marching columns. . . . Something utterly incredible a year ago.

Saturday, 29th

The end of an extraordinary week of despair and recovery; now, in incredibly few days, people's mood has changed again. In spite of the fact that it becomes clearer and clearer that what has happened in France is a *putsch* by the Right (though obviously the Army was beaten), now that all our troops are home, people's spirits rise: if we die, we shall die in our own fields and near our families and friends, and we need only consider ourselves. All our English obstinacy and xenophobia comes into its own. One gnawing question nevertheless: are there Petains here too, among our own Government ranks?

Sunday, 30th

I saw my Slovak friends, Marina Pauliny and Fedor Hodža (Dr. Hodža's son) again: Fedor had escaped from Paris and Bordeaux, and returned in a Dutch cargo boat, very bitter and disillusioned. I said: But you have no need to worry, your friends the Russians are at your gates, and will always get there first. And they both agreed that from their point of view there might be something in it. Fedor said he thought Russia was going to get Warsaw in the end. He also said he'd been with General Prchala at Czech H.Q., and all the time he'd pointed out how hopeless the position was after the breakthrough.

I begin to see the war in a new light: as an European experience, quite independently of sides and winners, with my Austrian friends for instance in it just as I am in it. And this is in some curious way comforting and strengthening.

One of the most poignant things I have experienced, that brought the war home to me more than anything else, was hearing the French wounded in this country send their messages across the wireless to those at home.

Saturday

London is an extraordinary place in this pause between battles. On the streets and in the pubs you see Canadian, Australian, New Zealand soldiers; French sailors, air-officers, legionnaires; Dutch officers, Norwegian and Dutch sailors; Poles and Czechs. . . . It quickens one's interest and excitement in the moment: it seems almost impossible to contemplate that one should fail them all.

Leonard, up in London for a few days and obviously in a more optimistic mood, produced a wonderful story of Virginia insisting in a stage-whisper that an innocent and embarrassed nun who got into their carriage was a German spy.

Mlle. X comes to see me, with the story of how she joined de Gaulle. It's difficult to get a picture through it all of what's really going on there, but she assures me that at present the movement is "purely military," politics are frowned on, that more and more influential people are rallying to the General, and also that an important French colony has definitely declared its support. She lets slip that de G. used to be associated with the Action Française, though he left it in disgust.

If obscurity reigns there, it is even thicker around the Czech National Committee. I asked Fedor Hodža out to lunch at the Café Royal — I find him more sympathetic each time I meet him — and managed to persuade him to give me some picture of what is going on. It is a gloomy picture, and he is profoundly *déçu*. He asserts (I am still uncertain what part he and his father are really playing) that Beneš and those around him still refuse to make the Committee properly representative, and that the Slovaks are still very badly treated. He accuses Beneš of *idées fixes* and vanity, and fears that the Committee cannot command much respect in the Protectorate itself until it is radically reorganized. He's lenient towards Hacha; and maintains that stories I've heard about Czech officers not commanding the confidence of their men are in many cases true. Finally, he promises me some literary stuff from Czech authors already over here or very soon to arrive.

July 23

Yesterday Fedor brought a young Czech writer, by the name of Mucha, in for a drink. He is now in the Czech forces here: he gave a fascinating account of Paris life just before the end. I asked him about the French writers, and he said: One didn't realize how decadent (!) France really was, a great writer was apt to be respected as a great artist whatever his political past. . . . Malraux was said to be in the south and unmolested. Gide and Mauriac were together at Mauriac's chateau in the south, getting on one another's nerves. Romain Rolland was dying, too ill to care. Giono had formed a party *"de la paix hon-*

teuse" at the last moment. Jules Romains had slipped away to Lisbon with all the PEN Club records. He knew nothing of Chamson, and I fear he may only too easily have been submerged, either at the Front or in the Daladier debacle.

Later in the evening I fell in with some French sailors, both merchant marine and navy. How bitterly they talked of the way their officers had sold them, how lost they seemed, in spite of their determination to *"vaincre ou mourir,"* not knowing what had happened, what would happen to their wives and sweethearts, not certain that the English would play fair with them. One boy from Bordeaux, half-Spanish, was almost in tears as he described how he'd never heard from his girl, whom he'd left in May seven months gone with a baby from him. At one moment he was saying that the English were far more kindly than the French, far less each one out for himself, and the next he was suspecting that the English themselves were torpedoing the shiploads of returning sailors . . . and absolutely certain he could never endure to go back.

Friday, 26th

The supreme lesson of the past seven years, if one has been in the thick of it in one way or another, is that the most difficult and at the same time the most important thing for a writer or artist is to maintain integrity as an artist and to make no concessions where truth is at stake.

A letter from Virginia about her "Leaning Tower" lecture, in which she says:

I handed on your message to Leonard, and we are both very sorry you couldn't come to Monk's House, and that your mother's ill again: please give her my sympathy. We could have offered you a great variety of air-raid alarms, distant bombs, reports by Mrs. Bleach who brought a stirrup pump (installed, needless to say, in my bedroom), of battles out at sea. Indeed it's rather lovely about 2 in the morning to see the lights stalking the Germans over the marshes. But this remains on tap, so you must propose yourself later. And let me know if you want to meet the Major and hear about — what was it? — why the crab walks sideways?

Leonard's tackling Mrs. N. downstairs — showers of confidences and complaints, also children's letters make the room almost uninhabitable, he says; and he's teaching Miss Griffiths how to mark off. I'm quite pleased with the sales of Roger Fry so far — L. is binding more. Don't bother to read it now, but some day I should value your opinion very much. . . . I'd like you to print the Leaning Tower, if I can bring myself to revise it, which I loathe. Also, when would you want it — also, what about America? I mean can I print simultaneously there? But at the moment I can't stop reading Coleridge — thanks to you, I'm lured back to the ancients, and read a William Morris, Chants for Socialists, with immense pleasure. So I can't bring myself to do anything I ought to do. Forgive this long letter.

Friday, August 9

Yesterday I finished my Pelican,* and sent it off to Lane. I find myself hardly able to believe it's been possible to get it done, with invasion and the Rumanian (or Russian?) job still vaguely lurking in the background. And now, I have to admit, the war is sometimes narrowed down for me to the question: will it be published in time? Which is vile, I fear, but natural, I hope.

Monday, August 12

"I couldn't stop laughing," said the grinning young Coldstreamer, recounting his experiences at Dunkirk in broad Yorkshire. "I didn't like seeing the lads popped off, underneath it all I was sorry, of course, but I couldn't stop laughing. I was scared of being killed all right, scared stiff I was, but what the f—— hell, I thought. And when I saw all the lads who'd talked so big pushing me aside on the beach in their hurry to get into the boats, I just couldn't stop laughing." Some day I must try and get down on paper his whole story of how he and thirty others held a barrier on the road, let what seemed to be a refugee car through and were machine-gunned by the occupants immediately afterwards, twenty-seven of them being killed. And how he tried to take some loot — wine-glasses — back for his sister's sideboard, and how it was all blown to pieces . . . and how he couldn't stop laughing through all this. And how the guns of the destroyer made the whole ship quiver and shake, and how that made him laugh too.

A letter from John Sommerfield, now in the R.A.F., in remotest Cumberland:

What is happening about *New Writing?* I do hope that you will manage to carry it on. Let me know will you, and it will be nice to hear from you anyway. The planes themselves are very lovely, and incredibly civilized, but nothing else in this life is.

* *New Writing in Europe* (see p. 282).

September 3, 1940

A year has passed since the beginning of the war: it seems quite extraordinary that I should be sitting out in the garden at Fieldhead, reading my books and fairly at ease. Did one ever imagine one would come to accept so much so quickly? The nightly, daily danger of death from the skies? The defeat and subjugation of beloved France? The whole of Europe ranged against us? And no word, no sign for twelve months from all my friends in Vienna? And the narrowing of the shutter of one's response into accepting the hourly toll of victims and destruction on both sides as the key of one's life? London bombed — Berlin bombed — picking up any day's paper, if one could have had it shown to one two years ago, wouldn't one have thought: No, this can never be, this is too mad? Yet it *is*, and one has been in it, and one goes on — if one is one of the lucky and older like myself — with one's own pursuits — I even go on with *New Writing*.

But the bombing of London hasn't been nice, I won't pretend that, nor will what is still to come be nice. Only one finds one adapts oneself so much more easily than one thought possible. And some instinctive mechanism in oneself prevents one thinking too much of the worst: prevents me remembering Vienna too often — prevents me realizing too logically that I also can be wiped out any day, with so much unfinished and unattempted — prevents me following too far in imagination the lines of destiny of all my many friends in uniform.

Another very odd transformation of war: the young Czech novelist Mucha, sitting in my flat in a private's uniform of the free Czech Army, discussing something to write for *N.W.*; and Fedor at Fieldhead, planning the new Slovakia from this country. How much water has flowed under the bridges since we first met in Bratislava, and yet how natural it already seemed that he should be here and preparing for Den Tag — *Our* Day.

One incident of these air-raid nights sticks in my mind. Alexis had arranged to look in some time during the evening, was delayed by friends and caught by the sirens. Hours passed and still he didn't come; and night came down and the searchlights swept the sky and raiders zoomed like angry blue-bottles overhead. . . . Then it was quiet again, and suddenly down the road in the utter darkness and silence I heard a well-known step and the clicking fingers like castanets for a Spanish dance — and a minute later he arrived in the highest spirits, bursting with news, not of the raid or anything to do with it, but of the Polish Ballet being started.

Sunday, September 8, 1940

Last night (in Wiltshire) Helen was at the canteen and Mounty and I were talking hard together after dinner, when the telephone rang and a military priority call came through — but it turned out to be for the real (and absent) owner of the house. Both of us thought the same thing, but we said nothing; then only a few minutes later the call from the A-Striking Force came through for Mounty. He rushed up to put on his battledress and pack, and I rushed round picking up field-glasses, cigarettes and anything else I could think of for him. In the middle of it a confirming call came through, and then Helen returned from the canteen. We rushed Mounty into the car, splashed some petrol wastefully into the tank by the light of a torch, wished him good luck — and off he went. Directly after, a third confirming call came through. The night was deadly still, no sound of aircraft. It seemed impossible to doubt that something big had begun. When we heard at midnight that gigantic raids were taking place on London, we felt absolutely certain. Yet no church bells had been rung, and the stillness was unbroken. It was an odd feeling, really something impossible to credit, that the enemy was at last at hand, here and now, yet the feeling was more of dramatic excitement than of alarm, or confusion, or even anger.

Later, we heard that church bells *had* been rung in some places in England. . . . But Mounty came back for luncheon, and said the whole thing appeared to have been just a flap.

Wednesday, 11th

I am writing this at Fieldhead, after three of the most extraordinary days of my life. Yesterday I was ordered to evacuate my flat, and came down to Bourne End after looking Beatrix up at her new flat (Julia Strachey's) in Charlotte Street, to make certain she was leaving for the country. She told me the strangest of stories, how she had wandered through London in the early morning, trying to find out what had become of me.

Mecklenburgh Square was a pretty sight when I left it. Broken glass everywhere, half the garden scorched with incendiary bombs, and two houses of Byron Court on the east side nothing but a pile of rubble. Clouds of steam were pouring out of one side, firemen still clambering over it and ambulances and blood-transfusion units standing by with A.R.P. workers and police. The road was filled with a mess of rubble muddied by the firemen's hoses, but the light-grey powder that had covered the bushes at dawn had been washed off by the drizzle. The time-bomb in the Square garden sat in its earth crater, coyly waiting. The tabby Persian cat from No. 40 picked her way daintily and dishevelledly among the splinters of glass on her favourite porch.

The night of Sunday was my first intimate contact with war. What surprised me was not to have been frightened, but to have been frightened so little; also that the actual noise of the bombs exploding was not nearly so bad as I'd expected. At the same time I felt rather ashamed not to be among the A.R.P. workers and firemen: they were really magnificent. . . . I left Salisbury in the afternoon. About 5:30 P.M. the train ran plumb into an air-raid. Blinds down, we went slowly on, then stopped: overhead a battle was going on, with sudden zooms and the rattle of machine-gun fire distinctly audible. People rushed to the windows in spite of all warnings, shouted that they could see the battling machines — but against the dazzling blue I certainly couldn't. Then the all-clear went, and the girl next to me sighed with relief and giggled. We went slowly on, then stopped at a signal outside Clapham Junction. Time dragged on, still we waited there, light began to fade. Passengers began to think of their lost appointments — the soldier of his date in a pub at Gravesend — the little fuzzy man of his work at 9 P.M. — but also of darkness and raids and being caught there. The fuzzy man's fat wife began to show signs of hysteria, the girl of pathetic agitation. Then soldiers began to jump off the train and slip through people's backyards into the road for buses: the old, very irate guard tried to stop them — nothing like it had been known in his fifty years' service with the company — but they went on, and civilians with their luggage began to follow them. At eight o'clock the signal light was still at red against us, though electric trains for London Bridge were still roaring by. I decided to make a dash for London. Luckily a 77 bus stopped only a few yards away, and I packed into it with a young R.N.V.R. officer. Only a few minutes later the inevitable sirens went again — but the bus sped on through the moonlit streets. Over the Thames and up into Kingsway it raced, and still there was no gunfire to be heard: I had an eerie, tense feeling after the week-end reports, eerier still when I jumped off the bus to get to my flat and saw the glow of fires in Holborn. But I got home, and dined off half a bottle of wine and an apple and some chocolate biscuits in my shuttered bedroom. Then I lay down, fully dressed, on my bed, and began to read *Père Goriot*.

I didn't get far. Gunfire began to rumble in the distance, and now it seemed to get nearer, with the persistent, maddening sound of aircraft overhead. Then I could distinguish bombs dropping. Then suddenly three whistling, ripping noises in the air, as if directly overhead, getting closer, and each time violent concussions followed by the sound of tinkling glass. . . . When the noise of the aeroplanes seemed to be getting fainter again, I went to the window and looked out on the Square: I found — underneath the black curtains — that some of my panes had been smashed, incendiary bombs were burning merrily in the garden, and an enormous blaze was developing beyond the Balloon station in the Foundling grounds. My first feeling was: how curious and almost incredible it was that this should have happened so near me. There was no searchlight: when I went downstairs the man from No. 46, who was just getting out of his car, said he thought the searchlight had had it. Then I went to shout to my landlord in the basement shelter, but he only answered sleepily and I left him. I hung about the ground floor for some time, a little dazed, went to the door again and heard the shouts of the A.F.S. men as they tackled the blaze beyond the Balloon site: suddenly it struck me that it looked alarmingly close to Stephen's flat over on the other side. "Well, poor old Stephen's the first to go" — was the odd, sad, resigned thought that went through my mind. A little later, as I was standing by the stairs, there was another tremendous explosion, the house seemed to clench itself like a fist for a moment, then silence. It struck me as strange that I had heard no whizz of a descending bomb, and I went to the door again and peered out: the sight that met my eye was an enormous bellying cloud of grey dust advancing down the road towards me like a living thing, and a man in pyjamas curiously walking across it to his flat. There was dead silence; but it struck me that it might be as well now to go to a shelter. Hardly had I got myself ready when I heard a crowd of people moving out of the garden: I opened the door, and met the man from No. 46 again, now in a tin helmet, who said there was an unexploded time-bomb in the garden and they were evacuating the shelter there, also that the houses on our side had rocked badly — he advised me to go. When I turned round I thought part of Byron Court looked rather odd: it was only a few seconds later that I realized I was looking at a tree beyond — Byron Court had simply been blown to bits.

As I passed it on the way to the shelter, the presence of death and murder seemed very vivid to me, to fill the atmosphere, as a thing now at last *perceived* in this war behind "the furious words" and all the stories I'd heard. The Guildford Street fire was still very violent, but seemed to be more under control, there was a red haze away in the direction of the City — but our searchlight sword was striking across the sky again.

And in the shelter: the hours passed by and one longed for the dawn, knowing the Nazis would retreat from it and our ascending daylight fighters. I sat on a step, scarcely under shelter, and talked to an A.T.S. girl in uniform, on and on. Girls lay sleeping clasped by their young husbands, women and children were down below, someone produced a Dostoevsky novel, a group of young women huddled in an angle of the stairs with what looked like powdered hair — but they had just been rescued from the ruins of Byron Court and it was rubble dust. Then more bombs whistled by — and the banging of the lavatory door sounded like bombs too — incendiaries were dropped outside — a warden came in and whispered to us that a flare had been dropped. . . . At last, in the grey light of morning, the all-clear went.

Sunday, September 15, at Fieldhead

It is nearly three o'clock, and an air-raid warning has just gone. Each time it goes now, one can't help wondering whether it's the prelude to the so long threatened, so long delayed invasion. The A.R.P. workers and their ambulances are gathering below, and the sky is overcast with rainy clouds. When the warning went, I began to think of my friends, waiting at their posts scattered over England. There's a feeling that if it were to come now probably the whole war would be decided one way or the other, and that's a good thing; and also a feeling that vies with it, that if only this winter the war would shift to the East, one would be ready for anything next spring.

But this is the epoch of surprises, of bombs that crash not merely through ancient buildings, but carefully built-up systems of thought and belief.

And now the all-clear has gone again.

On Thursday I went back to London to try and get back to my flat, but in vain: it was still cordoned off. I met Willy Goldman, who told me that what the East End had been through was indescribable: he had been down himself and seen the ruins of Stepney and Commercial Road, and knew several people who had been killed; there was scarcely a Jewish family that hadn't lost someone. Then I suddenly met Stephen with Peter Watson and Cyril C., who came up later; it was a relief, after my fears, to see Stephen as well and as wild-looking as ever. They told us nothing had been spoilt in the flat except one pane of glass — a miracle, considering how close the bomb and the fire had been. Both Stephen and Willy said the terrific new A.A. barrage the night before had put astonishing heart into people. I think we were all wondering how much of London would soon be left standing.

Up on Friday again: a far worse day, which showed that low clouds — we were all longing for the weather to change — gave the raiders a devilish chance to dodge and make a nuisance of themselves. The first air-raid warning started while the train was waiting outside Paddington, and it didn't finish till after lunch. All that time, intermittently, you could hear aeroplanes overhead, occasional crashes of bombs or bursts of A.A. fire, and suddenly catch a glimpse of a bomber as the clouds parted, sailing cool and high overhead. In spite of all official threats, people just stayed in the Underground stations, piled up with their newspapers against the walls: the dislocation of ordinary life seemed complete. In the middle of it I met L.S.W. and Virginia wandering along Guildford Street in their car after a fantastic journey from Rodmell. Leonard rather agitated with the confusion of everything, also in a mood of rather unhelpful bravado that slightly annoyed me when we were discussing plans for starting up the wheels of the Hogarth Press again. Virginia very smiling and apparently collected, the only gesture she allowed herself being later on; while we were viewing the Mecklenburgh Square damage from afar, she touched Leonard's arm and said quietly: "Leo, there are aeroplanes overhead, don't you think we'd better take cover?"

The worst was in the afternoon. I was about to round off my day by a quick visit to Charlotte Street, to see if I could get in and inspect the rooms below Beatrix's. There had been no air-raid warning; there was no sound of aeroplane engines; but suddenly, directly ahead of us, three screeching noises from the clouds and bombs burst — it can't have been more than twenty-five yards away in Howland Street. Window glass flew splintering in all directions; dense black smoke arose covering the whole area of the hits; people ran in all directions and the trolley buses piled up against one another; my taxi skidded violently from side to side and then drew up in a side-street. The astonishing thing was that in that side-street people were gazing quietly and curiously out of their doors to see what was happening. . . . After wandering, slightly dazed, in search of a shelter, I finally jumped into another taxi and made for Paddington. The sirens, incidentally, went about one minute after the attack was made.

Later, on reaching home, I discovered that Beatrix had by chance been in town and had an equally nasty experience at the same moment in the Euston Road. She rang up from Rosamond's, rather shaken.

September 19

A couple of days ago, when we were at last let into M. Square, we found that the exploding of the time-bomb had caused further damage, smashing the Hogarth's windows and bringing down part of the ceiling of the basement front room. Everything was covered with dust and plaster and splinters; Miss P. and I went round collecting things, dusting and sorting, while more sirens wailed outside. My flat has a chalk cross on the door to mark it unsafe — I thought of the Plague Year — but I got in, and found that though the shutter fasteners had been split and more front windows broken, there was no other damage. Yet it was uninhabitable, like the Press: and I suddenly felt very sad, standing by the windows and looking out on the ruin of the lovely old Square — and what had been for me a happy life there.

« 6 »

THE plan that Leonard and I discussed after the bombing of Mecklenburgh Square — we had had it in mind for some time — was to remove the operations of the Hogarth Press to our chief printers, the Garden City Press in Letchworth, a town which seemed an adequate distance out of London and not likely to be a target for a bomb. I therefore arranged to have the minimum of necessary files put on to the van, and went down to supervise the move-in.

The plan I eventually adopted, and kept to for the next six months with some regularity, was to spend two or three nights in the middle of each week in Cambridge, forty minutes further down the line, stop off in London with a friend or at the Athenaeum for one night going and one or two nights returning, and make my base and week-end refuge at Fieldhead. This may sound complicated, but it worked extraordinarily well and gave me the agreeable opportunity to renew friendships in Cambridge and get to know what the undergraduates were thinking and writing.

Thus were the bounds of my wartime world drawn, though I did not then foresee how constant they were to remain, and for how long. As, by a piece of luck, my lease of the Mecklenburgh Square flat only ran to the end of September, I decided to evacuate it at once and take

my books and furniture down to Fieldhead, as soon as I had removed
the Hogarth Press to Letchworth. I shall never forget the faces of the
removal men. They had, I suppose, been at work without pause and
probably with little or no sleep ever since the raids started, ignoring
sirens and bombs and making as much haste as they could through
cordoned-off roads that changed every day: they had the trance-like
expression of utter exhaustion as they went mechanically through the
movements of packing and loading. I have always thought they were
among the unremembered heroes of the blitz. I felt ashamed to hurry
them, though I was that morning acutely conscious of the vulnerabil-
ity of human chattels and human bodies, having been caught in my
bath at the top of the Athenaeum by an unexpected raid and violent
barrage, with the prospect, so I pictured it, of cascading naked in a
torrent of soap-suds down the grand staircase if the august building
were hit. I wondered whether Air-Marshal Joubert, a familiar imperturbable figure in the Club at this time, would even have lifted his
head from *The Times* as this fleshly bomb landed in front of him.
Only a week later clubland *was* hit, and it was with a shocked sense
that this time the Nazis had definitely gone too far, that I arrived at
the Athenaeum to find the liveried staff sweeping away debris while
disconcerted bishops stepped as delicately as cats over the litter of
broken glass.

It was a relief to unpack everything into the comparative calm and
shelter of Fieldhead. I considered myself remarkably lucky not to have
lost anything, luckier still as the months went by and the casualties to
my friends' dwellings mounted, while many who had managed to send
everything they possessed overseas had scarcely ceased to congratulate
themselves before they heard that a torpedo had sent the lot to the
bottom of the ocean.

Days of perfect early autumn weather succeeded one another in the
valley: the skies were clear, there was an idyllic stillness among the
yellowing leaves and on the glassy water, a fresh sweet tang in the air
and a faint mist that never entirely cleared. The memory of bombed
London might have faded in such surroundings, if this very beauty
had not turned to treachery every night. The moon, that "lucid friend
to aerial raiders, the brilliant pilot moon," was bringing the bombers
overhead every night, and as the sirens went my mother's Pekinese,
who had acquired air-raid sense with astonishing speed, jumped up to
lead the procession to the old wine-cellar. One night a stick of bombs
fell a mile or two down-river near Cookham gasworks, and the rever-
berations in the valley made it sound as if they had fallen in our

kitchen garden. I dressed and ran out, and saw one of the raiders drop a flare, so pretty in the moonlight that one could not believe it signalled danger: softly it floated down, while the only noise that now disturbed the night was the familiar roar and clanking of the mill away in Cores End, so loud in the dead hush that I thought at first there had been an accident there.

One week-end Cuthbert Worsley came down to rest from the air-raids. We took a walk that has always remained in my mind: down through the rain-softened garden, heavy with ripe apples and already looking a little untidy-autumnal with the ragged dahlias flopping over the beds and the leaves scattered over the lawn, and along the river, basking in the late September sun, to Marlow Island. We were both under the feeling, half-melancholy, half-exhilarating, that the events of the past few weeks had marked a great divide between our lives as they had been and as the war would now shape them. Our friends across the Atlantic, Christopher and Wystan and others, seemed to have grown far more remote, as if they had suddenly gone out of hearing; and the old days of the Spanish War and the early enthusiasms of *New Writing* seemed to have become at last definitively the past. We talked of the shape of society after the war, and the spiritual thinness of politics and political slogans; of the need for a total reassessment, a new kind of philosophy evolving from artistic and religious experience; everything, both within and without, seemed at the beginning of a great transformation scene.

One result of my spending week-ends at Fieldhead was that I began to take a more active part in the local Home Guard, which I had joined in the summer while the L.D.V.s were being formed. My responsibilities consisted in little more than parading on Sunday mornings, with instruction in the fantastic spigot mortar which was supposed to lob grenades at the advancing tanks of the invaders, but was so primitive and slow — so it seemed to me — that it would have been spotted and smashed to pieces by a tank's guns long before it could have taken a second aim. There were also guard duties on Sunday or Monday nights to fit in with my week-end routine. Absurd it all may seem in retrospect; but we were, in fact, an essential part of the delaying tactics envisaged if the enemy actually were to land in England, and we were uneasily conscious at the back of our minds that, with our totally inadequate equipment, there would be precious few survivors if the Nazi armour were to thrust up from the west, in spite of concrete road blocks and gun-emplacements disguised as cow-byres and pig-sties. The guards were generally mounted at the H.Q. in a little converted shop between the local branch of Lloyds Bank and the cinema. I took a volume of poems or a novel by Conrad with me, but there was little chance of either reading or sleep with the electric light and the electric fire blazing and the local characters gossiping and arguing away without pause. I learnt, however, a great deal about the village that would hardly have come my way through any other activity. Cars and motor-bikes and radios and the various ways of growing vegetables were exhaustively discussed by the carpenter, the plumber, the builder and the owner of the sweet-shop down the road, but the fortunes of the war and political alignments scarcely ever. Lying wrapped up in an army blanket on the floor, I would listen with innocent amazement to dramatic details of the more intimate side of village life that had been shrewdly and silently observed by the carpenter or builder in the course of their work; I began to wonder with a slightly anxious amusement how much they had noted of our own family life at Fieldhead through the years, while mending bell-wires or painting window-frames with apparently total absorption in their work. Gradually, the quiet, humdrum respectable façade of the neighbourhood dropped away, and I had glimpses of violent passions working to tragic ends in boat-houses, appalling vices flourishing on the further side of cabbage-patches, reckless ambitions thwarted in diabolical intrigues behind ribbon counters, and innumerable fantastic evasions of the law: one of the village mechanics confessed to having a secret bootlegging tobacco farm, on which he grew Virginian, Turkish and Egyptian varieties of the leaf and smoked the raw, exotic products in cellar orgies with a few chosen confederates. Sometimes, too, I was detailed for guard duty on the railway bridge with a young locomotive fireman: I remember how one still, moonlit night, the river smooth as a looking-glass reflecting the softly irradiated sky through a sleeper's open window, the drone of aircraft passing far overhead rose and fell in regular rhythm for several hours, though no siren sounded: in the morning we learnt of the destruction of Coventry.

« 7 »

MEANWHILE, during these months of tension and violence, an event of some importance had taken place in my career as editor. One day, in the fatal May of 1940, I received a letter from Allen Lane asking if I would be interested to follow up my Pelican *New Writing in Europe* with a selection of the best contributions from *New Writing* for the Penguin series. I immediately saw the possibilities in this suggestion for reviving the influence and usefulness of *New Writing*. I wrote back enthusiastically agreeing, and at the beginning of June, Lane informed me that his Editorial Committee were keen to back the idea and that he would come and see me about it. The following Wednesday he arrived in my office in Mecklenburgh Square, very much on top of the wave, announcing that the sales of the Penguins were steadily increasing, that he had confidence they would go on increasing even if the war got worse, and that he had a scheme for opening an office in Canada — just in case. His sanguine mood made our discussions extremely harmonious, and the very next day a draft contract was sent off to me. I had persuaded him that I could as easily produce two selections as one, out of the abundant riches of the old volumes of *New Writing*, and by the time the contract arrived I had already sketched out a provisional contents-list for both of them. The selections pleased him, and I had little more to do than write to the authors and explain the terms that Lane was offering them. All agreed, and a few weeks later all the MSS., with my own introduction and brief history of *New Writing*, were in the printer's hands.

The publication of the first volume was fixed for the first week in November. I had been anxious, in the early summer, to work on the selections as fast as possible, partly from fear that the threatened invasion would begin and the Penguins be forced to take wing for Canada, partly because it seemed likely that one of the war jobs I had been discussing with the authorities would materialize and I would have to go abroad any moment. "Perhaps," observed Julia Strachey in a letter to me at this time, "even as I write you will be sitting with your curly Balkan hat on, upon the hotel terrace at Sarajevo." But as the months went by and the Battle of Britain was won, and the mooted job and the curly Balkan hat receded even further into improbability, and the bombardments by night took the place of the battles by day, one began to anticipate a long period of siege and staying put. At the beginning of October, an idea that Allen Lane had put into my head during a conversation in which he had talked of the possibility of Penguin Books sponsoring a monthly magazine, suddenly crystallized. Why shouldn't the Penguin selections from *New Writing* be continued? Why shouldn't they appear monthly, with half of each number entirely *new* material — stories, poems, articles about books, and discussions?

I wrote off to Lane at once, and was happily surprised to get an immediate answer telling me to go ahead with the scheme as fast as I liked. The details were settled with what — considering the difficulties that were cropping up on all sides from the intensification of the attack on Britain — seems to me now incredible speed, and a new contract for six numbers of a monthly *Penguin New Writing* was signed by the end of October.

This was a signal that I felt I had long been waiting for without being entirely aware of it. The book volumes of *New Writing* had never been read as widely as I would have liked, and I believed that in its sixpenny format it would carry its message to thousands who had never heard of it before but in whose minds, especially in the revolutionary circumstances of the war, it would almost certainly strike a responsive chord. First of all, however, its contents had to be redesigned to make it more of a monthly, and to allow space for several regular features it seemed to me the times demanded. I set to work with an elation I had not known since the early days at the Hogarth Press: the new venture occupied most of my thoughts on my continual train-journeys, on walks by the Thames and along the Backs at Cambridge, and I discussed it at every opportunity with the friends who had been closest to me in the old days of *New Writing*. I think the air-raids and the appalling precariousness of the country's situation would have shaken me much more deeply if my hopeful schemes had not dominated my mind. I began by writing a series of letters to the contributors I valued most, such as George Orwell, V. S. Pritchett, Tom Hopkinson, William Plomer and the poets, telling them what was planned and asking them not to sign away any second serial rights in their old contributions without letting me know. (I had heard that several commercial magazines, in the dearth of new stories at the time, had been carefully scanning the files of *New Writing* for material they could use.) At the same time I reminded them how anxious I was to have new contributions from them. George Orwell I had already written to about this, and received a self-revelatory reply from him in July:

I am very sorry I have written nothing for you after promising I would. I began something, then the war began to get serious. I just can't write with this kind of thing going on. I have written nothing except book reviews etc. for a long time past, and also my time has been rather filled up with helping with the L.D.V. What is so terrible about this kind of situation is to be able to do nothing. The gov't won't use me in any capacity, not even a clerk, and I have failed to get into the army because of my lungs. It is a terrible thing to feel oneself useless and at the same time on every side to see halfwits and profascists filling important jobs. However, things *are* moving a little. I was informed at the W.O. that it is no longer held against a man to have fought in the Spanish Civil War. Of course you can use the elephant sketch again if you like. Two guineas would be very handsome. As to the photo referred to in your other letter, does it have to be a real portrait or will a snap do? I don't photograph well as a rule. . . . I have been living in London because I am now doing theatre criticism for *Time and Tide*.

The reply I had from Victor Pritchett put me in good heart:

A monthly issue is just the sort of thing that ought to catch on [he wrote to me at the beginning of November]. I imagine the shortage of creative writing will gradually go as we adjust ourselves to the war. The blitz has been a good thing in a way, because it is decisive in making everyone part of the war. One of the difficulties I have felt in writing is that I had the feeling of writing against the current of events. However the past despondency caused by the blitz seems to have passed; so it appears to me when I go to London. I don't even react with great horror when lovely things are destroyed, for the house-breakers in the last twenty years destroyed far more beautiful things for loathely profit than the blitz has done. At any rate, though often sick with disgust and gloomy with forebodings, I think the paralysis of the last years is passing. One *feels*. I had felt nothing for a year, had been a mere telegraph exchange for ubiquitous anxiety. I say all this with caution. One can only observe day by day.

One of the first people I approached was Stephen Spender, who was teaching at a school in Devon at the time, and had had some difference with the other editors of *Horizon* which made me feel it might be possible to enrol him as a regular contributor to *Penguin New Writing*. After some thought, I had chosen him as the first person to ask to do the monthly article about books, which I envisaged as an essential feature: my idea was that it should not be the usual "middle" about books in general, though current books would occasionally be reviewed in it, but rather a continuing discussion on the relations between literature (and the other arts) and life, especially those aspects which the war made to seem so important. I believed that such a series of articles could provide food for the thoughts that were stirring — as I had already discovered — in the minds of innumerable people who had hardly taken literature seriously before, or felt any need to go to the great poets and novelists for answers to the problems that now obsessed them, and at the same time could be valuable and interesting for the highbrows and professionals; and I believed that Stephen was one of the few writers of our generation who could undertake them successfully. I found him very eager to tackle the job, and after some discussions with Cyril Connolly and Peter Watson, in which a frontier line was drawn between the work he would do for *Penguin New Writing* and the work he would after all continue to do for *Horizon*, he agreed.

Another feature, which the manuscripts that had recently been coming in for *Folios of New Writing* made me believe might answer a growing need, was a series of articles, part reportage, part story, based on personal experiences of people plunged into new circumstances by the upheavals of the war. For this, which I decided to call *The Way We Live Now*, I wrote to several of my old contributors; but as the war went on my "hunch" proved right and contributions arrived increasingly from quite unknown writers. Indeed a great many of the first-person-singular war stories that we published without including them in the series would have suited it almost as well. And to balance these, I felt I needed fairly regular, rather personal stories that came out of the deep exploration of the past that so many people had found, since the war broke out, gave meaning and spiritual fortification to the dissolving present. My sister Rosamond's perfectly evoked story *The Red-Haired Miss Daintreys* had been so warmly received when I published it in *Folios*, was to me so exactly what I had in mind at its best, that I persuaded her to write several more stories for the Penguin in the same vein. Each story was a difficult birth, Rosamond being one of those complex imaginative artists whose whole creative being wilts at the merest hint of the regular production-line obligations of the journalist, as surely as a dahlia at the first touch of frost; but I was rewarded for my persistence, and more than adequately consoled for the disfavour I frequently found myself in as merciless editorial slave-master, by the eventual appearance of those beautiful stories *When the Waters Came*, *A Dream of Winter*, *The Gypsy's Baby* and *Wonderful Holidays*, which were at a later date collected in one volume with *The Red-Haired Miss Daintreys*.

It was very soon clear that Rosamond's methods of work would not allow her to produce one a month, as originally projected, and I realized that I could not count on these contributions coming very frequently. In order, therefore, to be certain of being able to strike this note fairly regularly — for the confusions of the war made me feel it vital to plan well ahead — I took a step for which I was sharply criticized on some sides, though I never regretted it myself, as it led to an unexpected and exciting discovery. I had been an eager admirer of Dylan Thomas's early poems, but rather less so of those (with certain outstanding exceptions) which had followed them, as their obscurity and over-elaboration seemed to me to be leading him into a cul-de-sac; when, however, I received *Portrait of the Artist as a Young Dog* to review for *Tribune*, I realized with a shock of delight that Dylan was a wonderful prose artist as well as poet. I wrote at once to ask him whether he was at work on any more stories or sketches such as he had included in the *Portrait*. He wrote back:

I'll be very glad to be a contributor to the Penguin *New Writing*. Thank you for writing. I haven't finished any new stories yet, but I hope I will have by the time you've finished the publishing details.

I'm glad you liked my *Portrait of the Artist as a Young Dog*. I'm going to start soon to write a continuation of it: one long story about London.

The months passed, however, and no new stories appeared. I therefore thought of another plan. I knew from conversations with Dick Church (whose persistent advocacy and encouragement of Dylan's work can never be praised too highly) that sales were small and that these stories of genius were not reaching the public I felt was there for them. So it was that I suggested to Dylan and his publishers that I should reprint some of the stories from the *Portrait* in *Penguin New Writing;* at the same time I urged him to let me see as much as he had written of the new long story as soon as possible. He wrote back from Bishopston at the beginning of March 1941:

Thank you for writing, and for wanting to know about my new book. I'm afraid I haven't got anything much of it done; I'm still looking for somewhere to live on extremely little — do you know of anywhere? — and have been so homeless and penniless and uncertain lately that I've only been able to write little bits of the story; I hope very soon to find a place to live in, really to live in for perhaps even two months, and then I can get it going. I'll let you know as soon as there's enough to print. I'm very glad you want it for *New Writing*. Staying, on sufferance, with parents and unfortunate friends, wanting to get away but quite unable, it's hard, I find, to settle to writing anything continuous.

And I'm very glad that you want to print some of the stories from *Portrait of the Artist as a Young Dog*. I wish I had sent some of them to you in the first place. I'd like, a lot, to see them come out in *New Writing*. Will you let me know which ones you're thinking of printing? I'm sure Dent won't raise any objection. The book sold hardly at all. Three or four hundred copies, I think. And if Dent do agree, any chance of a few quid soon?

I don't know when I'll be in town next, but I'll drop a line to Athenaeum Court when I do come. I'd like to see you.

After a good deal of coaxing, I managed to persuade him to let me see the sections of the "long story about London" which he had finished, and to which he had tentatively given the title of *Adventures in the Skin Trade*. I was enchanted with them when they came: they seemed to me to promise an entirely original work, with an unique mixture of humour and fantasy, and a strong vein of Dylanesque poetry running through it. How freshly it read, how alive it was compared with some of the more earnest "reports on war experience," authentic though they might be, that were beginning to come into the *New Writing* office at the time. I was a little worried that some of the passages in the version he showed me might be thought by a printer to be too obscene, but I decided to print the opening section at once in *Folios of New Writing*: it appeared in the autumn 1941 volume as *A Fine Beginning*. And from that moment I decided to make it one of my main objectives to get Dylan to finish it. If only he could be assured of a small regular income, he said, the thing was in the bag. I therefore agreed to pay him a few pounds every week. And every week we met in a Shepherd Market pub, Dylan generally bringing with him a silent, good-looking young man in a London Irish kilt who seemed to be assuming the office of personal body-guard; and to the accompaniment of drinks, general gaiety and many vivid descriptions of how the work was progressing, the notes were handed over. The work, however, did *not* progress; I began to realize that Dylan was treating all my cajolings and homilies as a huge joke (to which I was privy), and that while he was getting more deeply involved in war work or scripts for documentary films, the writing of *Adventures in the Skin Trade* was running down like a clockwork toy. Or was it that the experiences of the blitz made him feel it impossible to carry on with this innocent vision of a pre-war London? Gradually our meetings grew rarer. Eventually my letters remained without an answer. I deeply regretted this, not only for the loss of *Adventures in the Skin Trade* but also because it put a spoke of embarrassment into our relationship for many years, during which I should only have been too happy to publish his poems.

That was all in the future. Meanwhile, I felt that another feature was necessary: something in rather lighter vein, part commentary on the war scene, but allowing full play for fantasy, humour and imagination. I first of all turned to William Plomer, whose descriptions, in

conversation, of people he had come across and remarks he had overheard since the beginning of the war had delighted me with their feeling for the touching and the eccentric, their humour and their sharp
observation of basic traits of the national character revealing themselves under stress of war. I suggested to him that he should write a
series of articles in a form loose enough to admit any of these stories,
any moral he wished to draw and any satire on England-under-
bombardment he wished to indulge in. He finally agreed to this suggestion, but proposed that as he was now a (temporary) civil servant
in an important Service Ministry, he should write them under the
pseudonym of Robert Pagan. The secret was, I believe, well kept, and
only an extremely small handful of intimates and initiates were told or
guessed who the real author of the articles was. Even in our correspondence we kept up the pretence: I was always urging William to
tell Bob Pagan that I was in a hurry for his next article, and William
reported that Bob had just had a new idea, and did I think it was
suited to the odd fellow's talents, etc. All the new series started in No.
2, William's very gaily with *You Must Have Two Hats*, a satire on
civil service bureaucracy and a tongue-in-the-cheek defence of anar-
chism, which struck, in my opinion, exactly the right note to prevent
Penguin New Writing falling into the sins of gloomy routine bitterness and the over-earnest attitudes of may-light-break-through-our-
darkness. The Pagan contributions were extremely varied, evocations
of the past and reminiscences of childhood as well as vivid glimpses of
the extraordinary present, but through them all ran the sense of living
in a revolution that gave them a kind of unity and common perspective. Looking back on them, I see that one might have thought *A Dodo
in Every Bus*, for instance, to have been written by a spirited new
writer who knew how to grind an axe without losing his sense of humour, but I find it almost impossible to understand how anyone who
had rejoiced in the unique Plomer touch in the past failed to spot it in,
say, *Happy Days* or *Pas Avant*.

At the same time, I wanted another lighter feature, something in a
purely fantastic vein. I hit on the idea of asking George Stonier. He
immediately created the mask of "Fanfarlo," and a whole world of imaginary blitz-bound London characters began to take shape in his
mind with astonishing speed. To treat the bombardment as something
inconvenient but somehow absurd, a settled background for inconse-
quential comedy, was too sophisticated for certain minds, and no
doubt would have been incomprehensible to the young Teutons up
aloft who were the cause of it all, but it just suited a mood of the time.

Re-reading the sketches in the volume in which they were eventually collected, it seems to me that they continue to exist in their own right, preserved from the fate of most of even the best topical journalism by their qualities of wit and style.

While these preparations for the monthly were going forward, I was correcting the page proofs of my Pelican *New Writing in Europe*. This had been commissioned at the beginning of January, long before even the first *Penguin New Writing* had been conceived, but as it took me some months to write, it appeared at the turn of the year, at the same time as No. 2, the first of the monthly series; a useful conjunction, but not part of a wicked commercial plan to boost the new series, as some hostile critics immediately imagined.

New Writing in Europe was an attempt to give a bird's-eye view of the whole new movement that had grown up in the 'thirties, to analyse the impulses that had set it in motion, and to suggest what might happen to it after the disillusionments of 1939. Parts of it seem to me now absurdly simplified, some authors, inevitably, over-estimated, some misinterpreted or unfairly neglected; but there are many passages that I would not want to change now, except in the shift of emphasis that must occur as an author's *oeuvre* reveals itself more completely. For some years I continued to receive letters about it which showed in a most interesting way the varying reflections that such a history of a movement can stimulate in the minds of those who took part in it, or observed it at fairly close quarters: I felt that I had helped them to clarify their judgement while trying to get my own clear, and reading their letters my understanding was in its turn deepened, my judgement slightly altered. One of the first and one of the most entertaining that reached me was from V. S. Pritchett:

I've just been reading the Pelican, a most gratifying book. You have made the 30's blush with pleasure. . . . It's hard to imagine what will become of the poets but I suppose the future has always been their enemy, which only a few have surmounted. Prose writers rise and fall like the waves of the sea; unless some catastrophe or aberration strikes one, one goes on like a cork on the waves, sometimes in a trough, sometimes on a crest, but still going on. Of course I suppose poets go on too — Sturge Moore sturged more and more as the years went by — but prose writers do not have to suffer so much from the contempt of the public. Poets, like sopranos, are supposed never to sing flat. I'm on the outside of the Auden-Spencer family circle, and am not racked by its inner ecstasies and storms. Among them I feel like some coarse taxi-driver who has picked up a lot of eccentric fares who are all going to different places. This letter is going to be full of similes and there must be one more. You, I see as a sort of Simon Legree of letters, the slave-master, whip in hand, who drives us all to work with an air both flattering and threatening. Editors must threaten. I don't know how you manage your own writing — do you threaten yourself?

But seriously, I've been glad to be published by *New Writing*. No one else would publish me consistently and the idea of belonging to a "generation" or "school" has been very helpful to me. Being a few years older than most of the *New Writing* contributors I was too young for the war lot, and was quite homeless and isolated as a writer. Something has crystallized in *New Writing*. I loved the photographs. Wm. Plomer was frightening. There was a real writer at work, pen in hand, paper, blotter and desk. But what a fraud — for he never writes! — I thought.

Another letter which I valued particularly, full of sound criticism of "proletarian" writing as it had been practised in the 'thirties, came from E. M. Forster, who had from the beginning shown a sympathetic interest in *New Writing:*

It struck me as a real clearing up of the matter for the benefit of some future chronicler of the decade, or indeed for yourself if you take on that job sometime, and you are well qualified to do this. And it also helped to clear up *me*, and I now see better than last week where I stand in relation to all this left-wing stuff. I'm very glad the relation isn't a remote one, and I thank you very much for what you say about me. My difficulty with working-class writers is that they don't make the working-class come alive — Leslie Halward is an exception. . . . They give one information as they give their comrades gratification, but that's all: gloom, indignation, aspiration in plenty, and plenty of stains on the table-cloth and coal-dust in the milk — but no living beings to experience them. Consequently I find a lot of what you have (very rightly) published dull. Or put it another way: I find that we middle-class do demand that people in fiction should seem to be alive, and I realize too that this demand may not be as important as I think, and that there may be a fiction I am not conditioned to appreciate, in which Ted at the table, Ed in the mine and Bert at the works need not be differentiated. But I can't look at them in that way myself, and the working-class people I know don't seem so to look at them either, though their judgements are different from mine because it is more important to them than to me whether a man has money or not.

What's so good — among other things — is the way you relate the literature to the heaving political background. In connection with this, Christopher's *The Lost* stands out as it didn't before. Something lost for us, I fear, no one'll ever mirror the whole flux now — it's splashed too much of the mirror. A certain awareness (nice word, yes) is possible, though, and you help one to exercise it.

[283]

Many small points occur to me. Auden and Wm. Plomer are the poets I like best, and I particularly like what Auden wrote in the China book, which I think you don't mention. . . . Don't Marx and Engels like Balzac because he gives them so much material appropriate to a decaying society? — A section needed on the Conference spirit? — the only sort of literary life these new little international authors had access to. I wish I had been to more conferences. They were very strange things.

You'll make me read some new people — particularly J. Gibbon whose letter was splendid. Also John Lepper, who wrote very kindly to me once. . . .

In connection with this little book, the old row about Auden and Isherwood blew up again in an unexpected way. Sir Hugh Walpole was at that time writing regular literary reviews for the *Daily Sketch*, which had considerable influence with the reading public. Hugh had always prided himself on showing a generous sympathy towards the young, and had before the war written many appreciative reviews of *New Writing* and the authors who were associated with it. He could not, however, stomach the absence of Wystan and Christopher in America, and when *New Writing in Europe* came out he wrote in the *Daily Sketch:*

This is a wonderfully compact summary, generous and appreciative, and I feel that it is ungrateful to criticize it. But the harsh fact is that time relentlessly moves on. The leaders of John Lehmann's *New Writing* are no longer new at all. The leaders are all well over thirty. They are already old-fashioned. There is a new generation of new writing, and it disregards Auden, Isherwood, and the others altogether. The fact is that this war has, at one stroke, deprived most of Lehmann's "New Writers" of their contemporaneity. They belong to an earlier age, with their pessimism, their cynicism, their apprehensions, their despair. After Dunkirk new poets were born.

I had sent him a copy of the book, and at the same time as the review appeared Hugh wrote me a letter in which he said:

I'm afraid you will be cross with me after yesterday's *Sketch* but I have to write what I feel. I don't think you realize the harm done by Auden, Isherwood, MacNeice fleeing to America. I'm not blaming them but it has *killed* their influence here. The men you write of seem to me to belong in the main to the Spanish War. The young writers of this war have an outlook quite different. Anyway that's what I feel.

It was clear to me that what stuck in Hugh's gullet was the famous imaginary "flight" to America. He was determined to prove that the three writers (and the rest of their "group" as well) were old-fashioned, dead, without influence, because he didn't like what he fancied they'd done. The new poets who were born "after Dunkirk" — only six months back — were a fiction of Hugh's imagination. Perhaps it was a pity that there were no rousing backs-to-the-wall singers in England, but the more interesting young poets who had appeared since the beginning of the war showed no signs of filling the role: too many, for one thing, were deeply absorbed in what Auden had been doing. I wrote and told Hugh what I thought, and suggested that he was a little premature in sketching the poetic character of the 'forties in such bold outlines. (If he had lived to see that character emerge he would have been truly dismayed; and fancy boggles at what he would have made of Wystan's triumphant return fifteen years later as Oxford Professor of Poetry.) I also said I would not go over the whole dreary question of whether Wystan and Christopher did actually "flee" again, but pointed out that Louis MacNeice was in fact back in England, as he had always intimated that he would be.

I remembered that a year before I had had a long talk with Hugh in his Piccadilly flat, where every inch of wall-space in all the rooms was covered with exquisite water-colours and drawings, a large number of them precious Old Master sketches of the male figure. He had been at his most amiable, and full of compliments for *New Writing*, but extremely indignant about the "flight." I had tried to persuade him then that he was being unfair to Wystan and Christopher, whom he had always admired and liked personally. I could, however, see from this correspondence that my attempt to put the other side of the argument had been in vain: he had sensed, I am inclined to think, that I, too, bitterly regretted their absence, and believed that it would be a loss as much to them as to ourselves that they should not experience what we were experiencing — what we were going to experience; and took the rest of my attempted justification as loyalty to friends. I never saw him again.

By the time No. 2 of the *Penguin New Writing* came out, in the new year of 1941, the first number had already had a startlingly swift success — and that was before the real wartime run on books began. By the end of March two printings had been sold out, making 80,000 copies in all; and Nos. 2 and 3, the first two of the re-planned monthly series, had also exhausted their first printings of 55,000 each. Allen Lane was as jubilant as I was, having found that what he had originally envisaged to some extent as a "prestige" publication was in fact making him a profit. Very soon he agreed to increase the advances to me, so that I could pay out more money to the contributors and engage a regular reader to help with the ever-rising flood of manuscripts that were arriving: my sister Rosamond became that first reader. Nevertheless, there were difficulties about the monthly plan: difficulties of production, which the blitz had been making more and more hazardous and more liable to delay, and difficulties of paper-rationing, which had begun to make itself felt. I passed some anxious weeks in which it looked as if the new monthly was going to die almost as soon as born. I bombarded Lane with letters, and in the end my advocacy — and the growing evidence of *P.N.W.*'s success and popularity — won the day. It was a near thing: before going down to Harmondsworth for the crucial interview I passed a sleepless night on Home Guard duty, rehearsing all the arguments I could muster while the guns banged away almost without pause and the door rattled to every reverberation. We decided to carry on, and five tons of paper a month (at that time roughly the whole ration of paper for the Hogarth Press in a year) was set aside to produce approximately 75,000 copies of each number.

My recollection of those early months of *Penguin New Writing* is of continual train-journeys accompanied by a suit-case full of manuscripts and proofs which I worked through; of frequent halts on the line during an alert, the progress in and out of King's Cross or Paddington sometimes being as slow as the game of Grandmother's Steps we used to play in front of the Pavilion at Fieldhead, sudden spurts while the Nazis weren't looking, dead stops when aerial eyes were upon us; sometimes dusk fell over the darkened train and reading had to be abandoned, and passengers in silent gloom reflected that their plans to arrive — or leave — before the evening blitz were going to be in vain; guns started to bark and the far-away thump of bombs changed, disagreeably, to the swish-swish-swish of a stick of them swooping down close by. And all the time the letters and manuscripts poured in, chests of drawers at Fieldhead were desperately requisitioned, old rowing vests, mountain-shoes, lederhosen and anti-fascist newspapers, maps of Prague and Vienna and A.A. itineraries of long-ago car trips across Europe flung out, to make room for the ever-increasing offerings of every day's post. More and more were coming in from young authors who had been drafted into the Army, or the Navy, or the Air Force, and some of them so interesting that before long I began to see that it would be possible gradually to reduce the proportion of contributions reprinted from the old *New Writing*, and make the Penguin a completely contemporary magazine.

One of the most interesting of the new authors who came my way in those early days was Alun Lewis. He had sent me some of his poems in the spring of 1940, none of which I liked as much as the poem — his first to be published in London — which had appeared in the *New Statesman*. He had, however, let out that he was writing short stories at the same time, and I managed to persuade him to let me see some of them. I was struck at once, not so much by his technical skill, which was still, I felt, immature, but by the warmth of feeling and by the atmosphere in which they were soaked, the atmosphere of the recruits in the ranks in the months of waiting, which I had believed must eventually find its poet. My letter telling him that I wanted to publish *The Farewell Binge* followed him from camp to camp, and after some weeks he wrote back:

I am delighted you like my *Farewell Binge* enough to use it for *New Writing*. It's an honour I don't undervalue. Especially now, when I find myself under a regime which is so hostile to everything it is fighting to preserve. It's odd, the mixture there is in the Army. Centralized and socialized in distribution and production of goods, monastic in its celibacy and its veto on private property, communal as hell: and yet absolutely crucified by repression, regimentation, precedence and the taboos of hierarchy. I have been trying incessantly to humanize and fire the unit I'm with: I've started a weekly magazine, a debating society that holds mock parliaments and peace conferences: I've put forward a scheme of lectures in nineteenth and twentieth century world affairs: and all I have earned is suspicion, resentment, a petty charge and reduction to the ranks. *Tiens!*

His letters to me after this all sounded the same note: boredom, restlessness, impatience to make the war the first act in a social revolution. "The staleness of this particular unit is my most immediate enemy and I've been doing a lot of educational work, building up a library, getting decent weeklies and monthlies and Penguins and Pelicans included in it, and trying to persuade soldiers to read intelligent stuff in cinema and canteen," he wrote in March 1941. "It's hard work! Fighting will be easier." And again, a few days later, "I have been in trouble with the diehards at the top here, serious trouble. But I think I am winning my case. I was called a liar by a colonel when I was lecturing to 500 recruits on Germany and war. He promises now to apologize before the same 500 next time I lecture — on the League of Nations and war. *Enfin, c'est dur ici.*" While he was struggling to make enlightened crusaders out of his fellow-soldiers, he was hard at work at his stories and poems, and finding a sympathetic response among editors and publishers. What gave me such a strong belief in his future as a writer were the glimpses of passionate devotion to his art that came through the letters: "The story I'm sending you now I *must* send it. Will you please read it and tell me it's much too big a theme for such a little writer, and then I'll pipe down and go to bed at lights out instead of staying up hidden behind black-outs trying to write better and better, feeling for the truth, and not being able to sleep when I do go to bed." In the end I sent this particular story back to him, feeling that he had indeed tackled a job too big for his equipment at that stage; but my conviction was already forming that, moving though many of his poems were, his real originality and power as a writer were going to show themselves in prose — in short stories.

One of the more unexpected centres of literary and artistic activity, as the war got under way, was in the Fire Service. Easy enough to foresee that, sooner or later, stories and poems would be written out of the experiences of the new, articulate soldiers, sailors and airmen, born from the shock of hitherto intellectual lives suddenly thrust into the alien environment of barrack and airfield, the mix-up of all social classes, and a great, shrouded adventure beginning — as if our whole civilization was a giant liner that had left its berth and was slowly sailing into unknown waters under a thickening fog; but that in the fighting of the fires in the target cities, an adventure to prove as dramatic as any that the war provided, so many writers and painters should find the material through which to express the strangeness of this journey we were all embarked upon, was one of the surprise developments that had no precedent in any previous war. It appeared also a lucky chance (lucky, that is, in terms of the vitality of art) that one of the most subtle and complex literary personalities of our generation, Henry Green, should have volunteered for the A.F.S. at the very beginning of the war, and plunged into all the arduous dangers of the London blitz, should nevertheless have succeeded in keeping a detached creator's eye alert in his inmost being to record his experiences and turn them, even while the raids were in full swing, into the art of his unique rococo prose. He began to write out of his A.F.S. experiences in the late autumn of 1940, working with extraordinary speed, first at the opening chapters of his novel *Caught* and then at several short sketches or episodes. He sent me *The Rescue* early in January and followed it with *Mr. Jonas* very soon after. When I look back on it, it seems to me even more astonishing than it did then, that a fireman liable to be called out any night and at all times of the night, drained as he must have been by the sheer physical effort of tackling vast conflagrations among collapsing buildings with bombers still overhead, not to mention the nervous tension, could have produced a piece of descriptive writing as elaborately wrought as *Mr. Jonas.*

When he sent it to me, Henry wrote:

I have just let a girl read it and she laughed herself into a state of tears she thought it so bad. . . . In fact she laughed so much at the first page that she put it into her mouth as you can see from the lipstick on the first page. . . . On the other hand another one three days ago liked it. Anyway I thought I'd put some commas in this time. I've tried to do it in a more spectacular way to suit the more spectacular blaze. It's true, of course, as the other one was.

By the time *Mr. Jonas* appeared in *Penguin New Writing*, another regular feature had been added. I had persuaded Cecil Day Lewis, who also found himself on the crest of this curious wave of creative energy that had begun to gather, carrying so many writers and painters with it since the Battle of Britain, to let me have one of his new poems every month. We had just published his famous retort to the still repeated cry "Where are the war poets?" with its lines so exactly expressing the mood of the "anti-fascist" intellectuals of the 'thirties, a mood that was already giving way — as Cecil's own poetry showed — to something more positive though no doubt very different from what the clamourers expected and thought proper:

> It is the logic of our times,
> No subject for immortal verse,
> That we who lived by honest dreams
> Defend the bad against the worse.

« 8 »

SINCE the bombing of Mecklenburgh Square and the final evacuation of their belongings to Rodmell, Leonard and Virginia had left the running of the Hogarth Press almost entirely to me. We worked in greater harmony than ever before, and all problems which we discussed in our letters seemed to settle themselves with miraculous ease. From time to time Leonard would arrange to meet me in London, to exchange views about manuscripts and devise the best publishing plans for the future that we could envisage on our extremely minute paper ration. Virginia I rarely saw, but one day towards the middle of March they both came up for the day, and we all met for lunch at St. Stephen's Tavern. We had a table in the window on the first floor, looking out on Parliament Square and Big Ben, and I can clearly remember how brilliant the spring sunshine was in which the whole scene was steeped.

The week before, I had sent them Terence Tiller's first book of poems, with a strong recommendation that we should publish it. They had brought it with them: Virginia liked it, and declared that in her opinion the Press should accept it. Leonard grumbled about the obscurity of the young poets, and taking a sheet here and there out of the folder, challenged me: "But parse this poem, John, *parse* it!" Virginia came to my rescue, maintaining that he was being too logical, that there was music and imagination in the poetry that was rare for a first book. Leonard's objections, however, were only a rear-guard feint, and I soon saw that he had made up his mind to yield to our majority opinion — that in fact he agreed with us more than he had been prepared to admit at first. This was the last book Virginia was to read and approve for the Press.

During our argument I noticed that she seemed in a state of unusual nervous tension, her hand shaking slightly now and then. I began to feel that there was some awkward subject they intended to bring up. I had been aware for some time that Virginia was at work on a new book, but I had no inkling what it was, and knew her well enough not to press for details she was clearly reluctant to give. Then Leonard revealed the secret: she had written a new novel, which had been given the tentative title of *Between the Acts*. This was exciting news for the Press as well as for me as a devotee of her work, but when I turned to congratulate her she began to talk about the book in great agitation, trying to damp down my enthusiasm and saying that it was no good at all and obviously couldn't be published. Leonard rebuked her gently, telling her that she ought to know that it was one of the best things she had written. They went on arguing for some time, Leonard trying to calm her with the firmness of his conviction, until I pleaded to be allowed to read it and give my opinion. I could not believe that under any circumstances a new novel by Virginia, particularly after her triumph with *Roger Fry*, could be "no good." Finally she agreed to think it over when she got back to Rodmell, and let me see the typescript if she was in any doubt.

Before we left, she suddenly said she had nothing to do now, and could I send her some reading. I told her I would gladly pick out some manuscripts from the latest batch that had arrived for *Folios of New Writing*, if she really meant it. She eagerly agreed. Looking back on that request afterwards, when the tragedy was over, I realized that her need to have something to occupy and steady her mind was desperate.

A few days later the typescript of *Between the Acts* arrived at Fieldhead, where I had gone for my Home Guard night duty. With it came a letter, dated March 20:

Dear John: I've just read my so-called novel over; and I really don't think it does. It's much too slight and sketchy. Leonard doesn't agree. So we've decided to ask you if you'd mind reading it and give your casting vote? Meanwhile, don't take any steps.

I'm sorry to trouble you, but I feel fairly certain it would be a mistake from all points of view to publish it. But as we both differ about this, your opinion would be a great help.

Yours

Virginia

I hope you're sending the manuscripts — I should like to do them.

I plunged into the book at once, and finished it before I went off into the night with my rifle and tin hat. The typing — even the spelling — was more eccentric than in any of her typescripts I had seen before: that, and the corrections with which each page was splashed, communicated an extraordinary impression, as if a high-voltage electric current had been running through her fingers. But I was deeply moved: it seemed to me to have a quite extraordinary imaginative power, pushing prose to the extreme limits of the communicable, further than *To the Lighthouse*, to be filled with a poetry more disturbing than anything she had written before. I sent off a telegram the next morning, and followed it with a letter telling her that as far as I was concerned there was no question at all: *Between the Acts* must be published.

Her reply came at the week-end. It wasn't at all what I had hoped; and it was enclosed in a letter from Leonard that shocked and dismayed me, in spite of all the warning signs I had seen. Virginia, he told me, was on the verge of a complete nervous breakdown; she was so seriously ill that she could not possibly revise the book; we must therefore put it off indefinitely. He asked me to send the typescript back to her, with a letter to say how sorry we were that we could not publish it in the spring, but would hope for the autumn. I was touched that even in the midst of this terrible personal crisis he could add a few words to say what bad luck it was for me as a publisher. This was the letter he enclosed:

Dear John: I'd decided, before your letter came, that I can't publish that novel as it stands — it's too silly and trivial.

What I will do is to revise it, and see if I can pull it together and so publish it in the autumn. If published as it is, it would certainly mean a financial loss; which we don't want. I am sure I am right about this.

I needn't say how sorry I am to have troubled you. The fact is it was written in the intervals of doing Roger with my brain half asleep. And I didn't realize how bad it was till I read it over.

Please forgive me, and believe I'm only doing what is best.

I'm sending back the MSS. with my notes.

Again I apologise profoundly.

> Yours
> Virginia.

By the time this letter reached me it was all over. On the Monday I had another letter from Leonard, breaking the incredible news of her suicide. He had taken her to a doctor against her will, as many of the old symptoms that had in the past preceded one of her attacks were returning. They had already started the precautions that had become routine with them, even though, strangely enough, the nightmarish head-aches from which I remembered her suffering when she was finishing *The Waves* had been absent. On the day after the visit to the doctor she told Leonard that she was going for a short walk. The walk seemed to take a long time. Disturbed, he went down to her room, and discovered a note on her desk addressed to him: in it she said she knew she was going mad and had decided to kill herself. He ran out in the hope of overtaking and preventing her at the last minute; but all he succeeded in finding was her walking-stick lying on the river-bank. Just after she disappeared the tide had turned and poured out to sea. Her body was not found for several weeks.

The news broke in the papers on the Thursday, as Leonard had decided that the best thing to do was to give the facts to Geoffrey Dawson at *The Times:* he had delayed a few days in the hope that the body might be found. In the last letter he wrote to me on the subject he said, apropos *Between the Acts:* "She was very pleased when she got your letter about it. I still think it a very remarkable book. I had expected from what she said and feared to find a loss of vigour. I may be wrong, but it seemed to me the opposite, to be more vigorous and pulled together than most of her other books, to have more depth and to be very moving. I also thought that the strange symbolism gave it an almost terrifying profundity and beauty."

About a fortnight later, Leonard came up to town and lunched with me at the Athenaeum. I was struck by his fortitude in discussing all that had happened, and the changes Virginia's death would make in his own life and our future as publishers, though it was perfectly clear from one glance at him how much he had suffered. It relieved me, for his sake and for my own sake too, to hear him speak with such decision: everything was to go on as before, he looked to me to manage the affairs of the Press from London and Letchworth, while he went on working mainly at Rodmell. He already saw there would be a great deal of work for him to do as Virginia's literary executor: she had scarcely ever stopped writing; when it was not a long work it was essays or articles or short stories, and in addition to all such manuscripts left in finished or half-finished state in her desk there were many volumes of her diary and her enormous correspondence. First of all, he would do his best to get *Between the Acts* into shape, and we would then publish it as soon as war conditions allowed. We talked a little about her illness, and he confirmed the conclusion I had already come to myself: that the air-raids and the tide of war that had been flowing so long against us were far from being the main cause of her breakdown. Once again, and this time fatally, in her labour of imaginative creation she had strained the delicate mechanism of her mind beyond what it could endure.

When Leonard described all the posthumous works of Virginia that he intended to bring out, a programme that would obviously extend over a long period of years, I had a curious feeling of solace, as if Virginia the writer was still to be with us; but the prospect was only a small consolation for the absence of Virginia herself from the activities of the Press. Apart from my grief at her death as the loss of a friend, I was oppressed with melancholy at the thought that she who had seemed as essential a part of the spirit of the Press as Leonard, and whose retirement from partnership in the early months of the war had been little more than a formality, would no longer be there to discuss the manuscripts and their authors, to plan new anthologies and new series with us, and to laugh over the day-to-day alarums and excursions in our business life. It seemed to be yet another nail in the coffin of the hopes I had had when I started my publishing career, the worst discouragement yet.

« 9 »

ONE of the consequences of the arrangement I had made to spend part of each week in Cambridge was meeting the young Greek poet and critic, Demetrios Capetanakis: for that alone I should hold it one of the most fortunate decisions I ever made.

We were only friends for three and a half years in the middle of a war, a time when people are apt to embark on friendships which fade away when more normal times return; but I cannot conceive that Demetrios could ever have ceased to be my friend if he had survived into the peace, because he had a genius for friendship such as I have never known. If he wanted to be your friend, he entered into your mind and heart with an uncanny power of imaginative understanding that he never allowed to become jealously possessive. His tact was as unique as his perceptiveness, and because he had certain very profound and unusual feelings about the meaning of life and what was valuable in it, he would read your behaviour and the pattern of your existence as if interpreting a secret language that revealed a far deeper significance than it had been possible for you to see before. If he saw you disheartened or confused, he could restore your faith in yourself in the course of a brief conversation. So it was that being with him was almost always an astonishingly stimulating experience: he would, as it were, hold up a looking-glass in front of you in which you saw not the face you had become accustomed to accepting as your own for so long, but a new face with all sorts of potentialities you had allowed yourself to ignore or forget, or had been discouraged into disbelieving, and perhaps with scars on it you had long ceased to be aware of, clues which explained many things that had puzzled you in your relations with the world. And he would talk of mutual friends in the same way, so that you saw them in a new light too. It sometimes happened that the clarity of this strange X-ray power of his was clouded by temporary infatuations and repulsions; but this was rare, and again and again I found — and I think his other English friends had the same experience — that if I tested these intuitions of his, they proved accurate and capable of transforming the climate of a life.

I had not been established in my little room in St. Edward's Passage long, before I began to collect a small group of young men interested in writing, who would come and talk over drinks before dinner during my weekly sojourn. One of these, Adrian Liddell-Hart, a freshman from Eton and son of the distinguished military historian, I had met in the rooms of George Rylands, whose pupil he was; and one evening he appeared at my door in his sky-blue polo jersey with Demetrios in tow. He introduced him as a fellow-pupil of Dadie's, a fabulous connoisseur of modern literature and a fan of *New Writing*. As far as I remember, Demetrios did not say very much that first evening, contenting himself with sitting quietly amongst us, his enigmatic smile playing over his strangely mobile features and giving them the look of an archaic Greek statue, and occasionally breaking in with an absurdly humorous or enthusiastic observation that would immediately evoke Adrian's convulsive laugh. It was not long, however, before we began to see a great deal of one another, and his tongue was loosened to discuss every conceivable aspect of books and their authors, mutual friends and Cambridge figures about whom he could be extremely amusing and malicious in the most unwounding of ways, his experiences in Germany as a pupil of Jaspers and among the disciples of Stefan George, modern Greece and Greek civilization, and the meaning of the war for his own hard-pressed countrymen. He used often to come up to the evening gatherings of the young poets in St. Edward's Passage; sometimes we would meet for dinner at the Arts Theatre Restaurant, or go to see a particularly interesting play that was on. When he came to live in London about a year later, and to work for the exiled Greek Government, I saw even more of him, and scarcely a day passed when, if we did not actually see one another, we failed to ring one another up.

From the very first he showed an immense interest in *New Writing*, the back numbers of which he had managed somehow to swallow whole since his arrival in England the year before. The enthusiasm and passionate curiosity which he lavished on every detail connected with it buoyed me up and gave me fresh confidence at times when practical difficulties, emotional complications and jangled nerves seemed about to overcome me. He was always keenly ready to discuss general plans or special contributions for coming numbers, and I cannot remember a single occasion on which he failed me when I asked for his advice or assistance. He was particularly helpful in connection with the European contributions, as his knowledge of the European literature and thought of our time was enormous and disciplined; and, of course, above all in connection with Greek literature. He it was who first introduced me to the great achievements of modern Greek poetry. He would talk for hours about Cavafy, about that noble sage of

Athens, Angelos Sikelianos, and George Seferis, who was a close personal friend of his and happened at that time to be Greek Consul in Cape Town; and I persuaded him to translate some of the poems of these poets and others, such as Pantelis Prevelakis and Odysseus Elytis, which I could publish in *New Writing*. Thus began an association with Greek poetry which lasted all through the war and into the first years of peace, one of the features of *New Writing* that gives me the greatest pleasure to look back on; and one of its results was that Demetrios himself began to write poems and articles for *New Writing*. Fascinated by the way he talked about Rimbaud, Dostoevsky, Rilke and other "ancestor" figures, I persuaded him to write studies of them which would reveal the extraordinary quality of his thought.

Then came the day when he brought me, out of the blue, his first poem in English, *Detective Story*, which under the deceptive simplicity of its form and statement, concealed some of his deepest philosophical speculations:

> The stranger left the house in the small hours;
> A neighbour heard his steps between two dreams;
> The body was discovered strewn with flowers;
> Their evenings were too passionate, it seems.
>
> They used to be together quite a lot;
> The friend was dressed in black, distinguished looking
> The porter said; his wife had always thought
> They were so nice and interested in cooking.
>
> And this was true perhaps. The other night
> They made a soup that was a great success;
> They drank some lager too and all was right.
> The talk, the kisses and at last the chess.
>
> "It was great fun!" they said; yet their true love
> Throbbed in their breasts like pus that must be freed.
> The porter found the weapon and the glove,
> But only our despair can find the creed.

The easy, conversational tone worked into a tight stanza pattern was an altogether astonishing achievement for a foreigner whose intimacy with our language was little more than a year old; the dramatic concentration, the metaphysical overtones in a poem of only sixteen lines — something that very few English poets of the time, straining as they were after far-fetched effects, were capable of; it made a deep impression on all who read it, and seemed to me to offer the promise of a new break, of infinite possibility, in the poetry of our time.

The appearance of his poems and articles in *New Writing*, however, troubled Demetrios as much as it delighted him. He wanted our friendship to be so entirely without a shadow that the thought of my professional, editorial self bent over them, blue pencil in hand, agitated him. He had, I suppose, carefully noted my obstinacy and what he called my "ruthlessness" in dealing with the contributions of even very close friends, and he dreaded the tension that might arise between us over his own work. Some months before he actually started writing for me, he sent me the beginning of a (never finished) novel, and said: "I want you to read it as a friend — not as a critic or a publisher. I hope you will never be a publisher to me. It is perhaps ridiculous to make such distinctions, but I shall always be only your friend and nothing but your friend."

As it turned out, his fears were unjustified and some of the most delightful times we spent together were in discussing possible modifications and developments to poems and articles he wrote for *New Writing*. Partly this came from the fact that I was genuinely excited about them, partly because I had started writing poetry again myself, and found him the most acute and stimulating of advisers — though a great deal too indulgent to my faults. So the criticism was mutual; and I am convinced that if it had not been for his endless, insistent coaxing and enthusiasm, his absolute rejection of my own doubts about my very minor gifts as a poet, his habit of ringing up and reporting to me the favourable things he had heard other people say about my work, I might never have found the power to go back to poetry in the middle of all the strains and responsibilities of life in London under siege. That he was a dangerous flatterer to those whose work he admired, other people can testify besides myself; but perhaps even the humblest artist needs the kind of faith and encouragement to work his tiny territory that Demetrios gave me; that breathes from his letters to me when I told him that I had some new poems of my own ready: "I hope I will be one of the first people who will read them. Don't forget that, please! I believe I have the right to ask for this privilege, because I feel that I understand your work so well."

« 10 »

THE new turn of the war provided another revelation of spiritual change in our familiar world. All kinds of people, especially young people, were continually astonishing one by displaying qualities of endurance and stoic fortitude that one had not suspected, that one had never thought likely they possessed.

One day, in the train between Letchworth and King's Cross, I found myself alone with a night-fighter sergeant-pilot, a stocky pleasant-smiling boy of twenty-one. He immediately got into conversation with me, and told me that he had already had one crash and had also had to bale out on another occasion. It had shaken his nerve, yes, but he was O.K. now: pilots often lost their nerve for a time after a bad experience, but generally recovered it fairly soon. He warmed to the subject of the class distinctions between officer-pilots and sergeant-pilots in the R.A.F., so rigidly insisted on by the hierarchy and yet so absurd when they were both doing the same job. He told me how difficult it was to get on to the track of the enemy at all at night, and how they all prayed for bad weather to keep the Germans away. There were no false heroics about his story. I found it difficult to believe that such an unaffected, frank and even awkwardly schoolboyish type was actually one of the intrepid pilots whom we civilians looked up to with such humble respect as our guardians and avengers. His remark that death became very matter-of-fact, not to be worried about too much, haunted me for a long time after he had said goodbye to me at King's Cross.

The scientists tell us that during this period we were all doped with self-secreted adrenalin that marvellously helped us to endure things that had appeared totally unendurable in prospect. For me, and for many of my friends still carrying on professionally or assimilated into the war bureaucracy, I think work was the real adrenalin. To have to answer letters, to have to go on reading manuscripts, to have to go on making one's business plans and calculations, whether bombs were falling in the distance or not, prevented the imagination from straying too far and steadied the nerve quite remarkably. Actors and dancers found, I believe, the same; in fact, if the sirens went, it was more difficult to remain unconcerned when one was a spectator in front than while one was performing on the stage; and I remember marvelling at the coolness with which a group of dancers pursued their precise and delicate evolutions one evening when a bomb happened to fall quite close to the theatre — and shook me as well as the walls of the building.

As the spring advanced, the raids grew more violent. The bunks in the tube stations, to which a multitude of old people and women and children had fled, ignoring official objections, when the raids began in

September, were packed every night: a phantasmagoric troglodyte
population, never to be forgotten even if it had not been recorded, with
profound imaginative insight and tragic power, by Henry Moore in
his *Pink and Green Sleepers*. One was conscious every now and then
of a dangerous increase of strain, of one's reserve tank of strength
falling precariously low. One knew that the war at sea was intensify-
ing, though rationing still functioned smoothly enough. One was
bleakly aware that the enormous resources of America, in spite of the
active sympathy of the Roosevelt administration, were still not wholly
committed to the British cause. One put these thoughts away from
one.

In order to have a more permanent pied-à-terre in London, I had,
early in the year, taken an apartment in Athenaeum Court in Piccadilly, overlooking Green Park: it had many advantages, not the least
of them being its solid modern structure of steel and concrete. On the
evening of Saturday, May 10, I got home from Soho to my apartment
about eleven o'clock. Almost immediately the bombardment began; it
did not stop until dawn. Sleep was out of the question, with the continuous barking of the guns, the whistle and roar of the bombs, the deafening unheralded explosions of the parachute-mines, the whining
zoom of dive-bombers. The whole building swayed as if on a pivot,
while the windows shook and the furniture trembled. From time to
time one heard incendiaries clatter down, and soon the air was filled
with the smell of burning from behind the house: the lurid glow, as
one peered between the black-out curtains, revealed that Park Lane
and Shepherd Market were a raging fire. In the early hours of the
morning I went out to the fire-escape several times, to see the blazing
fragments floating through the air over our roof. There were too many
calls on the N.F.S. that night, and it was not till long after daybreak
that the fires were brought under control. Athenaeum Court was, astonishingly, unscathed; and the best thing to do in the morning
seemed, as usual, to change the water in the flower-vases. But I felt as
if I had had a very bad Channel crossing.

A few days later, I had to find a small street in the City, and was
taken by my taxi on a long zig-zag drive through many of the worst
bombed areas. The impression of devastation was stupendous; and yet
it struck me as having a kind of fantastic beauty. If London had to be
abandoned one day, and stillness descended on the wreckage, with
green branches showing through the blank windows of church walls
— walls still standing when roofs had fallen in — with the tangled
girders of office blocks, the jumbled heaps of masonry, the broken

statues, the bisected rooms, and weeds and flowers thickening through every crevice, it would, I thought, be a more extraordinary sight than eighteenth-century Rome as one sees it in the old prints of Piranesi and his followers.

If London had to be abandoned one day. . . . That thought was a little more real in those days than one likes to remember now. How many more raids like the one we had just experienced could the functioning of the city stand? And if they were stepped up, as seemed to be happening? What comfort was it if the German cities were also being smashed to bits? How much longer would the morale of the exhausted ants who still lived and worked in London hold?

But the raids, except for a rare and sudden retaliation for an attack of ours on Berlin, were over for a long time, though we could not know it then. That strange period in the life of wartime Londoners, the three-year breathing space, had begun, while Hitler's forces turned and massed themselves for the blow against Russia that even Stalin refused to believe was imminent.

The Other Dimension

AT about this time I went through a severe emotional and spiritual crisis, about which I still find it difficult to speak coherently. I emerged from it, I believe, in many ways a different person; not different, perhaps, in what is called character — for the mixture of virtues and weaknesses in my nature remained much the same, and my will remained dominant, though only just, over my senses and emotions; but different in the way I interpreted our human existence in the world, and in my whole scale of values. Like someone who has hitherto been deaf to certain notes at the end of the scale, I began gradually to be aware of possibilities in experience that I would never have admitted before, and at the same time to find the universe immensely more mysterious. The change was not simply due to a sudden revelation, but was, I can now see, something towards which my thought had been tending for some time; the emotional crisis precipitated and completed it in rather a violent and frightening way. It is possible that if my upbringing had been different, and if some very persuasive and perceptive missionary had been at my side at the time, religion would thereafter have played a large part in my life.

The main record I have of this crisis is in a sequence of prose-poems I wrote while I was experiencing the full force of it: I called them *Vigils*. I chose this form partly because I had for years been interested in experimenting in prose-poems, which I believed from my study of modern French and German literature to have possibilities that English poets had neglected; but more, at this moment, because I felt that the argument I was embarking upon was complex and difficult, that I would not know its outcome until I came to the end of writing the poems, and that it was absolutely essential not to falsify even the smallest detail in the interests of musical harmony, rhyme or metrical balance. It is in fact a measure of the limits of my strength as a poet that I did not dare subject my thought, in the midst of my spiritual upheaval, to the rigorous formal demands of any poetic stanza, even of the most accommodating kind.

Three elements came together at the same time to make this crisis acute: an unhappy love-affair, an entirely new sense of death as nothingness in the midst of life, and an almost unendurable anxiety about a younger friend who had gone to sea in a state, I knew, of despair. These three elements interacted to draw up the tidal wave which engulfed me for some months. It was an experience of the deepest confusion and agony of spirit; and yet when the waters ebbed and I gradually began to lift myself, with the aid of friends and work, out of the submerged and glaucous state of being so unhappily in love, I felt, paradoxically, that the ordinary dry-shore life to which I was returning, with its smiling reassurances and solidity, the sun shining on all the routine activities and daily preoccupations of men, was almost ridiculously trivial and empty of meaning. It was as if I were coming to from the effects of a drug, and though the state of mind the drug had induced had been mostly painful, and in a quite unprecedented way, the pain had nevertheless had some intense meaning which was all that mattered.

The partings of lovers during the war were especially hard to bear, because of the danger which lurked everywhere and the fear that every goodbye embrace would be the last; but when suspicion and jealousy suddenly began to play their evil role in the midst of these partings, the naked dependence of one soul on another, which is the extreme of love, made the suffering all but intolerable. Then the need for absolute certainties became desperate, and the more desperate it became the more impossible of satisfaction it revealed itself. One had opened a trap-door to a shaft of blackness that stretched down beyond knowing: everything seemed insecure and capable without warning of turning into its opposite: and the result was, of course, the total destruction of the relationship while one floundered and twisted in the accelerating panic of insecurity. And yet probably the love was there all the time.

Now this terror began to mesh in a diabolical gyration with the feeling I had of guilt and inadequacy in having let my friend, who had joined up on a sudden impulse earlier than he needed, go to sea in what appeared to me, from what he had said before leaving and what his subsequent letters revealed, to be a state of total unbelief and despair; with no conviction to hold on to, and no ideal to live for. The sea itself became a symbol of his despair; and I was filled with horror at the thought of his possible death, in the dangerous convoy work in which he was engaged, before this void of the spirit could be filled. The desire to be destroyed seemed no better than the desire to destroy; and as I had in the preceding years come to see that the latter arose in our time from a vacancy of belief, so I now saw the former as a direct result of the same despair.

In this double agony, it was as if I were holding a thinly constructed door against a great tornado of nothingness. And at the same time the continual facing of death, that had become almost as much the civilian's lot as the soldier's, at least if he lived in any of the target cities of the warring nations, made me realize that every one of the notions of survival or restitution with which men comforted themselves was, if closely examined, a deception or without certainty or proof. Not merely the notions of after-life, but the notions also of surviving as part of the thought of one's friends among scenes and objects impregnated in some degree with one's personality. In the war in which we were engaged, one had to envisage the total destruction of a civilization, as it had not been since the remote past:

But if the pounding of the guns, the plunging of the massed bomb-racks rubs out, not just this house and that, but the whole monument of love and history? Sands have covered cities, every stone lost and skulls forgotten. . . .

All of this long internal torment I tried to state, in its dialectical development, in *Vigils;* coming to the affirmation at the end, almost without knowing that I was arriving there, that even if the insistent presence of death was the trigger of the whole crisis, one could not construct any worth-while philosophy without the experience of that presence. Demetrios was, very soon after, to put it exactly as I felt it, in words I can never forget, at the end of his essay on Rimbaud: "Nothingness might save or destroy those who face it, but those who ignore it are condemned to unreality. They cannot pretend to a real life, which if it is full of real risks, is also full of real promises."

I had learnt a great deal; and seen through a great deal. I knew now that existence was a mystery which it was presumptuous ever to pretend fully to understand. And that even if we must try to understand it, and construct a working system of values on that understanding, we have to realize that our organs of perception are imperfect: there are forces in life that defy our attempt to grasp them, and no construction was so certain that we could be justified in forcing it on others. Certainty, indeed, was a mirage; the desire for the absolute the most dangerous as well as the most useless of human pursuits.

At the same time, I had come to a very curious conviction, or rather, perhaps, intuition; curious, that is, for one of my sceptical and agnostic habit of mind. In the midst of the nightmares into which jealousy and the discovery of falsehoods and infidelities in the loved one plunged me, I became haunted by the feeling that these cruelties were, in a sense, involuntary. I could not, I found, honestly say any longer that the person I loved was callous, cold, evil or calculating in intent: in an extraordinary way it seemed to me that this person was suffering as much as I was, was a *victim* as I was a victim of extraneous forces that worked against love. So it was that I began, in my tortured confusion, to believe in demons, spirits of evil that could capture and possess a human being, child of love, an eternal soul exposed to the cross-fire of the battle of life.

I am trying now only to put down, as faithfully as possible, my mood and reasoning of the time. But my future thinking, my future action during the war years was conditioned by these new discoveries and intimations. In the poems I began to write a little later, I was constantly trying to explore and enlarge them, and to find adequate images for them. They gave me, above all, a new belief in poetry, in all art; for only in that supra-rational activity of the imagination did it seem to me possible to express, and convey to the general mind, the complexity and paradox of the truth. I wanted to bring that belief to all those young people who, like my friend at sea, were looking for something deeper than a political faith, something more accessible than a religion hedged with dogmatic tenets; and at the same time to make their voices heard as they really were, in the authentic accents of their generation.

If I could do something towards this, I thought, I should not be wasting my time, in the midst of the destruction and the destroying creeds. As I struggled out of the unhappy love-affair, as I was lifted from the sucking mud of nihilistic doubt and confusion, it seemed that positive energies, inverse in strength to what had pulled me down, had been released in me to devote to these tasks that lay before me.

Years of the Airgraph

B Y the middle of 1942 my life had acquired a fairly regular, busy rhythm, very different from the kind of life I could possibly have envisaged for myself when the war broke out. We had lost Europe, we had been attacked with all the fury of modern aerial warfare, but we had survived the attack and kept our shores inviolate; and above all we had gained two gigantic allies in Russia and the United States. And now, after nearly three years of war, one was living in a not uncomfortable or uncivilized way, with minor deprivations and sacrifices but many compensations in stimulus for the mind and imagination; the chief one being the discovery that it was possible to go through "all the dreaded cards foretold" and still exist, still be sitting at one's desk and even booking a table at the Ivy for luncheon. There were dangerous moments when one was almost lulled into thinking that, as far as our own little islands were concerned, the Four Horsemen had ceased to ride; only one's constantly renewed anxiety for friends at sea, or in the African battles, and — in my own case — the awareness that my Austrian friends were bound to be involved in the sickening, never-ending slaughter on the Russo-German front, kept at bay the illusion that war could become a tolerable, settled way of life. Reason now as well as faith began to assure one that one's own side was not going to lose; one only pretended still to believe in invasion or a renewal of air-raids on the 1940–41 scale; Hitler's "secret weapon" had become little more than a joke, and my unscientific mind — like the minds of most of my friends — did not see as far as rockets and flying bombs.

After Michael Nelson was called up early in 1941, Sonia Brownell became my secretary, but left after some months to work in the Ministry of War Transport. I had a great fondness for the pretty, blonde-haired, vivacious Sonia, with her darting, gaily cynical intelligence and insatiable appetite for everything that went on in the literary world: her revolt against a convent upbringing seemed to provide her life in those days with a kind of inexhaustible rocket fuel. Later still, she joined *Horizon*, in which she played an increasingly vital role as Cyril's assistant, and provided yet another intimate link between the two supposedly hostile camps; and at the end of his life, after the war, married George Orwell. Her place on *New Writing* was taken by Barbara Cooper. She quickly became devoted to *New Writing*, which she had not known before, and began to display three qualities which from the point of view of a literary editor were almost — in combination — too good to be true: a near-fanatical loyalty, an infallible memory and an unquenchable zest for reading manuscripts, no matter how dreary, pompous, silly, ill-writtten or ill-typed.

Meanwhile, at the end of 1941, I had moved from Athenaeum Court to a flat high up in Carrington House, just behind it in Shepherd Market. With the end of the raids, it seemed not unreasonable to take a three-year lease on a flat; and the gain, with my increasing work and the opportunity it gave me to entertain as well as to spread my books and papers around me, treating it partly as an office, was immense. It became so useful, and I became so attached to it, that when the raids did start again three years later, I stayed on. It seemed as good a place as any in which to face mutilation — or death — though definitely not in the official shelter, which was in the deep basement, amid a formidable tangle of huge hot-water pipes next to the oil-fired boiler. Instead, I used to drag a mattress out into the passage, which was protected at least from flying glass.

As far as the war itself went, the tribute I paid still consisted in part of week-end service with the Home Guard at Bourne End. The local allegiance appealed to me, and the early volunteers began to feel the warm bonds of being old soldiers together as the lads from the valley factories were drafted in. As time went on, however, Sundays when work was too pressing for me to slip away to Fieldhead became rather more frequent, and to salve my conscience I arranged to do occasional fire-watching in London as well. It consisted mainly of being "on tap" for the night, with spells of patrolling on the roof of Carrington House and observing the stars.

In addition, I had my work for the B.B.C. and the Ministry of Information. Apart from occasional broadcasts on English literary subjects in the Overseas Service, I did some war-propaganda broadcasts in the German Service, and then, finding I suppose some measure of approval, was asked to start a regular series of broadcasts in the Austrian Service. These services were controlled at the top by Graham Greene's brother, Hugh Carleton Greene, who had come from the foreign staff of the *Daily Telegraph*. I never ceased to find it a strange and rather thrilling experience to be launching my voice into the ether, to be caught in the darkness (the transmissions were always at night) by an absolutely unknown, secret audience, which perhaps included some of my own special friends of the past. "*Lieber Pepi* . . ." they began, addressing an imaginary Austrian I might have known; but the single person one knew for certain would be listening was the monitor in Berlin. Anonymous, invisible, he became almost a friend, as one imagined his technical appraisal night after night. I learnt a lot about broadcasting in this hard school, and I do not think that without the wartime training in problems of pitch, pace of delivery, clarity of expression and knowledge of my own voice, I should have come to literary broadcasting after the war with a certain confidence and craftsman's pleasure.

My work for the Ministry of Information was all to do with Russia, and started quite unexpectedly, a few months after the Nazi attack on Russia, with a sudden barrage of telegrams from my old pre-war acquaintance Timofei Rokotov, editor of *Internationalnaya Literatura* in Moscow. He had decided to TAKE OPPORTUNITY GREET LONG-STANDING FRIEND COMRADE IN ARMS AGAINST NAZI TYRANNY; he wanted regular information about the wartime activities of English writers, and regular reviews of outstanding English books as they came out; and he demanded that the latest issues of *New Writing* should be sent to him, if possible by aeroplane. I did not at first see how I was to comply with all these urgent requests; but it was at least clear to me that a door had been opened through which one might be able to push some very useful propaganda for English literature and the war-effort with the minority but influential public that would be reading Rokotov's monthly. Soon after, however, something equally unexpected happened; the new British Ambassador at Moscow, Sir Archibald Clark-Kerr, who had made friends with Christopher and Wystan on their trip to China, and had long been a keen reader of *New Writing*, suggested in high quarters that I ought to be used in some way to further Anglo-Russian relations. Peter Smollett, head of the newly organized Russian Department in the Ministry of Information, got in touch with me, and I took Rokotov's telegrams along with me to the meeting. The result was that he gave his enthusiastic backing to a scheme by which I sent an article each month to Moscow dealing with all the points that Rokotov had raised. I was to be allowed 5,000 words free cabling for every article, and could keep the fee the Russians promised to send. Rokotov appeared as pleased as I was.

It was fun to do, but involved a great deal of gathering and sifting and reading, and snags of an awkward nature kept on cropping up, mainly due to the entirely different conceptions of the role of imaginative writers and artists in wartime which existed in Churchillian Britain and Stalinist Russia. Some idea of these snags will, perhaps, be conveyed if I quote the telegram I received from Moscow after I had sent off the fourth article in the series:

FOURTH ARTICLE RECEIVED SURPRISED ABSENCE FACTS ABOUT MOVE-MENT AMONGST ENGLISH INTELLECTUALS FOR QUICKER OPENING SEC-OND FRONT PLEASE GIVE ITS RIGHTFUL SPACE TO THIS IN YOUR NEXT ARTICLE KINDLY FORWARD INFORMATION ABOUT ROBERT GREENWOOD AUTHOR BUNTING AWAITING MATERIAL SENT

Of course there was scarcely such a thing as a "movement" amongst English intellectuals (apart from the small group of Communists and fellow-travellers) for a quicker opening of the second front, and I had to put up the best show I could by enlarging on the enthusiasm and admiration of the British for the way the Russians were fighting in their desperate campaign, and on the importance of the war at sea and the African campaign to us. The work was further complicated by the fact that the Russians appeared to know practically nothing about the literary scene in England. Early on I was abruptly bidden to send

DETAILED CHARACTERIZATIONS WORK OF MANY WRITERS MENTIONED UNFAMILIAR TO US HENRY GREEN NORMAN CAMERON LAURIE LEE WAL-TER ALLEN EVELYN WAUGH ELIZABETH BOWEN WILLIAM PLOMER.

Coping with this kind of request began to sap my morale; and at the same time, by a curious process of empathy, something of the high fervour of Soviet propaganda began to creep into my style and made me wonder whether I had actually written the articles that were sent off under my name.

If for nothing else, the experience was extremely valuable to me because it brought me the friendship of Archie Clark-Kerr. He was an unconventional figure among career ambassadors, the very opposite of the kind of stuffed-shirt diplomatist that the Left delighted to carica-ture before the war; forthright in speech, shrewd in judgement, impa-tient of red-tape and red-tape-minded people, a polished wit when he liked but also of an extremely earthy humour when he knew his company, he seemed to me at times to belong in temperament more to the eighteenth-century world of squire and laird than the high diplomatic and social circles in which he moved. His most valuable asset, at the moment in history which coincided with the peak of his career, was, I believe, a certain restlessness of temperament, which might by some strict judges have been thought to be a flaw in a public servant: it gave him at any rate a keen interest in the lives of people far outside his own class bounds, a freshness of response to new ideas and new attitudes and an intuitive awareness of changes in the spirit of the age. It was, I feel fairly certain, this quality that made him such a success as Ambassador in China in the late 'thirties.

He arrived in London on leave in December 1942, and announced that he wanted to take back with him to Russia as big a collection as possible of the works of young English writers and books about new trends in modern literature. He asked me to help him in the choice, and we arranged to meet at my flat one morning to discuss the details. In a few minutes we were as if old friends, and it was with some difficulty that I dissuaded him from demanding of authority that I return with him to Moscow. He described to me vividly the tribulations of the situation he found himself in, with the Russians so hard-pressed by the German armies and so little appreciative of our inability to launch an immediate attack in Europe to relieve the pressure. I am inclined to think that one of the chief reasons why our relations with our new ally were not worse than they were, was the forcible conviction with which Archie put our case across, and his determination to get into direct, man-to-man relations with Stalin. It seemed that he had succeeded — as far as it was possible to succeed with the suspicious Oriental despot that Josef Djugashvili had become — to judge from his account of long sessions at the Kremlin during air-raids, when they retired to the deep shelters and swapped (through interpreters) dirty stories. Molotov, I gathered, was sometimes present, and not particularly amused. "They call him Stone-bottom Molotov in Moscow," said Archie, "but as far as I'm concerned he's stone from top to bottom."

He flattered me gracefully by saying that the only book he had with him on the aeroplane, when he was rushed to Moscow, was my *New Writing in Europe;* and we made out the memorandum of books to be sent to him by adding to and subtracting from the list recommended at the end of that volume. I was impressed at once by his open mind and liberal ideas, and also by the speed with which he was summing up an England he hadn't seen for years.

Archie was extremely anxious to meet the young poets in person, and I managed to arrange a party in my flat which was attended by Stephen Spender, Louis MacNeice, Cecil Day Lewis and others. Most of us sat on the floor, while Archie discoursed on Russian war problems and the Russian attitude to writing in wartime, and questioned us about our own views and the work we were doing within the war bureaucracy: I think he was particularly interested to hear Stephen's account of the new technique of discussion groups that had been started in the N.F.S. since the end of the raids. It was an unusual kind of gathering for a British Ambassador to ask to attend; and as he left Archie closed it by an unusual remark, going up to Louis MacNeice and saying to him, as one Celt to another: "You are descended from a seal!"

Meanwhile, a mysterious silence had fallen on *Internationalnaya Literatura:* my last article had not been acknowledged, and copies of the magazine failed to turn up. It was not, however, until March that Archie, back in Russia, sent me a letter of explanation:

In case nobody has told you, I take it upon myself to report to you the demise of "Internationalnaya Literatura." Some say that it was euthanasia, others that it was a painful end. It cannot have been lack of readers, for it was the most sought after publication in the country. Nor can it really have been lack of paper, for new publications appear. It looks as if some of old Peter's windows on the West are being banged. I shall tell you if I can get at the truth. I am doing what I can to settle down after the terrific stimulus of those few weeks at home, to which you, by the way, made so handsome a contribution. They have left me restless and even rebellious. . . . As the years rattle by and I get nearer and nearer to the museum I find it harder and harder to feel grown up, and hardest of all to be tolerant of my own preposterous way of life . . .

Soon after, the Ministry of Information arranged for me to do much the same kind of work for *Britanski Soyuznik*, the British propaganda newspaper which the Russians allowed us to publish over there, and which had a phenomenal success: its circulation was severely restricted by a meagre paper-ration, but copies changed hands on the black market at high prices.

« 2 »

FOR most of the war, running the Hogarth Press was hardly more than a kind of holding operation. Our paper ration was extremely small, and when the calls on it for the reprints in most urgent demand had been satisfied, there was very little over. It was essential to keep the important volumes in Virginia's Uniform Library in print, as also Freud's works in the International Psycho-Analytical Library (in ever-increasing demand in America). Only occasional new novels or biographies or works of criticism could be published. Virginia's posthumous papers were, of course, the most important: after *Between the Acts* we went on to another miscellaneous collection of essays and critical studies, *Death of the Moth*, and then decided to do the volume of collected stories, including the earliest stories in her "new manner" published in 1922 as *Monday or Tuesday*, which she had been on the point of preparing at the time of her death. After some debate, Leonard decided to call it *A Haunted House*. Next in importance, to my mind, were Henry Green's novels, a sequence which seemed to me to be excitingly exploring new territory as they came out of his workshop, beginning with *Caught* in 1943. For a long time I hoped that I should also be able to publish more of Christopher's books, and the possibility of a new novel from him was always at the back of my mind when I was making my jigsaw-puzzle calculations about our paper-ration. But as he became more deeply involved with the Yoga movement in Hollywood, that hope began to fade. Early in 1943, in response to my persistent questioning, he wrote:

What am I writing, you ask? Well, before the sudden call to the movie-swamp stopped it, I was beginning a study of Berthold working at Gaumont British, which I intend to call *Prater Violets*. And after that, I want to do the story of Heinz. And, after that, a somewhat modified version of *Paul is Alone* (remember?). Three novelettes, to make a volume. Is it just a dream? I don't know. I was as excited as hell when I got ready to start: the only trouble is that I'll have to find a new *tone of voice:* because the ventriloquist has changed somehow, and needs a new dummy. . . .

The war was over, and I had already left the Hogarth, when *Prater Violet* arrived; and neither of the other two stories was ever completed.

Within these very narrow bounds, it seemed to me that the best way to show that our interest in the work of the younger writers was as keen as ever, was by keeping going the New Hogarth Library of cheap poetry books which we had started in 1940, and by continuing to produce the hard-cover editions of *New Writing* twice a year: they were at least a nursery for talent which we might be able to foster in times to come when paper-rationing was abolished. Between 1941 and

1942, however, these hard-cover volumes underwent yet another metamorphosis.

More and more, as the war went on, Leonard left the running of the Press to me. He remained for most of the time at Rodmell, but full reports went to him several times a week; and sometimes I went down to visit him there. My first visit after Virginia's death has left an indelible impression: I was haunted all the time by the feeling of her presence in the house, and it was difficult to believe she would not appear at any moment, and light one of her home-made cigarettes in her long holder, and say, "And now, John, tell us a little scandal. . . ." It was on that visit that Leonard told me that he had discovered six different typescript copies of Virginia's last essay on *Mrs. Thrale*, and further variants of some passages. Another occasion I vividly remember was about eighteen months later. We had had the idea of preparing an anthology, selected from all the poetry the Press had ever published, to celebrate the twenty-fifth anniversary of its foundation. We were going to call it *The Silver Anthology*, and we even announced it in our advance lists for 1944. As Leonard had a complete collection of the publications of the Press at Rodmell, we decided to do the work down there. When I arrived, I found him at the back of the house, sawing wood in his corduroys and what I used to call his "French poacher's" coat. The house was cold and damp, but filled with a great litter of books and apples and papers and jars of honey and jam that gave it a friendly feeling. We tackled our routine Hogarth work directly after tea, and went on steadily with only short breaks to dinner. After dinner, we had already begun our work on *The Silver Anthology*, when sirens sounded, followed swiftly by a noise of gunfire on all sides and a droning of aeroplanes that scarcely stopped for several hours. One or two extremely violent bursts of firing shook the house. It flashed into my mind that perhaps the Nazis were raiding London as a reprisal for our raid on Berlin; and sure enough this proved to be so, for I rang up the B.B.C. and found all the Austrian section down in their shelters. The raid died down again before midnight, while Leonard and I conducted one of our long, tussling arguments about the future of Germany and the organization of Europe after the war. In the middle of the night it began again, with violent, house-shaking gunfire and the continuous, mosquito-persistent droning of aeroplanes. We learnt next morning that there had been two attacks on London, not heavy but an occasion at least for a gala warning display of the terrific new London barrage that had been developed since the 1940–41 blitz had come to an end. Most of the morning we again spent crouching over the fire in the sitting-room at the top of the house, with all the Hogarth books of poetry spread out around us. From time to time Leonard exclaimed: "No, he's a hopeless poet," or "You know, we really *did* print rather well," or "That was one of Dotty's* insane choices. . . ." By lunchtime we had broken the back of the job, and I left on the afternoon train for London.

I have already described how my interest in the refugees from the Czech lands and from Slovakia brought me into contact with a young Czech writer by the name of Jiři Mucha, who had been in France at the time of the collapse and was a close friend of Dr. Hodža's son Fedor. Jiři, because of his passionate interest in contemporary literature and art in France, as well as in his own country and the other Slav lands, was just the person I felt I needed to have as a collaborator if the ideas of the old *New Writing* were to be kept alive during the war. His Bohemian charm, his lively mind, his family roots in the old Czech-French artistic association — his father's signature can be found in the corner of many a famous Parisian theatrical poster of the early part of the century — made him one of the most delightful of companions, and we soon became firm friends, with ambitious plans for developing the cultural side of the new exiled alliances. Jiři told me that there were not only a number of interesting Czech writers, poets, critics and dramatic experts in London, but also several distinguished Poles who cared for the same things of the mind and who were European in spirit rather than chauvinistic. Could we not get together to produce a magazine which would provide a place for the Czech, Slovak and Polish intellectuals to meet their English colleagues, and also their French colleagues whenever possible? I told him that one of my best friends was a young Greek poet who was in touch, in various roundabout ways, with all the Greek intellectuals of his generation; and after meeting Demetrios, Jiři was enthusiastic that the Greeks should play an important part in the projected magazine.

There were technical problems, of course; we needed more paper and more financial backing than the Hogarth Press could provide; and I dreaded stepping into the quagmire of inter-allied bureaucratic priorities. Jiři, however, managed in the end to arrange a meeting with Jan Masaryk, witty, imaginative and thoroughly westernized, who must (I remain convinced) have been the nicest man ever to become a politician in our time. He saw the point of our plans at once, and showed

* Lady Dorothy Wellesley, later Duchess of Wellington.

himself personally enthusiastic. Very soon after, I received a telephone message that he was going to give me all the support possible, and our problems for the launching melted away in an instant. We decided to call the new magazine *Daylight*, and Jiři set about organizing contributions from the Slavonic side with all his zest and persuasive powers, while I handled the Anglo-Saxons, the French — as far as we could get them — and the Greeks.

The first volume of *Daylight* came out in the new year of 1942. As it turned out, the English and the Czechs were most prominent in the volume; so much so that we felt obliged in our Foreword to say that we hoped in future to represent in juster proportion all the "other European peoples who have a common cause with the Anglo-Saxon world." It is true that the eager co-operation of Demetrios provided not only an admirable piece from his own pen, *The Greeks Are Human Beings*, but also some translations from the poetic sequence *Myths of Our History*, one of the major works of his friend George Seferis, and two poems of a younger Greek poet, Pantelis Prevelakis.

Daylight was well received, and sold well; but it soon became clear that to make it a regular publication was going to be even more difficult than we had thought. The support that the Czechs could give us over paper supplies was not unlimited; and in any case I did not want to be constantly dependent on the goodwill of one only of our European allies. The question of Czech predominance came up again over contributions. Jiři managed to organize a big flow of Czech material, some of it excellent but a great deal of it little more than topical journalism; contributions from the other East Europeans, however, were scarce. I began to see that if I insisted too much I should be asked by the Czechs why they should give assistance to propaganda for the Poles — and so on. Again, owing to supply difficulties, our original plan to make of it a regular magazine, rather in the manner of André Labarthe's *La France Libre*, had collapsed, and it looked as if *Daylight* could only come out twice a year, as a book, just as *Folios of New Writing* had been coming out. If that were to happen, both I and the travellers for the Hogarth Press felt that the two publications would be too similar to arouse much enthusiasm from the booksellers or the public. I did not want to give up *Folios*.

All these arguments increased in force the more I thought about them. So it was that *New Writing and Daylight* — a title that always seemed curiously clumsy to those who did not know the history, and was sometimes asked for in the shops under wildly garbled names, the one I savoured most being *New Writing in Moonlight* — came into being. It lasted until 1946. The new contacts I had made with the exiled European writers in London, the new scope in articles on the theatre, ballet and the plastic arts that the preparation of *Daylight* had suggested, restored to *New Writing* something it had lost since the outbreak of the war. However different the animating spirit, in scope and planning the first number of *New Writing and Daylight* in 1942 has more in common with the last number of *New Writing* (new series) in 1939 than any of the volumes of *Folios*.

At the same time, some far-reaching changes were taking place in *Penguin New Writing*. Allen Lane's enthusiasm about its prospects as a monthly were soon clouded by rapidly increasing difficulties of production and paper supply. Some printing works in England had been worse affected by the blitz than others, but all had been slowed down by the drain of their younger workers into the armed forces; and though Penguin Books had started the war with good stocks of paper and a ration just a little larger than their estimated needs, the stocks had been used up by the middle of 1941 and the ration had been cut again.* Allen Lane's suggestion was that we should turn *Penguin New Writing* into a quarterly at once. The struggle for its future went on for many months, but by Christmas it had been agreed between us that it should go on as a monthly — though the name had already become a misnomer and the interval between numbers was slowly stretching out — until No. 12 had appeared in the early spring of 1942. No. 13 was, then, to be the first of a new quarterly series.

The change-over to a quarterly seemed to me to be the opportunity to do something much more ambitious. The number of pages in each issue was increased, and the page itself redesigned to accommodate a good many more words: clever work in the Penguin office made the page look much more elegant in spite of being more crowded. But in some ways the most important to me of all the new developments was the addition of a section of photogravure illustrations. It was the realization of an ambition that had been growing in me for some time: not just to have pictures in *Penguin New Writing*, but to extend its range to cover contemporary theatre, ballet, music, cinema and painting, with illustrations from all these other arts. It seemed to me — as it seemed to many others — that under the most unlikely conditions, in the middle of a total war, something like a renascence of the arts was taking place in Britain. I was excited by the revival of the romantic,

---

* By December it was down to 37½ per cent of the pre-war standard figure of annual consumption.

visionary tradition in English painting, stemming from Blake, Palmer and Calvert, in which Graham Sutherland was undoubtedly the leading figure, and by the revival in stage-design which accompanied it. I was excited by the extraordinary development that was taking place in ballet, especially at the Sadler's Wells, where the choreographic work of Fred Ashton, Ninette de Valois and Robert Helpmann was creating a new intensity of imaginative discovery, so that with the new stage-designers and the new composers assisting, one could for the first time envisage a vigorous British style and school in that complex coming together of many arts to make a whole greater than any one of them. I also believed that extremely interesting things were happening in the film world, where a new kind of realism was being developed, that exploited for wartime purposes our pre-war skill in documentary, but without falling into crude propaganda or losing sight of the individual and his human reactions. And I had watched with passionate approval a revival of interest in our dramatic classics, especially Shakespeare, on which new ideas on production were being brought to bear with, it seemed, almost limitless possibilities. All this I wanted to be pictorially illustrated and critically discussed and interpreted in the new quarterly, and having obtained Allen Lane's ready agreement to the photogravure section, I planned to get several experts to write for me under the cover names of "Dance Critic," "Art Critic," "Theatre Critic" and so on. . . . And all for a tanner, and in an edition of between 70,000 and 80,000, I kept on saying to myself, slightly disbelievingly.

As so often before in my life, as the war went on I began to be obscurely aware of forms I believed poetry, novels, art should take to respond to the mood, the undefined spiritual impulses of the time; forms I imagined I could almost seize from the inchoate mists, but not quite, and so must find other poets and artists to create. I had for long felt that the mood expressed in the letters I was getting from young men in the Forces, and in their talk when I met them, had no correlative in art; when a curious chance put me in touch with a new artist, who had only just begun to realize that he was an artist. Among the many descriptions of war experience that were now arriving in my office by every mail, one struck me as soon as I read its opening sentences: it was an account of the unloading of a Red Cross train full of wounded, among whom was a German. It was written by a young man who signed himself Keith Vaughan. What particularly interested me was the quietly expressed but deep human compassion that filled it, as well as the sense it showed of how to use words: "The stretchers were held up level against the bunks and the men coaxed, like animals, to brave the crossing on to their steel meshes. Some moved suddenly and clumsily, hoping to make the journey before pain had observed their going. . . ." I wrote at once to find out more about the author, and learnt to my surprise that he had done very little writing previously, that he had been a photographer before the war, and would like to let me see some drawings of life in the army camps that he had been at work on. When these drawings arrived, I was immediately and deeply struck by them. Here at last, I thought, was a pictorial expression of the mood of the new Army, with its young recruits from every level of civilian life; a mood of resignation and sadness that, in the midst of alien surroundings, regimentation and squalor, was illuminated with a sense of spiritual adventure, with the chance of catching sight of some great truth about human life, some great hope for the future. Undeterred by the distinctly cool reception they received when I showed them to a distinguished and influential art-critic, I determined to publish reproductions of some of them in the photogravure section of the first *Penguin New Writing* Quarterly.

One immediate result for Keith Vaughan was that a large number of his drawings was bought for the War Artists collection. I think that after this he became convinced that his future was as an artist.

« 3 »

IN the long interim between the early blitz and the renewal of persistent raiding in the new year of 1944, the literary world of London became, paradoxically, something like a stable society. There were not a great number of us; most of those who were destined to spend at least part of the war in uniform had already gone; nearly all of us who remained knew one another (or very soon got to know one another) personally, and living more or less under siege conditions with very little opportunity of movement far afield, we were continually meeting to argue and discuss together, so that ideas were rapidly absorbed into the general bloodstream, and hostile camps and intellectual schisms never lasted for long or remained very serious. We were united in a this-has-got-to-be-seen-through attitude towards the war, which was taken for granted, and also in a determination to guard the free world of ideas from any misguided military encroachment. We *needed* one another, and for purposes larger than our own security or ambitions.

This sense of cohesion was extraordinarily stimulating. In peacetime it might well have produced staleness and preciosity; but in the grand transformation scene of the war exactly the reverse, I think, was true, at least until nearly the end; and, as I have already described, our small and closely integrated society dissolved at the edges when our thoughts, day and night, reached out in longing and anxiety towards friends, lovers and relations involved in the fighting in distant countries and oceans.

The bonds that held us were not, however, an elastic that refused to stretch. Most of us, inevitably, because of our age group, had already established ourselves in the literary world; but from time to time a younger recruit joined us, a poet or novelist who had just begun to attract attention, and was living in London or within easy reach of it because he had been posted to the Fire Service, or the Censorship, or the Ministry of Information. Of these, there were three who seemed to me discoveries of especial interest; Laurie Lee, of whom I have already written; William Sansom, and Henry Reed.

Bill Sansom has described, in his *Coming to London* article, how in the advertising agency in which he worked just before the war, a "comfortable rugger-bred middle-class youth" who scribbled away but thought of the arts as "something godly and distant, unintelligible and a bit dotty," he found himself one day sharing a new room with a young man called Norman Cameron; how Norman transformed his vision of painting and literature; and how, having joined the Fire Brigade at the beginning of the war, he started to write in his Hampstead station, met William Makins, business manager of *Horizon*, who told him to send one of his stories in to the editor; how the story — to his astonishment — was immediately accepted, and how, at Stephen Spender's instigation, he sent another one to me; which I promptly took for *New Writing*. After that first story, *Through the Quinquina Glass*, Bill continually sent me batches of the stories that now began to pour out of him; many of them I accepted straightaway, but many others I sent back with critical letters trying to explain where I thought the weak spots were. Sometimes he re-wrote them, and I eventually printed these, too; others he scrapped, others were printed elsewhere. It was extremely stimulating for me, whatever it may have been for him, because I had rarely before, if ever, had to do with an author so eager to learn from his experiments and to perfect them, and so little disposed to bite the hand that wanted to feed him — with the satisfaction of print. There were long periods of disappointment, when he seemed to be off the scent, but there was never a complaint about my sorrowfully posted return packets; then he would suddenly pick the scent up again, and another extraordinary, original, poetic story would arrive to delight me and the rapidly growing circle of his admirers. These pleasures were crowned when I persuaded Leonard Woolf to accept his first volume of stories, *Fireman Flower*, for publication by the Hogarth Press.

Of the stories in that volume, only one, *The Wall*, was a straight reportage of a fire-fighting experience. In the rest, if he used the setting and paraphernalia of the London fires it was to illustrate some subtle problem of psychology or to establish some symbolic truth. The pleasure his writing gave me came from the strange imaginative world he created, so that in *The Peach House Potting Shed*, for instance, one was immediately drawn as into an intense dream; this world of fable and symbol owed something, inevitably, to Kafka, something perhaps also to the contemporary examples of Edward Upward and of Rex Warner; but Bill Sansom gave it a flavour and quality of his own, creating some of his most ominously compelling effects by, as it were, arresting the motion of life for a minutely described and timeless moment, as if a cinema operator had suddenly stopped a film at a point charged with transforming significance. Sometimes he attempted a more deliberate and elaborate fable, as with *In the Maze*, but even when his symbols as explicit fable did not entirely convince, this imaginative power remained. And his success, of course, came from the fact that he loved language; that he was inexhaustibly interested in what could be done with words, in renewing their force in experimental combinations and coinings.

I first became aware of the name of Henry Reed as the signature under an article about Auden's work in the Birmingham University magazine, *The Mermaid*. I was so struck by this article that I immediately wrote off to the author and asked him if he would care to contribute to *New Writing*. Many weeks passed without an answer, and I had already given up hope of hearing, when, in the summer of 1941, a letter arrived from 10557689 Pte. Reed, H., in Squad 48 "B" Coy. No. 3 Training Battn. R.A.O.C., whither my letter had followed him. He promised poems as soon as he could get down to completing several he had drafted out, and articles, too, if later on I suggested themes to him, adding: "If this seems a poor response to your charming note, you will blame the Army, where so much of my time is taken up with marching, drilling, bayonet-fighting, the Bren gun, heavy-charing and learning to be a clerk. If you write again, as I hope you will, perhaps you wouldn't mind addressing the letter in a plain envelope. I don't want anybody to notice me more than they must."

It was a year, or more, before the poems began to arrive, but as those few which had already appeared in *The Listener* suggested, they were worth waiting for. A purity and exactitude of diction, a technical skill concealing itself under a perfect clarity and ease of statement, a cool, ironic intelligence keeping under faultless control a romantic imagination and an immense pressure of nostalgia: such gifts are rare in any young poet, rarer still in a young poet's first poems. The long poems, most of which were published in *New Writing and Daylight*, dramatic meditations or monologues by figures of classical or Arthurian myth, were, I thought, in spite of an echo of Eliotesque music now and then, an imaginative and technical triumph, though the wit and fierce ironic tension of the shorter pieces on army life — *Naming of Parts*, *Judging Distances* and *Unarmed Combat* — have made them the obvious favourites. As in Roy Fuller's poetry of this time, the sense of alienation and uprootedness is the dominant emotion in these *Lessons of War*: they are rejection-of-war poems more emphatically even than Roy's. But the two long poems on classical themes, *Chrysothemis* and *Philoctetes*, are dominated by a similar emotion, a sense of exile and separation, desolate or bitter, and while the protagonist in each is an entirely valid dramatic creation, they would not have made their extraordinary impact if one had not been aware of overtones arising out of the poet's personal emotion; if one had not felt that at a deeper level they were also parables of the artist's predicament in a world given over to violence.

During these years, in spite of the difficulty of obtaining drink in adequate quantities, some of us managed to keep up the pre-war tradition of gatherings for cocktails or wine before or after dinner, sometimes inviting only a handful of friends, sometimes a couple of dozen, but never great throngs or routs; and because they could not be huge or miscellaneous, these parties, in which the central, most permanent circle was enlivened by visitors from the country, together with soldiers, sailors or airmen on leave or in transit to a new posting, have left a very happy and intimate memory. At my own gatherings, in my new abode on the sixth floor of Carrington House, I endeavoured to bring together old and more recently discovered contributors to *New Writing* and Hogarth Press authors, and other friends in the publishing and literary worlds. If I had an exact record of these parties, I could give a composite picture that would illuminate the anatomy of our wartime society in the most truthful detail. As I have not, let me describe an imaginary but nevertheless imaginable party attended by some of those who at one time or another, though not necessarily the same time, did in fact accept my invitations. . . .

First of all, I see friends from the various swollen departments of the bureaucracy, especially (and inevitably) from the Ministry of Information. Graham Greene is there — if the party takes place before he leaves for West Africa — full of sardonic stories about muddle and maze-like confusion of action, wheels that refused to revolve in the press of logs being assiduously rolled and axes furiously ground (one delicious glimpse of this he was to contribute to *Penguin New Writing* under the title of *Men at Work*). Cecil Day Lewis is regaling us with similar stories, finding more entertainment than bitterness, reliving the dottiness, the Alice-through-the-looking-glass atmosphere that sometimes seemed to close in on him, roomful after roomful on all sides of his office, floors and floors of it above him, floors and more floors below. Laurie Lee, who now works with him in the Publications Department, is standing by the window, endeavouring to evade my demands that he not only write more poems for *New Writing* but also sketches of his Cotswold village childhood for *The Geographical Magazine*. From the bomb-proof depths of the Admiralty, where he is engaged on secret work with Ian Fleming, William Plomer has arrived with a crazy story of a general who never recovered from learning one day that human beings consisted 95 per cent of water, and had to be retired. George Orwell is present: the keen eyes suggest more melancholy than humour, and the deeply etched lines round his mouth only rarely stretch to a smile. He is working now in the Indian section of the B.B.C., and, planning a series of talks on the English poetry of our century, urges me to do the one on the poets of the 'thirties. Later, I overhear Orwell speaking, in rather different tones from those employed by Mr. Churchill, about Stalin as war leader and about Soviet diplomacy to Demetrios Capetanakis, who has come over a little late from a long day at the Greek Ministry of Information. Louis MacNeice, also from the B.B.C., is there, looking more seal-like than ever and talking about problems of the recitation of poetry over the radio to his fellow-poet Henry Reed.

There is a big contingent from the Fire Service: Henry Green, telling extraordinary stories of his fellow-firemen, at present bored and restless and getting on one another's nerves in the "lull" (about which he has just written a sketch for *N.W.D.* to publish), and forbidding me to use a photograph of him in the Penguin, for fear a fellow-fireman should recognize him and give the game away — "I should never hear the last of it," he says; Stephen Spender, full of eager information about the organization of discussion groups in the N.F.S., which he claims as a great discovery in democratic education; and William Sansom, not saying very much, not (one suspects) from hauteur but rather from stiffly controlled shyness.

Some of my fellow-publishers and literary editors have also joined us. Cyril Connolly, who still ingeniously succeeds in giving literary dinner-parties of a quality astonishing for wartime, discusses the problems of *Horizon*'s and *New Writing*'s paper ration with me; Roger Senhouse, oldest of friends and a director of the publishing house of Secker and Warburg, is talking to my sister Rosamond and to Raymond Mortimer, at this time literary editor and *eminence grise* of the *New Statesman*. The three of them form a group under the painting of Charleston by Duncan Grant, which hangs at the end of the room; and they are joined by Nancy Mitford, mistress during all these years of Heywood Hill's bookshop in Curzon Street, where she performs her skilled office of marrying the exactly desirable book to each questing customer and purveying the gossip of the town with her unique Mitford wit.

On the sofa my mother, who has come up for the occasion, is conversing with Veronica Wedgwood. At the other end of the room Elizabeth Bowen, smartly turned out as ever in spite of wartime restrictions, is discussing novels with Philip Toynbee, lately released from the Army. Elizabeth is as usual in high spirits, radiating charm and vitality, the slight impediment in her speech giving an attractive touch of diffidence to the eager flow of her wide-ranging conversation: her stories of London in wartime — she was an air-raid warden all through the blitz — are just beginning to come out. Near them, Victor Pritchett, brilliant raconteur and wit, has enticed George Stonier out of his shyness: their hilarity has affected a tall, burly figure whose name I have suddenly, distressingly forgotten (I am subject to such moments of total amnesia). My sister Rosamond informs me, with raised eyebrows, in response to a whispered question as she passes, that I ought to be ashamed of myself for not recognizing the distinguished author of *The Aerodrome*, especially as I have recently given a talk to the Sixth Form at the school in Wimbledon where he teaches. Rose Macaulay, symbol of some dauntless, indomitable quality of moral and intellectual integrity in the pre-1914 generation — you would never guess she has recently lost her most precious heirlooms and working manuscripts in a fire-raid — breaks in upon my confusion, asking why I don't get the authorities to allow the war prisoners to write for *Penguin New Writing;* but Derek Hill, up for the day from the Wiltshire farm where he works, suggests that it would be far better if she were to come down and interview some of the Italian prisoners who provide the labour there — and then write their stories up herself. Derek is not the only artist present: Laurence Gowing, who has recently received high praise for his still-life canvases of green apples (that set the teeth on edge) and shadowy, exquisitely poetic landscapes, is there; and Keith Vaughan, on leave from his pioneers, smiling and quiet.

Jiři Mucha has just turned up, a little late, and has brought another war correspondent in uniform with him, American or Canadian; and there is a sprinkling of younger men in uniform, one or two with their wives or girl-friends, all contributors or would-be contributors to *New Writing.* Later on, picking a party from these, and having seen my mother to her taxi, I go off to the White Tower in Percy Street, where I find that Cyril Connolly, with Lys Lubbock and one or two other guests, has preceded us; and glimpsing out of the corner of an eye the vast patriarchal head of Augustus John that seems to float over the room as in a drawing by Blake, and at another table the bowed, reverie-sunken head of Norman Douglas with Nancy Cunard beside him, I climb upstairs to find a corner table behind a huge, hilarious party mainly consisting of G.I.s celebrating the wedding of one of their number to an Anglo-Cypriot bride.

All during these years, Cyril and I used to meet from time to time, not only at such parties but sometimes at my club, sometimes at his home, to exchange gossip and compare notes. I think the characters of our two magazines were very different; and yet there was a broad area of agreement between us, and an unplanned common policy; particularly about the need to defend the independence of the world of literature, and to provide young writers in uniform with a place where they could let off steam about their grievances, experiment exactly as they wished, and be gloomy about the way the war was being waged and its probable outcome, if that was how it took them. *Horizon,* it always seemed to me, had a chancy brilliance: chancy because there seemed to be long periods when Cyril lost interest in it as an editing job, but made up for this by the wit and flavour of his own contributions. *Horizon* also had less interest in theatre, theatre design and ballet than *New Writing,* and pursued a very different course about art. I think

[323]

there was bitterness sometimes between us, but much of it could be put down to the malicious gossip-mongering of mutual acquaintances, who liked to invent a rivalry more remorseless than ever could have existed between two heirs of Bloomsbury with their backs to the wall. And sometimes an author who had started in *Horizon* came on to *New Writing* and thence to the Hogarth Press, for the further scope and opportunities with which we could provide him. William Sansom was an outstanding example. There was certainly plenty of room for both of us; and when I said one day to Michael Nelson that if ever *Horizon* was in serious straits I would subscribe £100 at once, I was in dead earnest.

To complete the picture, I must also mention those luminaries of our literary world, who, though established by choice or direction in regions of our islands fairly distant from London, seemed to be very much with us even if their visits were rare. John Betjeman had taken on a cultural liaison job in neutral Dublin at the U.K. Representative's office, and fulfilled his duties with immense aplomb and zest, charming the most suspicious among the local intelligentsia into at least keen interest if not whole-hearted engagement with what writers and artists were thinking and doing in war-shattered Britain, and keeping an easy lead over his Axis opposite numbers all through the course; thus proving, not for the first or last time, that in such a job a dram of personality is worth a hogshead of bureaucracy. He acted, in fact, as a two-way channel between the countries, providing at the same time Irish intellectuals with a much-needed outlet into the wider Anglo-Saxon world of letters, the normal passages of which censorship, shipping dangers and every other kind of wartime restriction had all but dammed up. He managed to arrange a mutual exchange of *New Writing* and *The Bell*, and elicited stories or poems from some of the more interesting Irish writers which he sent over to me, with accompanying letters that would suddenly break mysteriously into Gaelic and were sometimes signed *Seán ó betjemán*. I tried in vain to get him to send new poems of his own: "only Tennysonian blank verse pours out of me," he wrote in the spring of 1942; but a few months later: "I feel as though I shall never be able to write again."

Early in 1942 we had published in the New Hogarth Library poems by Robert Graves, Norman Cameron and Alan Hodge in one small volume called *Work in Hand*. This brought me into correspondence with Robert Graves, who was living down at Galmpton in Devon; and having read and much admired his famous *1805* in *The Listener*,

I asked him for a poem for *New Writing*. He replied that he didn't mind contributing several poems, but didn't want to contribute one, as a single short poem was apt to lose its taste and smell if surrounded by other people's work. To explain the single appearance of *1805*, he said: "This was shown to Ackerley by someone else, and he asked for it, and I used to be a neighbour of his so I said all right. I have also contributed a poem to the next number of the *Eugenics Review* beginning "Come, human dogs, interfertilitate" because the editor is my tame physician. . . ." Tantalized by this hint of what the next number of the fortunate *Eugenics Review* would contain, and hoping that the same vigorous spirit would inform all his work of the moment, I readily agreed to publish a batch of his poems. By return of post I received his *Satires and Grotesques*, six satires which contained that mordant comment on contemporary war communiqués *The Persian Version* and the miraculously free-and-easy song *The Oldest Soldier*, and his "grotesques," the oddest of which contained a reference to a certain Dr. Newman (who was unknown to me) and his "black imp, a sooterkin" which he drew out of his pocket at a concert. I was puzzled; but Robert Graves anticipated me: "In reply to unasked questions," he wrote, "Dr. Newman's 'Sooterkin' is, or was, a Dutch imp caused by the impregnation of women by the fumes of charcoal when they stood over a brazier in their wide hooped skirts. He is mentioned by Sam Butler in *Hudibras* and has the characteristics of a gremlin: probably now in service with the Free Dutch Air Force. . . ."

One of the most remarkable articles I ever published — in fact, I believe, one of the most important published anywhere during the war — was the first article of all in the first number of the combined *New Writing and Daylight:* Edwin Muir's *The Natural Man and the Political Man*. Edwin was in Scotland during these years, in St. Andrew's and then in Edinburgh, where he worked for the British Council in a job that brought him into close contact with the Czech, Polish and French forces in Britain. He was therefore particularly interested in the experiment of *Daylight*. "I think that it is splendid that you have managed to start it just now," he wrote to me, "that is at the right time for it — and the most difficult time for it." And very soon after, he sent me the article, saying that he thought it "an inadequate treatment of a real question, which would need a volume to do justice to it." *The Natural Man and the Political Man* was an analysis, in philosophical depth, of precisely that problem which had loomed so large for the writers of my generation as disillusion with the political developments of the 'thirties grew; it showed, more clearly than any of us had ever succeeded in showing, why fascism and Communism had come about through a change in the traditional Western attitude towards man during the nineteenth century — a change from the idea that an individual's life was a conflict to the idea that it was a development — and why fascism and Communism, beneath their violent surface opposition, were really so alike; and how this way of thinking had permeated a large area of modern literature, the novels of Lawrence, Montherlant, Hemingway most evidently:

What has gradually been brought into prominence by the religion of development is the primacy of *things*. Control things and you control mankind. In this conception the moral struggle which possessed the imagination of other ages, and was strong even a century ago, recedes into irrelevance, and becomes like one of those vestigial organs in the body which no longer perform any useful function, but exist merely to plague us: a vermiform appendix. . . . What has taken place in literature is a simplification of the idea of man, connected with this notion of natural process and development. The simplification is a general tendency; literature has not initiated, but merely reflected it; and only those writers who are deeply rooted in tradition, and possessed with the idea of time, have been able to make headway against it; such writers as Proust, James Joyce and Virginia Woolf, to confine ourselves to the novelists: there are similar figures in poetry. The obsession of such writers with tradition was called out by this human crisis.

From time to time Edith and Osbert Sitwell came down from Renishaw, and entertained on an unwontedly lavish scale. It was Demetrios who brought Edith and me together: he had conceived a profound admiration for her wartime poetry, and, when mutual friends introduced them, an equal admiration for the bold Renaissance outline of her personality. I myself had been deeply moved by many of the poems collected in *Street Songs* and *Green Song*, but I rather doubted whether the meeting would be a success, feeling that Edith saw in me one of the more political of the "gang" of the 'thirties, whose Left Book Club radicalism, I knew, had been unsympathetic to her and whose excursions into revolutionary agitator's verse she despised. Demetrios, however, overruled my doubts, and took me along with him one day to tea at the Sesame Club. His instinct was right (or had he prepared the ground very carefully without telling me?): Edith and I took to one another very quickly, and from that afternoon she became one of the elder literary generation I saw most of and felt most sympathy with. I was struck at once by the sculptural beauty of her oval face, her fine

intellectual profile and her aristocratic dignity of bearing and manner.
A first, hasty glance might lead one to suppose her haughty and cold
— and indeed Edith could be freezing to bores, enemies of the arts
and all inconsiderate vulgarians; but I recognized at that earliest tea-
party what was in fact perfectly clear from her poetry, and could not
be concealed even by the shower of shafts of satiric wit that sometimes
filled the air around her: that her response to any genuine emotion was
immediate and that she was extremely sensitive, especially to all forms
of suffering, human or animal.

Osbert Sitwell I came to know more gradually, but was impressed
early on by the contrasting sides of his personality. It was impossible
not to be charmed by him if he set himself to win your friendship;
impossible not to appreciate the warmth and generosity of heart and
the passionate caring for art and artists, whether they were poets, musicians, painters or dancers; but the first impression he made, as he
came into a room, was of princely apartness, of soldierly authority;
and the quick hawk-like glance he directed over the company seemed
to bode ill not only for foolish importances and gushing climbers who
presumed on his impeccable manners, but also for the shy and simple.
Their early struggle for recognition, their rebellion against both their
upbringing and the accepted fatuities of the time in the arts, had
marked both Edith and Osbert. Like all revolutionaries who win their
way against great odds, they were, it sometimes seemed, too ready to
suspect conspiracy and even treachery, a reaction that often baffled
and dismayed younger critics whose cracks were fundamentally inspired by a form of the same need to defy one's successful elders that
the Sitwells themselves had felt. And yet the hand that seemed, at one
moment, to hover threateningly over the proscription list, the next moment was extended in unreserved support and friendship to some
struggling poet or painter, or other fellow-artist who found himself
persecuted by bone-headed authority. The Sitwells' out-and-out partisanship of free experiment in the arts, the battle they never ceased to
wage against philistinism and bureaucratic insolence, was of priceless
importance during the war.

Morgan Forster, too, in quite a different manner, with an appearance of retiring diffidence, of a desire only to be gentle, and charming,
and amusing, while in fact taking deadly aim, continued to wage his
long-standing battle against the pretentious, the insensitive and the
intolerant. He used to come up from Abinger Hammer briefly, but
quite often, to broadcast on the overseas services of the B.B.C., mainly
to India, and from time to time he would come for tea, or a drink, or

supper after the ballet with me. I remember one occasion, in the Athenaeum, when he was at the top of his form, making fun of everything. We talked of *War and Peace*, and he remarked how brilliantly Tolstoi understood what went on in the world of public affairs, the sort of things that were happening again today; for instance, all the little men rushing about, talking and writing about the importance of *problems* that have to be mastered. "As soon as you've mastered one problem, there's always another!" he exclaimed with an astonishing chuckle. The fact that he was appalled by the dictators and their cruelties, that he thought the war had to be fought, did not mean that he gave an uncritical assent to everything our side did as necessary or right. In his pamphlet *What I Believe*, which the Hogarth published just before the war, he had written: "Hero-worship is a dangerous vice, and one of the minor merits of a democracy is that it does not encourage it, or produce that unmanageable type of citizen known as the Great Man. It produces instead different kinds of small men — a much finer achievement." I think he was well aware that war conditions were the enemy of that "minor merit." There was too much power concentrated in too few hands, and, as he wrote shrewdly in the explosive little pamphlet, "as soon as people have power they go crooked and sometimes dotty as well, because the possession of power lifts them into a region where normal honesty never pays."

Morgan Forster was always anxious to hear the latest news I had had from Christopher, to whom he had remained unswervingly loyal through all the public outbreaks of hostility. We were both conscious of the distance between us and Christopher slowly increasing: with the most sensitive sympathy in the world it was as difficult for Christopher to follow the changes that the war was gradually making in our attitudes as it was for us fully to understand Christopher's new leanings towards pacifist mysticism. I showed Morgan a letter I had had from Christopher early in 1943, about the piece I had published in *Penguin New Writing* No. 14, describing his work in the Friends' Service Committee Seminar in California:

I was very embarrassed by my La Verne thing: it reads like the parish magazine; but I'm sure you did right to print it. It administers a kind of sour sip of quinine flavoured with prigdom. I wouldn't feel I had to do so much apologizing, now; or be so gloomy. I sound as though I were being exiled to the salt mines, instead of starting a new life of the most absorbing interest and adventure, which this has actually been and is being. . . . I'm now temporarily free from the U.S. draft, because I'm over 38: they recently lowered the age-limit, so I'm going to live at the Vedanta "monastery" here in Hollywood, as from next month: more about this in another letter.

None of us were particularly enthusiastic about the news of the move to the Vedanta "monastery," fearing that it would increase the gulf between us, perhaps even to a point of total non-comprehension.

These social exchanges lightened the strenuousness of hard working days and short nights, and gave relief from the speculations that never ceased to gnaw at the back of our minds; even though it was just beginning to be possible to believe seriously in the turn of the tide. One day I was in the middle of preparing one of my scripts for the Austrian Service of the B.B.C., when Patrick Smith, in charge of the programme, rang up to tell me: "In a few hours you're going to hear terrific news, the biggest and best news to break for a long time. You can scrap your script; there won't be room for anything else except the news." The Battle of El Alamein was on, and the news of the victory came through, as he promised, the next day.

« 4 »

THE literary and artistic life of London in the middle of the war had also its grand salons, where skilful hostesses brought writers, actors and painters together with politicians, soldiers and other men and women in public life they might otherwise never have had a chance of meeting. These salons flourished in spite of the hazards of bombing, the scarcity of good food and drink and all the absences and removals.

The chief of them, the most famous and the best frequented, were undoubtedly those conducted by Lady Colefax and Lady Cunard. Sybil Colefax's had survived since pre-war days, and all through the war Sybil not only managed to keep her smart interior-decorating business going, but also to pursue her social mission with an indefatigable showering of indecipherable invitations on novelists, poets, theatrical stars, cabinet ministers, influential civil servants, visiting American celebrities and distinguished survivors of the European debacle. It was an heroic, scarcely credible phenomenon. I had had the privilege of being on Sybil's invitation list from before the war; but it was Archie Clark-Kerr who introduced me to Emerald Cunard's salon. She had only returned from America towards the end of 1941, and had established herself on a high floor in the Dorchester, in a suite which she adorned with her famous Marie Laurencins and Berthe Morisots and some of the most precious and beautiful of her bound books: the great house in Grosvenor Square, setting of the parties of her heyday, had become a melancholy, deserted casualty of the blitz. In her Dorchester suite she began again to entertain, sometimes to tea and cocktail-parties, but mainly to dinner-parties, keeping up the spirit and tone of an already vanished epoch with astonishing courage, attack and verve, although in her late sixties and giving the impression of great physical fragility.

An aristocratic (but also American) audacity, intelligence, wit and, beneath it all, an almost tragic sense of disillusionment were the keynotes of her character. She gave a superficial impression of being cold and hard, where Sybil Colefax was so obviously warm-hearted and vulnerable. If she disliked or was displeased by something, she said so at once and without concealment; even in wartime, the staff of the Dorchester trembled before her complaints about service and cooking. I could not break myself of the habit of arriving at her parties punctually at the hour proposed, with the result that I often found myself alone in the suite, and then alone with her, for a considerable space of time. It was a testing time for the shy new-comer, for Emerald always seemed to be in a state of nervous tension before a party began, complaining of windows being open or not open, curtains drawn or not drawn, or the table for dinner not being properly laid. As the party progressed her tension relaxed and her gaiety and charm increased: her capacity for putting her guests at ease, but at the same time for communicating a certain glittering vivacity, for challenging one to be at one's best, was extremely stimulating. Her values, one felt at first, were worldly, even snobbish, buttressed by the brazen assumptions of money and power that survived in England from Edwardian days of Imperial supremacy; conversation at her table was often ruthless, sometimes coarse, but never dull; reputations were mercilessly investigated, wealth probed and shrewdly assessed; nevertheless, if the arts rather than people were under discussion, she showed a quite different side of her nature. Her understanding of literature, and especially of nineteenth-century novelists of many nationalities, was deep, and her judgement acute. It was only when the subject of poetry was broached that she seemed deliberately to defer to me; and I can remember evenings when she persuaded me, after all the other guests had gone, to read Shelley or some more modern poet to her, and unburden myself of my own enthusiasms about poetry. It was at those midnight moments that her mask of diamond heartlessness slipped: one had

[330]

glimpses of a pathetic and suffering creature below, a woman to whose heart wounds had been dealt that refused to heal. She dreaded being left alone with the night: she slept scarcely at all (as she ate scarcely at all), and spent long hours reading in bed after the last dinner guest had departed. She once exclaimed to me, when we were by ourselves: "No man, John, has ever said to me, 'I love you!' But I have had letters — I have had *letters!*" It was natural to assume that by this enigmatic and tantalizing remark she was referring to the letters she had received from George Moore, and of which she was sometimes ready to talk: but perhaps not only to those. I did not dare to ask.

Emerald's salon had an unqualified right-wing bias. The politicians one met there were, with rare exceptions, Conservative, the outlook entirely Conservative, the prejudices almost at times a caricature of the conventional aristocratic class-consciousness, though sustained with a wit and vigour of mind that were delightful to anyone with an ear for dialogue. That winter and spring I remember as frequent guests Duff Cooper and the beautiful Diana. I had not met Duff before, and wondered whether, as powerful head of a "hush-hush" committee on internal security, he had been told by Archie to discover for himself that I was not the dangerous agitator I still appeared, it seemed, to those who controlled appointments in the war bureaucracy. My first impression of Duff was of a small man, puffed up with his own importance, extremely choleric, self-indulgent and narrow in outlook; but it was not long before I saw that I was misjudging him, and that under the all too easily provoked outbursts of temper lay a complex personality, caring deeply for the things of the mind, extremely well read, especially in French literature, and capable of displaying quite extraordinary charm in intimate conversation when once his distrust was dissolved. By Diana I was completely captivated, once and for all. Even with her great and genuine enthusiasm for music, the theatre and the ballet, Emerald showed a conventional reserve towards artists who did not come out of the same social drawer as herself, or who had not at least enriched themselves into it; Diana, I saw very soon, had no such prejudices, liked bohemians, and, helped by the fact that she had been an actress herself, could get on at once with every sort of person who lived by and for the arts. This absolute indifference of Diana's to class and political allegiance in the world of the creative imagination, was to be the cause of fervent admiration, dismay and amusement at a later date, when she became Ambassadress and dazzling hostess of the British Embassy at Paris. I was struck by the penetrating sense of her observations on people and events; but above all by her beauty, which exercised, and still exercises, an hypnotic power upon me.

I only saw Sybil and Emerald together on one occasion, and that was in the spring of 1943, when the first of the famous Poetry Readings took place, in aid of some wartime charity. These Readings were patronized by Royalty, packed with celebrities from both the literary and social worlds, and the scene of contretemps and scandal that provided stories to dine out on for weeks after. To this first Reading the Queen had agreed to come, and bring the two young Princesses with her. Edith Sitwell had been appointed one of the organizers, and a few days before wrote to me, on the brink of despair:

The shades of — less the prison house than the lunatic asylum — are drawing ever nearer to me. The Reading — the Reading! The letters to poets about their collars, the threats to faint on the part of one female poet, the attempt to (*a*) read for 20 minutes instead of 6, (*b*) change the time of rehearsal, (*c*) be rehearsed all by herself *by me just* before the Reading, (*d*) read a funeral eulogy of Yeats — on the part of another female poet. And other troubles of this sort! Life is very difficult.

Her fears were justified on the day. Lady Dorothy Wellesley was one of the poets invited to read, but in spite of a momentary, distraught appearance on the platform about ten minutes before the Queen arrived, failed to take her place. The poets performed in alphabetical order, and as the end of the alphabet approached, Vita Sackville-West slipped into the wings, only to return a few minutes later with a look of great shock on her face — but without the missing poetess.

The poets were ranged on either side of D. L. Murray, at that time editor of *The Times Literary Supplement.* No greater contrast could be imagined than between Tom Eliot, looking wearily benign and noble, Edith in her black robes and green hat shaped like a laurel wreath, as dominating as a Roman emperor, and Walter de la Mare, a wizened gnome king. Nearly all of them, with the notable exceptions of Tom, the Sitwells, and Vita, gave very bad performances, and reduced the professional verse-readers, of whom there were a number in the audience, to a state of squirming misery. And yet I found it impossible to agree with Eddie Sackville-West, who, at the back of the hall, was suffering more acutely than anyone else, that it would have been far better to have had only professionals. The gathering of so many notable poets on one platform was exciting in itself, and even when they were difficult to hear and showed little or no understanding of an audience's natural expectations, there was a fascinating juxtaposition of personalities and styles, and every now and then, even in the bad performances, moments that shed a new illumination, precious as coming from the creator himself, on poems one had always loved. This was not, I fear, true in the case of W. J. Turner, who went on monotonously reciting inaudible verse long beyond his strictly apportioned ration of time, and seemed quite incapable of taking the hint implied in the continual bursts of applause that interrupted him ever more violently as the recitation proceeded. The Princesses appeared delighted by this atmosphere of near-riot that developed so spontaneously, and so unexpectedly enlivened their poetry lesson. But the Reading would have been worth-while, apart from its comedy aspect, if only for the opportunity it gave us to hear Tom reciting *What the Thunder Said* from *The Waste Land*, starting on a deep, incantatory note and working up to a climax of superb passion and drama.

Emerald had invited me to join her party, which included Duff Cooper and Leslie Hore-Belisha; it was as we left the hall, passing the distressed figure of the future Duchess of Wellington at the head of the stairs, that I saw Emerald and Sybil come together and talk animatedly for a few moments. But Emerald was in one of her most ebullient moods, and as we emerged into Bond Street she pranced away from Sybil and up to Hore-Belisha, crying: "Leslie! Recite me some Ronsard! — You do it so beautifully!" The former War Minister, however, did not oblige.

« 5 »

SOMETIMES, after these excursions into the salons at the top, where still, through its disintegration, one could catch glimpses of what an older beau monde had been like, the need came over me to plunge to the other end of the social scale.

So I would sally forth into the black-out, to visit the pubs of Soho and the Fitzregnum, the French pub, the Swiss pub, the Fitzroy Tavern, the Wheatsheaf and others in remoter districts; or if it was after hours, the cafés and late-night snack-bars into which the stragglers emptied themselves. There a floating population of bohemians, actors, firemen, soldiers, sailors and airmen on leave or of the London garrison, and of many nationalities, poets and artists sometimes in uniform and sometimes in civvies, drifted together in chance and ever-changing groups: never have the London pubs been more stimulating, never has one been able to hear more extraordinary revelations, never witness more unlikely encounters.

The Fitzroy Tavern has changed now: gone are the dusty rows of naval cap badges pinned up above the bottles near the ceiling, famous names enough to conjure up a mighty fleet, the military caps and strange barbaric weapons beside them even more deeply dust-encrusted, too sacred and no doubt too fragile for a broom to touch; gone the cartoons of the proprietor and the recruiting posters of the First World War with their period pathos; gone all the famous old soaks, male and female, the groups of battledressed guardsmen like plants that had got more than their fair share of fertilizer and shot up above the rest, the Canadian and American sailors honeying with the painted girls of the town, the stray, argumentative intellectuals, the quiet couples, the squeaking hard-as-nails pansies who would only have made a facetious "camp" joke if a bomb had fallen next door, the tinkling piano and the jingling box handed round for the pianists' collection — all that came to mean a kind of invincible London spirit in those years. And yet in the middle of the general warmth, the tough high spirits, the thought of something very different was never far absent. One night, alone with my own ruminations there, I pulled out of my pocket and re-read a letter that had arrived that morning from my ex-secretary John Lepper in the Middle East:

While out in our truck the other day we were caught in a hell of a sand-storm which blew up without any warning. It almost seems at times that Nature gets irritated by the death-like silence which hangs over these wastelands and sends a sudden wind to disturb the stillness. It was about three hours before we could see sufficiently far ahead through the dust haze to risk a move — knowing that there was a minefield somewhere in the vicinity, we were not disposed to take any chances. It continued to blow very strongly all that night; towards two o'clock our tent collapsed and we had to fight devilish hard to prevent the whole issue from being blown all over the maidan.

I began to wonder whether John, and all the other soldiers and sailors who had known these pubs in the earlier phases of the war, thought of them nostalgically sometimes in the middle of the desert or in the wastes of the Arctic Sea. Somehow to be arguing, laughing, singing there was a vote of confidence in them; and the printed sign that hung up above the counter, WE ARE NOT INTERESTED IN THE POSSIBILITY OF DEFEAT, was not just a piece of bravado or a warning to spreaders of "alarm and despondency," but the statement, nine-tenths of the time, of a simple truth.

« 6 »

IN a letter to Christopher at the end of 1942, I told him that the ranks of the regular *New Writing* contributors and the new young authors in uniform who were apt to turn up in London on leave, or passing through from one posting to another, were gradually growing thinner: "airgraphs to Africa take the place of invitations to pilchards and cheese." It was in fact a time when the lines of communication between *New Writing* and its contributors and would-be contributing enthusiasts were stretched to their most tenuous, across all the oceans and continents where theatres of war were to be found. Letters came in every day by airmail letter card or by that ingenious, handy invention of the war years, the airgraph, from Kenya, Persia, Egypt, Palestine, Cyprus, India, Burma and every other country of the Middle and Far East that was still in Allied hands, reporting the at-long-last arrival of copies of the Penguins that had been sent off months before, or complaining of their failure to arrive, anxiously enquiring after manuscripts entrusted to the precarious surface mail, and disputing or agreeing with points of criticism I had made of manuscripts that had arrived safely and made their slow way through the increasingly congested editorial machine. My contributors could not see the bulging files (additions to which were so difficult to obtain), the heroic attempts by Barbara Cooper and her occasional assistants to find room for newly arrived manuscripts in inadequate chests of drawers already stuffed beyond capacity, or the struggle to correct proofs by airgraph texts, for some of the poets at least had begun sending their poems in this way to save time and danger. Punctuation in these minute photographic reproductions was sometimes extremely difficult to decipher; and occasionally, when the poem was long, or one of a series typed out over a whole sequence of airgraphs, the middle version would mysteriously fail to appear until a few weeks later, causing meanwhile odd misapprehensions in Carrington House about the jumps of thought, the pregnant sense-gaps that modern poets appeared increasingly to indulge in.

One of the chief contributors with whom I kept up a long-distance conversation in this way for many months, and even years, was Roy Fuller in the Fleet Air Arm unit at Kilindini. The editor-contributor relationship with Roy was in some ways the most satisfying of the war for me. He had been an interesting "second generation" poet of the 'thirties who, in spite of obviously strong intellectual equipment and deep feeling for poetry, had never quite emerged with an individual voice to catch and keep one's attention. Then, early in the war, he was drafted into the Navy and began to write a new kind of lyric about his training and the mood of his fellow-recruits, behind the straight simplicity of which extremely sharp observation, irony and deep emotion were closely packed in:

> Once as we were sitting by
> The falling sun, the thickening air,
> The chaplain came against the sky
> And quietly took a vacant chair.
>
> And under the tobacco smoke:
> "Freedom," he said, and "Good" and "Duty."
> We stared as though a savage spoke.
> The scene took on a singular beauty.
>
> And we made no reply to that
> Obscure, remote communication,
> But only stared at where the flat
> Meadow dissolved in vegetation.
>
> And thought: O sick, insatiable
> And constant lust; O death, our future;
> O revolution in the whole
> Of human use of man and nature.

When I read this poem, and the others he sent me which were written at the same time, I felt at once that they were the answer to the disgruntled old buffers and impatient well-wishers who were still complaining that there were no war poets, though the disillusioned, anti-heroic note might well not be to their taste; a more promising answer than the still rather soft, nostalgic poetry that Alun Lewis and Sidney Keyes were writing at this period, and far more effective than the rather tediously inflated verse that some members of the so-called "Apocalyptic" school and their fellow-travellers were producing at the same time. Several of Roy's new poems were published in *Penguin New Writing*, and were quickly noted by the connoisseurs. After he had finished his naval training, Roy was drafted eventually to his land-job in Kenya. He wrote at the time:

I feel more and more that I ought to develop in some way those simple things I was writing in England. The trouble is I seem to have escaped the war again — it must be fated that there shall be no war-poets. I just have the disadvantages of noise and gregariousness without the stimulant of action. I shall have to do some nature poems — there is certainly enough nature. For the rest, discipline is sensible and the Navy, as usual, in its rather bearish, clumsy way makes us as comfortable as it can. Six-pence a day colonial money, 50 cigarettes, 2 boxes of matches and a cake of soap free every week — it is like a kind but poor and vulgar aunt. I wouldn't be in any other service for 5s. a day more! And I still find my fellow-ratings witty, kind and simple. A man in the next bed to me, an airgunner, regular service, one long service badge, announced his intention of going to a concert in the town last night. They asked him what it was. "A Bach concerto, Mozart, Brahms." A howl of derision. But he howled too — "I've heard the bloke that plays the piano — and he's SHIT HOT." "Shit hot" is our catchword at the moment — it is the highest adjectival praise known to the F.A.A.

Out of Roy's feeling for East African nature, the sudden, fresh impact it made on him, came such beautiful poems as *The Giraffes*. But his mood of irresolution about the future direction of his poetry did not last long. He began to write poems of more elaborate organization and of even greater intensity of feeling, in which were mingled his vision of an African tribal life, horrible but satisfying to the primitive mind and spirit, now ruined by the corruption of white civilization, which gives material benefits but has destroyed the meaning, and the meaninglessness of the lives of the soldiers involved in the war, symbols of whose grotesque pathos and suffering he found in the animals he watched — crabs on the beach or captive monkeys. All through these poems is a sense of almost terrifying despair, an apprehension that something — which once existed in the world and can somehow be put back in it — is absent, drained out of life:

> . . . It says the human features
> Are mutilated, have a dreadful lack.
>
> It half convinces me that some great faculty,
> Like hands, has been eternally lost and all
> Our virtues now are the high and horrible
> Ones of a streaming wound which heals in evil.

It is the mood of the first book, but far more powerfully expressed, without sentimentality or rhetoric and with a marvellous control of language and use of poetic shape and rhythm to heighten his effects:

[337]

> For what is terrible is the obvious
> Organization of life: the oiled black gun,
> And what it cost, the destruction of Europe by
> Its councils; the unending justification
> Of that which cannot be justified, what is done.

It was, I think, exile — exile from intellectual companionship and the world of argument and discussion — that most writers in uniform minded more than any other aspect of the war. Norman Cameron, sending me three "travel-sketch kind of poems" from North Africa, wrote:

In a letter I got from you some time ago, you said something about living in mud and cold. I'm afraid I can't claim to be suffering any hardship, except lack of sheets. I live in comfort. I did do a trip recently to a comparatively forward area, and there I was more comfortable than ever, since soldiers in the field look after themselves as well as they can, when they can. In a Polish mess, for example, I had the best meal since 1940 — all made out of ordinary British rations, but quite unrecognizable.

What else? I'm beginning, despite all this comfort, to feel the effects of exile. As Robert Graves remarked about his stay in Egypt, one can live on one's hump only for so long, and my hump is not large. I want to meet some friends again. . . .

Then there were the younger poets, like Roy Fuller, struggling to hold on to the literary world of England by the frail capricious threads of airgraph and air letter, poets to whom the connection was even more important, as they were at the beginning of their careers and in danger of having no career at all at the same time. Alan Ross, slim, dark-haired poet of twenty from Haileybury and Oxford, sent me a batch of poems one day from a destroyer which he had recently joined as a sub-lieutenant. He had already, I discovered, had a smash in the Fleet Air Arm that nearly cost him his eyesight, and had since taken part in the Arctic convoys, which were among the most dangerous operations of the war. A combination of freshness of lyrical feeling and sophistication of approach in the poems appealed to me, and I accepted one at once. On his next shore leave he came to see me, and I found him bursting, not with stories of the hair-raisingly horrible adventures he had been through (I found out about them afterwards) but with ideas about poetry and pictures and plays. Every time his ship came back to port, he threw off his naval disguise and put on corduroys and a brightly coloured shirt, and made for the first bookshop he could find, to emerge with his arms full of volumes of poetry, new novels and biographies. He informed me, to my amazement, that on board his destroyer as many as thirty people, officers and ratings, read *Penguin New Writing;* and though they had begun to read it casually and dubiously, persevered perhaps because one particular story appealed to them for a background they recognized or for a character who might have come out of their own lives; so that they had now reached the stage of holding highbrow discussions about Auden and Lorca.

I used also to have a lively correspondence with Terence Tiller, who was teaching at Cairo University and was one of the leading spirits responsible for *Personal Landscape*. This was, in my opinion, by far the most interesting of the many briefly flowering literary magazines that appeared in Egypt during the war; indeed one of the rare "little" magazines that have made literary history in our time. "Environment and personal friendship, and not a specific poetic practice was the bond," wrote Robin Fedden in introducing the *Personal Landscape* anthology after the war, and described how he and Lawrence Durrell and Bernard Spencer had all got to know one another previously in Greece. Robin and Bernard were, of course, of my own generation; Larry, a little younger, had begun to make his name in Paris just before the war; Terence, the youngest of the original contributors, had attracted my attention a few years earlier, as I have already described, and had appeared in *Poets of Tomorrow* while still at Cambridge. "His tensity of style and piercing metaphysical eye," wrote Robin, "added something that none of us had got and emphasized just that variety of approach and absence of poetic *parti pris* that we felt was desirable." Beside the qualities Robin Fedden noted, Terence's poems had a remarkable verbal music and subtlety of rhythmic life; they particularly delighted me because, almost always carefully wrought, often arcane and yet never guilty of the confused grandiloquence that disfigured so much poetry of the time, they seemed to me the nearest thing to pure poetry to come out of those years.

Side by side with the young poets came the prose writers of the future: none more promising, more full of exciting possibilities in the context of the time, than Julian Maclaren-Ross. In 1940, he had sent me some stories which I had just not liked well enough to accept, because, for all the skill they showed, there seemed to me something a little *made up* about them (subsequently he sold several of them and made a success, especially with *A Bit of a Smash in Madras*, which appeared in *Horizon*). Apparently harbouring no resentment about this, he suddenly wrote to me in July of 1942, from the Beach Café,

Bognor Regis, in his extraordinary neat, marmoset's handwriting — he never then and never since used a typewriter — to say that he had started writing again. This was the beginning of a long literary relationship with an eccentric, brilliantly gifted author who sometimes seemed as if possessed by a demon whose satanic mission it was to thwart and wither at the root all the uniquely valuable talents Julian had been born with. The first story he sent me was *Y List*, an account of his own experiences in an army hospital, done with a wit, a story-telling flair, and a kind of dry pathos of characterization that marked it out at once as the work of a highly original writer; but not the masterpiece of humorous observation that I was lucky enough to publish for him a couple of years later, *The Swag, The Spy and The Soldier*. Julian's greatest gift, in these war stories, was, I thought, his intuitive sympathy for those who have fallen foul of The Machine; for those who are too simple in their eccentricity as well as for those who are too complex and sensitive, to fit into the conventional set-up; a passionate feeling for life, on the edge of despair, informed the best of them. He had, I reflected when reading these stories, the makings of a Dickens in him — a Dickens who had read Dashiell Hammett.

My main object, in the stories and sketches of wartime life that became a central feature of *New Writing* during these years, was always, I think, to find the writers who could reveal a truth more authentic, more intimate in detail than the propaganda to which we were (ever so gently) subjected could admit, something that slipped through the coarse nets of the journalists. Sometimes, however, it was the journalists themselves who provided it, breaking away in a moment of illumination from the uncommanded conventions of their calling.

In the British Navy, the drafted or volunteer ratings who had joined up only for the duration, were known as H.O. — "Hostilities Only" — sailors. In the world of letters also there were "Hostilities Only" writers. Some of them, like Rollo Wooley, might have taken up writing as a serious occupation after the war; one can never know, because they were killed so soon after having written their two or three stories or poems, evidence only of their intention of the moment and not of the unrevealed strength of talent and will-power. Rollo Wooley, whom I only met once for half an hour very shortly before his last flight, was a sensitive, good-looking boy of twenty-three from Rugby and Oxford, the dreamy look in whose eye was reflected in the slight but haunting story *The Search*, which I published in *New Writing and Daylight* in the winter of 1942–43. A crew go out to search for an aeroplane reported missing. But is it really for this aeroplane they are looking? Loch, mountain and ocean take on a sad, timeless, symbolic aspect in the young airman's eye:

What did they expect us to find? No we had seen nothing. All our lives we had been searching and had found nothing. Only the whitewashed cottages and some strands of seaweed. Only some fragments of cloud and the blueness of the sea. Only the thinness of the empty glittering waves. I felt too weary to remember the original object of our search. Certainly it had been quite clear a little while ago: a plane was missing: one of our pilots had not returned. But that was only the previous night, and surely we had been searching for longer than that? Ages and ages before we had begun the search . . .

Who can tell whether Rollo Wooley would have been able to develop the delicate poetic vein which these three pages revealed? Slight though they are, they have a curious perfection of expression in their time and place: an achievement which has nothing to do with bulk and complexity, and is rarely granted, even to those with far greater ambition, will-power and luck in survival.

From all the Services, from every front, manuscripts poured in. One day there would arrive a satirical ballad from a young man serving in the Royal Marines, who had already been in many of the most spectacular naval engagements of the war: it came in an envelope stamped *On Active Service*, and as I read it I was aware he might well be about to make a descent on some secretly chosen beach in enemy-occupied territory. Another day would arrive the story of a leave spent in Cairo from a gunner in the Long Range Desert Group: long before the MS. had made its slow way to London, he could have been captured or wounded in a furious sudden encounter with Rommel's tanks. A Monday morning's batch would include some reflective poems from a nurse in Malta, poems that had survived in a convoy that had had to fight off enemy attacks for days and nights without stop; an airgraph from a newly-gazetted lieutenant in PAI-Force, which contained a neat epigram on the meeting of Russian and British soldiers; a rather battered-looking packet, with Indian stamps outside and an unknown aircraftsman's diary inside, which had taken nearly four months on its way by the long sea-route; and a letter from a prisoner-of-war camp in Germany, containing elegies and sonnets written in the endless tedium of that remote, flat landscape of Northern Europe.

[341]

There were times when, looking through all these works so precious to the young men and women who sent them off, I felt as if I were in a telephone exchange in which confused, half-audible messages were being sent pell-mell, in a never-ending stream. The human appeal of these manuscripts was nearly always immense, but how vastly their literary value varied, how rarely the authentic gift revealed itself! The more of them I read as the months went by, the more pity I thought it that these burning shrapnel fragments of experience and reflection-in-action, from places where the meaning of the war was most keenly felt, so many of them so much more real and significant than what normally got into our wartime newspapers, could so seldom be used. The messages were too confused, too incomplete, the thing that needed so urgently to be said lost before the end in a tangle of clichés.

From the window of the room where I worked in Carrington House, the eye was directed, by high flanking walls to right and to left, southwards through a gap between the top floors of steel and concrete buildings, over the trees of Green Park to a confused ridge of chimney-pots and domes, in the middle of which rose a slim tower of vaguely Oriental aspect, the tower of Westminster Cathedral. Every now and then a white plume of smoke puffed up into the air somewhere along this ridge, indicating a train arriving or departing in the terminus concealed there. On a clear day a further line of wooded hills appeared behind the tower, the extreme limit of the view. To reach that line of hills, the eye had passed over the hidden chasm of Piccadilly at the foot of the steel and concrete buildings, the only evidence of which was the faint continual rumble and rustle of traffic, too faint for the ear to distinguish depth or distance; and the more remote chasm of the river, which only reminded the ear of its presence when the busier sounds of day had ebbed and the mournful hooting of a tug was heard to echo hollowly against the early morning or late evening sky.

The sofa table which I used as desk was always piled with manuscripts waiting to be read or re-read, and letters waiting to be answered. Often, trying to make up my mind whether a poem or a story was really worth accepting, or what to write to an author who seemed to me just not to have made the grade, I let my gaze stray out into the landscape, losing the thread of thought for a moment, letting the changes of light stir strange irrelevant imaginings. Sometimes the arrangement of trees and buildings, the haze of a fine day mounting towards noon, would begin to obliterate the vast city; as the sun illuminated a concrete wall to a certain tone of pale-gold against the pale-blue atmosphere, one could for a moment fancy that out there, only two or three hundred yards away, a curling line of foam was cooling a beach of sifted, white sand, and fishing boats of a shape and colour no English sea-side knew were sliding across the sparkling satin of the water. . . . Even in London the spring smells of the earth cannot be altogether effaced by smoke and petrol fumes; and straying on a light breeze through the open window they evoked disturbing mirages in the mind, sudden half-glimpsed memories of other, peacetime springs in other places, chestnut leaves unfurling against baroque porches and balustrades.

After working in London for several years of war with scarcely a break, one's mind was particularly susceptible to these transformations. Everything in the war seemed to be happening on a distant rim; and the two illusions underwent curious identifications in moments of extreme nostalgia, so that the fighting in Africa or the East, where so many of one's friends had been transported, appeared to the imagination not as the exile and ever-renewed danger of those friends, but as the fortunate experience of a younger self.

There was a great deal of weary work in the sifting and judging of these innumerable manuscripts, in spite of the keen pleasure of the occasional authentic finds; but it was constantly relieved by the eccentricities and unconscious humour of a certain proportion of the would-be contributors. I always intended to make copies of the dottier poems and "yarns" for the amusement of myself and my friends in the darker days that might be coming, but neither I nor Barbara Cooper ever seemed to find the time. Even if we had, I could not have quoted them here, for fear their authors might still be alive. In spite of the prevailing anti-heroic tone of wartime poetry, these eccentrics proved to me that the spirit of Sir Henry Newbolt was still alive, and when I read the clarion-call of a first line, "Day Lewis, arise!," I realized that the mood of defending "the bad against the worse" was chagrin and disappointment to at least one patriotic songster.

One day, a clipping came in from the *New York Herald Tribune*, in which the reviewer, Babette Deutsch, wrote of a batch of *Penguin New Writing*s which had just arrived from Britain: "These small books, thin, unbound, printed on shabby paper. Yet one handles them respectfully; they have come through. There is a challenge in the determination that got these pamphlets printed and distributed and shipped across the Atlantic." And I thought of a line in a poem I had published by Norman Hampson, written while serving in a corvette, on convoy duty, on the high seas:

. . . We keep
The truest course by the best light we know.

« 7 »

IT was clear, as soon as the first number of *New Writing and Daylight* had been published, that it was liked, and was going to be able to maintain itself: and I could therefore indulge in some long-term planning for its future. For the rest of the war, I suppose that scarcely a day passed without my two *New Writing* offspring being in my thoughts: and at week-ends when I could get away to Fieldhead, I used to take long walks by the river, evolving schemes for a special feature or a symposium for the next number, deciding whom I would invite to write for it, or how I would arrange the authors I had already accepted.

There were obvious similarities between *New Writing and Daylight* and the Penguin, and these increased when the former, like an elder brother at school passing on blazer or bat to a younger brother, gave some of its most successful contributions a second life at a year or so's interval in the Penguin. Nevertheless, I always saw the chief function of *New Writing and Daylight* as providing an international meeting-place of the arts, as the original, pre-war *New Writing* had, and I was constantly trying to find new foreign contributors among the exiled writers in London, or to extract from those in privileged places copies of new poems or stories that had been written abroad. So it was that I managed to publish some of Aragon's most beautiful *Crève-Coeur* poems in a skilful translation by Louis MacNeice; a short story by Nikolai Tikhonov, whom I had met in Russia before the war; poems by Czech poets still in the Protectorate, which Jiři Mucha obtained for me; Polish and Portuguese contributions, and many from occupied Greece through Demetrios and his Greek friends in many parts of the world.

But I also intended to devote more space in *New Writing and Daylight* to critical studies, with all the arts within their range. My most cherished aim was to find and give encouragement and scope to the kind of critic who has always interested me most, and has always seemed to me most capable of acting as a creative agent on the making of literature: the poet or poet-novelist whose intelligence is constantly exploring the philosophical raison d'être of his art, testing his conclusions by examining them in relation to the great artists of the past or his more formidable contemporaries, the writer with a bent for con-

[344]

structing systems out of the ideas which have filled his own mind for the time being; who is miles apart from the pedantic critic awarding marks and arranging schools, or the clever talker-critic with nothing new to say, who treats a book as a sort of tennis-court in which to play a brilliant game. Good — that is, stimulating and persuasive — philosopher-poets of this kind are unfortunately rare; and many hopes I entertained (though not all) were disappointed. In spite of this, and though I was well aware of the dangers of trying to "impose a line" on my contributors, a tone, a direction of thought did, I believe, emerge from *New Writing and Daylight*, and more recognizably as it went on; largely because the writers I went to for critical articles were generally friends with whose thought I was intimate through many a discussion, but also, perhaps, because there was a "spirit of the time," a sense of the need to emphasize the human and, to put it at its simplest, the overriding importance of humankind-ness, which all of us to some extent shared.

In these critical studies, I was also anxious to provide some kind of commentary on contemporary literature; and as it seemed to me that there were hints of some very interesting, indeed exciting developments, and my head was teeming with them, I undertook this job myself, in a series of articles which I called *The Armoured Writer*. I spent a great deal of the war years in reading, not only manuscripts for the Hogarth Press or *New Writing*, but also the newly published books that stood in any relation to imaginative literature, perhaps more than ever before or since; at the same time I read and re-read the great classics, looking always for some new relevance to the times we were living through. I should give a false picture of my life and mind at this time if I were to leave out all this reading and the restless experimental reflections it gave rise to: the continuous, rather undisciplined laboratory-researcher's testing and speculating.

In writing my article *The Heart of the Problem* for the first number of *Daylight*, I had complained of the fragmentariness, the imaginative inadequacy of the prose fiction of the period to deal with the crisis of civilization in which we found ourselves. In those early days I was thinking mainly of the novels that had come out of the experience of the 'thirties, each illuminating a small area of experience powerfully enough, but failing to provide the complete X-ray of the *sickness in the bone* of our time. But the first years of the war had, it seemed to me, given us even less than this; and in poetry, too, there was as yet nothing to compare with Auden's *Look, Stranger* and what it had done for the English left-wing fermentation of the 'thirties.

This was still the central theme of my *Armoured Writer* articles. I realized, of course, that I was asking rather a lot in expecting a Tolstoi to appear at once: *War and Peace* was written years after the end of the Napoleonic Wars, though the fighting scenes were based on Tolstoi's far more recent experiences in the Crimean War. Nevertheless, Malraux and Silone had written in the full tide of events, and written well, and Yeats's superb poems on the Irish Civil War had not had to go through more than a few months of incubation. What was beginning to disturb me was that the impulse of writers to wrestle with the real under-the-surface material of their time seemed to be flagging. The relationship of literature and life is complex and obscure, and the experiences of the 'thirties had warned me of the dangers of thinking that it should or could be immediate and realistic; but I still believed profoundly that if literature is to exert all its potential power as hidden healer in our lives, it must speak about the problems of the day in the language of the day, even if indirectly or by allegory and symbol. I did not think there could be any going back to purely esoteric literature after what had happened in the 'thirties, and while we were still in the middle of the revolution that the 'thirties had begun and the war was accelerating. I wrote in my first article: "What one has a right to anticipate is a work of art, whether it is written in prose or dramatic verse or some new mixture of both, which will cover all the ground that the Marxists and the Freudians opened up, but much more as well, a novel (to use a term which already embraces works as different as *To the Lighthouse, The Castle, The Counterfeiters* and *The Plumed Serpent*) that will have profited from the deeper insight that disappointment or disillusionment brought to those who pinned their faith to the formulas of the 'thirties." There was little enough to bolster this confidence when I wrote that article; nevertheless there were a few signs and portents, and in the course of the next two or three years they gathered strength and frequency.

Novels which had the conditions of wartime life as their setting were already beginning to appear. By far the most interesting to me was Henry Green's *Caught*, which describes the life of an auxiliary fireman, Richard Roe, in a London sub-station, from the period of his pre-war training down to the time when he is recuperating for a few days in the country after the great air-raids of the autumn of 1940. *Caught* contains two unforgettable characters: Pye, the unlucky, unhappy officer in charge of the sub-station, and Mary Howells, the cook who goes "adrift" and so, by chance, sets in motion the machinery of the trap in which Pye finds himself caught indeed in the end. It also contains two brilliant character sketches on a smaller scale: Piper, the toadying old soldier, and the ex-seaman Shiner Wright who, in the superbly described dockland fire at the end, sheds a light of almost superhuman courage on a resolutely anti-heroic book. What impressed me so much about Henry Green's developing art in this novel was the way the characters are defined and exposed by their dialogue. Again and again I found myself re-reading passages to savour this rare and marvellous gift: no one in his generation, even when one remembers that it includes Christopher Isherwood and V. S. Pritchett, has so accurate an ear for the way people talk, for the peculiar conversation patterns and word choice of every type of person, and above all for the element of the absurd and the irrational that is always cropping up in uninhibited English talk.

Caught mirrored, with something like genius, the compound of tragedy and comedy that was the truth of the war, the heroism that showed itself in spite of an extreme distaste for and distrust of heroics; as a work of art it was more satisfying to the spirit than any amount of simpler literature, whose consciously morale-building authors would not have dared to show the auxiliary firemen, the "heroes" of the blitz, as selfish, mean, coarse, absorbed in petty intrigues and petty anxieties about their careers, when they were not chasing girls in the black-out. This was a distinction that was impossible for our state-controlled Russian allies to appreciate; but of that more later.

It seems to me that the novels which appeared during these middle years of the war were all important in the degree they got away from the propagandist-heroic. For all the skill and expertise brought to bear on them, books like C. S. Forester's *The Ship* were, I thought, radio-actively dead, and did far less to support the will-to-victory and heal the breach in our culture than books like *Caught*, which had no propagandist design on their readers at all. Even when writers were laudably determined not to write *for* the war, it often managed to worm itself into their work in some concealed way. The stress of wartime life, the continual sense of danger and effort were still there even when they had become too habitual to be remembered; and they introduced twists to one's judgement and one's emotions, streaks of hysteria and sentimentality, without one being entirely aware of it.

As in warfare, the direct assault, the direct approach was yielding little enough, but there was also the indirect approach. By the middle of the war, a handful of novels had appeared which, though not immediately concerned with the war, had been written or finished at least under its influence, and had a deep symbolic or allegorical relation to it. The two most important were undoubtedly Virginia Woolf's *Between the Acts* and Rex Warner's *The Aerodrome*. Though the time — the late summer of 1939 — and the place — the countryside of southern England — are precise in *Between the Acts*, I find it difficult to believe that its poetic overtones, its intensely charged and haunting imagery will not be as full of significance twenty or thirty years hence as they were to the wartime generation. Like all works of genius, it is timeless. Nevertheless, there is, I think, an unmistakable sense all through the book of being on the brink of catastrophe, and of the themes that run below the surface being all the more acutely urgent because of the particular predicament of that time.

Rex Warner began *The Aerodrome* before the war broke out, but evidently at a time when the collapse of the Republican cause in Spain had started the process of reappraisal in disillusionment, which had affected all the writers of the 'thirties. If one compares *The Aerodrome* with Rex Warner's first "novel," *The Wild Goose Chase*, one sees at once the distance he had travelled in thought and feeling; the difference between the two books can stand for the journey taken by so many of his more sensitive contemporaries. *The Wild Goose Chase* is a success story, an anti-fascist fairy tale of the simplest basic pattern, subtle and imaginative and dramatic with the intensity of nightmare though many of the details are. In *The Aerodrome*, in contrast, there is a deep sense of inescapable imperfection, of good and evil fatally intertwined in life, which is the essence of tragedy and the very opposite of the fairy tale. The Air Vice-Marshal is obsessed with the possibilities of power that the science of our age puts into the hands of men who are daring and intelligent and ruthless enough to grasp it; he is an idealist, dreaming of the perfect organization for controlling the lives of human beings for their own good; but even when it collapses, because it demands an inhumanity from man that his moral nature cannot in the end acquiesce in — because the ends do not justify the means — even then, when a future order is envisaged arising out of a fusion of the old order with what was good in the Air Vice-Marshal's dream, there is still no certainty, life is still "most intricate, fiercer than tigers." *The Aerodrome* seemed intensely relevant to what was happening in the early years of the war; but the battle betwen the Air Vice-Marshal and the Village is still going on, is in fact the central conflict of our century. It was not surprising that the book caused such a stir in foreign countries when it was translated after the war.

In both these remarkable books, poetic symbolism was used in various ways *against* surface realism. There never could have been a village pageant like the one that took place at Pointz Hall; nor could there ever have been a village inn like the one near the aerodrome, where the rat-catcher bites off the rat's head to amuse the company. Another author, writing at very much the same time, was using poetic symbolism in much the same way for similar ends, but he came from the other side of the war lines, and his book had come by devious routes into the hands of a friend who lent it to me. It was a most curious and exciting experience to read Ernst Jünger's *Auf den Marmorklippen* in the middle of the war, in an edition openly published by a famous German firm, with Jünger's note opposite the title-page that it had been finished in 1939 *"beim Heer";* for it could be read as a scorching condemnation of the Nazi state, and, though one could deduce from it that the author approved of fighting and war under certain circumstances, as a kind of recantation of much that he had stood for in the eyes of the German people.

A hundred touches in the development of the story suggested to us then that the Nazis were being described: Wotan riding again from the ever-unquiet depths of the German soul, as the great philosopher Jung later imagined it. And yet, I would not be so sure today; obviously Jünger could not have written *Auf den Marmorklippen* without the story of Hitler's rise to power in mind; but some of the symbols in this extraordinary book may well refer to other levels beside that of the political and social order; and now, thirty years later, one sees that it can almost equally well allegorize other manifestations of our Grand Guignol century; an imaginative criticism of all those anti-moral upsurges of the lust for power in which one country after another seems forced to take the victim part. The Air Vice-Marshal of *The Aerodrome* is a distant relation of the Head Forester of *Auf den Marmorklippen;* and both had been nurtured on what Edwin Muir, in his article *The Natural Man and the Political Man,* had called "the religion of development," on the idea that if you control *things* you control mankind.

I was already becoming convinced that the great theme of our time was this problem of power running amok, power without moral sanction or restraint; and that there was something in the claim that the real image of the world we lived in was to be found in a certain class of detective and spy stories. A ceaseless murderous struggle for power, in which the protagonists are always, in peace or war, retreating behind more and more elaborate barriers of concealment and camouflage; a struggle which uses the individual with utter ruthlessness, and in which, if he is luckless or foolish enough to become too closely involved, he has no more chance than a sparrow hitting a high-tension cable; the world of industrial secrets and espionage networks and war — this, the world of the modern thrillers, seemed to me the truest picture of our own inescapable environment. And for this reason, I was particularly drawn to Graham Greene's *The Ministry of Fear*, which appeared in 1943. Graham called it "an entertainment"; but the basic difference between his "entertainments" and his novels has always been a little difficult to discover. The "entertainments" can, perhaps, be classed more easily as thrillers, though there is a "thriller" element in many of the best novels; but *The Ministry of Fear* is certainly as serious as *Brighton Rock* or *The Power and the Glory* as a criticism of the world we live in and the life we lead, and has moments of astonishing, poetic illumination about the pursuit of power in an unstable civilization. The passage that has always haunted me is where Arthur Rowe, sheltering in an Underground station during an air-raid, has a half-waking dream in which he imagines himself talking to his dead mother:

"This isn't real life anymore," he said. "Tea on the lawn, evensong, croquet, the old ladies calling, the gentle, unmalicious gossip, the gardener trundling the wheelbarrow full of leaves and grass. People write about it as if it still went on: lady novelists describe it over and over again in books of the month, but it's not there any more." His mother smiled at him in a scared way but let him talk: he was the master of the dream now. He said: "I'm wanted for a murder I didn't do. People want to kill me because I know too much. I'm hiding underground, and up above the Germans are methodically smashing London to bits all around me. . . . It sounds like a thriller, doesn't it, but the thrillers are like life — more like life than you are, this lawn, your sandwiches, that pine. You used to laugh at the books Miss Savage read — about spies, and murders, and violence, and wild motor-car chases, but dear, that's real life: it's what we've all made of the world since you died. I'm your little Arthur who wouldn't hurt a beetle, and I'm a murderer too. The world has been remade by William le Queux."

The contribution that the poets were making to the understanding — the cathartic interpretation — of this world "remade by William le Queux" was beginning, by the middle of the war, to show itself far greater and far more significant than one could possibly have expected in the first twelve months. In retrospect, in fact, it seems to me that in the whole field of what was written during the war, English poetry comes out on top.

« 8 »

NOT long ago, I was asked to address a school society on "something to do with poetry," and though I could not at the time make the journey, the following letter, addressed to one of the young members who (as I happened to know) wrote poetry himself, formed itself in my mind. . . .

"Dear Poet of Tomorrow," I began, "the Secretary of your Literary Society (as I'm sure you know, as you put him up to it) has asked me to come down to your school and talk to you about poetry. I receive quite a large number of such requests, and do my best, in the midst of a fairly busy life, to say yes as often as possible. On this occasion, however, I just can't make myself free, being surrounded by what my great-grandfather Robert Chambers called 'a botheration of articles to be finished and proofs to be corrected'; but as I fancy I detect from the tone of the Secretary's letter that he is kind and even genuinely interested (unlike those secretaries of youthful societies who only invite their speakers down in order to send them up), and as I know *you* are, I propose to try and put down in a letter the gist of what I should have liked to say. The subject I was going to choose was the poetry of the 'forties, or rather of the early 'forties, and my idea was to talk about it from my own point of view; that is, not from a historian's point of view, but rather following what particularly interested me as a literary editor working in London at that time, what seemed to me promising or significant, and what disappointing, boring or meretricious.

"To begin with, I feel fairly certain I shall need to dispel an illusion, or myth, about the poetry that was being written during the war, which has, in one form or another, been assiduously spread about in recent years, even by intelligent and gifted young critics who ought to know better. . . .

"Like all myths — as you will know from your classical studies or at least from Mr. Robert Graves — this particular myth has a number of forms which vary from locality to locality, or rather from critic to critic. The main features, however, seem to be fairly constant. The first is, I think, that the poets of the 'thirties were entirely absorbed in social-political problems and wrote only when inspired by what they read about in the newspapers. This is assumed to be one hundred per cent reprehensible, though it would appear to condemn a large number of sonnets by Milton and Wordsworth and such famous poems as Yeats's *Meditations in Time of Civil War*. I won't go into that at the

[351]

moment, because it is the rest of the myth which I am interested to demolish for you. For what is alleged is that the most remarkable poet of the 'thirties, Mr. W. H. Auden, saw through all this before the end of the fighting in Spain, washed his hands of it and left for America. Auden's departure and the outbreak of international war, which followed a few months later, were, according to the myth, crushing blows for the whole generation of the 'thirties (which was, as you know, my generation), and stunned it into silence. They never, it seems, recovered sufficiently to utter a single squeak again. Instead, they abandoned the field of English poetry to Dylan Thomas, his followers and his feeble imitators. Thus, apparently, the poetry of the 'forties became sententiously vatic, hysterically apocalyptic and pretentiously emotional overnight, in fact turned into the most recklessly undisciplined pseudo-poetical raving.

"Now it is perfectly true that, as the war went on, and everyone began to read more and more, as if hoping to find in literature an explanation of the mess that the modern world had got itself into, almost any young poet of the most moderate promise could get a volume of his verse published; and in this way a great deal of quite horribly feeble stuff appeared. . . . A decade, however, has a right to be judged by its best poetry and not by its worst, for — as any literary editor knows only too well — there is always an enormous amount of bad poetry being written in any decade or (as I would rather put it, since this division into decades is a slightly absurd modern mania) at any time. And the first thing that my experience with *New Writing* made clear to me was that, so far from the poets of the 'thirties having fallen silent, dispersed like a routed army when their general has fled to exile and safety, several of them were writing better than ever. Some of the most beautiful and intellectually vigorous work of Louis MacNeice, Cecil Day Lewis and Stephen Spender appeared at this time. I did not find in it any violent break with what they had written before the war, but rather a not illogical maturing from it. They had certainly shed some political illusions — that, as I am sure you know, had begun before the war broke out — but these political ideas had never dominated their poetry to the exclusion of everything else; and if one was conscious of a fairly thorough-going revaluation of values, the fundamentally human preoccupations of their wartime poetry had in fact been there from the beginning. The poems in *Word Over All* (1943) — I will chance my arm over this — still seem to me far and away the most striking, taken together, that Cecil Day Lewis ever wrote, more remarkable technically and more profoundly felt than what went before or what came after. Stephen Spender's *Ruins and Visions* (1942) and the wartime poems later collected in *Poems of Dedication* had moments of illumination more extraordinary than anything since his earliest work, the period of *I think continually* and *Oh young men, Oh young comrades*. Louis MacNeice, too, attained a greater depth and power in the poems he wrote between 1941 and 1944, after his return from America — and they include the dazzling *Brother Fire* and *Springboard*.

"At this point, you will, of course, be impatient to ask me how Dylan Thomas fits into the picture. Was he, in fact, with the 'Apocalyptics' and in opposition to the older poets of the 'thirties? Must he take a large part of the blame for the more disastrous manifestations of poetry during the war? Now the truth is that Dylan had no wish that I could ever discover to put himself forward as the leader of any school, and he did not write (or at any rate publish) a great many poems between *The Map of Love* in 1939 and the end of the war; but some of them, in particular his wonderful *A Refusal to Mourn*, are among his most complex and brilliantly controlled achievements. These poems certainly had nothing to do with 'poetical raving' or the 'fluent and windy word-stringing' that I deplored myself in the bad verse-making of those years. Nor had the poems which David Gascoyne presented in his romantic, Sutherland-decorated volume of 1943. . . .

"Inspired by your Society's invitation, I have been looking back through the pages of *New Writing*, of Cyril Connolly's *Horizon*, and of *Personal Landscape*, and I see that the dozen or so names of poets in their twenties which stand out are not those of wordy ranters, but of fastidious artists: for instance, Roy Fuller, Lawrence Durrell, Keith Douglas, Terence Tiller, Alun Lewis, Henry Reed, Norman Nicholson, Laurie Lee. All these young men have a perfectly sound claim to be considered poets of the decade, even though Roy Fuller and Lawrence Durrell had begun to publish before the war. And I also see that it was precisely their respect for form and tradition — so sweepingly denied by those who were boosting the wares of the young poets of a later date — that I was at pains to emphasize in my critical discussion of their work. . . . Nothing had struck me more in the wartime work of the poets I admired than their effort towards a new integration — their attempt to map some system of thought and feeling wide enough and deep enough for our culture to exist in. The crowded and terrifying events of only a few years had not only shaken a great many cosy settled beliefs and assumptions, but they had also done something

more exciting. It was as if some hills that had always blocked the view
had subsided in an earthquake, and given one a sudden glimpse of
great mountains behind, whose existence had been forgotten — if ever
known. The imagined and the fantastical seemed on the verge of becoming true. It was these new conceptions that I saw the poets endeavouring to assimilate and to embody in their poetry.

. . . And this apocalyptic sense was everywhere in the poetry that
was being written at this time. In Stephen Spender's lines, for instance:

> Yesterday you built those towers
> Of your money making
> In the city of bought doom,
> With workers barked at by the hours,
> And in the safe of heart-breaking
> The rich locked with their boredom.
>
> Break locks! Burn fire! It
> Penetrates interstices
> Of a skeleton of stones:
> The concrete lid over the spirit
> Laid by a century of successes
> Is stripped bare from the bones.
> How new you are! And real!

"It was really extraordinary how widespread it became. I remember
how struck I was by the sense of old certainties dissolving under the
pressure of some deep upheaval of the spirit, when I first picked out of
its envelope the long poem *The Jungle*, which Alun Lewis sent me
from India shortly before his death, with its — to me unforgettable
— last lines:

> A trackless wilderness divides
> Joy from its cause, the motive from the act.
> The killing arm uncurls, strokes the soft moss;
> The distant world is an obituary,
> We do not hear the tappings of its dread.
> The act sustains; there is no consequence.
> Only aloneness, swinging slowly
> Down the cold orbit of an older world
> Than any they predicted in the schools,
> Stirs the cold forest with a starry wind,
> And sudden as the flashing of a sword

[354]

> The dream exalts the bowed and golden head
> And time is swept with a great turbulence,
> The old temptation, to remould the world. . . .

"I think you ought to remember that Alun Lewis had started off as a convinced, proselytizing Socialist, in order to understand the distance he had journeyed to *The Jungle.*

"The younger poets were not alone. Before his death in 1943, Laurence Binyon was also at work on a small group of poems, in which he suddenly seemed to free himself from whatever had kept his work so polished technically and yet in fact so empty of any real content. What was so deeply moving about the whole sequence of *The Burning of the Leaves* was its combination of passionate vision and intellectual honesty. Binyon didn't try to find any easy, sentimental way to escape the shapes of death and destruction in whose shadow they were written; but recorded, with a dignified simplicity, how they made some things in life appear suddenly quite tawdry and shallow, and how other things, suggesting hope and renewal, seemed to endure against them. And in the fragments at the end, the sense of approaching revelation and of darkness is sketched with an extraordinary intensity:

> Horizon opening into unguessed horizons
> And I with the earth am moving into the light
> The earth is moving, the earth is rolling over
> into the light. . . .

"The more I think about it, as a matter of fact, the more convinced I am that the early years of the 'forties were — the pundits of the 'fifties notwithstanding — exceptionally rich in poetry. Don't forget that T. S. Eliot completed his great sequence of meditations on the meaning of time, art and God — the *Four Quartets* — during those years. *East Coker*, *The Dry Salvages* and *Little Gidding* were as exciting to me, as they came out, as news of great military victories. (I was all the more staggered, therefore, when, in answer to a request for a poem for *New Writing* in the summer of 1944, Tom wrote to me: 'I am pleased by your request for a poem, but I literally have written no verses at all since *Little Gidding*, and I cannot say with any confidence that I shall ever again write anything worth printing.')

"T. S. Eliot was not the only poet of an older generation who seemed to be stirred to new vigour and beauty of achievement in those years. To most of us in London it seemed, when *Street Songs* was published early in 1942, that another great event had taken place in English poetry. I had been delighted as a young man with Edith Sitwell's *Façade* and *Troy Town* poems; I had been moved by the brilliant violence of her satiric *Gold Coast Customs*, remote though it was in technique from what particularly interested me in the 'thirties; but I had not, I must admit, expected that she would make such a big leap forward. In her new poems all the gaiety of the early work was gone, but so was all the extravagance and unreality, and all the romantic private-world dreaminess of the poems that came after that; the poems in *Street Songs*, and *Green Song* that followed very soon, were tragic, and often bitter with a kind of savagery of bitterness, and they were written with an astonishingly easy-seeming mastery of her medium and an assurance of voice that was deeply impressive. I still think that *Still Falls the Rain* and *Lullaby* are two of the most original poems *about the war* that were written during the war; but I was even more struck by the series of great odes, or elegies, wrought with an infinitely subtle and sensitive technical virtuosity. In my opinion they were in the truest sense war poems, though the war itself was only alluded to indirectly, through symbol and myth, because they were inconceivable without the background of the war — without the impact of the world-wide tragedy on a poet capable at the same time of passionate grieving and sublime praising. I have heard some young people of about your age complain that there is a kind of wearying excess in these odes, that there are too many of them, on the same note, using variations of the same symbolism. But that is a criticism made in the light of Edith Sitwell's *Collected Poems* many years later, and I am not concerned here to rebut or admit its truth or partial truth; what I want you to understand is how exciting these poems were when they first began to appear during the war. It was a great moment for me, when for the winter number of *New Writing and Daylight* in 1943 she offered me *Invocation*, with its marvellous opening diapason:

> I who was once a golden woman like those who walk
> In the dark heavens — but am now grown old
> And sit by the fire, and see the fire grow cold,
> Watch the dark fields for a rebirth of faith and of wonder.
> The turning of Ixion's wheel the day
> Ceased not, yet sounds no more the beat of the heart
> But only the sound of ultimate Darkness falling
> And of the Blind Samson at the Fair, shaking the pillars of the
>   world and emptily calling

For the gardeners cried for rain, but the high priests howled
For a darker rain. . . .

"This, like Tom Eliot's *Four Quartets*, was poetry, I thought, equal
to the spiritual demands of an apocalyptic age.

"My Greek friend, Demetrios Capetanakis, used to say to me sometimes that, in some unexpected way, the war *physically* was not frightening enough; but that *metaphysically*, for anyone who cared to think,
what was happening was so disturbing that poetry of a high order
must come out of it. To have death standing constantly next to one is
certainly no situation to breed conventional thoughts, but rather such
lines as Demetrios wrote in his best-known, most extraordinary poem
Abel:

> And then he chose the final pain for me.
> I do not blame his nature: he's my brother,
> Nor what you call the times: our love was free,
> Would be the same at any time; but rather
>
> The ageless ambiguity of things
> Which makes our life mean death, our love be hate.
> My blood that streams across the bedroom sings:
> "I am my brother opening the gate."

"Certainly death sat uncomfortably close to Alun Lewis when he
wrote *The Jungle;* and to Keith Douglas when he wrote the poems by
which I believe he will be chiefly remembered, *Vergissmeinnicht* and
How to Kill:

> This sorcery
> I do. Being damned, I am amused
> To see the centre of love diffused
> And the waves of love travel into vacancy.
> How easy it is to make a ghost.
>
> The weightless mosquito touches
> her tiny shadow on the stone,
> and with how like, how infinite
> a likeness, man and shadow meet.
> They fuse. A shadow is a man
> when the mosquito death approaches.

"And the chilly, imagined proximity of death inspired the best lines that Sidney Keyes ever wrote:

> I am the man who looked for peace and found
> My own eyes barbed.
> I am the man who groped for words and found
> An arrow in my hand.
> I am the builder whose firm walls surround
> A slipping land. . . .

"There were war poets in the end, all right. The nostalgic elderly schoolmasters and the vulgarians of what is now called The Establishment, whose cry in 1939 had been 'Where are the war poets?,' were answered; but the answers were not the answers the young Rupert Brooke had given or the young Laurence Binyon; and I can only say that I deeply regret that some of the more reckless, simplifying critics who gained the ear of the public in the early 'fifties seem to have become allies of these tone-deaf gentlemen.

"I make no apology, as you see, for the poetry of the war years, in which I was fairly intimately involved myself. That poetry, in fact, was one of the things that made that time tolerable. I am not talking of the dross; but of the authentic vein of precious metal. And if you would like me to try and sum it up, and define what I find impressive about this poetry, I would say that it is not only its technical vitality, but above all its deep seriousness. The poets took a good look at death without hiding their faces: they saw how easy it was to kill without thought, how cheap the individual's life had become. They were aware that they were living in an age in which human affairs were getting increasingly out of control. They saw that civilization was reaching a point where monsters could be born more terrible than had ever been imagined possible in the modern world, but that this danger also evoked the possibility of the rediscovery of great spiritual affirmations to counter it. They saw that what was needed was a restatement of faith: faith, if you like, in imaginative creation, but above all in the value of the individual and the reality of moral choice against man-made machines of organization and the crudity of material 'Progress': against a world based on values of power only. . . ."

« 9 »

AN irony that every literary editor knows is that just when one believes that the time is ripe for, say, a Tolstoi, a Firbank writes his first book. Byron, one feels, could never quite forgive Keats for not writing like Crabbe. In a closed society, of course, such mutations and eccentricities are kept well out of sight or throttled at birth — if recognized in time. Woe betide the author in a totalitarian Marxist country at war (as I was about to find out) who dares not to write on the approved pattern of patriotic heroism; but in an open society there should be no *ought* and *must* in the realm of the arts. What one hopes to preserve — or to develop — is sufficient suppleness of imagination to recognize what is good when it is quite different from what one had been looking for so expectantly and so long, with one's field-glasses trained on the distant passes.

One day, early in 1943, a young man who signed himself Denton Welch sent me a story called *The Barn*. His name was not new to me, for some months earlier I had read a quite extraordinarily vivid and irreverent description of a visit to Walter Sickert in *Horizon;* and only a few weeks before the MS. reached me, his first book, *Maiden Voyage*, had been published, with an introduction by Edith Sitwell. As so often happened during the war with books that were not expected by their publishers to have more than a limited sale, but were nevertheless enthusiastically received by the critics, it had become unobtainable almost at once. I had not yet been able to read it: but this story struck me immediately, by an altogether unusual quality in the writing and in the observation it recorded. With a medieval miniaturist's clarity and precision, the author described a slight episode in the life of a young boy at home; he is bored and lonely, and overhearing his father give a tramp permission to sleep in their disused barn, decides to join the tramp secretly during the night and set off with him in the morning. The tramp allows him to sleep in the hay beside him, but sends him back contemptuously when he leaves. Nothing very much; but the sensuous impact of everything was so minutely and freshly described, and the author seemed to be able to see himself from the outside (for obviously the story was autobiographical) with such extraordinary detachment and truth, that it was clear to me that the admirers of *Maiden Voyage* had been right when they said he was a born writer. It was a rare and exciting experience to come across a passage like this:

I was in darkness, which smelt of dust and mist and hay. Chinks and cracks in the walls shot beams of light into the blackness.

I climbed on to some boxes, then caught hold of a beam and swung there, like a monkey. I gnashed my teeth and contorted my face. I gibbered and hung on with one hand as I scratched under my arm with the other.

I grew hot, swinging in the darkness, and my arms began to feel the strain. I broke my last imaginary peanut between my teeth and spat as disgustingly and coarsely as I could on to the invisible floor; then I sank down on to the boxes and thought that I was miserable and lonely indeed.

And as I lay there, I decided to be a slave who had to sweat and labour in the barn all day. . . .

I wrote to Denton Welch accepting the story, but suggesting that it could do with a little re-writing and pulling together. He replied with a letter that was shrewd, sympathetic and revealing; telling me that he had already re-written it twice, but that he'd go over it again if I really thought it necessary. "Do you think its lack of very perceptible shape is due to its being, almost completely, a plain statement of fact? Whether this is a good thing to attempt or not, I tried very hard to keep it only to this; and consequently I may be a little more inept in some passages than I would otherwise have been. I do hope you will use it, for although I too thought it was clumsy, I still liked it for some reason; that is why I sent it to you."

I wrote back and told him I certainly didn't want him to change it unless he was convinced himself that it could be improved. A fortnight later he did, in fact, send me a slightly revised — and certainly improved — version. "I did not like one or two sentences and adjectives, they did not really express my true feeling," he wrote, and added: "I could, of course, have changed it a great deal more, but I resisted this temptation, as I knew that I would make it into something quite different and perhaps worse if I persisted."

The truth was that practically everything Denton Welch wrote was autobiographical. He had a passion for exact accuracy about thoughts and feelings, and therefore he was always up against the problem of accommodating the artistically feasible to this strict conscience about his own experience. Even when writing in the third person, he admitted to me, it made little or no difference; and it is for this reason that I have sometimes wondered whether, if he had lived, he would have gone on writing fiction. I see him, rather, developing into the most disconcerting diarist of our day: an English Gide, but a more delicate and exotic bird than the (sometimes a little self-important) *cher maître* of the Rue Vaneau.

His fantasy, curiously enough, seemed to go almost entirely into his exquisite little drawings and decorations, and the rare paintings of his mature style, so full of strange, poetic symbols; of which one of the most beautiful and mysterious, the cat with the arrow, hangs beside me as I write.

At the time when he sent me *The Barn*, Denton Welch was only twenty-six, but had already been for eight years a cripple, slowly wasting from the disease which had followed the accident when he was knocked off his bicycle by a passing car. Many years after the war, and after his death, I was destined to publish his own story of that time of almost intolerable spiritual and physical suffering, in his third "novel," *A Voice Through a Cloud*. Perhaps it was the conviction, which must have come to him sometimes, that his life was going to be short that made him want to record every detail so exactly. And perhaps it was the pain, from which he was seldom free, that was the cause of the streak of slightly cruel malice which sometimes appears in his portraits of people: as in *The Judas Tree*, a story which I printed very soon after in *Penguin New Writing*, where he so brilliantly and so mercilessly exposes the old schoolmaster. On the other hand, it is possible that this appearance of cruelty came from a tension in his spirit between the need to be loved and to lavish affection, and his hatred of all pretension and sentimentality, including sentimentality in himself; as if he had to over-compensate a little for the quick warmth of response that was natural to him. It was revealing, I thought, that he was afraid (as he told me in a letter) that the critics might sneer at *Maiden Voyage* as the story of just one more rather sissified boy who couldn't fit into school life and was bad at games; and believed that Edith Sitwell's Foreword had prevented such a reaction. Edith certainly did him a good turn, just as she had done Dylan Thomas a similar good turn a decade before; but I think that only the most crudely philistine critics could have failed to spot, in *Maiden Voyage*, the sharp critical intelligence at work and the expert appraisal of beautiful things.

« 10 »

ONE thing is quite certain: the Russians would never have understood the case of Denton Welch. This was brought home to me by the tremendous hot water I suddenly found I had got into with our Red allies.

My work for *Internationalnaya Literatura* and *Britanski Soyuznik* had, I suppose, directed Russian attention to my own writings and to the progress of *Penguin New Writing*. They did not fail, therefore, to read in one of the numbers an article called *State Art and Scepticism*, in which I discussed the difference between the Soviet and the British attitudes to imaginative literature during the war.

I had told Archie Clark-Kerr how keen I was to be kept posted about developments among the Russian writers, and from time to time he had digests of articles and controversies of particular interest to me sent through the Bag to London. In one of these I found a summary of a long article by my old friend Nikolai Tikhonov, from the magazine *Bolshevik*, on *The War and Soviet Literature*.

To explain how I reacted to this article, it is perhaps necessary to repeat that though British writers managed successfully to keep regimentation and censorship at bay all through the war, the battle was never finally concluded in their favour: sentries had to be posted in continual vigilance. And as the perfectly reasonable and justified boosting of Russian achievements proceeded, some of us began to feel a little nervous lest our own bureaucracy grow jealous of the firm control under which the Soviets appeared to keep their writers.

It seemed time to fire a few warning shots from my own small corner of the redoubt. It struck me that this article of Tikhonov's provided an excellent opportunity.

Tikhonov, who had contributed to the very first number of *New Writing* in 1936, and whose wartime sketch *The Apple Tree* had been sent me for *Daylight*, had become Chairman of the Union of Soviet Writers: he was, thus, Headmaster of a school with very rigid rules and intolerant Governors, and he had to keep the boys in order. His article in *Bolshevik* was obviously of considerable internal significance. A grand summary and analysis of Soviet literature since Hitler's invasion, it reminded me of nothing so much as the children's *Krampusfest* I had often witnessed in Austria on the eve of St. Nicholas's Day: presents for the good boys and birch-rods for the bad ones. Only it was in earnest; and the unfortunate humorous writer Mikhail Zoschenko, one of the few who was known and appreciated in the West, was one of those who had clearly had it . . . for "serious ideological mistakes." "The voice of the writer," Tikhonov announced in ringing tones, "is a power in our country. It accompanies the soldier to battle, and helps towards victory in the front and in the rear." With this inspiration illuminating his countenance, the Soviet writer was evidently expected to square his shoulders, seize his ideological rifle and thank Stalin for the glorious opportunities vouchsafed him. Most of them, however, I could not help feeling, must have experienced a slight shudder, devoted patriots though they may well have been. Poor Selvinsky happened to write in one of his poems — obviously doing his best — that Russia was "a land with a serene smile." Down came the thunder at once: it was a bad poem, a slander on the Russian people, riddled with ideological faults. Dovzhenko, admired author and film director, was also sent straight to the Headmaster's study for "serious mistakes of a fundamental character" in his story to which he had so hopefully given the name *Victory:* neither eminence (and world fame) nor good intentions saved him from being told that his story was "in essence a slanderous estimate of the struggle of the Soviet peoples." Even the luckier authors who got past without castigation had the cane rattled warningly on the desk at them; Vera Inber, for instance, who had written a long poem commemorating the terrible siege of Leningrad, was reminded, after brief words of praise, that in the past she had "sinned on the side of aestheticism." The Headmaster's talk ended up with a terrifying bellow of authoritarian menace: "It is the writer's responsibility to mould the coming generations. Soviet literature *must* deal with moral problems, *must* strengthen the ideas of the state, the great ideas of socialism, it *must* build up the moral health of the people." Remembering the fate of such people as Prince Mirsky in the past, many a poet and novelist must have felt that only the most flatulent praise of Stalin or the corniest kind of black-and-white propaganda writing about the war could save his skin.

Comically enough, the Governors of the school did not appear to see where all this would lead them — or why it had led them where they found themselves. "The young poets," observed Tikhonov, "still show faults of triteness, wordiness, insufficient care." And even more wistfully: "The style of our authors rarely gives that impression of freshness and easy clarity, which so captivates one in the classics." That there might be a connection between the brutal and narrow State imperatives and this result, did not seem to occur to him; or at least he could not admit it.

In my article, *State Art and Scepticism,* I tried, without indulging in polemics, and without in any way suggesting that heroic exploits were not an excellent theme for writers in wartime, to point out the absurdity of the Soviet attitude, the extreme unlikelihood that such imperatives would produce any masterpieces, and their total incompatibility with the sceptical British temperament. "The Russian writer," I said, "has been expected to 'take his part' in the national war effort in a very emphatic way. We — if we think about it at all — are apt to conclude that the writer is most successfully 'taking his part' if he pursues his researches into the truth about human life and fate according to his own inner light; and if our leaders bade us 'take our part' in the way the Russian writers are bidden, would feel that the words had been given a most shallow and philistine interpretation. For the

[363]

Russian writer is expected to write exclusively about what is happening in the war, and his story is expected to conform to a pattern in which the Soviet citizen triumphs by unparalleled endurance, devotion and heroism on whatever front he is fighting, in which the enemy is always a brute and the lesson learned is flaming hatred against him and fanatically reinforced love of the Soviet Fatherland, Stalin, and the local Commissar (who always does prodigiously better than anyone else). Such rigid rules of creation are unknown and indeed unthinkable in our country. . . ."

If I had left it at that, perhaps my sin might have been overlooked; unfortunately, I indulged in a little fun directly afterwards. I ought to have remembered that joking is the worst of all crimes when one is criticizing a dictatorship or totalitarian set-up. "Let us imagine for a moment," I continued, "what it would be like if such standards were applied here. I'm afraid very few of our more distinguished writers would escape censure for weakness of 'ideological-political approach,' in Tikhonov's phrase, or for absence of the 'proper high patriotic note' which the Moscow correspondent of the *New Statesman* tells us the official mentors insist on. Soviet authors are, in addition, apparently expected to travel everywhere and produce like rabbits. Suspicion falls on E. M. Forster for having transgressed these rules quite flagrantly. The case of the Sitwells is worse. 'Some of our writers,' says Tikhonov, 'imagine they can sit in their burrows and watch events go by. If the writer takes no part in life, in its stormy and heroic doing, then he condemns himself to barrenness. He begins to write beside the point.' Renishaw Hall is no doubt a large burrow, but neither Sir Osbert nor Miss Edith can expect mercy for that reason. Tikhonov goes on: 'Many writers have lived for long periods far in the rear, but have written nothing, or next to nothing, about the hard work of people in the rear.' Where are Sir Osbert's Odes to the Gallant Miners in the Derbyshire pits? Where are Miss Edith's Songs for the Sheffield A.R.P. workers? The more one thinks of it, the worse it becomes. Robert Graves, too, is wasting his time writing facetiae and prose epics about the Argonauts way down in Devon. There is no connection with the present struggle at all, as far as one can see. His proper study should be the British Land Girl through the ages, or a rollicking tale of Sir Walter Raleigh's boyhood. As for the charge of 'aestheticism' or 'formalism,' which rouses the peculiar rage of the Soviet pundit of today, I'm afraid British authors have a record that could hardly be worse. T. S. Eliot, with his *Four Quartets*, is hopelessly lost before his case opens; and is followed into ignominy by Walter de la Mare (for his poems in *Orion*), Laurence Binyon (for the title poem of *The Burning of the Leaves*), Dylan Thomas (most emphatically, for his recent poems in *Horizon*), George Barker, Stephen Spender and Terence Tiller for their love poems ('erotic in the worst sense,' as *Komsomolskaya Pravda* furiously complained about some verses by the unfortunate Joseph Utkin), and a whole cohort of the young. Prose writers are in no securer position. Elizabeth Bowen, in particular, beware! Subtle descriptions of atmosphere in the Irish countryside are no substitute for a healthy pugnacious note against the foe. William Sansom, again, what is he up to with his distempered fantasies of potting-sheds and phallic lighthouses? And that 'high patriotic note'? How does it happen that Day Lewis has been allowed to talk about defending 'the bad against the worse'? To write a poem about an album? And Mac-Neice one about alcohol? What frivolity towards the great issues of the day!"

Of course this article was not really aimed at the Russians, but, as I have explained, nearer home; partly to expose the uncritical nonsense that was being written in some quarters about heroic Russian war literature, partly to ridicule in advance any attempt in the last phases of the war (or first phase of the peace, for that matter) to tighten bureaucratic control of writing. In an effort to make my standpoint quite clear, I said at the end of the article that I had heard (which was quite true) that in top Kremlin circles the absurdity of some of the results of the official line had begun to be recognized, that it seemed possible that a much greater freedom would be restored after the war, and that I believed "the genius of the Russian people, now so magnificently displayed in feats of organization, endurance and military élan, is bound to reassert itself in the creative arts as well."

All in vain. Some months later I was shocked to discover, from the press service which was sent me, that the article had been read, marked and totally misunderstood in Moscow (or Kuibishev); and in spite of the fact that not a single Russian intellectual (other than the privileged Party high-ups) was in the least likely to read the copy of *Penguin New Writing* in which the article appeared, a ludicrously wrathful offensive had been launched against me. I had become overnight a decadent, a reactionary, an ally of the Brown Beast, a calumniator of the heroic Red Army: all the clichés of Communist rage, were trotted out, all the dented old cannon balls came hurtling over in my direction. It went on for years — was still going on long after the end of the war.

The whole episode amused me; but saddened me far more, because it seemed to point to the impossibility of an intellectual understanding developing between the Russians and our own people, as long as no one of their side dared to reject the rigid and deforming Stalinist tenets about art and literature. I saw it as a thoroughly bad omen for the future, that after three years of alliance the rigidity was totally unchanged. And the pressure was kept up to make it seem that if one did not accept the Soviet view about Soviet literature, one was being disloyal to the common cause. Only a few weeks before the end of the war in Europe, I was shocked to hear the incomparable Desmond Mac-Carthy, at a crowded memorial meeting for Alexei Tolstoi in the Curzon Cinema, maintain — on no evidence that could possibly have come to him from his own observation — that Alexei Tolstoi only began to achieve greatness as a writer when he decided to "accept the Bolshevik régime." Did he really believe this? The speech was woolly, even for Desmond at his most absent; it would be charitable to assume that he was speaking from notes prepared for him by someone else, and had not had time to go through them.

Desmond did not live long enough to hear of the event that exposed this horrible claptrap once and for all: the suicide of Alexander Fadayev, so long the cruel executor of the official Party line among his fellow-writers, when the Khrushchev thaw began. Nor the hysterical persecution of that great writer Boris Pasternak (contributor, as it happened, like Tikhonov, to the first number of *New Writing*), when the freeze-up started again so soon after; an event that was to prove, in the most public and sensational way possible, how power without check allied to false dogma can warp and poison men's minds.

« 11 »

AND then, gradually, the war began to change and enter its last phase. All the preparations that had been going on in secret while the surface of life in England remained so calm, all the campaigns on distant frontiers, were coming to harvest. Our hallucinatory fortress life of the three-year breathing-space was over.

Now the raids on London began again: the "tip-and-run" raids and the fire-raids of the winter of 1943–44, which could not be compared with the earlier raids because they were made by isolated aircraft, defying in high-speed sallies the massed barrage of London's new ack-ack defences, for no worth-while reason that one could comprehend except to demoralize, to maintain the idea of the imminence of the enemy — in which no one seriously believed any longer. Up on the roof of Carrington House, in my tin helmet, I would watch, fascinated, all the beams of the searchlights waving about like the antennae of some threatened giant insect, finally to converge, in the clear darkness of the sky which they pierced, on the little silver-winged cabin streaking away, while the clanging, cracking and reverberation of the guns increased and concentrated itself with winking explosions in the raider's path. These attacks were disagreeable because of the suddenness of their violence, which broke up sleep; but considered from the dramatic-aesthetic point of view, they were rather beautiful, and the actual damage they did was comparatively small.

Meanwhile, Africa had been conquered at last, and the sunburnt victors began to trickle back to London, to infiltrate, with their bleached hair and dark-tanned knees, among the now almost entirely American soldier crowds in the pubs, to appear suddenly in their home villages, despising the tinned pilchards and Woolton pie that seemed to appear ever more frequently on our tables, but rejoicing almost with unbelief in the greenness of fields and gardens: at the back of their eyes, as they told their stories of desert camps and tank encounters in the sandstorm and smoke, and evening carousals along the boulevards of captured cities, there still seemed to linger a dream of Oriental horizons, a fading glimmer of something timeless, an adventure that did not quite belong to the iron schedules of industrial war, the tiered bunks in grimy tube stations and the squalid rubble of the bombed insurance offices, mercantile banks and A.B.C. shops.

Among my own friends, John Lepper returned after long service with the Fourth Indian Division all through the desert campaigns, as full of admiration for the Indian soldiers with whom he had fought as he was of contempt for the Arab inhabitants; Harold Acton from India, bringing refreshment with his sparkling affectionate courtesy and his chippendale flatteries, and describing for hours on end, with an inimitable flowery wit and Proustian eye for social comedy, goings-on in the bizarre, evanescent world that official India had become: compounded of the mixture of old-time colonial administrators with newly arrived generals and air-marshals and admirals, surrounded by their temporary staffs and an outer fringe of Hindu and Moslem politicians, prospering business contractors and frustrated intellectuals; Roy Fuller from East Africa, happy indeed to be home with Kate and his young son John but indefinably suggesting that some inspirational ghost of himself had been left behind; and many others, in their vizor-peaked caps and worn battledress, veterans now who were once the

[367]

companions of drinking nights in the first winter black-out of all; whose absence, though only two or three years in fact, already seemed to have lasted half a lifetime.

At the same time, as a result of these triumphs in North Africa, the intellectual silence between ourselves and the French began at last to dissolve again. It had never been complete: that excellent monthly *La France Libre*, directed by André Labarthe with the aid of Moura Budberg, had kept some devious contacts with Vichy France, some of Gide's *Figaro* articles even found their way into *Horizon*, and Louis Aragon's *Crêve-Coeur* poems had reached us and made a deep impression by their powerful nostalgia, their lack of even concealed Marxist propaganda, and the beauty of the imagery that evoked simultaneously the agony of still almost unbelievable defeat and the splendours of the past.

The victorious armies discovered an intellectual life in Algeria which had maintained itself with some dignity in spite of Vichy prohibitions, and which immediately expanded under the sun of liberation and developed an immense thirst for news of what had been going on in England. This opening of windows was good for us too; it must be admitted that the air in London was by now getting a little stale, and the malice that is normal among denizens of the literary world when they talk about one another would suddenly erupt in absurdly distorted fantasies of envy and suspicion. Max-Pol Fouchet, the young editor of a notable new literary review, *Fontaine*, was brought over to London by the British Council, and with his chubby countenance, his enthusiasm, his Miranda-like air of continually exclaiming to himself, "O brave new world!," charmed all of us, who were indeed happily excited to make contact at last with a Frenchman in the same line of business.

Very soon after, I must admit to my immense pleasure, Jiři Mucha came back from Algiers to announce that he had met André Gide there and found him reading a volume of *New Writing and Daylight*. The sage, cordial as ever and unruffled apparently in his dignified seclusion by the tides of war that had swirled around him, had cross-questioned Jiři with voracious curiosity about all that was going on in England, and had presented him with a volume of his wartime "interviews," *Attendu Que*, adding that if I wished to translate and publish them in London he would be delighted. Thereupon a long exchange of letters and cables ensued, of the most flowery sort, but as the Americans had got a jump ahead of us, and Gide's pre-war publishers, Secker and Warburg, were already in touch with them, in the end I

Christopher Isherwood, 1938; photo by the author

J. L. with
Leonard Woolf,
at Rodmell, 1939;
photo by Virginia Woolf

Virginia Woolf at Monk's House, 1939; photo by the author

J. L. in 1939

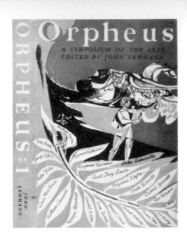

A montage of John Lehmann Ltd. book jackets

J. L. at Carrington House, circa 1943

Demetrios Capetanakis

Alexis Rassine, Christopher Isherwood and Gore Vidal
at 31 Egerton Crescent, 1949

*Alexis Rassine and Beatrix Lehmann with Carlotta and Taffy
at Lake Cottage*

J. L. at Lake Cottage, early 1950's

The London Magazine *Launching Party, 1954:* above, *E. M. Forster,*
Rex Warner, William Plomer; below, *Louis MacNeice, Rose*
Macaulay, Edmund Wilson

regretfully abandoned the idea of taking Gide at his word, especially as the directors of Secker and Warburg were my friends; and in spite of the fact that Gide in one of his letters to me observed (I think untruthfully) that he had never heard of them.

In the middle of the fire-raids, Demetrios's death took place, an event from which it took me a long time to recover.

He had been ill for several years, without knowing exactly what was the matter with him. Before he left Cambridge to work with the Greek Department of Information in the autumn of 1941, he had been told by a local doctor, to whom he complained of persistently feeling out of sorts, that it was all nerves and imagination. He even managed to convince himself for a while that this was in fact so; coming up to London and entering into a wider literary and political world acted as a tonic, and it was some months before he began to feel his illness gaining on him again. At the same time he went through a violent personal crisis, which brought on a complete collapse: when I went to see him in hospital, he kept on speaking to me of "experiences that can't be described" when he was on the brink of death, of a state of mind he could not even entirely remember, which had transformed his whole outlook on life and death. "I'm afraid," he wrote in a letter, "although I don't like it, that I am becoming a mystic. It was wonderful to prepare oneself never to wake up again. I longed so much for a night of freedom and rest, in which there is no memory, no right and wrong, no suffering. But I had to wake up again, and I shall go on and try to make the best of it. But I doubt if the foretaste of the night I experienced will ever leave me alone. . . . My new contact with this night reminded me that one must never be too categorical with the things in the world. Everything is changing in it. We have the right not only to fear the worst, but also to hope the best."

When he came out of hospital, his courage returned, and spurred on by the immense interest his first English poems and articles soon began to arouse among his friends and acquaintances, and by my persistent urging and planning, he settled down to what he intended to be a long period of literary work. Again his spirit triumphed; but again the disease, which his new London doctor had realized was a dangerous sickness of the blood, broke the new élan down. By the autumn he was feeling very ill again, and was sent away for a rest and change in Devon. "Today," he wrote to me on November 12, 1942, "I feel much better, and people tell me that I do not look ill any more. In spite of that I must stay here a little longer; I am not quite prepared yet to face

London again. My days here are pleasant and peaceful, but my nights are full of terrors: full of the most exhausting nightmares. In the morning I get up extremely tired and I need all the peace of the day to forget the terrors of the night. I know that it is ridiculous to get so much affected by 'things which are not,' but I also know that my fate will always be to succumb to these things. That is what destroys or threatens with destruction everything positive given me by life."

It was against this background of continual spiritual and physical struggle that Demetrios, in the brief space of three or four years, conquered the English language as poet and critic.

It would, however, be wrong to think of him as a predominantly melancholy and dispirited character. Not only did his conversation sparkle when his literary enthusiasms were under discussion, but also, when he was well, he displayed the liveliest sense of fun and of teasingly malicious observation in his social life. After Devon, he made his last and most extraordinary recovery. He was suddenly very much happier in his personal life, and for a time, in spite of what I was now privately told about the almost incurable nature of his disease, I believed he might be on the way to getting well. During the meals we had together two or three times a week, and the afternoon walks we sometimes took across the park, past the statues of Byron and Achilles, he would occasionally speak with horror of the oppression and starvation in Greece, of which nauseating accounts reached him direct; but often his mood was gay, and he would talk brilliantly of his latest discoveries in English or American literature, and make witty and penetrating comments on our mutual acquaintances.

The recovery did not survive his return to London. He began to have long fits of dizziness and increasing nightmares, and knew at last that his only chance was to be treated in hospital. He waited in vain, however, for a hospital bed: they were as difficult to come by in those days as a bunch of bananas. In the end, it was only by deliberately causing himself to collapse and be found unconscious on the floor of his room in Prince's Gate that he brought the emergency service into action and so gained admittance to Westminster Hospital. He was given every kind of treatment, including an extremely painful operation, which consisted in drawing all his blood out and pumping new blood in; but the leukaemia slowly wasted him away. It gave him great pleasure that all his friends visited him there, not only his devoted Greek friends but also the circle of English literary friends he had gathered about him, including William Plomer, Joe Ackerley and Beryl de Zoete, but he could never talk to them except briefly. He kept

[370]

on telling me how unhappy he was to have disappointed me, because he had not written the many poems, essays and stories we had planned together. His essay *A View of English Poetry*, which had cost him such an enormous effort just before he was taken to hospital, he thought could only be considered as a series of aphorisms, as there was so much more he would have liked to say; and, as I have related in my own study of his work, *A Greek Poet and his English Language*, he felt that his last poem *Lazarus* was far too unpolished to be published at all. In general, I believe that the wishes of the dying should be respected, but as I was sure that he was wrong in his view of it, I thought that he would have forgiven me for printing it. Nothing he wrote haunts me more.

> . . . Love is slow,
> And when she comes she neither speaks nor hears:
>
> She only kisses and revives the dead
> Perhaps in vain. Because what is the use
> Of miracles unheard of, since instead
> Of trying to remember the great News
>
> Revealed to me alone by Death and Love,
> I struggled to forget them and become
> Like everybody else. . . .

Of his last days, while the nightly fire-raids were taking place — they were far too much of this world to trouble him — of his funeral, of my hunt through his papers and the essays and fragments I found there, and all that I did not find, I have given an account in *A Greek Poet and his English Language*. It would have been inappropriate there to speak of what I personally lost by his death; but I do not suppose that even now I have ceased to feel the wound of it. Without his belief in what I was trying to do, as an editor and publisher as well as a poet, I have often thought that in the stress of war, in the torment of uncertainty about where one was going and what it was worth, in the baffling periods when one seemed to be misinterpreted even by those one thought to be one's closest friends and colleagues, I would have been tempted to throw everything up. Not heroic, certainly; but I am not one of the cold men of iron will-power; and even after Demetrios's death my natural pertinacity would sometimes have failed if I had not been able to think of things he had said to me — to hear as if his living voice, making a whole of all the disordered fragments.

Not very long after Demetrios's death, I was rung up one day by the *Manchester Guardian*, and asked if I would like to say anything about Alun Lewis, as news had just come in that he had been killed on the frontiers of Burma.

I have written elsewhere, in my essay *A Human Standpoint*, of the shock this caused me, of my admiration for the way his poetry was developing and of my greater admiration for the stories he was beginning to write. I was immensely proud to be able to publish the mysterious and beautiful last, long poem, *The Jungle* (which reached England after his death), but his two short stories, *The Orange Grove*, which appeared in *Horizon*, and *Ward 03 (B)*, which I printed in *Penguin New Writing* No. 18, showed him maturing, I thought, as a writer of fiction more rapidly and remarkably than as a poet. In announcing the dispatch of the latter story, in the late summer of 1943, he wrote on an airgraph to me: "Life follows Hobbes's description: excessively strenuous and brutish. There are however friends, and sometimes a gramophone, and I find a solid basis for myself in the Welsh colliers of my regiment. In many ways I'm glad I'm not in England. I'm sure I can see straighter here. Human behaviour is as clear as the lucid climate, and as hard and immutable. Change seems less simple than it did at home. Everything was possible there." These words were the first foreshadowing to me of the profound changes that were taking place in his mind, that emerge so significantly and so disturbingly in *The Jungle* and the two stories, as if he were suddenly moving out of a narrow room into the open air of an experience of the universe of which he could not discern the limits.

And now he was gone, with his passionate sense of instinctive truth and elemental love that withstood the questioning of everything else, the "tangled wrack of motives drifting down an oceanic tide of wrong," only just on the threshold of becoming that kind of imaginative creator the world so badly needed. Sidney Keyes had vanished one day into the desert, with the whole of his dawn patrol. Drummond Allison had been killed in Italy just as his first and only collection of poems, *The Yellow Night*, was being brought out. Drummond, in a long letter asking me to tell him what I really felt about his poetry and how he could improve it and pleading with me to persuade the Hogarth Press to take it on, had said, "I expect Sidney is dead, you know, although, as John Heath-Stubbs says, 'he may be wandering in some remote part of the desert disguised as a holy man.'" (But his grave was found in 1945.) I was suddenly filled with dread that what had almost incredibly not yet happened was going to be our doom in the last stages of the war. There were no miracles; the poets were going to be killed as they had been in the earlier war; how foolish we had been to think we could escape without the massacre of all that was best in our generation.

Then the sickles of war flashed out, reaching murderously across from either side of the Channel. The long-awaited news of the Normandy landings under General Eisenhower came over the radio one June morning. And waking early another morning, sleepy and bewildered Londoners heard a strange spluttering noise, that grew louder, and then stopped, to be followed by a distant explosion: the first of the doodle-bugs had fallen.

This Theme, Their Hope

I THINK it was largely owing to Demetrios's encouragement and quite extraordinarily intense perceptive interest that during the lull I began to write poetry again, after an interval of several years. It surprised me to find the springs flowing as in my pre-Vienna days, to be covering page after page in my exercise books with notes and arguments and images for poems; but there was suddenly so much I wanted to say, and only in poetry, for the "mysterious agency in the inmost chamber of my imagination" had begun to co-operate again. Then, the very fact that one's life was so narrowly ordered and distractions were so rare — above all, no travelling abroad and no motoring about — made it, I found, possible to draw a poem out of its sheath of invisibility by slow stages, adding perhaps a stanza every other day, two or three in a week-end, while remodelling others. Nevertheless, without the extra impetus that Demetrios's continual eager demand for new poems gave me, I doubt if much would have got beyond the scribbling and fragmentary stage.

Some of this work was done in London, in late afternoon intervals of other work; but a great deal more in the country, at Fieldhead, or staying with Rosamond or Helen, both of whom had cottages in the south, or on brief holidays by the sea. So it happens that the poems are filled with the imagery of English gardens and river-valleys, bluebell woods and sheep-cropped downs, cliffs and chines and sandy beaches of the Channel; but not all. Several of the earlier poems, for instance, evoke the Alpine landscape of Austria, *The Last Ascent* and *The Summer Story* most vividly, for at that time I would often find myself day-dreaming about the country I had loved so much; a nostalgia I worked off partly in my broadcasts, and partly in these poems. I remember one winter evening, reading manuscripts alone in my flat, I tuned in by chance on my portable wireless to a German station, and

[374]

let it run on for an hour or so while I prepared my supper. The massive Allied raids had just begun, and they gave a long list of places that had been bombed during the previous week: as I heard the name of each Austrian town, the place itself and the country round it became almost unbearably vivid to me, and my memory was flooded with images of holiday expeditions and explorations, all with friends who were now officially my enemies. The feeling that oppressed me during the whole of the war, of the tragic absurdity of a situation that turned friends into murdering enemies as quickly as a thunderstorm blows up on a sultry day, began to crystallize into verse:

> O in this cloud of darkness that endures
> Better by far, the guns say, greeting ill
> To barricade us for eternity
> Where the green wave the island dream immures
> And the Armed Guardian of the Cliffs can be
> Our classic, unrelenting stance, and kill
> The wandering birds of love that brave the sea . . .

The Summer Story came out of the same nostalgia at an earlier date, but transposed and blended with other elements to make a whole that is still mysterious even to myself: I can only testify to its inner coherence and truth, which cost me many hours and days of slow work. Though it would appear to be about despair and death, it seems to me to cover much more spiritual experience than that: inevitable, as it was in a sense a concentration into forty short lines of an idea I had for a long story or play, and as it went through the process of condensation and transmutation it attracted to itself unexpected images and phrases (in the musical sense).

By the middle of the war Fieldhead had been turned into a Red Cross home, with some of the wards in the downstairs rooms, but we still had the dining-room and the library as well as several bedrooms upstairs, and were in general fortunate because my mother had had much to do with the local organization before the war and was held in considerable awe by the commandant (who was devoted to her) and the other officers. In face I often got the impression that it was my mother who was running the whole show, having for so many years been accustomed to run every show in the neighbourhood and get her own way. In addition, with the touch of sly New England canniness she never entirely lost, she took full advantage of the fact that she was partly crippled since the accident in the library when she broke her thigh, and was thus at the same time Supreme Patient and Grey Eminence of the home. She saw the joke of this herself, I think, and didn't mind being teased about it by her children. She had in any case grown a very tough skin, years before, against our teasing, which she treated as a kind of harmless half-witted fooling — an attitude no doubt justified by the fact that even then, when we were all in our thirties or early forties, we were apt to converse in a childish private language that dated back to the First World War. The long rest in bed did her good, and she looked extraordinarily young and beautiful when her worries cleared: even ten years later, when the cross-hatchings of age were far more minutely etched on her face, she retained a freshness of colour in her cheeks, a sweetness of expression and a sparkle in her grey-blue eyes that someone much younger might have envied.

As the summer of 1944 advanced, and the battle of Europe developed in intensity, a strange and terrifying contrast developed between earth and sky. Where I walked, thinking out my poems and articles, all was peace and fruitfulness, the great garden of Fieldhead in its imperturbable and changeless seasonal rhythm bringing flowers to bloom and fruit to ripening as it had when I had been a small boy before the First World War. The mottled red and yellow colours of the apples deepened in the branches, the windfalls dropped into the heavy-dewed grass where the wasps attacked the bruises, and hedgehogs crept among them, snouts to earth; in the borders asters and dahlias and snapdragons flamed in many-coloured fires, yellow leaves began to appear among the limes in the drive and the crimson drippings of the Virginia creeper over the library walls; squirrels leapt and swung from aromatic branch to branch among the walnut-trees, and late butterflies could be observed asleep in window corners. Then, as sunset darkened into twilight on cloudless nights, slowly great armadas of bombers rose over the horizon and the tops of the chestnut-trees, and their clustering formations, heading for the Continent, filled the sky for hours on end with their steady whine and roar. . . . One began to wonder whether one would ever live under quiet skies again: it was an awe-inspiring spectacle, this gigantic concentration of death-dealing power moving off to the kill, but appalled though one might be at what this revealed that war had become, for us they were there to protect. I could not help contrasting them with the outnumbered battles of our fighters in the same skies four years before, and the ceaseless humming of the enemy bombers towards Coventry that moonlit night when I mounted guard by the railway bridge.

Gradually the sense of a civilization that had lost its way, a world out of control, began to dominate my thoughts. I think this was a not unusual experience among reflective people, as the ingenuity of modern technology revealed itself more and more diabolically in the last phase of the war. At the back of one's mind grew the still tiny but ominous apprehension that the conquest of the Nazis might only mean a pause and a change of partners before the process of destruction began again: the sense of something accelerating that should never have been set in motion. This, surely, was the impulse behind the revival of interest in archaeology and the science of vanished civilizations that began to be so marked at this time: not merely the new, still scarcely believable idea that our own civilization might join the rubble of the past without leaving a trace, but also that somewhere in the speechless mounds and crumbling stones, faint landmarks in a time-space stretching out far beyond Rome and Greece, a secret might be found that would tell us where we went wrong, what belief or intuition we had lost. Perhaps it could be found in the patient, cunning unriddling of the buried fragments; perhaps in the legends that had come down to us through the civilizations we knew. These ideas crystallized first in my poem *Invocation:*

> . . . When the lone mounds and mazes on the downs
> And shards dug up from ruins of old fires
> That blazed where Kings of Logres built their towns,
>
> Seem on the point of utterance, with lips
> Unlocked at last from their unreckoned sleep. . . .

I went down during a brief holiday period to stay with my sister Helen near Salisbury. At that time her husband Mounty was still in the Middle East, both her daughters, Maureen and Nancy, were engaged in war work and Simon was at Eton. She occupied her energies, as a member of F.A.N.Y., in driving for the American Army, but so far from being tired of sitting at the driving wheel during her days off, she was eager to jump at any excuse to get back there. It is no doubt merely a masculine prejudice that leads men to judge women at the wheel as unreliable, unpredictable and irresponsible; but Helen at least is one of the few women I would unhesitatingly award a certificate of exception to. I had, therefore, little difficulty in persuading her to drive me to Stonehenge, which I studied with a new curiosity and excitement. American G.I.s were wandering in and out of the rings, or nonchalantly lying against the trilithons, chewing gum: a ripple of the world storm had frothed up just to touch the unfathomably ancient temple. I noticed for the first time the megalith burial mounds to the

west, and the traces of the tracks on the downs where the stones had
been dragged up from the river. All around were the gigantic horizons
with their suggestion of measureless realm and air. The visit stirred
me deeply, and I began to find the first phrases and images for the
long poem, *The Age of the Dragon*, in which I tried to define the
mood of this time of massed Anglo-American raids, the contrast between the violence of the present and the symbols of permanency, the
reapers in the fields and the megalithic burial chambers and temple
stones above:

> . . . The marble hands imploring from the past,
> The cities and the symbols are dismissed,
> And history, our home, is changed too fast
> Till all our lives grow thin as autumn mist;
>
> O give us words, as strong as the ringed stones
> That still outlast forgotten priest and name
> Counting the years by thousands on the downs
> To cage the Dragon and transmute our shame.

In this poem I felt I had most nearly captured the tranquillity of
tone, combined with intensity of image, that I was always aiming at;
with the exception of *The Sphere of Glass*, it was the poem in which
my own fragile-winged Muse seemed most completely to have inspired
me to transform the disorder of living, feeling and thinking in a world
cataclysm into the calm and order of art.

The Sphere of Glass came out of a spring visit to Rosamond, who
had taken a cottage at Aldworth in the Berkshire hills. As the bus
from Reading wound up and down the country roads, the fields looked
so fresh and restful and softly green, the bluebells a swimming ground-
mist of azure-violet in the copses, that my longing to have a cottage of
my own in such a landscape one day became a determination. Later,
Rosamond and I went for a walk in the woods. The light fell on the
young leaves of the trees, so that some of them looked like a shower of
pale green-gold coins pouring to earth. I told her about the poems I
was trying to write; and she excited me very much by describing the
new novel she was at work on, to be called *The Ballad and the Source*.
Then we began to talk about the war, and the struggle that was going
on at the time between the Poles and the Russians, which seemed so
ominous for the future. As we talked, the air was filled with the distant, ceaseless humming of aeroplanes; and I was aware of some
strange counterpoint between those aeroplanes with their constant re-

minder of the war in which we were engaged, and the Roman dyke, still visible as a lumpish heaving under the soil, beside which we were walking. All this I tried to distil, to bring into harmony in the poem I began when I returned to London, starting from the key line that came to me almost of its own accord:

So through the sun-laced woods they went. . . .

I was conscious during the walk, in a quite extraordinary way, of the power of poetry, or rather of tragic art in a more general sense, to resolve the discords of hope and despair, of agony and triumph recurring in an eternal pattern in life, so that the imaginative artist who dared to look far enough into the truth was given a new dimension of being, as strong as — and for an agnostic world stronger than — the consolations of religion:

> Within the wood, within that hour
> It seemed a sphere of glass had grown
> That glittered round their lives with power
> To link what grief the dyke had known
> With voices of their vaster war
> The sun-shot bombers' homing drone,
>
> And make one tragic harmony
> Where still this theme, their hope, returned,
> And still the spring unchangeably
> In fires of its own sap was burned
> And poetry, from love and death,
> The peace their human contest earned.
>
> It might have been all history
> Without the sphere of wonder lay
> And just beyond their colloquy
> Some truth more pure than they could say,
> While through the bluebells and the ferns
> Sister and brother made their way.

As the tempo of the war quickened, and Europe became the main battlefield, the tempo of publishing activity quickened also. More countries were being liberated, more opportunities appearing for entering the foreign field again: not only sending one's own publications abroad, but getting hold of the most interesting books and authors from abroad to introduce to an English audience. Gradually my work for the Hogarth Press and for *New Writing* began to increase, and my other, more official work grew more complex; gradually the hours I could spend with my poetry exercise book grew fewer, and I sadly recognized that the old division of my life was making itself insistently felt once more.

⤳ V I ⤶

The Last Phase

LIFE in London during the V-weapons offensive was not particularly
pleasant; and yet it went on very much as before. The trouble
about the doodle-bugs was that they came over at all hours of the day
and night, and were continually interrupting work, meetings, parties
and sleep with their disagreeable splutter, like an aerial motor-bicycle
in bad running order. If one was not in the open, and could not see
which way the beastly flame-tailed thing was heading — having escaped all the obstacles erected in its path between London and the
coast — one had only the noise to go by. Gratefully one heard the
splutter fade away into the distance; painfully one heard it grow
louder, until it seemed directly overhead; tensely one waited for the
cut-out. If the splutter stopped at the moment of maximum noise, one
dived — if one had anything to dive into or under, shelter entrance,
archway or table. After all the years of war, Londoners were tired, and
the doodle-bugs frayed their nerves abominably. To me, they seemed
far less frightening than the all-night raids of the spring of 1941 with
their massed bombs, land-mines and incendiaries, because the area of
fear was so much more precisely charted; but I know that many people
felt them to be the worst trial yet, and there were moments when it
seemed that human existence was not much better than beetle or ant
life. Even so, the alarm and despondency they caused was never anything like as great as Hitler's propagandists gloatingly reported.

Life went on: though the approach of a doodle-bug had a markedly
freezing effect on conversation at the luncheon- or dinner-table. I remember a luncheon that had been arranged at the Savoy, in a private
room, to discuss whether funds could be raised to create a permanent
memorial for Demetrios, in the form of a poetry prize or some similar
award. Sir Kenneth Clark was there; the Greek Minister, Monsieur

Romanos; George Seferiades,* poet-diplomat and friend of Demetrios, over from Cairo and one or two other interested friends. It was the first time I had met Seferiades, whose poetry I had begun to publish in *New Writing and Daylight*, and I was deeply impressed by his charm, by his immense knowledge of everything that was going on in poetry all over the world, and by the look of brooding, philosophical reflection in the large dark-brown eyes under the domed brow: a true egg-head, if ever there was one. I was deep in conversation with Kenneth Clark about the war artists: he seemed surprised at my interest in and admiration for all he had done to help them individually and to make it possible for an imaginative vision, and not merely a factual record, of the events of the war to be preserved for posterity, and he promised to show me some of the latest stuff that had just come in from Normandy. At that moment the familiar splutter began to be audible in the distance; as it grew louder, we all became a little more thoughtful; conversation faltered, dried up here and there for some seconds though the thread was never entirely lost; gestures were inhibited, not a fork was lifted to a mouth for the brief span of time that seemed an eternity. When the machine had evidently veered away again, it was satisfactory to observe that no member of the party had actually disappeared under the table.

There was another, famous occasion at the Churchill Club, in the autumn. I do not imagine that anyone who was present will ever forget it. The three Sitwells were reading from their poetry. This attraction had drawn the whole of the smarter artistic and literary world, from Emerald Cunard and Sybil Colefax to those dapper young Americans in uniform whose war aim seemed to be to compete for the social place of "The Sergeant" (now absent in Normandy). Apart from the last-named, there seemed very little room indeed in the hall for the ordinary members of the Allied forces for whom the Club was supposed to be run. As Edith got up to read, and began with her poem about the air-raids in 1940, *Still Falls the Rain*, the warning whistle was sounded in the Club. She had, I believe, never experienced a doodle-bug raid before; but she seemed quite unperturbed. As she reached the passage:

> Still falls the Rain —
> Still falls the blood from the Starved Man's wounded Side:
> He bears in His Heart all wounds —

* As poet, George Seferiades has always taken the name of Seferis.

the rattle grew to ominous proportions, and it was impossible not to think that the monstrous engine of destruction was poised directly overhead. . . . Edith merely lifted her eyes to the ceiling for a moment, and, giving her voice a little more volume to counter the racket in the sky, read on. It was a magnificent performance, worthy of a British admiral coolly dictating orders from the bridge in the middle of a fierce naval engagement. She held the whole audience in the grip of her discipline, the morale of her unspoken asseveration that poetry was more important than all the terrors that Hitler could launch against us. Not a soul moved, and at the end, when the doodle-bug had exploded far away, the applause was deafening.

One grew hard about other people's misfortunes: one had to. One did not try to picture the scene when a doodle-bug had fallen, if it was sufficiently far away, out of sight and out of hearing. One registered a moment's relief at not having been present, shut it out of one's mind, and carried on. One Sunday morning, looking out of my sitting-room window in Carrington House, I saw one fall in the middle distance, at a point that seemed to be somewhere between the Palace and Big Ben. A small column of black smoke arose: it was extraordinary how little it affected the general view. It was only the next day I heard that I had witnessed one of the most horrible disasters of the doodle-bug offensive: that particular bomb had hit the Guards Chapel just when it was full for morning service.

Life went on, in a way that would have seemed incredible if one had imagined the situation before the war. The theatres and cinemas remained open: most people bought tickets and went, whether there was an alert or not. The performances of the Sadler's Wells Ballet always drew full houses. I remember one evening that autumn going to see *Giselle* with Alice Harding (who had been born an Astor and became an Obolensky, a Hoffmansthal, and later a Pleydell-Bouverie, as well as a Harding), always a devotee of the ballet and a profound admirer of Fred Ashton's work with the Sadler's Wells. Margot Fonteyn and my friend Alexis Rassine were dancing the principal roles, and as they completed the famous love-dance in Act I, Alice murmured: "They dance like a dream, they dance like a dream. . . ." Indeed the spell of a great ballet like *Giselle*, with music and movement and colour and physical charm all acting together upon one's mind and senses, did draw one into a dream-like trance where even all memory of the doodle-bugs was lost until the curtain came down.

The rockets — the V2s — which began a few months later, were, to my mind, much worse than the doodle-bugs. There were not many of them, and by the time one heard the after-roar it was too late to worry. But there was something singularly disturbing about their unpredictable imminence; it was uncomfortable to feel that one might at any moment, perhaps without even a second's warning, be hurled in fragments into eternity. Sometimes on a dark night, after one or two had fallen in the distance, perhaps at intervals of only a few hours, I must confess I found it difficult to concentrate on my work. There was one particular, grim winter night, which remains in my memory. Beatrix had been appearing in *Uncle Harry* with Michael Redgrave, giving one of the most electrifying performances in her career: so powerful was the effect she had upon the audience when she appeared in her prison clothes in the last act, that I was ready to believe that for the first time it had become exactly true and not a figure of speech, that one could have heard a pin drop. Suddenly one night, on leaving the theatre, she was taken seriously ill, and a very dangerous operation had to be performed. My mother came up to be at hand, and stayed with me in Carrington House. The drear, iron-chill winter afternoon darkened into night, and the operation began. We waited and waited for news: the time when it was supposed to be over passed, and still there was no news; in the distance the roar of a V2 falling could be heard, and still the hours passed; and another V2 fell, seemingly nearer; and still we waited. It was a tough endurance test for all of us, most of all for my mother, who first heard a V2 fall that night, when distraught with anxiety for her youngest daughter hovering between life and death under a surgeon's knife.

Another winter evening which remains engraved on my memory had a more comic side. Owing to the *Crève-Coeur* poems, which had made such a deep impression on English intellectuals, Louis Aragon had become a major symbol of suffering France for us. When, therefore, it was announced that he was intending to visit London, great excitement prevailed and every effort was made to receive him with festive honours. Cyril Connolly arranged an evening party for him at his flat in Bedford Square, and the most distinguished authors then in London were among the guests, with Tom Eliot at their head. Aragon quickly showed us that he had lost none of his skill in charming people when he talked to them individually, but perhaps the position he found himself in after the Liberation, as chief rhetoric-monger of the left-wing Resistance, had somewhat blunted his sensitive responses on more public occasions. After we had talked over drinks for some time, the word was whispered round that he wanted to give a recitation of his poetry. Several of us took the cue and pressed him to let us hear him recite some of the poems which had so profoundly moved us while France was occupied. Flattered and happy, Aragon settled himself by the fireside: the rest of us found chairs or cushions on the floor and grouped ourselves round him with an eager reverence that English intellectuals, so far less insular than the intellectuals of most other nations when it comes to the arts, rarely fail to show on such occasions. The recitation began with some of the favourites from *Crève-Coeur*, delivered by their author without a single hesitation and without a glance at the book. There were murmurs of appreciation and pleasure from round the room. Then Aragon announced that he would like to read us some more recent compositions that we were less likely to be acquainted with. As if by magic, he produced a sheaf of slim volumes from outer and inner pockets. Do you know this volume? he asked, holding one up. Or this? — holding another up. Murmurs of regret from the cushions, noises expressing eagerness to hear them recited. Without waiting a moment, Aragon, casting aside the texts, lifted up his voice and began. . . . Time passed, the declamation went on . . . and on. . . . In the distance the dread, familiar roar of a rocket falling could be heard by English ears attuned to these reminders of mortality. A frozen look began to come over the faces of the audience, unable to banish problems of home-going from their minds as the quarter-hours ticked away. It is doubtful if Aragon, intent on his rhetoric, was aware at all of what was happening; but he certainly heard what happened next. An intrepid young author, arriving late, endeavoured to steal in through the kitchen, could not find the light switch, and crashed into a row of empty bottles on the floor. He then joined us, looking somewhat ruffled, and conducted a running commentary on the recitation, in what was not exactly an undertone. Sweat broke out on our host's brow. Faces reddened: even Tom Eliot's look of kindly, enquiring attention seemed to freeze into something more like a smile of embarrassment. I do not know how Aragon interpreted this disturbance: but the flood of poetry rolled on.

That winter had the peculiar terror of a recrudescence of struggle and uncertainty, just when the worst had seemed to be over. In the late summer the great events had followed one another with mounting excitement — Paris liberated — Marseilles liberated — Rumania suing for peace from Russia — and success feeding upon itself, every day's news confounded the prognosis of the day before. Nothing appeared to stand in our way: Allied troops would soon be deep into Germany, and all the sites of the rocket-weapons cleared. At Fieldhead we witnessed the astonishing armadas of aeroplanes with gliders in tow setting forth for the invasion of Holland. "Dare one begin to say 'Till we meet'?" Christopher wrote at the end of a letter in September. . . . Then the checks began to occur. As the shortest days of the year approached — a time for me of strange perturbation, for I have always for some unknown reason felt that the dying year was dying *in* me — the savage Greek crisis between the Communist-dominated E.A.M. and the West-sympathizing partisans broke out. I was glad then that Demetrios had not lived to know of it: during the last months of his life, he had been very gloomy about the role that political factions were beginning to play in Europe on the eve of liberation, and especially in his own country, where he felt that embittered political division was a curse that had been laid upon it from earliest times. And at the same time the Germans launched their counter-offensive in the Ardennes, the last gesture of a nation at bay, to remind the world of the greatest military tradition of Europe. At Christmas at Fieldhead, my mother, Beatrix and I sat huddled over a fire blazing as high as the fallen bough of one of the poplar trees could make it (the boiler for the central heating had burst). A thick rime covered the grass and the trees, and through the french windows we watched a transformation scene of extraordinary beauty develop, as the mist cleared and the feathery white tree-tops were touched by the wan yellow rays of the sun, against a blue sky. There was even frost on the back of a solitary swan that came for food as Beatrix and I, wrapped to our noses, stood on the raft to watch the white sparkle of the willow-trees all down the further bank. Behind us in the locked Boat-House, the harvest of apples and potatoes lay snugly massed in the gloom under its straw and sacking, with the long-unused racing craft resting on their racks above them. Here all was peace, and the unchanging winter sleep of nature: but our thoughts were darkened by the news of the German breakthrough that had begun a few days before, the lengthening prospect of slaughter and ruin it seemed to foreshadow, and the suffering of many friends involved in the fighting. Some, including Jiří Mucha, Harold Acton and Lincoln Kirstein, I knew were out of harm's way in Paris, but the news they sent me was not reassuring: the French intellectuals were indulging in an orgy of accusation and counter-accusation, private vendettas were being worked off, and the Victor Hugos of the Resistance, in the intervals of soaking the public with their fountains of trumpery verse, were denouncing their distinguished but more reserved elders as all but collaborationists.

Only Malraux, fighting under De Lattre de Tassigny in the Vosges, they told me, kept a dignified silence.

« 2 »

TWO other visitors who caused some commotion arrived in our midst during the early months of the spring, before the war with Germany was over. Both were from America: Edmund Wilson and Wystan Auden.

Edmund Wilson had long been one of the favourite American authors of the English intellectuals: an odd irony, as he was to prove himself singularly Anglophobe — at any rate in the English eye of disappointed love. I could remember what a stir *Axel's Castle*, which Wilson published in 1931, had made in Bloomsbury and Cambridge. Generally acknowledged now, I think, as one of the key books in modern literary criticism, this study of seven writers of our time, all in the symbolist tradition, profoundly impressed us at once not only by its intellectual energy, but also because of the confident attempt it made to see these writers in their deeper perspective, as part of a movement in the mind of man that had been going on for decades. *Axel's Castle* was followed in 1939 by *The Triple Thinkers*, in which Wilson brilliantly used his favourite X-ray apparatus, combining Marxist analysis with Freudian intuition, on Kipling, Henry James and other authors of the immediate past, with startling if not always entirely convincing results. The capacity of his mind, the restless movement of his thought, the vigour and bite of his writing were unexpectedly displayed in a totally different sphere when he wrote an elaborate — but immensely readable — study of the development of modern revolutionary Socialist ideas, from an independent left-wing point of view, in *To the Finland Station*. Edmund Wilson explained the inter-war literary generation to itself more completely than any other philosophical critic: it was natural that there should be eager anticipation when we learnt that he was to be one of the first from the other side of the Atlantic to break through our intellectual isolation. Again, as in the case of Aragon, the red carpet was laid down; again a certain dismay clouded the occasion, and seeds of bitterness were sown where the flowers of a happily renewed understanding should have sprung up. Hamish and Yvonne Hamilton laid on an evening party, to which everyone was invited; the literary "top brass" were on their best behaviour, but the little man in the drab clothes who was the guest of honour lurked rather silently in corners, was difficult to draw out, and gave a distinct impression of displeasure. "He's just like a business executive," sourly exclaimed a distinguished literary figure, who had hoped for a warmer and wittier response. A few days later, however, he came to luncheon with William Plomer and myself at my flat, and after a rather chill and wary start began to thaw, unable to keep up his reserve under the bubbling of William's grotesque stories and comic observations. For the first time I saw him laugh, and during an increasingly relaxed conversation he made a number of extraordinarily perceptive and incisive remarks about books and people, not all of them destructive, though the sharpness of a passing judgement on Willie Somerset Maugham (whose work enjoyed an unusually fervent highbrow vogue at the time) made me wonder whether part of the trouble at the evening party had not been that he was coming to the conclusion that the war had turned us all soft in the head. We parted on the friendliest terms. A few days later I saw him hurrying past the Poets' Fountain in Hamilton Place, coat flapping in the breeze, eyes on the ground, too absorbed in his own thoughts to recognize me or anyone else. Perhaps he was already composing in his head the *New Yorker* articles that caused such offence — in which the unkindest cut of all was his comparison of the atmosphere in post-war London to that of pre-war Moscow.

A week or two later Wystan Auden turned up. His arrival, of course, was of crucial interest to all of us who had been associated with him before the war. He had torn up his English roots and replanted himself in America without, it seemed, a lingering glance of regret: he had been reviled and indignantly defended in public on numerous occasions since 1939; but whatever doubts some of us may have entertained about the poetry he had written since leaving England, not only did we still think of him as *the* leading figure in our literary generation, but also we knew that he had established himself as an admired poetic master in America. Lincoln Kirstein had written to me that he thought the Prospero poem and the *Oratorio* "the finest verse since the death of Yeats." How much had he changed? How much was he aware that he had become a controversial figure in his native country? Edmund Wilson had discussed his transplantation with William and me, with shrewd understanding and sympathy; but, perhaps inevitably, could not give us much idea of what alteration to expect.

I very much doubt if there is such a thing as a completely detached point of view: one cannot change countries without changing one's outlook, even if only ever so slightly. Christopher Isherwood had written to me in the autumn about *Penguin New Writing:*

In Number 20, I thought the best things were the Stern story, your poem about the boy on the shore, the Gottlieb story (*What Are We Waiting For?*) and Plomer on Forster. I like that poem particularly: better, almost, than any others you've written. And I must frankly say that the Gottlieb story seemed to me to stand head and shoulders above the British reportage — so bold and warm, after the half-tints and wavery lines. I do hope I'm not getting prejudiced in favour of my adopted idiom. I don't think so, though. Because I find the great mass of that kind of American writing boring and unsubtle; whereas the English nearly all have undertones and some sort of inner awareness. Of course the exhaustion of the war-mentality is apparent in all the English writing, as it should be. But a good writer can be exhausted and still maintain all his qualities. In fact, the best of the stuff in *New Writing*, and in Forster's letters, for example, has special qualities which perhaps only come with exhaustion; an extreme relaxation, a wider scale of values, a special kind of humour . . .

At a distance of fifteen years, this seems to me an intelligent piece of criticism; but at that time one was hyper-sensitive to any kind of implied slight or note of detached superiority. I had felt a tiny prick of dismay on reading Christopher's letter; when Wystan appeared, however, the dismay was more like a jab with a blunt hypodermic needle. He had been sent over by the Strategic Bombing Survey to study the effects of bombing on the civilian population in Germany. A slight shudder went through me, as one who had also been bombed, at the coolly clinical implication of this mission; but unjustly, because I knew that in reality Wystan had longed for an excuse to get back to the country which had meant so much to him before the war. He arrived at my door one Sunday morning, complete with new American officer's uniform and new American accent. A little overpowered by this, I was at a loss how to get the conversation going; but it did not matter, for without much beating about the bush, he launched into a long lecture, quoting detailed statistics of pig-iron production and the industrial man-power graph, on the world power position after the war. Great Britain, her Dominions and Empire had apparently been liquidated, while the two giants, the U.S.A. and the U.S.S.R., towered over the world. Britain, in fact, was lucky to have survived the war at all. There was no word from Uncle Sam Auden about what we had endured, the various skills, the faith, the unremitting industrial and military effort without which the fortress of Western civilization could never have been held; there was not even a personal word of sympathy to a former friend about the discomforts of flying bombs and flying glass and trying to work while a whole building shook and swayed about one under the impact of high explosive. On the contrary, the second part of the lecture consisted of an exposé of the superiority of American culture, and a sharp calling to order of myself when, as a kind of desperate gesture of defence, I made some mild criticisms of recent American fiction.

Of course I was wrong to be so furious. Wystan's prognosis of the post-war situation was more than partly true; and I had forgotten how impersonal he was by nature, and how habitual it was with him to deal with a situation, when he felt uncertain or shy, by immediate attack. Stephen Spender told me later that he had had a violent row with him because of a similar lecture, but had made it up almost at once and found Wystan sympathetic and human as soon as the air was cleared: once the idea that we were going to be morally superior with him was out of the way. Indeed, I was disarmed myself when he told me at parting, with a pleasure that found an immediate response in me, that the American Navy had ordered 1,100 copies of his collected poems.

« 3 »

THE long vigil of that winter of torment and durance came to an end at last: the miracle month of April arrived, when one after the other the walls of Hitler's empire were breached, and the Allied troops poured in to their victorious meeting among the ruins.

One evening I attended a recital of Edith Sitwell's poems at the Polytechnic. Edith herself spoke very quietly and very movingly, with a face twisted with pain in the war poems; a singer then took over, in a group of poems set by William Walton; and the programme concluded with a choral work by Michael Tippett, the composer himself conducting. During the choral singing, I began strangely to feel that history itself had become like music: almost in a trance I perceived the freeing of the concentration camps that was taking place in Germany as against all expectation fitting and just and even sublime with the sublimity of great music; the revelation of degradation and bestiality not triumph of horror and darkness, but resolved at last, incredibly, in a final movement, an act of deliverance that repaid and justified all the struggle and suffering we had been through.

The trance-like feeling continued as the fantastic drama was being played to its close across the Channel, while the daffodils came out in the parks, where people walked freed at last from the fear of sudden death from the skies. The reality of the last days of Hitlerism seemed to eclipse the wildest imaginings of the fabulists and doom-warning dreamers among the poets and story-tellers. Only Shakespeare seemed to match the times: Birnam Wood was marching to Dunsinane while Hitler-Macbeth was dying in the flames of his bunker, and the theme that runs all through the last plays — of what seemed lost for ever being found, of the rejected in the fulness of time restored and wickedness foiled by some mysteriously working power of justice and faith — was being daily illustrated. I tried to work these themes into a poem I began to write, using an image from one or other of the plays in the last line of each of the four stanzas, and picturing the swastika as the great axle of some primeval car that had tried to drag the world back to barbarism:

> Reunion and reprieve: the words like suns
> Blaze on the day these garland bells acclaim,
> And the great axle of doom that seemed to run
> Backwards forever to the unlucky dead
> Palpable over them as tank or gun,
> Dissolves in mist beneath those words instead —
> See: the veiled statue wakes, resumes her breathing name.
>
> The soldier drops his weapons at the door
> And from his forehead wipes the brand of Cain,
> The toasts are raised, the dancing shakes the floor,
> And that tall stranger with the eyes of ice —
> Look round, and laugh, for he is there no more
> To drain the tankard with the skull device —
> For the green springing host has come to Dunsinane.

The announcement of the victory over Nazi Germany had been anticipated for so many days before it actually took place that the celebrations seemed to go off at half-cock, and there was none of that sudden wild relief from unendurable tension that I remembered from my boyhood in 1918. It so happened that Stephen Spender was with me in my Carrington House flat when Churchill's voice came over the radio at three o'clock in the afternoon of Tuesday, the 8th of May; and the coincidence struck me only when he left that he had also been with me, in my now charred and shattered Mecklenburgh Square flat, when the announcement was made of the German attack on Poland, six years before.

Even though we knew we had entered the age of hideous, death-dealing marvels, no one outside the innermost war-waging conclaves, during those three months between May and August, imagined that the end of the war would come so suddenly and in the way it did. This is what I recorded in my Journal at the time. . . .

"The explosion of the atom bomb over Japan has made me feel physically sick for two or three days. I wonder how many people reflect that it may cast doubt, not merely on the way the world is going to be run now, but also on the whole course of human *aspiration* for the last two hundred and fifty years. That is the thought that won't leave me alone.

"The atom bomb announces beyond argument that the supreme need of today, with priority above all other needs, is that each living person should become aware of the reality of every other living person in the world. Unless the imagination, the human imagination is at work, and can create a close moral connection between the act and its result — in war, in commerce, in government — modern Satanisms will surely continue to flourish. . . .

"On the first V.J. day, the Wednesday, I suddenly decided, in my bath, that I would like to have some special memory of it. So I raced through my shaving, and hurried in the light drizzle across the Park to the Palace, where a sizeable crowd was collected to see the State procession set off to open Parliament. The Guardsmen lining the route seemed to be in the same happy, informal mood as the crowd: then the sudden clap and rattle as arms were presented all down the Mall, the clatter of the black chargers of the Life Guards as they pranced out of the Palace courtyard heightened the tension. They were followed by the open barouche in which were seated the King, looking rather nervous and leaning forward in his Admiral's uniform, with the powder-blue Queen waving and smiling beside him — a cheer from the crowd — more Life Guards — more barouches filled with officials — no cheers, but ' 'oo are these?' from my side — and it was all over (though long after they had passed a fussy explaining mother nearby kept on warning her schoolboy son that it might be difficult to see, he'd better keep a sharp look out, and so on, and so on). As I walked back, I passed a shabby little old woman stumbling along by herself, a beatific smile on her face, and muttering 'lovely dresses . . . lovely dresses. . . .'

"The evening was perfectly clear, warm and still: it was impossible to resist going out to see how London was celebrating, to join in somehow, somewhere. We went down from Carrington House by Whitehorse Street, and as we emerged into Piccadilly, we were confronted by an extraordinary sight: the brilliantly lit street — that was strange enough in itself — was packed with people as far as the eye could see, in both directions, with no wheeled traffic to be discovered anywhere, except one slowly moving car on to which people kept climbing and crowding. As we walked towards the Circus, the mass turned out not to be so impassable as it seemed, because everyone was quietly, happily, aimlessly on the move. One longed for bands and music everywhere; but it was, after all, a totally unrehearsed occasion, and people found their own haphazard way of giving vent to their feelings, as if scarcely able to believe that the long, long horror was over at last, bemused in their joy, with exhaustion suddenly coming over them. There were sailors giving girls endless, passionate kisses in the middle of the street; here and there people threw fire crackers; climbed lampposts; occasionally burst out singing; exclaimed to one another delightedly at the display of the searchlights; and most extraordinary of all, suddenly made dancing rings, performing strange, impromptu, atavistic steps, as they might have when the news of Waterloo or of the Armada's defeat came through; then wandered on again. We made our way past the Athenaeum, where torches were flaming over the portico and all around the Clubs were blazing with lights and hung with flags, down into the Mall, where we were confronted by the same perspective of massed crowds, thickening up to the Victoria Memorial: at the end the great illuminated façade of the Palace, with an enormous, raw half-moon hanging over it. As we came nearer, the noise of singing increased; the crowds were finally jammed beyond movement, and on the Memorial itself people were clustered as thickly as swarming bees. Every few minutes the singing would pause, and the chant would go up: 'We want the *King* . . . *We* want the *King* . . .' Until at last the french windows on the far, red-draped, fairytale balcony were opened, and the King and Queen, diminutive but glittering figures — the Queen's diamonds flashed into the night under the arc-lights — came out to wave and be greeted by cheer after cheer, waving of hands, and the singing of 'For he's a jolly good fellow.'

"Then many dispersed — though many others, insatiable, waited for a later reappearance — and the squashed but happy crowd poured through the gates into Green Park, where the sudden soaring of fireworks lit up the innumerable couples on the grass and under the trees."

I thought that night, on returning home, of the dark moments, the sinkings of heart that had inevitably occurred during the past six years, when vital fires were low and doubt was strong and no such happy ending as we were at last celebrating seemed possible. As our side, after 1942, had gradually gained the advantage, the intimations these moments brought were not so much of defeat and catastrophic humiliation — Britain after the gigantic proscription and the gas chambers reduced to the status of a helot colony of the world-dominating Third Reich — as of an endless stalemate, war continuing for all our lives with only the briefest respite leading to ever more feverish and exhausted efforts on both sides to reach an absolute conclusion. Henry Moore's drawings of the sleepers in the Underground stations were perhaps a prophetic vision of a condition that would become perpetual . . . while we sank into a darkness without hope or joy, only machines would grow more ingenious and more devilishly powerful. Perhaps the destiny of mankind was not to listen to the angels, but to go on perfecting machines, giving birth to machines in our own death, until machines were indistinguishable from life — in everything except mercy, pity, and love. . . .

It would be as well, I thought, even while the bells were ringing, not to forget that one had had these waking nightmares.

ᥱ VII ᥲ

Taken at the Flood

B EFORE V.J. day arrived, I had begun to plan a visit to Paris,
whither Cyril Connolly, Raymond Mortimer, Eddie Sackville-
West and other literary lights of the London wartime firmament had
already managed to get themselves officially invited, not without slight
twinges of envy on my part. At last, with the assistance of the Publishers' Association, the British Council and in particular Enid MacLeod,
who had put all her Scottish determination and intelligence into the
task of re-establishing cultural links between France and Britain, and
with the miracle-working approval from Duff Cooper and Diana, already established in the British Embassy, I managed to convince the
authorities that my mission was urgent and found myself in possession
of the necessary permits, orders and allowances. I left in the first week
of September: a long, slow journey, the discomforts and delays of
which, including hours of waiting for the right tide to float us into the
still rather makeshift port facilities on the French side, were dissolved
in a mounting excitement as the train jolted through the familiar
landmarks which announced the approach of Paris. For a moment it
seemed almost incredible that Paris had survived as mistress of itself
and not as the subjugated second city of a triumphant Nazi empire,
that one would see it almost untouched by bombs, and that one had
actually survived oneself to be on this journey, after six years that
were more like sixty.

Among many vivid memories of that first post-war visit, many wonderful occasions of reunion with friends, many moving sights, discussions and discoveries, one moment of deep emotion stands out. We
arrived late in the evening, and tired, but before going to bed I went
for a walk by myself down past the Madeleine to see the Place de la
Concorde and the Champs Elysées again: I could not wait till the
morning for that. There were still very few street lamps burning, but

enough for me suddenly to notice that many of the chestnut-trees were already shedding their leaves, while new, spring-green buds were appearing in their place. I had completely forgotten this peculiarity of the chestnut-trees of the Champs Elysées: and as when, after many years of separation, one meets a person one has loved very much and one catches one's breath on seeing again some intimate individual mark or trait, a dimple or a pucker of the eyes or a one-sided smile, that had slipped out of the picture one had tried to keep in one's mind, so I caught my breath on noticing this second burgeoning along the blackened branches, and tears started to my eyes with all the memories that came tumbling back.

At that time, Paris was still a city of austerity, suffering and want. The weather was mild, but the Parisians already knew that they would have little or no heating for the winter, and that thousands of old and sick people, especially those who relied on savings and pensions in depreciated currency and were far too poor to buy on the flourishing black market, would die from cold and hunger and neglect. To bring to one's friends, or one's friends' friends, a pound of coffee, a bar of chocolate or a cake of soap, was acutely embarrassing, so overwhelming was the gratitude and relief. Very few restaurants or cafés were open, and those that were only provided the most meagre nourishment against the little ration-stamps with which one was provided. The Allied occupation authorities had requisitioned a number of the best and most famous places, the British in particular having brought off quite a coup by collaring Maxim's and turning it into the British Empire Club. The bill of fare was not especially varied there but the cooking of course was first-class, and one felt slightly guilty, avoiding the eyes of passing Parisians as one slipped in for luncheon or dinner. Not that one came across any bitterness or envy; on the contrary I was deeply impressed by the warmth of the welcome one received from nearly all the French people one met, the fervour with which they spoke of our war effort, our aid to the underground Resistance in the cities and in the maquis, and the almost sacred veneration in which the B.B.C. was held. Duff Cooper and Diana were, I believe, the most popular figures in Paris at the time: applause greeted them whenever they left the Embassy. The French made it quite clear that they believed we were the only nation among the Allies really to understand them: already a slight anti-American tone was discernible, which was unfair considering how much the Americans with their unlimited resources had done and were all the time doing for them; it arose perhaps inevitably from a thousand small occasions when some Americans unconsciously failed (in French eyes) to conceal the fact that they were not Europeans, that they considered themselves the new world-bosses, and that Paris had been created for the sole purpose of unlimited sexual gratification.

I found the literary situation in Paris even more confused than it had appeared the other side of the Channel: on the spot the opposing groups seemed more embittered, the accusations and counter-accusations more violent, and I was shocked by the power the extreme left wing appeared to wield in deciding whether an author should be allowed to publish (except in a hole-and-corner way) or not. It was sad also to see so much effort, money and space being lavished for largely political reasons on the floods of rhetorical "Resistance" poetry that filled the magazines. André Gide, however, François Mauriac and Paul Valéry held aloof from the more sordid public squabbles and still had their honour and their incense. The hour of the badly compromised Montherlant's return had not yet arrived, but Jean Cocteau, who had been in Paris during the Nazi occupation and friendly with the intellectuals among the German authorities (as Ernst Jünger's note-books clearly demonstrate), had managed by another astonishing display of his natural conjuring powers to present himself as a poet of the Liberation. I even heard a story (no doubt apocryphal) that as the last German lorries and armoured cars roared away and the population poured out on to the approaches from the west to greet the arrival of the liberating Army, the first jeep that emerged out of the clouds of dust was found to contain the figure of — none other than Cocteau, in Allied uniform, happily acknowledging the cheers of his fellow-Parisians.

The scene, however, had changed radically in many ways. Among the now immensely influential Communists, Aragon was bidding to be a kind of literary dictator, but Paul Eluard, former surrealist and a man of the most seductive charm and subtle artistic gifts, was already recognized as the Party's outstanding exhibit in poetry. Jean-Paul Sartre, who before the war, at the time when I had published his short stories in *New Writing*, had been admired by only a comparatively small highbrow circle, had become the leader of the younger generation, high priest of the new cult of atheistic existentialism; his lectures and writings, one was immediately told, were driving hundreds of young people to despair and suicide, and his new novels and plays *Les Mouches* and *Huis Clos*, were all the rage. Among those who were ranged with him as his disciples, one new name was, I found, repeated on all sides as a close competitor in influence: Albert Camus, a young writer-philosopher from North Africa, with two plays, *Le Malentendu* and *Caligula* — for which Harold Acton had already the year before whetted my appetite, describing them as "of immense intensity and stark beauty" — and a first novel, *L'Etranger*, already published.

I made a special pilgrimage to see André Gide, whom I found writing in his huge library in the Rue Vaneau. He greeted me with great warmth and enquired very keenly about our mutual friends in the literary world, about what people were reading in England, who the new authors were, and also about *New Writing*. As we were talking, the door-bell rang and a very small young man with a drawing block under his arm was ushered in. In a low, reverential voice, he reminded Gide that he had an appointment to make a drawing of him. The Master thereupon settled himself at a table by the window in a suitable pose, with a book in front of him, and the young man started feverishly to draw. While this was going on, Gide did not for a moment stop talking to me, discussing the Strachey family and asking about Virginia Woolf's death. Finally the drawing was done, and was presented to Gide for his approval. "*Pas mal! Pas mal du tout!*" he exclaimed, interrupting his conversation with me for a second. "*Merci, cher maître,*" murmured the little fellow, almost prostrating himself to the ground; and then, as Gide turned back to me, bowed himself slowly out. Before I left, other young worshippers had already arrived.

André Chamson, the meeting with whom in the last days before the war broke out had remained so vividly in my mind, was not in Paris, but André Malraux had returned from the Eastern Front at the end of the fighting to become General de Gaulle's "*chef de Cabinet.*" I managed at last to arrange an interview, and went to see him at the Ministry of War the day before I left. I was shown into a large room with a thick pile carpet and a huge Empire desk: a young secretary who was busying himself with papers in a corner, offered me a chair and whispered: "*Le Colonel viendra tout de suite.*" Ten minutes later Malraux came in, welcomed me with great cordiality, and dismissed the secretary. As soon as he had gone, Malraux hurried to the door in conspiratorial fashion, made certain that it was properly closed, and then turned eagerly to me and demanded at once to know what had happened to his English friends of the time of the Spanish Civil War. Had they changed their views about the Communists? I tried to describe the evolution of most of my contemporaries, who had been agitating anti-fascists a decade earlier, from direct political engagement to a more detached and reserved attitude, and an increasing preoccupation in their work with the deeper and more permanent problems of the human situation. Malraux kept on nodding vigorously as I spoke, and murmuring how he, too, with his closest friends were now completely disillusioned, at least with extreme left-wing ideology and agitation. He then suddenly asked me whether I thought there had been *progress* in Britain. Rather surprised, I replied, after a moment's hesitation, that in literature, art and music certainly exciting new developments had taken place, but that, in a more general sense, perhaps the recovery of a sense of national community — the non-party planning of a Welfare State — could indeed be described as progress. He nodded again, and said: "*En France aussi on a fait beaucoup de progrès.*" Anxiously, I enquired in what specific direction. "*Dans la reproduction en couleurs!*" he hissed triumphantly, and with his characteristic unsmiling nervous enthusiasm immediately launched into a long description of a plan for having the hundred greatest masterpieces in French painting reproduced in colours, life-sized, and chucking everything out of the provincial museums of France to make way for them; so that, whether one went to Lille or Lyons, Toulouse or Bayonne, one would still see the same hundred masterpieces. . . . Malraux was out of office before this ambitious and disturbing scheme could be realized.

France's intellectual vitality was, I thought, as remarkable as ever, but it seemed to me to a large extent to be turning in a void. Whether it was the result of the shock of defeat and the humiliation of Nazi occupation, or of some deeper reason that went further back, the dominant spirit was, I thought, anti-humanistic, even nihilistic. It was the very reverse of what I had hoped to find, remembering Antoine de St. Exupéry's noble *Letter to a Hostage*, which I had published in *New Writing and Daylight*, with its cry: "Human respect! Human respect! There's the touchstone! . . . If human respect is established in men's hearts, men will certainly end by establishing in return the social, political or economic system that will sanctify this respect."

Human respect: was it not precisely this quality that emerged so strongly from what had been written in England during the war? Some weeks before the German surrender, I went down to Salcombe on the Devon coast for a few days' rest. I had been there for a holiday earlier in the war, but since my first visit the little harbour in the estuary had been turned into an American naval base, and in spite of the still continuing black-out in London, repairs on the ships went on all night under blazing arc-lamps. The little homely pubs were now filled with flushed and raucous young American sailors: to go in for a

drink in the evening seemed at first like visiting the orgiastic celebrations of some strange barbaric tribe in Africa. To the limey eye they
appeared exactly alike in their manner, their reactions, their thoughts;
but as one got to know them one found that their ancestry was as
varied as the map of Europe. The original suspicion melted quickly
down into an immense friendliness, and on the third or fourth night an
attempt was even made to persuade me to sample and praise a "wun-
nerful" drink they had concocted, which turned out to be spirits of
turpentine and soda-water. In the midst of this weird transformation
scene portending the future, I was jerked back into the past by meeting an old waiter in the hotel, who told me, his voice trembling with
emotion, that as a young man he had been steward in a sports club of
which my father had been a leading light, and produced ancient letters
to corroborate his story. My thoughts churned up by these contrary
encounters, I took a long walk in the spring sunlight out along the
cliffs, up the slopes of which armies of bluebells and primroses had
marched, thinning out only where great broken ribs of grey quartz
rock broke through the soil: sea-gulls perched and strutted on them,
every few minutes planing off to dive and swoop and circle with piercing squawks over the blue-green, clear-as-jewels ocean sparkling and
foaming in a slow rhythm round the rocks far below. The sharp sea-
breeze buffeted the meadow-brown butterflies in the nodding bluebell
stems about my feet, and gathered as if to lift me from the cliff-top to
an element of exultation and prophecy between past and future. I was
suddenly filled with a kind of sublime joy in the knowledge that victory was approaching, that all our resolution and our tears had come
to harvest, in the intuition that we ourselves had been changed in the
process. Now at last in the new world that was taking shape behind
the guns, we had, tested in a fire so different from, so much fiercer
than anything we had envisaged, purged and strengthened ourselves
to seize, if we would, a spiritual leadership out of the chaos. Surely
now all the lack we had felt in our civilization before the war was being
filled, the split in our culture healed; we had waged the war endeavouring not to loose our hold on the ideals of justice and humanity we had
invoked against the Axis power; surely all the best that had been written in poetry and story, all that had been expressed in a thousand ways
in articles and letters and speeches by those who were to inherit the
peace, the spirit that more and more had come to inform all the pictorial
and musical arts, pointed to a new awakening of the moral imagination,
a new dedication in our islands to human respect. . . . Such was the
inspiration that came to me on my cliff-top walk among the bluebells,

promising so much in defiance of the chagrins of history; while the hammering and welding on the warships went on without pause in the estuary below.

In the last months of the war, I had thought a great deal about my future as a publisher and editor. I had gradually become aware that I had started something that looked like growing too big for me unless I did some drastic reorganizing.

Both *New Writing and Daylight* and *Penguin New Writing* were flourishing, the latter in particular bringing in an ever-expanding mail from writers and artists, from young people in the Forces who had been fired by it to enthusiasm for books and paintings and the theatre, or had begun to write and paint themselves. It kept up a circulation — it seemed incredible at the time — of 80,000, and sometimes, when Penguin Books could find the extra paper, of 100,000. The copies were gobbled up the moment they reached the bookshops, and so many addicts began to complain to us that they couldn't get copies, that with No. 21, in the summer of 1944, we introduced a subscription scheme. At the same time, we made a second and this time effective promise to appear quarterly: since our first promise, with No. 13, we had not in fact produced more than three numbers a year, but by the middle of 1944 the labour position in the printing works had begun to improve. Allen Lane's enthusiasm remained keen, and at the end of the war we began to plan a bigger development: enlarging the format, improving the layout, introducing colour plates as well as photogravure reproductions, and a new three-colour pictorial cover design of enchanting beauty by John Minton. The first number (in fact No. 27) in this new series appeared in the spring of 1946. By then we had also, in gradual stages, increased the number of pages again, using the additional space mainly for more critical articles — on all the arts — and more poetry. So many stories had been coming in that were fiction and yet had a background of war experience, that I decided to keep them separate from the first-person reportage: "Report on Today" was therefore abolished and the reportage sketches put at the end under the new name of "The Living Moment." I have always believed that the end of a magazine should be as strong, in a different way, as the beginning, and this change was in no sense intended as a down-grading of the reportage, or as a turning of the section into a nursery for unknown first-triers. The newly designed *Penguin New Writing* cost one shilling, but I doubt if such value for a bob had ever been offered before in a serious magazine of all the arts.

New Writing and Daylight also had its enthusiastic following, and sold out very quickly, sometimes going into a second impression: but of course on a much smaller scale. I certainly did not want to give my editorial work up when it appeared to be beginning to yield so promising a harvest; but the combination of that work and running the Hogarth Press, as all the opportunities of peacetime publishing began to open up again, was, I could see, going to become a rather formidable burden, leaving me very little time indeed for my own writing. If I were to go on as both editor and publisher — two aspects of the same purpose — I realized that it would be essential to run the Hogarth Press in a different way: to expand in order to carry a proper staff, to have the opportunity to train managers who could take as much as possible of the complex and time-wasting detail off my hands. I feared that Leonard Woolf might want to go back to what I considered the bad habits of the old days: that system of running things on a shoestring that had persisted because of the way the Hogarth had grown up from a hobby and a small personal venture. Never again, I vowed to myself, those damp and grimy basements of Bloomsbury houses, the homespun method of accounting and salesmanship, which had (I admit) charmed me so much in my early days when the business of publishing was illumined with almost as sacred a radiance in my eyes as the actual persons of Leonard and Virginia Woolf. The war had turned the Hogarth Press into a moderately valuable property, and it would, I thought, certainly be possible to find the capital for expansion. Before the war I had wanted to use it to complete the work of presenting the most interesting of the authors who came to *New Writing*, and to some extent I had succeeded. Quite obviously, with the large body of young authors *New Writing* had accumulated round it during the war years, the opportunities now were very much greater. In my more confident and energetic moments, it seemed to me not only folly from my own point of view to neglect these opportunities, but also a failure in responsibility towards the poets, story-writers and critics I had brought forward. And I was already catching glimpses of new European and American authors who could be added to a list that aimed at discovering and gathering together the most significant talents, the most vigorous creative impulses of the time.

I was not absolutely certain I would decide to have a shot at expansion, still seeing the advantages of quietly exploiting what we already had, still hearing the plaintive call of all the poems and books I wanted to write; but turning more and more towards it. There was, however, another element in the problem. In the first year or two after Virginia's death, as I have already related, Leonard was content to leave most of the running of the Hogarth to me, and a greater harmony had been established between us than ever before. This halcyon period did not, unfortunately, last. I do not know why, but by 1944 our disagreements were beginning to grow more frequent and more difficult to resolve. In particular, Leonard appeared to me to be setting his face against allowing me to publish the new authors in whom I had invested so much capital of encouragement, appreciation and faith; and Virginia was no longer there to moderate between us. I had to remind myself all the time that I might have felt just the same suspicion and anxiety if I had been in Leonard's shoes; but it was frustrating at that particular moment when I felt convinced the tide was running so strongly with me.

Meanwhile I took one decisive step. I was tired of flat life, and rents were already beginning to shoot up. I remembered what Leonard had always said: to live in a house is really no more expensive than to live in a flat, and infinitely preferable. . . . I had accumulated an enormous mass of books and papers during the war, and had laid the foundation of an interesting collection of modern pictures. Most of my prewar library was still down at Fieldhead. I wanted to have a place where all these possessions could be housed; and I wanted it to be large enough for me to entertain there on a fairly generous scale. I had grown more and more to believe that bringing authors together in social contact was an essential part of a good literary impresario's job; besides, it was fun. Vienna had grown too far away, under the long separation and the emotional pressures of the war, for me ever to make my home there again. In spite of the intimate nostalgic colouring my memories had acquired, I was quite clear about that; and equally clear that in London, not in Paris, Rome or New York, I had the best chance of combining, as I had always hoped I could, my spiritual and physical homes. I therefore discussed my plan of looking for a house with Ernst Freud, son of the great doctor and father of Lucian. He was not only an extremely able architect, but a man full of ideas and enterprise. We were still in the early months of 1945, and I hesitated a little to commit myself while the chance of bombardment by various forms of V-weapons still existed. He brushed my doubts aside, with eager and persuasive arguments: the war was as good as over, the risks were negligible, I must grab one of the many excellent properties still going cheap before everyone else joined the hunt. So off we went, whenever we could find an hour or two, exploring as many of the likely houses as possible;

Ernst Freud sniffing for dry rot, pulling at peeling wall-paper, shifting piles of rubble-litter with his foot, calculating with lightning speed the cost of mending a roof damaged by incendiaries or a stairway shaken by explosions next door, remodelling interiors to my liking with a conjuror's dazzling patter — and dismissing the whole vision at once with a slightly diabolical laugh, when he saw me reluctant.

Eventually we decided on a house at the western end of Egerton Crescent, which was in a comparatively undamaged state, and with its fine interior proportions promised both room for all I wanted to bring there, and a welcoming, dignified setting for hospitality, in parties large and small. Besides, it had trees on all sides — an advantage that counted for much with me — including a tree of heaven, an acacia, and a pretty little laburnum leaning over the front door-steps. I was doubtful whether we could get a generous enough building licence to make it habitable in the way I wanted, but Ernst produced at once the most ingenious plans for making do with what was already there. The result was that the estimate was low, and was passed fairly soon; and work had already begun before I left for France. "Where are the builders?" was the despairing cry often raised in the Press at the time; but Osbert Sitwell, passing by one Sunday morning at the end of August, announced that he knew the answer: "at work on John's new house."

In the late summer, I finally decided that Leonard and I had reached a point of no return: if our partnership remained the same, with each of us able to veto any project the other proposed, not only would the Hogarth Press come to a standstill, but my own career would finally be frustrated. As I saw Leonard only at intervals, and communication even then was rather restricted, it was difficult for me to know what was in his mind: it was possible, I thought, that he might be glad to be relieved altogether of publishing preoccupations; was, in fact, inviting me to buy him out. I realized, however, that even if this was so, he might hesitate at the last moment, baulking at the thought that the handling of Virginia's books would be removed from his control. So I took the only course that was open to me. Our partnership agreement had a blindfold hazard in it: if either of us announced to the other that he wanted to terminate it in its present form, the other could within three weeks buy him out; if within those three weeks he made no move, the original challenger could make the same offer. I therefore tried to find some way of exploring Leonard's mind before taking the final step. I suggested a modification of our partnership agreement, allowing me to be associated with some other small publishing venture through which I could present my new authors, thus leaving our exiguous paper ration entirely for the reprinting of Virginia's works and other important Hogarth books. Perhaps it would not have worked; in any case it found no favour at all with Leonard.

I did not actually write my letter telling Leonard that I was now convinced to my sorrow that our partnership would never work, and formally giving notice to terminate, until the end of January. I hoped that he would agree to a quiet tête-à-tête discussion, because I wanted to propose a scheme I had at the back of my mind, by which, if he allowed me to buy him out, I would arrange for him to keep absolute control over Virginia's books, including the posthumous works not yet published. Remembering how often he had spoken to me of literary work he wanted to complete, and political work he wanted to develop, I had some hope this would appeal to him. Leonard, however, immediately wrote a letter telling me he proposed to buy me out; and my subsequent attempt to put forward my scheme in writing was in vain. If this result was a shock to me, if I felt more than a little chagrin when I thought of all the work I had put into the Press, and the authors I had brought to it; if I never ceased to regret not having anything more to do with Virginia's books, I realized that I had known that the course I had taken involved this hazard. I have often, however, wondered since whether the whole crisis may not have been due to a simple misunderstanding; the letter Leonard wrote to me later about the problem that faced him (he had received an offer from Chatto & Windus) gave colour to this idea.

Once more the confusing choice was before me. Temptation? . . . Or opportunity? I could at this moment have decided to say goodbye to publishing, and explore at last what I could make of all the other chances that offered themselves to me. One precious child, however, I was extremely loath to give up: *New Writing and Daylight.* Perhaps I could make an arrangement to keep this going in some way, while I thought over what was best to do in a more general sense. My friends in any case were eager to see me carry on as editor and publisher, pointing out (perfectly accurately) how much was in my grasp and how many young people were looking to me; and my mother, my sister Rosamond and my brother-in-law Mounty, with a loyalty and readiness that moved me, promised support. But in order even to keep *New Writing and Daylight* going, I needed paper. And paper was still very strictly controlled.

One is found out by one's illusions in the end. Because *New Writ-*

ing had had such a success; because all the official and semi-official authorities, the Ministry of Information, the British Council, and the rest had shown such interest in it; because already I had received invitations from liberated France, Greece and Czechoslovakia to go and lecture on the young writers — on literature in wartime England — on my problems as a literary editor; because I had always dealt, on the official level, with people who knew exactly what I was doing, I fondly imagined that I would have little or no difficulty in getting the tiny allocation of paper I needed to keep *New Writing and Daylight* alive. I had failed to realize that the Paper Control, that Olympian body in Reading on whose decisions the fate of publishers, great and ancient, little and striving, rested, was not concerned with literature except in the smallest and most indirect way: cardboard cartons, wrapping paper, lavatory paper, official paperasserie and newspapers were the chief subjects of its weighty deliberations; and long after them the problems of the great publishing houses, the huge lists of technical and educational handbooks; after all those demands had been satisfied there remained a tiny area in which *New Writing and Daylight* was a pinpoint invisible to the naked eye of the Reading bureaucrats, whose previous lives had been spent, not reading books but manufacturing paper from esparto grass, wood pulp, rags and salvage.

Full of optimism, I made an appointment with a Paper Control official for a Monday in February 1946, and went down to stay with Rosamond at Aldworth for the week-end. She drove me into Reading herself, and waited down below while I went upstairs for my interview. It was all over in five minutes. . . . *New Writing?* Never heard of it. Are you still a partner in, er, let me see . . . the Hogarth Press, Mr. Lehmann? No, but. . . . Ah, in that case, I'm afraid we can't do anything for you. . . . Sorry, but we have our regulations, and it would be most irregular to allow any such exception. . . . No, Mr. Lehmann, I can't suggest anything you could do about it. Good day to you, Sir.

It was then that my natural pride and obstinacy came into play. The choice was quickly made. I was not going to knuckle down under this refusal. As we motored back to Aldworth, I told Rosamond, who was full of indignant sympathy, that I was determined to carry on as a publisher. I hadn't the slightest notion how I was going to set about it.

BOOK THREE

The Ample Proposition

New Beginnings, New Journeys

THE time, it seems to me as I look back, was one of hope and confidence. Against all odds, we had, with our allies, destroyed the Nazi and Fascist tyrannies, and a ruined Europe lay at our feet. The cost had been enormous, in lives, wealth, effort, but the full effects of that spending were still to a large extent concealed from us. An atmosphere of triumph as well as of relief reigned, not crude triumph, but a feeling that faith, under inspired and magnanimous leadership, had been fully justified, and that we had taken the key part in freeing the world from the latest monsters the twentieth century had spawned to enslave mankind. The proud bearing, the smiling faces of the soldiers, sailors and airmen one passed in the streets seemed to reflect the mood of the hour. We would rebuild our battered country, remoulding it and our society nearer to the heart's desire, in the image of justice, humanity, and un-self-seeking prosperity. Liberated Europe waited for a lead from us. Wherever I went in my travels, I found, or seemed to find, admiration for, gratitude to, and expectation of the British people. A chance, such as had not been ours for more than a hundred years, lay before us; if only we had the nerve to grasp it and the vision to make the most of it.

In literature and the arts, too, I felt almost convinced that a great epoch lay before us. The enormous increase in interest in literature, drama, painting, sculpture, music, ballet, that had grown up during the war years, the new vigorous talent that had emerged in all these arts, promised surely a magnificent harvest. It seemed to me that as editor and publisher, with the immense goodwill that *New Writing* had attached to itself, I could play a not unimportant part in the new developments I looked forward to so keenly.

I still had control of *New Writing and Daylight* and *Penguin New Writing*. Books and literary magazines were still selling in quantities that would have seemed incredible when the war broke out. The only difficulty was that I had just been deprived of my position as a publisher. I had been paid for my share in the Hogarth Press, and I therefore had a little money to risk on a new venture; I had plenty of authors willing, in fact eager to throw in their lot with me; but I had been refused a paper quota. I was a rider without a horse, a beaver without a single tree that he could get at.

« 2 »

THERE were only two courses open to me in these circumstances. Either I could try to persuade a big publisher with an ample paper quota to take me in; or I could beg, wheedle or cajole a printer to let me have just enough to start off in a small way with the books I thought most urgent.

I must admit that as I went the round of printers' offices, my task seemed to me almost hopeless, and I began to doubt whether I was entirely sane in encouraging the authors who wanted to be published by me to wait just a little longer. If it had not, perhaps, been for the rage into which the refusal of the Paper Control to help my desperate condition had put me, and the sense of injury under which I smarted from Leonard Woolf's decision to drop his wartime pilot, I might have given up. Both, no doubt, had excellent reasons for their actions; but my pride had been wounded, my obstinacy aroused.

Nevertheless, in those first winter months of a peace that was proving austere indeed for Britain, I did manage to extract small quantities of paper (in exchange, of course, for printing orders) out of half a dozen sympathetic firms, and also out of a sympathetic paper supplier. I was thus able to send to press an assortment of books I thought would make a good start, at least in order to show my intentions.

Then the first lucky break came my way. I had heard that there was one west country printer, Purnell, who had an exceptionally large quota, and had ambitions to expand into book-publishing. They already had one firm, Macdonald, under their control, and I was able to arrange an interview with the son of the chairman of Purnell, Eric Harvey, who was at that time managing Macdonald. He received me in very friendly fashion, and startled me at once by warning me that they couldn't arrange for very large editions, a run of 10,000 copies at the most. Surely there was some gap in our discussions? A river — *the* river — seemed to have been crossed before I knew where I was.

I left Eric Harvey's office with a tentative agreement, which he ex-

[410]

plained would have to be confirmed by the chairman and the works at Paulton in Somerset, to help me with a few books. For the first time I felt real hope, and the stirring of excitement. A *few* books! As if I had the money to finance any more than a few at the start.

And that was precisely where the crux lay. After the interview, negotiations were taken over by another of the directors, Clifford Gibbs. He came to see me, he was kind, he was encouraging, he promised me support. He explained to me that Purnell had had a rough time before the war, as many printers had, but by a stroke of genius the chairman, Wilfred Harvey, had in 1939 bought up various concerns, not book-publishers, which were able to claim large paper quotas. This move had set them on the road to prosperity; they planned to expand and instal the latest machinery, especially for colour printing, and they wanted to work with publishers in a way that would make it possible always to keep their staff fully employed. This meant, in fact, that they wanted financial control of *my* business. And they weren't particularly interested in *small* publishing.

The temptation was enormous after my setbacks. The dilemma was almost intolerable. I saw that if I wanted a decent start, I had little choice except to work with Purnell, but I struggled hard to keep as much independence as possible. Discussions went on all through February and March, a large part of them devoted to the name my new publishing venture was to have. Innumerable suggestions were made, and rejected on both sides; the Pericles Press seemed in the last lap to be leading. I finally agreed to giving Purnell 51 per cent control, if full editorial control was left to me, and I was allowed — provided I could find the paper — to go elsewhere for a small number of books.

Then suddenly, perhaps made uneasy by the obstinacy I had displayed, the chairman said they must have 100 per cent control or nothing. Of course I could have all the finance and all the paper I wanted; but I would become a salaried employee.

I decided to gamble. I refused. I knew the risk I was taking, but I had got on sufficiently well with the directors for them to temper the collapse of negotiations with an agreement to print, and produce paper for twelve books in each twelve months. I had represented to them as strongly as I could that they had at least not dissuaded me from committing myself to a number of books that I should now not be able to publish if they cut off all assistance. Purnell were also probably gambling at this point, that I would bite off more than I could chew and have to come back to them. For me, however, the respite was extremely precious, because it gave me the opportunity to establish the character of my firm before any crisis broke.

There was much to be done, and as fast as possible. I decided to throw in the best asset I had in the literary world, my name, and call the firm John Lehmann Limited. Then came the problem of finance. The money due to me from the sale of my partnership in the Hogarth Press seemed to me to be fairly divisible into the original sum advanced by my family trust (of which my mother was life-tenant), and other sums advanced by my mother and my brother-in-law, Mounty Bradish-Ellames, to help with *New Writing* at one time or another. I therefore proposed that they should be made shareholders and directors in the new firm. My sister Rosamond was keenly interested to take part in the venture, provided some more capital, and also became a director, as well, of course, as an important literary adviser. All told, I don't think we had as much as £10,000: an absurdly inadequate sum by present standards, but in 1946 we were still in the middle of the book boom, and my friends, both in the writing and bookselling worlds, were confident that my literary reputation would carry the day. Even so, in spite of my own sanguine hopes and the optimism that surrounded me, I frequently had qualms. I knew I would need a lot of luck.

In the matter of authors, there were three things to be done without delay. First, to pick up those authors from the Hogarth Press who were not tied by long contracts and whose loyalty was rather to me than to the Press. I tried without success to get Henry Green to follow me: I had been responsible for his coming over to the Press, and had nursed him, as publisher-editor, through the swift career that had already proved so dazzling. Rightly, however, though full of sympathy for me, he pointed to ineluctable contracts and the awkwardness of leaving half a dozen of his books behind him when there had been no quarrel. He was indubitably *my* author, but I recognized that the loss of him was one of the sacrifices I had to make. I experienced the same disappointment with William Sansom: the appearance of his first novel, *The Body*, under the Hogarth Press imprint a few years later was a painful pleasure to me, for it confirmed me in my consistent conviction, from the start, of his immense original talent, and at the same time aggravated my sorrow at having lost him. No use to say that as things turned out it was better for them to stay as they were; because if I had had Henry and Bill on my list perhaps the catastrophe of 1952 might never have occurred.

With Roy Fuller and Laurie Lee, I was luckier. When Roy agreed to come over, he produced not another book of poems (which came later, as *Epitaphs and Occasions*), but a brilliant adventure story for boys, *Savage Gold;* a marvellous card in my hand for the poker-game with Purnell. Laurie promised me a new book of poems, which came out as *The Bloom of Candles;* and I talked him into promising an autobiography. This took many years in gestation, and my career as a publisher had long been over when *Cider with Rosie* came out, and was an immediate best-selling success. Laurie inscribed my copy: "This is really your book and you are responsible for it, but I won't blame you." Another painful pleasure.

Quite apart from *New Writing and Daylight*, which remained my own, there were more than these two authors to pack in my bag when I left the firm. During my last few months there, a remarkable first novel came to me from America, by an unknown young author: *Dangling Man* by Saul Bellow. I was immediately struck by its unusual power and promise, but I did not persuade Leonard Woolf to see it as I did. Saul Bellow had, I thought, a beautiful, incisive style, a penetrating wit, and a wonderful understanding of the solitary imaginative life. As soon as the decision to dissolve the partnership had been taken, I raced after it again, and found to my great satisfaction that it had still failed to find a London publisher. I followed this with *The Victim*.

Then again, I had always been deeply impressed by the work of Ivan Bunin, whose *Gentleman from Francisco*, in the translation by D. H. Lawrence, Koteliansky and Leonard Woolf himself, the Hogarth Press had had the distinction of publishing way back in 1922. His autobiographical book, *The Well of Days*, followed in 1933, and had long been out of print. I made up my mind to reissue it, managed to buy the rights from Leonard and got in touch with Bunin himself, an old and almost starving exile in Paris, who though often (I understood) was quietly approached with invitations to return to Russia, continued to treat the Soviet régime with hostility and contempt. This small coup had the fortunate result of bringing into my hands, a few years later, one of the most masterly collections of short stories in modern literature, Bunin's *Dark Avenues*.

The second thing to be done was to tie up one or two of the other authors I had supported in *New Writing*, who had either broken with their former publishers or had not yet got a publisher at all. John Sommerfield's wartime stories of the R.A.F. had made a deep impression when they appeared in the Penguin, and I persuaded him to collect them for me to publish under the title of *The Survivors*. I had made rather a speciality of publishing the younger New Zealand writers in *New Writing*, and I now arranged with the most gifted of the prose-writers, Frank Sargeson, with whom I had carried on a lively correspondence throughout the war, to publish his short novel *That Summer* in one volume with a score of his short stories. In both cases I hoped, as all publishers do when they publish short stories (at least in the Anglo-Saxon countries), for further progeny from the marriage in the more profitable form of novels.

In poetry, Hamish Henderson's *Elegies for the Dead in Cyrenaica*, some of which I had published in *New Writing*, was one of my first choices: I had long felt they were among the most original and beautiful poems to come out of the actual fighting. I also decided to make a volume of John Heath-Stubbs's translations from Leopardi, many of which had also appeared in *New Writing*.

Fulfilling a deep personal debt and an obligation as literary executor at the same time, I set about producing a volume of the poems and essays written in English by Demetrios Capetanakis before his death in 1944, together with appreciations of him by a number of writers he had known. It appeared as *A Greek Poet in England*, and is now completely out of print. Another part of that debt was to continue the translations of the Greek poet to whom Demetrios had introduced me, George Seferis. The team of translators, consisting of Bernard Spencer, Lawrence Durrell and Nanos Valaoritis, went ahead, and when *The King of Asine* was ready Rex Warner wrote a brilliant introduction.

Third, I felt it extremely important to emphasize the European and international line of the new publishing house, in fiction as well as in poetry, by having at least two or three books of living continental novelists, apart from Ivan Bunin. I remembered the success I had had with André Chamson's stories from *Les Quatres Elements* in the earliest volumes of *New Writing*, before the war, and I therefore decided to publish the book as a whole (only four of the five sections had so far been translated). This was to be called *A Mountain Boyhood*.

I have described the excitement which the arrival in England of a copy of Ernst Jünger's *Auf den Marmorklippen* caused during the war. One of the first things I did was to go after the translation rights in this book. Negotiations were slow, as they had to be conducted through the British Control Commission in Germany, but I found an ally in Gerard Hopkins, who was working for them at the time, and eventually landed the fish.

I had long wanted to publish a translation of Jean-Paul Sartre's *La*

Nausée, a key book for the understanding of his philosophical inspiration — and perhaps the best book he ever wrote, except for the short
stories in *Le Mur*. When I found to my delight that Jamie Hamilton,
who had bought the English rights in his new trilogy, *Les Chemins de
la Liberté*, was not interested in *La Nausée*, I wrote off to Gallimard,
obtained the rights, and published it a year or two later as *The Diary
of Antoine Roquentin*.

All these translations of novels and short stories went into what I
decided to call my Modern European Library. But I had an idea for
another "library," a series of reprints of books which, either because
old slow-selling editions had been exhausted during the war or for some
other reason, were unobtainable. In the book-hunger of the time, I
thought that well-printed and reasonably priced editions of such books,
many of which commanded high prices in the second-hand shops,
should go well and at the same time cater for an important cultural
need. I planned to include not only famous novels, biographies and
even long poems (such as Byron's *Don Juan*), but also specially prepared selections and anthologies. Henry James was riding high. His
early and middle period works had for long been special favourites of
my own, and I immediately set about negotiating the permissions
(they had just come out of full copyright) with Innes Rose, the English agent for the Henry James estate. I called the series the Chiltern
Library, and, perhaps rather perversely, started off with William Adlington's famous translation of *The Golden Ass* of Apuleius, for which
I persuaded Louis MacNeice to write an introduction. In the distance,
I envisaged reprints of Mrs. Gaskell and Herman Melville.

I was lucky in being able to exploit the good relations I had established with contemporary English artists through *Penguin New Writing*, to persuade them to collaborate with me in illustrating and designing book-jackets for my first batch of publications, which came
out in the autumn of 1946. At the time, very few original artists
were employed for book-jackets, most of which were carried out by
designers in commercial studios. Remembering the success I had had
with John Banting's designs in the Hogarth Press before the war, I
made up my mind that the work of the younger English artists of the
day was to be one of the characteristics of my publishing house. Some
of the booksellers objected, as they always appeared to object to anything novel; but I think I set a style.

My first book of all, an anthology from the poems which had appeared in *New Writing* during the ten years since it had been
founded, had a jacket designed by John Minton, who was also respon-

sible for the jacket of *That Summer*. The seventh (and in fact the final) volume of *New Writing and Daylight* had Keith Vaughan as its jacket designer, as did also *Poems from Leopardi* and the miniature edition of Melville's *Billy Budd*. Robert Medley illustrated with line-drawings and designed the jackets for *Savage Gold*, *Dangling Man* and *The Golden Ass*. Stephen Spender's brother, Humphrey, tackled the jacket for *The Well of Days*.

With these nine books, John Lehmann Limited opened its campaign in the autumn of 1946. A recklessly audacious offensive it seems to me now, as all the books were literary, most of them highbrow or near-highbrow. And yet the circumstances of the time, the success of the literary standards set in *Penguin New Writing*, lured forward with promise that would be ludicrous today. My difficulty had not been to find authors or books to suit my ideals, but to get the venture going at all in the face of the bar by the Paper Control, the unlikelihood of the control being relaxed for some time, and the enormous difficulties of staff and materials in which all printers found themselves as accumulating war-born obstacles piled up on one another in the first years of peace. I even sent two small but important books of poetry to New Zealand to be printed by my old friend Denis Glover at his Caxton Press: Laurie Lee's *The Bloom of Candles* and Edith Sitwell's *The Shadow of Cain*.

« 3 »

MY life in London now became fuller than ever, but I made a point of getting down to Fieldhead for as many week-ends as possible, to talk things over with my mother, and to do some quiet thinking and planning during walks by the river with my mother's large white poodle, Chico, and a new addition to the household in London, an enchanting golden spaniel with a white muzzle and a white flash on her forehead, who was given the name of Carlotta (and called Lottie for short). She was, I think, the sweetest-natured dog I have ever known, and captured all hearts. There was, I fear, a bar sinister somewhere in her ancestry, for she had rather shorter legs than a lady of her breed should have developed, but her ears were exceptionally silky and her coat was exceptionally lustrous, points of beauty which made what she lacked in height off the ground, of trifling significance. She was, so to speak, the toast of the dogs of SW 3. When, twice a year, she became "strangely beautiful," her suitors, of all shapes and sizes, assembled from far and wide on the pavement outside the house: Carlotta would appear to them on the first-floor balcony, a Juliet fluttering her eyelids at a dozen or so impatiently whining canine Romeos.

My friend Alexis Rassine, the dancer, discovered one day by chance that she was a singer. A Sadler's Wells colleague of his was imitating a prima donna, when suddenly to their astonishment Carlotta cocked her head, then lifted it and produced a remarkable accompaniment to their imitation, emitting a note of the utmost purity, long sustained and without a quaver. From that moment, one had only to act as her tenor for her to join in the duet after a few seconds' rather coy hesitation. Her performances became famous, and she was much in demand at parties. In particular, Osbert and Edith Sitwell were fascinated by this gift of hers, and she was frequently invited with me to dinner at 2 Carlyle Square, in order that she should sing to the guests over coffee and brandy. In almost every letter she wrote to me, Edith sent messages. "Please stroke Carlotta's head from me. What a fancy I have taken to that most sweet dog." "I hadn't realized that Carlotta *sang*. But I heard about it from Osbert and David. It is very 1890 of her — I don't think girls do sing much nowadays, do they — I mean as amateurs." "Please stroke Carlotta from me, wish her a happy Christmas, with plenty of hunting, and thank her for singing so beautifully at my ghastly supper party." "Tell that beautiful (if now somewhat full-figured) young matron who inhabits your house, charming you with the songs the Sirens sang, that I am sorry I hit her, inadvertently, with my bracelet and I hope it won't cause a breach in our friendship." "Tell Carlotta I think some of the solos — the arias — from *Wozzeck* would suit her. The girl is a tragedian, in the Grand Operatic manner." Soon after, however: "Osbert thinks I am wrong to have recommended *Wozzeck* for Carlotta. He says the girl has a pure melodic line, and ought to keep to *The Bride of Lammermoor*, *The Somnambulist*, and so forth." "Tell Carlotta that Tosca is indicated, and should be one of her greatest roles."

Carlotta and Chico galloped through the grounds of Fieldhead, chasing largely imaginary squirrels and rats, while I wandered round with rather melancholy thoughts oppressing me. For the moment had come to say goodbye to this home that had meant so much to us all in our childhood and youth. It was far too large for my mother, with her crippled thigh and reduced means, to cope with alone, and various plans that were mooted for myself and my sisters to divide it up and live, as it were, in flats there came to nothing. The Red Cross hospital would be closing down, but the W.V.S. was interested in carrying on with the place as a home for disabled old folk. One thing, however, my mother was quite certain about: she would not share her home with an organization any longer. It had been all right, an emergency obligation, while the war was on; but she had lived at Fieldhead too long and loved it too much to endure having numbers of strange invalids wandering through the flower gardens, orchards and vegetable beds, sitting out by the Pavilion, or the lily-pool, or down by the river under the wych-elm, indefinitely into the future, in spite of the respect in which she was held and the influence she wielded. She decided to be ruthless, and sell as soon as possible, even though it was the worst time for getting rid of property such as Fieldhead, not really large but large enough to have serious staffing and fuel problems.

So in 1947 we put it into the hands of house agents, and set about looking for a smaller property roughly within a ten-mile radius. Disillusioned though my mother was with the inroads of national political parties into local administration which the 1945 upheaval had brought with it — staunch Liberal though she was, she had always believed in the old tradition of unpolitical, unpaid service by those who could afford the time to devote themselves to these local problems — she wanted to keep her ties with various county council committees and other bodies where her work had for so long been appreciated.

Eventually we found a house on the high ground just outside Beaconsfield to the west, which she could run with the help of her devoted housekeeper, Maud Deeley. The grim business of sorting through cupboards and drawers and chests in a house that had been lived in continuously for fifty years began. What papers to destroy? What furniture, curtains, carpets to take with us, what to sell? My mother faced all these problems with a slow, steady New England patience, sometimes looking desperate and exhausted, but sustained by her sense of humour and the feeling that life would be easier when the task was done. To move house at any time is a burden, but to have to go through the experience in old age — my mother was over seventy — is especially hard. It is as if one is packing up everything for the grave. She had already done a great deal of work on family letters and diaries (from which I was to benefit many years later, when I came to explore the family past for my book *Ancestors and Friends*), but odd and often rather poignant mementoes of my father's athletic, political, and writing life would continually turn up: old rowing photographs, medals, cuttings about famous regattas, drafts for political speeches, illuminated addresses of thanks, menu cards of notable *Punch* dinners, and bundles of clippings of poems and articles. And then there were the memorials of the childhood of my sisters and myself: lockets of

[418]

hair, laboriously written fair copies of compositions produced before we had even reached our teens, the earliest school reports, Girl Guide badges, photographs of amateur theatricals in which we had taken part, and programmes of afternoon entertainments we had put on ourselves; all preserved by our parents with a fond and amused piety. Many went into the wastepaper basket, only those with the rarest flavour were preserved. And then, the forgotten, stuffed-away toys, albums, christening presents going back several generations, dog-collars, treasures of every sort fit only, for the most part, for Autolycus's tray. In dismantling the defences of the wine cellar, which had pretended to be our air-raid shelter during the war, my mother discovered in the remotest recesses an overlooked bottle of Château Margaux 1870. Alas, its contents, unlike its label, did not conjure up the "fine dew, sweet yet tart," that glistened on the boy Rimbaud's brow as he wandered through the war-ravaged French countryside that year; they were pretty well undrinkable.

Curiously enough it was the hidden corners of the garden that moved me with the sadness of parting rather than the formal flower-beds, the ornamental centres of urn, bird-bath and sundial set in their expanse of green cropped lawns and paved rose enclosures, the long vistas of pergola dripping their purple clematis, pink rosebuds and never-ripening vine clusters. I went down and talked to the old head-gardener, Mr. Goodman, in his pungently smelling garden shed that was also an apple store, and encouraged him to tell me of his boyhood days in the valley. I crept up the wrong side of the bank at the end of the garden, planted with poplars, from which I had, with my chums, busily noted the numbers of engines as they thundered across the bridge in my childhood, and tried to recapture a long-lost magic and dreams of being an engine-driver. I sniffed for the last time the peculiar, mixed, musty smell of the long Boat-House, and let my fingers slide over the punts, canoes, skiffs and slim rowing craft I should never see again. I looked up to see the martins speeding out of their nests in the rafters beside the blades of the closely ranked oars, as I remembered them doing for years and years into the past. I opened the kennel gates that had once housed Great Danes, St. Bernards and mastiffs and had then been made into "houses" for my sisters, and tried to find some fragment in the scattered straw and broken boxes that would bring those days back in a vivid flash of memory. I lingered in the now rankly overgrown dogs' cemetery, re-reading the engraved names of animal friends just remembered from earliest childhood, and others buried before I was born and part of my sisters' mythology, and trying to put names to those "sad little hummocks in the ground," which had never received a stone.

The lilac and laburnum came into flower in the shrubberies in front of the house. Gradually the bookshelves in the library were emptied of their gold-lettered sets of famous authors, leaving a dusty, bookless vacancy behind them. The ancient apple-trees were in pink-and-white blossom once more, the walnut-trees putting out their tender leaves, but we should not crop the fruit. My mother dug up a few plants especially precious to her, and put them in boxes, ready for the van. Yes, the time had come and we must be off.

Rosamond wrote: "I went over to Fieldhead last night and looked my last on the garden with feelings indescribable."

The departure from Fieldhead was the cause of almost the only poem I wrote in those years, *The House*, which I described as an "Eclogue for the Air, on themes suggested by living in an age of transition." It was commissioned by Robert Gittings at the B.B.C., as one of a series of long, semi-dramatic poems by living poets. My life was too fully absorbed again in hunting for other authors and looking after their work, as it had been in the early days of the Hogarth Press, for me to be able to listen more than fitfully to the small voice of my own Muse.

« 4 »

ONE event of the winter of 1946–47 brought the contrast between past and present into sharp focus: Christopher Isherwood's first visit to England since he had left with Wystan Auden almost exactly eight years before. It made me, and I think his other friends, suddenly see the distance we had travelled since before the war, in certain experiences that had perhaps matured us and others that had undoubtedly impoverished us.

Christopher wrote from Santa Monica in December, announcing his coming visit towards the end of January, and asking if he could stay with me for a couple of nights before going up to Cheshire to see his mother at their old family home. He added: "I'm a Yank now — but don't be alarmed — you'd never know it." Perhaps he didn't realize that his accent and some of his mannerisms had changed as much as we noticed at once. These changes did not, however, show themselves continuously: I had the impression, talking to him during the three months of his visit, that he was, in spirit, being pulled to and fro across the Atlantic all the time.

In his article in the *Coming to London* series, published in the *London Magazine* some years later, he writes of his arrival at my house the night he landed: "There a welcome awaited me that I shall never forget. Looking around me at the faces of my old friends, I discovered a happy paradox — namely that, while England seemed fascinatingly strange, my friends and our friendship seemed to be essentially what they had always been, despite the long separation. That was what was to make my visit so wonderful and memorable."

Christopher was excited, during those two days, a little confused by the changes he had already noticed, and nervous about the way he would be received. I think we soon put him at his ease: a company consisting of as many of his old friends as could be mustered to meet him in person, and others who were on the telephone almost at once. None of us had joined the scapegoat chase in which politicians and journalists who had never known them had tried to vilify him and Auden as "escapers." We had been sorry not to have him with us during the weird, sometimes apocalyptic and frightening experiences we had been through; we had been a little sceptical, while the bombs fell, of his mystical exercises in Yoga temples; we were immensely glad to have him back, even in this slightly transmogrified form. We noted that the face, tanned by the California sun, was a little more lined; but that the deep-set eyes, though opened wide in respectful amazement or horror at the tales we had to tell, would twinkle with the same old impish appreciation of anything comical or fantastic. We noted that his favourite talk was of Hollywood and movie stars; and we wondered sometimes whether he didn't in fact see us as characters in a film — an American film of little old England heroically carrying on through all trials and tribulations.

Christopher's sharp observation of the altered London he encountered made us see ourselves more objectively. We realized that we had become shabby and rather careless of appearances in our battered surroundings. That we had become crushed as civilians to accept the ordering about of officialdom. That we had become obsessively queue-forming, and were priggishly proud of it.

That winter was in any case worse than anything that had been experienced since the first winters of the war — and it was worse than that. It was also worse because we were no longer sustained by the sense of shared danger in the face of an enemy we were determined to destroy. The adrenalin was no longer being pumped into our veins. We endured with misery and loathing the continual fuel cuts, the rooms private and public in which we shivered in our exhausted overcoats, while the snow blizzards swept through the country again and yet again. Were there to be no fruits of victory? The rationing cards and coupons that still had to be presented for almost everything from eggs to minute pieces of scraggy Argentine meat, from petrol to bed-linen and "economy" suits, seemed far more squalid and unjust than during the war, when we knew at least what they represented in the mortal perils of ships and sailors.

Before Christopher left in mid-April, he came down for a final party at my house, at which I managed to gather many friends with whom he had not yet been re-united, and many others, younger people who were eager to meet the legendary "Herr Issyvoo." I had introduced him in particular to John Minton and Keith Vaughan and their paintings, some of which he had already seen in reproduction in *Penguin New Writing* during the war. He became a keen fan of Keith's, and carried off with him several samples of his work, which he intended to show to everyone in California. And he promised to act as an unofficial talent scout in America for my new publishing firm, a promise he never forgot, as many letters of tip-off advice (and warning) about the younger generation of American writers witness.

On arrival in New York, he wrote: "Just to let you know that I arrived on Friday, after a bugger of a voyage, with strong head-gales. I avoided being sick by doggedly over-eating and dosing myself with whisky. We were all vaccinated, which made me a bit sick after landing but I'm fine now. . . . In a few days I hope to start driving the plough over the terrain for my new novel. I have terrible stage-fright about this, but the only thing is to make a start. At all costs, I'm resolved this time, not to be funny. I don't care how dreary and boring it is, as long as it isn't the kind of book anybody could possibly read for pleasure on a train. People resent being amused more than anything, I've decided."

The World in the Evening was interrupted by his journey to South America and the writing of *The Condor and the Cows*, and seven years passed before it appeared in England.

« 5 »

WITH the nine books I had published in the autumn of 1946, and with the others I had signed up at about the same time, I had at least made a blue-print for the future pattern of my publishing venture. I now had to consider very carefully how to go about laying down more solid foundations. I had gobbled up what had been lying about for my picking in the aftermath of my career with the Hogarth Press. And I had started the Chiltern Library as a medium for the more highbrow reprints which particularly interested me, and which seemed to be in demand.

Now I had to lay my snares beyond what I had already taken on, for (1) the new British writers, (2) the new writers in Europe, and (3) the new American writers. I began to believe that my "nose" would lead me to where they were lurking in the coverts.

It was not only literature in the shape of fiction and poetry I envisaged, but new writers of travel books, autobiographies, biographical criticism, and experts on the theatre, the opera and the ballet. In fact I wanted the list of John Lehmann Limited to look, in some ways, not unlike one of the recent copies of *Penguin New Writing*, with all the arts given their place. Novels cannot be commissioned: you can only encourage the authors to carry on. Commissioning, however, is more or less essential to those other books that need research and illustrations. I therefore urged Norman Marshall to write what turned out to be one of the most successful books we ever published, *The Other Theatre*, an account of the avant-garde theatre movements in England since the end of the First World War.

This was the first of a number of books I published about plays and actors. Meanwhile I encouraged William Chappell who had written so well for *New Writing* while he was in the Army, to write the book about ballet he obviously had in him. *Studies in Ballet*, when it was ready, was less history than what in fact its title indicated, a series of essays on the art of ballet, on the dancer's physique, and on the problems of the association of music, plastic design and choreography; but it was valuable on both counts, was written in an uniquely personal style and had the considerable advantage of being illustrated not only with precious photographs from Billy's archives but also with his own imaginative line-drawings.

My friend Eric Walter White had, in my earliest Hogarth days, written a short but remarkable book called *Stravinsky's Sacrifice to Apollo*. He now undertook to write a much longer critical study of the composer's developments and changes of style, which was published, also by the end of 1947, simply as *Stravinsky*.

Finally, in this department, I suggested to Alan Ross that he and John Minton should go off to Corsica together and write a travel book, illustrated by John. This was in many ways the most ambitious of my early projects for a single book, for it was to be an extremely lavish, anti-austerity production. Without the magnificent facilities put at my disposal by Purnell, I could not, of course, have attempted it. *Time Was Away*, more a poet's note-book on holiday than a conventional travel book, is a very beautiful book, with its lavish black-and-white and four-colour illustrations, an evocatively sultry and arcadian jacket by John, and its elegantly original typography and spine design by Keith Vaughan. It is also now a rare and much sought-after book.

« 6 »

I HAD for some time been feeling that the formula of *New Writing and Daylight* was wearing a little thin, and that something new was needed. I have always been aware of the danger of carrying on with one formula too long, of letting things slip into a rut. In contrast to this, Barbara Cooper, who had come over to work with me in the new venture, hated any kind of change, and I think she was shocked and deeply disappointed when I announced that I was going to kill *N.W.D.* and start a new book-magazine in its place.

If *Time Was Away* had been planned as a book to startle with beautiful design and brilliant colour in the drab hour through which we were passing, *Orpheus* was to be even more an out-and-out anti-austerity production. I handed over the designing in its entirety to Keith Vaughan. He was to be responsible not merely for the three-colour jacket and the decoration of the whole cover, including the spine, but also for the general decoration in the form of black-and-white almost abstract tail-pieces to go wherever there was space at the end of a contribution. The result, I think, was exceptionally beautiful. When I opened the first advance copy to reach me from the works, I experienced a thrill of pleasure; a thrill that is still renewed today, whenever I take the volume out of the shelf. And at this point I must pay tribute to the work Keith did for my publishing house in the early years as a transformer of what can so easily remain the plain informative utility of the spine of a book — that is, what is seen when the jacket is taken off and it is put into the shelf — but in his hands became an enchanting series of imaginative inventions. Set side by side in a long row, they are poems: but when, alas, except in a publisher's library, are they set side by side?

My idea was that *Orpheus*, which I had originally thought of calling *The Nine*, should be a magazine of *all* the arts; an expansion of the idea that had been developed in *Penguin New Writing*, in the later years of the war, beyond the limits that a paperback was held to at that time, and without the element of topical semi-reportage that had been so popular when its readers were scattered over all the continents and all the oceans and were looking for some common denominator of spiritual experience. "There are admirable magazines devoted to literature, or drama, or music separately," I wrote in my Introduction. "There should be more when they can all come together in a *Festspiel* of the printed page, proclaiming their kinship by proof and lighting one another with interlinked fires." Deep down, I think, I still hankered after the equivalent in a magazine of what the ballet had achieved under Diaghileff: the marriage of several arts in one coherent creation — music, dancing, decoration, painting, even spoken poetry. Only of course a magazine could never be as unified as a ballet or theatrical production, and could only *suggest* the coming together of the arts by indirect means. Nevertheless, even this limited ideal, even this Dionysian illusion, seemed to be worth attempting and celebrating, a little defiantly, in the face of the prose of our age. "The deep need today," I wrote in the concluding paragraph of my Introduction, "is to assert the lyrical and imaginative spirit against materialism and the pseudo-sciences. This is not new, for it is what Shelley and the other great creative minds of his time were proclaiming one hundred and fifty years ago, but it is even more urgent in our own lives upon which the same dangers can act so much more frightfully and more swiftly. Nor is it new that it should be equally urgent to assert the rights and dignities of the individual human being against the pretensions of the State. It is one of the oldest of wars, but the enemy has returned to the offensive armed with far greater powers than the spies of the Inquisition ever knew, and the encroaching sahara of his paperasserie is far vaster and more chokingly arid."

Bunin — Seferis — Elytis — Supervielle — Queneau: contributions from these European authors, together with an article by Bernard Denvir on modern French tapestries, another by John Fleming on the Roman artist Renzo Vespignani, and a third by Harold Acton on modern painting in Mexico justified the claims I had made that *Orpheus* would "know no national boundaries, but will everywhere choose what is visionary rather than what is merely realistic, what rejects the dogmas and looks at truth every day with fresh eyes." The programme did not, however, find favour in Moscow, where literature and art were groaning at that moment in the deepest Stalinist darkness. A certain Comrade Zenkevitch, writing in *Soviet Literature*, threw a good bucketful of abusive words at *Orpheus*. He called it artificial, reactionary, useless, epigonic, decadent, stale, stilted, a hopeless void, just a phantom, and a plateful of gilded nuts. It was exhilarating to have hit the target so exactly, particularly as a fellow-crusader against the decaying culture of the West, Comrade Elistratova, was weighing in against *Horizon* in the same number, and unmasking the hideous face of American imperialism behind it.

The gilded nuts did not last beyond a second helping. The press notices of *Orpheus* were good, some very good indeed, and private comment was enthusiastic; but the sales did not seem to me to justify the heavy expense involved. If I had been personally rich, and had had no other irons in the fire, I might well have devoted myself to it; but my decision to abandon it after the second number, albeit with a heavy heart, was also influenced by changes that were taking place in the world of books as a whole and in the fortunes in particular of my own publishing venture.

« 7 »

By the middle of 1947 I became aware that dangers were looming ahead. I had known too well the publishing conditions of the 'thirties not to sense a change of wind early on. The fuel crisis of the long winter, the breakdowns in production at the factories which were still short of labour, meant that one had to space out the publication of books whose profitability had been calculated in a more concentrated form. At the same time the conditions of bookselling, far too good to be true during the war, began to change back to normal. The returning soldiers were putting money aside to buy new homes, new equipment for living, though leisure had not yet been exploited by mass travel and television. No longer was it possible to calculate that an edition of 5,000 to 10,000 of a new book of any merit whatsoever would sell out on publication — or within a few weeks. The empires were breaking up. Hard and harder work in selling lay ahead. And stocks would have to be held longer. That meant money, capital locked up.

I had embarked on an ambitious programme in 1946, partly because I felt the conditions to be favourable, partly because I knew that to take full advantage of my literary position I must move fast. Authors cannot be kept waiting for long, however loyal or grateful they may feel to one personally. To a certain extent my advantage was mean: with no back list to keep in print like the big established publishers, I had been given the chance to exploit a fairly large allowance of paper to bring classics back into circulation. Seeing, however, how the dice were loaded against me in other ways, I did not feel oppressed by guilt about this; particularly as I noticed no striking impatience among the relevant publishers to do anything about the authors I was interested in.

The programme, then, was building up; but my capital, in the changing situation, was running out. Between the wars, an ambitious new publisher had once observed that in order to start a publishing house one needed £100,000 — and that would only serve to establish one's imprint in the first five years. With my Hogarth Press background, I had always considered this a bit of an exaggeration; but I now saw, only too clearly, that even so the £10,000 odd I had mustered was far too little. What was I to do? I considered that I had made all the demands that were fair on family and friends. The problem was urgent: to slow up my plans even more than the fuel crisis had made necessary might risk the whole grand design. I had never dealt with capital finance problems before in so isolated a position, and I passed many anxious hours of reflection, many sleepless dawns in trying to decide on the best course. I realized in the end that I was, in a sense, at the mercy of Purnell, however unwilling they might be to put the screw on: my paper came from there, and I had no quota right to a single ounce of it. If I found new backers from elsewhere, how should I answer their reproaches if Purnell for their own good reasons suddenly cut down on the paper they allowed me? My room to manoeuvre was small, but if I went to the directors now, at least I was in a stronger position than I had been eighteen months before. The publishing house was *there*, it had established its character, it had had its successes and its honours. All these were strong arguments I could use in order to be left in full control of editorial and artistic policy. I decided — I should really write "it was decided for me" — to swallow the bitter pill.

I found that Clifford Gibbs was very willing to reopen negotiations. He acted, during the autumn months of 1947, as liaison between myself and Wilfred Harvey, and very soon brought me the news that Harvey was indeed still interested in backing the firm with the full resources of Purnell, but only on the terms which had caused the collapse of our discussions at the beginning: 100 per cent financial control. This was no surprise to me, and I did not, could not object. The agreement that was finally worked out allowed me to pay my relations, my mother, my sister, my brother-in-law, in full for the money they had so bravely put up. That at least was a tremendous load off my mind. It allowed me to remain as managing director on a fixed salary, and to engage Rosamond as a salaried reader. Two good advan-

[427]

tages. Another advantage was that it allowed me still to have one or two special books produced from time to time outside the Purnell group — books that would only be a nuisance in a factory designed for straightforward, large-scale operations.

I could now go full steam ahead with my plans for extending the Chiltern Library, and for founding two other libraries, or series. The first was to be called the Library of Art and Travel, and was to consist of reprints of notable books, long unobtainable, as elegantly produced as possible. The other, the Holiday Library, was also to consist of reprints, but of between-the-wars fiction and biography in a small-sized format such as had been popular for reprints before the war.

I am inclined to think that the Holiday Library was my great mistake. Purnell were very keen to acquire, through me, as many copyrights as possible, and I let my judgement be swayed too easily by their enthusiasm. The publishers were very much more reluctant to let these titles go, and in many cases I only acquired a licence limited to a short term of years. There was, I believe, nothing much wrong with the choice. Nor was there anything wrong with the look of the books: they were extremely pretty, both inside and outside, and I considered the design one of Keith Vaughan's outstanding successes. Unfortunately, however, there was something wrong with the whole conception — as a money-making proposition. Even three years before, I think, they would have sold out; but as things gradually returned to normal in the publishing world, it became clearer and clearer that the time was over for such reprints. The future was with the paperback revolution. Too much of the capital sunk in the Holiday Library was to remain locked up.

The prospect ahead of me seemed full of exciting possibilities. Perhaps, as the new year of 1948 dawned with its rosy hopes, I was a little too ready to ignore the fact that the powerful tanker which had refuelled me in mid-air had also hooked me. It was the end of the beginning. But a small voice somewhere inside me could sometimes be heard whispering: "Is it also the beginning of the end?"

« 8 »

EVER since the excitement of my first post-war visit to Paris in September 1945, I had dreamed of following this up with visits to the countries beyond the Rhine that I had come to know so well before the war, especially Austria, which had for so long been a second home to me. In immediate post-war conditions, the idea seemed far harder to realize, more exciting but much more alarming also. What would Vienna and Prague look like after the bombardments and the battles? How many of my former friends should I find alive, and what would be their attitude towards me? Would they have become embittered by all the anti-English propaganda they had been forced to swallow by the Nazis, and by the possible sufferings they had endured at our hands? Or would they greet me as a long-lost friend whose return they had steadfastly hoped for through all the silence? I dreaded yet longed to know.

Luck favoured me in a remarkable way. It seemed that *Penguin New Writing* had followed the troops into the occupied countries, and the British Council decided that I was just the chap, especially with my knowledge of Central and South-Eastern Europe, to go and lecture for them in the centres they had already set up in the main cities. As a matter of fact, the first visit, to Czechoslovakia, came as much from the Czechs themselves as from the British Council. It came in the late summer, and I set off in mid-November in an uncomfortable, semi-converted bomber, with a contract from a Czech publisher for an anthology of stories from *New Writing* in my pocket.

My first shock of pleasure was to find that Prague, like Paris, had been practically unharmed by the war. The allied bombers had done some efficiently destructive work in the great industrial centres, Brno, Pilsen and Kolin; but in Prague the main damage seemed to be confined to the gutted town hall where the Germans had put up a desperate last fight, and a tall building in the Wenceslas Place that had been ripped open by a random American bomb. It was more than I had dared to hope. At night the city was illuminated for an international students' congress, and as one rattled down the hill in the tram (with about fifty people standing — and always room for half a dozen more) all the famous domes and towers glowed against the night sky. I thought to myself: the evil dreams and murderers have gone, and the rightful owners are back. This impression of the all-smiles ending to the grim story, of living happily ever after, was increased when I went to a big reception and was able to meet Jan Masaryk again, home at last in the Republic his father had created. He was his characteristic cheerful, joking self, but I thought he looked unusually care-worn.

Then the doubts began. The euphoric mood of my arrival faded, to give place to a more anxious, uncertain assessment. I began to notice that too often there was a green look about people's faces, and their clothes were appallingly threadbare. I learnt that fats, vegetables and many other foodstuffs were terribly scarce, real coffee and tea and chocolate almost unknown. The gas only came on two or three times a day, just strong enough to cook a meal, but not to have a hot bath. Transport had broken down. Not enough lorries, not enough rubber, not enough petrol; rolling stock smashed in the railway sidings, bridges blown up and lying (as I saw with my own eyes) in jagged chunks in the valleys and streams. All this was understandable enough. But there was something worse.

The Red Army was leaving. Or so they said. The joke in Prague was that they left in uniform, with bands playing, at one gate, and came back stealthily, in civvies, at another. One or two people I met muttered despairingly: Why, why did the Allies allow the Russians to occupy Prague? With the Red Army had come the indoctrinated Czech Communists who had spent the years of exile in Moscow. They were powerful, strongly favoured by the Russians, in spite of the coalition National Front Government that seemed so democratic and amicable on the surface. They were deeply suspicious of the *other* Czechs, such as my friend Jiři Mucha, who had spent the war fighting with the Allies in the west. Totalitarianism is a disease that lurks in the bloodstream when the spots have gone. After nearly seven years of subjection to the Nazis, one may find it easier, and even natural, to substitute one kind of police control for another rather than breathe the difficult air of democratic freedom. Gradually, I found that some Czechs, of a fine record untainted by any form of collaboration, still looked over their shoulders to make sure that no one else could hear when expressing criticism of the way things were going. Perhaps it was a hangover from the days of the Gestapo: perhaps *not*.

What left a particularly nasty taste in the mouth was a story I heard in the British Embassy, where my old friend Philip Nichols, brother of the poet, was doing his best to further British interests in a situation which he obviously considered extremely tricky. A guest at luncheon talked of the case of a certain count, a young man belonging to the old aristocracy, of partly German origin, who had been flung into prison on charges of collaboration. I was assured that these charges were entirely trumped up, and he had never been brought to trial. The real reason, my informant asserted, was that the Communists wanted to confiscate his estate, which they thought would make an ideal rest-home for writers. I discussed this story with several non-Communist writers, and found that they knew it and were deeply shocked. It is important to remember that this was before the Communists actually took over the Republic lock, stock and barrel, and before Masaryk's tragic suicide when he saw that he had been cheated of all that he had worked for.

The story had a disagreeable if slightly ludicrous sequel. I was asked if I would like to be taken to the castle, and refused. A couple of mornings later I was visited in my hotel by a woman of cold and sneering aspect. After a certain amount of beating about the bush, she revealed that her mission was to persuade me to visit the castle after all. My refusal, she explained unsmilingly, might be misinterpreted. If I didn't . . . She astonished me so much that I was at first tongue-tied. I could not imagine what she, or those who sent her, thought they could do to an Englishman and an officially invited guest. Then I pulled myself together and told her to go away. I thought a great deal about the incident. It seemed to me a very bad omen.

I flew to Bratislava very soon after reaching Prague. There, even more than in the west of the Republic, my first impression was that Russian influence was far stronger than British or American. I had been warned by Jiři that the trauma of Munich had not yet been overcome; and I remembered Beneš's words during the war about the great Russian brothers, friends to all the Slavs in their tribulations. When flags were out in Slovakia, in nine cases out of ten they were the Russian and Czechoslovak flags alone. From shop-windows still decorated for the Liberation (and for want of goods to put in them) huge portraits of Beneš and Stalin stared out at me — not of Churchill or Attlee, not of Roosevelt or Truman. But the further I scratched below the surface, the more evidence I came on that, so far from having rejected us, these people were keener than ever to be our friends.

In Brno and Bratislava I was lecturing on the European idea in English literature during the previous ten years. Not a subject, I realized, for everyone; and I spoke in English. The arrangements had been hurried, owing to a change of date. We expected quite small audiences, but in fact the halls were filled to overflowing. I did not flatter myself that more than a few people in my audiences followed what I said at all closely. I soon understood that the applause that greeted the lectures simply came from their happiness at hearing an Englishman speak to them at last, in the flesh, after the long separation. And I was moved to discover that everywhere there was an enormous interest in everything Anglo-Saxon, and a great keenness to learn English. If I were asked to name the major responsibility for this state of affairs, I would say unhesitatingly: the B.B.C. European Service.

I had often spent week-ends in Bratislava when I was living in Vienna, and knew it well. I went up to where I could look along the Danube into Austria. There, in the haze, was the city I longed most to visit again. I felt a terrible pang of nostalgia. But directly before my eyes was an astonishing sight that drew me sharply back to the realities of the present. Some rough pontoons had been thrown across the river in place of the shattered bridge, and there, lumbering slowly over, with what seemed an infinite patience, was straggling column after column of Russian troops, fur-capped and dishevelled, with their carts and camp-followers. I might, I suddenly thought, have been watching the hordes of Genghiz Khan or Tamburlaine. Asia had at last broken through, where nearly three hundred years before Prince Eugen had held the Turks at bay and rescued the Western civilization to which Austria and Bohemia truly belonged. Vision and fantasies of a November afternoon in 1945 . . .

Some years later, when the last of the frail bastions of genuine democracy had collapsed in Czechoslovakia, I met one of the innocent people who had suffered, a prince of the old aristocracy, at an international gathering of writers in Venice. He had been flung into prison and vilely treated, merely for the accident of birth, though he lived to tell the tale in freedom. I questioned him about his experiences, and he said: "You may be surprised to hear me say it, but I came out of prison more convinced of the worth of human nature than when I went in. Whatever the cruelties we endured at the hands of our gaolers and on the instructions of their political bosses, the prisoners themselves were wonderful. They were from all walks of life, and it was the poorest and simplest who showed the greatest kindness to one another — and to me."

« 9 »

IT was two years before I was able to visit Vienna again. Meanwhile, as soon as peace in Europe was declared, I had been able to get in touch with my friends who still remained in Austria; above all, with my friend Toni, who had been my secretary and chauffeur in the old days, and his family.

The first letters were full of excitement and relief. He was alive — we were both alive — and he now had a little boy who had been born to him and the art student, Gretl, whom he had married at the beginning of the war. They had lived all the time in my old flat in the Invalidenstrasse, right up to the last moments when Vienna came into the firing line between the Nazis and the Russians. All the family were alive, his mother, his sisters; it seemed almost incredible. But their survival had not been easy.

When I got to Vienna, he was able to tell me the story. I had been fearful, when I left in the summer of 1939, that the Nazis might turn suspicious of his connection with me. If their intelligence was efficient, they would surely know that I had been associated with the international anti-Nazi movement. In my experience, however, the secret police of totalitarian states are, contrary to what is generally believed, remarkably inefficient. Not a rat stirred for a long time. Toni joined the Reichswehr, did his training successfully, and had a good posting. It was months before the blow fell. He was suddenly arrested, and while under guard found it totally impossible to discover what the charges against him were. Finally he was brought before his judges, and accused of having been closely associated with "the notorious British agent John Lehmann."

Luckily, Toni had the Viennese gift of the gab and of bluffing it out developed to a high degree. He was able to persuade the court that the charges were ridiculous, that he had only been my secretary without any knowledge of what I was doing. He was released, marched with the German troops on their entry into Paris, then later with the first wave of troops that invaded Russia. For a long time he was stationed in Minsk. He told me some of the horrible things he had witnessed. He would never forget, he said, seeing Russian partisans bundled into a lorry. Gallows were set up beside the lorry, nooses were fixed to their throats, then the lorry drove off at full speed, and they were left dangling.

Later still, he was invalided home, owing to ill-health. By then the nightmare disaster of Stalingrad had overtaken Nazi arms, and enthusiasm for the war, which had never been remarkable among the Viennese, dropped almost to zero. Eventually I was to learn that two or three of my former friends, including Richard, the art student who had painted my flat, had "never returned from Stalingrad." Toni told me that he discovered a secret organization had been created in the city to cause crippling accidents to soldiers, on ordinary leave or on sick leave, who were about to be sent back to the Russian front. A friend of his, revolted by the senseless slaughter, had got in touch with them. He had been taken to a room where he was laid out on a table, and his leg smashed. He was then bundled into a taxi, with a helper on either side, and driven to one of the bathing-places on the old Danube. There he was told to walk as normally as was possible for him in his acute pain, jump into the water and then call for help. To all appearances he had broken his leg by stupidly jumping in at the shallow end. He got away with it.

When the Russian armies were approaching Vienna, Toni was still in my flat with his wife and little boy, Peter. As the fighting raged over the Danube bridges and in the Prater, once the scene of carefree summer amusement and amorous encounters among the twilit bushes, he decided to evacuate his family to his father's home on the other side of the city. Gradually the gunfire died down; and one day he felt it was safe enough to return to the city and attempt to get back into the flat, in order to collect various belongings he had left behind. Scarcely had he reached the city boundary when the fighting flared up again, now in the more central districts. With infinite difficulty, dash by sudden dash, and using the knowledge of Russian he had acquired in Minsk in order to get past the Soviet posts, he made his hazardous way to the Invalidenstrasse. To that day, he told me, he didn't know how he had managed it.

Dusk was falling when he reached the flat. He found that in their flight they had left a basket of eggs in the kitchen, and he cooked himself what he described as "the biggest omelette I have ever eaten or am ever likely to eat in my life." He sat in front of the great circle of windows looking out over Vienna north and north-westwards, the same windows from which I had watched the torchlight procession of the jubilant Nazi youth in March 1938, and later, in the summer of 1939, the trains rolling through the Hauptzollamt Station just below, crammed with troops for the Polish front. Bombs and shells were falling. Fires were blazing everywhere, and he saw the Stefansdom suddenly ignited like a giant torch. "I couldn't bring myself to go away," he told me. "The whole war, all we had experienced seemed to be summed up in what I saw before me. What an end that fiery panorama was to the mad, stupid adventure that had started when the Nazis took over, how ghastly a tragedy it had been for our beloved Vienna."

Finally, he decided that he must make an attempt to get back to his father's home. As he opened the front door of the house, a bomb whistled down nearby, and blew open the iron shutters of a bicycle shop, revealing several glittering new machines. The temptation was irresistible: he seized one of them, swung himself on, and made off. He had hardly gone a few hundred yards when he heard a Russian voice challenging him. He looked round, and could just see a Soviet sentry with a raised rifle. "That's a nice machine, just give it here." He had no option, and proceeded gloomily on foot. At a big cross-roads a few minutes later, he saw coming down towards him two Soviet soldiers on horseback, very drunk and singing noisily. He took a chance, shouted to them in Russian, and was told to jump on behind. So, swaying through burning Vienna, he eventually found himself on the western outskirts, jumped off, waved the drunken soldiers goodbye, and made the rest of his way on foot.

When the fighting was at last well and truly over, he went back again, his wife Gretl pushing a cart made out of a wooden crate in which their little boy Peter was installed, and found that the flat had been commandeered by an officer of the Russian Danube Fleet. He never got it back. One day the Russian officers left, as the Invaliden-strasse was declared part of the British zone. Immediately, however, his neighbours on the same floor, whose flat had been damaged by shrapnel, broke through the wall and occupied it. If I had arrived in uniform in some capacity attached to our occupying forces — and almost everyone seemed able to do this at that time — I could no doubt have bundled the man out and reinstated Toni and his family. As it was, I had no time, and could only find Toni a good lawyer to help him through the labyrinthine complications of the laws about living space at that time. The case went on for years, and Toni eventually won it, only to be deprived of the fruits of victory by the Wohnungsamt, where the bureaucrats decided that as he already had a flat he couldn't have his old one back. How they imagined he could have lived in the interval without a flat, they didn't explain.

So I never saw my Viennese pied-à-terre again. Toni had, however, taken the books I had left and one or two pieces of furniture with him. It was curious to look through those English books, and to think they had been waiting for me behind the enemy lines all through the war.

Apart from the wrecked Prater, the damage in central Vienna was confined mainly to a few outstanding buildings, which had suffered in the very last stages of the war: the charred and collapsed roof of the Stefansdom, the Opera House and the beautiful baroque elegance of the Albertina Museum behind it, and the Burg Theatre. It was strange that these dominant symbols of Austria's civilized past should have been hit in the orgy of destruction that Hitler had willed, thus completing — so it seemed then — the ruin of a once great country. I had been given a room in the British-occupied Sacher Hotel, through whose corridors mad Nijinski had wandered after his rescue from Hungary two years before. Even under military occupation it had not completely lost its atmosphere of a vanished aristocratic world. What had happened to that world? Who had survived the war that destroyed the Habsburg Empire, the inflation that followed it, the economic misery in which the grim and pointless struggle between Dollfuss and the Social-Democrats took place, the Nazi terror against Jews, Socialists, Roman Catholics and humanists, the new war and the bombardment and the street fighting, the Russian invaders and the terrible new inflation? One step after the other in the descent to the hell of the present. It seemed impossible that Central Europe would ever recover. Those Viennese who still held on to any decent life were selling their last possessions to buy food on the black market. They seemed dazed and adrift. They hadn't much time to think of rebuilding the shattered world of the mind and the spirit.

One day I went exploring through the Third District, where I had lived and which I knew so well. I walked through a square in which I had once had my earliest flat. It had been a charming square in those days, inhabited by middle- and upper-class families, many of whom had come down in the world from grander abodes after the inflation of the 'twenties. In the middle of the square, among the trees, had been a *Kinderfreibad*, one of the attractive open-air bathing-places for children that the enlightened Social-Democrat Municipal Government had built all over the city. I was looking forward to seeing it again; but when I came into the square I saw nothing but ruin. There was no bathing-place, there were no trees, and the houses had been half-destroyed by bombs or shells. What sent a shudder of horror through me, however, was an anti-aircraft tower that rose, a monstrous growth of green concrete, where the bathing-place had been. With its smashed searchlights on top and the battered, deserted shelters at its base, it was a vision of pure nightmare.

Just before the war, the Swiss philosopher Jung had written a remarkable essay which he called *Wotan*. One of the most striking passages came back to me: "Germany is a land of spiritual catastrophes where certain facts of nature never make more than a pretence of peace with the world-ruler reason. The disturber is a wind that blows into Europe from limitless and primeval Asia, sweeping in on a wide front, from Thrace to the Baltic. . . . It is an elemental Dionysus that breaks into the Apollonian order. We call the creator of this storm Wotan." Jung saw the Nazi movement as the latest and most destructive storm created by Wotan. The Austrians had been caught up in this tremendous primitive storm and tidal wave; and then the counter-wave that it provoked in Asia had come crashing down on them. It was Wotan's own tower, I suddenly thought, that stood before me.

After I had given my two lectures in Vienna, to the English Seminar of the University and to the Austro-British Society, I took the British military train down to Graz and Klagenfurt, passing out of the Russian zone and into the British zone at the Semmering. This was a comparatively simple operation compared with my final journey, from Vienna to Innsbruck by the ordinary international express. Nothing could have illustrated more vividly the ordered chaos of the aftermath of war and the jealous way the four powers stood on their rights. I had to show my *laissez-passer*, the well-known "grey card" issued to visiting foreigners and stamped by the four separate authorities, three times during the night, once at the Russian demarcation line, then at the American line, and again at the French line before we reached Innsbruck. The longest and most anxious wait was, needless to say, at the Russian line, at the cold and sleepy hour of 3 A.M. The young Russian frontier guard was brusque, suspicious and disagreeable. I do not think he could read, because he appeared to be looking at some of the travel documents upside down, but he spotted something that seemed to him to be wrong — perhaps the colour — in the permits of an Austrian couple sitting opposite to me, poured out some violent objections in Russian which they did not understand, and then bundled them off the train. I was glad that I was not an "enemy" national.

It was not on this occasion, but on a second visit a few years later, when life, at any rate on the surface, was beginning to return to normal in Vienna, that I had a curious experience, a moment of agonizing vision, complex and yet heart-rending in its meaning. I was strolling through the streets on one of those soft, golden September afternoons that I have always associated with Vienna. On the opposite pavement, coming towards me, were a group of friends, young men in lederhosen (they had not yet discarded them in favour of jeans), with their girl-friends in dirndls, looking exactly as they might have done twenty years before when I first came to know the city. At that moment, bells began to peal from churches nearby, and in the familiar music of the bells I became conscious, almost simultaneously, of two sensations. I imagined, for the flash of a second, that I was my younger self, and that these young men approaching me were the friends I had known two decades ago. In that same instant of transformation, "instant of knowledge and despair," I realized that those friends were lost, had vanished without trace, had "never returned from Stalingrad," were leading crippled lives somewhere, and the young men confronting me on the other side of the pavement, though so bewilderingly like them, were their sons, a new generation that had never known what we, their fathers and myself, had known and been through.

[437]

I walked on, feeling more ghost-like than real, conscious almost unbearably of the wreckage of the age in which I had lived, and of the bitter fruits of allowing one's affections and interests to be divided between two countries. I was also, not altogether happily, conscious of the speed with which the appearances of things are mended. But it was not the appearances that worried me. Had something been fatally changed and ruined deeper down, in the spirit of men?

« 10 »

In between those two excursions into the past, I had visited Greece for the first time. This was certainly a highlight of the post-war years for me. I had always been deeply interested in everything Greece could mean to an imaginative Englishman brought up in the Classics, her art, her civilization, the impression she had made on our great poets of the Romantic period while she was fighting to free herself from the long Turkish domination. My visit to the Naples museum in my last year at Eton had brought this idealization to its highest point of enthusiasm but, unlike so many of my Greek-struck contemporaries, I had never set foot in the country itself. Partly this was due to my obsession with Central Europe and the social scene of the 'thirties, partly to the fascist cloud that hung over political Greece at that time. By 1946, however, I had learnt a great deal about modern Greece. Owing to the chance of meeting Demetrios Capetanakis at Cambridge during the winter of 1940–41, I had discovered not only the heroism of her resistance to the Italian and German invaders, but also her contemporary literature and art. Sikelianos, Seferis, Elytis in poetry, Ghika, Tsarouchi in painting, seemed to me among the most important and exciting names in the creative arts of the time — not to mention Demetrios's own writings. I had had the opportunity during the war of publishing translations of their poems, illustrations of their paintings and studies of their work. Now I was keyed up to meet them in their own country, to experience the effect of Greek light and air on my own senses. Demetrios had taught me to keep my mind and imagination open to Greece, not as an isolated far-away phenomenon of the sixth century B.C., but as a constant, ever-changing but fundamentally unvarying presence throughout history, right down to our own day, in which the battle with the fascists, the occupation and the famine, the Liberation and the civil war that had accompanied it, were merely new manifestations of the eternal Greek struggle for identity. "What matters," he had written in 1941, "is not history as history, but

[438]

human beings. What matters is the Greeks of today and what will become of them. . . ."

The opportunity came when, during the summer of 1946, the British Council, at the suggestion of Steven Runciman, who was their Representative in Athens at that time, invited me to travel out to give some lectures. Some tentative suggestions had been made by the Greeks themselves at about the same time. So I knew that I would be welcome. In addition my friend Rex Warner had been appointed Director of the British Institute in Athens the year before, and I knew that he would see that I had at least a good and probably a thoroughly uproarious time, as far as local conditions permitted.

My plans and papers were finally in order by the end of October, and I arrived in Athens on November 1. I have always regretted that I did not keep a diary of this visit, because it was one of the most passionately interesting episodes in my whole life, so crowded with incident that only a day-to-day journal would bring everything back to mind. Though I left in a state of total exhaustion, which was, alas, not entirely sober, it acted as a terrific tonic on a war-wearied citizen of London, thirsting for renewed contact with the vibrant, life-enhancing sources of the Mediterranean world. In my mind, as a keynote of my expectation, ran the opening lines of Odysseus Elytis's *Age of Blue Memory:*

> Olive trees and vines spreading to the sea,
> And, beyond, red fishing-boats as far as memory,
> The golden sheaths of August over our midday sleep
> Full of sea-weed and shells. . . .

Undoubtedly my visit was made by Rex, and the band of young ex-soldiers, lecturers and enthusiasts all for Greece, who were working with him or in one of the offices of the British forces still encamped on Greek soil to help the Greeks put their country into order after the ravages of the German occupation and the murderous civil war that followed it. They were supported, on a higher level, not only by the worldly-wise, amusing, scholarly personality of Steven Runciman, who was *persona grata* with the Greek Royal Family, but also by the Ambassador, Sir Clifford Norton, and his wife "Peter," who had a passionate interest in modern Greek art and also in the art of young Englishmen, in particular John Craxton, who were in love with the Greek scene. Gigantic, brilliantly coloured pictures of young Greek shepherds, in curious perspective with their sheep and the Greek landscape, decorated the august walls of the reception rooms in the British Embassy, where elegant eighteenth-century portraits had hung before. Britain was fortunate in having these men and women to represent her at that particular time: if their appointment was not the result of extremely skilful choice by some anonymous genius in the Foreign Office, it was certainly an exceedingly lucky chance. They had managed to make themselves intimately popular with the Greeks, and indeed gave the impression of being on holiday with them rather than working in their midst as members of a foreign mission. Those were the halcyon days of the Anglo-Greek honeymoon, darkened before a decade had passed by the bitter Cyprus dispute.

Rex took charge of me at once, introduced me to all his Greek friends, who always seemed in the highest spirits when in his company, arranged my expeditions and lectures, frightened me by the glowing terms in which he described me as I sat cowering beside him on the platform with a sea of unknown Greek faces before me, and took me off to carouse in tavernas when official duties and ordeals were over. His good humour never failed. The atmosphere in his office when visitors called — and they called very often — was indeed more like that of a taverna than a centre of administrative organization. This the Greeks immensely appreciated, knowing that they could argue exactly as they pleased in his presence, on politics, literature, history and sex, while Rex chuckled continuously at the quips that flew around and made genial but shrewd ripostes whenever necessary. He imposed authority as much by his sturdy physical build as by his obviously deep classical learning, his devotion to Greek civilization, and his reputation as an outstanding imaginative author. In his *Views of Attica* Rex observes that when offered the job originally, he felt neither particularly interested nor particularly well equipped for it. Perhaps that is the way to start on an exceptionally successful mission.

I have been to Greece several times since 1946, as a simple visitor and as a member of the British team at the meetings of the Anglo-Greek Mixed Commission, and on each occasion I have seen more and learnt more about that wonderful country. But on each occasion I have found tourists in even greater swarms, and the countryside, especially in Attica, a little more spoilt by frenzied and graceless building, of hotels, residential suburbs, factories, bathing establishments and petrol stations. And on each occasion, therefore, I am even more grateful for the invitation that allowed my first impression to be so unencumbered, at the time when, for instance, the coast-line between Piraeus and Sunium and the scenery along the road to Eleusis and

Daphni could be appreciated in all their natural and awe-inspiring beauty, and fragments of prehistoric pottery could still be picked up from the tangled flowers and weeds in the excavations of Mycenae's citadel. In fact it seems to me now extraordinary that I was able to visit some of the most beautiful sites with no one about at all, except for our own small party and perhaps a shepherd piping in the heather of a nearby mountain slope. The roads were often atrocious, and the accommodation simple in the extreme: but the gods were at home.

This numinous quality, which is now so rapidly vanishing as the eager young students clamber in their hundreds every week over the ruined columns of the temples, and the Ministry officials in Athens seriously discuss the possibility of removing them altogether and substituting concrete replicas, affected me very deeply. I had a dream the night before visiting Sunium that a strange creature, like a winged insect and yet indefinably resembling a human being at the same time, appeared to me. Inexplicably, in my dream I knew it was the goddess Demeter. The next day, while strolling through the grass that surrounds the floor of Poseidon's temple, I suddenly observed a creature at my feet that recalled the dream with a shock: I had never seen a praying mantis before. Again, after visiting Eleusis, I dreamed that I was present, as a ghost or in some former incarnation, at a ceremony of initiation in a huge theatre-like cavern below the rocks. Music, with an insistent hypnotic beat, was rising to a climax, while on a stage lit by streaming torches and in front of awed, upturned faces crowded row after row into the darkness at the back of the hall, actors in gigantic effigies as gods were performing a mysterious dance.

I was even more deeply affected by my visit to Delphi. At the best, even today, the journey from Athens is long and tiring. Then, in 1946, the roads were full of pot-holes and shell craters, some of the bridges were in an extremely precarious state, and for long periods a car was only able to crawl, throwing its passengers violently up and down as they attempted to fix their thoughts on timeless art and myth. At first the authorities were unwilling to let me go, muttering about the dangers of bandits on Parnassus. I replied that I had long been familiar with this situation and did not care. Eventually we set out one morning early, lunching in Thebes (which seemed to me then, my head full of Oedipus and Aeschylus, a totally absurd thing to do), and gradually penetrating deeper into the wild and lonely country beyond. My head swam, my pelvis ached, my conversation became more and more monosyllabic and inane, and I wondered on several occasions whether I could restrain myself at the next pot-hole from scrambling out of the car and taking to the maquis. Then, on the last lap, amid the increasing grandeur of the mountain scenery while twilight fell, my spirits began to revive. A thunderstorm was gathering over the peaks, and opaque black clouds seemed to be whirling ahead of the car like manifestations of spirits from Pluto's kingdom. As we came round the bend of the road, that suddenly reveals on one's right the gigantic arena of the mountains which the ancient Greeks looked upon as the navel of the earth and chose as the stage for their most sacred religious ceremonies, the storm broke. Lightning played on the broken columns of the temples in livid searchlight flashes, and thunder-claps reverberated with deafening echoes. For that experience alone the journey, a long operation without anaesthetics, would have been worth-while. It was, I thought, as if Apollo were revealing himself in all his terrifying majesty: I could well imagine the effect the phenomenon would have had on pilgrims in ancient times approaching the famous shrine from distant parts of Greece, to consult the Pythian Oracle.

The next morning, the scene was totally changed. A dazzling November sun of Greece blazed in the cloudless blue of the sky, and below me I discovered one of the most amazing sights of my life. Far, far away, down beyond in the southwest, a tongue of hazy blue sea indicated the edge of the Gulf of Corinth; and I saw descending towards it, in almost unbroken multitudes, forest after forest of olive-trees like a vast silver-green glacier. On the other side, like the back of some great cyclopean theatre, rose the sheer wall of Parnassus, and over it, as it seemed in the remote depths of the sky, eagles were slowly circling and gliding, keeping up their ceaseless search for prey.

We met no bandits on our journey, nor did any partisans descend to encircle and kidnap us. But the warning we had received before we left was a sharp reminder that the unhappy country was still not entirely at peace. In Athens itself it was difficult to believe that the orderly streets one saw had so recently been the scene of a ruthless, brutal civil war. If you swallowed the free fantasy of the Paris left-wing Press — and even some of our own — you pictured restaurants closed, papers outlawed, armed police with British troops beside them patrolling the streets and preparing to fire whenever two or three starving people gathered together for what might be clandestine plotting, lorries mounted with machine-guns racing past under the shadow of the Acropolis, and picking up defenceless, struggling victims for the next fusillade against the barracks wall. What I found in Greece was so different, at the same time far better in some ways and rather worse in others, that I found it difficult at first to adjust myself to the reality.

There was no famine in Athens. The shops were full of goods, many of the kind that had been unobtainable in London. The restaurants, even quite small ones on the outskirts of the city, were capable of producing dishes that devotees of Greek cooking pronounced delicious, washed down with *retsina* (poison to me). You could buy papers of Socialist or even Communist leaning at the kiosk outside your hotel — if you could dodge the attentions of eager small boys with their shoe-shine apparatus — and voice any opinion you liked at your café table. I never saw or heard of a policeman threatening anyone with a revolver while I was there, nor did the British troops cause anything worse than mild traffic jams when changing the guard outside their headquarters. The Athenians in fact seemed thoroughly grateful to the British Police Mission for having taught their own police to handle difficult crowds and demonstrations without firing on them.

This was the first surface impression; but of course one soon saw that there were qualifications underneath. The smell of the police-state *did* sometimes creep under the door, though far less noisomely than my well-trained nostrils had recognized in countries before the war. If the royalists were criticized for harshness, they could with reason point to the massacre of the anti-Communists when ELAS was in control in Athens, to the seizure of hundreds of innocent hostages who had disappeared for ever with the retreating Communists, to the foreign fingers pulling the strings. Greece had simply become one of the chief battlegrounds for the new war that had supplanted the old, the war for world power between the Soviets and the West.

There was, as I have said, no famine in Athens; everyone had enough to eat, but for the majority it was the simplest fare, and if the shops were loaded with luxuries it was because only the rich and those who had profited on the black market could afford them. Against that, one had to make an odd counter-qualification. The rich were not always those you would have expected to be rich. The retired civil servants and widows with pensions were the worst hit, while the dock labourers in Piraeus probably earned more in that topsy-turvy time than most employers who were trying to run their own small businesses.

Nevertheless, the mood in Athens was exuberant enough, at least when Greeks and British met together. If I had known the country before the war, perhaps I would not have been so surprised that social intercourse seemed so animated, so full of enjoyment of life and interest in all things intellectual and artistic. How different, I thought, from the atmosphere in Paris, in Vienna or even in Prague. I fell under the spell.

My friends took me down to the Piraeus to see the sailors dancing in some of the simple tavernas. I had never seen Greek dancing before, and even managed to consume a large quantity of *retsina*, so hypnotized was I by the insistent rhythms of the *bouzouki* music, the clapping of hands and the waving of handkerchiefs, the strange leaping and twisting of the linked performers as if in a trance, now surging in line to and fro like waves on a beach, now a pair caressing one another as if half in an agony of love, half in sensuous hate, now a single sailor breaking away to perform a spontaneous *pas seul* in utter oblivious concentration, as if every step had a symbolic meaning, as if in their sequence they were lines of a poem he was creating from his imagination that had its inspiration far, far back in history. In comparison, all dancing I had ever seen before (apart from pure classical ballet) seemed almost empty of meaning and degenerate.

I was introduced to George Katzimbalis, the liveliest talker and most fantastic raconteur in Greece (and perhaps in the world), stout, balding, formidable yet entirely charming, with a voice that was more like a roar when he reached the climax of one of his incredible stories, and a chuckle that reverberated through any room where he was entertaining his friends. He was at that time editing the *Anglo-Hellenic Review*, under the benevolent eye and with the financial support of the British Council; not a propaganda sheet but a serious cultural review with first-class contributions, and a larger circulation than any other similar paper in the country.

One evening in a taverna I was brought to the great poet Angelos Sikelianos, whose *Death-Feast of the Greeks* I had published in *New Writing*. He was in the company of Rex and Lawrence Durrell, the latter over on a visit from Rhodes, where he was working for the British Mission. Sikelianos's health had been undermined by his privations during the war years, but his talk, of poets and poetry and experiences of his life, was full of fascination and wit, and I was struck by the dignity of his bearing, the sweetness of his expression, and the gentle warmth of his manner. He had been a legendary figure in his generation, organizer of great poetic festivals at Delphi before the war, in 1927 and 1930, and an inspiration to his countrymen during the Italian invasion and the German occupation. The story was often told how, during that grim time, he and George Katsimbalis had led the

singing of the Greek national anthem — then of course forbidden —
as the poet Palamas was carried to his grave.

Larry took a number of photographs of the occasion, and wrote
from Rhodes afterwards: "The meeting with Sikelianos will have
some of that smoky historic poignance that one gets from the Manet
painting showing them all there, Rimbaud, Verlaine, etc. — or do I
mean the Toulouse Lautrec?* I feel the locale was perfect with the
wall of gaudy biscuit tins behind, and the once great Sikelianos — a
sort of phoenix huddled in the ashes of his overcoat."

The poetry of Sikelianos is deeply impregnated with a sense of
Greek history, of Greek religion and myth, as a responsibility and
consciousness that the modern Greek cannot escape; in that resembling, though more mystical (his belief has been called Christian or-
phism), the poetry of the younger George Seferis, who has now received international recognition as recipient of the 1963 Nobel Prize. I
had already published some of the latter's poems, and had in mind the
volume that was eventually to appear as *The King of Asine*. During
that autumn he was resting, in an interval of his diplomatic labours,
on the island of Poros, and the miracle-working Minister of Information, Baltazzi Mavrogordato, managed to get a gun-boat of the Royal
Greek Navy put at our disposal to take us all out there.

On the way, we put in at the island of Hydra, and saw the cliff-built
villa (now alas destroyed by fire) of the painter Nico Ghika, and were
able to observe how lovingly he had used the features of his island
home in his paintings, so that they seemed to combine, in one impression, modern Greek island landscape and classical and Byzantine
idiom. How far away from the work of his elegant contemporary Tsarouchi, with his Matisse-like sailors and bicyclists, their muscles and
masculinity bulging out of the framework of his canvases.

When we reached Poros, we found the poet awaiting us in genial
mood. He discoursed to us learnedly, wittily, endlessly, and showed us
his remarkable collection of walking-sticks, many of them *objets
trouvés* from his walks inland and along the shore. He looked more
relaxed than he had at the time of the Damaskinos episode, and more
relaxed, too, than he was to look during his difficult London mission as
Greek Ambassador at the height of the Cyprus troubles. Then, as before and later, I was struck by the high-domed head and the look in
the brown eyes when at rest, as if brooding over the destiny of his
country and the ruin of modern Europe — the Europe of his so-
admired T. S. Eliot's *Waste Land* — like the mask of an Ionian mer-

* He meant, in fact, the Fantin-Latour "Le Coin de la Table."

chant captain, one thousand, two thousand, or three thousand years ago, a Tiresias who had seen everything and known too much.

On the way to the islands George Katzimbalis, standing up in the gun-boat like an archaic statue that had been dressed in modern clothes for a lark and was being transported to a museum, made an impassioned oration on the subject of the great past of Greece, claiming that in Alexandrian times 80 million people had spoken Greek — "a nation of 80 millions!" he roared, not entirely consequentially, to the waves and the wind and the uncomprehending, rather scared young sailors. Thinking about this when I woke next morning, I wondered whether we British too would be filled with such intense, proud, almost intoxicated national consciousness if the order of history had been reversed and *we* had fallen from a nation of 50 millions with a glorious past to a small nation of 5 millions, pawn of the intrigues of greater powers, upstarts in the longer historical perspective. Demetrios had said that the Greek had an "unheard-of pride." Was it that pride that made the air of Attica so electric, or something in the climate, or both? Reflecting on the great poets of modern Greece I had met, and on the violence of political life that all my friends had made me aware of since my first contacts during the war, I began to see the Greeks as bearers of a double identity: on the one side the heroically inspired, unforgetting heirs of the great civilization from which our own evolved; on the other, a passionately politically-minded people who were capable of pursuing the power game with a blind Balkan ferocity and disregard of any rules — except winning.

« 11 »

THE success of *Penguin New Writing* crept on in a way that astonished me as much as my publisher, Allen Lane, during the last year of the war. A new series, with more pages, improved lay-out and colour plates as well as photogravure illustrations, was launched in the spring of 1946 with No. 27. By this time the first printing order had been increased to 100,000 copies, which could easily mean a readership of least 250,000, a figure which made me feel rather dizzy. Nothing seemed able to stop it; and yet the tide was already imperceptibly turning here too.

Underneath the surface of mounting success, there were often difficulties, struggles and even heated exchanges between myself and Penguin Books — which were as often amicably resolved within a few weeks. Partly this was due to my continual pressure in favour of making *P.N.W.* a regular magazine, appearing at least at fixed quarterly intervals, if not six times a year, or even at best as a monthly. Allen Lane rejected the idea of making it a monthly, and, later, a bi-monthly, on the grounds that such regular publication did not suit his organization, and was not in any case feasible under the still rather higgledy-piggledy conditions of post-war printing and binding. In these decisions I think on the whole that he was right (in a cautious fashion); but the disappointment at my end was great. It was not only that I had always wanted a monthly or bi-monthly but also that I felt certain it would be much simpler and cheaper for me to organize on that basis. In addition, the material that was now pouring in at a tor-rential pace would have provided enough contributions for at least six numbers a year, even if only a minute fraction of it were used.

As well as arguments about how often *P.N.W.* should appear, there were also arguments about its price, about whether advertisements should be included to help the finances, and whether it should be avail-able on subscription. Perhaps everyone's temper had been a little frayed by the long war. We were, certainly, all more exhausted by then than we realized. It seems a little absurd that everyone who was in-volved in handling a literary and artistic publication whose circulation had reached six figures should not have been wreathed in smiles; but in fact almost immediately after the climax that was reached in the spring of 1946, some of the great success began to slip away. Other magazines were feeling the same change, but I had hopes — and I think Allen Lane had shared them — that we had discovered an un-tapped source of mass appreciation; that given the right formula, an enormous public was now ready to devour what would have been con-sidered almost entirely highbrow fare before the war. But war is like one of those machines that build up terrific temperatures, under which certain substances are transformed into others. Without the pressure the substance remains obstinately as it always has been. In 1947 the printing figure had dropped to 80,000. Eighteen months later it was 40,000, and in spite of all the new features we had introduced the circulation was still falling.

To have a readership that can be estimated as somewhere between 50,000 and 100,000 is something most editors of literary magazines in Britain during the last half-century would find intoxicating. If, however, you have tasted the keen air of the peaks, the lower slopes are apt to be disappointingly unstimulating. As we toiled away at the huge piles of MSS. at our desks in Egerton Crescent, as we read through the still so enthusiastic letters that poured in from all over the world, it seemed very difficult to believe that the change was taking place, that the temperature which had altered so much during the war years was dropping fast. It was not that the hard core of enthusiasts had abandoned us, nor the true converts we had made. What we had underestimated was the ease with which the great outer circle of those who had become readers, and often eager readers, when there were few competitors for the occupation of leisure hours, would slip away. I do not think I am speaking from a purely selfish or injured point of view, or for literature alone, if I say that the low level commercial exploitation of the increased leisure that the British people have won themselves since 1945 has been one of the great post-war disappointments.

By January 1949, Penguin Books decided that they must reduce the number of pages to 128, with 16 pages of photogravure, and some months later they felt that they could only produce two numbers a year. From my end, with an assistant and office expenses to cope with, however much shared with my other professional earnings as broadcaster and journalist, this decision meant — as my accountant was not slow to point out to me — that I was actually losing on *Penguin New Writing*. Publishing was taking up more and more of my time, which meant there was less time for profitable journalism.

By the beginning of 1950, Penguin Books had come to the decision that they could not under any circumstances produce *P.N.W.* more than twice a year, and perhaps only once. I did not doubt their good faith; only I was bitterly disappointed that they did not share my belief that it could still be saved by a change of publishing conception. I knew that I could not continue to run it on the basis they proposed. I also felt that even if I could find the money, to do so would spoil my chances of finding backers for a monthly or quarterly elsewhere.

So it came about that No. 40, published in the later part of 1950, was the last. We had survived, in our hectic, extraordinary and rather romantic career, as a "little magazine" that had had the public of a very big magazine indeed, for ten years.

This last number was rather interesting. In the photogravure plates, we had not only reproductions of new paintings by John Minton, and new sculpture and drawings by Barbara Hepworth, but also photographs of some of our American contributors. These were Lionel Trilling, Paul Bowles, J. F. Powers, Tennessee Williams, Saul Bellow, Nelson Algren, and Eudora Welty. Not a bad roll-call, I think, of the names that were making American literature at the time — and several among those who are still making it vigorously today. The text itself was remarkable for a first story by a new English writer of clearly outstanding gifts, Frank Tuohy, and an extract from a first novel by a new American writer, William Goyen. I am glad, looking back, that our last number kept up so well our reputation for introducing the future. Perhaps the most striking contribution, from this point of view, was the last of all: an article by the twenty-five-year-old John Wain, scarcely known at that time outside University circles, on the poetry of William Empson. This was, in fact, a revolutionary appeal that was deeply to influence the new "Movement" of poetry that started not long after *Penguin New Writing* came to an end. The concluding words were as follows: "Whether Empson will ever write any more poetry is not my business. If he does, it will be interesting to see whether the landslide in English literary taste has left us with a public capable of appreciating him. For the plain fact is that many of the reputations which today occupy the poetic limelight are such as would crumble immediately if poetry such as Empson's, with its passion, logic, and formal beauty, were to become widely known. . . ."

The long-enforced ban on the publication of new magazines had come to an end earlier in the year, and it seemed to me that new groupings and new attitudes — such as John Wain's article foreshadowed — were bound to emerge soon. The doubts I had were whether in the changing climate that was withering *Penguin New Writing*, a purely literary magazine would be able to survive.

With No. 27, *Penguin New Writing* had at last become what we had always hoped it could be: a magazine primarily devoted to literature — and offering opportunities to young writers above all — but also covering the other arts, with articles on the theatre, the ballet, music, cinema, radio, as well as on literary themes, and illustrations to complement those articles. All this, of course, on an international, not merely British scale.

This more ambitious scope added considerably to the work of preparation, but enormously increased the fun of it at the same time. Later on, when new magazines could be started, it was obvious that more specialized reviews would appear; but at the time we were moving in to what was almost a vacuum, and the response we found, from artists, producers and choreographers was correspondingly eager and cooperative. I think I have enjoyed all my days as an editor, but no period more than this, when my house was filled, not only with huge piles of MSS. but also with drawings, paintings and photographs of plays, operas, ballets and their creators, all waiting their turn for selection and reproduction. I doubt if we missed any development of real significance of those years. What is curious to reflect is that this marvellous opportunity came my way at a time when I was most truly in sympathy with what was going on. Ten years later, at the height of the vogue for non-representational painting, and for the Marxist theatre of Brecht, for instance, I could not have felt the same afflatus or had the same imaginative understanding to guide me.

Barbara Cooper was in tears when the decision to call it a day was made, and tears continued to flow while the depressing business of sending back the MSS. that could no longer be used went on. I do not think they were tears only for the end of an enterprise she had so whole-heartedly identified herself with. She felt, as I did, that with *Penguin New Writing* added to the lengthening list of literary magazines that had folded, the future for young writers looked decidedly black. "Already," I wrote, "the creeping frosts have claimed *Horizon* and *Life and Letters* as their victims, and a number of other less talked-about magazines that performed a specialized but valuable function. . . . Soon there will be hardly any address at all to which a young poet or writer of short stories can send his MSS. in the hope of advice and publication — and that immediate and so necessary settling of roots that publication can give. Such a state of affairs cannot be endured for long, because a healthy literature demands a centre of growth and ferment, of appreciation and criticism by intelligent and imaginative standards. . . ."

When the story broke — within hours in the London Letter of the *Manchester Guardian* and in the *Evening Standard* — the letters and telephone calls of regret began, and soon swelled to a flood. Stephen Spender wrote: "It is the worst loss so far, and for the greatest number of people. Isn't there anything we could do? Isn't the failure of these magazines partly due not just to the public but to the failure of talent? Wouldn't it be possible now to start a magazine of all the talents? Couldn't we, say, try to draw up a list of those who are simply the best writers in England and try to get the collaboration of all of these, old as well as young and new? . . ." This idea was, indeed, very much the inspiration of the *London Magazine* three years later, but by then Stephen had branched off in a new direction of his own.

I may perhaps be forgiven for remarking on the extraordinary legend that *New Writing* appeared to have created. I have continually come across people hitherto unknown to me who have been eager to tell me how much it meant to them. Of course this pleased me; but it also, quite genuinely, astonished me. Once, when I was lecturing in Copenhagen, some years after *P.N.W.*'s decease, a young West In-

dian got up, and announced that he didn't want to ask me anything —
but to tell me something. As usual I was galvanized into despairing
attention, bracing myself for denunciation on count after count. The
young West Indian, however, plunged at once into a panegyric of
New Writing, informed the audience that he and his friends in Ja-
maica had been keen readers and had followed it throughout its career. He wanted me to know how much they had appreciated it, and he
was sure they would be pleased to know that he had had the opportunity to thank me personally. Taken completely by surprise, I blinked
and stammered, while the audience clapped and Her Britannic Majesty's Ambassador gave me a huge grin from the front row.

Equally astonishing has been the number of letters I have received
over the years from people who wanted me to know what an important
part *New Writing* played in their lives at one time or another. As I
write this — so many years after the appearance of the last number
— a letter has come in from someone I have never met, in Canada,
who writes that at the age of eleven, during the war, he was given a
copy by his father, and was "literally dug out from the pages of *Big-
gles* and *The Wizard* and *The Hotspur* and transplanted into the
world of literature. A world that occupies all of my free time now."

« 12 »

ONE of the first bonuses that came to me from the new arrangement
with Purnell was the opportunity to visit the U.S.A. A group from the
firm was going over in April of 1948, mainly to study printing methods and machinery, and they managed to get me included without
difficulty. This immensely simplified the problems, peculiarly complicated at that time, of permits and allowances. Also if I had still been
on my own, I rather doubt whether I would have thought the heavy
expense justified.

I was very much excited about the visit. I had many friends in
America, especially in the publishing and literary world, and I knew
that they would make my introduction to the novel scenes and experiences of their country as pleasant and stimulating as possible. I hoped
that both John Lehmann Limited and *New Writing* would derive considerable profit from it. But above all I was excited by the thought of
at last getting to know my mother's homeland and seeing the places
where my New England ancestors had spent their lives.

It is, I think, a common experience of British publishers visiting
New York that the first few days are a delightful round of handshakes,

drinks, invitations to lunch and dinner and to the theatre, and an occasional passing reference to a book, as something quite on the side. Then it begins to get serious. Catalogues that have been slipped into one's coat pocket have to be carefully examined, items are marked for further enquiry before one switches out the bedside lamp, and the second time round the discussions begin to turn professional. Advance copies of "winners," proofs of novels or biographies that their publishers are convinced will break the sales records, arrive in parcel after parcel at one's hotel. One struggles to cope with them all, but as by this time hospitality has got under way with a vengeance, it is a losing battle. The telephone never stops ringing, one reads later and later into the night. In the end one abandons many of these offerings unread, and arranges for the bulkiest of those others that seem to promise something special to be sent on by post, after having made desperate attempts to pin down options on them. Like many other visiting Englishmen, I found there was some champagne quality in the Manhattan air that makes the burning of the candle at both ends tolerable, and even enjoyable. It is when one leaves the city that the kick-back hits one, and one is suddenly prostrate.

I shall always be grateful for the way in which my New York publishing friends — who turned out to be far greater in number than I realized — initiated me into their extraordinary closed society. I could not have had more marks of attention and affection lavished upon me if I had been a long-lost brother or son. I marvelled at the ruthlessness of their behaviour to one another, and at the same time at the way they kept together in spite of their cut-throat scheming. I marvelled at the way in which authors were treated as if they were mere raw material for editorial and sales departments to work on, if necessary entirely transforming original, cherished versions. I marvelled at the tremendous organization involved in promotion campaigns. After all, was it not true that far too much money was involved for anything to be left to chance? Since then, British publishing has gone some of the way down the same road; but in 1948, I felt like a cottage weaver confronted by the vast machinery of modern textile industry.

Before I left, I had already made up my mind to capture as many of the new post-war generation of American writers as possible. They seemed to me to have qualities of vitality, self-confidence and keenness to explore new territory that were much rarer in Britain, where the exhaustion of the long struggle still appeared to inhibit experiment and invention. A reputation for talent-spotting and disinterested encouragement of youthful adventurousness, founded on my record as editor of *New Writing* and associate of Leonard and Virginia Woolf in the Hogarth Press, had preceded me; sometimes I felt it was a little difficult to live up to, but it opened all doors to me, and I found it far easier than I imagined to pounce on the authors I wanted. In some cases I had been anticipated by a shrewd colleague. Little Truman Capote shook his head, or rather his fringe, and announced that he was very very sorry, honey, but he had already had a very grand interview with A. S. Frere of Heinemann's, so grand that he had felt obliged immediately to agree to go on Heinemann's list. I regretted this because I felt that *Other Voices, Other Rooms* showed an extraordinarily original poetic talent; but perhaps it was as well that he was engaged elsewhere, because I decided to take a chance on Gore Vidal, whose homosexual novel *The City and the Pillar* had just caused a considerable stir. Gore, I discovered, considered himself to be in an unique rivalry relationship with Truman, almost like infant prodigies banging away at the piano against one another in different parts of the same concert hall. Later, when Gore came over to London and I was preparing the publicity for his book, I asked him whether it was true that he was only twenty-three. "No, John," he said, with a pained expression on his face, "I'm twenty-*two*. It's Truman who's twenty-three."

I was taken to Tennessee Williams's *Streetcar Named Desire*, which was running with great success on Broadway with Marlon Brando as Stanley Kowalski, and felt at once that he was too good an author to be missed, even though the publication of plays has never been a very profitable line of business. I was amazed to find that the English rights were available, settled the contracts when I returned to London, and started the series with *The Glass Menagerie* the same year. We did well with them; we did even better with his short novel, *The Roman Spring of Mrs. Stone*, which we published in 1950, causing a furious division of opinion among the critics, some of the female critics being uncompromisingly hostile. Like Rosamond, however, Barbara Cooper was enthusiastic from the beginning, saying that she thought him "the Puccini of modern literature." *The Glass Menagerie* was produced a few months after I returned at the Theatre Royal, Haymarket, by John Gielgud, a production which brilliantly inaugurated Tennessee's reputation on this side of the Atlantic.

In general, my American trip was more valuable in getting to know publishers and agents, and in clinching deals that had already been proposed, than in actually finding new authors. I already had Saul Bellow on my list, and I had already taken a short story by J. F. Powers, whose work remains unique in the American scene and in his generation, and tentatively agreed to publish his remarkable first collection of stories, *Prince of Darkness*. Calder Willingham's *End as a Man* and Chandler Brossard's *Who Walk in Darkness*, the first "hip" novel of all, were to come a little later, though I heard much about Calder's reputation on the trip. There were, however, notable exceptions.

Before I left New York, my agent Mike Watkins told me of a novel that had great difficulty in finding a home, though James Laughlin of New Directions, famed for encouraging "far-out" highbrow and experimental writers, had at last shown interest. The author of this novel, however, was not in his twenties, but had known Christopher Isherwood in Berlin in the 'thirties. He had just had a remarkable and macabre story, *A Distant Episode*, published in *Horizon*. He had also written the incidental music to *The Glass Menagerie*. Paul Bowles, in fact, was a musician by reputation, and *The Sheltering Sky* was his first novel. "It's a pretty strange book," observed Mike. "And I'm not going to say anything more than that. Except that I don't see it on anyone's list in England except yours!" When the typescript arrived, I read it with mounting enthusiasm: I had not been so struck by an American novel since Saul Bellow's *Dangling Man*. We all agreed that it must be on our list, whether it could have been on anyone else's list or not. It proved one of our greatest successes.

The second notable exception was Theodore Roethke. Donald Elder at Doubleday, whom I had got to know well during his stay in Europe, showed me some of his poems which they had published, a *succès d'estime* but not much more. I was immediately attracted by the earliest group, and felt that if a young writer (but he was in fact, as I learned later, only a year younger than me) could create so completely convincing a poetic world out of greenhouses, potted plants, camellias, weeds and moss, he was a poet indeed.

We made a book out of these and a selection of the later poems, and published it under the title of *The Lost Son*. Roethke, who was a Professor of English at Washington, was soon to be recognized as one of the most gifted poets of his generation. His early death, only a few years ago, was a disastrous loss to American literature.

As my aeroplane took me away from the fabulous city, I made a small inventory of things that had particularly struck me. I noted the rather grim, quite definitely not contented look on the faces of the crowds that poured in and out of offices four times a day. Keeping up with the Joneses seemed especially difficult amongst the skyscrapers:

however well you did, there was always somebody richer and more amply endowed with the material furniture of success. I noted the smart modernity and cleanliness of apartments and offices; and the filth that blew through the narrow canyons of the streets. I noted the prevalence of a cynical, wisecracking habit of comment, often very witty and semantically inventive; which nevertheless co-existed with a spontaneous, warm-hearted concern with the plight of friends in trouble. I was touched by the generous impulses that were aroused in people the moment they heard one was a "limey," and the rather awe-struck respect they had for our sufferings in the blitz; and amused by the way these impulses struggled with a traditional suspicion of our diplomatic and commercial craftiness and of concealed, unassuaged imperial ambitions. I was appalled by the habit of drinking several extremely dry double martinis before a meal, and of subsequently tak-ing iced coffee and water with it. Any knowledge of wine was as rare as the classification of orchids. I was driven mad by the inability to get my shoes polished by putting them out in the corridor when I went to bed. And I was more entertained than perturbed to find that the gen-eral criterion of worthiness, the alpha plus in the examination for American excellence, was the ability to *sell* — whatever it was to whoever it was. I shall never forget going into a shop to buy a pair of socks, and the look of despair on the face of the young salesman when he failed to sell me at the same time two other pairs of socks, several drip-dry shirts and a dozen underpants. It was, for him, as if all thumbs had been turned down against him in the American arena.

My expedition into the New England countryside began a few days later. I stayed in Worcester, where my mother had lived as a young girl, with my cousin Harry Ransom Davis and his family. His wife Eleanor made me feel at once as if I had known her all my life; a gift I think peculiar to the nicest kind of Americans — even when they are not one's relations. They took me out to their little beach house in Montauk, far up on the north-eastern end of Long Is-land. There was a light sea-fog when we got there, but the sea made itself known by the endless beating and toppling and foaming of the waters: Harry's wife said she could never have enough of it. And the moment the fog lifted and I saw the house on the sand-cliff, I felt it was exactly the kind of house I had been looking for myself. I became much attached to them all, and was horrified when tragedy struck some years later. A typhoon came raging inland, and the alarm was sent out that it was approaching Worcester. Dear, kind, gentle, responsible Harry went up to the roof of his business offices to see that everything was battened down, and was whirled off into the street, as if by a demon of destruction, and was dead in a few moments.

I was taken to see cousin Forest, an eccentric, extremely rich old bachelor who lived alone in what looked like an enormous Greek temple. He greeted me genially, but with a certain canny reserve, as if he thought I might well be a conspirator in some plot against his possessions. I could not help remembering that many years before, on a lightning visit to England, he had come over to see me as a young boy at Eton. In those days an Eton boy when visited by a rich relation expected a tip to be pressed into his hand as goodbyes were said: a £1 note at least, to be spent in an orgy of banana messes amongst his friends the next day. Cousin Forest demanded almost at once to be taken to my hosiers, the famous shop of Devereux. He then proceeded to indulge in a riot of spending, ordering practically every item of clothing he set eyes on, in half-dozens, dozens and more. The assistants raced around the shop almost hysterically, and my hopes rose higher and higher. £1? £5? Perhaps even more? But there was absolutely nothing in the hand that so fondly shook mine as he went off to catch his train.

I stayed in Milton with Rosamond Hamlin, one of the two Peabody girls my mother had been teaching when my father first met her, and still deeply devoted to her. I spent a night in Exeter, with my mother's sister Aunt Jessie and her husband Jack French, in their home, one of the beautiful clapboard houses that seem to me one of the great architectural achievements of Anglo-Saxon civilization. I had never seen them before, and they prepared an enormous repast for me the next morning, with eggs and meat and waffles and every other conceivable delicacy of the American breakfast. I felt ashamed not to do justice to it with my war-shrunken English stomach. They drove me up into the mountains beyond Concord to visit the old family farm of Cliffhead, on Saddleback, wild, lonely and romantic among its overgrown orchards, with a famous pink quartz fireplace in the living room that my grandmother had added; an expedition that moved me deeply, for it had loomed very large in my mother's childhood memories of endless summer holidays, picnics, blueberry picking and burning juniper bushes on the mountain at night.

My farewell week in New York passed in a haze of parties and last interviews with authors, publishers and agents. No one could be gainsaid: neither my cousins Georgene and Helen, living together in a smart apartment on Fifth Avenue, nor my new American friends, nor any of my London friends who seemed to have gathered there at that moment in abundance. I had one small, but important agent's job to complete myself on behalf of Rosamond. I went to see Katherine Brown at M.C.A., and broke to her the fact that the sales of *The Ballad and the Source* in the U.S.A. had now passed well beyond 600,-000. This meant that a new clause in Rosamond's film contract with Walter Wanger came into operation, by which she was due for a further very large sum in dollars. Katherine Brown took this news gallantly, but not without flinching; for the project had run into trouble and one after another of the great film stars had failed to agree, or be free, to play the leading role. Bowing her head for a moment she quickly turned to another topic. Did I know, she asked, what her favourite book was? Why, of course, *Dusty Answer*, and Walter Wanger agreed with her. They renewed their agreement on this matter every time they rang one another up on the long-distance telephone. What a film it would make! They agreed enthusiastically on that, too, but . . . if only the young people in it, so lovable, could enjoy a little *human happiness* at the end. . . . Judging it not to be my business to recommend my sister to make the answer less dusty, I sighed and took my leave.

Amid Pleasant Opportunities

LOOKING back on those years of the late 'forties and early 'fifties, it seems to me that some of the chief focal points of metropolitan intellectual and artistic life were created, first, by the French Embassy under the dazzling régime of René and Odette Massigli; by Edith Sitwell, supported by her brothers Osbert and Sacheverell, and, of course, by Sibyl Colefax.

Sibyl's strength, however, was failing. The famous "ordinaries," the dinners to which one was invited but for which one paid one's own bill later on — still went on for some years, and, naturally, the cocktail-parties in Lord North Street. Then came the time when one only saw Sibyl in bed, looking frailer and frailer, as if she were made of match-sticks and old wool, but somehow or other keeping up her appetite for celebrities with heroic determination. Her latest enthusiasm was for the Oliviers, Larry and Vivien. I think Sibyl almost literally wor-shipped them. I remember one occasion when I was bidden to visit her in hospital, and found when I arrived that a large assortment of her friends had already arrived in her sick-room. She enquired, as ever, with eagerness about my doings, and began introducing me to other people whom I already knew. Then, suddenly, the door opened, and Larry and Vivien came in. Even in her enfeebled state, Sibyl's eyes brightened as if a hundred-watt bulb had been switched on behind them. Instinctively, the rest of us retired to our corners, turned our backs and engaged one another in conversation, while the ceremony of worship began.

Sibyl died at the end of September 1950. I went to the memorial service, at 12:30 one morning, in Wilton Place. There was gathered a large company, many familiar faces and many known to me only be-cause I had seen them time and again at Sibyl's parties. Even with those intermittent acquaintances I felt I had a kind of bond, and I was sad because I knew in my bones that I should rarely, if ever, see them again. Rose Macaulay was beside me, and just before the singing began she whispered to me: "This is Sibyl's last party."

It is said that when that other great hostess of the time, Emerald Cunard, departed a few years later, she was under the impression as she lay on her death-bed, that she was making her way into the crowds of a large party. "I can't make out," she said, "who the host is."

Brilliant ambassadors of France, and ambassadresses who made brilliant hostesses, have come and gone in London; but for those of us who were fortunate enough to be in town at the time, and on the French Embassy's invitation list, there will never be a period as brilliant and stimulating as the long reign of René and Odette Massigli. The champagne-parties, the evening receptions, often with music, the great luncheons and the intimate dinners, at which the food was always delicious, were a tonic that all thirsted for, whether politicians, financiers, newspaper magnates, duchesses, women of influence in full sail, or mere actors, musicians, and writers like myself.

On one occasion, Odette arranged a "private" dinner at the Embassy, as she said when she invited me, "for the Queen Mother to meet some intellectuals and literary people." There were about thirty of us gathered there when the Queen Mother finally arrived; but Rosamond and I murmured to one another in slight dismay that dukes and duchesses, earls and countesses appeared to be in the majority.

After dinner I sat in the little circle round the Queen Mother with Harold Nicolson, Kenneth Clark, Lord Salisbury, the Duke of Wellington and the Duke of Buccleuch for the last hour and a half. Harold managed to steer the conversation round from the inter-relations of the nobility to Byron and Shelley. The Queen Mother showed herself intensely curious, amused and intelligently interested, and suddenly professed the strongest views about not putting any more busts in Westminster Abbey. I remember one incident in particular. The Duke of Wellington turned to Harold Nicolson, and said: "Tell me, Harold, have we got to take this chap Dylan Thomas seriously?" Harold replied: "Yes, of course" — and was firmly supported by the Queen Mother.

Edith Sitwell still used as a base for her sallies on London from Renishaw the Sesame Club in Grosvenor Street, and there she would hold what she called her "monster tea-parties," her more intimate luncheons and occasional suppers after a theatre or a concert. She was an exotic figure in this respectable middle-class ladies' club, and as she swept through in her long dresses and bizarre hats designed to emphasize her patrician looks, strange gold ornaments round her neck and enormous semi-precious stones on the rings that covered her fingers, a hush would descend on the conversation at tables where other members were entertaining their guests, and eyes would be raised from newspapers where ravaged solitaries were huddled in decrepit armchairs. They did not look in the least imperial figures or pioneers — the full name of the club was the Sesame Imperial and Pioneer Club — but Edith *did*, and curiously enough the two words, so grotesquely associated with the club's name, represented the two sides of her nature: the aristocrat always conscious of background and breeding, and the daring, iconoclastic pioneer in the arts, who had shocked conventional London with her early poems and the public presentation of them.

Edith's policy at these gatherings was to mix old friends and almost total strangers who happened to have written to her about her poetry — or *their* poetry — with visiting relations and the inevitable toady or two who could not be got rid of; and hope for the best. Osbert and Sacheverell, with his Canadian wife Georgia, were nearly always there acting as stiffeners, to liven the conversation in those parts of the room geographically remote from Edith, to encourage the shy and to rescue friends from bores when they perceived that good manners had reached snapping point. Poets, from Tom Eliot, Stephen Spender, Louis MacNeice and Dylan Thomas, to some penniless unknown young man whose verses had caught Edith's attention, were always to be found in abundance; publishers, literary agents and editors (except those whose papers had been guilty of printing tepid or slighting notices of the works of herself and her brothers — Alan Pryce-Jones, then editor of *The Times Literary Supplement*, was constantly in hot water and as constantly extricating himself with his usual deft savoir faire); her favourite critics, talkers and wits, especially Maurice Bowra, Kenneth Clark and his wife Jane; her favourite actors, especially John Gielgud and Alec Guinness, and sometimes the leading lights of the ballet world, Fred Ashton, Robert Helpmann and Constant Lambert. Edith's magnetic personality and fame had an extraordinary attraction for near-lunatics, and sometimes one of these managed to get himself or herself in, causing the utmost confusion, alarm — and comedy.

Edith liked to discuss feuds in the literary world with the greatest zest and most unqualified partisanship, sometimes being very funny indeed in a totally ruthless way. Her own enmities would change into or back into friendships with extraordinary suddenness, leaving those who weren't entirely up-to-date breathless and bewildered. By nature she was combative — how could she have surmounted the obstacles of her early life if she had not been? — but her capacity for forgiveness was as unlimited as her impulse of kindness towards those she discovered were in trouble or difficulties. But as she once confessed to me, she liked, "for a lark," to sharpen her wits on wooden heads "in the way that cats sharpen their claws on the legs of kitchen tables."

One of the most remarkable traits of Edith Sitwell, I have always thought, was her capacity for making comedy out of things that happened to herself, occurrences that must, at the time, have been embarrassing, exhausting and even dangerous. She wrote to me from San Francisco, on one of the major triumphal tours that she and Osbert carried out in America after the war, that

as a result of fatigue, I got bronchitis, for the second time in three months. I had to give three readings here, coughing my head off. However, the reading in Hollywood was a great success, I do think. Lots of film stars, including Harpo Marx came. And during my reading of the *Macbeth* sleep-walking scene, I was just announcing that Hell is murky, when a poor gentleman in the audience uttered the most piercing shrieks, and was carried out by four men, foaming at the mouth. As one of the spectators said to me, "you ought to be awfully pleased. It was one of the most flattering things I have ever seen. . . ." * We also met Miss Ethel Barrymore, who was delightful, although Osbert ascribes my bronchitis to her, as she was breathing heavily. I must say I couldn't have enjoyed Hollywood more. We think all the waiters at the hotel there were suffering from the effects of smoking marijuana, their conduct was so strange. They would shriek with laughter, suddenly join in conversations, and lean on the sofa on which we sat for our meals, putting their heads between ours.

At that time Edith was preparing an anthology of American poetry to be published by my firm. She had, from the outset, shown the greatest interest in and enthusiasm for our venture, and hearing no doubt that we were not without our difficulties, she wrote, with great generosity: "I am very distressed to hear about the proofs and the expense of the American anthology. Now look here. I have for very long wanted to make a present to the firm of Messrs Lehmann. Please allow me to make a present of this book. By which I mean, with the

---

* In *Taken Care Of*, Edith Sitwell ascribes this remark, or something similar, to Ethel Barrymore.

exception of David Higham's fee, I don't want a penny from the book. In fact I won't take one."

One's memory selects episodes, moments, glimpses to retain with an unusual intensity, according to some mysterious law of its own. I have a vivid recollection of Edith coming to tea at my house one summer's day about this time, while I was writing my British Council booklet about her work. She answered a number of questions I put to her about her early life and how she started writing poetry, and told me what a horribly dark and painful time she had had while nursing Helen Rootham through her last illness before the war. She sat on the sofa in the green-and-gold light of my library, the green deepened to a darker glow by the tall spreading plane-trees outside in the Crescent gardens, and the light from the western window caught in the prisms of the chandeliers and reflected off the plum-red, orange and gold of the books in the shelves on either side of the fireplace, like a sombre priestess of prophecy and poetry. Her wide, dark, floppy hat overshadowed her strangely luminous, pale, oval face, the greenish eyes narrowed in their huge rings, the noble nose reminding me of the profiles of Roman emperors set in their marble medallions along the chimneypiece. As she talked very quietly of bitter experiences in the past, the ends of her lips turned slightly down in a mask of suffering and sorrow. Then Carlotta came galloping into the room, and Edith's expression changed at once to delight and amusement as she greeted her and demanded an aria.

I shall always see Edith as I saw her that afternoon, a vivid image I put beside the dramatic memory of her reciting *Still Falls the Rain* at the Churchill Club during a doodle-bug raid.

« 2 »

WHEN she was made an Honorary Doctor of Letters at Oxford, Edith celebrated by giving a large luncheon-party to her friends. I found myself nearly opposite Tom Eliot, and became entirely absorbed towards the end in contemplation of his face: the rather grey lava-like landscape it presented, the furrowed brows, the deep-set eyes behind the spectacles that associated so well with the deep, slow voice. Most striking of all, I thought, was the large mouth with its kindly humorous "set"; a reminder that this impressive tall figure, with the slightly bowed shoulders that added to the distinctly venerable general look, was the author not only of some of the greatest religious poetry of our time, but also of *Old Possum's Book of Practical Cats*.

As poet and editor and publisher himself, Tom Eliot had constantly shown the friendliest interest in my career and various ventures. From time to time we used to discuss professional matters together, as well as gossip about our friends. At that time he was President of the Alliance Française in Great Britain — a post in which I was to succeed him a few years later — and I remember that I was sitting beside him one afternoon during a long and exhausting meeting at the French Institute. In the intervals we talked about the state of literary magazines. He revealed that at its best his well-known quarterly, *The Criterion*, sold under 1,000 copies and lost its publishers about £500 a year. When he packed it up at the outbreak of war, the circulation had dropped to a couple of hundred — an ironic fact when one considers the historic fame it has since acquired on both sides of the Atlantic. He told me that he had enjoyed the experience very much, all the seventeen years of it, but added regretfully that he had never been satisfied: he should have spent more time on it, and he should have travelled more abroad to study what was going on there. He criticized various contemporary survivors for making what he considered the fatal mistake of trying to combine a "popular" appeal with a "highbrow" appeal. But he agreed with me when I said that I found authors often made a similar mistake, in trying to write popular pot-boilers when their talents were really for difficult books that could not appeal to more than a minority audience. It was only later that it occurred to me with dismay that he might have thought I was indirectly referring to his first essay in popular play-writing: *The Cocktail Party* appeared in London very soon after. I certainly did not intend that; and yet for all Tom's skill in evolving a medium to carry both social conversation and high poetry, I am not sure that his plays are not flawed, fundamentally, by exactly that contradiction.

Tom had a ruthless streak in him, which came out sometimes in his judgements of his contemporaries. When I had finally agreed to succeed him at the Alliance, we lunched together at the Athenaeum, and he gave me some useful hints on the problems and personalities of the organization. I particularly remember him saying to me: "You will, of course, have to deal with the President of the Alliance in Paris, Monsieur Emile Henriot, a charming man who has written a great many books that will soon be forgotten."

A couple of years later, on Tom's sixty-fifth birthday, *The New York Times* asked me if I could persuade him to give me a special interview. In the course of our conversation, I reminded him that some years before he had written to me to say he felt he would never write poetry again. "Well, I was right," he said, chuckling, "because I haven't." When I asked him how, in that case, he accounted for the plays, he immediately replied: "That doesn't count, it's quite different. It's what you might call *applied* poetry, and if real poetry happens to get into it by the way, that's just something to be thankful for!"

He went on to give the information, which I found quite extraordinary, that he had felt as if he was never going to write poetry again several times before in his life. The first time was after writing *The Hollow Men*. By chance Faber's had just started the little series of separately published *Ariel Poems*, and persuaded him to contribute. "Writing those *Ariel Poems* released the stream again, and led to *Ash Wednesday*. Then I remember feeling I'd written myself out just before *The Rock* was commissioned. I had to write it — I had a deadline — and working on it began to make me interested in writing drama, and led directly to *Murder in the Cathedral*."

Again, he told me, he felt pure poetry had dried up in him for good; but — most extraordinary of all — there were some lines and fragments that were discarded while *Murder in the Cathedral* was being rehearsed, and out of these fragments he gradually saw a poem shaping itself. "That was how *Burnt Norton* came to be written. But it might have remained by itself, if it hadn't been for the war. I was very much absorbed in the problems of writing for the stage, and might have gone straight on from *The Family Reunion* to another play; but the war destroyed that impulse for a time, the conditions of one's life changed, and one was thrown in on oneself. So I wrote *East Coker* to follow *Burnt Norton*. And in writing *East Coker* I began to see the poems as the first two in a set of four."

Such was the series of chances that led to the writing of a masterpiece.

When I said to him: "But if such random chances have led so often to new poetic creation for you, isn't it possible it might happen again? If someone, for instance, made you promise a poem — for a special occasion?" He laughed and said: "I'd like to think that . . . but I don't want to repeat what I've already done. It has always struck me as very curious the way certain poets, Browning for instance, have gone on writing in their old age without taking any step forward, making any new discovery. Why go on and on doing what you've already done well? I myself want each poem or group of poems to be different, a separate creation. Even Milton seems to me to have made a mistake in writing *Paradise Regained*. *Samson Agonistes* is different, it's something new, a new victory."

I have a vivid recollection of him, a year or so later, after the end of my publishing, at the ceremony which was held to unveil the "blue plaque" on Oscar Wilde's house in Tite Street. Just before Compton Mackenzie started his moving speech, he arrived in an old slouch hat and raincoat, pushing the bath-chair of his friend John Hayward. He became a close friend of Nora Wydenbruck, one of his German translators and author of an excellent book on Rilke, which I had the pleasure of publishing. One evening I met him at her house in his gayest form, and I reminded him of the Oscar Wilde ceremony. We talked about Wilde as a writer, and he said that in his opinion the poems were, of course, hopeless, though *The Importance* was a masterpiece; but he remembered being very much excited and stimulated as a young man by reading *Intentions*, and still thought it was a good book for young people to read who intended to be writers. When I drove him back to Cheyne Walk after the party had broken up, he said to me suddenly how much he wished I was still a publisher and could relieve him of part of the responsibility he felt of publishing the work of new poets.

All that was before his sensational elopement with his attractive secretary, Valerie Fletcher. To be capable of slipping off in a taxi with a new bride one morning, as one is approaching the age of seventy, and just leaving a note on one's desk to astound one's employer, gives every sensible author hope. Browning, after all, was only in his thirties when he eloped with Elizabeth Barrett.

« 3 »

THERE was a third guardian angel among my elders and betters, to whom I looked for advice and whose interest in and approbation of my doings was extremely important to me. I have described the sympathetic encouragement I got from E. M. Forster over *New Writing*, and the tireless battles he waged, in his devastating, impish way, against the philistines and power-maniacs to whom the war was such a golden opportunity.

He used sometimes to come to tea at No. 31, and we would exchange gossip about our mutual friends, Christopher Isherwood, William Plomer, Joe Ackerley and John Morris in particular. He always thought it very funny that William, to whom he is devoted, had a habit of being extremely secretive about his telephone number. He told me that when he was laid up with a broken ankle in London in the autumn of 1951, William had at last relented and offered it to him;

but he had refused to use it because he felt it was taking unfair advantage. As he told me this, he became incoherent with laughter over his tea-cup.

He had broken his ankle in the tower of Aldeburgh church, and had it in plaster for some weeks. It gave him an opportunity, he said, to do some reading for me if I wanted. I immediately seized the opportunity to ask him to read and advise on Denton Welch's *Journal*, which had just been sent me. I had only to write to him, he told me, and he would do more if he could. Sometimes, however, like every other distinguished literary figure, the importunities of others, especially strangers, overwhelmed him. In the summer of 1952, in reply to a cautious feeler I put out, he replied: "Yes, it's long since I sat on your nice, low soft sofas and chairs, and I should much like to do it again soon. Will ring in hopes. I'm afraid I can't undertake any little job though yet awhile. I'm snowed up as it is with others' MSS., and no nice big St. Bernard to dig me out. There are: a novel by a friend's daughter-in-law, a study on Czechoslovakia by another lady, a translation by a Bengali scientist of Tagore, a short story about child-birth, and a thesis on myself by a Copt. And there is my own work on a Mahratta prince, with which I must say I manage to proceed, despite all. . . ."

When he came to visit me, he often used to ask me to read him some of my poems, among which he had one or two special favourites. I shall never forget that at a moment when the blows of fate seemed to be raining particularly cruelly upon me, he wrote me a marvellous letter of comfort out of the blue. I cannot refrain from quoting it here, because it seems to me an example of the true aristocracy of friendship:

I have long been minded to write you a line of esteem and affection, and if there ever was a special moment for such a letter perhaps this is it. I do so appreciate what you have done for literature through publishing and the way you have done it. And also — though this you already know — I appreciate your own work, and I was re-reading only the other day your *Dark Lieutenant from the Sea*. . . .

« 4 »

ONE of the advantages of being an editor and publisher, if one's friends happen to be mostly in the world of literature and the arts, is that it gives one a reason to work with them and see them intensively from time to time. The longer I live, the more it appears to me that life is disagreeably devised in such a way that friends can hardly fail to drift away from one another, unless special ties of work or contiguity bind them together. The circle of one's intimates in one decade imperceptibly changes, until one realizes in the next decade, with a shock of sadness, that half — perhaps nearly all — of those one loved and enjoyed to be with so much have slipped out of the circle; others have taken their place.

Pleasant, then, have been the opportunities that arose from my calling as editor and publisher to grapple a friend closer to my soul for a while. Such an opportunity arose from the scheme of Hallam Fordham to compile a picture book on the subject of John Gielgud. Hallam put it up to me in the autumn of 1951, and the three of us had a first luncheon to discuss the project, which appealed to me very much, almost immediately after. This gave John an opportunity to talk about his life, his ancestry, his favourite roles, in an extremely fascinating and amusing way, speaking at high speed and scarcely drawing breath. He is one of the most delightful talkers in the world; not so good, however, as a listener. He can be extremely witty in talking about his colleagues, but seldom malicious, a rare gift among actors. I have admired him ever since I saw him as Richard II in 1929, and every time I have heard him in Shakespeare my conviction has deepened that no one can equal him in the speaking of verse on the stage. Though Macbeth cannot, perhaps, be counted as one of his greatest parts, I do not myself think anyone will excel him in giving tragic conviction to the transition of Macbeth from the proud and triumphant warrior to the guilt-ridden murderer haunted by his own imagination. Equally, there will never, for me, be any other Jack Worthing in *The Importance of Being Earnest*.

When the book was all but ready for the press, he came to lunch at my house to discuss the final touches. Though rattling away with great vigour, sitting at the table with an Edwardian straightness of back, he was in more reflective mood, and began to talk about the future of his career. Emlyn Williams had recently had a notable success with his recreation of Dickens readings: a bold and brilliant venture that delighted the public in spite of many gloomy prophecies. I suggested that he should do something of the same sort with readings from among his great Shakespearean roles. John seemed at first very reluctant, taking the line that it was the kind of thing one only did at the end of one's career (I did not say that the case of Emlyn Williams seemed to contradict his view). What he really liked, he said, what satisfied his deepest desires as a man of the theatre, was the *whole thing*, a whole play, the entirety of a production through which he

[467]

could express his creative spirit adequately. After some further discussions, he yielded as far as to say that he might one day do Shakespearean readings, perhaps for television in the U.S.A. Many years were to pass before he did in fact adopt this idea, with overwhelming success.

One day, at the beginning of 1950, David Gascoyne suddenly rang the door-bell of my house. I had not been in touch with him for some time. The figure I saw when I opened the door shocked me: his unshaven, quivering, grey-green face looked ravaged by nervous tension, perhaps by waking dreams of persecution and prophetic alarms. All the worst forebodings of the sick age in which we live seemed to writhe like snakes in his ever-changing expression. He came in, and poured out a fevered story of his recent life, a Cassandra-like cry into the void. I calmed him down as best I could, and suggested he should collect the poems he had written since the appearance of his wartime, Sutherland-illustrated volume, and let me publish them. The idea appealed to him, and resulted in the publication of *A Vagrant* at the end of the year, one of the rare books I feel it was a deep privilege for me to have brought to the light.

One day he brought Carson McCullers to dinner. Tennessee Williams, who had just arrived in London, joined us. As usual, Carson and David talked across one another, and at one moment I rather rudely told him to shut up, as I wanted so much to hear what she was saying. He jumped up and made off, and I had to wheedle him back from the front door and ask his forgiveness. I was particularly struck by the tender and affectionate consideration Tennessee showed Carson. He knew exactly how to handle his erratic and brilliant friend, and revealed an impressive side to his character of which I had, I confess, not been fully aware before. Afterwards, we all jumped into the car, and drove round and over the river bridges to see the lights of the Festival of Britain and the Fun Fair in Battersea Park.

Tennessee expressed regret that the Fun Fair sported no ferris-wheel. We had published *The Roman Spring of Mrs. Stone* the year before, and he had written to me from Rome:

Rome is now the hottest it has been for 100 years, so Mrs. Stone and I are leaving Tuesday night for Vienna. Mrs. Stone says she wants to find "the Fourth Man," and I want to take a ride in that big ferris-wheel. . . . If we sail from a northern port this time, I will make every effort, but no promise to get over to London. I want to see you and your sisters, and the

Christopher Fry plays I have heard so much about. Peter Ustinov is here doing Nero in the great new M.G.M. spectacle *Quo Vadis* which has already cost 8 million dollars and given employment to almost every street-walker in Rome. . . . They have a pack of lions, about 30 of them, a herd of fighting bulls, a brace of cheetas. The *poveri ragazzi* are quaking with terror of the scenes they have to act with this menagerie. Ustinov did not look so happy when the pair of cheetas walked on, supposedly pets of Octavia's, but perhaps he was only afraid they would steal the scene. A *Vogue* photographer wanted to take our picture together on Nero's throne and Ustinov said, "I don't share my throne with anybody! . . ."

Tennessee informed me that evening that he had seen something of Paul Bowles's new novel, *Let It Come Down*, and was very much excited by it. It arrived by air from Tangier about ten days later: a descent into hell by a master of infernal landscape, with a dry macabre humour running through it that seemed to me an important gain over his first novel, *The Sheltering Sky;* a book not to be put down till the very end.

Paul had first appeared in England in the late autumn of 1949, just as *The Sheltering Sky* was being published. In his early middle-age, with his shock of gold hair, slightly curled and as stiff as if made of nylon bristles, he still looked like a slim Greek athlete who might have had a nervous breakdown and taken to an intellectual, bohemian life after just failing to win the discus championship. Neatly dressed, with imaginative eyes, over which he wore a shade in the early morning, he was much more reserved than most of the Americans of his generation I had met. In fact the long years he had spent away from his country, in Europe, Central America, and North Africa, had, I thought, left a deep impress not only on his behaviour but also on his writing: he seemed to me far more like an European writer, in thought as well as in style, than an American writer of his generation. He struck me at once by his quiet charm and intelligence, his shrewdness about the ways of the world, and — when the reserve melted — a sharp wit that did not spare his contemporaries, of some of whom he could give very funny imitations.

His books reveal a highly developed gift for descriptive writing, especially in exotic scenes, and also an intuitive understanding of abnormal minds and abnormal states of mind bordering on madness. The same gifts appear in his letters. From England he went on to India and Ceylon, where he had plans for buying an island. In April I had a letter from Trivandrum, in southern India, in which he wrote:

Madura temple I thought completely wonderful; I've never seen anything remotely like it. As if a madman had conceived a meeting-place for people who automatically went mad on entering it. And of course one does. After you've been in the temple for a couple of hours you begin to feel people tinkering with the inside of your mind, and that leaves you feeling strangely empty afterwards. They literally sit there in their rags, looking straight at you for twenty minutes or half-an-hour at a stretch, and scratch around inside your head; I suppose it is one of their daily exercises. And the bells ring and the flutes and drums play and the priests look and act exactly like bouncers in a low bar, and the people jiggle wildly in front of Sri Ganesh, the elephant god, which in this case is spotted with obscene white patches and wears an enormous dirty sarong of ordinary cotton over its loins, and the "water" in the tank is brilliant green and thick as paste and bubbling with putrefaction, and the place is as big as Grand Central Station, with huge courts where loud-speakers blare and two or three thousand people sit around on the ground under the trees listening, and there is an entire section full of shops which sell everything from sandalwood statues to lollipops, from kitchenware to artificial flowers, from Japanese dolls to postcards. . . . I wish I had come twenty years ago.

In some ways Paul Bowles's short stories, a collection of which we published under the title of *A Little Stone*, are, I am inclined to think, more remarkable than his novels, enlarging the imagination with strange images of primitive vision and belief, of passion and horror entirely beyond the Christian categories of good and evil; stories that have no parallel in modern literature as far as my knowledge goes. I cannot speak of his talents as a musician, but I am certain that he has the capacity to be one of the greatest modern writers; a gift that general opinion is likely to fight against to the last, because he has the quality that geniuses, great and small, so often display, of being profoundly disturbing to the deeper conventional assumptions and patterns of value — and not merely shocking (which he also is) to established codes of behaviour already more or less abandoned by free-thinking people.

For the jacket designs, I gave each of Paul Bowles's three books to a different artist. *The Sheltering Sky* to Fred Uhlman (because he had just been to North Africa), *Let It Come Down* to John Minton, and *A Little Stone* to Keith Vaughan. If I valued the opportunities my publishing activities gave me to be in closer touch with author friends, I was just as happy when the same thing happened with my artist friends. Keith Vaughan, as I have already related, was regularly employed by my firm in its early days, and continued to design spines and jackets and illustrate various books long after.

Very different in temperament was his friend John Minton, whose death so early in his career, and in the way it happened, was one of the most saddening things I have known since the war. As mercurial as Keith is level-headed, even in his most extravagant moods of gaiety he could not conceal the melancholy that lay, a dark unstirring pool, in the depths of his nature. I had met him through Keith towards the end of the war, and was captivated at once by his warmth, sensitivity and sense of fun; perhaps too, and more intuitively, by the melancholy that I know lies not far below the sanguine and practical surface of my nature also. I can remember gatherings of friends, evenings when his tearing high spirits and absurd clowning infected all the rest of us and made us far wittier and merrier than our normal selves. I can also remember tête-à-tête meetings with him when he would express some of the restless dissatisfaction he felt with his own work, with the way painting was going in our time, and his need to get away from Europe for long periods, to refresh the springs of his creative activity and to sort out the problems of his personal life. It was inevitable, with his temperament, that he should feel strongly that art needed, in our age above all, a close relationship to and meaning in human life as it is lived. The danger of the world, the despair that must at times overcome even the most cheerful people when they stopped to think, were too pressing, he used to say, for any enclosed, cerebral or mathematical art. And it was, I think, because he saw art all over the Western world moving towards abstraction, and knew that he could not sincerely follow it himself, that his despair increased as the years went by and his gaiety became more forced and frenetical.

With another young author-artist I much admired, my relations were, unfortunately, posthumous in this period. Denton Welch came into my editorial life in the middle of the war, when he sent me a short story, *The Barn*, for *New Writing*, and I encouraged him to design some tail-pieces for the Penguin. I shall always regret that I never went down to see him in his Kentish home, and how a series of mischances kept us from meeting on his rare visits to London. He was killed, as everyone knows, by the lingering illness that afflicted him after he had been knocked down by a car. Soon after his death in 1948, I was surprised to find that his previous publisher did not appear to want the novel he had left in an all but completed state. I read the MS. and was deeply moved: scarcely veiled autobiography, it seemed to me a marvellous piece of work, not merely as a story but as literature, and I immediately accepted it. I gave it the title of *A Voice Through a Cloud*.

A year later, I published a volume of his still uncollected short stories and poems, together with reproductions of the best of his very small but immensely engaging and rather mysterious work as a painter, as *A Last Sheaf*.

The reviews for *A Voice Through a Cloud* were among the most enthusiastic I had for any book. They spoke of "writer born," "a work of genius," "a tragic and unforgettable book," of "sunshine blazing through a leaf, showing up every vein," "a triumph." And Stephen Spender wrote to me from Cornwall: "It's one of the most wonderful and terrifying books I've ever read. Certainly the first three-quarters of it make a masterpiece. Poor Denton Welch. How dreadfully sorry I am. I feel it will be impossible to think of anything else for days. I am very shaken by it." I agreed with him; but I have now to reflect sadly on the chances of so small a literary output, and in a way so specialized, surviving the importunate and ever-thickening crowd of new names and new reputations urgent for lasting recognition.

From time to time Stephen and I used to meet for a lunch or an evening together, though not so frequently as before, as he was travelling abroad a great deal, lecturing in America, and involving himself ever deeper in the politics of the Committee for Cultural Freedom, which had just been formed after the Congress of Writers in Berlin, and which was eventually to be the publicly declared power behind *Encounter*. In spite of the impression he was apt to make of boyish fluster in public debates, Stephen was really very good at these congresses, showing a strength of will and a political flair that was obviously in his blood. He would sail into a congress like a demolition expert arriving to inspect a row of old cottages that had outlived their usefulness. Before the inhabitants had grasped the significance of his presence, bricks would be thudding to the ground and lorries roaring away with the rubbish. It is always good to see an expert at work, but personally I regretted this particular expert was not at work building poems, a skill which came to occupy less and less of his time.

I have already written of the close ties I had at this time with a number of writers, apart from Stephen who were not published by my firm; especially William Sansom, Henry Green, and Elizabeth Bowen. Among my friends in the literary world, Elizabeth was one of the most consistently sympathetic with what I was trying to do, urging me at one moment not to neglect my own poetry, and at another to see that *Penguin New Writing* filled the gap that was growing ominously larger among English literary magazines. She was, I think, beginning to feel increasingly restless in England, and wanted to settle in her ancestral home at Bowen's Court in County Cork, whither she invited me to stay at any time when I happened to be passing, by air, to or from the United States. When her husband, Alan Cameron, died in 1952, even that plan proved too ambitious for her, and she decided to sell Bowen's Court and live in England.

Elizabeth's anxiety about the state of English literary magazines was certainly timely. In the autumn of 1949 Cyril Connolly let it be known that he was thinking of retiring from *Horizon* for a year. "Cyril must have a rest" was the theme of his helpers. I knew, however, that one cannot "retire" a magazine for a period and start again where one has left off. This was clearly the end of a great and memorable venture, though Cyril Connolly found it difficult to admit it. A few months later he offered me *Horizon*, over a bottle of champagne at the Athenaeum, at a reduced price. Though I was aware that the magazine was as completely *his* as *New Writing* was mine, I was tempted, owing to the difficulties I was encountering at that time in my negotiations with Penguin Books. I suggested to my backers in Purnell that it would be well worth-while buying for the small sum involved; but nothing came of it.

After this, Cyril, newly married, was eager to devote himself to writing, and also, it seemed, to the planting of shrubs in his Sussex home. I had recently been planting my garden at the cottage I had just bought near Three Bridges, and one day he challenged me to a contest of Latin names of the most desirable rhododendrons, magnolias and camellias. I had delved as deeply into the catalogues as he had, and I think I held my own fairly well, perhaps to his surprise. He already had plans to write a novel, a successor to *The Rock Pool*, and he told me that he had invented a new "internal daydream" technique. He confessed, however, to a snag: his imagination conjured up the scenes he intended to create so vividly, and they appeared so funny to him, that he just lay on his sofa and chuckled at the brilliant show his fancy was putting on for him. It was difficult, in these circumstances, to put anything down on paper.

« 5 »

My life in London during those years was very busy indeed. Not only did I have the work of directing my publishing firm and myself reading the manuscripts that Rosamond or Barbara or Julia Strachey recommended to me, of keeping up as far as I could with what was going on in literature in America and across the Channel, of keeping going and then winding up *New Writing*, but I also had other commissions and responsibilities. I broadcast from time to time on various services of the B.B.C. — Home, European and Overseas. I edited (and published) a series of anthologies of contributions from *New Writing*, apart from *Poems from New Writing* with which I had started, including *French Stories*, *Pleasures of New Writing* (which combined fiction, poetry and articles) and *English Stories*. From time to time I was invited by the British Council to lecture for them abroad, and edited for them, in 1949 and 1950, their pamphlet guides to *The Year's Work in Literature*. At the same time I was invited to join the Council's advisory panel on publications, and later became its chairman. I was a member of the General Committee of the Royal Literary Fund, which hands out thousands of pounds every year to authors in need (after a pretty severe scrutiny), and fought there the battle to permit *young* authors in need to apply and not merely those in their bath-chairs or on the point of receiving a telegram from the Sovereign on their 100th birthday; a contest which the supporters of the young won (on points).

At the same time I lived a full social life. I entertained my friends and authors in my own house. I tried to arrange luncheons or evening gatherings whenever any interesting author came from abroad, in order to introduce them to the English literary world, and parties to celebrate the publication of any special book. And I remember a party to celebrate the appearance of my hundredth book (this was *The Dark Peninsula* by Ernest Frost), in September of 1949, with fourscore guests packing my library and study.

I won't pretend that I didn't enjoy all this social life, in spite of the effort it cost me and in spite of the feeling that it postponed even further into the future the time I could spend on my own writing. I try to look at it objectively, and I think I can say that the fact that the fortunes of my publishing house depended more than those of other publishing houses on myself and my own assumed flair for finding and fostering new talent, made it almost obligatory for me to create such a social centre, where new acquaintances and friends could be made among authors, painters and exponents of the other arts. I wanted all those with whose work I was dealing to feel that they were as much part of a band of friends inspired by common ideals, as involved in a commercial venture (which in any case would never make my fortune).

My interests were by no means confined to the literary world. I have always had a special interest in painting and painters; the theatre, not merely because my sister Beatrix is one of the great tragic and character actresses of her time, has always evoked in me a thrilled and expectant response; and during the war I began to find a deep artistic satisfaction in the art of ballet.

I was an early spectator when any new ballet by Fred Ashton or Robert Helpmann or Ninette de Valois herself was put on by the Sadler's Wells Company, and was in the audience on that exciting evening when they graduated at last to the reopened Royal Opera House, in their performance of *The Sleeping Beauty*.

Their greatest post-war triumph was, I suppose, their first tour as a company of the United States, in the autumn of 1949. This triumph came at a good moment for national morale, when we, the victors in the recent war, felt poor and humiliated, floundering in a bog of misfortune out of which it seemed we might never be able to struggle. It was especially satisfying, as many American ballet folk, who had come over after the end of the war, had been rather lukewarm and patronizing — or so we thought. My friend Alexis Rassine, who accompanied them as one of the chief male soloists, kept me regularly posted with accounts of the rapturous critics and audiences, and their almost royal progress across the continent in their special trains.

The members of the company loaded themselves up with gifts for their (in comparison with the austerity-free Yankees) underprivileged friends in Britain: food, shirts, nylons, sweaters, ties, scent and anything else their dazzled eyes lit upon in the great department stores of the American cities. As far as I could make out, the British customs, on their return home like a flock of twittering swallows with the spring, gave one look at their toppling luggage, despaired, and chalked them through without a word.

« 6 »

IT was just about this time that an event occurred which acted like a small but violent earthquake in the fairly closely knit intellectual world of our generation, reminding us that the past could suddenly strike out at us and that under the surface a subsidence of earth could have taken place without anyone realizing it.

In the first week in June (1951) the Foreign Office suddenly announced that two members of the service had been missing since May 25, and had been "suspended with effect from June 1st." Their names were Donald Maclean and Guy Burgess.

The shock was terrific, because it became clear almost immediately that the two young officials had not merely gone off on an unauthorized holiday but were in flight, and heading pretty certainly for Moscow. The *Daily Express*, which was on the scent at once and soon had the whole pack of its top reporters in full cry, announced simply: "There is a possibility that they may have important papers with them."

Guy Burgess was an Etonian, several years my junior, whom I had got to know through mutual friends some time in the late 'thirties. He was an extremely intelligent, sanguine character, with a boisterous sense of fun and a malicious edge to his tongue. Not creative himself, he nevertheless had an immense interest in the writers who were my contemporaries, particularly Wystan Auden and Stephen Spender, and in his own way had tagged along with the pre-war anti-fascist movement of which they were the leading literary lights. He was an old friend and devoted admirer of Rosamond.

Donald Maclean was not known to me personally, though I may have been introduced to him at some party during the 'forties. He was, however, well known to many of my friends, including Cyril Connolly, Goronwy Rees, and Philip Toynbee, and also to my cousin Sir Ronald Campbell. Ronald had been the British Ambassador at Cairo when Donald, who had been appointed Head of Chancery at the Embassy in 1948, had what was euphemistically known as a "breakdown," the culmination of a long series of drinking bouts. Ronald, it seems to me, treated him with great tolerance and consideration, and had had him quietly sent home a year before the dramatic flight.

During those early post-war years it so happened that I saw very little of Guy, and I knew neither of his close association with Donald Maclean, nor of his crazy behaviour in America, which had led to his recall by the Foreign Office.

At a French Embassy reception the day after the news broke, nobody seemed able or willing to believe in the full implications. The theory was even canvassed that the story was a double bluff on the part of the Foreign Office.

As far as my own particular part in the story is concerned, the first thing that happened was that, by pure chance, very soon after the French reception, I happened to ring up Humphrey Slater about something to do with his writing. He told me, to my amazement, that he'd been almost certain for a long time that Donald had been a secret member of the Communist Party, and had wondered whether he ought to turn him in. The second thing was that, the same day, Rosamond told me, over the telephone, an extraordinary story. She said that ever since the news of Guy's flight had come out, she had been trying to recall everything that Guy had said and done in the years before 1945 when they had seen much of one another. She had been uneasy for a long time; now she was completely convinced not only that Guy, originally out of pure idealism, *had* become a Communist agent, but also that even if he had wanted to he had been unable later to get out of the one-way lobster-pot, and that his flight — she felt sure — was due to the fact that the security net was closing round him. She further told me that she had already got in touch with the security authorities, and though she had been mystified by the lack of urgency with which an eminent military figure had appeared to treat the whole affair, she had managed to obtain an appointment and was going to tell them all she knew — and all her deductions.

On June 10 the *Observer* carried an interview with Stephen Spender, who was at that time holidaying in Italy. In it he said that he found it very difficult to believe that Guy was a Communist sympathizer, because only very shortly before he disappeared Guy had rung him up to praise his autobiography *World Within World*, which had many disillusioned things to say about Soviet Communism.

The same day, by coincidence, I wrote to Stephen about something entirely different. Here is my letter in full:

I wonder whether you can help me. I wrote to Wystan (c/o your address) before I went to Paris, asking him to help me land the British rights for *The King and the Corpse*. Do you remember if he ever got the letter?

I am rather anxious to take action about the book as soon as possible. What is Wystan's address?

Just a word, after reading what you said in this morning's *Observer* about Guy's disappearance. I was in touch yesterday with someone whom you know very well, who told me she'd worried for *years* about Guy, owing to a piece of information that came her way during the war; and now that all the pieces fitted together, she was absolutely sure.

And exactly the same information about D.M. — from someone else we both know; who had seriously thought during the last few months of denouncing him.

Assuming what these two people said is correct, it can't be long before the news breaks.

Hope you and Natasha and the children are having a lovely time.

On the evening of Friday, June 15, there was a ring at my doorbell. Two reporters from the *Daily Express* were on the steps. They asked if they could interview me about the Burgess and Maclean affair. I told them I didn't think I could help them very much, but if they wished they could come in and talk for a few minutes. I was not at all alarmed; if anything I was slightly amused, as it had become a joke in our circle to say, "Poor so-and-so hasn't been interviewed yet about Guy and Donald." I was still very green about the methods some of the popular newspapers were prepared to employ in order to get their story.

They asked a few routine questions about my acquaintance with the two missing men, and then suddenly said that they understood I had written to Stephen Spender with some important information. Startled by this, I began to say that there was nothing of any great importance in the letter except to urge caution on Stephen in his public pronouncements, when one of them cut in: "Mr. Lehmann, we have been talking to Spender on Lake Garda, and we have a copy here of your letter to him. May we read it to you?"

I listened in speechless amazement as my letter was read out verbatim. It seemed to me almost incredible that Stephen could have let them have my letter to copy. I had to think quickly, as it seemed to me essential that Rosamond's name should not come out, not only because she was now in contact with our counter-espionage people, but also to save her from being plagued by telephone calls, requests for interviews, and photographers.

The two reporters tried to press home their advantage, but I refused to be drawn about the identity of the woman I had referred to in my letter. They told me it was in the national interest that I should reveal her name. I replied to this extraordinary observation that she was already in touch with MI5, and that seemed to me to be that. After a little more nagging and needling they left, one of them remarking casually and charmingly, "If I were you, Mr. Lehmann, I would leave my telephone off the hook tomorrow morning."

The reason for this menacing piece of advice became clear next day. Splashed across the front page of the *Daily Express* was the headline: DIPLOMATS — THE SECRET. "Known to two people in England." MYSTERY WOMAN 'PHONES MI5. . . . As I began to read the story that followed, I was suddenly horrified to see that the third paragraph of my letter to Stephen had been photographed and reproduced in the middle. So Stephen had actually *given* them my letter. My bewilderment and anger were now boundless. I sat down at once and wrote what is generally known as a "stinker" to Stephen. And I arranged an interview with my lawyer for the Monday morning, for it seemed to me that at the very least the *Daily Express* had committed a gross breach of copyright in publishing extracts from my letter without getting my permission.

My letter to Lake Garda crossed one from Stephen. He was coming to from the anaesthetic of his excitement, and beginning to have qualms. If he could have known what persecution from the Press my sisters were already undergoing when he wrote, his letter would have had a very different tone. No, he had trustingly given my letter to the *Daily Express* and was only just beginning to grasp what use they might make of it. Already, before my "stinker" arrived, however, he had seen the full reports in the Italian Press of the repercussions of his indiscretion, and was "appalled and frightfully sorry." At the same time he believed that "fortunately these agitating things are soon forgotten."

Over in England the *Express* was doing its best to prevent that happy conclusion. My lawyer had already succeeded in getting them to admit breach of copyright. After some haggling they agreed to pay token compensation (a cheque for 100 guineas which I handed over to the Royal Literary Fund), and insert an apology. Perhaps this swift action prevented further exploitation of the episode in the paper, but the damage had been done. For days the only women the Press could think of as likely to be known intimately to myself and Stephen, i.e., my sisters, had been pursued by reporters in an inhuman and intolerable fashion. They sat on their door-steps, they rang their telephones without cease, they even besieged Beatrix in the theatre where she was appearing at the time.

Meanwhile Stephen's letters from Lake Garda grew more and more agitated, as he became fully and distressedly aware of the chain reaction he had set off. I did not write to him again; but my lawyer did, informing him that I still held him firmly responsible for what had happened. Stephen was certainly all penitence and anxious to present himself publicly in sackcloth and ashes. Unfortunately none of the schemes he proposed nor letters he drafted for publication could satisfactorily explain, to any averagely shrewd person following the case — or indeed to anyone who had not got the necessary key to Stephen's so often child-like psychology — one simple fact: why he had casually handed over my private letter to a reporter he had never seen before and of whom he had no knowledge. (It is only fair to say that, as he told me later, he expected my letter to be given back to him the same day.) He was advised by sage mutual friends to drop it, for fear of making matters worse. A year later, at my request, he got the *Ex-*

press to return the letter to me, thus setting at rest many unfair rumours that had for a time been rife.

Everyone, of course, is capable of insane-seeming actions in situations that knock them temporarily off their perch; people of highly strung artistic temperament perhaps more than others. Stephen's aberration, which I am now absolutely convinced had no malice about it, set back our friendship for a long while.

The hullabaloo that the *Daily Express*, as self-appointed substitute for the security services they considered incapable, made about the letter did not advance their desperate chase in search of the truth about Burgess and Maclean in the slightest. It only caused a great deal of pain to several totally innocent people who were trying to keep their heads and do their duty.

Friends rallied round with exemplary loyalty, deeply shaken though most of them were by what already looked like a deliberate act of treachery on the part of Guy and Donald. I remember with especial gratitude a letter expressing bewilderment and sympathy from Harold Nicolson, one of Guy's friends in an older generation, who was most deeply upset by the flight. When, some years later, the Soviet authorities eventually allowed Guy and Donald to admit to the world Press that they were living and working in Moscow, Harold, loyal to his friends above all things, did get in touch with Guy. But I myself never saw him nor spoke with him again. When I visited Leningrad and Moscow in 1963 for a congress of European writers he was already seriously ill, and the tragedy — for tragedy I continue to think it — was nearly over.

The "someone else" I mentioned in my letter in connection with Donald Maclean was, of course, Humphrey Slater, whose novel *The Conspirator* I had published two or three years before. The whole affair was as if the story of *The Conspirator* had taken on actual life among his friends.

« 7 »

ONE of the pleasures of living in London during these years was that I had friends and relations in country houses not too far away, and could make visits to them at week-ends, and during occasional longer spells of absence from my office. Manuscripts submitted by authors, known and unknown, were always in my suit-case. Sometimes I would devote almost the whole of a week-end to them; sometimes the hours passed away in pleasant discussion, walks and festivity.

From 1947 my mother lived in her new home outside Beaconsfield, where the most precious possessions from the old family home at Fieldhead, and all books, pictures and other objects, from statuettes and rowing trophies to Chinese candlesticks and walking-sticks, most of them loaded with associations of the past had, somehow or other, been rearranged in a far smaller space. As the years went by, my mother's lameness (from her accident) increased, and she gradually gave up many of the extraordinarily varied public interests she had had. Thus, she settled into an ever more detached calm, viewing us, I think, with occasional amusement as well as love: her ship seemed to sail into serene waters as she approached harbour, and people would remark not only on a freshness of complexion remarkable in an old lady of eighty, but also on the spiritual incandescence that underlay it.

She followed my publishing career with intense interest, reading all the books as they came out, and finding especial delight in the series of Henry James reprints in the Chiltern Library. We would sit for long hours of a Saturday or Sunday evening in her drawing-room, I with a pile of typescript on my lap, she with a copy of *Roderick Hudson* or *The Bostonians*, reading quietly together.

In the Isle of Wight, that still drew us all irresistibly as it had drawn us in our childhood, and our grandfather and grandmother a hundred years before, my beloved godmother, Violet Hammersley, still had her exquisite little early Victorian house at Totland Bay, only a few yards from the crumbling cliffs, with a glimpse of blue sea between the fuchsia bushes and the Spanish gorse.

To this abode she would invite me each year for bathing and (for she was a determined and almost indefatigable walker even in her seventies) climbs over the heather downs, past the abandoned forts of Napoleonic times, to the coloured cliffs of Alum Bay and the Tennyson Memorial above Freshwater. Even after my mother's death, some years later, it was impossible to think of Violet as old, except for her deafness and the sudden illnesses which overwhelmed her — and from which she seemed to arise so swiftly with indomitable vitality restored. With her dark hair that never turned white, and her voice as musical and vibrant as ever; with her enormous curiosity about people, politics, art and literature, her sense of humour, her dramatic retelling of stories from past and present, her habit of asking for immediate answers to the most profound and anxious problems, she still appeared to me as I had always known her.

Beyond Beaconsfield, on the road westwards, Rosamond was living in her beautiful, rambling Georgian house at Little Wittenham, under the shadow of the Clumps, with the upper reaches of the river only a few minutes away across the meadows. Beatrix had also installed herself in the large, picturesque barn in the same grounds, so a visit to one was always pleasantly a visit to both. From there it was easy to make sallies upon Oxford, and friends further north; in particular Rex Warner (after his return from abroad) and his second wife Barbara, daughter of Mary Hutchinson and previously married to Victor Rothschild, who occupied first of all a small but elegant country seat (there is no other word for it) in the village of Tackley, and then took a smaller house, with a long narrow flower-garden behind, in the little town of Woodstock, just outside the park precincts of Blenheim.

Some of my happiest memories are of those westward expeditions — which often turned into evening visits to the theatre at Stratford — between 1949 and 1952. I find in my diary the following extracts.

At the end of July 1951:

Yesterday I motored from Beaconsfield where I had spent two nights with Mother, down to Woodstock to see Rex and Barbara. Behind the unassuming but very attractive Georgian grey stone façade of this house, only a few yards from the gates of Blenheim Palace, I found tremendous preparations afoot: hammerings, sawings, paintings, a large house with handsome rooms already with beautiful wall-paper laid on the walls and beautiful furniture stacked everywhere; Barbara in the midst of it all, looking pretty and desirable as ever, but a little more matronly, slipping out from time to time to keep an eye on her new baby Lucy, who has the brightest blue eyes and the most remarkable society smile, in a pram in the long finger of garden behind; Rex returning from the pub, as rugged, jolly, imperturbable-seeming and delightful in conversation as ever. We had lunch at the "Bear," talked a great deal about the Burgess-Maclean business and cracked jokes at one another for a solid two hours. I persuaded Rex to join my "reading panel," and then under the apple-tree he read me passages from his new translation (for the Penguin Classics) of Thucydides.

After that I left for Banbury, Sulgrave and Weston, to stay with Sachie and Georgia Sitwell, through the silvery-green rolling landscape (I had almost forgotten how beautiful) into the very heart of rural England — green-golden fields of corn, starred with poppies and cow-parsley and vistas criss-crossed with hazy dark-green hedgerows and blobs of elms. When I arrived, I found Sachie and Georgia out in the garden. We sat there and talked, again about the Burgess-Maclean affair, and then about the Sadler's Wells and the Oliviers. Sachie showed me his old-fashioned roses, an enormous collection in bed after bed, intensely perfumed but looking rather in need of dead-heading. In the morning I took some colour-pictures of the old house and the two of them, and then set off for Stratford, while the earth slowly turned to its iron-red Warwickshire colour; lunch at the "Falcon," a deep inhaling of the air of beloved Stratford; and then back to Oxford and Little Wittenham to stay at the Barn with Beatrix.

During the years while Rosamond was reading for the firm, our editorial discussions took place, of course, mainly in London. Sometimes, however, we continued them at Little Wittenham, on walks up to the Clumps and down along the river. Her daughter Sally and her son Hugo were often there. There had been talk of my nephew coming into publishing with me, but when he discussed it with his grandfather, Lord Milford, the idea had not found great favour. His clinching remark was, according to Hugo: "Your Uncle John's got a good business head, I've always known that — but publishing is a spiv's game."

It was not only to Lord Milford that publishing sometimes seemed a spiv's or at least a mug's game. I find in my diary at about the same time the following entry:

Who would be a publisher? I sometimes wonder how much longer I can stick it, second nature though it had become after all these years. It's not merely the endless MSS. to be read, translations to be vetted, drafts about which advice must be given; the administrative and financial job that comes on top of the literary and artistic job; but the endless anxiety about each book, the letters and telephone calls to critics and editors that go with proofs and advance copies; and, following that, the strain of disappointment and worry if certain books are not reviewed soon enough in the right places, a feeling as if the result of a crucial lottery was about to be declared when one opens the *Sunday Times* or the *Observer* each week. And then the problems of other publicity continually going with it: there is never a moment when one of the current books, one's children, is not giving anxiety in one way or another. . . . Far too much of the last three weeks, afternoons and evenings, I would gladly have devoted to reading the multitude of books I long to get my teeth into — let alone preparation for my autobiographical book and the poems that begin to swim again into my mind — instead has had to be devoted to reading, with that word-for-word care they demand, the translations of Stendhal's *Aux Ames Sensibles*, Malraux's *Les Noyers d'Altenbourg* and Pavese's *La Luna e i Falo*, which have just come in. Proud to have them, yes indeed, but when shall I find someone I can trust (and pay) to do just this special kind of work for me?

In the autumn of 1951 Rosamond, deeply troubled in her personal life, decided to leave Wittenham and live in London. I felt extremely sad about it, as I had always thought of her house as a dream fulfilment of my ideal of Thames Valley manor, with its purity of design, its warmly mellowing brickwork, and ancient history embedded in every field around. As bad, it meant that Beatrix would be leaving the barn. The last Sunday night I spent there, at the end of November, Hugo and his new wife Margaret were there, and Rosamond was working at her novel *The Echoing Grove* until Rex and Barbara arrived for dinner: the party then went with a roar, and we shouted and laughed till long after midnight.

I took Rosamond back to London with me, and we discussed what we had touched on the evening before with the Warners — the comparative failure of new writers to materialize on this side of the Atlantic, the continuing sense of war exhaustion, the empty despair that seemed to characterize (at that moment) the war generation, and the need of our generation, who had stronger roots, to hold on against all in the coming years. Rosamond then said something that touched me deeply: "All our friends think the work you are doing is almost superhuman, but I think you ought to be editing *the* literary magazine . . . of course you can't, with all the problems of publishing on your shoulders."

Meanwhile, as I have already mentioned, I had bought a cottage in the country, on the northern borders of Sussex, not far from Three Bridges. It had once been part of the Montefiore estate, which began to be broken up and built over in the 'twenties. Originally a farm building, or forge, it had been converted soon after the war into a habitable house by an architect for his own use. No sooner had he finished it, however, than he decided to leave for South Africa — perhaps appalled by the restrictions and generally black outlook of the winter of 1947. I was therefore the first to live in it.

What immediately appealed to me and made me feel that I must acquire it was not so much the house itself, which was attractively painted white and as unlike as possible the usual modern bungalow of the Home Counties, but the situation. The two acres or so of its grounds were filled with huge trees, nearly a score of great spreading oaks at least two hundred years old, beeches with mighty trunks and conifers as well, and a host of willows, aspens, silver birches, sycamores, poplars, yews, hollies, cypresses, portugal laurels, old twisted hawthorne and crab-apple-trees. This zoo of trees was mainly grouped, except on the side of the cottage, round a large pond or miniature lake which had originally served as a hammer pond in the far-off days when all that part of the country had been almost continuous forest. We soon discovered that it was chock-full of fish, though unfortunately not of a very interesting sort. It was also full of the most grotesque junk, relics of its wartime use as a dump by a Canadian regiment stationed nearby. This was also true of parts of the garden — if one could have given the name of garden to the overgrown wilderness out of which the cottage rose like a miniature version of the castle in which the Sleeping Beauty was discovered by Prince Florimond.

I have always had a deep need to live near water, whether river or sea or lake, and I had a vision at once of a smooth lawn made from the cottage to the banks of the lake, planted here and there with flowering shrubs and crowded on the edge of the water with bulbs to flower from early spring to late summer: crocuses, jonquils, irises, day lilies and montebretias. When my friend Alexis Rassine saw it, he also fell in love with it and was eager to become part-owner, envisaging it as a place in which to repose and enjoy garden pursuits in the intervals of the long tours which stretched ahead of the now world-famous Sadler's Wells Ballet. Carlotta approved, to judge by the excitement of her furiously wagging tail sticking out of the undergrowth and the reckless plunges she made into the water in pursuit of moorhens. I decided to buy.

The immediate tasks were to remove the junk, cut down dead trees, hack away undergrowth and sprawling laurels, and create lawns, orchard, rock garden and pathways out of the waste. The work went on all during autumn and spring. Lorry after lorry was loaded with broken bricks, rusted coils of barbed wire, huge oil-containers that had been wallowing in the water like hippopotami, shoals of old cans and soggy, discarded army boots, and were driven away to return with good earth to moderate the heavy clay, paving stones, gravel, and young bushes of every sort: aucubas, rhododendrons, azaleas, magnolias, camellias, hydrangeas, cotoneaster, veronica, berberis — and roses. Gradually the vision took shape: it was an intoxicating time, and I have rarely enjoyed myself so much.

Now that I have owned Lake Cottage for two decades, I still look on it as a source of inexhaustible interest and pleasure: a refuge for work, a place to entertain friends and relations and refresh one's own petrol-filled lungs with country air and garden scents, and a centre for expeditions. There is never a time, except in the brief depths of winter, when some flower or ornamental leaves or sprays from a blossoming shrub cannot be gathered from the grounds. As much as anything, I have enjoyed observing wild life there. At the beginning, we were surrounded, in the fields and copses just outside our limits, by rabbits and hares, and had to buy fences to protect our tender young fruit-trees from them; now that myxamatosis has wiped them out, I would gladly sacrifice a row or two of lettuces to have them back. Hedgehogs and moles hide themselves in the woodland, squirrels spring from branch to branch, and steal stealthily across the lawns thinking to evade canine pursuit on their way to raid the peach- and pear-trees. There are old inhabitants, a vole and a pair of grass-snakes who can sometimes in summer be seen swimming across the water. For years a large toad lived behind some flower-pots in the greenhouse I built to house a vine, feasting on the insects that would have feasted on the plants, and became almost a friend.

Above all, as the housing estates of the new town of Crawley have crept ever nearer, the place has become a bird sanctuary. Year after year, moorhens have never failed to build their nests under the trees on the opposite side of the lake. From time to time mallard duck settle in the evening on the water, and are gone at the first opening of a window in the morning. Until recent years herons used regularly to come and fish under the branches: once in the woodland I managed to catch one that had been wounded in some way, and dumped it, hissing, over the fence, which it was unable to climb or fly over. Now I think they have gone, frightened by houses pressing ever closer to their old nesting-places on the lower lake beyond my boundary. Kingfishers still haunt, however, flashing in sudden sapphire from branch to branch. Owls hoot almost nightly among the tree-tops, and once I found one dead, inexplicably, under a magnolia-tree on the lawn. Robins have divided up their territory and sing with piercing sweetness to defend it. The dawn chorus in early summer is deafening, and in winter crumbs thrown on the hard ground bring, beside the robins, hedge sparrows and house sparrows, cole-tits and blue-tits, blackbirds, thrushes, chaffinches (and sometimes even a bullfinch), woodpeckers, nut-hatches, tree creepers and wrens, and swooping down for sudden forays, jays and magpies, rooks and jackdaws and pigeons.

In the first spring I spent there I noticed to my delight that clumps of aconites and wild anemones appeared at the foot of some of the trees in the woodland. Later, the whole untamed area was carpeted with violets, interspersed with primroses and bluebells. Nearer the house, at the foot of some of the tallest oaks, I planted dog-tooth violets, wild cyclamens and autumn crocuses, which now have a hard time to survive against the pouncing and rolling of Carlotta's successor, my golden retriever Rudy, who has chosen this particular corner to amuse himself with his ball.

Perhaps the most interesting of all the encounters I had in Paris during those years was my interview with Ivan Bunin, which was arranged by a friend and agent, Dr. H. I felt not a little emotion at the thought of meeting this remarkable genius, whose work I had admired for so long, the last living representative of the great line of pre-revolutionary Russian novelists. I saw before me a little goblin king of a man, with skin yellow as creased parchment, blowing his toothless cheeks out as he talked — a little in French to me, and a great deal in Russian to Dr. H. He was in his eightieth year at the time, but he could, I felt, have been a hundred and fifty years old. His eyes, his whole face — that reminded me at moments of Leonard Woolf, though more elfin — gave an impression of fatigue and illness. And then suddenly a smile of great fascination would flash across it, and his eyes be lit by a wicked spark of lightning, especially when speaking of the misdeeds of editors and publishers, and the inhumanity of the tax laws. Only shortly before, I had arranged to publish an English translation by David Magarshack of Lydia Avilov's story of her relationship with Chekhov in the 'nineties, *Chekhov in My Life.* I mentioned this to him, and he immediately said that I should not read too much into this romantic story. He had known Lydia Avilov well, and he was fairly certain that she had been more in love with Chekhov than he with her. In any case, their affair had never been intimate in the true sense of the word.

I have described my long discussion with André Malraux when he was *chef de cabinet* of General de Gaulle directly after the war, and my first encounter with him during the Spanish Civil War. I had always been haunted by the slightly bulging greenish eyes in the pale unsmiling face, the long French nose and the finely sculptured hands, and the strange *other* sound (due to an old wound), as if from a second person, that accompanied his voice as he poured out his theories on politics, war, literature and art. Humourless, obsessively romantic about danger and daring, a mythopoeic believer in destiny to the point of absurdity, Malraux seemed to me the same twenty years later on as when I first knew him. I have nevertheless always thought of him as one of the key writers of our time, and brilliant though the coruscation of ideas may be in the great works of aesthetics he devoted himself to before he rejoined his hero general when he came to political power

[487]

again in the 'fifties, I have never ceased to regret his abandonment of the novel. I now had designs on him. I knew he had refused to allow the first volume of his unfinished trilogy, *Les Noyers d'Altenbourg*, to be translated, on the grounds that it was but a fragment and would not properly be understood without the other two, unwritten volumes of what was to have been called *La Lutte Avec l'Ange*. He had told me that if the Gestapo had not taken away the notes he had made, he would have completed the work and revised *Les Noyers d'Altenbourg* in the process. Nevertheless, it seemed to me a work of such profound interest and power that it ought without question to appear in an English translation.

I went to see him in his home in Boulogne-sur-Seine, in the hope of persuading him. He received me in a study leading off a large, modern, white-painted music-room studio, looking I thought rather iller than usual, though in the intervals of the hoarse spasms which as usual punctuated his conversation, I seemed to detect — for the first time — an occasional faint ghost of a smile. He talked a great deal of his *Saturne*, which he seemed very keen that I should have; but I gradually worked him round to the subject of *Les Noyers*, and at last extracted a half-promise that I should have the English rights. At the same time, to my great surprise, he told me that another project that was waiting for the completion of his great series on the Psychology of Art was a sequel to *l'Espoir*, and suggested that I should agree to take that too. Nothing could have suited me better, but though I did very soon succeed in publishing *Les Noyers*, in a translation by Xan Fielding, as *The Walnut Trees of Altenburg*, the sequel to *l'Espoir* is still, alas, to be written.

Many years later, when he was already Minister of Fine Arts, we had a long discussion one evening in his office after all his officials had left. I reproached him for neglecting *his* destiny as a novelist, more important than politics, or even theories about art. He then told me that he considered it essential for a man if he was to remain truly alive, to be where the central stream of his time was running. Nevertheless, he said, in some part of his mind all that he was witnessing and all the drama he was taking part in, as one of the General's closest collaborators, was being quietly and secretly digested into the cud of art. The rest of our talk — which was, indeed, mainly a monologue with promptings from me — about the future of France and the world, though of the utmost fascination, cannot be revealed here. André Malraux has a rooted objection to being reported, and would certainly not have spoken as freely as he did if I had not made a promise to keep silence.

André Malraux has suffered so many abrupt, unbelievably unkind blows of fate in his private and family life, that it would not be surprising if he treated political ambitions as a way of deadening the pain. Nevertheless I feel fairly certain that his close association with de Gaulle arises from a deeper, anterior need in his nature. Viewed from a certain angle, what one can perhaps admire most about him is his refusal to play in with the inbred Parisian world of inflated intellectuals, of *cher maître* this and *hommages* that. During one of our discussions in the 'thirties, I asked him what he thought of Gide's *Au Retour de l'URSS*. He immediately replied that the trouble with Gide was that during his Russian trip he had only met the boring Soviet intellectuals. Now if he had only met some of the glorious Soviet airmen. . . .

One day, on one of these visits, I persuaded André Gide to let me bring young Gore Vidal to be introduced to him. This was an event that Gore had dreamed of for years, and he was in a high state of excitement as we rang the door-bell in the Rue Vaneau. The master was in his most cordial mood, and questioned Gore closely about the restraints on frankness about sex in American writing. At the end Gore rather nervously mentioned that he had sent Gide a copy of his *The City and the Pillar*, though he had received no acknowledgement. Gide replied that he remembered perfectly well; and then immediately switched the conversation to the stranger perversions that were prevalent, he was told, among rich spinsters and widows in New York. Afterwards, Gore sighed and said he supposed that just meant that Gide had not read his book. I was not so sure. Roger Martin du Gard has told the story how Gide came to visit him once at the sea-side, and appeared delighted when he suggested he should read him his latest play. While the reading was in progress, Gide took up a pair of field-glasses and studied two young men, who were bathing naked on a distant part of the beach, with minute attention. Roger Martin du Gard, furious, finally stopped reading. The same evening Gide, pretending not to have noticed the painful impression he had made, launched into a detailed critique of the work — which showed that he had followed everything.

In the winter of 1949–50 I was again in Paris, and rang Gide up. He was not at all well, he said, but he would make a special exception and see me. When I entered his room, I was horrified and wished I had not taken advantage of his kindness: his face was grey, his cheeks were sunken, he was unshaven and gasping for breath. Nevertheless, rather miraculously, he showed his usual animated curiosity about friends and events in the literary world of England. He was particularly interested in the new, unbowdlerized version of *De Profundis* which had just then been published. He told me that he remembered once witnessing, in Algiers, a terrible quarrel between Oscar Wilde and Bosie, which left Wilde white and shaking. Afterwards, Wilde turned to him and said: "Everyone imagines I am in the midst of joy and carefree happiness — and you see what has just happened — it happens all the time."

Two years later, I went to see Dorothy Bussy, Lytton Strachey's sister, whose translation of Valéry's *Dance and the Soul* I had just published, in her home in Nice. She told me the saga of Gide's funeral: how infuriated Mme. Lambert and Roger Martin du Gard were to discover, on arrival in the little village, not only a deputation of "*anciens combattants*" but also a Protestant pastor who actually read out some passages from the *Journal* and followed the recitation by prayers at the grave-side. Roger Martin du Gard kept silence until it was all over, then could contain his indignation no longer and made a terrible *esclandre* about this insult to an immovable atheist. "It seems destined," said Janie, Dorothy's daughter, "that funerals should always be either unendurable or comic." Gide, I believe, would have found it comic, as he kept his sense of humour and his defiance of the Churches to the end, as his remarks on his death-bed about Cardinal Mindzenty show.

« 8 »

ONE of the most exciting things, for my generation, after the war, was the rediscovery of Italy. Englishmen have, I believe, a natural affinity for that country which goes a long way back into history. The stupid interlude of Fascism did not kill that affinity, but made intelligent islanders, particularly those of artistic leanings, miserable that a place they had loved, and continued to love, had been as it were requisitioned and scrawled over by a gang of interlopers who were using it for evil purposes. When Fascism had at last been brought to its absurd and bloody end, I think that most of us were only too eager to resume a relationship that had brought so much happiness, and had been so fruitful in the past; to revel again in the idyllic nature of that country, to make friends again with a naturally friendly people whose temperament seems so precisely complementary to our own, and to revisit the inestimable masterpieces of art of which Italy is the treasure-house and cornucopia.

In addition to this deep-welling readiness to forgive the wrongs and forget the bitterness, we had a new interest, full of surprise and pleasure, in the post-Fascist Italy that began to emerge from the ruins. I am not speaking of politics, but of the vigorous ferment of creative ideas that we increasingly discovered as the natural genius of the people reasserted itself: new artists, new poets and novelists, new movements of thought and feeling that appeared not merely in Rome but in all the other great centres: Milan, Venice, Florence and Naples. In those early post-war years, Italians had not yet had the chance to show that they could compete with the cleverest and most inventive brains in the world in engineering and design, particularly in cars and men's as well as women's fashions, but there was already a sparkle in the intellectual air that made one feel that anything was possible. While some millennial quality or virtue seemed to remain almost untouched, the process of change was accelerating. Not merely the grotesque Italy of Mussolini, but also the other Italy of E. M. Forster and D. H. Lawrence was whirling away into the past.

For myself, who had scarcely visited the country at all since my teens, to the pleasure of discovering the new Italy was added the pleasure of getting to know, with immensely increased understanding and appreciation, the ancient Italy that I had neglected for so long. My ignorance was not so great as in the case of Greece, but I found that even when I had become acquainted with classical ruins, architectural splendours, frescoes, sculptures and dazzling landscapes all those years before, I was seeing them with new eyes and with as great an intensity of aesthetic response as I saw what was hitherto entirely unknown to me except through photographs and descriptions.

The first post-war encounter with Rome was perhaps the supreme moment for me. It was the beginning of June, the oleanders were out, the flower-sellers' stalls at the bottom of the Spanish Steps were piled high with spring blossoms, and the late spring light was making the characteristic rose-pink and golden-orange tints of the city glow with what seemed to be a soft internal illumination, so that one was surprised to see it fade with the fading of the day. I wandered about, exploring Roman ruins and baroque churches, feeling that to walk among the pines of the Borghese Gardens and the mazy walls and tessellated floors of the Baths of Caracalla, or through beckoning side-streets where palm branches curled luxuriantly over high walls topped with white statues against a deep-blue sky, was like awakening into a new kind of happiness. Ever since, Rome has retained for me something of that first shock of delight. In spite of not particularly caring for Italian food, I feel better there, more alert and impressionable than anywhere else. Each time I visit it, I find new beauty, a church façade or interior, a vista, or corner of ancient ruins incorporated in later building, an Egyptian obelisk sticking up improbably in the middle of a sun-drenched piazza, a flight of steps or a curiously carved fountain I had not noticed before.

About eighteen months earlier, Rosamond and I had been very much struck by a novel by a new Italian author called Ennio Flaiano. The title of the novel was *Tempo di Uccidere*, the story of an Italian officer in Abyssinia whose brief affair with a native woman entangles him in a web of guilt and fear that seems to become more intricate the more he struggles to free himself from it. What impressed me was not only the extraordinary dramatic power of the telling, but the psychological insight, the compassion and irony. We published the novel as *Mariam*, in a translation by Stuart Hood.

As I was extremely keen to find out more about this remarkable author, I got in touch with him as soon as I arrived in Rome. It was a lucky throw: he turned up at my hotel in a little Fiat, and offered himself at once as a guide round Rome. He proved a delightful, witty, intelligent friend, and a tremendous asset in my sight-seeing. Without those hair-raising sallies, by day and by night, into the infinite confusion of Rome's geographical lay-out I do not think I should ever have approached an intimate understanding of the city and its treasures.

One evening, he introduced me to the Trastevere district, a world in itself that I had not been even aware of during my visit as a young Etonian more than two decades before. We bounced through its winding cobbled streets, passing as if in a fairy tale (to me) in and out of little piazzas with bubbling fountains and silver baroque church fronts and crumbling palaces. Everywhere the inhabitants were sitting out in the streets, round tables and lights, arguing and drinking wine, sometimes, as Flaiano pointed out, between two broken Roman pillars, or under an old Roman carved shop sign. When I asked my guide whether they would be discussing politics or family affairs, he replied: "No, no, just football — nothing but football."

Soon after the war, I had made the acquaintance of the redoubtable Marguerite Caetani, who became Princess Bassiano and then Ducesa di Sermoneta. An American heiress, born Marguerite Chapin in Connecticut in 1880 (and therefore only a few years younger than my own mother), a true-life Princess Casamassima married to an Italian aristocrat of extremely ancient lineage, with inflexible will-power and a passion for the arts, she had before the war — between 1924 and 1932 — run a literary and artistic magazine in Paris called *Commerce*. In this she had the help of some of the most notable French intellectuals of the day, including Valery Larbaud and Leon-Paul Fargue. St. Jean Perse translated T. S. Eliot (who was related to her) for *Commerce*, and Valery Larbaud some early passages of *Ulysses*. It was a most distinguished venture.

Since the war, she had started in Italy a multi-lingual literary magazine to which she gave the picturesque name of the street in Rome where the ancestral Caetani palazzo stood, *Botteghe Oscure*. Every number of this bulky occasional magazine had an Italian, a French, and an Anglo-American section, each under a different editor or rather sub-editor. She wanted to enlist my help in finding young British contributors, and I was able to suggest to her various names of poets, to some of whom she afterwards became a most generous patron. *Botteghe Oscure* never made anything but a large loss, and was heavily subsidized by her own private fortune. She ran it on the admirable system of paying her contributors — who included Dylan Thomas, Vernon Watkins, Theodore Roethke, Robert Lowell, Tennessee Williams and Burns Singer for the Anglo-American section — what she thought, or found out that they needed; and when she became particularly interested in a young poet she would give him additional support by providing him with free accommodation somewhere on her family properties. In some curious way Marguerite managed to retain the puritan New England prejudices of her upbringing, while publishing avant-garde authors who flouted them all.

She was at her country estate of Ninfa, south of Rome in the hills, on the occasion of my visit, and invited me out for luncheon there one Sunday. I remember in particular how she told me that during the war when rumours came that the Germans were approaching, the entire population of Ninfa, with their household goods and beasts, with Marguerite and her husband at their head, removed themselves to the mountain fastnesses of Sermoneta — which we could see in the blue distance as we drank our coffee — and locked themselves in, in true medieval, feudal fashion.

On my way to Rome, I had stopped off in Florence to visit my old friend Harold Acton at his treasure-filled family villa, La Pietra, on the Via Bolognese. I spent a great deal of time with Harold, for whom, ever since Eton days, I had had a deep affection. During the 'thirties our ways had parted. While much of my time was spent in Central Europe, he had settled in Peking, to enjoy the happiest period of his life, in the last days of a society to which his own extraordinary sense of Oriental courtesy, his erudite and mischievous wit, and his devotion to the ancient Chinese way of life instinctively drew him. In his autobiography, *Memoirs of an Aesthete*, he has described how, after the London house he shared with his brother had been sold, he decided that Fascist Italy was too stifling for him, and set out on his travels. As Odysseus was ensnared by the spells of Circe, so Harold in these travels fell under the spell of China. He did not return till 1939, when I began to see him again. I have described how we wrote to one another continually as he was moved about the world in his R.A.F. postings, until he finished up in liberated Paris. Fond and loyal, with a clairvoyant understanding of my deepest impulses, he would say to me, in moments when I was discouraged or ruffled by passing setbacks: "Don't be defeated by things of no importance. Believe in your star, my dear John, believe in your star."

I remember my first evening with him in the city as one of especial delight and illumination. Florence, absurd though it sounds to say it, was still strange to me — in my early forties. Engrossed in conversation, we suddenly came upon the floodlit façades, of baptistry, campanile and duomo, and I caught my breath at the unexpected splendour of chequerboard marble in that dramatic light.

La Pietra, of which I had had a romantic mental image ever since I had read Harold's autobiography, was no disappointment: in fact the reality appeared more beautiful than the dream. His father had filled the spacious rooms with priceless, often ravishingly beautiful quattrocento works of art — he had begun collecting in the far-off days when masterpieces were to be had for a (comparative) song. Outside, terrace after descending terrace of formal garden overhung the distant view of the city. Amongst these bosky terraces one continually came across weather-worn garden statues, mostly Venetian in style and very much to my taste. But the features that perhaps struck me most powerfully on his first visit were the lemon garden at the back of the house, and the great, narrow dipping avenue of cypresses that led from the front to the park gates.

It was not till two or three years later that I met Bernard Berenson, the sage of I Tatti, the princely villa further up in the hills. Rosamond had become a close and much-admired friend; and I was invited up one day in spring. I saw him sitting on the sofa in his drawing-room, a frail little man with a small head and a neat white beard. I found him very genial and charming and welcoming, though his conversation on this occasion was not very witty or very profound. He was surrounded by adoring American, English and Italian women, who treated him as a mixture of the Oracle of Delphi and God the Father. I must confess that this atmosphere dismayed me (though I should have been prepared for it), and I could not entirely resist the question rising in my mind: whether all this reverence and adoration would have been lavished on him if he had not made a great fortune by his transactions in the picture markets of the world. The next day I confessed these doubts to Harold. He calmed them by saying that he himself found that the cult sometimes reached nauseating heights (or depths), but there was no doubt in his mind that B.B. was a great intellectual figure of our time, especially in his far-reaching, continuous work of art-attribution; though he had certain reservations about the whole Duveen phase.

I must add that B.B. himself started off by mocking his raison d'être, observing to me that "art is a vast department in the empire of humbug." And he followed this by some very uncomplimentary references to Duveen.

The main object, or rather the starting point of my visit to Italy that spring, was to attend a meeting in Venice of the Société Européenne de Culture, to which I had been invited as an English delegate. This society was the brain-child of a young Italian professor of Padua University, Umberto Campagnola, full of demonic energy and slightly inchoate dreams (which I found characteristic of post-war Italy) of creating a cultural society where intellectuals of the European nations of the West could sit down at the same table with their dittos of the eastern iron-curtain nations, and engage in a prolonged *dialogue*. This *dialogue* was supposed to resolve differences of outlook, contribute to peace and international amity, and make of the intellectual world an effective force independent of politics — or rather *influencing* politics by its independent harmony — but unfortunately, at this stage of the cold war, took no account of the fact that iron-curtain intellectuals permitted to attend such gatherings were bound to be Marxist propagandists incapable (on the surface at any rate) of being influenced or deflected in any way at all. One either played their game or remained glaring as before. Another difficulty was the incapacity of the post-war Italians (and to a lesser degree of the French) to understand the English mind, our unshakeable preference for pragmatic rather than dogmatic solutions, and our deep suspicion of rhetoric. This failure in understanding was made worse by the fact that we had gone through no experience of German occupation and largely Communist-led resistance movements, and had not been landed with large Communist parties in our body politic. The result was that distinguished Latin intellectuals would release torrents of rhetoric couched in Marxist or pseudo-Marxist jargon, while the Anglo-Saxons looked more and more uncomfortable, bewildered and bored; sometimes (I am afraid) sniggering at one another behind their hands. Nor could French or Italians understand the absolute lack of status of writers in Britain. They were inclined to regard our diffident apologies on this subject, our attempt to explain that high-sounding declarations and denunciations of this or that (which we all signed) would cut no ice at home, as further examples of Anglo-Saxon duplicity.

Nevertheless, I must admit that in spite of the stifling and largely useless *séances de travail*, these congresses and assemblies attracted me, not merely because one received free and generous hospitality abroad, but also because it gave one the opportunity to meet many interesting writers from many countries *outside* the conference-room. And what more entrancing city to hold a congress in than Venice?

After a few days, I wrote in my diary:

I find it almost impossible to define and capture the effect Venice has on me. The multiplicity of impressions confuse and stimulate me beyond measure, the beauty of the buildings, the history within the buildings, the beauty of sudden passing youthful features — surely the young are more beautiful here than anywhere else in Italy except Rome. And always there is the appeal of the sea beyond anything one is doing or saying, beyond anywhere one is, the invitation to the light, the colour, the freedom of the lagoon — and then the open sea. What is wonderful in this city at night, as one crosses the silent bridges over the side-street canals, is to see the *sleeping* gondolas, perhaps very gently rocking on a water into which a little moonlight has been shaken. And at dusk, as I go down the Grand Canal, I keep my eyes open in tense anticipation on the *piano nobile* of the palaces, for most probably someone inside will just be switching on the lights, and chandelier after chandelier will begin to sparkle and dance, with all their exquisite fantasy of silvery and coloured glass leaves and sea beasts and stars. The little, shadowy creeper-festooned *calle* seemed more mysterious and inviting than I remembered them, the ringing, clanging, chiming, booming of the bells more enveloping, the mood — with an English destroyer in and Italian sailors everywhere as well, tourists beginning to pour in — more recklessly than ever; the pagan gods winking behind every pillar. But *not* a city for serious conferences, because nothing can be serious here, nothing has been serious for generations, the atmosphere of fantasy and frivolous merry-making is far too strong. Perhaps one should write something to examine the demoralization caused by water if brought into the very veins of our daily life. . . .

As I listened to the sonorously intoned platitudes of the speakers at our inaugural session, I was aware all the time of the louder voice of the dazzling golden surroundings, the glittering reaches of the lagoon outside the windows.

One of the most interesting people I met during this Congress — or rather, met again after many years — was Louis Guilloux, novelist of Brittany, author of an excellent book before the war, *Le Sang Noir*, and a leading figure with Malraux, Sartre, Nizan, Cassou and Chamson in the intellectual anti-fascist movement of the 'thirties.

One evening he hauled me off to the piazza to "*boire une coupe*" with him, and discuss what had happened to us in the twelve years since we had last met. Looking rather like a miniature Lloyd George, with many rhetorical gestures and smoothings back of his disordered greying locks, he told me about his war experiences: the German terror in Brittany, the dangerous chance encounters, heart in mouth, with German soldiers late at night. He also told me for the first time of some remarkable episodes during the famous tour of the U.S.S.R., on which he and Jef Last had accompanied André Gide. In particular, he described, with humour but not without a certain touch of horror in his detachment, how Gide used to prepare "little games" to amuse and entice the adolescent boys he met in the various cities where they stayed. One evening in Tiflis, in the Park (of Culture and Rest) Gide had started cuddling an especially attractive young Georgian in his teens, when the Ogpu arrived. They asked Gide for his papers, let him go, but hauled the boy off. When Guilloux asked Gide whether he didn't feel guilt, and a certain distress for the boy's misadventure, he thought for a moment and then said: "*Presque*. . . ."

We made many entrancing expeditions to Padua, to Torcello and elsewhere in the lagoon in the intervals of our official reunions. Among the delegates was an elderly Swedish professor, of clearly exceptional erudition about Venice and the Veneto. Whenever we came to an outstanding *sehenswürdigkeit*, whether church or palace or piazza, he would plant himself in the middle and deliver himself of a learned lecture — in French. He was ignored by the Italians, not without reason, and by the French out of their usual bad manners; but I was pleased to note that some of the English felt it incumbent on them to hang around, even if sheepishly; thus reinforcing my view that in international gatherings our countrymen, though often lamentably ignorant and tongue-tied, nearly always display the greatest sense of human decency.

Once upon a time Venice was filled with Englishmen, lovers of Italy, who rented dilapidated palaces for a song and lived a life enclosed within a dream of eighteenth- and nineteenth-century cultivated indolence. By 1950 this dream was coming at last to an end. England no longer commanded the world. More Americans than ever Henry James imagined were competing for the palaces, and Englishmen encountered difficulty in finding the foreign exchange for rapidly rising prices. I was privileged to visit on this trip two of the survivors of the Venice-loving English settlers: Leslie Hartley in the Palazzo Boulini and Victor Cunard in the Palazzo Foscarini. In spite of the gaiety of our meetings, and my enthusiasm for Leslie's works, a profound melancholy seemed to emanate from them, the last representatives of a dying princely race who had lived surrounded by their gondolieri, their books and pictures, their fading painted ceilings that one could almost see in the exterior views of Canaletto and Guardi.

How the Blow Fell

M Y publishing career lasted until the end of 1952. I had therefore
— though I did not know it — only four years to accomplish
the best I could from the moment when, in 1948, the printers who had
taken over my firm gave me the green light to go ahead without thinking (for the time being) about capital problems. As I have already
mentioned, my state of mind was extremely ambivalent about this development. I felt that great opportunities, of a rare lucky kind,
stretched before me. At the same time, I had my doubts about the
freedom I had been promised. Did my new backers realize the difficulties of building up a list, which would be successful financially, on a
mainly literary basis? I believed I could do it, but not at once. Again, if
the administrative pressure and the effort involved in keeping up with
competition increased — as it seemed almost certain they would as
free supply conditions returned — was I prepared to make sufficient
sacrifice of the other, creative side of myself, the self that wanted to
write poetry?

I remember a long, late evening discussion with Blanche Knopf,
who remained all through one of the most intimately sympathetic of my
many well-wishers on the other side of the Atlantic. She objected that
I was taking too much upon myself; that the load would break me; and
that I ought in reality to be chief literary adviser to a big and established firm, and not to have to bother with the rest. In my heart, I half-
agreed with her; but my New England and Scottish blood urged me
on to dangerous adventures, where the prizes — not of money but of
reputation — still beckoned almost irresistibly in the distance. I
thought not only of the success I might have as personal to my own
career; but also of what I could do — so it presented itself to me —
for English literature.

So it was that when Donald Klopfer of Random House came to see me (in 1951), and said quite simply: "I was told you were the best publisher in England today, so I thought I must come and pay my respects before I go home," I felt a glow of pleasure and surprise; and simultaneously a kind of guilt and an urge to say to him what I could not possibly have given utterance to: "You touch me and flatter me, but if only you knew what doubts and anxieties I have about being able to keep it up . . ."

By the beginning of 1952, I could look back on six years of hard, exciting and on the whole surprisingly productive work. I had an impressive group of the most promising young Americans on my list. I had made a success even beyond my early hopes of my Modern European Library. One of the last of my "scoops" had given me especial pleasure: Nikos Kazantzakis's *Alexis Zorba*, which I re-christened *Zorba the Greek*. I had always wanted to build up a top list of contemporary poets, as I had begun to do at the Hogarth Press with the great reputation in that field of Leonard and Virginia Woolf behind me. The list was already very much to my liking, though I wanted to go much further. I had not the slightest doubt, which my experience with *New Soundings* later confirmed, that the new post-war poets who began to appear at this time would have come to me.

I have already described the specially commissioned and illustrated books which gave me particular pleasure, to which I should add Michael Ayrton's edition of Nashe's *The Unfortunate Traveller*, with fifteen of his own lithographs in illustration. I planned a series of authoritative biographies of great figures in the background to modern literature, and had begun with Countess Wydenbruck's *Rilke*, Ernest Simmons's *Tolstoy* and *Dostoevsky*, David Magarshack's *Chekhov the Dramatist*, and Ronald Mason's study of Melville, *The Spirit above the Dust*. In addition, in this branch, there were the books on drama and ballet.

Another and deeply satisfying opportunity that came my way when the printers offered me very handsome supplies of paper, was the bringing back into print of English and American classics. When I started the Chiltern Library, in 1946, the scarcity of editions of the classics was desperate; but I saw that I ought in general to concentrate on special authors, just a little apart from the popular stream. Sooner, probably, rather than later, the Oxford University Press, Collins and Everyman would bring their most popular classics back on to the market, using plates that already existed. Rosamond had a particular enthusiasm for Mrs. Gaskell, so we planned a series of her chief books, if possible to include everything if we were successful. The revival of

Henry James, one of our favourite authors, was reaching its height; Graham Greene at Eyre and Spottiswoode was planning, we heard, to republish the later novels of "James the Old Pretender," so we decided to start on the novels and stories of the early and middle periods, which were, with very rare exceptions, totally unobtainable and likely to remain so. We began with *Roderick Hudson*, and by the end had ten volumes in print. I decided to add to this some of the unobtainable works of Herman Melville, interest in whom had grown very rapidly during the war. Curiously enough, they included *Billy Budd*.

These reprints gave me the chance of commissioning new introductions by leading contemporary writers. I was, for instance, glad to have William Plomer, Peter Quennell, Elizabeth Bowen and V. S. Pritchett on my list in this however minor way. When the end came, though the rewards of reprinting the classics had already become far more difficult, I had many extensions of the Chiltern Library still in mind.

Our plans for bringing, or bringing back, foreign classics into English translation did not stop there. I discovered that *Lucien Leuwen*, Stendhal's great unfinished novel, had never been brought out in English; we published it in two volumes, *The Green Huntsman* and *The Telegraph*, in H.L.R. Edwards's scholarly version. We followed this by *To the Happy Few*, Norman Cameron's translation of a selection of Stendhal's letters, which had recently been a great success in France. Later, I also found that Benjamin Constant's autobiographical novel, *Cecile*, a kind of sequel to *Adolphe*, which had only been discovered a few years earlier, had not yet been taken for translation into English. I published it among my last books, again in Norman Cameron's version. Being a great admirer of Balzac's cycle of Vautrin novels, I managed to get Kathleen Raine to re-translate them, with Philippe Jullian contributing illustrations for which he seemed to me so admirably suited. Alas, we only managed to do the first half, *Lost Illusions*, as a bumper volume; but we planned to follow it by another bumper volume containing *Splendeurs et Misères des Courtisanes* and *La Dernière Incarnation de Vautrin*.

I should perhaps apologize for devoting so many pages to a recapitulation in detail of what we had achieved before the end; but only so, I feel, can I show what impetus we had managed to attain in those few, hectic, stimulating, pioneering years. A publishing firm is only different from any other business in that it deals with the precious substance of art. But serious publishing, unless in the exceptional periods such as have been produced by war and social upheaval, needs heavy capitalization. And I was to learn that success and a growing reputation, in normal times, are not enough. What is needed is *great* success, the big best-seller *every* season.

By the middle of 1951 the printers had obtained the lease of a house in Gilbert Street, and offered us accommodation there, together with other associated companies in their group. We moved in during July. I had a comfortable ground-floor office, with room in it for an assistant's desk, which Barbara Cooper took over. Higher up were the general offices, presided over by Clive (John) Hall, and a special room at the top, where Julia Strachey could devote herself to reading and preparing reports about the MSS. which were piled high on tables and shelves. Val Biro, our new production manager, an immovably good-natured, sturdily built, good-looking young Hungarian-born artist, with glossy black hair, a disarming intelligent smile (and a glamorous wife), also had his own room, where he prepared lay-out and specimen pages for each accepted MS. as it came to him, and also designed spines and jackets.

One day, as we were discussing the work, Julia Strachey exclaimed to me what a happy family we all were in the office. And this was indeed true: we all had our appointed jobs, and none felt subordinate to any of the others beyond what smoothly working routine required. I was, I suppose, conductor of the orchestra, but most of us were creative in our own right — Barbara and Julia as prose-writers, Clive as a poet, Val as an artist — and there was absolutely no office "bull." We were all friends who met one another outside office hours, and all were there because we were seriously interested in what we were trying to do. I made it clear from the beginning that anyone could come into my room whenever he or she liked, to discuss any problem that had arisen, without the fuss of knocking or asking permission through a secretary. Perhaps it would have been impossible in a larger office; perhaps it was too good to last; but I remain firmly of the opinion that it was the *right* way to run a literary publishing office.

Every week some young man or woman would come to see me, looking for a job in publishing. I found this part of my duties nearly always engrossing for the human interest of the stories I was told, but also often rather heart-breaking. So many young people saw publishing as a happy compromise between commerce or finance and a highly risky life devoted to writing or painting; so few of them realized how small the number of available jobs was, compared with the number of young people like themselves looking for them. So many of them were ready to risk a couple of thousand pounds, all they or their parents could scrape together, to get a junior directorship; so few of them knew how hot the stove of publishing was to make these little drops of capital disappear in steam in the twinkling of an eye. Unless they were clearly well-to-do, I used to advise them against these adventures; but I also used to tell them that if they had a real passion or obsession with publishing, it didn't matter where they were slipped into the tank, how humble the starting job was. If they had the right gifts, they would sooner or later be able to swim over to the sunny side.

Towards the end of 1951 I was invited to give a talk to the Society of Bookmen. As usual with my talks and lectures at this period, I did not or could not set aside enough time to plan it properly, and found myself the evening before with only scattered notes. From 10 P.M. I worked feverishly, through half the night, to give body and coherence to these notes. I called the talk *A Post-War Publisher in the Narrows*, and tried in it to get to the root of the difficulties which beset someone in my position, caught in the cross-winds and cross-currents of the book market in the first seven years after the war. I was overwhelmingly conscious of its deficiencies. On arrival at Kettner's restaurant, where the dinners of the Society of Bookmen were always held, I was astonished to find an enormous gathering, including most of my friends and acquaintances among the publishing fraternity. I was told it was the second largest gathering they had ever had. Pure sweating panic seized me, as I sat down between Ian Parsons of Chatto & Windus and Bertie van Thal. However, wine was flowing and gaiety abounding, and in that genial and tolerant atmosphere I was inspired to make the most of my miserable script, and relieved to find that it appeared to go down very well. A vigorous discussion followed, in which my old friend Rupert Hart-Davis rose gloriously to my defence. When I reached home I was completely exhausted as well as tipsy.

Looking back I am inclined to see this evening at the Society of Bookmen as symbolizing the high-water mark in my career as a publisher. I had reached the moment of deepest understanding of the problems with which I was wrestling. And, in some way or other, I had managed to touch the imagination of my colleagues and friends in the world of books, so that they had the highest hopes of me and were generously willing to wish me well on the dangerous voyage ahead.

Danger indeed was gathering, like ominous little livid clouds on the horizon. The gods may shower one with gifts, but the more abundantly and suddenly they offer them, the more likely it is, it seems to me, that one crucial gift will be left out. The unknown Carabosse who had been forgotten among the invitations to my christening as a publisher had condemned me to a fatal lack of free access to the materials of my trade. It was for that lack that I had mortgaged my independence. I have often thought that if I had merely lacked capital, the judgment upon me of my great-grandfather, Robert Chambers, would have been severe. He would have told me that one must accumulate capital before one takes to risky business ventures; and that one only accumulates it by caution and patience as well as by unremitting work. Robert Chambers, however, was never stumped for paper to print his books on.

The plain fact was that my relations with the printers, who now controlled the fate of John Lehmann Ltd, were deteriorating. Wilfred Harvey was getting restive about the failure of the firm to show a clear profit. I was charged by the works the normal price which they tendered to any outside firm, which included of course profits at every stage of the operations: composition, supply of paper, printing and binding. It was therefore, after these had been debited, that my success or failure in making a publishing profit was reckoned. It was my contention — it would be better described as my guess, perhaps — that even if I was still in the red on that reckoning, there was almost certainly a concealed profit, apart from the fact that I always endeavoured to supply the works with my jobs when they were comparatively slack, thus keeping the wheels turning. It was even more seriously my contention that the kind of literary publishing house it was my aim to create needed time for the fruits to ripen, far more time than I had yet had for development; and that the unusual proportion of prestige successes I had had were exactly what was needed to bring eventual financial success as well.

The chairman, however, was not impressed, even though some other members of the board were more sympathetic. He was used to quick success and big profits, and the appearance of a laggard in his team, and a laggard obstinately set on going his own way, clearly discomfited him. I do not believe he understood what I was after. There was no very cogent reason why a business genius of his calibre should, though he had given me the impression at the start that he welcomed the addition to his empire of a small highbrow principality.

The geniality of our meetings began to evaporate, the temperature of our exchanges about the accounts to drop to glacial. In a way they were very funny, because of the total incomprehension, but I was too anxious most of the time to see the funny side — except in those moments of pure philosophic detachment which have throughout my life saved me from despair and dispersed at last the bile of extreme bitterness. One thing I should make clear: I never, until the final show-down, pleaded that the loss my accounts showed on their reckoning was a trifle in their huge profit-making operations, though in my opinion it was a fact. It was for them to say that it was worth it; not for me.

I should not give the impression that Wilfred Harvey found no merit at all in the endeavours of John Lehmann Ltd. No doubt he realized that the leading Press reviews, the praise and the controversy, the Book Society Recommendations, the *Evening Standard* choices, the public acclaim for production and design, were marks of some kind of achievement; but they were strange to him. When he praised a book we had taken on, it was generally one that was a little outside our usual range, such as *Miracle at Carville*, or *Victory in My Hands*. In spite of this, until nearly the end he did not try to control our editorial judgement. It was when he began to show signs, as I thought, of wanting to interfere in that department that I knew the game was — all but — up.

In April 1951, after a very brief discussion he said drily that he'd carry on for another year and then see how things had shaped. I had never before had to do with the head of a complex business empire, who could only spare ten minutes for small fry like myself. I felt rather like Alice, when she found herself asked to show a ticket in the railway carriage in the Third Square, and the voices all said together, "Don't keep him waiting, child! Why his time is worth a thousand pounds a minute!" Leonard Woolf was not a tycoon. He belonged to the same intellectual world as myself, and I had a great respect for him, even when I differed strongly from him in judgement or thought he was being unreasonable. Leonard liked long, wrangling arguments, and could always find time for them. When he greeted some remark of mine with: "But, John, it's *grotesque* . . . ," I knew that the bell had gone for the next round. Allen Lane was nearer to tycoon status, and always had too much to do; but he would listen and be swayed by arguments I put up. I always felt that Harvey had made up his mind before the five minutes had started.

The pressure increased in the early part of 1952. Before a crucial interview in February I determined not to yield any ground. I had decided that figures were the only thing that interested the chairman, and had prepared a string of clear and exact calculations to prove that our results for the previous year weren't so bad after all. This was the only occasion I can remember on which Harvey listened with attention, but I rather doubt whether his attention was in fact due to my demonstration. I had found a new ally. Eric Harvey, his son, who directed Macdonald's, had obviously put in a plea for me; and when Gibbs, who was as usual present, started on his well-worn theme of the need for economies — in what I considered essentials — he was sharply opposed by Eric. I went away feeling astonishingly calm; but the calm came not so much from having gained a reprieve, but from the sudden realization that in my long previous broodings I had crossed the Rubicon and was prepared for the worst.

When I told Christopher Isherwood about this interview, he remarked: "In Hollywood one starts by saying yes, but gets to the top by saying no."

Though I told Christopher, and of course Rosamond, what the situation was, I knew that it was extremely important not to let anyone else have an inkling. I was already beginning to cast about in my mind for drastic solutions. Assuming I found one, I realized I should only be worse off if a whisper of disaster had got around before.

Rosamond was very divided in her attitude. She saw how much the publishing of good books and the building and fostering of promising authors meant to me. She saw that I had put myself in pawn to some extent by the sanguine gesture of giving my own name to the firm. She knew that its reputation was riding higher than ever, and had a golden opportunity of carrying everything before it. At the same time, she was convinced that if I had to go on with the kind of struggle that building the first storey had involved me in, I would cripple myself as a creative artist. She would have liked me to be relieved of most of the administration and financial care. If only a substitute could be found for Purnell, a group with equal resources but run by people who understood and sympathized with my aims. Perhaps then I could write poetry again. Perhaps I might even be able to start a literary magazine in the place of *Penguin New Writing*.

At this juncture, it occurred to me to go and see a new man in the book world. His name was Robert Maxwell. He had the keenest ambition, immense energy and drive, resourcefulness, and a brilliant organizational mind. I had taken a liking to him, because of the audacity and pluck he showed in challenging the conservative British book world with his new ideas. I also found his story romantic: born of the poorest parents in a remote part of Europe (which I had travelled in myself just before the war), he had escaped from the Nazis as a youngster, joined the Czech Army in France and on the collapse of France had managed to get away to England. He acquired a new name, a commission in His Majesty's forces, and very soon after an

M.C. We had met and discussed publishing on a number of occasions. I found that my liking for him was returned. The publishers and booksellers of London, however, were cagey. They thought that his pluck was cheek, and found his methods too unorthodox. We met several times, and he listened to my story with patience, interest and occasional comments. He knew of my reputation in the literary world, and gradually let me see that he was tempted to help me. By the late summer we had formed a rough plan: I would offer to buy back my firm from Harvey, he would supply the finance up to an agreed limit, and we would then reorganize John Lehmann Ltd with more opportunity for me to devote myself to the literary side.

Maxwell's support heartened me immensely. At the same time I had a curious feeling, as if I were imprisoned in ice; so numb had the long struggle with Purnell made me.

By the beginning of November we had all agreed on our tactics. I asked for an interview with the chairman, who sent word that he could see me at Paulton on the first Thursday of the month. By chance it so happened that Thursday was the day on which I had arranged to give a party for John Gielgud's book. I had therefore to make all arrangements for the party beforehand. I got my helpers to come in on the Wednesday, explained to my loyal and understanding housekeeper, Mrs. Crew, exactly what had to be done, and arranged with my sister Beatrix to start it off if I were to be late. I calculated that as Harvey was expecting me, he would be able to see me before lunch, and I could catch the 3:18 from Bath back to London. Plenty of time if so.

The only person I sounded out in Purnell beforehand was Eric Harvey, to whom I outlined my plans on the Tuesday. On the train down to Bath I let Gibbs into my secret, and managed, I thought, to persuade him that the project was reasonable.

On arrival at Paulton, however, we found to our consternation that Harvey had retired incommunicado into a close huddle with one of the Woolworth high-ups. No one dared disturb him. Lunch-time arrived. During lunch, Harvey, at the head of the table, gave us a lecture on "the kind of book the public likes." The rest of the table sat eating their peaches and cream in reverently squashed silence. The lecture, I felt, was aimed obliquely at me. As we broke up Gibbs was able to collar him, and make him promise to come down and talk to me for a few minutes as soon as he could. Time trickled by. . . . I saw that catching the 3:18 was a lost cause, and sent a teleprinter message up to London to warn Beatrix and Barbara Cooper. At last Harvey appeared in the front office, and as succinctly as I could and as politely as I could, I said my say. He appeared to listen with care, and promised to study the figures I had brought down. He would give me an answer within a few days. The interview was over in ten minutes. Ten minutes, I thought, to plead for my life.

The party went with a bang. I have never had a stranger feeling at a party in my life.

A week later the blow fell. Soon after the interview at Paulton, Harvey had sent me a letter, setting out the calculations by which he had arrived at what he considered a fair price for John Lehmann Ltd. I was stunned. It was far above anything I thought he would ask. I failed to understand why, if he considered it worth all that money, he was so hostile to it. I had a series of interviews with Maxwell and my accountant, to decide on a counter-offer, and the tone of the letter I should write. When we agreed, I wrote my letter, got Maxwell's 100 per cent approval, and then took it to Eric Harvey. It was couched, I thought, in the most reasonable and courteous terms, and fully recognized the value of what they had allowed me to do. Eric became very agitated, and told me he was personally appalled at the thought of winding up the firm. He feared that his father would sweep my counter-offer aside, but at the week-end he would try to influence him to make a compromise.

At the same time I sent a copy to Gibbs. He hurried into the office next morning, and told me he very much doubted if the "old man" would bite at all. We argued about the price. At last I said what had been in my mind for so long: "My new backers, who are hard-headed business men, take the view that your price is several thousand pounds more than what the company is worth at break-up value. They also make the point that whatever the profit-and-loss account may have shown, they doubt whether you have lost over the operation, because a firm like mine does not occupy more than a fraction of your production capacity, but merely keeps the machines turning in the idle moments between big jobs. Some might even go so far as to say that my books have only cost the materials and the electric current. And if your chairman is a man of generosity and vision as well as of supreme business acumen, he will see that the sums involved over John Lehmann Ltd are as nothing in the big total of his consolidated accounts, whereas my name is of the greatest importance to me."

For the first time, Gibbs seemed shaken, and appeared ready to admit much of the truth of what I said. On Friday evening, however (the 14th), he rang me at my house to say that Harvey rejected my counter-offer altogether. He proposed to wind up the company in due course, and gave notice to terminate my service agreement on December 31.

This seemed to me a most brusque and ruthless gesture, following my appeal, and it made me, of course, very angry. If I had misunderstood the position, Harvey could have taken the trouble to explain it to me. If his claim for a far higher price was well founded, he could have expounded it to me. But no; he rejected the idea of negotiation or discussion altogether. It was this total refusal to negotiate when so much was at stake for me that stuck in my gullet then — and still sticks. I had no intention of keeping my mouth shut, as I might have if more consideration and respect for my feelings and the plight I found myself in had been shown.

I saw that the adventure was over, and my hopes lay in ruins. I must extricate myself as best I could. In that operation my first duty lay towards my staff; my next towards my authors. I must give the former as long notice as possible that they were going to need to find new jobs. And I must see that none of the latter were tied, if I could help it, against their will.

The next step was to prepare a brief announcement for the Press on December 1, and let my most intimate friends in the publishing world and in Fleet Street know by telephone or by letter. I made my announcement quite brief and bold:

Mr. John Lehmann announces that on December 31st he will cease to have anything to do with the publishing company of John Lehmann Ltd, which he founded in 1946 and has directed ever since. Owing to differences of opinion over future policy, Messrs. Purnell, who own the controlling interest, have informed him that they will not require his services beyond the end of the year.

Val took the announcement to the Press Association in his car in the morning. By the afternoon it was on the front page of the *Evening Standard*, and from that moment my telephone never stopped ringing. Next morning the news was in the *Express*, the *Manchester Guardian*, the *Daily Telegraph* and the *News Chronicle*. It was at that point that I had agreed to go to see some of the Purnell directors at Maddox Street to discuss various technical points about the contracts with authors. I found them in what seemed to me a state of mingled rage and confusion. It was wicked of me, apparently, to have told my staff what had happened; and even more wicked to have let the Press know.

Clearly, I was another case of the *"animal méchant . . . quand on le bat, il se défend."*

After that, the letters began to pour in; from intimate friends, from authors, from publishing colleagues, and from a host of other people I hardly knew at all, all expressing shock, indignation and solidarity. The *Observer* invited me to lunch, in order to prepare a paragraph about the event. Edmond Segrave of the *Bookseller* invited me to dinner and promised all support. Henry Green wrote to say that he was going to organize a luncheon party in my honour, and Rose Macaulay that she was going to get signatures for a letter to *The Times*. I was overwhelmed and deeply moved by the general sympathy my misfortune evoked. I had never imagined that it could be so widespread.

In the midst of all this almost embarrassing solidarity, I must confess to have had an extremely uncertain and ambiguous feeling about the future. I wrote to all my friends that I felt myself to be a "publishing animal," and would sooner or later reappear, somehow or somewhere, in the publishing world. I made a final effort to launch myself into a continuous future by asking Purnell if I could purchase from them, at cost, the eight or nine books which were currently in production. This request was curtly refused. I contemplated, with a kind of agonized detachment, the column advertisement which appeared in *The Times Literary Supplement* reviewing the year's successes in our publishing programme: Malraux's *The Walnut Trees of Altenburg*, Paul Bowles's *Let It Come Down*, Nikos Kazantzakis's *Zorba the Greek*, Jean-Louis Curtis's *Lucifer's Dream*, Benjamin Constant's *Cecile*, John Gielgud's biography in pictures, Annette Hopkins's biography of Elizabeth Gaskell and my own anthology, *Pleasures of New Writing*. What would it all lead to? Would I ever again, in spite of my brave assurances, be able to make the tremendous effort of building up a new publishing firm? In the almost impenetrable fog that settled on London that week-end, completely exhausted, I settled myself by the fire in my library, with Lottie beside me, and read *David Copperfield*.

The letter which appeared in *The Times* read as follows:

The news that Mr. John Lehmann has severed his connection with John Lehmann Limited will have been received with regret, and even with dismay, by writers and readers in many parts of the world. There can be few people of literary interests who, during the last fifteen years, have not often been grateful to Mr. Lehmann for the breadth and fervour of his enthusiasms; and there must be very many writers, both in this country and abroad, who can bear witness to Mr. Lehmann's qualities as an inspired encourager. In France, Italy, Czechoslovakia and Greece his patron-age has been particularly well-directed; and since he founded in 1946 his own publishing house, he has contrived to give an idiosyncratic flavour not only to the contents of his list but also to the appearance and decoration of the books themselves. Thus it is that many young painters will also have reason to regret the departure of one who has chosen to neglect his own considerable gifts as a writer in order to devote himself, unselfishly, and unsparingly to furthering the gifts of others.

It was signed by Freddie (A.J.) Ayer, Patrick Leigh-Fermor, Henry Green, Graham Greene, John Hayward, Arthur Koestler, Rose Mac-aulay, Raymond Mortimer, Harold Nicolson, Simon Nowell-Smith, John Russell, Roger Senhouse, Stephen Spender and Angus Wilson.

Thinking of this wonderful tribute, the leader in *The Times Literary Supplement*, and the repeated notices in the *Bookseller*, I began to have a curious feeling that I had died, and was leading a ghost-like posthumous life. And sometimes I felt that all this was about someone else. How could I answer all the letters, except in the terms of a brother or son of the deceased?

I was pulled up to reality again by the final days, before Christmas, at Gilbert Street. We spent them sorting out, packing up and tearing up. There were tears, dramatic demonstrations, and laughter too. We had been asked by Purnell to label everything very carefully before we left. The two typists, Pauline and Janet, determined to carry out this last demand with meticulous care. They completed their work by labelling the office tea-pot as "tea-pot," the table as "table," the window as "window" and finally the floor as "floor." By lunch-time on Christmas Eve, they had all gone, after many affecting farewells, and my car was at the door, loaded up with various parcels of books and papers that belonged to me. Barbara, with smiling but tear-stained face, saw me off.

The luncheon that Henry Green organized for me took place at the Trocadero on January 14. Tom Eliot took a leading part, and there were nearly thirty of my fellow-writers there, including, of course, Rosamond, and to my great delight, E. M. Forster. I enjoyed it, although I felt almost unbearably keyed up and nervous about my own speech. Henry muttered to me: "This is the first occasion authors have given one of their own kind a *meal* since Coleridge organized a dinner for Leigh Hunt on his release from prison." Cyril Connolly, who was obviously enjoying himself very much, likened us all to Harley Street surgeons and doctors, and suggested as we dispersed that we ought to form ourselves into a monthly luncheon club. Alas, nothing came of this excellent idea. Tom Eliot warmed up as the occasion warmed up, and described to me the technique he himself had developed to deal with stage and film tycoons.

My mother had written to me: "I have had you very much in my thoughts since the crisis and I know you have been under a hideous strain. But how splendid to have so great intellectual support: it does prove that true culture in this country is not commercial."

I did not know at the time that it was the end of my publishing career. Only my sanguine temperament, like a machine that insists on whirling on in spite of sand thrown into the cogs, carried me forward to the next stage, the next events.

⋘ IV ⋙

A Leap into the Air

IN the meantime, another development had taken place which was to give me one of my most exciting opportunities to discover and present new authors and new literary ideas. I had become editor and compère of the first B.B.C. "literary magazine of the air," *New Soundings*. It was the continuing existence of this programme that softened a little the blow that the extinction of my publishing firm had dealt me; though only for a few months.

One day, a few years before, a very young poet, who happened to be doing his military service in the R.A.F., came to see me with a sheaf of poems in his hand. His name was David Hughes. Tall and slim, with curly black hair and a cupid's bow of a mouth, he seemed almost improbably the type of the romantic young Shelleyan poet. He was an ardent fan of *New Writing*, and was bitterly disappointed when the Penguin came to an end. I encouraged him in his writing, though his poems did not appear to me ready for publication as yet. At the end of his time in the R.A.F. he went up to Oxford, and we kept in fairly close contact. He touched me by showing an almost greater concern for a successor to the Penguin than I had felt myself. Eventually, he conceived the idea that, in order to achieve as wide an audience as possible, the successor should be a radio programme produced at regular intervals like a quarterly or monthly magazine. I liked the idea, as it came out of our constant repeated discussions, and encouraged him to try and convince the B.B.C. of its worth. I was nevertheless astonished and impressed when he told me that he had managed to interest the novelist P. H. Newby, at that time one of the leading Third Programme producers, to the point where he thought the B.B.C. would definitely buy the idea.

Sure enough, Howard Newby came to see me one day towards the end of September 1951, and told me that the scheme was on. The

B.B.C. wanted me to organize and edit it. The terms and facilities they offered seemed to me to provide immense opportunities in what was an entirely new field. I accepted with little hesitation. Even if I had not been personally eager to tackle the experiment, I knew that it had to be done.

Once more into battle. When the details were finally fixed, I started contacting all the authors I thought might provide appropriate contributions, particularly the younger poets and novelists whose work had only recently come to my notice. I had been given forty-five minutes once a month on the Third, with a repeat. The arrangement at the beginning was that I should confine myself to British authors; I intended to mix new work by authors already known, more or less of the *Penguin New Writing* generation, with the younger hopefuls, and have occasional comments by older writers. David Hughes, who was already editing *Isis*, was beginning to grumble, not unnaturally, that the B.B.C. was leaving no room for him in a programme that was his brain-child; but his loyalty to me was unshakeable, and he eagerly agreed to arrange an Oxford party for me, at which I could meet all the budding undergraduate writers.

This was an exciting moment of discovery and fermenting dreams. Word began to get around even before January with astonishing speed, and unsolicited typescripts began to arrive almost every day. I saw all sorts of pitfalls looming, especially in the amount of difficult allusive poetry listeners would be ready to take, and the length of the prose literature contributions; but I felt that I must plunge in, make the first two broadcasts as stimulating as possible in spite of whatever technical blunders I might commit, and learn from them as quickly as I could, before the permissive enthusiasm — if I succeeded in generating it — began to evaporate. I knew at least that the dearth of literary magazines since *Horizon* and *Penguin New Writing* had come to an end put much initial sympathy on my side.

When the evening of the first broadcast came, I felt extremely nervous, though Howard Newby had been encouraging and optimistic about the authors I had chosen and the editorial comment I had woven around them. I always felt keyed up and at my most alive on entering a broadcasting studio; but this time I began to wonder whether I hadn't bitten off more than I could chew.

This sense of dismay was increased as I observed Henry Green on the other side of the microphone table, looking as if he had reached the ultimate point of dislocated world-weariness. Punch in the attack, however, and variety in the material seemed to carry the day.

It is perhaps worth quoting my introductory flourish, as it reveals all the thoughts that were stirring in my mind at the time:

"In comparatively recent years, a new disease has attacked rhododendrons in this country. It is called 'bud blast,' and it causes the buds to turn brown and rot during the long period of incubation between their formation and their opening.

"Something of the same sort seems to have been happening in the arts, especially in imaginative literature. Most of those who have been concerned, in one way or another, with the fostering of young talent will agree with me, I think, when I say that during the last seven years or so there has been a tragic failure of fulfilment. A young poet has written two or three poems of promise and originality; he has appeared to be just about to find his voice; then two years later he has made no advance, but rather sunk into the clichés of his time and the repetition of the first tricks he learned. A young novelist has excited all the critics with a first novel in which a fresh eye seems to be viewing the world, and the attitudes of a new generation defining themselves. Alas, his second novel tries to recapture in melodrama what his first created from passion; and his third is still going the rounds of the publishers. Worse still — and this is the true 'bud blast' — many young would-be writers who have just reached the time, at their universities or in their first explorations of the world, when they should be experimenting with vigour, making slap-dash mistakes but fizzing over with something to say — even in a passion of imitation of someone else's style — these young writers show themselves timid, confused and imitative without passion.

". . . The poets of the 'thirties were carried forward on a great wave of belief, or hope, that they could remould the world. The poets of the war years were strengthened by that deep searching of the roots of our spiritual life that was an instinctive reaction in this country from the first shock of the ending of peace. The poets of today have as their inheritance a peace that has never succeeded in becoming real, a ruined economy, and a thick atomic fog of insecurity over the future of Europe, of the world.

"No wonder that they find it difficult to open up a clear path of advance for themselves. No wonder they wrestle almost vainly with the problem of defining an attitude, or discovering the symbols of a philosophy. And yet, even though fallow periods are inevitable in the history of a literature, there never was a time, a challenge, to which art, poetry, could not find an answer.

"But the search requires weapons and equipment, and one of the most important items of equipment is a magazine: a place to be published in, a place where reports can be pooled of new soundings that are being made, new ideas stirred into life and old arguments brought up to date. Alas, very few such magazines exist today. . . .

"In this new series of programmes we are going to try to do something that has never been attempted before. We want to provide in the spoken broadcast word a substitute that may, with luck favouring, turn out to be something very much more. . . .

"The air provides, I think, an excellent medium for this purpose; and a medium whose discipline is to my mind altogether beneficial. It demands a certain clarity and definition, a certain immediacy of impact either by thought or image or rhythm, and will hardly tolerate the intellectual mists and verbiage in which young writers all too often try to escape the searching eye of judgement.

"This may sound rather sternly commanding; and I am reminded that in the battle of literature it is the business of an editor not to order his troops about, but to follow where the most spirited lead. . . ."

In spite of my panic doubts, the programme went over exactly as I hoped it would. The Press was good, and a few days later I had a letter from Howard Newby, in which he said: "I have now been able to gather a few opinions about *New Soundings I*. Everyone here is pleased with it . . . the general summing up is one of warm approval."

The result was that, while I was collecting material for the second programme, and dealing with the immediately accelerated pouring-in of letters and manuscripts, I was invited to lunch by Harman Grisewood, the director of the Third Programme at that time. He was so pleased with the launching that he offered me another quarter of an hour for each programme (making sixty minutes in all), gave me permission to use American and other foreign contributions in translation, and extended the run to six months. I told him that, as far as authors went, I had everything my own way, provided I could find the right material. After all, *New Soundings* was not just another highbrow literary magazine come in to fill a vacuum, but a broadcast programme with a national audience running into six figures, well paid, with — for the poets at least — the possibility of reprinting in the *Listener* for another good fee.

And indeed I was getting some first-class recruits. Geoffrey Grigson wrote in to tell me that John Wain, who had contributed the last article to the last number of *Penguin New Writing*, was also a poet, and had a small volume of poems, *Mixed Feelings*, privately printed at Reading University. When I eventually got hold of a copy, I at once liked the clarity, the wit, the pithy concentration with its romantic undertones to the classical manner, and took several of them for *New Soundings*.

About the same time, another contributor appeared who inspired in me almost exactly the same feeling. In the autumn a friend had shown me a small volume of naval short stories, which had just been published, written by an ex-sailor called Charles Causley, who was now a schoolmaster in Cornwall. I discovered that he was also the author of a very slim pamphlet of poems published (with their usual courage) by the Hand and Flower Press. I liked them so much that I wrote off to him at once, and after some correspondence received from him a poem or ballad, *Ou Phrontis*, which not only delighted me but seemed quite admirably suited for broadcasting. This was the beginning of a long association, friendly and professional, with Charles Causley, a poet with a style and inspiration that have remained utterly unlike anything else in his generation.

The second programme, however, ran into a road block. The script was ready, the performers all booked, when the news came through of the death of King George VI. All scheduled broadcasting programmes were immediately cancelled, even on the Third. Nevertheless we recorded it at exactly the same time that evening, just as if it had been going out. Louis MacNeice, who had scarcely recovered from a chill, pulled himself together to give a remarkable reading of several sections of a long harrowing poem about a cat which had belonged to him in Athens, all the more moving for the strange, lazy drawl in which he spoke. I was always glad when contributors were accomplished enough to read their own works, and this poem was one of our outstanding successes. Christopher Isherwood, who happened to be in England again at this time, also gave a highly characteristic performance in reading a piece he had written for us on six up-and-coming young American writers: very confidential in manner, serious and yet subtly managing to give his audience the impression that he could hardly refrain from chuckling, that he found some of the information he was giving peculiarly funny. He chose Ray Bradbury, Truman Capote, William Goyen, Speed Lamkin, Norman Mailer and Calder Willingham. I can still hear the relish that gradually came into his voice as he spoke about Truman Capote and the southern school of writers that seemed then to dominate the American literary scene:

[517]

There are, in fact, two souths that people write about. One of them is the real contemporary south; a land where industrialization is increasing, education is spreading and considerable progress is being made towards solving the Negro problem. The other is the gothic-romantic, macabre south of decaying mansions, degenerate families, despair, drink, Spanish moss, sexual atrocities and lynchings. Truman Capote writes about this second kind of south, and makes it just as gothic, funny and macabre as he knows how. I must confess that this second kind of south bores me utterly — its cult can in some respects be compared with the cult of a romantic Ireland which flourished at the beginning of this century — and the greatest tribute I can pay to Capote's talent is to say that nevertheless I sincerely admire his two novels. . . . He can be very funny and very touching. But I can't help feeling that he is often guilty of playing with the reader, as if trying to see just how much weirdness he can get away with. . . .

By the time I had prepared these two programmes, I had a fairly clear idea of the chief difficulties that confronted us. First of all, I saw that the speaking was the supreme priority, especially with poetry. All the poems we included were new, or at least only known to the readers of magazines with very esoteric circulations. It was therefore extremely important that the reader should not only make the sense of the poem as clear as possible, but also — in particular when dealing with unrhymed poetry — by his control of the rhythms and the slightest of pauses at the end of a line that carried no stop, suggest to the listeners the shape in which the piece was written. With a poem like *Ou Phrontis*, for instance, or the ballads by Vernon Watkins which we broadcast, the problem was negligible; but many of the poems I chose had, inevitably at that time, a complex imagery and a compression of the steps of argument which was not at all easy to follow even in the best reading. Humpty Dumpty introduced Alice to the conception of portmanteau words; much of modern poetry has consisted, since the publication of Hopkins, of portmanteau or concertina poems. These are poems that need, after having made their original imaginative impact (if they are good poems), to be quietly unriddled with the printed page beside one. This problem dogged us to the end; but later in the series I tried the experiment of having a poem read once, then trying to give a few words of elucidation myself, then having it read again. The main objection to this method — apart from the danger of my missing the point — was the time it took.

The other bedrock limitation was in the length of the prose contributions. If as much as half my sixty minutes was devoted to prose, that only meant time for about 4,000 words, to be divided between

two or three writers. Two was the minimum; but even three prose
pieces were all too few to represent new imaginative writers and new
critical thought. In *New Writing* the most successful prose contributions, whether short stories or documentary reports or critical essays,
had nearly all been between 3,000 and 6,000 words in length. In fact,
in *New Soundings* we had to jettison serious criticism almost entirely,
as I took the view that critical themes of any importance could not be
properly elaborated in 1,000 or 1,500 words. We confined ourselves
to more general comment, such as Christopher's examination of young
American writers, Cyril Connolly's confession of infatuation with Petronius's *Satyricon*, or a later display of typical French fireworks by the
young French novelist Roger Nimier on being a writer and twenty
years old in Paris directly after the war. The only exception, I think,
was André Maurois's presentation of the newly discovered early novel
by Proust, *Jean Santeuil*, which we sent a van to record in his country
home in France.

In spite of these limitations, I think we managed very soon to see
how to give weight without stodginess in the comments, and dramatic
speaking effect without losing lyrical depth in the poems, as well as
how to choose the short fiction extracts without appearing too fragmentary. The problem of variety was always in the forefront of my
mind. I was immensely helped by an excellent team of B.B.C. readers;
also by many of the authors who were reading their own work and
practised in it, each, like Christopher, giving his own special flavour to
the performance. I think this was particularly important, as the listener to a radio magazine can't browse and pick and choose as the
reader of a printed magazine can, but must listen through to the end if
he is to hear all. Some of our recordings became pretty hilarious when
good performers were round the table. I remember, during the fourth
session, William Plomer, who was reading a piece he had written on
the tribulations of being a publisher's reader, the grotesque zest in his
voice, the gestures and facial expression he used to help his performance; Laurie Lee's rendering of an extract from a book about Spain he
was writing, with no gestures at all but a sly humour suggested all
through by the inflexions of his voice; John Betjeman, whose pre-
recording of the now famous "Song of a Night-Club Proprietress,"
Sun and Fun, came suddenly booming out of the loud-speaker, transfix-
ing us all by its harrowing absurdity:

> There was kummel on the handle of the door,
> The ashtrays were unemptied,

The cleaning unattempted,
And a squashed tomato sandwich on the floor. . . .

The only other writer I saw use the same accompaniment of gestures as William was Dylan Thomas, when he recited his *Prologue* in No. 8. In his case the gestures were even more pronounced and extraordinary, as if he were trying to wind up a very heavy bucket from a very deep well. No one who heard only the melodious, magical voice that came over the air could possibly have imagined what went on in the studio.

By that time great interest had been aroused in America. Victor Weybright, the publisher of the paperback series New American Library, had just started *New World Writing* in frank imitation of *Penguin New Writing* (which he handsomely acknowledged), and wrote to ask if he could see the script of No. 1 and publish it in his country if a scheme could be worked out. I happened just to have prepared a composite programme out of the first three or four programmes for the North American Service of the B.B.C., and sent a script over as an alternative. He and his co-editor, Arabella Porter, received it with acclaim, and it appeared in *New World Writing* a few months later.

« 2 »

EVERYTHING seemed to be going even better than I could have hoped at my most sanguine. The B.B.C. agreed to commission a further six programmes, making twelve in all. The Press as a whole had turned from encouraging to enthusiastic. By the time No. 4 had been broadcast, *New Soundings* had even been called (in the *Observer*) "the most interesting programme in British radio." I was therefore startled (to put it mildly) when I received a letter from Howard Newby confirming the extension for a second six months, but at the same time telling me that the programme had been such a success that they wanted to go on with it beyond that — but not with me as editor. The very success of the programme, he told me, was partly the reason for this decision! They didn't want to give the impression that any one person had a corner in the market.

This reasoning on the part of the B.B.C. baffled me. The more I thought about it, the more indignant I became. I feel sure that if they had said they wanted to introduce another editor, give him a six-months run, then come back to me for another six months, and so on, I would have seen a good deal of sound sense in the proposal. But to dismiss an editor completely because the magazine he had created, organized and kept going had been a resounding success seemed to me, well, out of a looking-glass world. I knew that Howard, who had been a sympathetic ally from the beginning, was only handing on to me the decision of his committee, in which he had only one voice, but it was to him that I had to send my reply and my protest. Because I had made a success of an entirely new venture in broadcasting, I asked him, must it promptly be given to someone else? "If Allen Lane had said to me in the old days, '*Penguin New Writing* is a great success, therefore we're giving it next year to ———— to carry on,' where do you think I would have told him to ———— ?" I said I saw the point of this monopoly, but if that worried them, why didn't they start more magazines-of-the-air? I ended up, a little intemperately, "To hell with such cant."

Howard replied: "Your rocket has arrived, still giving out sparks." He proposed we should let emotion cool, and then discuss the situation. I agreed, and we did so. But neither then nor at any of my subsequent discussions with him, or Harman Grisewood, or at the very end with John Morris, who had succeeded Grisewood, or Mary Somerville, did I succeed in deflecting the B.B.C. from their unholy decision. If I had not continued, quite unreasonably, to hope that they could be reasoned out of it, those last months of *New Soundings*, containing as they did the blow of the end of John Lehmann Ltd, would have been dark indeed.

My reaction to my dismissal was echoed in the Press. The *Sunday Times*, which had said in the autumn that I had made my radio magazine "compulsory listening for all who care for creative imaginative writing," now commented tersely that I had "exceeded one's hopes for a year. His curious reward is to be dropped." While the last programme was being recorded, I heard that the so-called "Listener Research Coefficient" for the programme had gone sharply up to 74 per cent from the 68 per cent it had been in the autumn.

Looking back on that series of twelve programmes, I am particularly glad that *New Soundings* gave the first *national* platform to so many poets who were to make names for themselves in the 'fifties: John Wain, Charles Causley, Elizabeth Jennings, Norman McCaig (brought to my notice by Louis MacNeice); Donald Davie, with a beautiful early poem called *North Russia in the Fall;* John Holloway, with his *Apollonian Poem*, which electrified all who heard it, including Edith Sitwell; Thom Gunn, who was still at Cambridge, with the *Secret Sharer* and *Incident on a Journey*, and James Merrill, a gifted American poet little known over here at the time. All these poets came on with me to the *London Magazine*, and I was therefore rather amused when some of the more strident propagandists for "the Movement," a chimaera which popped up with teeth bared a few years later, and to which many of them were said to belong, claimed that old has-beens like myself couldn't possibly appreciate what it was all about.

The main problem for me all through was to find an appropriate critical "envelope" for the contributions I accepted; more difficult than the task I faced later, of writing a Foreword to each number of the *London Magazine*, because my introductory remarks to a *New Soundings* programme had to be far more directly related to what was coming than the foreword to a number of a printed magazine; and I had to continue, in between the separate items, to pursue any theme, or let it slide naturally into another. I harped continually on questions of language and style, because they seemed to me far and away the most important at that time; and I am inclined to think they still are. Rosamond echoed my own thoughts when she said, in a contribution she made: "Why is so little attention paid nowadays to words? What makes some novelists suppose they can get by without caring how words are arranged, what ring is given out by them?" Raymond Queneau spoke in similar vein about changes in the French language that was spoken all around him: "A new language calls forth new ideas, and fresh thoughts need a fresh language. . . . Contemporary French will not become a real and fruitful language until it is used by philosophers themselves and, of course, by men of science. Here, therefore, I hail the first mathematicians who shall write a text-book of algebra in this new tongue, which is one of the few good things still left in this country."

Many other phrases, epigrams and words of wisdom by my contributors still ring in my ears. Cyril Connolly, for instance, on the chance of finding the lost books of Petronius: "I know that I would sacrifice everything a space-ship could bring us back from Venus or all the minerals on the moon for a sight of those rolls in their charred cases, and a few more episodes of those aesthetes in adventure." And again: "In the picture gallery Eumolpus said that in an age that worshipped drink, sex and money there could be no more great art; people would no longer take the trouble to write well and would rather earn a gold ingot than own an old master. Like many whose gaze is fixed on the past, he was apt to find himself looking into the future." Iain Fletcher, on the intellectual snobbery of little magazines: "Poetry does provide the peaks of literature, but we can reach them only by the foothills." And William Plomer, in talking of the decay of regional novelists:

"There are no longer fairies at the bottom of the garden — only a bus route."

New Soundings, of course, was only a makeshift on the way to new literary magazines, which eventually turned up. Nevertheless, I am pretty certain that, given the existence of those magazines, the B.B.C. could have organized a magazine-of-the-air, a variation from *New Soundings*, which would have been of great value and given great pleasure. I cannot applaud the directing spirits of that great Corporation for having, after two brief experiments that followed my editorship, given up the enterprise entirely.

My successor, I learnt eventually, was to be John Wain, one of the new authors I had been happiest to push forward. He wrote me an extremely nice letter about this. I wrote back to him to say how sorry I was I should not be in London to hear the first programme he had put together, as I was going abroad.

I was badly in need of time to lick my wounds.

Mediterranean Reflections

I HAD long promised myself a Mediterranean holiday, on which I could relax and see if the springs of poetry would start flowing again. I decided on Cyprus, with a visit to Rome and Amalfi on the way. I took with me, as far as Amalfi, a young actor friend, Spence Coulter, who had never seen Italy before.

Rome, in the brilliant rose-golden light, seemed more beautiful than ever. Revisiting the famous classical sites of Rome, Michelangelo's capitol, the Baths of Caracalla and the Pantheon was an especially exciting experience with a companion whose youthful ardour and interest burned so intensely as Spence's. For the first time, I was struck by the strangeness of the fact that Trelawney lay beside Shelley in the Protestant Cemetery, as Severn beside Keats. I lunched with Ian Greenlees, the engaging mandarin figure who was at that time in charge of the British Council in the city, in a dining-room crowded with Guttuso paintings of startling vigour and beauty, and directly afterwards bumped into my old friend, the painter Derek Hill, and Elizabeth Bowen in the Piazza Colonna. I have found that paradoxically enough, one sees more of one's English friends and gets to know them better when one meets them on holiday abroad. I had to tell Elizabeth and Derek the whole story of the crisis and climax in the fortunes of my publishing firm, and of the honour and comedy of the luncheon organized for me by Henry Green. Elizabeth, who was collecting material for a book on Rome and soaking herself in the atmosphere of the city, suggested that I should go over and stay with her in her family home in Ireland to finish my autobiography, while she finished her book; an invitation I was eventually able to accept, with very happy results.

We reached Amalfi from Salerno, by a coast road of extraordinary beauty, on the mountain-side of which the Judas-trees were already in full, pale-magenta bloom. Osbert and Edith Sitwell had recommended the hotel to me, a converted monastery perched dizzily on the rock face above the sea. As they appeared to be almost the patron saints of the place, we were received with great deference, and given a room that might once have been a superior kind of monk's cell, with views over the great welcoming haze of the blue-grey silky sea from the huge windows looking south and west.

Amalfi plunged us into a world of drama and poetry at once, because the day after our arrival was, though we had forgotten it, Good Friday; and a great procession took place, as it had for centuries. As dusk gradually fell with its orange and violet light, the whole population of the little place seemed to be gathered in the area around the cathedral. The lights came on, and then, in the distance, in the square, we heard the singing grow louder as the procession approached. First came the ranks of the white-sheeted, white-cowled and -hooded ministrants, their eyes appearing through the slits in their hoods, their heads bound with what was surely a symbol of a crown of thorns: they carried lighted lanterns, and one in the middle a black crucifix. There followed the pall-bearers of the golden bier with the image of the dead Christ upon it, flanked by rows of dark, silent sailors who seemed a reminder of the far-off greatness of Amalfi's past, when the Republic, incredibly enough, was one of the richest and most powerful of the Mediterranean world. It suddenly came to me what pride of history was compacted into that great cry from Webster's tragedy: "I am Duchess of Malfi still!" After the sailors came the boys' choir, with their haunting high-soaring chant; and as that faded into the further streets we went up the wide climbing steps into the huge cathedral, all lit by hundreds of candles which threw their quivering light over the marble-faced pillars and the great ceiling with its painted and gilded carvings. Gradually we heard the procession returning, and saw the white ministrants mounting the steps on the final stage of their symbolic journey, with the solemn music ringing all around them. I am easily moved by beautiful ceremonial; but I had never before been so moved by a religious drama, nor was again until I saw the same Good Friday procession, many years later, pass through the darkened streets of Athens.

Amalfi in spring seemed to me exactly what I had longed for through all the time of struggle. A thirst for the open Mediterranean world, for living in the sun on a coast where scarcely any moment of the year was without its beauty of nature, for sensing around me a rhythm of life that had changed so little through the centuries, of a people simple and passionate with direct roots to the ancient world, had grown in me since the war. I began to rise like a piece of grass long crushed under a heavy stone: words and phrases of poems did indeed begin to move in my mind: perhaps the old power, tiny but with its ever-potent spell over my life, was not dead, but merely sleeping.

I revelled in the rose, violet and blue-green tones of sky and sea, changing all day long under the hot spring sun, the translucent depths that washed the grey rocks of this volcanic coast that we watched from our windows and from the high peaks of Ravello, to which we clambered. And I saw that the steep declivities on the edges of which Amalfi had been built might have suggested, if bare and untouched by the civilizing hand of man, terror and violence; but instead, terrace after terrace from the sea to the peaks displayed sprouting vines under protective awnings of dried leaves, lemon groves with their abundant globes of yellow and golden fruit and their intoxicating scent, cherry blossom and plum blossom and in the gardens of the white-washed villas with their contrasting shutters of pale-green and salmon- or shell-pink, fuchsias and geraniums and stock, stonecrop, violets and primroses covered every inch of ground upon which plants could flourish. So Amalfi, defying its gloomy origins, appeared like a storm-bird perched on the danger of the world. After nightfall, as the scent from all the luxuriance of leaf and blossom grew more intense, fire-flies darted hither and thither, disappearing like sparks from a burning as one approached.

I was charmed by what seemed to me the unhurrying patterns of traditional southern life; but I was to learn, by rude shock, that modern Italy had another face. As I have said, we had become a little vague about times and seasons. Startled to find Good Friday taking place on the day after our arrival, we failed to work out that Easter Sunday would be followed by Easter Monday and its holiday. We had booked a car to take us on Monday to Paestum, the Greek temples and half-excavated ruins of which had long been one of the goals of my dream-voyaging. Nothing could have seemed more promising. The sun freed itself from the white mist early in the morning, very soon the air was as warm as the most perfect June day in England, and the distant villages along the coast became clearer than ever, picked out in all their sun-golden colours. We left in highest spirits.

When we reached Paestum, my dream world of lonely temples quivering in the heat haze of midday, with wild flowers clustering round the bases of the columns, and a shepherd piping to his flock between half-revealed mosaic floors and the sea, fell to pieces. There

indeed were the honey-coloured time-chewed pillars of the greatest
temple with its perfect Doric proportions, rising still triumphantly on
the edge of the lightly foamed ripples, with fresh green of little tufts
of plants sprouting between the coigns, birds singing on the pedi-
ments, larks twittering high in the blue sky above, and electric green
lizards flashing when a shadow fell on them to their immemorial
hiding-places in the stones . . . but one had to detach these elements
by a conscious effort of the mind from the uproarious paraphernalia of
an Italian bank holiday that surrounded, swamped and dominated
them: innumerable charabancs, baby Fiats, motor-bikes, Vespas, pony
traps and bicycles parked everywhere and still arriving, raucously
honking, down the coast road to discharge their swarming families
and courting couples and gangs of youths, with their picnic baskets,
their transistors, their record players bellowing out jazz tunes and
Neapolitan songs, their dolls and games for the kiddies and packets of
sweets. Why, I asked myself, in a moment of disgust and dismay, do
all this at *Paestum*, when you can't appreciate what it means, don't
want to appreciate it, and spoil it for those who do? These uncharita-
ble, undemocratic thoughts were not to be suppressed, even though I
recognized that the scene might have had its charm for me anywhere
else along the coast at all; but equally not to be entirely suppressed or
submerged was the voice that rose from the antique ground, celebrating, like the larks, these pure memorials of the Other Time, the time
of source and vision and beginning, with its mystery and its joy.

Some friends and acquaintances I have met during my life, endowed it seems with second sight or some form of what is now called
extra-sensory perception, have claimed that in a long-ago pre-
incarnation I played some important part in the world of ancient
Greece. I do not know about this, as I am sceptical and agnostic by
habit of mind; but I do know that every time I meet face to face with
the sublime monuments or ruins of Greece, I am profoundly shaken,
even to the point of having violent dreams.

Before I took off for Athens, I had another encounter in Rome with
unexpected English friends whom I had not seen for a long time. I was
invited to a party where I found Jennie Graves, Robert's daughter;
Benedetto Croce's intelligent Anglophile daughter, Elena, who appeared to be much more au courant with what was going on in the
intellectual and artistic world of London than I was myself, and those
two great luminaries of the Oxford firmament, Maurice Bowra and
Isaiah Berlin. Both of them being inexhaustible talkers and entertainers of sparkling wit and recondite knowledge, they had as it were di-

vided the company between them, Maurice holding court in one corner of the room and roaring away like a Roman fountain when the wind suddenly blows the noise towards one in a greater roar; Shah in another corner, sufficiently far away from Maurice for the two platforms not to impinge, holding forth on the eccentricities of Bertie Russell and the philosophical fashions of the young men at Oxford with a nervous intensity like a diesel engine ticking over at a station halt.

I had scarcely arrived in Athens when my friends began to gather round me, immersing me in the tonic fountain of their welcome; but this time they were Greek friends, and not long-lost English friends. Very early on my first morning I picked up the telephone to hear the jovial voice of George Katzimbalis, immediately proposing a trip out to the country with the new Director of the British Institute, Wilfred Tatham, and his wife; a party the next evening for me to meet again all my available Greek friends, and a carousal at a taverna afterwards. The "country" turned out to be Sunium again, but a Sunium — and the road to it — transformed by innumerable spring flowers, white and yellow marguerites, moon-white and pink rock-roses and little magenta moonflowers and purple vetch, then cushions of spurge and tiny Virginia stock and clusters of diminutive wild iris, the inner fields covered with red anemones — which small brown-limbed peasant boys held out to us in tight-fisted bunches on our return — and all against the dazzling sea-prospect, blue this afternoon as a Brazilian butterfly's wing, a-glitter with a million sparkles of sun, the "curly golden head" of the Aegean, with the pale blue-purple silhouettes of islands in the distance. Again I felt the numinous atmosphere surrounding me on that sacred headland, that I had been so powerfully aware of on my first visit, but as it were in a different key to suit the different season.

I climbed down the cliff-side, and saw as if in a dream fragments of pillar and pediment among the rocks, quivering white under the water, like Shelley's ruins of Baiae. We lunched on sea-food by the rocky edge of all this pure translucence, under a group of olive-trees, while George held us all willing prisoners under the fountain of his talk, pouring out his stories and quips. He was at the top of his form during my whole sojourn. Especially memorable was a visit with him to the National Museum, not yet entirely finished, where the hall in the basement was filled with prostrate archaic *kouroi* awaiting their definitive placing. This sight inspired George to a lyrical outburst in praise of the *kouroi* — "hundreds and hundreds of these beautiful young men dug up all over Greece" — of eternal Greek youth and

Greek sculpture of the great age; at the end of which he confessed to me that when young he had been told he looked exactly like a *kouros* himself, but now, alas, felt old, overweight, and castrated.

There was only one sad moment for me. The family of Demetrios Capetanakis had been at great pains to conceal the fact of his death from his mother, who was old and had long been in poor health. She had, nevertheless, as I had always felt in my bones that she would, eventually make the discovery. It had been a greater shock to her, it seemed to me, than if she had been told at the time. She had written me a deeply moving letter; I therefore hoped that I would be allowed to meet her and talk to her on this visit. Demetrios's brother John promised to think this request over, and discuss it with the rest of the family. Eventually he rang me up, and suggested I should come to see him in his flat, which was also his consulting-room. The ever-kindly Odysseus Elytis shepherded me there. As we waited for John, or Yanni as his intimates called him, in his book-lined inner room, I was suddenly startled to discover on one of the walls an enlargement of a photograph of Demetrios, taken before he left for England, his eyes lowered over a book; it was so natural that I imagined for a moment he might lift his eyes and look at me again, speak a word. When John came in, I noted especially clearly how like Demetrios he was: all his brother's gentleness and sensibility showed in his face, but there was no trace of that impish malice that sometimes would illuminate Demetrios's features when he was in his gayest form. He told me that when their mother had found out, she had suffered a tremendous shock, almost a stroke, and symptoms of the same kind recurred every year on the anniversary of his death; therefore he could not bring himself to accept the responsibility of letting her see me, or know that I was in Athens. As John had struck me as a most sincere and sensitive person, I had to accept his verdict, though not without much inner doubt and protest. A few years later she died, so I was never able to tell her in person of all that Demetrios had meant to me and to my English friends.

« 2 »

I was lucky to visit Cyprus when I did. Only a few years later it was plunged into the terrible *enosis* struggle that cast such dark clouds over the traditional Anglo-Greek friendship and swept away (luckily only for a time) all the special warmth of sympathy that was immediately aroused between members of the two nations in their post-war encounters. It was a bitter time to live through if one had come to love and admire the Greeks as I had. Extremism in Athens and terror in the island were so rabid that one could only feel the deepest admiration for those among one's Greek friends who kept their heads. During this visit, I came to realize that, mixed in blood as the Cypriots are, an amalgam of primitive races and conqueror after conqueror — Persians, Romans, Byzantines, Franks, Venetians and Turks, those who spoke Greek *felt* themselves to be Greeks, just as much as the inhabitants of Rhodes or Crete. It was absurd to imagine that we British could hold in any kind of subjection any branch of the Greek people for more than the briefest interim period of adjustment. Unfortunately, it seemed to me, those who pleaded this just cause most eloquently were apt to forget that there was a Turkish side to the question, which had not been manufactured by us. So the wire-pullers in the international power-game found their opportunity, and the slide into violence and confusion began. All this has since been written of with a sorrowing restraint, a love crossed by despair, by Lawrence Durrell in the best, most real of his books about the Greek world, *Bitter Lemons*.

Let my diary take over for this visit:

Thursday April 16: Platres in the mountains.

A rough air crossing in a small aeroplane from Athens to Nicosia, which I did not care about, with head-winds buffeting the ridiculous little machine high up in the vast blue empty sky, and children being sick around me. How *does* one keep up on this invisible element? A most disagreeable sensation of trapped insecurity. I tried, but failed totally to take any pleasure in the sight of the islands far below, rocky foam-fringed oases appearing suddenly in the expanse of sea beneath the wisps of scudding cloud. Ganymede could not have felt more helpless on his talon-gripped flight to the world of the gods. The dark, mountainous, deep-cliffed coast of Turkey to the north-east could so easily become a permanent symbol of the dispossessed stomach.

But the journey from Nicosia to Platres was sheer delight. We drove first of all across the flat plain between the mountains to north and south, so green with its luxuriantly growing corn, the earth showing up rust-red between, the mountains so purple-dark, so ominous in the thundery light. The roads were utterly lonely, bordered by mimosa-trees in flower. Every so often the car had to slow down to pass or let pass a flock of sheep with long dragging tails and black heads, sometimes with skipping lambs beside them; or now and then, in the villages where peasants were leading the paniers of their donkeys, goat-flocks with golden-brown goat-kids with floppy ears and intelligent eyes. The shepherds had a timeless look, as old as Homer and the Bible, and recalling too the England of King Richard Coeur de Lion's day, where also the hills were swarming with sheep. Then the climb into the mountains began, up twisting roads among deep-eaved, long-balconied villages, passing a roaring torrent or slender forms of ghost poplars; up into the pine-trees and the darkness, the pure cold of the night air of the peaks gaining upon us. . . .

Suddenly, at midday, a great throng of house-martins started circling and twittering outside, almost flying in at my window. I watched them, fascinated, for some time before I realized they were building their hard mud nests under the eaves.

My first walk was down on the road to Limassol and Paphos, past Judas-trees not so far advanced as at Amalfi or on the road to Sunium, with a vision in a sweeping semi-circle of azure-blue sea between fold after fold of dryish mountains where vines will soon be growing. Far off, I saw little valleys and villages in them and tiny Byzantine churches in between with tall, dark cypresses around them and then the brilliant green again of cornfields. All these settlements looked as if newly washed and scrubbed in the crystal-clear air. As afternoon advanced, I met, at a crossing, two R.A.F. boys in a lorry, almost the only traffic on the roads: they had lost their way to Paphos.

Friday 17th

Maurice Cardiff, now Representative of the British Council here, came to me early in a Council car, and we set off for Curium and Old Paphos (Kouklia) under a hot sun and cloudless sky. Maurice I find a delightful companion, much easier to be friends with than when we last met in Athens — we have both moved on — sympathetic, with a sharp and interesting mind, amusing and amused, expressing concern and indignation at the story of my firm, discussing the literary situation with intelligence and acute judgement, surprisingly in accord with me on many points where we differ from the current and fashionable view; expressing too, great enthusiasm for Demetrios's poems. He had before this been in Milan for the Council, where he had seen much of [my niece] Sally. He was sour and witty about the well-to-do Italians of the north: he had found them superficial, and quite empty in their depths; hopeless in their attitude towards artists and writers, whom they treated as social ornaments and pets; and suffering from a confused Anglophobia under their surface blandishments, which he felt arose from a deep-down, not entirely conscious refusal to forgive us for destroying Mussolini's régime.

Curium, on its hill-side looking out over the intense peacock-blue of the sea, now with tones of vivid green in it, gave me an impression of great confusion: it is, of course, a fairly recent excavation, under the devoted care of a brilliant young American archaeologist, and apart from some beautiful mosaic floors with Greek inscriptions and a temple of Apollo, has still to reveal most of its secrets. Nevertheless, there is much evidence of a big and flourishing town. Peasants were digging away for more, up above us, as we wandered round what had been uncovered. Perhaps because the sandstone here is so crumbly, I had a strong feeling of the ruins wanting to hide themselves, of refusing to speak.

Everywhere, between Curium and Old Paphos, there was green corn massed in the fields, with scattered red poppies peeping through, and olive- and carob-trees breaking up their expanse. The roads were bordered with masses of big yellow daisy flowers and mauve-pink convolvulus. Wherever the cultivation stopped, the rocky heaths were a mass of myrtles and rock-rose bushes densely tufted together.

Old Paphos has the same wonderful situation looking out over the sea to Curium, but is far more extraordinary. The ancient site, with its broken, fluted columns and cyclopean walls, is almost inextricably entangled with a little village, still lived in, an exquisite miniature Byzantine chapel built of lichen-splashed grey stone, and (most astonishing of all) a medieval sugar refinery with characteristic Cypriot arches. And village, chapel, refinery, all built out of the site, which was obviously much greater than its appearance now suggests, and of very great pre-Hellenic antiquity and veneration. The obliteration is profound here, but it still speaks in a faint wind-lost voice. Big dust-coloured lizards scramble over the ruins. There are old olive-presses in the chapel precincts.

Motoring fast along the coast road after leaving Old Paphos, we passed the bay where Aphrodite is supposed to have been born, bathed in the golden light of afternoon. The chauffeur, muddled and obstinate, refused — or failed — to let us stop, but perhaps even because of the speed of our passage it made a deep, in fact thrilling impression on me. On one side, I thought, it might have been Freshwater Bay or Lulworth Cove; on the other the two famous landmarks, the big rock and the little rock, and the full lines of foam creaming around them, gave it a more exotic appearance. . . .

As we motored back across the mountains, the scenery struck me as

more like the Georgian Military Highway in the Caucasus than anything else, in its loneliness and grandeur, in the way the road was
carved out of the midway rock, a shelf above the gorges.

Tuesday, 21st April

A letter from Christopher in Los Angeles, regretting that he had not
known about the luncheon that was given for me. "My blood boils to
think how you were treated: you who have done more than anybody
else for the things we believe in, and who have set an example which is
now, I'm happy to say, being followed by several different groups in
this country. . . . I have a rough draft of my novel [*The World in
the Evening*] finished and now I hope the whole thing will be done by
the end of the summer at the very latest. It has been more trouble than
anything else I have ever attempted and I'm not at all sure that this
means it is any good; but it has been a great discipline."

The Dome Hotel here at Kyrenia is the most extraordinary study in
human wreckage — one might almost say wreckage of a contracting
empire — a sort of Buxton-cum-Cheltenham by the Middle Sea.
Shaky old jossers in old school ties with arthritic wives; blue-haired
widows of incalculable antiquity gallantly keeping up appearances,
creeping along on sticks, only just held together (one feels) by pins;
booze-sodden ex-military men with aggressively flowering white
moustaches under purple noses, nagged by their women folk at every
meal; middle-aged suburban couples so nondescript they seem to fade
into the furnishings, with the smiling neuter Cypriots hurrying to and
fro to attend to their wants and soothe their plaints. Among these a few
holiday-makers from London, surprisingly a publisher and his wife
known to me, friends of Rosamond's, and an old gent in an O.E. tie,
who turns out to have known my father.

This morning I met Lawrence Durrell at a little wine bar, very
much bronzed but not so rotund as I remember him at our last meeting
in Athens. He introduced me to the artist Sigmund Pollitzer, charming, sensitive-faced, who in the afternoon took us over to his little
white-washed cottage by the shore, surrounded by a sea of yellow wild
chrysanthemums. It has an exquisite interior patio filled with flowers,
a fountain and fluttering white pigeons. Filled me with envy and longing. I was struck by his pottery, which seemed to me full of imagination, and his black-and-white drawings, a strangely austere (or neurotic?) reaction to this landscape of changing, burning colours.

Friday 24th

Larry Durrell has been a good friend, a very agreeable companion to find here. We talked endlessly (he is a great talker), in his place on the beach (where he settles himself in bathing costume every afternoon, with his 18-month-old little daughter and Diana, the attractive South African girl who accompanied him from Belgrade), in his favourite wine-shop, and on the expedition we made on Wednesday to St. Hilarion and Bellapais. Ideas bubble out of him continually, ideas for books *he* should write, ideas for books *I* should publish, and every other kind of literary scheme imaginable, some comic and quite impossible, some tempting, tempting. He appears, poor chap, to be in a pretty bad jam: his wife had a mental collapse and left him, and he says he can't work because he has to look after the child. All the same he seems in very good spirits.

He plans to settle here, and took me to see the little house he has bought in the village above Bellapais' honey-coloured abbey, a bargain, he says, will be very attractive — considered by itself — when he's done with it, but personally I couldn't stand the slummy village atmosphere encroaching so closely. Outside the abbey all the male population was sitting about, idle and contented, on chairs — the inevitable Cypriot chairs. He told me the peasants were extremely friendly and uninhibited towards him in the expression of political opinion. In his view, there's a great deal of emotional fantasy about the *enosis* business: natural enough, but he doesn't believe it goes very deep, and is only fanned into an unwilling flame by the implacable priests (priests meddling in politics have always roused my hackles.)

St. Hilarion is a staggering sight. The road rises so sheer out of the plain, it's like climbing in an aeroplane to go up, and I felt suddenly giddy and insecure. On the way up, a shepherd sitting under a tree, surrounded by his flock, greeted us gaily. Asphodels, and glowing yellow ranunculi within the keep. Again a very small boy emerged from nowhere and had just instituted himself our guide when the official guide turned up (much to his disgust). There are bewildering, beautiful views to north, west and east: Kyrenia looks like a tiny model harbour, a child's toy. How on earth did the crusader knights exercise themselves when they spent all the summer up here? As with so many medieval buildings, abbeys, cathedrals, forts, castles, I am amazed at the daring of the conception, the strength and thoroughness of the execution. Bellapais abbey is just the same.

After St. Hilarion, we went down to a little beach Larry and his friends have discovered, with a welcoming lap of sand among the rocks, the water warm, buoyant and flawlessly clear. As usual there were beachcomber dogs hanging about, panting for stones to be thrown for them. An immediate emotion of distress rose in me when I caught sight of them, but they did not seem to be starved or broken in spirit. My favourite is the one who always has a wet bottom, from sitting in the waves.

Tuesday 28th. Famagusta

Sunday morning I left Kyrenia for this place, driving along the coast with its dazzling panorama of rocky bays and blue water turning to green as it comes in shore. Then we turned south over the Levkoniko Pass, swiftly changing sharp outlines of hills with gnarled ancient olive-trees and shepherds with their flocks under them. Again we passed green fields of corn with purple primuli sword-lilies growing wild among the poppies, and everywhere banks covered with giant pink convolvulus and yellow wild chrysanthemums. At last we began to twist down into the plain, towards Famagusta and the other side of the sea.

We made a stop at Salamis, which stirred my imagination more deeply than anywhere else on the island. Salamis, a purely Greek town, was once — as early as the sixth century B.C. — the most important city on the island, boasting an excellent harbour and a flourishing mercantile community. All one sees at first is a scrub-waste of mimosa-wattle lying towards the sea-cliff; and sand dunes. Then one drives through the mimosa, and suddenly one comes to a hollow scooped out of the sand, to see marble pillars, some still standing with their carved capitals, some fallen, fragments scattered everywhere. And everywhere, if one scoops up the soft sand and sifts it through one's hands one finds broken shards and bits of marble. Further on, one comes upon half-excavated temples and a market-place, and more tumbled columns hiding in the mimosa. I can't believe that great treasures are not still lying buried only a little way below the dunes. Dust-coloured lizards and small snakes slither away. The sense of a forgotten, once-teeming city, a lost obliterated civilization, of something now for ever irrecapturable and stillness after clamour is almost oppressive. I went down to the beach, absurdly to see if I could glimpse the other ruins said to be still lying on the sea-bottom. No, nothing. I kicked the pebbles about, looking for more pottery shards, while a gipsy leading a donkey passed me.

On to Famagusta, the hotel edging on to the sandy beach and the surf. In the distance, down the coast, an army rest-camp (service men on leave from Suez) with its line of tents; and nearby a little bay with all the gaiety of sailing and fishing boats and bathing. From the window of my room I can catch a glimpse of the ruined sandy-coloured cathedral that has been turned into a mosque, the merchant ships and warships laid up in the port, and the pointy-prowed sailing boats in front of them. The line of Kyrenia's hills in the distance.

After dark, and before dinner, in the moonlight, I made a first prowl into the old town, in a different way almost as disturbing and strange as Salamis. There was scarcely anyone about — it might have been under curfew. I could only detect occasional movements and murmurs behind the shutters of the little houses which let out their chinks of light. All around me the towering massive fortifications, and against the moonlit sky the dark outlines of tall palms and the half-ruined, hollow shapes of abandoned churches and the buttresses of the cathedral. An extraordinary ghost-like impression of the East invading the West, of the skeletons of history.

Bill's friend, the gentle, good-looking young painter Valentinos Charalambous, who has studied in London, full of charm and fun, took me to see another aspect of life last night in the old town. Two young Royal Marines were sitting in Pop's Bar, getting steadily sozzled. One, from London, good-looking in a cheeky-boyish way, was full of grins and winks at me, while his friend from Yorkshire gave the barman advice on how to do his pools. Outside the door, two smudgily painted whores, of incredible squalor, kept on leering and beckoning to them. . . . Later, he took me on to the new town, to a street that reminded me of the "gut" in Malta, where we plunged into a bar called the Spitfire. A ridiculously bad fifth-rate floor-show was going on, displaying some wretched lost girls from (I would guess) Budapest and Vienna and Syria. Little tables and chairs were packed into the room, which was crowded with English soldiers in civvies, sailors and marines in uniforms, and a sprinkling of Cypriots. One big, heftily built black-haired young marine, of straightforward English good looks, was pretty far gone, happily and fatuously bestowing drunken smiles all round the room, and trying to imitate the movements of the dancers, allurements and wrigglings and mock embraces, offering to kiss his pal, who was desperately trying to keep him in order. Several times he suddenly collapsed on the floor, waving a feeble arm towards one of the girls, but was propped up again against the bar before the approaching M.P.s could spot him.

Here, in my new room, I am finding, as I hoped, that I can write poetry. I began roughing out some poems in Platres, and now suddenly they are beginning to flow, at a rate rather faster than my usual slow rate. I am working especially on a poem which tries to express the change in the nature of reality caused by the atom bomb — by the apocalyptic nature of our age. . . .

> The public voices make believe
> Reality is still as square
> As what our fingers fastened on
> When there was more in air than air,
> Too deep in consequence to see
> The cities where the treasures lie
> Have learnt the impermanence of leaves
> Under the spell of this goodbye. . . .

Friday, May 1

Yesterday I went out on the Salamis Road, to see Valentinos's family pottery workshops, where they have been working for generations. The old father and his assistants were busy at their wheels — I watched, feeling the eternal fascination of the pottery wheel and the shaping fingers — turning out jugs and bowls on an immeasurably old, traditional pattern: while inside, with his up-to-date electric kiln, Valentinos was intent on producing modern stuff, for a more sophisticated public (and yet V's designs were a subtle modernized version on ancient themes more often than not.) As usual, the atmosphere of a craftsman-artist's working-place completely captured me, seemed like home. Valentinos, in his blue jeans, took me down through the enormously long grove of oranges, lemons and bitter-oranges, to the water-tank at the end where he plans to make his own little secret hideaway out of a derelict outhouse. . . .

I am appalled to learn that when the Suez Canal was being built, enterprising get-rich-quick traders plundered Salamis (and perhaps other sites in Cyprus) and shipped enormous cargoes of marble off to Egypt. It is something to know that all that happened before we took over suzerainty of the island from the Porte, though heaven knows we haven't done much about the exploration of the sites since. Let sleeping dogs — and treasures — lie, seems to have been our Imperial motto for most of the time.

If I were to try to order my impressions of Cyprus for a serious article or broadcast, I would say that these are the features that strike me in the main. First, the extreme orderliness and quiet of the island. Whether the Cypriots like it or not (and there's no particular reason why they should like it), they are better administered than they have been since Roman times. The villages have been cleaned up, the farms are fruitful, the roads extended, the mountain forts protected, justice is uncorrupted. There are moments when it seems as if it is all but a little paradise. Second, when one gets out into the country, only a few miles from the towns, the absence of crowds. One motors for hours along roads where one meets almost no one, compared with the English countryside or even Italy or Greece, only flocks of goats and goat-herds and an occasional high-piled village bus, with the lonely, awe-inspiring ranges of mountains and isolated peaks on the horizon. And one finds bay after bay of heavenly warm golden sand where one can sunbathe and swim without a sign of another human being. Third, the extreme beauty of nature, the wild flowers in all their beauty at their season, the groves of oranges, lemons, tangerines, grapefruits, with the rich colour of earth, sea and sky burning through them. Fourth, the astonishing abundance of pretty little painted Byzantine churches wherever one goes. Fifth, the fact that the bones of everything that happened in history seem to be here: the ruins of prehistoric and classical Greek settlements, Roman aqueducts, Byzantine cities, crusader castles, Venetian forts, Turkish mosques. The folly and strangeness of all the imperial adventures that have passed across the island without it ever finding its true identity; down to the British, which has produced an extraordinary fusion or mixture of English and Mediterranean cultures, much more extraordinary than in Malta, with British orderliness superimposed on Mediterranean mess.

I am haunted by the ghosts of Richard Coeur-de-Lion and Rimbaud.* An odd pair. The saints here seem to have a peculiar brand of humour.

Saturday, May 2

Yesterday I had an almost perfect bathe, at Dhavos after visiting Kantara's ruined castle, perhaps the most marvellous bathe of my life, so that it transcended bathing and became a symbolic poetic act. . . .

I began to think again that I could *escape*. What prevented me keeping a small pied-à-terre in London, and coming out to Greece, to Cyprus, buying a plot of land and building a little villa in the sun, living as I had increasingly longed to live, in a Mediterranean atmosphere? I had no publishing firm to look after now, no magazine since

* Arthur Rimbaud worked as a labourer on the island for some months in 1879, and then again in 1880 as foreman in charge of a gang building the Governor General's summer residence.

the end of *New Writing*, no radio programme since the end of *New Soundings*. The literary world, the young writers could look after themselves, without any stirring and pushing from me. Instead of looking after others, I would look after myself at last, write poetry, memoirs, begin the novels I had long cherished as phantasmal shapes at the back of my mind. Instead of being de-humanized by the business rat-race and the artificial pressure of modern metropolitan civilization, I would rediscover the ancient rhythms of life in these countries where they had never been entirely destroyed. I had made myself miserable with fruitless struggles. Now I would be reborn and live in *le vrai*. I would grow my own grapes, figs, peaches, lemons, exotic flowers far more abundantly and simply than I ever could in England. I would acquire a mahogany-coloured body and a pagan calm of spirit. . . .

Yes, *what* prevented me? It was no good; or no good *yet*. My restless temperament, my tattered ambitions answered me: I had been defeated, or outmanoeuvred twice, three times, I must try my luck once more. I was still young enough, I still cared very much about what happened in the world of literature and art. I believed I could still influence and stimulate the creation of great work. That vanity had not entirely left me, nor had the voices of others telling me I was still needed. No, I had not done enough, done enough, done enough. . . .

So this internal argument has gone on during this holiday, reviving in the intervals between writing poems, in discussions that have followed marvellous expeditions, in reflections late at night as I have re-read letters from England. At Dhavos a moment of temptation or illumination had come to me, as it came to Mr. Lucas at Platanisti in E. M. Forster's story; but not on the road to Colonus. Dhavos was one of the stations where I might have changed trains, as at Heiligenkreuz before the war. My star has blessed me; but cursed me too.

Four days later, I returned to England. Before the end of the year, with the backing of Cecil Harmsworth King, grand panjandrum of the *Daily Mirror* and the *Sunday Pictorial*, I had founded and become editor of the *London Magazine*.

✦ VI ✦

Epilogue

WRITING as I do now, at an interval of more than a dozen years from the foundation of the new *London Magazine*,* I see that many hopes were fulfilled but many others disappointed: perhaps by my own deficiencies, perhaps by a real dearth of first-class new literary talent in our country at that particular time, perhaps partly also by sudden changes in taste and fashion, undercurrents over which the individual has very little control, if any at all.

The seven years during which I edited the *London Magazine* were full of stimulus and interest for me, if also bringing a share of vexation and discouragement. I like to believe that they were of value to the continuity of literary creation in our country. Equally, I am certain that it would have been unwise for me to carry on beyond 1961, even if I had found a Maecenas who would stoically have endured the lean years and judged with a sceptical eye the fat. One plays one's part on a certain stage; it is good if one can be aware of the signs which indicate that a new generation of players is impatient to take one's place. I never wanted to linger on as a grotesque from an earlier generation, held in place only by compassion and respect for past achievement.

The death of Dylan Thomas had seemed to mark the beginning of a new period, during which the writers of the 'thirties and the 'forties were spurned (at least temporarily, and with certain exceptions) by an up-and-coming generation who affected, in their early manifestos, to be scandalized by the romanticism and cosmopolitanism of their immediate predecessors. The vogue for a new kind of social realism and a picaresque style in the novel indicated much more effectively, I thought, a genuine shift in the social structure of our country, the first results of post-war Welfare State building, than the move towards a

* This was originally written in 1966.

kind of humdrum "consolidation" in poetry. In so far as both these tendencies were parochial and against the European mind, they seemed to me reactionary and to be deplored, even to be absurd in the circumstances of the world in which we have lived since the first atom bomb exploded. Already, however, the so-called "Movement" has disintegrated, and the authentic talents have pursued their own diverse paths, ignoring the slogans with which they were launched.

In curious contrast, the new movement in the theatre, which began with the first night of John Osborne's brilliant *Look Back in Anger*, rapidly expanded into an interest in foreign theatrical developments, the experiments of Brecht, Ionesco, Beckett and Dürrenmatt. There was a certain irony in this return to the symbolical and surrealist elements in our modern intellectual heritage just at a time when they appeared to be anathema to the novelists and literary critics.

I found this new phase in the theatre sympathetic and often exciting, and believed it could have a fertilizing influence on the whole literary scene. It was my constant regret while I was editor of the *London Magazine* that it was impossible in such a review as mine to do much to help or blow wind into the sails. I felt that for some years the most vital imaginative currents would be moving towards the drama, and that young authors who had something urgent to say would be much more likely to want to write plays rather than short stories or poems, perhaps even rather than novels.

This is not, however, the place or the moment for me to attempt to write in detail or pass judgement on those developments that coincided with the founding of the *London Magazine*. It is also, I must admit, still painful to me to write of years which saw the death of so many writers and artists, dear friends of mine, admired and often loved by me, who were prominent in the intellectual activity of that time. Even while I have been writing, their number has been swelled by the deaths of Tom Eliot, Edith Sitwell, and Louis MacNeice. If I were editing a magazine today, again and again when asking myself the regular question "Now who should write about this, or that?," I know that the names of the dead would come to my mind first.

My mother's death also took place in those years: my mother, who had helped me to support *New Writing* at more than one crucial point, who helped me to find the money to start my publishing firm, and supported me again when the *London Magazine* lost its original backers. She died in the fulness of years, in greater calm and detachment than she had known through all her middle age, but leaving such a gap that still today, years later, when I am abroad on a holiday I cannot change the impulse that makes me want to write the first postcard or letter to her.

I remember how we celebrated her eightieth birthday at Egerton Crescent. My three sisters, Helen, Rosamond and Beatrix, had taken her to the theatre, and late supper was laid out in my newly decorated dining-room, with its black and gold furniture, on their return. We drank her health in champagne from the exquisite cut-glass goblets that had been specially made for my grandfather in Bohemia in the last century, and ate from the Oriental dishes he had brought back from his Far Eastern trip nearly a hundred years before. She seemed at the top of her form, as young as any of us in comment and appreciation. It seemed to me that at the end she retired happily into a world of her own, reflecting perhaps with amused satisfaction on the phenomenon of being surrounded by all her children on such a night of celebration, after two world wars, in a London so much changed from the city she had known when she first came over from New England with my father more than half a century before.

Everyone who has enjoyed a game which he has played, with some success and effect, for over a quarter of a century, and who is eventually obliged to give it up because he finds the forces arrayed against him too great for him to control, must have some bitterness among his recollections of past pleasures and achievements. I must confess that a certain sour taste of frustration has been in my mouth, while I have watched authors, whose hopeful beginnings or revivals I encouraged, pass on to the lists of other publishers, or individual books of rare merit, which originally appeared under my imprint, be reissued with little or no mention of how they first came to the light. So the waves of time sweep away all the sandcastles we spend our mornings with such expenditure of energy and enthusiasm in erecting.

If I were not by nature a poet, endowed with some measure of philosophy, all this would be much harder to bear. But my career has made me reflect on the increasing difficulties which individual ventures in publishing and editing are bound to contend with in our time. Gone are the days when a young man or a young couple with keen literary interests and a feeling for the production of books could start a publishing business with a few hundred pounds in the bank, and with a certain amount of luck favouring could establish it as of national importance and make a modest living out of it within a decade. And yet those days are only as far away as the years between the wars. Gone are the days when it was not too difficult to find a private patron who would support a literary magazine. Heavy taxation, and the increasingly rigorous rules under which the Inland Revenue judges what can be allowed as expenses before taxation, have almost eliminated such patrons, except in the rare cases of great riches deliberately dedicated to such enterprises. My own career has, I think, been a kind of demonstration experiment of the problems of finding a patron in our time. I can only hope that in the future the only patrons left will not be public and official bodies. Immense though their value may be, I have never believed that they — or the great commercial enterprises which for prestige reasons care for a time and then lose interest — could in any way replace the private patron with a hunch.

I have written of the "fertile dilemma" which seemed to rule my life: the way in which the course of events, with diabolical and repeated ingenuity, made it impossible for me to decide to devote my energies finally either to writing, or to the presentation and encouragement of other people's writing. Part of my mind, when I was running a literary magazine or a publishing enterprise, always regretted the time I could have devoted to my own poems and books. And yet, as soon as such an enterprise came to an end, the opportunity arose to start a new one which I felt I could not refuse. A few weeks of creative work, and the note-books had to be abandoned again for the new editor's or publisher's desk.

At the same time, I would be both foolish and hypocritical if, having looked back, I pretended that I had not found great rewards in my life of tension between these two poles. I think of all the friends I might never have met, all the stories of adventure, suffering and joy I might never have heard, all the discoveries in other people's lives I would never have made, all the journeys I would never have set out on; above all, of those moments of pure delight when I found a book, a story or poem that I knew was the real thing and could be shown by me to the public to be the real thing. If it has been a weakness in me not to have been ready to accept the more restricted and austere life of the artist struggling in his own darkness, I cannot altogether say that I am sorry I failed to be strong.

Now I face a different life, with all those strange and turbulent ends and beginnings behind me. Only the future will tell whether I shall still find keys to other rooms along the long corridor that is always in shadow just ahead of one's steps; or whether my good angel will have at last to admit that both his hands are empty.

Index

Aberystwyth University, 170
Abinger Hammer (Sitwell home), 327
Abney (Hammersley home), 35, 36, 40
Ackerley, Joe, 325, 370, 465; *The Prisoners of War*, 87
Acton, Harold, 68, 75, 367, 386, 398, 425, 493–495
Adelphi, The, 160
Adlington, William, 415
Age of the Dragon, The (Lehmann), 378
Alberti, Rafael, 182
Albertina Museum (Vienna), 103, 435
Aldworth, Rosamond's cottage in, 378, 406
Algren, Nelson, 448
Ali, Ahmed, 170
Alington, Cyril A., 68, 77
Allen, Walter, 170, 308
Allison, Drummond, 372
Alum Bay, 49–50, 223, 481
Amalfi, 524–526
Anand, Mulk Raj, 170
Anders, Georg. *See* Soyfer, Yura
Aragon, Louis, 177, 384–385, 387, 397; *Crève-Coeur* poems, 177, 344, 368, 384, 385
Archer, David, 162
Arnold, Matthew, 65
Ashton, Fred, 316, 383, 460, 475
Ashton, Leigh, 252–253
Astor, Lady, 52
Athenaeum, 271, 272, 293, 328, 393
Athens, 439, 443–444, 527–529
Attlee, Clement, 187, 431
Auden, Wystan H., 112–118, 126, 170, 179–180, 204, 223, 284, 307, 339, 352, 387–390, 476; *Poems*, 116, 164; collaboration with Christopher Isherwood, 138, 201–203; *The Dance of Death*, 141; and *New Writing*, 151, 153, 156, 164–166, 167, 220–222, 245; and international writers' conferences, 173; and Spanish Civil War, 178; *Spain*, 179, 184; emigrates to U.S., 203, 222, 231, 273, 284, 420; *In Memoriam Ernst Toller*, 232; *Leaves of Life*, 232; branded as traitor by press in World War II, 240, 247, 284–285, 421; influence on post-Dunkirk poets, 285; *Look, Stranger*, 345
Authors' Society, 152
Austria, 127–130, 138, 139, 143–149, 185–186, 194–201, 228, 233–234, 237, 428–429; Anschluss, 199, 207–217, 227, 229; during Nazi occupation, 250–252. *See also* Vienna
Avilov, Lydia, 487
Ayer, Freddie (A. J.), 75, 511
Ayrton, Michael, 500

Balzac, Honoré de, 501
Bankhead, Tallulah, 78
Banting, John, 415
Barbusse, Henri, 144, 150–151
Barker, George, 162, 166, 365; *Four Elegies*, 232
Barnes, Alfred, 187
Barrymore, Ethel, 461
Bartlett, Vernon, 136
Bassiano, Princess. *See* Caetani, Marguerite